THE SOCIOLOGY OF SOCIAL PROBLEMS

PRENTICE-HALL, INC., Englewood Cliffs, New Jersey 07632

THE
SOCIOLOGY
OF
SOCIAL
PROBLEMS

SEVENTH EDITION

PAUL B. HORTON
Western Michigan University

GERALD R. LESLIE
University of Florida

Library of Congress Cataloging in Publication Date

HORTON, PAUL B
  The sociology of social problems.

  Includes bibliographies and index.
   1. Social Problems. 2. United States—Social
conditions. I. Leslie, Gerald R., joint author.
II. Title.
HN57.H6 1981   362'.042   80–25415
ISBN 0–13–821702–5

10 9 8 7 6 5 4 3 2 1

Editorial/production supervision by Fred Bernardi
Interior and cover design by Walter Behnke
Manufacturing buyer: John B. Hall

PRENTICE-HALL INTERNATIONAL, INC., *London*
PRENTICE-HALL OF AUSTRALIA PTY. LIMITED, *Sydney*
PRENTICE-HALL OF CANADA, LTD., *Toronto*
PRENTICE-HALL OF INDIA PRIVATE LIMITED, *New Delhi*
PRENTICE-HALL OF JAPAN, INC., *Tokyo*
PRENTICE-HALL OF SOUTHEAST ASIA PTE. LTD., *Singapore*
WHITEHALL BOOKS LIMITED, WELLINGTON, *New Zealand*

CONTENTS

6 CRIME AND DELINQUENCY: CAUSES AND TREATMENT 130

7 FAMILY AND GENERATIONAL PROBLEMS 160

8 RELIGIOUS PROBLEMS AND CONFLICTS 194

12

RACE DISCRIMINATION IN AMERICAN LIFE 309

13

SOME OTHER DISCRIMINATIONS 353

14

URBAN AND RURAL PROBLEMS 379

18

**CIVIL
LIBERTIES
IN AN AGE
OF PROTEST
527**

19

**ENVIRONMENT
AND
SOCIAL POLICY
563**

PART THREE

Conclusion and Future Prospects   *595*

PREFACE

A textbook should do at least three things: first, it should present both a body of data and interpretations of those data that will meet the reasonably critical demands of professional colleagues; second, it should fit those data into a framework of theory the student can use in interpreting data after the course is completed; third, it should present data, interpretation, and theory in a manner that stimulates and challenges the students who use it.

Built upon the assumption that modern social science provides the tools to permit significant, systematic, and consistent interpretation of social problems data, this book employs three separate, but related, frames of reference that have proved more than ordinarily useful. Social change and resulting social disorganization, the emergence of value conflicts, and the influences of personal deviation are brought to bear upon each problem. This is no "omnium-gatherum" of facts and varying interpretations of those facts, nor is it a narrowly particularistic interpretation.

Part one includes a chapter on the nature and definition of social problems, a chapter that outlines the three sociological approaches used in our frame of reference, and a chapter on logical and statistical problems involved in the interpretation of data. Part two includes 16 chapters devoted to the analysis of major social problems. Each chapter presents a body of the most relevant data bearing on the problems and interprets these data in terms of each of the three approaches. Such practical application explains and illustrates the concepts of social disorganization, value conflicts, and personal deviation. The chapter sequence presents first those problems traditionally recognized as social problems—crime, race relations, marriage and family problems—then moves into some problems of more recent concern, such as civil liberties, mass communication, and problems of the environment and social policy. A final chapter integrates and concludes the discussion.

Most students who use this book will be lower division students with fairly limited training in sociology. The book is written with these students in mind. It strives to be readable, yet sociologically sophisticated. It avoids unnecessary "sociologese" but seeks to explain basic sociological concepts thoroughly. It assumes that a textbook need be neither a "student's book" nor an "instructor's book," but may adequately meet the needs of both.

In preparing the seventh edition, we have been impressed by the many recent contributions in our rapidly changing field. The basic approach remains unchanged. We believe that instructors who liked the earlier editions will be pleased with this one. We hope that those who were less enamored may find some of our errors corrected by this edition. In the effort to please, however, we have not diluted controversy to the level of platitude. We have sought to make this textbook as interesting as possible so that it may stimulate students to seek greater understanding of the drama in which they are both actors and audience. We are grateful for many helpful suggestions and criticisms from our colleagues, and we owe a deep debt of gratitude to Dr. John F. Cuber for his encouragement and assistance, and to the editorial staff of Prentice-Hall for their tireless dedication.

We sought to document this book with easily available sources and references whenever practical. Obscure citations and foreign language references may spread the mantle of erudition upon a book's authors, but are of little use to undergraduate students who often depend upon meager library facilities. The descriptions of current social developments draw heavily upon such sources as *Time* magazine and the *New York Times*, since current developments are rarely found in academic journals. A list of audiovisual aids is found in the instructor's manual.

We share joint responsibility for the organization of the book, and each chapter is a product of mutual criticism and suggestion. In the actual writing, Horton prepared chapters 1, 3, 5, 6, 8, 10, 12, 13, 15, 17, 18, 19, and 20, while Leslie prepared chapters 2, 4, 7, 9, 11, 14, and 16.

THE SOCIOLOGY OF SOCIAL PROBLEMS

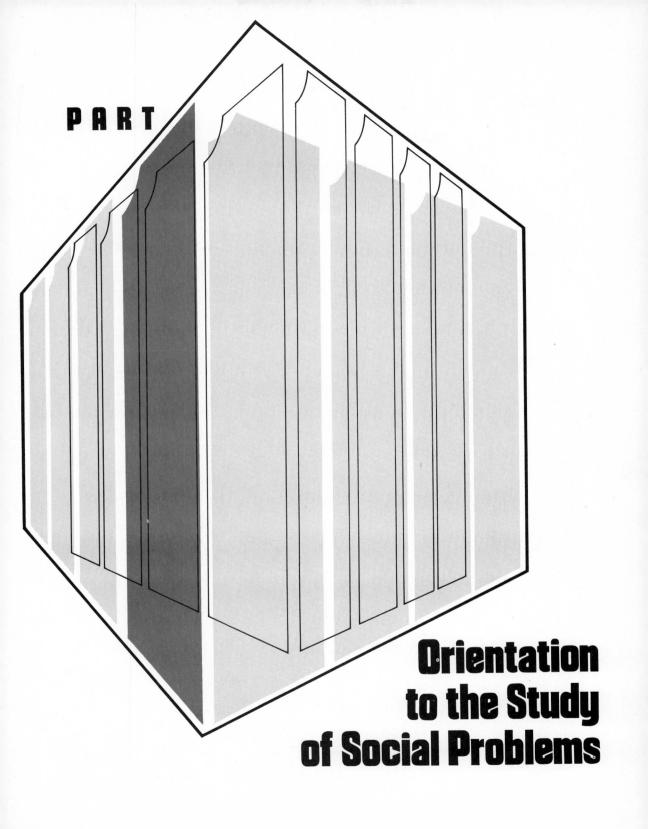

PART

Orientation to the Study of Social Problems

Marc Anderson

WHY STUDY SOCIAL PROBLEMS?

At the close of the Middle Ages, a sombre melancholy weighs on people's souls. Whether we read a chronicle, a poem, a sermon, a legal document even, the same impression of immense sadness is produced by them all. It would sometimes seem as if this period had been particularly unhappy, as if it had left behind only the memory of violence, of covetousness and mortal hatred, as if it had known no other enjoyment but that of intemperance, of pride and of cruelty.

Now in the records of all periods misfortune has left more traces than happiness. Great evils form the groundwork of history. . . . But in the fifteenth century, as in the epoch of romanticism, it was, so to say, bad form to praise the world and life openly. It was fashionable to see only its suffering and misery, to discover everywhere signs of decadence and of the near end—in short, to condemn the times or to despise them.[1]

3

The United States in the 1980s bears some resemblances to John Huizinga's description of European society at the end of the Middle Ages. The complacency and optimism of the 1950s were replaced by the conflicts of the 1960s and the polarizations, antagonisms, and falling expectations of the 1970s. Recent polls show a widespread feeling among Americans that the quality of life is deteriorating. They reflect both a growing anxiety over taxes, inflation, declining public morality, crime, drug use, disorder, and environmental pollution, a drastic loss of public confidence in American institutions, and a fear that deep recession and unemployment await us.[2] Clearly, the American people are deeply concerned about social problems today. Whether we like it or not, *social problems affect all of us,* so perhaps we should know something about them. What are they? Why do they exist? Who is responsible for them? How much do they cost? What can be done about them?

To ask these questions takes only a short paragraph; to answer them would require a library with half its shelves filled with books not yet written. Even the first question, What are social problems?, is much more complicated than it appears.[3]

Definition of a Social Problem

Whenever people begin to say, "Isn't it awful! Why don't they do something about it?" we have a social problem. A formal definition might read, *A social problem is a condition affecting a significant number of people in ways considered undesirable, about which it is felt something can be done through collective social action.* This definition has four distinct ideas: (1) a condition affecting a significant number of people; (2) in ways considered undesirable; (3) about which it is felt something can be done; (4) through collective social action. Each of these ideas needs to be examined in detail.

"A CONDITION AFFECTING A SIGNIFICANT NUMBER OF PEOPLE . . ."

One's pet peeves are not social problems unless they also disturb a good many other people. How many people? There is no exact number that must be affected before a condition qualifies as a social problem. But when a condition affects enough people so that many of them notice, talk, and write about it, a social problem exists. One way of measuring public concern about a condition is to count the number (and length) of magazine articles devoted to it each year as listed in the periodical indexes. For example, in all the magazines indexed in the *Reader's Guide to Periodical Literature,* only 1 article on environmental pollution appeared in 1940, 7 in 1950, 13 in 1960, 155 in 1970, 139 in 1975, and 67 in 1979. When numerous articles appear, the condition has clearly attracted widespread concern and has become a social problem. When the number of articles begins to decline, either (1) concern over the problem is waning, or (2) considerable policy agreement about it has been reached.

Doffer boy in a Georgia cotton
mill in the 1930s.
(Library of Congress)

"IN WAYS CONSIDERED UNDESIRABLE . . ."

Child labor was no social problem as long as most people thought child labor was desirable. Only when a considerable number of people decided that
child labor was harmful and began saying, "Isn't it awful!"—only then did
child labor become a social problem. Many people today consider marijuana
use a grave social problem. They believe that marijuana is harmful and
should be forbidden by law. The scientific evidence of harmful consequences of marijuana is inconclusive, but the widespread public *belief* that
marijuana is harmful and should be suppressed makes marijuana use a social problem. A social problem, therefore, involves *a value judgment,* a decision that the condition is "bad." For many centuries witches were feared in
Europe, and witchburnings were a common event. They ended when people began to suspect that the "witches" were merely harmless eccentrics or
annoying neighborhood scolds, totally unable to summon evil powers to do
their evil bidding. In view of today's growing interest in the occult, it is possible that witchcraft may again become a social problem.

These examples show how *values may define any condition as a social problem or prevent designation of any particular condition as a problem.* Suicide,
drunkenness, narcotic addiction, homosexuality, starvation, kissing on Sunday, beating one's children, not beating one's children—any of these may be
defined as a social problem by the values of the society, or they may be defined as nonproblematic because they are acceptable. No condition, no matter how dramatic or shocking to someone else, is a social problem *unless and
until* the values of a considerable number of people within the society define
it as a problem.

"ABOUT WHICH IT IS FELT SOMETHING CAN BE DONE . . ."

Everybody talked about the weather, but nobody did anything about it until
very recently. Conditions that cannot be changed or evaded must be ac-

cepted, usually with the aid of a supporting set of rationalizations. In much of the world, famine was not a social problem until very recently, because famine was seen as part of the natural and unchangeable order of things. Flood control became a social problem only when we decided that floods could be prevented; before that, floods were simply a misfortune to be endured. Now that we may exercise some control over the weather, the weather is becoming a social problem; debate has arisen over who owns the clouds in the sky and who may say where rain shall fall.[4] Now that techniques have been developed for mining the great mineral wealth of the deep seabeds, the lack of a suitable international "law of the sea" has become a serious problem.[5]

The nature of a problem also changes as techniques of treatment are developed. For centuries, the mental illness problem was purely one of protecting the sane and hiding the mentally ill; only recently (and to a lesser degree than might be imagined) has the problem become one of treating and curing the mentally ill. This is not because our ancestors were insensitive, but because they lacked means to treat mental illness.

A condition is a problem *when it is believed* something can be done about it. It is the belief in the possibility of treatment that causes people to consider it a problem. Whether this belief is correct can often be determined only by trial. Meanwhile, the *hope* of treatment is sufficient to lead people to consider a condition a problem and to seek ways of doing something about it.

". . . THROUGH COLLECTIVE SOCIAL ACTION"

If I am the only person who is unhappy over the lack of sitar concerts on television, my discontent creates no social problem. But if thousands of other viewers share my sense of deprivation and think we should do something about it, a social problem develops.

New social problems arise as people discover a condition they consider undesirable and correctible. Then there follow the processes of public discussion, crystallization of value judgments, exploration of alternatives, determination of treatments, and organization of pressure so that the problem can be treated. Social problems are those situations that are so widely disturbing that public concern, opinion formation, and pressure develop in the search for treatment.

Social problems, therefore, are *social in origin* ("a condition affecting a significant number of people . . ."); *social in definition* ("in ways considered undesirable . . ."); and *social in treatment* (". . . about which it is felt something can be done through collective social action").

Bias Implicit in Definition

A *bias* is an unconscious tendency to notice and interpret facts in a way that supports our value preferences. A totally unbiased definition of specific social problems is impossible, because each definition of a problem carries implicit assumptions about the causes of the problem and the kinds of policy outcomes that are desirable. For example, the student revolt in the 1960s against the rules governing campus life might have been defined as a problem of student disorder or as a problem of rule obsolescence. One definition implicitly accepted the rules as appropriate, and looked for the "causes" of the problem in the immaturities and psychological aberrations of rebellious students. The other definition began with the assumption that the student rebellion was a symptom of the obsolescence and inappropriateness of the rules themselves. Similarly, most research in criminology asks, "Why do people break the law?"—not "Why do societies make such laws?" The problem of poverty may be stated as, "What's wrong with the people who are poor?" or, "What's wrong with an affluent society that still has so many poor people?" The problem of homosexuality may be defined as a problem in sex deviation or as a problem of personal liberty. Most statements of social problems, research designs, and policy recommendations have a bias, which has usually been conservative. Their impact has been to preserve the major values and institutions of the existing society. Whether one views this as good or bad depends upon one's own degree of radicalism or conservatism.

Not All Problems "Belong" to Sociologists

In an article in the sociological journal, *Social Problems,* one sociologist scolds social problems textbook writers for not consistently following their own definition.[6] He charges that, after defining social problems as whatever people worry over, we then ignore their choices in organizing our textbooks. As shown by table 1–1, not all the problems listed as most serious by the public are chapter titles in this (or almost any other) social problems textbook.

There is a reason for this omission. Not all social problems lie within the sociologist's field of expertise. Sociologists are not specialists in everything

TABLE 1–1   Major Social Problems as Ranked in 30 Gallup Polls, 1935–1979

Problem	Number of times mentioned in 30 polls
1. War and peace	27
2. High cost of living, inflation	24
3. The economy, including unemployment	23
4. Civil rights and race	16
5. Labor problems	14
6. Crime and delinquency	13
7. Foreign policy	13
8. Taxes	13
9. Lack of religion and morality	9
10. Communism	8
11. Government spending	8
12. Atomic bomb	6
13. Poverty	6
14. Farm problems	5

SOURCE: *The Gallup Opinion Index,* various dates.

The Army recruiting office is a visible reminder of the ever-increasing threat of war in today's world.
(Irene Springer)

and should not act as if they were. Economists are better equipped than sociologists to analyze problems of inflation, unemployment, and taxes; while political scientists can better treat problems of war, peace, and foreign policy. Since no textbook can cover everything, we sociologists should concentrate upon those problems for which our training and experience best qualify us. Furthermore, the focus of this textbook is not upon selected problems themselves, but upon the *sociology* of social problems, that is, upon how and why social problems develop.

Fallacies About Social Problems

Although most people know something about social problems, their "knowledge" is generally unorganized, frequently contradictory, and often incorrect. A listing of some of the widespread fallacies about social problems will reveal that much of this popular "knowledge" is superficial and unreliable.

THAT PEOPLE AGREE ON WHAT THE SOCIAL PROBLEMS ARE

Although many people may agree that housing, poverty, and unemployment are social problems in America, many others emphatically disagree. Important real estate spokespersons have insisted that there has been no real housing shortage. Some religious sects claim that poverty is spiritually beneficial, while some wealthy people argue that poverty is good for people (for other people, that is). Some employers feel that some unemployment is a good thing, for it encourages workers to be quiet and work harder. To some, the marijuana problem is how to suppress marijuana use; to others, the problem is how to change public attitudes and policy and end the persecution of marijuana users. Although there may be considerable agreement upon some problems, agreement is never complete; on other problems there may be very little agreement as to their nature or even their existence.

THAT SOCIAL PROBLEMS ARE NATURAL AND INEVITABLE

To attribute a problem to "natural law" is a delightfully simple way to dispose of it without doing anything about it. The "natural law" cited usually turns out to be an a priori assumption that has emerged from the depths of an armchair rather than from scientific research. The "natural law" of self-interest—that is, that people work hard only for private gain—is easily disproved by data from dozens of other cultures, and hardly explains the motivation of Albert Schweitzer, Eleanor Roosevelt, or Martin Luther King; yet this "law" is often invoked to sanction the status quo. The "natural law" of the survival of the fittest, borrowed from zoology, where it has some application, can easily be shown to be inapplicable to human society, where customs and institutions interfere with the survival process; yet this "law" is cited as a "natural law of society" to sanctify the successful and to discourage sympathy for the unfortunate.

In the chapters that follow we shall see that problems are not products of natural law or physical inevitability. In only one sense are social problems inevitable—namely, that *certain social arrangements make certain outcomes inevitable.* But this is a totally different kind of inevitability, because it is somewhat under human control.

THAT SOCIAL PROBLEMS ARE ABNORMAL

Social problems are often viewed as some kind of breakdown in the established order. When established rules and procedures are ignored or violated, a problem develops. Thus, campus disorder became a social problem when students rebelled, sometimes noisily and violently, against traditional norms of student behavior. This definition fits some problems, but it obscures the important fact that many problems are the product of *normal* behavior, not of breakdowns or deviations in social behavior. For example, our pollution problem is not caused by people suddenly becoming slobs, any more than they always have been. We have a pollution problem because a growing population in an affluent society is creating a rising mountain of refuse, a lot of which will not rust, rot, or burn; consequently, our normal and traditional habits of refuse disposal—dumping it wherever handy—is poisoning our water and littering our land. There is nothing deviant about having babies, but the resulting population explosion is a serious problem. *The traditional, normal, and acceptable behavior of decent people contributes at least as much to the development of social problems as does abnormal, deviant, antisocial behavior.* Even problems that may be viewed as a result of breakdowns or deviations in behavior, such as alcoholism, crime, or drug addiction, cannot be analyzed purely in terms of behavior deviation, for the same social values and pressures that make a person competitive and ambitious may also create the insecurities, frustrations, and failures that encourage such deviations in behavior. Our high divorce rate is usually described, with much hand-wringing, as a symptom of social breakdown; it is much more accurately viewed as a perfectly logical expression of the high value our society now places on individualism and marital happiness. In short, *social problems are the logical, normal, and inevitable products of present social values and practices.*

THAT SOCIAL PROBLEMS ARE CAUSED BY BAD PEOPLE

That social problems are caused by bad people is probably the most widespread fallacy of all. In many ways we are conditioned to analyze problems in terms of a simple good-bad dichotomy. Nursery tales are filled with fair young princes decapitating fiery dragons or evil witches, whereupon all dangers cease and joy reigns forever. Most novels and television shows avoid offending any group by presenting all problems as simple contests between the good people and the bad people; with the defeat of the bad people the matter is happily ended. We shall see, however, that social problems are as often caused by good people who are minding their own business as by bad people who are being bad. For example, when nice people move to a pleasant suburb, carefully zoned to keep out the poor (who, besides, are often black), they help maintain the race and class segregation in housing that helps produce the urban ghetto, the crisis of the city, and a host of other problems. Nice people recoil in well-bred dismay from the squalid homes and festering violence of the urban ghetto, but their actions are partly responsible for these conditions. Social problems persist because nice people tolerate and support the conditions that produce them.

This conclusion is not easy to accept. Religious training has encouraged us to impute evil motives to those who do things we consider evil. To all this conditioning is added the fact that some of the people involved in social problems are doing some bad things—being selfish, brutal, exploitative, lazy, and shiftless. It is easy to conclude that the problem exists *because* some people are obviously at fault. When we observe that a drunkard is unemployed, our conditioning leads us to assume that he is unemployed because he drinks, not that he drinks because he is unemployed. Although either possibility may be true, our conditioning prepares us to accept one explanation without even considering the other.

Conditioning makes the average person's study of social problems an elaborate game of "I Spy," a search for the villain instead of a search for insight. To many people, doing something about a social problem means finding and punishing the "bad" people. The chapters that follow will try to show how *each problem is a product of existing social institutions and practices, not primarily a product of willful wickedness*. We shall see how the "evil" conduct of the persons involved is more properly viewed as a *symptom* of a problem than as its *cause*. We shall also see how merely punishing the "bad" people, although it may relieve our feelings, has very little permanent effect on the problem.

THAT PROBLEMS ARE CREATED BY BEING TALKED ABOUT

The belief that problems are created by being talked about takes the form of the suggestion that it is not entirely decent or "American" to talk about things like slums, poverty, inadequate medical care, or racial discrimination, because ignorant and irresponsible people may become dangerously inflamed. To talk about such things is to "stir up trouble," "foment class hatred," and so on. Of course, this belief is completely undemocratic and therefore "un-American," for it presupposes that the common people cannot be trusted to use responsible judgment. Yet democracy is based on the assumption that the common people *can* be trusted to make wise decisions most of the time.

The fear that talk is dangerous exaggerates people's excitability. Most people are more interested in ball games and television shows than they are in social issues. If you doubt this, try promoting a local forum or discussion group. Reformers have always found the task of arousing people exasperatingly difficult. Only when the problem deeply affects *them*, or sharply threatens *their* cherished values, are most people concerned enough even to listen, let alone do anything about it.

It is true that talk *is* dangerous when there are seething resentments and a sense of festering injustice that talk may inflame. An oppressive social system cannot tolerate freedom of dissent. But we know of no instance of a beneficent social system that was destroyed by criticism. Unless real grievances exist, no amount of publicity will create a problem. The absence of publicity, however, may perpetuate the problem and postpone any action on it, which is just what some people want.

THAT ALL PEOPLE WOULD LIKE TO SEE THE PROBLEMS SOLVED

When the British Admiralty built a string of lighthouses in the Bahamas a century ago, the Islanders were furious; this ended their plunder from the ships they lured onto the reefs with false signal lights.[7] For every social problem, there are some people *who do not want that problem solved*. This writer once talked to a women's group about racial discrimination; the women nodded in sympathetic agreement with each remark, but during the tea that followed, many were heard lamenting that black housecleaners were demanding as much pay as white workers received. Whatever their professed ideals might be, these women did not wish to surrender their genteel exploitation of blacks.

Plenty of well-paid, pleasant jobs for all would mean that the dirty, unpleasant work would simply not be done. The economist argues that unemployment cannot be ended without greatly reducing the income gap between the poor and the affluent—a prospect which the affluent view with no great relish.[8] The big conventions that put so much money in the cash registers of a city's hotels, restaurants, and stores are more likely to visit a city with "good" night-life (high-class prostitution, nude floor shows, "honest" gambling, and after-hours taverns). A too-determined enforcement of the laws governing such attractions would meet the opposition of powerful sections of the business community and of local citizens of all classes who enjoy these attractions. Genuine equality of opportunity would mean that successful parents could no longer pass on their advantages to their children. Should genuine peace between nations break out, the social and economic dislocations would be most painful to a great many people.[9]

For any social problem, a sizable array of groups can be found who do not want its solution. Either their values do not define it as a problem, or a solution would prove costly to them in money, status, power, sentiment, or something else they treasure.

THAT PROBLEMS WILL SOLVE THEMSELVES

A central element of the American ethos is a general expectation of progress. Although the formal theory of automatic and inevitable social progress has taken a beating in the carnage of recent decades, Americans seem to accept it piecemeal, if not in toto. Many discussions of a problem are sprinkled with such sage observations as "Of course, it's improving, and . . ." or

"It's not as bad as it used to be, and . . ." These statements are sometimes descriptively true, yet behind them often lurks the unspoken suggestion that such progress comes about naturally with the passing of time, like the growth of a tree or the melting of an iceberg. From this position it is but a short step to the belief that only patience is needed, for time will solve all problems. This belief rationalizes inactivity; it enables one to make a very creditable display of sympathetic feeling for the unfortunate without requiring the sacrifice of a penny of money or an hour of time. It enables one to be both humanitarian and thrifty.

The belief that problems will be solved if left alone is based on this theory of automatic, inevitable progress, a theory few if any social scientists accept today. To apply it to social problems is naive and unsound. Although some problems (for example, the migrant farm labor problem) may grow less pressing as time passes, others (crime, drugs, pollution) seem to grow more serious. To expect problems to solve themselves is unrealistic and ineffectual.

THAT "GETTING THE FACTS" WILL SOLVE THE PROBLEM

No problem can be treated intelligently without first learning the facts about it, but "getting the facts" is no guarantee that people will interpret facts in the same way. Facts in themselves mean nothing and lead nowhere. Facts must be *interpreted* before they have meaning. Does the fact that a manager earns $100,000 a year and the workers $10,000 mean the manager is earning too much or too little? Does the legalization of abortion illustrate social progress or moral decay? Does the fact that many respectable citizens gamble mean that the laws against gambling should be repealed so that their gambling will be legal, or enforced so that their gambling will be discouraged? Clearly, *a fact has meaning only as it is interpreted according to one's values.* When people have the same values, fact gathering may help resolve their disagreements. When people have differing values, fact gathering cannot possibly resolve their disagreements; it only helps people defend their values more convincingly. Since nearly all social problems involve conflicting value judgments, it is useless to hope that fact gathering will solve them. It is difficult enough for people to agree on means when they share the same ends or goals; when their goals differ, agreement on means is virtually impossible.

The process of getting the facts does, however, have certain utility. Carefully collected facts can demolish the rationalizations through which some people evade the problem. Statements such as "Only lazy bums are on welfare" or "Everyone has an equal chance to make something of himself in America" can be contradicted effectively with facts. Large masses of carefully collected and fully digested facts are needed before people who agree on values and objectives can work out practical modes of treatment. Facts are exceedingly important, but we need a clear understanding of what *can* and what *cannot* be accomplished by fact gathering.

THAT PROBLEMS CAN BE CURED WITHOUT INSTITUTIONAL CHANGES

Many people are like the fat person who wants to reduce without eating less. We would like to solve social problems if we could do so without changing anything. Social scientists are invited to produce a quick, painless social panacea that will solve the problem without anyone's sacrifice of money, power, or sentiment. This is impossible. A complete solution of nearly any problem would require sweeping changes in present institutions and practices. To cure the problem of poverty would require such extensive changes in our educational, economic, and governmental institutions that some of them would become unrecognizable. To solve the housing problem would probably require either a drastic reduction of building costs through new materials and processes or large government subsidies for housing; either solution would involve major institutional changes and exact costly penalties from many vested interest groups. Problems are painful, but so are solutions—and then the solutions create new problems.

Because the genuine solution of social problems nearly always involves sweeping institutional changes that require unpleasant sacrifices, it is unrealistic to expect that these problems will be solved easily or quickly. Most institutional changes come slowly, and therefore basic solutions of social problems will come slowly, if at all. Meanwhile, some *amelioration,* or improvement, may be possible without major institutional change. For example, better street lighting reduces street crime, scholarship programs reduce inequalities of educational opportunity, and welfare programs reduce the suffering of the destitute. Whether such halfway solutions should be attempted is a question that separates conservatives and liberals from radicals and revolutionaries.

Attitudes Toward Social Problems

Our attitudes and values determine the meanings that we find in the facts we observe. A study of some widespread attitudes toward social problems may help show why people react to facts so differently.

INDIFFERENCE

Possibly the most widespread attitude is that of unconcern. Few of us become agitated over anything that does not involve our personal welfare. There is never time enough for all the things we want to do, and there are many diversions more entertaining than boning up on the present status of the migrant labor problem. Pressures of home, family, friends, jobs, and other duties keep us so busy that in idle moments we crave amusement and relaxation, not social surveys and research studies. General interest in a problem is likely to develop only when people sense a serious threat to *their* welfare or a particularly shocking denial of *their* values. The drug problem, for example, became important to comfortable white Americans some years ago when they discovered that it had overflowed the ghetto and was lapping at the suburbs. Similarly, the peace movement among college students suddenly ran out of steam when the draft for service in Vietnam ended in 1971, although the bloodshed in Vietnam continued unabated. Most members of all races, classes, and ages are relatively indifferent to problems that do not appear as direct threats to them.

FATALISTIC RESIGNATION

Another common attitude is the passive acceptance of misfortune. Countless millions have endured great suffering, even starvation, with a calm, stoic resignation. One who believes the way to meet misfortune is to endure it quietly does not attempt to solve the problem. In fact, there *is* no problem—nothing that we should do something about—if one believes misfortune is simply an inescapable fate one must endure. It is not that these people *refuse* to do anything about problems; rather, the thought of trying to do something does not even occur to them. This is the attitude of hundreds of millions of the "wretched of the earth."

CYNICISM

To the confirmed cynic, all talk about social problems is a waste of time; the unfortunates aren't worth getting excited over, and the do-gooders are a bunch of hypocrites secretly grinding their own axes. The cynic believes that people are really a sorry lot, that all people are motivated purely by self-interest and other ignoble motives, and that those who are not completely repulsive are either amiable scoundrels or pious frauds. Since those in trouble are not worth saving, and since their "saviors" cannot be trusted, why not just let such persons stew in their own juice?

Marxists and other radicals often charge that liberals and reformers are merely trying to prop up an exploitative system by making minor concessions. They believe that the liberal reformer's professed sympathy for the unfortunate is a facade for either hypocrisy or self-delusion, behind which the reformer is seeking to perpetuate inequality and oppression. Marxists and other radicals therefore seek social revolution, not social reform.

The widespread indifference to the needs of troubled society members is a sad reality of modern-day society.
(Marc Anderson)

RELIGIOUS RETRIBUTION

The attitude of religious retribution views problems as God's punishment for sin. If there be drought, flood, war, pestilence, depression, high prices, low prices, or other calamity, some proclaim it God's punishment of human sin. If this is true, the solution for social problems is to be found not in social policy or institutional changes, but in penitence, righteousness, and prayer.

All questions about God's intervention in human affairs and the functions of penitence and prayer belong to the fields of philosophy and religion, not to sociology. These are questions for which there are no scientific techniques for seeking an answer. In the study of social problems, however, sociologists *as scientists* can analyze them in terms only of social, rather than supernatural, causation. Furthermore, we now have enough facts about social problems to realize that the theory of religious retribution scarcely does justice to God. It would cast God in the role of one who uses a punishment that is both unjust and ineffectual. The sacrifices of war, depression, and other problems are never equally divided; there is no evidence that only the "wicked" suffer. Neither is there evidence that those who suffer through being poor, ill, unemployed, or shot at become, in general, more godly, righteous, or noble as a result. Instead, there is some evidence that those who survive insecurity and hardship are likely to become selfish, callous, and insensitive. The modern conception of God as wise, just, and loving is not compatible with the theory of religious retribution, but is entirely compatible with the theory that social problems result from imperfectly harmonized social institutions.

ROMANTICIZING

In an explicit sense of the word, to romanticize means to see something the way one wants it to be, not the way it really is. For example, the romanticized view of the Old South presented in the novel and film *Gone with the Wind* was actually true for only a very few people in a very few places. The romanticist's attitude leads people to perceive social problems in a selective manner that is emotionally satisfying—they unconsciously screen their observations to make them fit the ideal world they imagine.

At present, right-wing romantics imagine that the rules and values of colonial America are fully applicable today, and that social problems would be solved by a rededication to individual work, thrift, and moral rectitude. In the romanticized view of many conservatives, virtually everyone gets what he or she deserves in our "free enterprise" system, and with few exceptions the poor are poor because they are lazy, stupid, and improvident.[10] Conversely, many contemporary liberals and radicals perceive the poor as helpless, innocent victims of a rapacious, oppressive society. The left-wing romantic will not concede that any of the poor bear *any* responsibility for their misery; blame is placed upon the middle and upper classes for maintaining their exploitation of the poor.[11] Left-wing romantics dispose of any unflattering characteristics or shortcomings of the "oppressed" either by simply denying them or by redefining them as virtues. For example, the inability of many ghetto children to speak, read, and write standard English well enough to qualify for good jobs or for higher education is romanticized by perceiving their language as a "beautiful" ghetto language, "just as good" as "middle-class" English. Or, as one observer notes, "ghetto romanticism says our [ghetto] home is traumatic to our children, but since we can't change it, let's say that having gone through it has made better adults of our children."[12]

The current literature in social problems contains a great deal of romanticizing, in which the dragon is the oppressive society, the noble oppressed are cast as the fair damsel, and St. George in the form of the radical activist dashes to the rescue. Virtually all sociologists would unhesitatingly agree that exploitation and injustice exist in all societies, including American society, and that blaming the poor and the sick for being poor and sick is futile and unwarranted. But practical solutions to the problems of poverty, ill health, racism, and urban decay will begin with rational analyses, not with romanticized delusions.

SOCIAL SCIENCE

The social-scientific attitude is distinguished from the other attitudes mainly by the social scientist's concern for withholding judgment until all available relevant evidence is assembled and studied. The social scientist asks, "What are the various definitions of the problem? What are the relevant facts? What are the various value judgments? What are the alternative policy options and their probable outcomes?" For example, the social scientist would reject as unsubstantiated the two romanticist views of the poor cited earlier, but would examine both to see what measure of truth there might be in either.

Should social scientists reflect a neutral and unbiased objectivity in the study of social problems? Or should they openly support the interests of the "oppressed" and devote their teaching and research to the promotion of the social policies they feel are desirable? This question—whether sociology should be a value-free science or an activist discipline—is hotly debated among sociologists.[13]

While social scientists are not agreed on value neutrality versus value commitment, there is widespread agreement that the social scientist should be as objective as humanly possible in the conduct of research and in the processing and interpretation of facts. Social scientists should be intellectually honest, should seek understanding rather than the placing of blame, and should not become so emotionally involved in any cause or group that their perception of reality becomes distorted. But some social scientists in all periods have lapsed from science into romanticism.

The social-scientific attitude is the most difficult of all to maintain. It denies us the luxury of allowing our prejudices and hostilities to masquerade as science. It rejects all simplistic, emotional answers to problems. In the social-scientific attitude, successful social policies are found only through painstaking, objective study. Rash conclusion-jumping and polemical posturing are much less work and much more emotionally satisfying (which may be why they are so popular.)

The several attitudes discussed above are not mutually exclusive. Each is an ideal type; that is, each clearly represents an *idea*. But the actual attitudes of each person are likely to be a blend of two or more of these ideal types. Thus, a person may be indifferent or cynical toward one problem, a romanticist regarding another, and social-scientific toward still another; or his attitude toward a particular problem may be a mixture. For example, in viewing the race problem, a person might be cynically indifferent to the anxieties and complaints of one race, a romanticist about another, yet social-scientific in data-gathering and -processing.

Objectives for Study

AWARENESS

Students should become aware of the main social problems. Have you ever visited a place and then been surprised at how often you heard or read about that place afterward? The place had been mentioned just as frequently before you visited it, but you never noticed these comments until you were acquainted with it; thereafter, you noticed each reference because it related to something you knew about. Similarly, an awareness of a particular problem causes us to notice things we would otherwise overlook. We notice each reference to it in the newspaper, possibly take time to read a magazine article, or prick up our ears when it enters conversation. In this way we may constantly increase our knowledge of a problem and the validity of our judgments about it.

FACTUAL KNOWLEDGE

All intelligent analysis must rest upon facts. Shared ignorance is still ignorance. To "discuss" a social problem accomplishes little unless some members of the group know what they are talking about. Although fact gathering will not automatically solve any problem, it is entirely impossible to analyze a problem intelligently until large masses of facts have been collected, organized, and interpreted.

UNDERSTANDING OF THE SOCIOLOGY OF SOCIAL PROBLEMS

To understand the sociology of social problems is to have *a general understanding of why and how problems develop, of how people are affected by them, and of what is involved in dealing with them.* These general understandings become a frame of reference within which data may be catalogued and problems studied. With a thorough understanding of the sociology of social problems, data on any particular problem can be organized quickly, and the problem can be analyzed intelligently. These general understandings help one decide which data are significant and which are trivial; they help one interpret new data correctly and fit them in place mentally to keep one's thinking up to date. The data in this text will become obsolete, and the complexion of many problems may change considerably within a few years; yet if you understand the *sociology* of social problems, you will not find it hard to interpret new data and understand new developments.

RELATION OF THEORY AND PRACTICE

To poke fun at theory and theorists is as American as hot dogs. Our frontier values, which rated skill with an axe and a mule team above skill with Latin verbs and metaphysical propositions, are mirrored in the present pride of the average person in being "practical, not a theorist."

The naiveté of this anti-intellectual bias is evident when one recalls that

17

in social policy, as in most other fields, theory and practice are inseparable. Every practical policy flows from some theory of causation, and every theory carries some implications for control or treatment. The person who tries to separate them merely reveals an ignorance of their relationship, and most self-styled "practical" people are simply unaware of the theories that underlie their actions. For example, the person who says, "Criminals should be punished, not coddled; give them long sentences on the rockpile and they will think twice before doing it again," probably imagines that this is expounding practical common sense untouched by "mere" theory. In truth, however, this person is subscribing to a number of theories. He is applying the 4,000-year-old theory that people are hedonistic creatures determining their actions on the basis of simple pleasure–pain calculations, so that if we make the consequences sufficiently painful, people will refrain from undesirable acts. He is also using the theory that each person is a purely rational being whose actions are determined not by habit or training or emotion, but by coldly rational and logical calculation. Still other theories about the existence of free will, the efficacy of punishment, and the process of learning influence him. Hundreds of pages would be needed merely to state the theories underlying this person's innocent remark, and thousands of books have been written to explain and debate them. Of all this, "practical" persons know nothing; they merely "know" that they have a "practical answer."

People who imagine themselves unmoved by theoretical considerations are, in fact, slaves to the theories of some dead economist or philosopher. Their stout denial of theoretical contamination only reveals their ignorance of the theories that guide their thinking. Both the conservative and the liberal support economic policies derived equally from economic theory; their main theoretical difference is that while one prefers policies based on the theories of classical economists like Adam Smith, Thomas Nixon Carver, and Milton Friedman, the other supports programs based on the newer theories of Thorstein Veblen, Karl Marx, and Paul Sweezy.

Of course, it is true that scholarly individuals may become so immersed in theoretical abstractions that they seem innocently unaware of the realities surrounding them. It is from such persons that the stereotype of the impractical theorist probably was drawn. Sound theory is proved by successful application. Not until it is shown that a theory "works" can we know whether it is sound. Vague theorizing or failure to test the theory at every possible point has no place in science, and a discipline that is guilty of these errors deserves no defense.

It is equally true that practice divorced from theory is not always practical; it may be merely guesswork, sanctified by precedent. One does not become "practical" merely by pronouncing oneself practical. Benjamin Disraeli once observed that the practical person is one who repeats the mistakes of his predecessors. But the truly practical persons, in the field of social policy, are those who know and understand the theoretical underpinning of their recommendations, who know how they have worked out elsewhere, and who have some factual basis for predicting their effectiveness.

To help the student gain a clear picture of the relationship of theory to practice is one of the objectives of this book. To recognize that sound theory is established by successful applications; that no policy is any sounder than the theory from which it flows; that only when one thoroughly understands the theories involved is one qualified to select a practical course of action; that much "practical common sense" is nothing more than guesswork and folklore—to recognize these guidelines is to clear one's mind of a clutter of myth and misconception that obstructs clear thinking.

A SENSE OF PERSPECTIVE

Some people find the study of social problems upsetting. Just as many people are frightened by all the diseases they see dramatized on television, some students are disturbed at the great amount of implied criticism of our society that is included in a social problems course. For some others, the awareness of social imperfections may become almost an obsession. They become so impressed with the suffering, frustration, and waste of a problem-ridden society that they dismiss all hope of reform and recite the litany that our "oppressive" or "sick" society can be cured only by wholesale revolutionary change.

The sick society cliché uses a biological analogy of society as an organism. But a society is not a living organism—it has no body, organs, birth, death, or life systems. Use of biological terms for social structures is a literary device that is inappropriate in a science. The sick society concept has no precise meaning and tells us nothing about the nature of the problem or the cure. It tells us only that the person who uses this concept is unhappy about the state of the society.

The oppressive society cliché, as applied to American society, is applicable only if one considers *all* societies as oppressive—whereupon the concept becomes meaningless. *All* societies impose restraints on people, treat different categories of people unequally (unjustly?), and punish deviation from established social norms. While the ideals of equality, freedom, and justice are far from perfectly realized in American society, any informed comparison will find very few if any societies that are more tolerant of dissent or deviation, more nurturant to the disadvantaged, more supportive of the indigent, or more actively in pursuit of the life enrichment of their racial and ethnic minorities. For each of these criteria one or more countries may be found that surpass the United States, but few if any surpass it in the combination of them all. The oppressive society cliché makes sense as a revolutionary slogan, but not in responsible social science analysis.

A sense of perspective means that present problems are neither evaded nor exaggerated. They are seen against a background of past realities, not of past myths. The popular complaint that "things aren't what they used to be" overlooks the fact that they never were: The past was rarely the tranquil, problem-free pastoral scene we sometimes imagine. Because history books rarely give full details on past problems, today we are simply unaware of how sharp and bitter they may have been. Several historians have recently undertaken to tell their readers what the "good old days" were really like.[14] If people who feel that "it would be unfair to bring children into the kind of world we have today" would read some history, they might be less timid. Some people will probably be amazed to hear that in earlier periods of American history, government was far more corrupt, vote frauds more common, war profiteering far more flagrant, graft more widespread, business methods less scrupulous, minorities more often mistreated, drunkenness more commonplace, hunger and misery far more common, labor violence less restrained, employers incomparably more ruthless, newspapers more often biased, police less efficient and more often brutal, riots far more bloody, and wife beating and cruelty to children more common than they are in America today. To cite one example, between 1790 and 1840, Americans downed nearly a pint of hard liquor per person per day.[15] Those who deplore today's immoralities and long to return to the pieties of the past merely reveal that they do not know their history very well.[16] In fact, some modern problems (for example, prostitution, racial inequality, newspaper bias, influence peddling in government, truth in advertising) have become

Traffic jam at Randolph and Dearborn Streets, Chicago, 1905. Seventy-five years later we still have traffic jams, but of a much more automated variety. (The Bettman Archive, Inc.)

problems because our values now define as undesirable certain behavior that earlier generations accepted without question. A century ago it was taken for granted that a senator had a personal financial interest in any legislation he sponsored (and he often did.)[17] President Nixon resigned in disgrace after actions which would have raised few eyebrows in most countries of the world, or even in the United States of a century ago. In a very real sense, some modern problems have arisen because our standards of public morality are higher than those of our ancestors. This is scarcely a reason for despair.

This text will strive to place each problem in a reasonable perspective, presenting it in its setting of past history, present trends, future prospects, and mitigating circumstances. In this way, it may help you develop an attitude of realistic analysis that avoids the twin extremes of complacent rationalization and naive exaggeration.

APPRECIATION OF THE PROPER ROLE OF THE EXPERT

Americans distrust experts. We want no one telling us what to do. We prefer the common sense of a "plain, practical American" to the theories of some impractical "expert."

Although in a democracy every person is equally entitled to an opinion, it does not follow that all people's opinions are equally valuable. If we want a useful opinion on why our head throbs or our car stalls, we ask an appropriate expert. But when we wonder why a child has grown obnoxious or how to reduce sex crimes, we often disdain to ask the expert and confidently announce our opinions, perhaps after discussing the questions with others who know more about them than we do.

Such inconsistencies arise when people fail to distinguish between *questions of knowledge* and *questions of value*. In matters of knowledge there are right and wrong answers, while in matters of value there are no right and wrong answers, merely differing preferences. In questions of value the layman[18] and the expert are equals, each entitled to his preferences. But in questions of knowledge the layman and the expert are *not* equals, and for the layman to debate a question of knowledge with the expert is futile and presumptuous. To illustrate, the question whether cigarette smoking is injurious to health is one upon which the experts are in general agreement and upon which lay opinions are not worth much; but the question whether the pleasures of smoking justify the risks is a question of value, upon which all opinions are equally legitimate.

Stated in its simplest terms, *the function of the scientific expert is to tell people how to get what they want*. When experts agree on the futility of one policy or the effectiveness of another, it is an arrogant presumption for the layman to disagree. Although it is possible that all the experts are wrong, it is much more likely that the layman is wrong. When the experts disagree among themselves, it is presumptuous for the layman to consider any answer as positive and final. To illustrate, since the experts in criminology agree that criminal behavior is learned and not inborn, laymen who talk of a "criminal instinct" or a "born criminal" simply reveal their ignorance. Since the same experts are not entirely certain what measures will most successfully reduce crime, laymen who confidently prescribe a particular treatment simply make fools of themselves.

In the field of social problems, a proper function of the expert is to provide accurate descriptions and analyses of social problems and to show laymen what consequences will follow each proposed treatment. Since people often want contradictory things (for example, lower taxes with more government services), it is also the function of the social scientist to show laymen wherein their values are incompatible, and where they must compromise or choose between them. More simply, saying to the layman, "If you do this, here is what happens," is the function of the social scientist. The task of students is to learn how to recognize an expert and how to guide their own thinking by expert knowledge rather than by folklore and guesswork.

Is it also the function of the scientific expert to tell people *what they should want*? Should the sociologist, as a scientist, seek to promote gay liberation, legalized marijuana, or income redistribution, and join in all other worthy causes? This is the hotly debated issue of value neutrality versus value commitment, mentioned earlier. The basic question is, "Should the social scientist, as a scientist, make value judgments, beyond his commitment to search for the truth?" Most sociologists of a generation ago said, "No. Sociology should be value-free, a pure science on the model of physics or chemistry, seeking to discover knowledge but not becoming involved in social issues."

Many sociologists today challenge this view, claiming that sociologists *should* state their recommendations in questions of public policy. They feel not only that sociologists should say what society *can* do about race conflict, urban blight, birth control, sex education, and so on but also that sociologists have a duty to say what society *should* do about such problems.

While this remains an unsettled issue among sociologists, the view that sociologists *should* make social policy recommendations and promote social reforms or revolutionary changes seems to be winning supporters.

PERSONAL ORIENTATION

In the course of a study of social problems, the student will probably react personally to them. Each student will have some attitude toward social problems, perhaps one of the attitudes discussed a few pages earlier. Some students have an active interest in social problems and an eagerness to find solutions, while some enroll for other reasons. Yet these students nevertheless find themselves developing attitudes toward the subject they study. To some, social problems represent a subject to be completed, a course to be passed, and not vital situations dramatically and tragically affecting the lives of human beings. To some, the study of social problems may be a depressing recital of miseries and woes, while to others it may be a catalog of suggestions and encouragement. A great many students may find that the continuous emphasis on the institutional setting of social problems fills them with a vast sense of futility—What can one person do? If a problem grows from the ponderous movement of impersonal social trends and forces, what is the use of one person's trying to stem the course of social change?

Granted that one person cannot do much, students who feel impelled to do something should remember that they are never alone. Changes in social policy grow from changes in the thinking of large numbers of people. Although a single person does little to bring about a change, each person is a necessary part of that change merely by being on one side rather than the other. As a famous clergyman has noted, one may avoid a depressing sense of personal helplessness by asking, "Am I part of the problem or part of the answer?"[19] Are you one whose ignorance, indifference, prejudice, and self-interest are obstacles to the building of a more humane society? Or are you one whose sympathetic interest, realistic knowledge, and open-minded receptivity place you on the side of those seeking to promote intelligent social policy? Even though one may accomplish very little alone, the belief that one is on the "right" side is a powerful antidote for despair.

Summary

This introductory chapter outlines the nature and scope of social problems. Social problems are defined as conditions affecting many people in ways thought harmful, but avoidable through social action. Some important social problems are not treated in this textbook, because they lie outside the sociologist's field of specialization. Contrary to widespread but fallacious belief, (1) people do not agree on which conditions are problems; (2) problems are not natural or inevitable; (3) problems are not abnormal, but are normal results of our social arrangements; (4) problems arise from social arrangements, not from "bad" people, and the "badness" of the people involved should usually be viewed as a symptom or result rather than as the cause of the problem; (5) problems are genuine, not illusions created by wild talk; (6) many people do not actually want certain problems solved; (7) most problems do not solve themselves or die out as time passes; (8) "getting the facts" will rarely solve a problem, because people hold different values and want different outcomes; (9) problems cannot be thoroughly solved without major changes in present social institutions and practices.

Different persons hold different attitudes toward social problems. Some are *indifferent* and disinterested. Some are *fatalistically resigned,* accepting social problems as unavoidable scourges to be endured with patience. Some are *cynical* in their belief that the victims of problems are not worth helping and that the reformers are corrupt and venal. Some consider social problems as *religious retribution*, as divine punishment for human misconduct. All four of these attitudes discourage any attempt at treatment. The *romanticists* are guided by emotional wish fulfillment into distorting reality to make it fit the ideal world which they imagine. The *social-scientific* attitude attempts to apply scientific technique to the analysis of a problem so that effective social policies can be developed.

It is our intent that through the study of social problems the student may develop (1) *awareness* of present problems; (2) accurate *factual knowledge* about some of them; (3) some *understanding of their sociological origins*, of the general way in which problems develop; (4) an intelligent understanding of the *relation of theory and practice* in which all theory is tested by practical application, while all practical policy is based on sound theory; (5) a *sense of perspective,* so that a problem is seen in proper relation to the past and present society without distortion or exaggeration; (6) an *appreciation of the proper role of the expert* respecting social problems, with some skill in locating and using expert knowledge and opinions; and (7) a *personal orientation* that is intellectually and emotionally satisfying to the student.

Suggested Readings

BECKER, HOWARD S., "Whose Side Are We On?" *Social Problems*, 14 (Winter 1967), 239–47. A highly sophisticated discussion of how the values and assumptions of sociologists influence their research.

CAUDILL, HARRY M., *Night Comes to the Cumberlands: A Biography of a Depressed Area* (Boston: Little Brown, 1962). A highly readable description of how geographic, historical, political, economic, and social factors have interacted to destroy the lands of the Cumberland Mountain region and to reduce a proud and industrious people to demoralization and apathy. Although the final chapter is somewhat outdated by recent developments, this book is most highly recommended.

DOUGLAS, JACK D., ed., *The Relevance of Sociology* (New York: Appleton-Century-Crofts, 1970). A collection of articles that argue that sociology can be relevant by abandoning value neutrality for an active commitment to social reform.

GOULDNER, ALVIN W., "The Sociologist as Partisan: Sociology and the Welfare State," *American Sociologist*, 3 (May 1968), 103–16. A critique of Becker's article listed above.

HORTON, PAUL B., and DONALD H. BOUMA, "The Sociological Reformation: Immolation or Rebirth?" *Sociological Focus*, 4 (Winter 1971), 25–41. A statement of the case for value neutrality and of possible consequences of value commitment.

LEKACHMAN, ROBERT, "The Specter of Full Employment," *Harper's* (Feb. 1977), pp. 35–40; reprinted in *Current* (Apr. 1977), pp. 13–20. An economist's view of what it would cost us to solve the problem of unemployment.

LEMERT, EDWIN M., "Is There a Natural History of Social Problems?" *American Sociological Review*, 16 (April 1951), 217–23. An attempt to apply the theory of stages of awareness, policy formation, and reform to the problem of regulating trailer courts.

MANIS, JEROME G., *Analyzing Social Problems* (New York: Praeger Publishers, 1976). A short paperback giving an alternative definition and classification of social problems.

Statistical Abstract of the United States (published annually by the U.S. Department of Commerce) and *The World Almanac and Book of Facts* (published annually by the Newspaper Enterprise Association, Inc.). These two books are not readings, but sources of statistical and factual information. They are the most easily accessible sources of data on practically any subject. Every student should thumb through these books to learn what kinds of information can be found in them.

STEINBECK, JOHN, *The Grapes of Wrath* (New York: Viking Press, 1939; Garden City, N.Y.: Sun-Dial Press, 1941; New York: Bantam Books, 1945), ch. 5. A famous and highly controversial social-problem novel dealing with the Okies, the marginal Midwestern farmers whom drought and farm mechanization displaced and converted into migrant farm workers during the 1930s. Chapter 5 raises and gives an answer to the perennial question: Who is to blame?

Footnotes

[1] J. Huizinga, *The Waning of the Middle Ages* (London: Edward Arnold, 1924), p. 22.

[2] Angus Campbell, Phillip E. Converse, and Willard I. Rogers, *The Quality of American Life: Perception, Evaluation, and Satisfactions* (New York: Russell Sage Foundation, 1976); Seymour Martin Lipset, "The Wavering Polls," *The Public Interest*, Spring 1976, pp. 70–89; entire Oct./Nov. 1979 issue of *Public Opinion*.

[3] Sociologists disagree on whether "social problems" should be defined by the general public or by social scientists— whether "social problems" are those situations over which a large number of the public are concerned, or those over which social scientists think the public *should* be concerned. See Jerome G. Manis, "The Concept of Social Problems: Vox Populi and Sociological Analysis," *Social Problems*, 21 (1974), 305–15; and Jerome G. Manis, *Analyzing Social Problems* (New York: Praeger Publishers, 1976). To the authors of this book, social problems are conditions that are socially recognized and socially debated: therefore, we shall follow the public's definition of social problems.

[4] See Robert G. Fleagle, *Weather Modification: Science and Public Policy* (Seattle: University of Washington Press, 1969); Howard J. Taubenfeld, *Controlling the Weather: A Study of Law and Regulatory Processes* (New York: Dunellen, 1971); E. B. Weiss, "International Responses to Weather Modification," *International Organization*, 29 (Summer 1975), 805–26;

Lowell Ponte, "Who Will Control the Weather," *Reader's Digest*, May, 1980, pp. 115–18.

[5]See John C. Siegeer, "Mining the Sea—The Unrealized Potential," *AFL-CIO American Federationist*, June 1979, pp. 1–6.

[6]Robert H. Lauer, "Defining Social Problems: Public Opinions and Textbook Practice," *Social Problems*, 24 (Oct. 1976), 122–31.

[7]See " 'Wreckreation' Was the Name of the Game That Flourished 100 Years Ago," *New York Times*, 30 Mar. 1969, p. 14.

[8]Robert Lekachman, "The Specter of Full Employment," *Harper's*, Feb. 1977, pp. 35–40.

[9]See Special Study Group, *Report from Iron Mountain on the Possibility and Desirability of Peace* (New York: Dial Press, 1967), for a grave discussion of these painful consequences, published in a tone of serious scholarship but soon found to be an elaborate hoax. While a brilliant piece of political satire, it raises genuine issues.

[10]See Edward C. Banfield, *The Unheavenly City* (Boston: Little, Brown, 1970), and *The Unheavenly City Revisited* (Boston: Little, Brown, 1974), for a modern statement of this venerable idea.

[11]For example, see William Ryan, *Blaming the Poor* (New York: Pantheon Books, 1971); James J. Graham, *The Enemies of the Poor* (New York: Random House, 1970); and Nathan Caplan and Stephen D. Nelson, "Who's to Blame?" *Psychology Today*, Nov. 1974, pp. 99–104.

[12]Linda J. M. LaRue, review of Joyce A. Ladner, *Tomorrow's Tomorrow: The Black Woman*, in *Society*, Feb. 1972, p. 59.

[13]See Alvin W. Gouldner, "Anti-Minotaur: The Myth of a Value-Free Sociology," *Social Problems*, 9 (Winter 1962), 199–213; Howard S. Becker, "Whose Side Are We On?" *Social Problems*, 14 (Winter 1967), 239–47; Paul B. Horton and Donald H. Bouma, "The Sociological Reformation: Immolation or Rebirth?" *Sociological Focus*, 4 (Winter 1971), 25–41; Dennis C. Foss, *The Value Controversy in Sociology* (San Francisco: Jossey-Bass, 1977).

[14]See Otto Bettman, *The Good Old Days—They Were Terrible* (New York: Random House, 1974); and Henry Fairlie, *The Spoiled Child of the Western World* (New York: Doubleday, 1976).

[15]W. J. Rorabaugh, *The Alcoholic Republic: An American Tradition* (New York: Oxford University Press, 1979).

[16]The sexual license of the later Roman Empire, the Renaissance, and the Restoration are well known. Yet even the Victorian period, supposedly so prim, was in fact indulgent. Most wealthy men had mistresses, and prostitutes in eighteenth-century London were at least 50 times as numerous, in proportion to population, as they are today. See Cyril Pearl, *The Girl with the Swansdown Seat* (Indianapolis: Bobbs-Merrill, 1956); or Steven Marcus, *The Other Victorians: A Study of Sexuality and Pornography in Mid-Nineteenth Century England* (New York: Basic Books, 1966), for a well-documented look beneath the surface of Victorian respectability. For more Victorian horror stories, see Charles Terrot, *Traffic in Innocents* (New York: E. P. Dutton, 1960).

[17]For example, Daniel Webster, eloquent senatorial defender of the National Bank, saw nothing improper in writing to the bank's director in the midst of Senate debate over renewing the bank's charter, complaining that "my retainer has not been received or refreshed as usual."

[18]With regard to social problems, the term *layman* refers to everyone except social scientists. Workers, farmers, business people, and government administrators are all laymen where social problems are concerned, just as the sociologist is a layman in the field of farm technology or medical diagnosis.

[19]Harry Emerson Fosdick, "Are We Part of the Problem or Part of the Answer?" *National Education Association Journal*, 36 (Dec. 1947), 621–22.

Marc Anderson

APPROACHES TO THE STUDY OF SOCIAL PROBLEMS 2

An Indian Tsar commanded that all blind men be gathered together, and when they were collected, he commanded that they be shown his elephant. The blind men went to the stables, and began to feel the elephant.

One felt the leg; another, the tail; the third, the rump; the fourth, the belly; the fifth, the side; the sixth, the back; the seventh, the ear; the eighth, the head; the ninth, the tusk; and the tenth, the trunk.

The Tsar called the blind men to him, and asked them: "What is my elephant like?"

And one blind man said, "Thy elephant is like a pillar." This blind man had felt the leg.

The second blind man said, "Thy elephant is like a broom." This blind man had felt the tail.

The third said, "It is like wood." This man had felt the rump.

The man who had felt the belly said, "An elephant is like lumps of earth."

The man who had felt the side said, "It is like a wall."

The man who had felt the back said, "It is like a hill."

The one who had felt the ear said, "It is like a handkerchief."

The one who had felt the head said, "It is like a mortar."

The one who had felt the tusk said, "It is like a horn."

The one who had felt the trunk said, "It is like a stout rope."

And all the blind men began to dispute and quarrel.[1]

Reprinted by permission of The Reporter, New York.

Each of the blind men was telling the truth. An elephant *is* like a pillar, *and* like a wall, *and* like a rope. Yet, anyone depending on blind men for a description of an elephant will undoubtedly be misled and confused. An elephant, like a social problem, may be studied from more than one point of view.

Some Oversimplified Interpretations of Social Problems

There are more people afflicted with intellectual blindness, or at least shortsightedness, than there are people whose eyes are sightless. Intellectually shortsighted people sometimes produce simplistic interpretations of complex social problems. We shall examine several widely shared, over-simplified explanations of social problems to show their inadequacies.

Simplistic explanations of social problems share a common characteristic: they all propose a *single main cause* for social problems in general. That single cause is often an important factor, and the interpretations of it that are offered are frequently partly correct. The proposed single cause emerges not from examination of all the relevant data, however, but as a revelation from some "inspired" theory or doctrine. Data are used, ignored, or twisted according to whether they harmonize with the doctrine. Such abuses of data are obviously unscientific.

EUGENIC INTERPRETATIONS

Some people believe that bad social conditions are caused primarily by bad genes; if only human reproduction could be properly regulated, most social problems would disappear. This faith is misplaced, however, for two reasons: First, genes are only one of many factors determining behavior. Second, we do not yet know exactly what behavior is genetically determined. Eugenic programs do not offer a basis for solving social problems.

RACIST INTERPRETATIONS

Many people believe that some form of race-related behavior lies at the root of most social problems. White racists blame poverty, crime, and urban decay upon the bad genes and slovenly habits of black people. Black racists, in turn, see white racism as the only cause of all problems that plague black people. As chapters 12 and 13 will show, both views are grossly oversimplified.

RELIGIOUS INTERPRETATIONS

Millions of Christians accept as an article of faith that the basic cause of social ills lies in the evil human heart. Consequently, they believe that all solutions must begin with the transformation of sinful human nature through divine redemption. Unfortunately for this argument, most of the evidence shows that the social behavior of religious people does not differ conspicuously from that of irreligious people.[2]

The history of religious schisms and conflicts reveals that even members of the same faith cannot always get along with one another. Moreover, periods of intense religious fervor have not been notably peaceful. As we shall see many times in this book, the well-intentioned behavior of decent, godly people is an important contributing factor to many social problems. Obviously, any exclusively religious analysis of social problems will be inadequate.

MARXIST INTERPRETATIONS

Although Marxists differ among themselves as much as Christians do, Marxist scholars generally agree that class exploitation is the basic cause of social problems. Thus, they view racism as a device to justify exploitation of one race by another. Poverty exists because the wealthy classes want it to, and wars persist because they are profitable to the capitalists who run the country.

Such Marxist analyses are neither entirely wrong nor wholly adequate, because they ignore all data that do not fit. They ignore the fact that racism has cultural and psychological roots as well as economic ones, for example, and that poverty has many causes. Finally, the naiveté of the war-profits thesis is revealed by rises in stock prices with each burst of peace news.

Marxists believe that the only solution to social problems is socialist revolution; all more moderate reforms are mere diversions, designed to preserve an exploitative system. They ignore the fact that socialist revolutionary regimes, such as those in Russia and Cuba, have as many and as persistent social problems as we do; or they explain this situation as the result of failure to apply socialist principles properly. Marxists, like Christian theologians, blame human failure rather than the unsoundness of their ideology for their inability to recreate the Garden of Eden. They are ingenious in blaming capitalist failures on the capitalist system, and socialist failures upon human imperfection.

Some sociologists employ Marxist analyses in the study of social problems, with varying degrees of balance and perspective.[3] The authors of this book do not view Marxist analyses as categorically wrong; in fact, we frequently note how our predominantly capitalist society operates to create and perpetuate social problems. But it is our conviction that exclusively Marxist analyses are invariably unbalanced and incomplete—one point of view to be considered, but not a set of absolute truths to be revered.

Sociological Frame of Reference

Students who have taken courses in sociology will be familiar with the sociological point of view. For others, it may be helpful to discuss certain aspects of the sociological frame of reference.

SOCIAL CHANGE

Although the change may be gradual and unnoticed, all societies are constantly changing. Social change may be planned, but more often it takes place without plan or intent. Virtually every act of every individual leaves a particular situation different than it was before the act occurred; even when the act is a conscious attempt to prevent change, some kind of change follows. Thus, the attempt of a farmer to resist the federal government's corn acreage allotment controls inevitably affects the government's authority over agriculture: if he can defy the government successfully, its authority is weakened; if he must eventually comply, its authority is confirmed. Either way, he has effected change. Thus, the actions of farmers, whether compliant or evasive, become elements in structuring a social problem. In like manner, people sometimes oppose new industry because they wish to "keep our town as it is now." Without new growth and opportunity, the young people migrate, the buildings age, so the town does *not* remain unchanged. People may be unaware of helping change the social group in which they live, but they do so nevertheless.

Not all aspects of a society change at the same rate, however, or even in the same direction. The automobile and our highway system, for example, have given youth an unprecedented opportunity to escape the watchful eyes of their elders. Profound changes in courtship patterns and in criminal behavior are only two of the unanticipated results. The translation of atomic energy into bombs has far outdistanced the development of political attitudes or skills adequate to handle the resultant problems. The principle implied here—that changes in technology often occur more rapidly than changes in customs and beliefs—has led to the formulation of the concept of "culture lag."[4] One eminent sociologist observed that technological change requires that adjustments be made in other (nonmaterial) aspects of the culture and that there is generally a time lag before such adjustments are made. Hence, the development of the automobile encouraged an earlier physical involvement among dating couples and showed that new social controls would be needed if the former rules were to be enforced. Whether these adjustments have yet been made is debatable. The time lag involved is the period of *culture lag;* the resulting breakdown in time-honored courtship practices would be called *social disorganization.*

The constancy of culture change and its different rates are two major principles in the understanding of human behavior; consequently, they are important in the analysis of social problems.

CULTURAL RELATIVITY

Social practices are almost infinitely variable. Governments are democratic, republican, oligarchical, or totalitarian; they are elaborate and formal, or they may operate informally under a chief, a headman, or a matriarch. The means of production may be privately owned and controlled, they may be privately owned and publicly regulated, or there may be substantial public ownership. People may worship one god or many—through fasting, meditation, and self-denial or through feasting, dancing, and orgy. Any of these cultural practices may meet the needs of a given society. This ability of human beings to devise endless ways of solving group problems stands at the heart of the concept of cultural relativity.

Societies are generally ignorant of the principle of cultural relativity. Instead, each society tends to believe that its ways of doing things are the most logical and proper ways—indeed, that they may be the *only* right and proper

The diverse cultural traditions present in American society today challenge us to seek viable approaches to accommodate all peoples into the overall community.
(San Francisco Convention and Visitors Bureau)

ways. Sociologists call this *ethnocentrism*. They recognize that ethnocentrism restricts the range of possible solutions that may be found for social problem situations.

The concept of cultural relativity implies that *a trait has no meaning by itself; it has meaning only in its cultural setting.* No custom is either good or bad by itself; it is good if it harmonizes with the rest of the culture in which it functions, and bad if it clashes with the rest of its culture. Thus, the immolation of the widow upon the funeral pyre of her husband may be "good" in a society that provides no place for widows in its social system. Polyandrous marriage, with several husbands sharing one wife among them, is very practical for a primitive people who *must* keep their population in check or face starvation in their environment. This is the meaning of cultural relativity: every idea or practice must be understood in terms of its relation to the other parts of the culture within which it occurs. This concept helps us understand some of the stresses within our society and some of the difficulties in finding agreeable relief from them.

LEARNED BEHAVIOR

The recognition that personality, or behavior, stems largely from the society and culture in which the individual lives is one of our most important discoveries. Whether one is sad or joyful at the death of a loved one depends on how death is defined by one's culture. Whether one shows grief by laughing or by crying is culturally defined. In one society boys are taught to be aggressive and domineering, while in another the male is supposed to be shy and dependent. In the United States, middle-class pupils seek the teacher's approval while lower-class children invite the teacher's censure;—both are seeking recognition from their fellow students. Biologically the human species is one, but human behavior varies strikingly from group to group and from culture to culture.

In the study of social problems, one frequently encounters the argument that proposed changes are undesirable because they are contrary to human nature or to the customary ways of doing things. They supposedly will not work because they are new, or different, or "radical." The student who understands the above principles will require more satisfactory evidence than such a priori statements before either accepting or rejecting proposed solutions to social problems.

Approaches to the Study of Social Problems

Because of the tremendous number and involved nature of social problems, no single approach to their study has proved wholly satisfactory. At least three relatively distinct approaches have proved useful in the study of various problem situations: (1) the social-disorganization approach, (2) the personal-deviation approach, and (3) the conflict-of-values approach. Each of these approaches will be employed in examining the specific social problems treated throughout this book.

THE SOCIAL-DISORGANIZATION APPROACH

All social life occurs in a setting of regulation. The behavior of individuals and groups is controlled through a vast network of rules or norms that define which behaviors are permissible, desirable, or mandatory. At the most formal level, that of *law,* the norms are codified; that is, they are written down, and punishments are specified for each violation. Thus the law prohibits the unprovoked killing of another person and specifies death or a long prison term for murderers; the punishment for illegal parking is a small fine; continued unsanitary conditions in a restaurant may lead to its being closed. Most of the norms in any society, however, are less formal than laws. They take the form of certain *expectations* about how people will act. We expect the police officer to enforce the law, the mother to love her children, and the worker to get to work on time. Such expectations pervade every aspect of life and operate unobserved—as long as they operate effectively.

This network of socially sanctioned expectations about personal behavior makes up most of what the sociologist calls *social organization.* These expectations are internalized by the members of a society and, except in the face of unexpected rapid change, they ensure the smooth functioning of the society. People usually act as others expect them to act, and moral concepts of "right," "natural," and "good" become associated with these customary ways of behaving.

Not always, though, do rules function efficiently. They are especially vulnerable to breakdown under the influence of social change. People try to adjust to the new conditions by adhering to time-honored ways, but instead of satisfaction, they reap frustration and unhappiness. The order and predictability of former days are replaced by confusion and chaos. This is the condition of social disorganization.

One of the routes to a competent analysis of social problems is via analysis of the social disorganization that accompanies social change. Whether one is talking about the problems that plague the modern family or the issues that surround racial integration, one needs to understand how the

Every society expects its people to exhibit some common social behaviors; a mother demonstrates love and protection of her child, for example, in this scene of North Carolina hurricane victims.
(American Red Cross photo by Ted Carland)

present issues have developed. The social-disorganization approach assumes that, at some time in the past, a problem did not exist or was not recognized. It assumes that a society once had a fairly stable equilibrium in which practices and supporting values were in harmonious agreement. Then social change of some kind disrupted this harmonious agreement. Change brought new practices or new conditions in which the old practices no longer worked properly, or new knowledge that made old practices look foolish, or new value judgments that declared old practices no longer endurable. In the resultant confusion, old rules were both debated and ignored, yet no new rules were generally accepted. Change had *disorganized— disrupted the organization of*—the former system of behavior. Eventually, according to this approach, new rules and practices will develop, and a new equilibrium will appear and be preserved until it is disrupted by another round of change.

For example, the development of the trailer, or mobile home, has created some new problems. "Home" normally means a fairly permanent abode enshrined in sentiments and values and embedded in a network of laws, regulations, and tax policies. Within the generation or so since the mobile home appeared, it has come to house over nine million people—more than live in our 13 least populous states. The tax laws, sanitary regulations, and other policies developed for conventional homes are not practical for mobile homes and mobile-home courts. Mobile-home dwellers are accused of avoiding their fair share of taxation, of overcrowding local schools and other public facilities, and of depressing real estate values. Many communities have sought to exclude mobile-home residents by legal regulations of various sorts. Yet the mobile-home population is growing constantly. Other communities have sought to revise their tax laws, zoning restrictions, and other regulations affecting housing in such a way as to take into account the different nature of the mobile home. Eventually most communities will come to terms with this new way of living, thus completing the cycle of organization, disorganization through social change, and eventual reorganization.[5]

There are no periods of complete cultural stability separated by cycles of change, for change, disorganization, and reorganization are going on continuously. Yet it is helpful in understanding a particular problem to look for an earlier period of relative stability, from which the present situation has developed. In analyzing specific social problems we always need to ask, "To what extent does this problem stem from social change and social disorganization?" and "What can the direction of social change tell us about the possible resolution of the problem?"

Specifically, in applying the social-disorganization approach to social problems, here are some of the questions we ask:

1. What were the traditional rules and practices?
2. What major social changes made them ineffective?
3. Which of the old rules have broken down? To what extent?
4. Is the social change continuing? How fast? In what direction?
5. Who are the dissatisfied groups? What solutions do they propose?
6. How do various solutions fit the trend of social change?
7. What new rules may be the accepted rules in the future?

THE "SICK SOCIETY" VARIANT   One variation of the social-disorganization approach is based on the concept of the "sick society." This concept was widely used by sociologists during the late 1800s and early in the present century, when the bio-organismic school of social thought was popular.[6] Recently, the "sick society" concept has been resurrected in a new form by the radical sociology movement. This group promotes a romanticized view of society in which corrupt institutions prevent basically good individuals and groups from acting with kindness and generosity as they share the good things of life. Blacks, women, the poor, and various minorities are seen as special victims of an increasingly dehumanizing system.[7]

But while organisms may get "sick" in ways that can be precisely described by scientists, societies are not organisms and do not suffer from maladies such as inflammation of the lungs or fibrillation of the heart muscle. Analogies are useful literary devices that should be viewed as colorful prose, not scientific description. Societal problems cannot be analyzed in medical terms, and the use of the biological analogy often confuses rather than informs.

Specifically, the advocates of the "sick society" approach have not been explicit either about how society became "sick" or about what can be done to restore it to "health." They generally call for a revolution on the assumption that corrupt institutions must be replaced by good institutions before corrupt people can become good, but they supply very few guidelines for accomplishing this goal. The social-disorganization approach that emphasizes the continuous organization-disorganization-reorganization cycle is generally regarded as more useful than the "sick society" variant of that approach.

THE PERSONAL-DEVIATION APPROACH

In employing the social-disorganization approach to social problems, one looks to the rules that have broken down, to the general social change that has accompanied the breakdown, and to the new rules that are emerging. In using the personal-deviation approach, one looks to the motivation and behavior of certain *people* who are influential in causing the problem, in defining its nature, and in proposing solutions to the problem or opposing them. These people are deviants whose deviancy is bound up in many ways with social problems. We need to know how personal deviancy develops and what types of personal deviation are frequently involved in social problems.

PSYCHOLOGICAL DEVIATION   Deviancy does not spring full-blown from germ plasm—at least in the vast majority of cases. Individuals ordinarily become deviant or nondeviant in the process of learning the norms (rules) of their societies. The development of deviancy is literally the development of personality. In the development of deviancy there may be either an inability to follow generally accepted norms or a failure to accept those norms.

Inability to follow generally accepted norms   Some persons are so constituted biologically, emotionally, or socially that they are incapable of adhering consistently to generally accepted standards. They are biologically, emotionally, or socially *deficient.* The socially deficient do not truly violate norms; rather they manifest an inability to learn and follow the norms. The existence of large numbers of such inadequate persons is, in itself, a social problem.

With the mentally deficient the cause of deviancy is often biological; however, several other groups are totally unable to follow generally accepted norms. Narcotics addicts, alcoholics, and compulsive gamblers, for example, have little power to alter their deviant patterns. Most of these individuals have internalized society's norms early in life, but they appear, for reasons that are primarily emotional or social, not to have the control over their behavior expected of normal members of society. These deviants constitute social problems, and they also add substantially to related problems; for instance, they often require medical treatment or are involved in criminal activities.

Failure to accept generally accepted norms   With some alcoholics, narcotics addicts, and the like there has obviously been a failure in the socialization process. Though many of them have learned the norms and have come to accept them as bases for judging right behavior from wrong, they cannot follow them. A different sort of deficiency in socialization occurs when a person fails to accept the society's norms in the first place. Some individuals never seem to be able to accept the standards of judgment of the conventional people around them. They never accept the values inherent in fair play, honesty, truthfulness, personal integrity, justice, cooperation. They are apt to lie, to cheat, to defame, to exploit, or even to kill when it suits their purposes to do so. Since they have never accepted society's norms in the first

Compulsive gambling—at the racetrack or otherwise—is often defined as a
social problem.
(Irene Springer)

place, their deviant behavior does not produce in them the guilt and shame that would be experienced by more adequately socialized persons. Psychologists use the general term *character disorder* to refer to the variety of symptoms that accompany the failure to develop a normal social conscience. Such people are often involved in social problems. They seek power, wealth, and personal aggrandizement. They may change sides completely on a social issue if it serves their purposes to do so. They care little whether social problems exist or whether they are solved, so long as the existent situation can be used to their personal advantage.

SOCIAL DEVIATION   While the basic inability of some persons to become properly socialized and the gross failures of the socialization process account for some deviant behavior, these essentially psychological explanations leave much of the deviance in modern societies unaccounted for. The bulk of deviant behavior probably stems from social causes.

Sociologists have identified three major ways in which social deviation develops and have constructed partial theories about them. They are called labeling theory, anomie theory, and cultural supports theory.

Labeling theory   One group of sociologists makes a sharp distinction between *primary deviance* and *secondary deviance*. The idea of labeling is central to the concept of secondary deviance.[8]

According to this theory, primary deviance refers to the occasional deviant behavior of people who generally conform. Violations of social norms are exceedingly common, and virtually all persons are occasional violators. Every person who eases through a stop sign without coming to a complete halt, every minor who buys a drink, and every person who hedges on an income tax return is a lawbreaker.[9] All such acts contribute in a minor way to the development of social problems.

Such primary deviance, however, is not so significant a cause of social problems as is the secondary deviance that may develop from it. Secondary deviance occurs when the person's deviant behavior is discovered by others and is *labeled* as deviant. Thus, the effects of pot smoking may be benign unless the person is caught and labeled a criminal. Similarly, a teenage boy who has sexual intercourse with a girl a year or two younger than himself may be discovered and labeled a rapist, even if the girl consents to the act. All kinds of deviance—drinking, homosexual behavior, prostitution, burglary, and so on—may be so labeled.

Once people are publicly identified as drug addicts, rapists, thieves, prostitutes, or whatever, they are treated differently by other people. They find themselves increasingly ostracized by the "straight" world, forced into association with other deviants who have been similarly labeled. What began as a simple deviant act sets in motion a series of forces that completely alter the individual's life organization. Labeling theorists assign primary importance to this process in the creation of the organized social deviation that is a major factor in the emergence of social problems.

Anomie theory   The term *anomie*, which means normlessness, refers to a situation in which there is widespread loss of respect for the normative order:

National Guardsmen during a Miami race riot and young Amish folk during a Whitsun Day party in Lancaster County, Pennsylvania—the contrast vividly highlights the extreme polarities that can simultaneously exist within a given society.

(United Press International and Jane Latta, Photo Researchers, Inc.)

people are ambivalent about conforming to and deviating from previously accepted norms.[10] The violation of norms occurs on a large scale.

The traditional use of narcotics by lower-class people in the United States as a way of escaping the pain and frustration of everyday living provides an example. Urban neighborhoods with high rates of drug use also tend to be characterized by low educational attainment and high rates of family breakdown. Anomie appears to be a consequence of slum living conditions.

Mental illness provides a second illustration. Statistics show that more men than women, more single than married people, more urban than rural people, and more ethnic and racial minority group members than native whites are committed to mental institutions. The explanation appears to be that both mental illness rates and commitment rates are higher as a result of the disorganized living conditions of the inner city. Financial hardships, overcrowding, anonymity, and frustration either produce mental illness directly or at least expose the deviant behavior of mentally ill people to public authorities.

Cultural supports theory   This theory employs the concepts of *subculture* and *counterculture*. Subcultures are essentially cultures within a culture, comprehensive enough so that people may live in virtual isolation from the norms of the larger society. (The ways of life of the Amish and the Hutterites provide illustrations.) Countercultures are a special type of subculture in which the subculture norms are in direct conflict with the norms of the larger society. Countercultures require their members to act in ways that are defined as deviant by the larger society. (Delinquent street gangs provide a good example.)

Both the labeling and anomie theories assume that norms are violated by people who accept those norms and are aware of the violation. Cultural supports theory does not. It assumes that some groups do not accept the society's norms and values in the first place.[11]

Cultural supports theory is most useful in the explanation of criminal behavior. Slum youth are indoctrinated with criminal norms as an approved way of life. Boys may develop deviant forms of life organization by moving up from petit-larceny gangs to hijacking or racketeering as naturally as middle-class boys move up from kindergarten through college to a profession.

Persons who are deviant by virtue of membership in a counterculture are not simply maladjusted people. They may be well adjusted to the expectations of their deviant groups, though they appear maladjusted to outsiders in the larger society. Moreover, it is doubtful whether many such people can live out their lives without having reference groups in the larger society. To the extent to which such conformist reference groups exist, persons operating in countercultures are exposed to emotional conflict. For at least some of them, such conflicts are severe.

Personal deviation is involved in social problems in several different ways. Some deviants are maladjusted people whose neurotic compulsions, enthusiasms, hates, and determination involve them in continuing conflict. Such fanatic people help create social problems, demand that their pet solutions be adopted, and are ruthless in their efforts to stamp out opposition. Other deviants become problems when they are stigmatized by a society that insists upon labeling their behavior and treating them accordingly. The breakdown of norms so characteristic of deteriorated inner-city areas both causes personal deviation and makes it more visible. Finally, deviant subcultural patterns are inevitable in complex societies.

In applying the personal-deviation approach to social problems, we ask the following questions:

1. What deviant persons and groups are involved?
2. Are the deviants basically maladjusted people? What motivates them?
3. Are deviants themselves the problem? In what way?
4. How much of the deviance is a product of labeling? Is the deviance harmful to anyone other than the deviants themselves?
5. Are counterculture norms involved? What are these norms?

6. How much of the deviance stems from breakdown of the norms for certain social groups? To what social conditions does this breakdown trace?

7. What alternatives are there for dealing with these situations?

THE VALUE-CONFLICT APPROACH

A society's values are its estimates of worth—its preferences and its rejections. A society derives its character from its values, whether they be monogamy, democracy, and practicality or opposite values, such as polyandry, theocracy, and impracticality. Modern societies, moreover, are characterized by diversity and heterogeneity. Rather than *one* set of values each society has *many* sets of values—which results in disagreements about values.

VALUE CONFLICTS HELP PRODUCE SOCIAL PROBLEMS   Value conflicts in modern society help produce social problems in the following two ways: First, they help produce problems through conflicting definitions of desirable social conditions; second, they foster moral confusion, which encourages personal deviation.

Conflicts over whether problems exist   Many of the most bitter conflicts surrounding social problems arise over whether a given condition is desirable or should be regarded as a problem. Given social conditions do not equally affect all parts of the society. Some groups profit from conditions that produce misery for others. And whether profit or advantage is involved or not, value differences that lead to conflicting definitions of social conditions remain. Prostitution and racial discrimination, for example, are subject to widely conflicting definitions in the United States. Prostitution is denounced from the pulpit, by the medical profession, and by many individuals and groups who deem it a moral threat to the family structure. Others argue that both history and biology amply demonstrate that the sex drive should not be denied. They view prostitution as a necessary evil that provides a temporary solution to sexual frustration. At the same time, some landlords, some tavern owners, and some highly respectable business people who want to "entertain" customers find that prostitution is highly profitable. To some, racial discrimination in the United States is a moral blight; to others, it is the inevitable result of inherent differences between the races. Some whites and some blacks profit more by preserving discrimination than by eliminating it. It is the exception rather than the rule when most groups agree that a given condition represents a problem to be eliminated. A problem is usually compounded because there is universal acceptance neither of its existence nor of a definition of its nature.

Value conflicts encourage personal deviation   Not all value conflicts in a society derive from the failure to accept a given condition as a problem. Conflicting values permeate the American social fabric and are internalized within the individual personality during its growth. People are taught that they should be scrupulously honest; at the same time, they are taught that it is important to be successful in their occupations. Yet complete honesty and success are not only *not* the same thing, they are fundamentally incompatible at many points. Similarly, church attendance, a certain humility, and concern with otherworldly things are religious values widely acknowledged in this society. At the same time, it is considered important to amass material goods and to conform to the demands of peers for cocktail parties or for golf on Sunday. One result of conflicts such as these is the creation of moral confusion in the society, which in turn encourages personal deviation. Constant exposure to conflicting values may lead to the individual's inability to hold to any values consistently. Such confusion fosters personal irresponsibility; it encourages one to define social problems strictly in terms of personal gain. Such confusion may result in enlarging problem areas due to the desperate efforts of a floundering personality to find certainty and security through pathologically becoming identified with a "cause."

THE NATURAL HISTORY OF SOCIAL PROBLEMS   Value conflicts are involved in the origin, the definition, and the solution of social problems. The idea of a regular series of stages through which problems pass in the process of being defined and solved was originated by Richard Fuller[12] and elaborated by Malcolm Spector and John Kitsuse.[13]

Stage 1: Private troubles into public issues   Many conditions that eventually are defined as social problems are not so regarded at first. Eventually, some groups begin to complain about the situation. The complaining groups may be the victims of the imputed problem condition, such as welfare recipients complaining about the demoralization that the system imposes upon them; or the complainants may be other interested groups, such as social workers or members of the clergy. In the first instance the complainants are developing interest groups, and in the second case they might be called moral crusaders.

Stage 2: Official recognition   The second stage begins when some governmental or other influential agency responds to the group's complaints. Official hearings may be held, with the complainant group invited to testify as "experts" on the problem. If the agency accepts the legitimacy of the problem, an organization may be created to deal with the complaints of the aggrieved and to afford them relief. On the other hand, the complaining group may be effectively "cooled out" by the appointment of a committee to "study the problem." This cooling out may be done at the highest levels of government: witness the refusal of presidents to accept and act upon the reports of presidential commissions on obscenity and pornography, marijuana, and violence.

Stage 3: The shifting of complaints   Regardless of the intent of the agency or agencies involved—that is, whether they seriously try to ameliorate the problem condition or merely seek to divert attention from it—the bureaucratic response is seldom successful or satisfactory. In the third stage, the complaints shift from the original ones to new ones about the agency response. Complaints originally directed at environmental pollution, for example, are redirected at the Environmental Protection Agency's formulation of policies favorable to industry. The complaining groups in stage 3 may be the same ones who complained about the original problem in stage 1, or they may be different groups who have become involved more recently.

The new complaints may lead to an altered bureaucratic response. There may be a personnel shake-up in the responsible agency, new procedures may be instituted, or a new and more specialized agency may be set up to deal with the problem. These efforts may lead to more effective ways of dealing with the problem, or they may simply increase cynical and hostile attitudes toward government and officialdom in general.

Stage 4: Pursuit of alternative strategies   If the original or revised bureaucratic responses to the problem are adequate, stages 3 and 4 may never develop. If they are not, however, and if public confidence in official agencies apparently is deteriorating, then the final stage of disillusionment with official responses and the pursuit of alternative strategies may be reached. Complainants may conclude that it is impossible to work within the system and may react to protect themselves by pursuing essentially private and local solutions to their problems. Those who complain of inadequate police protection, for example, may form vigilante patrols for their communities. Groups opposed to busing in the public school system may create private schools for their children. Such solutions may be either temporary or "permanent," depending upon the continued interaction between the development of complaints and the official responses thereto.

While the general logic of a series of stages in the definition and solution of social problems is clear enough, it is important to remember that it is only a general model and that the handling of specific problems will vary from it in greater or lesser degree. The concept of a natural history is a tool for the analysis of social problems and not the analysis itself.

Here are the questions we ask in applying the conflict-of-values approach:

1. What are the values that are in conflict?
2. How "deep" is the value conflict?
3. What groups in the society hold to each of the competing values? How powerful are they?
4. Which values are more consistent with other, larger values, such as democracy and freedom?
5. What value sacrifices would each solution require?
6. Are some problems insoluble at present because of irreconcilable value conflicts?

The Analysis of Social Problems

This book analyzes each of a series of current social problems in considerable detail. In each case, the attempt has been to marshal and present the most relevant facts bearing upon the origin and development of the problem, upon its present status as indicated by the findings of scientific research, and upon the various possible lines of future development. These data, considered in the light of our three approaches, provide a basis for evaluating the already proposed and yet-to-be-proposed solutions to various aspects of problem situations. Rather than advocate given types of solutions, the authors try to maintain the role of analysts who foresee and predict certain outcomes according to the policy followed. Remember from chapter 1 that it is consistent with the position of the social science analyst to say, "If these are your values, *then* this solution will work," or "This solution that you propose is not consistent with your other basic values," but they generally do not, *as scientists,* adopt the role of value advocate.

With our present social knowledge it is reasonable to expect that more adequate data will be available on some problems than on others and that, consequently, more precise and fuller analyses will be possible in some situations than in others. Each social problem is analyzed in terms of its relation to social change and social disorganization, in terms of the deviant behavior patterns involved, and in terms of the conflict of values among different social groups.

Summary

Social problems are not separate, clear-cut, uncomplicated, readily corrected situations; they are complex phenomena, endlessly interrelated, and difficult to analyze objectively. Their analysis requires that a frame of reference be adopted. Three major approaches—social disorganization, personal deviation, and conflict of values—are used in this book.

The term *social organization* refers to all the organized and customary ways of doing things in a society, and is characterized by order, stability, and predictability of behavior. Social disorganization, a product of social change, occurs when the customary ways of doing things break down or are no longer adequate. The resulting confusion and disorder are major elements to be considered in analyzing social problems. Analysis begins with a description of the original behavior patterns, traces their breakdown under the influence of social change, and finally moves to the consideration of current proposals for dealing with the situation.

The deviant behavior of individuals is also a factor in social problems. Some personal deviation must be explained in essentially psychological terms as the development of neurotic personality patterns. Much deviant behavior, however, is of social origin. When behavior is labeled as deviant, the alleged offenders may be coerced into adopting deviant lifestyles. Other deviant behavior is a product of the breakdown of social norms. Finally, some behavior that is deviant to the larger society is actually in conformity to countercultural norms.

Modern societies show great disagreement within themselves over basic values. These value conflicts create disagreement as to which conditions should be defined as actual problems and encourage moral confusion, which leads to personal deviation. There is a kind of natural history in the development of social problems. First, groups begin to complain about an imputed problem. Second, there is an official bureaucratic response to the complaints. Unless the bureaucratic response is adequate—which it seldom is—the complaints then tend to shift against the agency itself. Finally, a search for alternative problem-solving strategies develops.

Suggested Readings

DINITZ, SIMON, RUSSELL R. DYNES, and ALFRED C. CLARKE, *Deviance: Studies in Definition, Management, and Treatment* (New York: Oxford University Press, 1975). A judicious collection of readings on social problems from the deviance approach.

FICKER, VICTOR B., and JAMES M. RIGTERINK, *Values in Conflict: A Text Reader in Social Problems* (Lexington, Mass.: D. C. Heath, 1972). A current and systematic analysis of social problems employing the conflict-of-values approach.

GOVE, WALTER R., ed., *The Labelling of Deviance* (New York: Halstead Press, 1975). Provides a detailed evaluation of the utility of labeling theory in the analysis of alcoholism, physical disability, mental illness, mental retardation, crime, delinquency, drug abuse, and sexual deviance.

KINCH, JOHN W., ed., *Social Problems in the World Today* (Reading, Mass.: Addison-Wesley, 1974). A fascinating collection of readings from popular rather than standard sources.

LOWRY, RITCHIE P., *Social Problems: A Critical Analysis of Theories and Public Policy* (Lexington, Mass.: D. C. Heath, 1974). A sophisticated critical examination of the role of theory in the analysis of social problems.

McCAGHY, CHARLES H., JAMES K. SKIPPER, JR., and MARK LEFTON, eds., *In Their Own Behalf: Voices from the Margin* (New York: Appleton-Century-Crofts, 1974). Writings by and about people labeled as deviant. Provides insight into the development of personal deviation.

MAUSS, ARMAND L., *Social Problems as Social Movements* (Philadelphia: J. B. Lippincott, 1975). An unconventional but provocative analysis of social problems.

SURAN, BERNARD G., *Oddballs: The Social Maverick and the Dynamics of Individuality* (Chicago: Nelson-Hall, 1978). Explores the role of deviant personalities in social change.

Footnotes

[1] Based on Leo Nikolaievich Tolstoi, "The Tsar and the Elephants," in *The Great Fables of All Nations*, selected by Manuel Komroff (New York: Dial Press, 1928), pp. 439–40.

[2] Gary D. Bouma, "Assessing the Impact of Religion: A Critical Review," *Sociological Analysis*, 31 (Winter 1970), 172–79; and Andrew M. Greeley and Peter H. Rossi, *The Denominational Society* (Glenview, Ill.: Scott, Foresman, 1972), ch. 9.

[3] See any issue of *Social Policy*, the *Insurgent Sociologist*, or the *Berkeley Journal of Sociology* for examples.

[4] Otis Dudley Duncan, ed., *William Ogburn on Culture and Social Change* (Chicago: University of Chicago Press, 1964).

[5] For an incisive analysis of the appearance and public control of mobile-home courts in several California cities, see Edwin M. Lemert, *Human Deviance, Social Problems, and Social Control* (Englewood Cliffs, N.J.: Prentice-Hall, 1967), pp. 31–39.

[6] See Pitirim A. Sorokin, *Contemporary Sociological Theories* (New York: Harper & Brothers, 1928), ch. 4.

[7] For representative collections of readings from this perspective, see Leo Hamalian and Frederick R. Karl, eds., *The Radical Vision: Essays for the Seventies* (New York: Thomas Y. Crowell, 1970); and Frank Lindenfeld, ed., *Radical Perspectives on Social Problems* (New York: Macmillan, 1968).

[8] For characteristic writings from this perspective, see Howard S. Becker, *Outsiders: Studies in the Sociology of Deviance* (New York: Free Press, 1963); Erving Goffman, *Stigma* (Englewood Cliffs, N.J.: Prentice-Hall, 1963); and Erich Goode, "On Behalf of Labeling Theory," *Social Problems*, 22 (June 1975), 570–83.

[9] The President's Crime Commission reports that 91 percent of Americans

have committed acts for which they might have been imprisoned or jailed. See *The Challenge of Crime in a Free Society* (Washington, D.C.: Government Printing Office, 1967).

[10]The concept of anomie was developed by Emile Durkheim in *Suicide*, trans. J. A. Spaulding and G. Simpson (Glencoe, Ill.: Free Press, 1951). For contemporary analyses, see Robert K. Merton, *Social Theory and Social Structure* (New York: Free Press, 1957); and Talcott Parsons, *Essays in Sociological Theory* (New York: Free Press, 1954).

[11]Albert K. Cohen, *Deviance and Control* (Englewood Cliffs, N.J.: Prentice-Hall, 1966); Albert J. Reiss, Jr., "The Study of Deviant Behavior: Where the Action Is," in Mark Lefton, James K. Skipper, Jr., and Charles H. McCaghy, eds., *Approaches to Deviance* (New York: Appleton-Century-Crofts, 1968).

[12]Richard C. Fuller and Richard R. Myers, "The Natural History of a Social Problem," *American Sociological Review*, 6 (June 1941), 320–28.

[13]Malcolm Spector and John I. Kitsuse, "Social Problems: A Reformulation," *Social Problems*, 21 (Fall 1973), 145–59.

Irene Springer

THE INTERPRETATION OF DATA 3

The hemline indicator, despite its past successes, isn't currently telling investors a thing about which way stock prices will go.

This indicator, first noted by the late Ralph Rotnem of Harris, Upham & Co., shows an amazing correlation since 1897 between the ups and downs of the Dow-Jones industrials and the hemline of women's skirts. Both went down sharply in 1929 and again in 1937.

Later, stock prices moved up with hemlines and, after the miniskirt appeared in 1967, they went wild. Then came pants suits and maxi coats—and a new bear market.[1]

This is the only social problems book most of you will ever read. Whatever you learn about social problems after completing this course will come largely through what you read in newspapers and magazines, hear on the radio, see on television, and pick up in casual conversations. These sources rarely give an authoritative, objective, and comprehensive analysis of a social problem. Instead they offer bits of gossip, sensational incidents, offhand guesses, wild charges, and various kinds of propaganda. The extent to which you remain intelligently informed about the social world will be measured largely by how skillfully you recognize and interpret these scraps of social data. If this textbook has any enduring value, that value lies mainly in helping you develop skills in collecting and interpreting the scattered social data you will continually encounter.

A certain amount of the social data—the "facts," incidents, charges and countercharges, and so on—that one finds in popular sources is untrue. Other data consist of half-truths, distortions, and exaggerations. And all data need to be related to other data before they have meaning. Therefore, we need to know (1) whether to accept a report as true, and (2) what difference it makes even if it is true.

The Technique of Successful Lying as Practiced by Talented Liars

Most people have heard about the laws of libel and slander and have a comfortable feeling that "people wouldn't dare say what they say if it weren't true." Accompanying this assurance is the folk belief that "where there's smoke there must be fire," a statement fairly true in a folk society but not necessarily true in a mass society wherein propaganda is a fine art. There are many ways to plant a lie without running afoul of the laws of libel and slander.[2] A good way to learn how to recognize truth is to discover how liars go about their business.

LIE ABOUT A GROUP

A group cannot sue for libel or slander. An individual can sue, and under certain circumstances a corporation or organization can sue or prosecute, but an unorganized group of people cannot sue anyone who slanders them. To charge that John Jones is a robber would invite a libel suit. But to charge that bankers are a bunch of robbers, or cops are pigs, or Jews are a bunch of subversives is legal in most states. No particular *person* or *organization* has been slandered, so no one can bring a legal action. (Three states now have group libel laws, but in the other forty-seven there is still open season.)

Gossip is perhaps the most universal of all methods of transmitting and communicating data.
(Irene Springer)

LIE ABOUT THE DEAD

The dead cannot sue for libel. Their heirs can, but they seldom win. Edgar Allen Poe's reputation as a lecherous, drunken wastrel is a tribute to the hatchetry of the Reverend Rufus Wilmot Griswold, a mediocre and jealous poet who, after Poe's death, made a career of inventing and publicizing malicious biographies of Poe.[3] A public figure's death always spawns a rash of "revelations," some perhaps true and others false.

LIE ABOUT A PUBLIC FIGURE

The Supreme Court ruled in 1964 that false criticism of a public official is not libelous unless actual malice can be proved. It is very difficult to prove malice. And just who is a public official has not been precisely defined by the courts, although they seem inclined to include almost anyone who becomes a figure in "public debate."[4] Every president has been the victim of ferociously libelous attacks,[5] but a libel suit filed by a president would probably be legally unsuccessful and would certainly be politically unwise.

IMPLY GUILT BY ASSOCIATION

The attack on Jesus Christ for associating with sinners was neither the first nor the last use of the technique of implying guilt by association. Both President Nixon and President Carter have learned that when their favorite banker friends get into trouble, their own images suffer.

In instances in which two persons are in close *personal* association over some period of time, there is good reason to suspect that they may have similar ideas. But a purely *verbal* association, in which two people happen to have been on the same side of a particular question at a particular moment, is a very different matter. Consider this syllogism:

> The Pope believes in child-labor laws.
> The communists believe in child-labor laws.
> Therefore, the Pope is a communist.
>
> (or)
>
> Therefore, the communists are Catholics.[6]

49

The syllogism works either way. By this warped "logic" one can prove anyone guilty of practically anything.

IMPUTE WICKED MOTIVES, PURPOSES, OR CONSEQUENCES

Imputing evil motives or results is another way to lie by implication. To charge specific *actions* may be dangerous; it is too easy to prove or disprove such charges. Instead, one can be charged with *wishing* to bring about some despicable end. During the Vietnam War, instead of hearing that "Dr. Benjamin Spock and the peaceniks are a pack of communists and traitors," we heard how Dr. Spock and the peaceniks "want to help the communists win in Vietnam." As a case in point, Robert Welch, founder of the John Birch

Well-known public figures (such as Dr. Benjamin Spock shown here at a 1967 anti-Vietnam sit-in) are frequently powerful forces around which various opinions, political or otherwise, may be publicly disseminated.
(United Press International)

Society, for years insisted that former President Dwight Eisenhower was "a dedicated, conscious agent of the communist conspiracy,"[7] and devoted an entire book to "exposing" President Eisenhower's "treasonous" motives and actions. These are libelproof ways of accusing someone of being disloyal. Such inferences may, of course, be entirely true. The important thing to note is that merely because such statements do not produce libel suits is not proof that the charges are true.

For many years, the welfare system was accused of coddling loafers, encouraging illegitimacy, and undermining the capitalist system. More recently, however, the "welfare establishment" has been accused of exploiting and manipulating the poor for the purpose of depressing wage levels and maintaining the capitalist system.[8] Such imputations of motives and purposes belong in theology or mythology, not in social science.

USE "WEASEL" WORDS

A weasel is a small animal that can wiggle through a tiny opening. "Weasel" words are shrewdly chosen qualifying words that make a statement technically correct but very misleading. Thus the speaker has not actually told a lie but has just made it easy for you to infer one.

Weasel words abound in advertising. Federal laws forbid the claim that a pill will cure an illness unless there is some factual basis for the claim. So the seller must find some way of convincing buyers that it will cure them without actually saying so. This is done by using weasel words few people will notice or understand. If the ad says "Hoakum's Pills will cure your backache," the advertiser may be in trouble with the Food and Drug Administration. So the ad says "Hoakum's Pills, which have helped so many people . . . ," or "Try Hoakum's Pills and see if you don't feel better!" The television announcer reads, "New Dri-Up is twice as effective as any other deodorant tested," without saying how many others were tested or how their effectiveness was measured. Radio and television announcers who deliver such commercials have developed a technique known as the throwaway. This consists of sliding over the weasel words and emphasizing the others so that the weasel words will not be remembered. One highly successful announcer reported some years ago:

> Every sponsor has to put some weasel words in his copy that you've got to learn how to handle. Suppose an announcer has to say, "If you use Blank face cream you can hope for a more beautiful complexion." You've got to get that word, "hope" in to keep the lawyers happy, but as much as you can, you'll throw it away.[9]

A recent example of rather spectacular lying through weasel words is the 1977 Tylenol campaign claiming that "doctors recommend Tylenol

---

ARE THERE ANY WEASEL WORDS IN THIS ADVERTISEMENT?

Unwise eating or drinking may be a source of mild, but annoying bladder irritations—making you feel restless, tense, and uncomfortable. And if restless nights, with nagging backache and muscular aches and pains due to over-exertion, strain, or emotional upset, are adding to your misery—don't wait, try _____ 's Pills.

_____ 's Pills act 3 ways for speedy relief. 1—They have a soothing effect on bladder irritations. 2—A fast pain-relieving action on nagging backache, headaches, muscular aches and pains. 3—A wonderfully mild diuretic action through the kidneys, tending to increase the output of the 15 miles of kidney tubes. So, get the same happy relief millions have enjoyed for over 50 years. Large, economy size saves money. Get _____ 's Pills today!

more often than all leading aspirin brands combined," and that "hospitals dispense more Tylenol than all leading aspirin brands combined." This is technically true. Doctors know that all aspirin is alike and rarely recommend any *brand*; they just say, "take an aspirin." Hospitals generally use bulk aspirin, not branded aspirin. Including the weasel word, "brands," made the lie legal.

Weasel words are useful. Research shows that most people accept claims that are merely *implied* as readily as they accept claims that are straightforwardly asserted.[10] There is no easy way to detect weasel words. Sometimes the qualifying phrases are so obvious that the critical reader cannot miss them, but in other cases some special knowledge is needed to detect them. While an awareness of these verbal pitfalls is helpful, there is no substitute for an intimate and exact knowledge of a subject for spotting the misuse of language.

QUOTE OUT OF CONTEXT

The Bible says, "Let him who stole steal . . . ," clearly a subversive doctrine. Of course, if St. Paul's statement is quoted in full—"Let him who stole steal no more" (Ephesians 4:28)—the meaning is somewhat changed. By leaving out part of a sentence or omitting the sentences that precede or follow it, one can make the most innocent remark sound damning.

THE BIOGRAPHY OF A LIE

"You cannot bring about prosperity by discouraging thrift. You cannot strengthen the weak by weakening the poor. You cannot help small men by tearing down big men. You cannot help the poor by destroying the rich. You cannot lift the wage-earner by pulling down the wage-payer. You cannot keep out of trouble by spending more than your income. You cannot further the brotherhood of man by inciting class hatred. You cannot establish sound security on borrowed money. You cannot build character and courage by taking away a man's initiative and independence. You cannot help men permanently by doing for them what they can and should do for themselves."

The above quote, attributed to Abraham Lincoln, has been widely circulated by conservative publications and organizations. It was actually written by the Rev. William J. H. Boetcker of Erie, Pennsylvania, and published, as his own ideas, in 1916. In 1942 the statement was published by the Committee for Constitutional Government with a credit line, "Inspiration of Wm. J. H. Boetcker," along with an authentic quotation of Lincoln's on the other side of the page, entitled, "Lincoln on Limitation." When a later edition of the leaflet was published by the Committee for Constitutional Government they left off the name of Boetcker. This and later printings led readers to assume that the words on both sides of the page were the authentic words of Lincoln.

From *Lincoln Lore*, Jan. 1962, bulletin published by the Lincoln National Life Insurance Company, Fort Wayne, Ind.

Equally common is the practice of ignoring the time and situational context of words or actions. Thomas Jefferson the young revolutionary talked and acted differently from Thomas Jefferson the president.[11] Abraham Lincoln has been attacked in some circles because his views and actions on racial questions were not those of a twentieth century liberal.[12] To level charges of bigotry at Jefferson for owning slaves, at Martin Luther for suppressing dissent, or at Plato for being a male chauvinist would be as unfair as to label them ignorant for not knowing how to drive an automobile.

"DOCUMENT" ELABORATELY

Responsible scholarship is extensively documented. So are skillful hatchet jobs, giving them the *appearance* of responsible scholarship. Thus a slashing attack on former President Lyndon Johnson is very heavily footnoted.[13] Most of the citations are from the *Congressional Record* or from congressional committee hearings. This is highly impressive—except to those who realize that most of these citations are to totally unsubstantiated charges placed in the record by some witness or member of Congress. Many other citations are to right-wing journals, wherein similarly unsubstantiated charges are quoted back and forth. Critical students will not be impressed by the number of footnotes alone, but will want to know something about the quality of the sources cited.

REPEAT THE LIE AT EVERY OPPORTUNITY

Hitler argued that the bigger and more preposterous a lie, the more firmly it will be believed, *if it is repeated often enough.* Sometimes it seems as though Hitler was right. An American business executive sadly observed:

> Tell a big lie to millions of people, tell it over and over without bothering about facts or logic, without regard to how preposterous or ridiculous or vicious it sounds at first, and pretty soon it acquires the status of fact with those unhappy people who are not in a position to check the facts.
>
> Pretty soon even the injured and slandered parties, who know better, are panicked into fighting the big lie or negotiating over it, just as if it were the truth.[14]

A famous example of the "big lie" was the charge in 1970 that 28 Black Panthers had been murdered by police in "a national scheme by various agencies of the government to destroy and commit genocide on the Black Panther Party.[15] This figure and the idea of a police war of extermination against Black Panthers were accepted uncritically and widely quoted as fact by many responsible newspapers and individuals, and it became briefly fashionable for wealthy socialites to lionize Black Panther guests at fund-raising parties.[16]

Like most big lies, this one had some plausibility. Police brutality against blacks is far from unknown in American society, mutual hostility between police and Panthers was no secret, and instances of police harassment of Black Panthers were well documented.[17] But when a skeptical reporter critically examined the data behind these charges, the "28 police murders" turned out to be, at the least, a fantastic exaggeration, and the charge of a police war of genocide was totally unsubstantiated. Seldom has a single published article quashed a big lie so effectively.[18]

Tests of Reliability in Interpreting Data

It is clear that many reports cannot be accepted as true. Some are deliberate falsehoods, some are unintentional errors, and some are products of neurotic, irresponsible people who are emotionally unable to distinguish between facts and wishful thinking. Are there any tests or rule-of-thumb ways of evaluating reports and estimating their reliability?

AUTHORSHIP—WHO SAID IT?

Who makes the charge or reports the disturbing facts?

IS THE AUTHOR AN AUTHORITY ON THE SUBJECT INVOLVED?   Renown in one field often gives one the illusion of being an authority on everything. Thus, some extravagant nonsense on the presumed genetic basis for race differences has been broadcast by a Nobel Prize-winning physicist, whose views the American Physical Society felt constrained officially to repudiate.[19] Some people become "authorities" on government, foreign affairs, or the like, not through professional training, but through the ingenuity of their press agents. A continuous parade of "diet specialists" collect lecture fees and book royalties without displaying either scientific training or professional experience in dietetics.[20] The counseling field is cluttered with thousands of self-appointed "psychologists,"[21] "counselors," and "human relations experts" who have no professional training in these fields. This misrepresentation is a profitable racket, as long as there are people who do not inquire whether the "authority" is a reputable professional person.

Many people without college degrees have become recognized authorities through private study and experience, such as Thomas Edison and Vilhjalmur Stefansson. The question is, "Experience makes one an expert in *what?*" The obvious answer is, "Experience makes one an authority in the matter in which one is experienced; in unrelated fields one is not an authority." To repeat such an obvious truth seems unnecessary, were it not that this limitation is so often overlooked. A successful business executive has learned a great deal about the conduct of a business, but business experience is no qualification as an authority on diet, teaching methods, or government. The college professor of physics is unlikely to be an authority on the cultural patterning of personality.

We must also distinguish between the "familiarity with" and "knowledge about" phenomena. A bank cashier who handles millions of dollars does not thereby become an authority on government finance or banking legislation. Workers who bottle pills in a pharmaceutical house have some familiarity with many drugs but generally know little of their chemical structure or pharmacological action. A supervisor who has bossed many black workers may imagine that he "understands black people," when all this supervisor may really have learned is how to handle a certain group of black people in a particular situation. Yet this supervisor may talk confidently on all phases of black life. A superficial familiarity does not make one an authoritive philosopher upon a subject.

WHAT IS THE AUTHOR'S KNOWN BIAS?   Is the author known to be a liberal, a conservative, or a radical? Is this person an atheist, an agnostic, or a believer?

In which faith? *All persons have biases*, but some control them better than others. Knowledge of an author's biases is helpful in interpreting his or her statements.

IS THE AUTHOR EMOTIONALLY STABLE? This is exceedingly important. Most of the violent diatribes against government, against business, against the church, against the "establishment," against "radicals" are the products of neurotic, paranoid, or otherwise maladjusted personalities. Most extremists, both right-wing and left-wing, are maladjusted people whose bitter attacks stem from their inner emotional problems rather than from the realities of the situations they fret about.[22] Unfortunately, it is not always easy to detect a neurotic personality upon brief acquaintance. Many neurotics are brilliant, engaging people, who speak and write convincingly. But when a writer has a reputation for instability—for taking extreme positions, for changing sides and causes frequently—emotional instability may be suspected.

A CASE OF PHONY SPONSORSHIP

Judge Byron Arnold, presiding judge of the San Francisco County Superior Court, has a best-seller on his hands. It's the transcript of his decision on a 1962 case of political sabotage and misuse of campaign funds. If the charges sound like today's headlines, so do the names involved. According to Judge Arnold, a Republican, the effort was directed by the then-candidate for governor, Richard Nixon, and his campaign manager, H. R. Haldeman.

The caper involved a postcard poll of Democrats, purportedly sponsored by Democrats and proving that rank-and-file party members overwhelmingly rejected various "extremist" views attributed to Nixon's Democratic opponent Pat Brown. The postcards also solicited money to help the "Committee for the Preservation of the Democratic Party in California" wrest control from the radicals it said had taken over. In truth, the committee was a "dirty tricks" arm of the Nixon campaign committee. The postcards were sent only to conservative Democrats, the published poll results were misleading, and the money collected went toward Nixon's election effort. The Democrats sued, and won. In his decision, Judge Arnold declared: "The postcard poll was received, amended, and finally approved by Mr. Nixon personally," and that: "Mr. Nixon and Mr. Haldeman approved the plan and project . . . and agreed the Nixon campaign committee would finance the project." P.S. Pat Brown won anyway, and the rest is history.

The Business Week Letter, 7 May 1973. Reprinted with permission of the *Business Week Letter*, a biweekly personal finance service published by McGraw-Hill.

SPONSORSHIP—WHO PUBLISHES, DISTRIBUTES, OR SPONSORS IT?

The law generally requires that the publisher of printed materials be identified. Reputable publications are unlikely to publish grave charges or shocking reports without making some investigation. An article in the *New York Times* or the *Christian Science Monitor* will be widely accepted by discriminating readers, since these newspapers enjoy an excellent reputation for objectivity; certain other papers are notorious for distorting the news to make it fit their editorial policies. Labor newspapers and trade journals clearly reflect the biases and vested interests of their respective groups; while the *facts* they present will generally be true, the *selection* and *interpretation* of these facts reveal the bias of the publishers.

Sometimes the real sponsor hides behind an apparent, phony sponsor. The "kiss of death" sponsor is a standard political trick, in which a disliked person or group is presented as an apparent supporter of one's opponent. In the 1921 contest between James Curley and John Murphy (both Catholics) for mayor of Boston, Curley hired some clean-cut young men to go through (heavily Catholic) South Boston handing out leaflets in the name of "Baptists for John Murphy."[23] In another election, one candidate "was the victim of someone who sent a flatbed truck carrying a black band and black semi-nude go-go girls into a conservative white ethnic neighborhood, noisily urging his election. He lost."[24]

Sponsors are sometimes stolen without their consent. Communist-front organizations have listed on their "advisory boards" the names of many famous persons who had not given permission for their use. In an election some years ago the supporters of one successful candidate for Congress had four pages of flattering news and pictures of him printed in the style of a *Life* magazine article; these inserts were stapled into copies of *Life* and scattered throughout his district. This made it appear that the editors of *Life* had given this candidate a favorable write-up.

Organizational names are often chosen to conceal rather than to reveal the true goals of the organization. For example, opponents of Maine's bottle deposit law changed their name from "Citizens for Repeal of the Forced Deposit Law" to "Citizens for Litter Control and Recycling," carrying an environmentalist "good guy" image. And "Citizens for . . ." sounds better than "Citizens against. . . ." All organized pressure groups choose impressive titles, dripping with noble words ("freedom," "justice," liberty," "fairness"); thus, the title of an organization tells little about its purposes.

VESTED INTEREST—WHOSE AXE IS SHOWING?

The vested interest of a spokesperson can often be seen peeking between the lines of the arguments. In many attacks upon the "frills" of education, the desire to cut school costs is easy to sense, while the vested interests of wealthy people who oppose income redistribution are as obvious as are the vested interests of low-income groups who favor it. Of course, it is possible to collect and state facts with complete honesty, despite one's vested interest. But in evaluating data we must never forget that the author's selection of data and interpretation of it are almost inevitably affected by the author's vested interest.

FACTUAL CONTENT—HOW SPECIFIC IS THE AUTHOR?

Is the report based on established facts, or does it consist largely of unproved assumptions, imputed motives, and undocumented accusations? Are the "facts" really facts upon which all qualified observers would agree, or are they assumptions and accusations stated as if they were facts? Sometimes a number of people who share the same viewpoint will quote one another's opinions and accusations back and forth until they become accepted as facts. Sometimes a generalization is "proved," not by citing cross-sectional surveys but by citing a handful of examples. The repetition of a series of horror stories has convinced many people that most welfare clients are lazy bums, busily breeding children to increase their welfare checks, while many other people are firmly convinced that most police officers are brutal. Through the selected-example method, any group can be convicted of practically anything.

VERIFIABILITY—CAN IT BE CHECKED?

Unless one is not only a liar but also a fool, one will be careful about the accuracy of statements that can be checked easily by the audience. The statement that "wages (or profits) doubled last year" could be easily checked against the statistics; the statement that "workers today are a bunch of loafers who don't work like they used to" cannot be measured or tested easily.

The more readily a statement can be checked, the more likely it is to be reliable. There is no guarantee that it will always be true, however. The author may make an unintentional error or simply be careless about checking the facts. Or an author or speaker may lie in the belief that the truth will never catch up with the lie. Yet the general rule is that reliability will vary in direct ratio to verifiability.

RELEVANCY—DO THE DATA SUPPORT THE CONCLUSIONS?

When one confronts a distressing lack of evidence to prove one's case, an ancient dodge is to prove a different case. Irrelevant evidence can be cited as though it supported the original conclusion. For example, the maker of a well-known mouthwash wishes to promote it as a cold preventative. Since the cold germ has not been isolated and therefore there is no evidence that this mouthwash kills the cold germ, the advertisement simply tells how many millions of other germs this mouthwash kills. Or, to give another example, one argues that crime increases have been caused by parental permissiveness, or by pornography, or by television violence, or by anything else, and "proves" this by citing evidence on the crime increase, without showing how the alleged cause has operated to produce the effect. Fortunately, the test of relevancy can be applied easily, merely by asking how directly the data are related to the conclusions drawn from them.

STYLE—IS IT DESCRIPTIVE OR PROPAGANDISTIC?

ARE THE FAMILIAR PROPAGANDA DEVICES USED? Material that employs the standard propaganda devices *may* nevertheless be truthful and accurate, but is still suspect until its exact purposes and content are established. The standard propaganda devices include the following:[25]

1. *Name-calling*—giving an idea (or person) a bad name, so it will be rejected without examining the evidence—"socialized medicine," "slave labor act," "rich man's tax law," "communistic idea."
2. *Glittering generality*—associating an idea with noble words that have vague meanings: "the American way," "sanctity of the home," "the future of America," "patriotic support," "sound program."
3. *Testimonial*—linking a loved or hated person with an idea: "The Jeffersonian principle of . . . ," "Washington would be shocked at . . . ," "Russia will be happy if . . . ," "Our boys overseas pray that . . . ."
4. *Plain folks*—making one's ideas seem to represent those of "the people": "Your plain Yankee horse sense tells you . . . ," "The simple faith of my

mother tells me that . . . ," "I'm just a simple farm boy, not a corporation lawyer, and . . . ."

5. *Card-stacking*—using only selected facts, true or false, that support one's case. Supporting facts are emphasized, damaging fact ignored.
6. *Band wagon*—"Everybody's doing it," "Every thinking person now realizes that . . . ," "Join the rising tide of protest against . . . ," "Unite with that great army of patriotic Americans who . . . ."

IS THE STYLE ACCUSATORY AND CONSPIRATORIAL?   Does the material abound in cloak-and-dagger suspense, with a dark plot on every page and a subversive or a traitor or a bloodsucking capitalist behind every bush? If so, it is probably the work of a crackpot. Dependable, reliable reporting is usually written in sober, precise, cautious language, and any writing that departs from this should be very critically examined. Of course, a skillful propagandist addressing well-educated minds will assume a dignified style. So, while a melodramatic style suggests unreliability, a sedate style is no guarantee of reliability.

IS THE STYLE INFORMATIVE OR PLATITUDINOUS AND TAUTOLOGICAL?   A platitude is a statement of a truth so obvious as to be inane, such as "Our future lies before us," "The home is the cradle of civilization," or "The race belongs to the swift." Many a speaker's reputation, politician's career, and cleric's eminence rests on the ability to recite platitudes so eloquently that they sound original and profound. Tautology is the needless repetition of the same idea in other words, such as "audible to the ear," "visible to the eye." Attributed to Calvin Coolidge are the statements that "When there are not enough jobs for everybody, unemployment results," and "The cure for unemployment is work." Skillfully tautological writing sounds impressive but is devoid of meaning.

IS THE STATEMENT CLUTTERED WITH MEANINGLESS WORDS AND MYSTICAL EXPRESSIONS? The literature of some religious cults, flying-saucer fanatics, spiritualists, psychics, and some other unorthodox groups is filled with phrases like "levels of consciousness," "spectral self," "fourth-dimensional transmigration," and other terms that have no exact meaning. When pressed for definitions, the groups offer additional strings of meaningless words. Enigmatic and imprecise prose of this sort is the hallmark of questionable propaganda.

CONSISTENCY—DOES IT AGREE WITH OTHER KNOWN FACTS?

The test of consistency is perhaps the most useful test of all, *providing that one knows the other facts* regarding the matter. Health fads and frauds are most readily accepted by people who have very little accurate knowledge of physiology and medicine. The misleading Tylenol advertisement mentioned on p. 51 relied for its effectiveness upon people's unawareness that doctors and hospitals generally use *unbranded* aspirin. As stated before, there is no substitute for factual knowledge in interpreting data.

PLAUSIBILITY—DOES IT SOUND REASONABLE?

How to avoid radar speed traps. Fits all cars. Full instructions enclosed. Send $1.00 cash or money order.

This advertisement appeared in a popular magazine, and some people were naive enough to believe that a device that would neutralize a car against radar waves could actually be made and sold for a dollar. In return, these people received a small windshield sticker on which was printed: "Warning!!! Obey all Speed Limits," and in small print, "Place in a conspicuous place as a constant reminder."[26]

Dozens of gadgets are being advertised with careful, weasel-worded promises to increase gas mileage, boost power, and so on. If there really were a simple device that would boost gas mileage as claimed, its inventor would be an instant multimillionaire—unless trampled to death in the rush of auto manufacturers begging to buy the patent rights. Yet such devices appear in an unending series, confirming C. P. Barnum's sage observation that "there's another sucker born every minute."

To use the test of plausibility, ask: "If this claim were true, *what else* would be happening?" General Motors is now spending billions of dollars trying to boost gas mileage. If some simple device would do this, would not General Motors pay handsomely for it? If the oil companies had somehow suppressed a wonderful new gas-saver—a perennial rumor—would General Motors remain silent? Would not General Motors and Ford be clamoring for a congressional investigation? Would not the senators from Michigan be making eloquent speeches about the public interest? Would not the President fill the television screens with his indignation?

Some years ago there was a rash of "Negro Bump Day" rumors. People in several cities gravely assured this writer that every Tuesday, Wednesday, or Friday (the tale varied), Negroes would flock downtown to bump and push white people out of the stores and off the sidewalks. None of the informants *themselves* had been bumped but each "knew" of many who had been. If this absurd report had been true, would not store owners have complained? Would not fights and riots have broken out? Would not police have arrested hundreds, and a great furor resulted?

If spiritualist mediums can really communicate with the dead, why do they never learn anything important, such as the location of a missing will or hidden valuables? If fortune tellers could really tell the future, why are they not stock-market millionaires instead of penny-ante stage performers? If psychics can read other people's minds, why do psychics not win national bridge or chess tournaments? If psychics can transport objects by mental power (telekinesis), why are they transporting teacups and pencils instead of bank notes and diamonds? Is it plausible to believe that people who really have such powers would use them for such trivia?

How to Lie with Statistics[27]

Benjamin Disraeli once observed that there are three grades of liars: plain liars, damn liars, and statisticians. This unkind observation springs from the fact that statistics can be manipulated to support whatever point of view one wishes. But to dismiss statistics as misleading and confusing is pointless, for *statistics mislead and confuse only when one does not know how to interpret them.*

There are elaborate statistical formulas for determining the significance and reliability of a statistic, but this text is concerned only with some simple tests that the student can apply.

THE UNDERFED SAMPLE

A toothpaste maker breathlessly announces scientific tests that prove that a new miracle formula stops tooth decay. The "test" referred to was conducted on exactly *six* persons. Several small test groups were observed, and all the results were discarded until one of these small groups gave the desired results. One survey some years ago solemnly announced that one-third of Johns Hopkins University female students married faculty members. Very true. At the time Johns Hopkins had only three female students, and one of them married an instructor.

A sample *large enough* to rule out chance variations is called an *adequate* sample. It may number from a few hundred to several million, depending upon the rarity of the phenomenon under study. If we are studying something that appears in only one of several thousand people, we need a large sample; thus, a study of student suicides would need a larger sample than a study of student cheating. A sample is not considered statistically adequate until it is found that the addition of more cases does not alter the percentages established.

THE UNBALANCED SAMPLE

Two pollsters, one at a factory gate and the other at a country club, may report very different findings. A sample is useless unless it is *representative*. This means that each *kind* of person appears in the sample *in the same proportion* as that kind of person appears in the total population group under study. One would not obtain a representative sample by standing on a street corner quizzing passers-by, because not all kinds of people will appear on that street at that hour. A student sample collected at fraternity houses and campus hangouts would leave several groups underrepresented. A representative sample of the student body would have the same percentages of freshmen, of females, of science majors, and so on, as are found in the entire student body. Occupation, income, education, and several other variables must be controlled to poll a representative sample.

A very common shortcut is the *random* sample, which is constructed so that each person in the group under study has an equal chance to appear in the sample. Placing all names in a turn-cage and drawing out a number of them would be one way to obtain a random sample. When the group is listed alphabetically, as in a student directory, a random sample can be approximated by taking, for example, every tenth or every fiftieth name.[28] When people appear sequentially, as with persons appearing at a ticket window, the same procedure (every fifth, tenth, fiftieth) may be used. If every tenth house in the city is visited, this random sample would be highly representative. An *uncontrolled* sample is composed of whomever the roving pollster comes across, without any system or formula, and is of little value.

All *self-selected* samples are suspect. These are samples in which people become members of the sample through their own actions. Those who attend a particular meeting, read a particular magazine, or write letters on a particular issue are by no means a representative sample of the entire population. California's Governor Edmund Brown, Sr., some years ago received thousands of letters urging him, in a ten-to-one ratio, to stay the execution of convicted kidnapper Caryl Chessman; he did so, and promptly found his mail scolding him, by six-to-one, for his action. This does not necessarily show that people are fickle, but that self-selected samples are not representative.[29]

The respondents in a mail-return questionnaire study are a form of self-selected sample. The higher the percentage of returns, the more representative is the sample and the more dependable are the findings. A 90 percent return is fine; as returns fall below 50 percent, the findings are increasingly suspect. A recent best-seller (Shere Hite, *The Hite Report: A Nationwide Study of Female Sexuality* [New York: Macmillan, 1976]) is based upon a *3 percent* return of mailed questionnaires. Such a "study" is scientific garbage, although it may be a commercial gold mine.

THE LOADED BASE

More women are murdered at home by their husbands than are slain on the street by sexual psychopaths, but this does not prove that women would be safer sleeping on the sidewalks, since there are many more women at home than on dark streets at night. To be comparable, two statistics must have a comparable base. All statistics have some starting point in time or some universe of data on which they are based. A percentage, for example, has no

Employee of Association of Computer Machinery interviewing two passers-by during a promotional tour in New York City. Indeed, polls, be they sidewalk or of a more sophisticated variety, have become a consistently relied upon interpretative tool.

(Margot Granitsas, Photo Researchers, Inc.)

With today's rapidly rising food prices, the consumer has become more aware of the value of comparison shopping and of taking advantage of advertised sales and coupons.
(Irene Springer)

meaning by itself—it is a percentage *of* somthing. An advertiser's claim that "79 percent prefer Del Morte cigarettes" has no real meaning as it stands; 79 percent of *whom* prefer Del Morte *over what*? That women drivers are involved in fewer accidents than men, in proportion to their numbers, is inconclusive; it is not the *number* of women drivers, but the proportion and type of *driving* done by women that is the base against which the percentage of accidents involving women should be compared.

Percentage comparisons can also be misleading when drawn on a very small base. Occasionally one sees a "research" project in which the data consist of a small handful of cases, yet these have been fully analyzed in terms of percentages and other statistical procedures. A percentage based on two or three dozen cases or informants is not worth much—the base is too small. The same holds true when computing percentage of increase or decrease. For example, during recent years of rising crime rates, the *number* of female arrests increased far less than the *number* of male arrests, but the *percentage* increase in female crime rates was many times higher (67 percent for females and 16 percent for males between 1967 and 1976.)[30] The female crime rate was traditionally very low, so a modest absolute increase showed up as a huge percentage increase. These spectacular percentage increases fueled some wild speculation about the "female crime wave," and "women's liberation into crime" among sensationalist writers who overlooked the small base against which these percentage increases were computed. Any percentage change will be very misleading if computed against a very narrow base.

Table 3–1 shows what may happen when a constant percentage is computed on bases of differing size. Suppose that tax revenues were to be increased by adding ten percentage points to the income tax rates on all sizes of incomes. Although such a proposal might have the appearance of "justice," it clearly would not impose equal sacrifice upon all groups. Notice particularly how the same set of facts can be used to support opposite conclusions. If one wishes to make this look unfair to the poor, one will cite the percentages in Column B, which show that the "little fellow's" taxes are increased proportionately more than those of the wealthy person. If one wishes to make this look unfair to the rich, one will cite the percentages in Column D, showing how much this tax rate change would reduce the income he had left after taxes. Probably no one has proposed exactly this tax schedule; it is cited purely to illustrate how percentages can be used and misused. Much of the demagoguery in tax debates has made such questionable use of percentages to buttress anguished cries of outrage at such "injustice."

A General Accounting Office study of the profits of defense contractors found that "profit measured as percentage of sales averaged a modest 6.5 percent, but it soared to 28.3 percent when measured as return on total capital investment, and to 56.1 percent as a return on equity capital alone."[31] The nation's food store chains in 1978 showed a profit of either 2 percent or 16 percent—2 percent on sales and 16 percent on net worth.[32] All of these figures are correct, and all are useful—some for impressing stockholders and some for resisting wage demands or price cuts. It makes a difference which base is used.

An interesting statistical shell game uses a "wandering" base. In this game, the propagandist shifts bases in mid-argument. For example, an automobile advertisement showed two tables in which the maker's car, offered in only one basic model, was compared with the competition in both price and luxury features. Only by reading the fine print, however, could one detect that the tables compared the maker's car with the "bare" models of the competition in luxury features, but with the "luxury" model of the competition in price. Another auto manufacturer based a national advertising campaign on the claim that his standard car ran more quietly than a Rolls Royce. He failed to state that he had measured noise levels in a *new* model

TABLE 3–1   Would the Same Percentage Change in Tax Rates Affect Everyone Alike?

Adjusted gross income	Federal income tax at 1979 rates	Taxes after adding 10 percent to rates	Percent increase in taxes paid	Income left after taxes	Percent drop in income left after taxes
5,000	84	244	285	4,916	3
50,000	10,484	14,544	39	35,456	10
500,000	317,424	366,484	15	133,516	27
5,000,000	3,467,364	3,966,364	14	1,133,636	33

Taxes have been computed for married couples with four children, using standard deductions. The actual taxes paid on very high incomes are less than shown here, because of earned income limitation, tax shelters, and other deductions which affect each tax return differently.

of his car and in an *old* Rolls Royce.[33] Obviously, a comparison is valid only if its base remains unchanged throughout the comparison.

As with percentages, *the most important thing about an average is its base,* that is, the universe upon which the average is taken. As table 3–2 shows, very different "average" wage rates can be computed from the same data, depending upon what categories of workers are included and excluded from the base. Computing national averages becomes complicated. For example, in computing average family income, how does one define a family? If persons living alone are counted as a family, the average income will be reduced. Should part-time and unemployed workers be included in the total of income receivers? Should unemployment insurance, pension payments, welfare payments, and other such "income transfers" be included as income?

Trends are often shown through index numbers, and every index must have a starting point. The objective scholar picks a relatively normal year as a base year, while the propagandist looks for a base year that is particularly helpful for propaganda use. For example, if wages and prices are measured from 1960 to 1979, average weekly wages have increased almost 30 percent more than consumer prices, but if 1972 is chosen as the base year, prices have risen 12 percent more than wages.[34] It makes a difference where we locate the starting point. Most trends show some fluctuations. This makes it possible, by selecting either a peak or a valley as a base year, to show the trend as a crawl or a gallop, according to one's wishes. This is why the base

TABLE 3–2   Average Annual Earnings of Employees of the Blank Manufacturing Company

Management's figures

1,000	Regular employees @ $10,000		$10,000,000	
500	Trainees and probationary employees @ $5,000*			
500	Laid-off and part-time employees @ $2,000*			
100	Supervisors @ $15,000		1,500,000	
50	Engineers and technicians @ $20,000		1,000,000	
	Bonus payments and overtime pay—$2,000,000		2,000,000	
1,150		1,150	)$14,500,000(	$12,600 Average Earnings

Union's figures

1,000	Regular employees @ $10,000		$10,000,000	
500	Trainees and probationary employees @ $5,000		2,500,000	
500	Laid-off and part-time employees @ $2,000		1,000,000	
100	Supervisors @ $15,000*			
30	Engineers and technicians @ $20,000*			
	Bonus payments and overtime pay—$2,000,000*			
2,000		2,000	)$13,500,000(	$6,750 Average Earnings

*Not counted.

year or starting point of any comparison must be critically examined. Is it a relatively normal year or a highly abnormal one? Is the base period long enough so that season or annual variations are evened out? Frequently a base period of several years is used to obtain a base that is not distorted by peculiarities of a single year.[35]

THE TOP-HEAVY AVERAGE

One might say that the average yearly income of a person's graduating class is $50,000. He or she might also say that an average classmate earns about $10,000. Both statements can be entirely correct, for the "average" is often a top-heavy figure, inflated far above anything that is normal or typical of the group. One could divide last year's baby crop into the number of women aged 15 to 44, and find that the average woman had .069 of a baby, which shows that in some cases an average is meaningless. Or one could compute the average height of river vessels to decide how high to build a bridge; again, the average is useless. Or one might say that a person with his head in an oven and his feet in a freezer should, on the average, be very comfortable. An average is useful only when it is pertinent to the problem.

There are three standard "measures of central tendency." They are computed differently and have different uses. The most common one is the *arithmetic mean,* commonly called the average, found by adding all the values and dividing by the number of cases. It is simple to compute, and can be computed from the most easily available data. It is useful for many purposes, such as showing year-to-year trends. Its disadvantage is that a few extreme cases can pull this average so high that it is not at all typical. If the graduating class has one millionaire, this one case pulls the "average" far above what most members earn, which gives a false impression of their wealth. Because of this tendency of the average to become top-heavy, two other measures of central tendency are widely used. They are also occasionally referred to as averages. The *mode* is the value in a series that *appears most frequently,* and is therefore descriptive of the largest possible number of cases. The *median* is the *midpoint* in a series of cases, with half the cases above and half below it. Both mode and median are easy to compute if the values have been arranged in top-to-bottom order. The figure that appears most often will be the mode, and counting halfway through the series will locate the median. If only the total figures are known, without a frequency distribution or a top-to-bottom ranking, then there is no way to compute the median or the mode.

AN AVERAGE TELLS NOTHING ABOUT THE INDIVIDUAL

How to Make $100,000 a Year

1. Acquire a spouse and 16 children.
2. Compute the average per capita income (about $5,478 in 1977 in the United States).
3. Multiply by 18 (you, spouse and 16 children = 18 × $5,478 = about $100,000).

Adapted from Darrell Huff, *How to Lie with Statistics* (New York: W. W. Norton, 1954), p. 105.

When a frequency distribution approaches the normal, or bell-shaped curve, the three measures come out the same. If the distribution is *skewed*, or lopsided, they diverge, as shown in table 3–3. Whenever there are a few extreme cases in a series, one knows in advance that the arithmetic mean (or average) will be a misleading figure. The mode and the median are coming into increasing use, because they give a better picture of normal or typical cases. However, these calculations allow the propagandist some leeway in selecting whatever figures best suit his purposes.

THE MICROSCOPIC COMPARISON

Some years ago, *Reader's Digest* published research showing that at that time all popular brands of cigarettes contained about the same amount of tar, and that the small differences in tar content among brands were unimportant. A cigarette maker promptly launched a massive advertising campaign on the theme, "_____ has *less* tar than any other brand." Many people, when it suits their interests, can pump a flood of conclusion from a drop of scientific data. When two groups or cells differ by only a few percentage points, the serious scholar will base no firm conclusions upon such a small variation.

THE ELASTIC GRAPH

A graph can be made to distort data somewhat as the curved mirror in an amusement park makes one look grotesquely fat or incredibly lean. Each graph has two (or three) scales plotted along its axes. For example, time (decades, years, months) may be plotted along the horizontal axis at the bottom edge of a graph, while data (dollars, births, or whatever else one wishes to show) are plotted along the vertical axis. Both vertical axes can be used, as in figure 3–1, where earnings are plotted along the left axis and prices along the right axis. If the step interval along the vertical axis is great, then a great change will appear as a tiny jog on the graph. Making the step interval very small blows up a minor change into a massive sweep on the graph. The graphs in figure 3–2 show what interesting things can be done by varying the step interval on the scales of a graph. There are many other ways in which graphs and charts can deceive and mislead, but limited space prohibits their description.[36]

This does not mean that you should dismiss graphs as unreliable; instead, *study them critically* to see what they actually show. Read the title or

TABLE 3–3 Family Income in the United States, 1974	
Arithmetic Mean—"the average"	$18,269
Total income divided by number of families	
Median	$16,060
The middle case—half above and half below	
Mode	$14,781
More families at this income than at any other level	

Source: *Statistical Abstract of the United States, 1978*, pp. 43, 457, 458 (mode computed by interpolation).

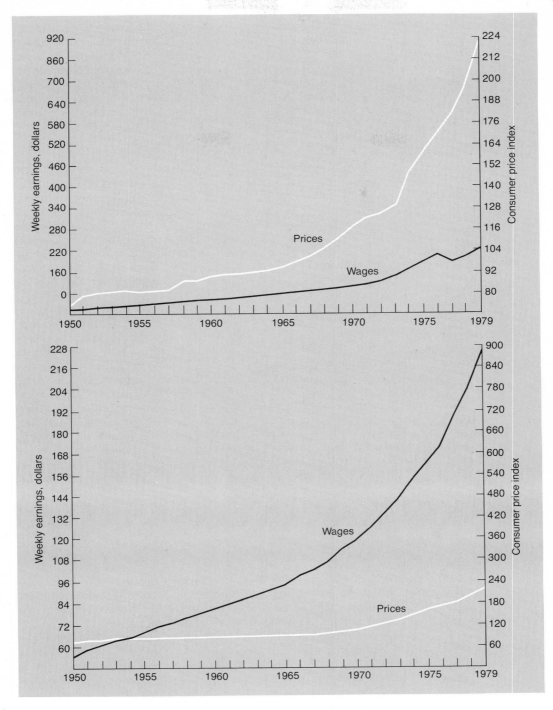

Figure 3–1
Which rises faster—wages or prices?
Source: *Monthly Labor Review*, various dates.

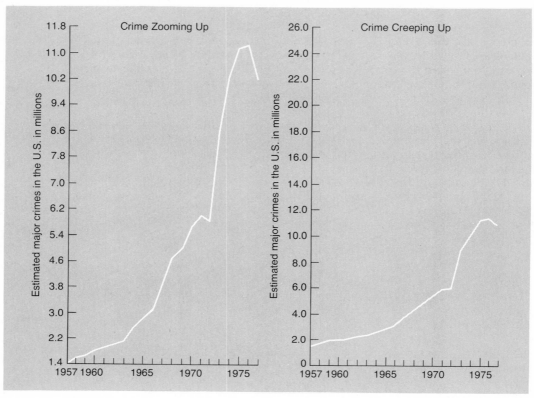

Figure 3–2
Is there a crime wave?
Source: *Uniform Crime Reports,* 1959–1979.

heading, study the scales along the axes, and see exactly what is shown and in what way. A graph is a *picture* of a body of data, and you must determine whether the picture is accurate or deceptive.

THE LEANING POLL

A complete study of the art of public opinion measurement would fill several volumes. Since public opinion polls are often cited in debates about social problems, students should be able to recognize the more obvious of the pitfalls that impair the accuracy of opinion measurement.

a. *Sampling errors* probably have ruined more opinion polls than any other error. The sample must be adequate and representative, as outlined earlier in this chapter. The first step, therefore, in evaluating any poll is to take a critical look at the sample.

b. *"Loading" the questions,* a second common error (often intentional), means wording them in such a way as to elicit a desired response. This is done deliberately when the "research" is intended as support for propaganda, but it may also be an unintentional result of carelessness or ignorance. In either case, an inaccurate measure is the result. Even when conducted with the greatest of care, the wording of questions affects the outcome. For example, in 1978, some 60 percent of a national sample agreed that "Every woman who wants an abortion should be able to have one," while in another poll, 60 percent agreed that "Abortion should not be legal if a woman is married and wants no more children." The most cautious of wording does not completely eliminate unintended bias.

c. *Limiting of responses.* If responses are to be tabulated, the informants must select one from a series of prepared answers. Among the few answers offered, some persons may find none that suits them. If this happens, the findings of the survey are not valid.

Highly reputable opinion measurement concerns, such as the Gallup and Harris polls and the National Opinion Research Center, generally avoid these errors. Many opinion surveys are made by less competent agencies, or are intended to provide support for a publicity campaign, and should be carefully examined for possible misrepresentation.

STATISTICAL ASSOCIATIONS AND CAUSATION

A favorite method of hunting for "causes" is to hunt for statistical associations. Associations, or correlations,[37] have been claimed between drinking and unemployment, broken homes and juvenile delinquency, drug use and school failure, and many other factors. What does "association" mean?

DETERMINING AN ASSOCIATION   The first step in evaluating a claimed association (assuming that the statistics themselves appear to be accurate) is to contrast the association with the total universe from which it is drawn. For example, suppose that 50 percent of the unemployed are "drinkers." This tells us nothing until we know how many of the general population are "drinkers." If 50 percent of the general population also drink, then there is no true association between drinking and unemployment; whereas if considerably more (or less) of the general population are "drinkers," then an association exists. *We have a genuine association only when the factor we are studying appears much more (or less) often in the observed group than in the general population.* Delinquency is associated with broken homes only if delinquents come from broken homes more often than do nondelinquents. Suppose that 50 percent of the delinquents came from broken homes. If only 25 percent of *all* children live in broken homes, then there is an association, since the broken homes are contributing more than their share; but if 50 percent of all children live in broken homes, then there is no association, since the broken homes are contributing exactly their proportionate share.

The step of contrasting the association with the total universe is one that students often have difficulty in grasping, so we shall give some further illustrations. The examples in table 3–4 may clarify the central point—namely, that a genuine association exists *only* when two things appear together *either more frequently or less frequently than would be normally expected.*

IMPUTING CAUSATION   Chanticleer the Cock crowed each morning and made the sun rise—or so he believed. Cause and effect are easily confused, so when an actual statistical association is found, the next step is to determine which is cause and which is effect. Whenever two factors are associated, there are at least four possibilities:

1. *A* causes *B*.
2. *B* causes *A*.
3. Both *A* and *B* are caused by *C*.
4. *A* and *B* are independent, and the association is accidental.

To be more specific, consider the well-established association between smoking and poor grades in elementary school. The possibilities include the following:

1. Smoking among small boys causes poor grades. (It upsets digestion, interferes with mental concentration, and has other ill effects.)
2. Poor grades cause smoking. (Boys who get failing grades smoke to show off, to rebuild ego, and to express defiance of school authorities.)
3. Both are caused by a third factor. (Boys who hate school are likely to smoke to express defiance, and get poor grades because they are uninterested; in the lower social class, both early smoking and a lack of interest in school are parts of the class subculture.)

TABLE 3–4   When Does a Percentage Indicate Statistical Association?

If:	We need to know:	Before trying to decide:
35 percent of college dropouts are regular marijuana users	what percentage of all college students are regular marijuana users	whether dropping out of college is associated with marijuana use
50 percent of fatal accidents involve drinking drivers	what percentage of all driving is done by drinking drivers	whether drinking drivers contribute more or less than their share of accidents
50 percent of all cancer victims have a relative or ancestor who had cancer	what percentage of all people also have a relative or ancestor who has had cancer	whether those with cancerous relatives are more likely than average to contract cancer
75 percent of delinquent children have fathers who do not go to church	what percentage of all children have fathers who do not go to church	whether paternal church-going is associated with delinquency rates
50 percent of relief clients are illiterate	what percentages of all people of similar age and race are illiterate	whether illiteracy is associated with relief status
20 percent of penitentiary inmates are mentally retarded	what percentage of all people of similar age and sex are mentally retarded	whether mental retardation is associated with criminal status
10 percent of convicted criminals are foreign-born	what percentage of all persons of similar ages are foreign-born	whether the foreign-born contribute more or less than their share of convicts
40 percent of former college athletes die of heart disease	what percent of all people die of heart disease	whether there is any association between athletic activity and heart disease

Above percentages are hypothetical, not factual.

4. They may be independent variables. (Some boys get poor grades because of limited intelligence and smoke because the gang does.)

This case shows how a statistical association never identifies the cause; it merely states that two factors move together, without indicating why. The difficult question of determining *what causes what* is only begun when a valid association is established.

A coefficient of correlation is a particular kind of measure of association used when associating two or more quantitative variables. For example, if height and weight of a group of people show a coefficient of correlation of +.80, this would mean that in most cases tall persons are heavier than short persons. This is called *positive* correlation, for both variables rise or fall together. In *negative* or *inverse* correlation, the two variables move in opposite directions. For example, as people grow older their hearing usually fades; age and hearing acuity, therefore, would show a negative coefficient of correlation, written with a minus sign preceding the coefficient.

How much does a coefficient of correlation mean? A coefficient of less than ±.20 (either positive or negative) is so low as to have scarcely any significance. Those between ±.40 and ±.60 have moderate significance; those between ±.80 and ±1.00 are highly significant. But even a very high correlation between two variations never *proves* that one causes the other; it only suggests that the two variables are related and that further study is needed to find out whether one causes the other.

Sometimes an association or correlation is highly significant, even though the question of cause remains unanswered. For example, one insurance company, after finding that smoking drivers had two to three times as many automobile accidents as nonsmokers, began offering a premium discount to nonsmokers.[38] While it is desirable to know *why* two variables are associated, the mere fact of the association may be sufficient for a policy recommendation.

Definition of Terms

Such terms as *liberal, conservative, moderate, radical, reactionary,* and *revolutionist* are often heard in public discussion of social problems. There is no complete agreement upon their meaning. When *liberal* appears in *American Opinion* (circulated by the John Birch Society), it refers to a procommunist, working (consciously or unconsciously) to undermine American free enterprise. When *liberal* appears in *Socialist Revolution,* it describes a spineless hypocrite, mouthing humane sentiments while helping to preserve capitalist exploitation.

In this text we shall follow the most common usage among scholars. While no simple definition is fully satisfactory, terms are often viewed as points along a continuum: reactionary, conservative, moderate, liberal, and radical or revolutionist.[39] They represent a progression of attitudes toward the existing society and toward changes in it. Reactionaries would like to return to the society of some earlier period (or, more correctly, to a romanticized image of society as they imagine it to have been). Conservatives wish to preserve the existing society with no great changes, but will accept some limited reforms that they see as necessary to preserve the society. The moderate accepts a few more reforms than the conservative. The liberal sees far more good than bad in the existing society, but advocates much more sweeping reforms than the moderate or conservative. The radical or revolutionist considers the existing society too rotten to be worth saving, and seeks a wholesale overturn of existing institutions and values. Not all revolutionists desire a violent, shooting revolution, but all seek sweeping changes in values and fundamental shifts in the power system. The term *neoconservative* has recently been applied to some prominent intellectuals who were liberal or radical in their youth, but who have developed a special brand of moderate conservatism as they have grown older (and more prosperous!).[40]

To illustrate these terms, consider attitudes toward business and government. Most reactionaries would like to return to a system in which business interests clearly dominate the government, while the main function of government is to serve business. Most conservatives would dismiss this as foolish romanticism, yet wish business to have a very strong voice in government, which would rarely if ever take any action that business interests would oppose. The moderate generally believes that government should balance the interests of business, labor, and other public groups, while no group would have veto power over government policy. The liberal is likely to believe that government should actively promote the public interest, ignoring any protests from business, labor, or other organized interest groups, and should actively assist the poor and the weak at the expense of the prosperous and the strong. The radical or revolutionary sees all such "public interest" programs and controls as ineffectual, as mere smokescreens for exploitation by the rich and powerful, and calls for control of the economy by "the people."

This brief sketch is imperfect in several respects. A person may be conservative on one issue and liberal on another. And in some respects the diagram should be a circle, not a straight line, because in some respects the reactionary and the radical are in agreement, not in opposition. Both despise the existing society, both view liberals and reformers with contempt, and both are disdainful of tolerance and civil liberties and distrustful of the democratic process. Both are ready to impose their views upon the majority by force and violence. But, despite the imperfections in the terms, one cannot discuss contemporary events without using them.

It is no easy adventure upon which you are invited. The interpretation of data is the most difficult task in social science. It requires a degree of objectivity that not all students have the will or capability to develop; it demands an awareness of common pitfalls such as those described in this chapter; it requires an accumulation of factual knowledge—plain, unvarnished, unspectacular, painstakingly acquired facts—without which no intellectual tricks or short cuts will bring the practical understanding of social issues that students presumably desire. Although the study of social problems will never be dull, neither will it be easy. The most difficult task of all will be to recognize and accept the truth when one has found it.

Summary

Data (facts) lead nowhere by themselves; they are quite motionless. Data must be *interpreted* before they have meaning. The first problem is to establish with reasonable certainty whether the data are *true*. The popular faith that "they couldn't say those things if there weren't some truth in them" underestimates both the skill of an accomplished liar and the unintended distortion inherent in one's frame of reference. Those who wish to falsify the truth are likely to

1. Lie about a group.
2. Lie about the dead.
3. Lie about a public figure.
4. Imply guilt by association.
5. Impute wicked motives, purposes, or consequences.
6. Use "weasel" words.
7. Quote out of context.
8. "Document" elaborately.
9. Repeat the lie until it becomes accepted as fact.

How is a fact to be recognized as authoritative? Among the useful tests for reliability in interpreting data are the following:

1. Authorship—who said it?
   a. What is the person's training and competence?
   b. What is the person's bias?
   c. Is the person emotionally stable?
2. Sponsorship—who publishes, distributes, or promotes it?
3. Vested interest—whose axe is showing?
4. Factual content—how specific is the author?
5. Verifiability—can it be checked?
6. Relevancy—do the data support the conclusions?
7. Style—is it descriptive or propagandistic?
8. Consistency—does it agree with other known facts?
9. Plausibility—does it sound reasonable?

In interpreting statistical data, it is easy to employ truthful data to reach false conclusions. Distortion may be suspected whenever a sample is too small to be *adequate*, or too carelessly controlled to be accurately *representative* of the groups and classes of people involved. The *base* on which a percentage or index number is computed, or which is used as a starting point for a trend or comparison, may be chosen to give a true picture, or may be chosen so as to conceal the truth.

In using averages, the *mean* will always be misleading if based on a lopsided, rather than a normal, distribution, whereas the *mode* or *median* will give a more nearly typical picture. A graph line can be flattened or sharpened by stretching or compressing the scales along the axes, and each graph must be carefully studied for possible distortion. Public opinion polls can be used either to measure or to manufacture public opinion. Sampling errors, loaded questions, or a limited choice of answers may give fallacious results.

Associations and correlations are most useful in suggesting hypotheses and indicating *possible* causes. But an association is real only when something occurs more often than chance would indicate; thus, every claimed association between two factors must be checked by asking how often these two factors normally occur together. When it is found that two factors *do* occur together more often (or less often) than can be accounted for by chance, it still remains to be shown whether either one causes the other. Neither association nor correlation proves anything beyond the *possibility* of causation.

Such terms as *reactionary, conservative, moderate, liberal, radical,* and *revolutionist* describe some alternative positions upon the causes and treatment of social problems. Each term suggests a fairly consistent outlook, which its holder is likely to apply to the world in general. While imperfect, these terms are useful concepts.

Suggested Readings

CAHN, ROBERT, "Buying the Voters' Minds," *Audubon*, Jan. 1980, pp. 105–112. Analysis of competing propaganda on the bottle-bill controversy, illustrating many of the techniques discussed in this chapter.

DUNHAM, BARROWS, *Man against Myth* (Boston: Little, Brown, 1947). A critical examination of some of the major myths and intellectual clichés of our time.

EVANS, BERGEN, *The Natural History of Nonsense* (New York: Alfred A. Knopf, 1946). A highly entertaining account of many popular myths and superstitions, which the author demolishes with a rare blend of wit and erudition.

GARDNER, MARTIN, *Fads and Fallacies in the Name of Science* (New York: Dover, 1957); earlier edition titled *In the Name of Science* (New York: G. P. Putnam's Sons, 1952). An extensive catalog of unscientific and pseudoscientific claims and theories.

HUFF, DARRELL, *How to Lie with Statistics* (New York: W. W. Norton, 1954). A breezy little book on the use and misuse of statistics.

MacDOUGAL, CURTIS D., *Hoaxes* (New York: Dover, 1958; 2nd ed., Toronto: Macmillan, 1940). Fakes and frauds in history, science, literature, art, journalism, and politics, engagingly presented and analyzed.

MONTAGU, ASHLEY, and EDWARD DARLING, *The Prevalence of Nonsense* (New York: Harper & Row, 1967). A highly readable exploration of widely believed nonsense.

SPEAR, MARY ELEANOR, *Practical Charting Techniques* (New York: McGraw-Hill, 1969). A brief, clearly written explanation of graphs and charts and their interpretation.

Footnotes

[1]Vartanig G. Vartan, "Probing the Market's Depths," *New York Times*, 24 Feb. 1974, sec. 3, p. 1.

[2]See Paul R. Ashley, *Say It Safely: Legal Limits in Journalism and Broadcasting* (Seattle: University of Washington Press, 1976) for an explanation of the laws of libel and slander. For a popularized account of deception and misrepresentation in advertising, see Sam S. Baker, *The Permissible Lie: The Inside Truth about Advertising* (Cleveland: World, 1968); or Ivan L. Preston, *The Great American Blow-up: Puffery in Advertising and Selling* (Madison: University of Wisconsin Press, 1975).

[3]John Carl Miller, *Building Poe Biography* (Baton Rouge: University of Louisiana Press, 1977).

[4]See "Private People," *Time*, 9 July 1979, and "Court Narrows the Defenses in Libel Suits," *New York Times*, 1 July 1979, Sec. 4, p. 7.

[5]See John A. Stormer, *None Dare Call It Treason* (Florissant, Mo.: Liberty Bell Press, 1964). For an entertaining example, see *New York Times Book Review*, 21 July 1968, pp. 1ff., for reviews of two books, one of which (Allan H. Ryskind, *Hubert* [New York: Arlington House, 1968]) attacks 1968 presidential candidate Hubert Humphrey as a "pink" who sold us out to the communists, while the other (Robert Sherrill and Harry W. Ernst, *The Drugstore Liberal* [New York: Grossman, 1968]) attacks him as a phony liberal who sold out to the conservatives. A more recent example of presidential character assassination is Philip Roth, *Our Gang (Starring Tricky and His Friends)* (New York: Random House, 1971), a satirical novel about a fictitious president named Trick E. Dixon.

[6]Adapted from Stuart Chase, "Guilt by Association," *New York Times,* 14 Oct. 1951.

[7]See Robert Welch, *The Politician* (Belmont, Mass.: Belmont, 1964).

[8]For example, see James J. Graham, *The Enemies of the Poor* (New York: Random House, 1970); and Frances Fox

Piven and Richard A. Cloward, *Regulating the Poor: The Functions of Public Welfare* (New York: Pantheon Books, 1971).

[9]Dick Stark, quoted in *Time*, 16 June 1952, p. 72.

[10]Richard J. Harris, "The Comprehension of Pragmatic Implications in Advertising," *Journal of Applied Psychology* (in press).

[11]See Leonard W. Levy, *Jefferson and Civil Liberties: The Darker Side* (Cambridge, Mass.: Belknap Press of Cambridge University Press, 1963).

[12]See Lerone Bennett, Jr., "Was Abe Lincoln a White Supremacist?" *Ebony*, Feb. 1968, pp. 35ff., for the accusation; see Herbert Miltgang, "Was Lincoln Just a Honkie?" *New York Times Magazine*, 11 Feb. 1968, pp. 34ff., for a reply.

[13]Stormer, *None Dare Call It Treason*.

[14]Philip D. Read, quoted in *The Progressive*, Oct. 1951, p. 8. Read was chairman of the board of directors of General Electric.

[15]This and a later statement that "the actual number of Panthers murdered by the police is many times that number" were made by Charles R. Garry, chief counsel for the Black Panther Party. See Edward Jay Epstein, "The Panthers and the Police: A Pattern of Genocide?" *The New Yorker*, 13 Feb. 1971, pp. 45–77.

[16]See Tom Wolfe, *Radical Chic and Mau-Mauing the Flak Catchers* (New York: Farrar, Straus & Giroux, 1970) for an amusing description.

[17]See F. K. Huessenstamm, "Bumper Stickers and the Cops," *Trans-Action*, Feb. 1971, pp. 32–34.

[18]When Edward Jay Epstein pressed Garry for the names and details, Garry provided only twenty names. Of these, one was killed by a storekeeper in a holdup and nine were killed by other blacks, leaving ten who were killed by police. In six of these cases, it appears that blacks initiated the shooting; only four were shot by police who had not themselves already been wounded; only two blacks were killed when they were not actively threatening the lives of police. While even two unjustified killings are two too many, the evidence for "police genocide" is unconvincing. See Epstein, "The Panthers and the Police," for a detailed account of each incident.

[19]Described in Robin Fox, "The Chinese Have Bigger Brains than Whites—Are They Superior?" *New York Times Magazine*, 30 June 1968, pp. 12ff.; see also Associated Press reports of the January 1972 annual meeting of the American Physical Society.

[20]For an account of how a person with no scientific training became a "national diet authority," see Ralph Lee Smith, "The Vitamin Healers," *The Reporter*, 16 Dec. 1965, pp. 18–25.

[21]In most states, anyone who can spell the word can adopt the label "psychologist" and collect fees for "psychological services" from the uninformed.

[22]See Harold D. Lasswell, *Psychopathology and Politics* (Chicago: University of Chicago Press, 1930); and Eric Hoffer, *The True Believer* (New York: Harper & Brothers, 1951) for classic statements of this idea.

[23]Letter in *Time*, 26 Mar. 1979, p. 5.

[24]See "Good Old Dirty Tricks," *Time*, 30 Oct. 1972, p. 12.

[25]Adapted from Institute for Propaganda Analysis, *The Fine Art of Propaganda*, eds. Alfred McClung Lee and Elizabeth Briant Lee (New York: Harcourt, Brace and World, 1939), pp. 23–24.

[26]*Motor Trend*, Mar. 1958, p. 86.

[27]This title, and some of the illustrations that follow, are taken from Darrell Huff, *How to Lie with Statistics* (New York: W. W. Norton, 1954).

[28]Most listings miss some people. The census misses several million, including many people who have no fixed address and many illegal aliens; a city directory misses the newcomers and the drifters. The telephone book would provide a random sample of telephone subscribers, but would not be representative of the entire community, since many of the poor have no telephone.

[29]See Robert Rosendahl and Ralph L. Rosnow, *The Volunteer Subject* (New York: John Wiley, 1975), for a discussion of self-selected samples.

[30]Lee H. Bowker, *Women, Crime and the Criminal Justice System* (Lexington, Mass.: Lexington Books, 1978), p. 6.

[31]*Business Week*, 6 Mar. 1971, p. 44.

[32]The Conference Board, *Economic Road Maps*, May 1979.

[33]Reported in *Moneysworth* (consumer newsletter published at 110 W. 40th St., New York), 27 Dec. 1971.

[34]Between 1960 and September 1979, the consumer price index rose from 88.7 to 221.1, an increase of 149 percent, while average weekly wages rose from $80.67 to $224.55, an increase of 187

percent. Between 1972 and September 1979, the consumer price index rose from 125.3 to 221.1, an increase of 66 percent, while average weekly wages rose from $136.99 to $224.55, an increase of 54 percent. Source: *Monthly Labor Review*, various dates.

[35]For example, the "parity price" formula used to determine federal price supports for farm products is based upon a five-year period, 1910–14. The Bureau of Labor's Consumer Price Index was based on prices of selected items for the 1935–39 period until 1953; on 1947–49 prices until 1963; on 1957–59 prices until 1971; and on 1967 prices since 1971.

[36]See Huff, *How to Lie with Statistics*, for other examples of graphic deception. For a brief, understandable explanation of various kinds of graphs and charts and their interpretation, see Mary Eleanor Spear, *Charting Statistics* (New York: McGraw-Hill, 1969).

[37]A *statistical association* is a relationship between two pairs of categories, such as drinker-nondrinker and em-

ployed-unemployed. A *correlation* is a statistical measure of degree of association between two sets of quantitative variables, such as amount of education and amount of income.

[38]James Ray Adams and E. Belvin Williams, *The Association between Smoking and Accidents: Overdependency as an Influencing Variable* (Safety Research and Education Project, Teachers College, Columbia University, n.d. Available from Farmers Insurance Group, Box 948, Aurora, Ill. 60507).

[39]Some would distinguish between *radical* and *revolutionist* with the revolutionist seeking more complete change in institutions and values than the radical, but there is considerable tendency to use the terms interchangeably. In strict correctness, *revolutionist* is a noun and *revolutionary* is an adjective, but these terms, also, are often used interchangeably.

[40]See Peter Steinfels, *The Neoconservatives: The Men Who Are Changing America's Policies* (New York: Simon and Schuster, 1979).

PART

Major Social Problems in the United States

Peter Southwick, Stock, Boston

VESTED INTEREST AND PRESSURE GROUPS 4

Tax law reform. Killed.

Labor law reform. Dispatched to die in committee.

Consumer protection agency. Killed.

Hospital cost containment. Gutted.

The crude-oil tax in energy bill. Stalled.

There is normally a complex of reasons for the failure of a major piece of legislation to emerge from Congress and sometimes it is simply that there is no clear national consensus behind it. But in these five instances, and others like them, the force that proved decisive in blocking passage this year arose out of a dramatic new development in Washington: the startling increase in the influence of special-interest lobbyists. . . .

The lobbyists have grown so able and strong that last week a mere handful of them was able to kill another bill, one of particular significance to them. It would have required the lobbyists to reveal who pays them, who they represent and what issues they have sought to shape. . . .

There was irony in the spectacle of some of the most sophisticated generals of the vast new army of lobbyists, so skilled at casting the special interests of their clients in terms of the broader national good, now pleading so persuasively to keep their own operations secret. It was evidence of the extent to which the increasingly independent members of Congress have let the clashing voices of a multitude of special interests obscure their own sense of the broader national good.

Lobbying as such is scarcely a sin. Quite the contrary. Without lobbying . . . government could not function. The flow of information to Congress and to every federal agency is a vital part of our democratic system. But there is a darker side to lobbying. It derives from the secrecy of lobbying and the widespread suspicion, even when totally unjustified, that secrecy breeds undue influence and corruption.

The . . . concern is justified. . . . While fewer than 2,000 lobbyists are registered with Congress under a largely ignored 1946 law, their actual number has soared from about 8,000 to 15,000 over the past five years. Their mass arrival has transformed Washington's downtown K Street into a virtual hall of lobbies. . . . It is estimated that lobbyists now spend $1 billion to orchestrate public opinion across the nation.

There is probably not a single major corporation that does not now employ Washington lobbyists. Ford Motor Co. . . . maintains a full-time staff of 40 people. Among the airlines alone, 77 have their separate lobbying staffs in Washington. . . . Of the roughly 6,000 national trade and professional associations in the U.S., 27 percent are now headquartered . . . in Washington. . . .

Apart from business and industry, 50 labor unions maintain their separate offices in Washington, often working independently from A.F.L.–C.I.O. Chief George Meany's 300-member staff. . . . Politically aware action groups also have their lobbyists in Washington, including 14 that pursue the special interests of the elderly and six that deal with air pollution. . . . Large staffs are maintained by such . . . public interest groups as Common Cause and the Ralph Nader organization. Grumbles House Speaker Tip O'Neill: "Everybody in America has a lobby."[1]

All of us know, in a general way, that powerful organizations lobby the Congress incessantly to secure the passage of legislation that is favorable to them, and to defeat bills that they don't like. What is not so often recognized is that lobbying is an inevitable accompaniment of the thousands of interest groups that make up modern society.

Special Interest and Pressure Groups

Most people in the United States believe in democracy, fair play, and proportional representation. People are expected to sacrifice purely selfish interests in favor of the general welfare, and representative government is supposed to protect us against those who would subvert the democratic process. If it worked this way in practice, this chapter need not—indeed, *could not*—have been written. This ideal picture of how society should operate fails to consider the operation of interest groups and pressure groups.

INTEREST GROUPS

One of the delightful, perplexing, and occasionally frightening things about modern society is its multiplicity of special interests. Some people obtain deep satisfaction from supporting a symphony orchestra; others "dig" only modern sounds; some don false mustaches to sing barbershop-quartet melodies; still others protest against any kind of music being piped into a public transit system or played, for the community's benefit, on church bells. People who could not care less about music may be vitally interested in cats, or peanuts, or local traffic ordinances, or stamp collecting, or right-to-work laws, or any one of thousands of other aspects of modern life.

Most people find others with similar interests, with whom they form an organization. The Philharmonic-Society, the Society for the Preservation and Encouragement of Barbershop-Quartet Singing in America, the American Feline Society, the Anti-Nicotine League of America, the American Medical Association, the American Legion, the National Association for the Advancement of Colored People, the National Council for the Prevention of War, the Vine Street PTA, and the North Side Neighborhood Association are a few examples of special interest groups in American society.

When people band together to further their common interests, they theoretically do so without threatening the interests of other groups. Actually, of course, this is not true. The interests of any group may conflict at many points with the interests of other groups. The interests of the peanut growers (who want high prices for peanuts) conflict with the interests of candy makers (who want cheap peanuts to put in their candy bars). And when the National Organization for Women and Zero Population Growth promote the right of women to secure abortions, they are opposed by the National Right to Life Committee and other such organizations.

Organization into special interest groups is a natural development of life in any complex society. Common interests reflect at least a few shared values, and it is pleasant and profitable to associate with others who share our values. The shared values that encourage comradeship and loyalty within the group, however, may possibly bring it into conflict with other groups. Actual or latent conflict implies that the success of one group in promoting its interest may have been at the expense of another group's interest. When groups become aware of the possibility, or the necessity, of advancing their interests at the expense of another group's interests, the stage is set for the appearance of pressure groups.

PRESSURE GROUPS

When special interest groups actively work to impose their wishes on others, they operate as pressure groups. Pressure groups exist to do exactly what the word *pressure* connotes: to apply strong influence whenever necessary to gain their ends.

Perhaps the sharpest examples of pressure group operation are found in the field of practical "power politics." Here, pressure groups encourage legislation favorable to themselves, combat unfavorable legislation, and attempt to influence the administration of laws already in existence. Accordingly, they seek the election of particular political candidates; they try to influence the appointment of public officials; and they conduct lobby operations in local, state, and national capitals and extensive "educational" campaigns designed to mold public opinion. Pressure groups are intimately associated with all extensive conflicts of interests in the contemporary scene.

Pressure groups, as well as the special interest groups from which they usually develop, are a natural consequence of the advantages of organization in our modern society in which organized power is the most effective kind. Few individuals possess enough power to attain their goals unaided, and the few people who do have such force become still more powerful when they band together. Pressure groups are natural in all areas of activity. The efficient conduct of religious, educational, civic, and business affairs requires organized influence.

Vested Interest Groups

So far, our discussion has treated interest and pressure groups as though they all had equal chances to attain their goals. In a certain formal sense, this is true. We have also emphasized the role of interest and pressure groups in promoting social change. Again, they do often promote change. But the situation is more complicated than that. Over time in a society, certain interests tend to be more successful than others. They manage to have their views accepted by the society at large, and they accumulate money, organization, and power. In so doing, they become *vested interests:* interest groups that derive special advantage from things as they are, that seek to protect their special advantages, and that oppose all further changes except those favorable to them.

To some degree we all have vested interests. Physicians have a vested interest in the practice of medicine. Parents have a vested interest in the local schools. Professors of sociology have a vested interest in the curriculum.

When vested interest groups turn to organized demonstrations, they are classified as pressure groups. One such effective use of pressure resulted in the FDA's 1977 investigation into liquid protein products, which culminated in warning labels being required.
(United Press International)

Students acquire a vested interest in the university that may grant their degrees. Furthermore, vested interests, when they pursue their interests, may either benefit the public interest or they may damage it. When physicians' organizations prevent quacks and untrained people from practicing medicine, for example, both the medical profession and the public are protected from injury. When they oppose mass immunization programs, however, as they have done in some instances, their action probably benefits the profession, but whether it also benefits the community is debatable.

SPECIAL INTERESTS AND VESTED INTERESTS IN COMPETITION

Special interest and vested interest groups continually oppose one another concerning social change. Special interest groups tend to be initiators of action, while vested interest groups are more often opponents of change. Objectively, vested interests possess many advantages. They are protecting what is already theirs by law and custom; they have power, organization, and often the weight of public opinion with them. Yet, the fact that vested interests find it necessary to marshal and employ their resources with ever-increasing skill indicates that the advantages are not completely on their side.

Vested interests compete not only with special interest groups and amorphous, unorganized masses of people who have no particular interests but also with one another. The number of vested interests in the United States, like the number of pressure groups, is unknown, but surely it is extremely large. Some groups are small, and some are huge; some are better organized and more powerful than others. The company that has a contract to supply coal for the boilers of a local institution and the people who manage to have truck traffic routed around their neighborhood, for example, have vested interests that are noncompeting but that bring them into potential conflict with other coal or oil companies and with other neighborhoods. Relief clients and the business community are large, powerful, and competitive vested interests whose purposes bring them into sharp conflict with many other segments of the community. Recipients of public assistance oppose measures that would interrupt the receipt of, or decrease the amounts of, their monthly checks. Hence, they oppose the enforcement of "need" provisions, economy drives, the opening of welfare rolls to public inspection, and so on. Other vested interests—chambers of commerce, local tax groups, and the like—further their interests by trying to have the welfare rolls cut. Whether the rolls go up or down at any time often is determined by the relative strength of these and other vested interest groups, such as professional social workers.

The struggles of vested interests must, however, take into account a latent power that is almost always greater than theirs. This is the power of the majority of the people, most of whom are members of various vested interest groups, but who are not immediately interested in a particular conflict. The interest of the quiescent majority may become focused on an issue; if it does, its judgment of the worth of the competing vested interest groups may completely shift the balance of power among them. Vested interests openly compete with each other at times, but they constantly compete—consciously or not—for public support.

Historically in the United States, the most visible and one of the most powerful vested interests was that segment of the population usually referred to simply as "business." The next sections will trace the rise of business as a vested interest and the challenges to that interest that have appeared in recent decades.

Business: A Primary Vested Interest

To understand the role played by business—especially big business—in the current struggle of interest groups, we must know something of the historical developments that resulted in the present situation. Briefly, it was the emergence during the eighteenth century of a set of principles concerning the relations of employers and employees and the right of individuals to acquire, hold, and use property that paved the way for business to become a major vested interest.

FREE CONTRACT

At the time business definitions were formulated, industry was still in the handicraft stage, and large-scale corporate organization was far in the future. Shops were small; worker and employer worked side by side and talked the same language. Employers and workers had approximately equal bargaining power, so neither could unduly exploit the other. The employer was essential to the workers, and the workers were essential to the employer. Each had to bargain with the other. This situation, in which buyers and sellers of labor bargained with one another, became embodied in the principle of "free contract." The right of workers to seek the best jobs and the best pay they could find and the right of employers to hire them at the lowest wages possible became integral parts of the philosophy of economics and government now known as laissez faire. Each person was a free agent with the right to enter into any contract. So long as the power wielded by employers and employees was approximately equal, free contract did indeed prevail.

PRIVATE PROPERTY

Owners and workers were free to make the best bargains they could, and each claimed the right to hold and to use the fruits of their labors in their own best interest. The acquisition of property was both an end in itself and the means for the acquisition of more property. Thus, the concept of private property developed along with that of free contract. Through diligence and thrift, workers might advance themselves eventually to the status of owner and/or employer. Then, by paying wages, they would enable others to climb the same ladder. The only restriction placed on the use of property was that it should not be used to infringe upon the property rights of others. As laissez faire became firmly entrenched in the political and economic life of Western European nations, property rights gradually became inviolable. Since property was a means for the acquisition of more property, its permanent possession and free use provided the cornerstone for the growth of modern industry and business.

Born of the twin principles of free contract and private property, business quickly took on the character of a vested interest seeking to maintain intact its parent principles. Further developments were the increased concentration of business power and the separation of ownership from control.

GROWTH AND CONCENTRATION

Even before the turn of this century the concentration of business and industrial power had led to the passage of antitrust laws. The Sherman Antitrust Law, 1890, and the Clayton Act, 1914, were the chief weapons of government in its attempt to prevent the growth of business monopoly. That they did not succeed, however, in preventing the spread of semimonopolistic conditions throughout the American economy is easily established.

Some early indication of the amount of industrial concentration in the United States was provided by information compiled by the Temporary National Economic Committee before World War II. It found that in the field of transportation and public utilities, fewer than one-twentieth of the total number of corporations owned 93 percent of the corporate assets. In manufacturing, fewer than 2 percent of the corporations owned 66 percent of the assets. Even in the construction industry and in agriculture, both of which are strongly competitive, the few multimillion-dollar corporations owned over one-fourth of the total corporate assets. The situation has not changed significantly since World War II. In 1970 four companies in each field accounted for 91 percent of all of the output of motor vehicles, 84 percent of cigarettes, 72 percent of tires, and 70 percent of detergents.[2]

The 1970s saw special growth and concentration in the food industry. United Brands, for example, controls over 50 percent of the United States banana market and, in addition, A&W Root Beer, Baskin-Robbins ice cream parlors, and John Morrell and Company, one of the four giant meat companies that sell most of the processed meats in America. The Safeway grocery chain owns more than 2,400 supermarkets, 109 processing and manufacturing plants, 16 bakeries, 4 soft-drink bottlers, 3 meat processors, 3 coffee-roasting plants, a soap–peanut butter–salad oil factory, a fleet of 2,100 tractor-trailers, 60 warehouses, and a half-interest in 25 Holly Farms fried-chicken outlets.[3]

The United Auto Workers has one and so does Coca-Cola Co. There is one called Speak Up for Rural Electrification and another named the Committee to Defeat the Union Bosses' Candidates. They are political-action committees, a bewildering assortment of more than 1,700 fund-raising groups that represent business, labor, single-issue advocates and political candidates. In short order, they have become a major factor in American elections. . . .

The trend has alarmed some politicians. PAC's "are multiplying like rabbits, and they are doing their best to buy every senator, every representative and every issue in sight," charges Sen. Edward Kennedy. The special-interest money further undermines the party system and atomizes the legislative process, critics say. "It's almost impossible now to create national policy in Congress because you have very powerful interest groups slicing up the pie," says Fred Wertheimer of Common Cause. "What we're headed for is the United PAC's of America."

A study released by Common Cause . . . provides some examples of PACification. Of the 22 House Commerce Committee members who voted to kill the hospital-cost containment bill—vigorously opposed by the American Medical Association—nineteen had received $85,150 over the past three and a half years from AMPAC, which is run by the AMA. . . . The AFL–CIO backed an amendment to the bill exempting the wages of hospital workers from cost controls. Of the fifteen committee members who voted for it, eleven had received a total of $61,250 from the AFL–CIO. "While substantial campaign contributions may not actually 'buy' votes, they do ensure easy access to public officials and create an unhealthy atmosphere of familiarity," the study says.

The power of PAC's stems directly from the election law reforms of the early 1970s. When Congress limited individual campaign donations to $1,000 per candidate per race, it permitted corporations, unions and other groups to become involved in making direct political contributions to candidates. Companies are still barred from contributing corporate funds, but through their PAC's, they may solicit voluntary contributions from employees and stockholders and then give up to $5,000 to candidates in each of their primary and general election campaigns. A business-oriented congressman on a key committee, for example, can take in tens of thousands of dollars from dozens of corporate PAC's. . . .

Source: *Newsweek,* 6 Nov. 1978, p. 57.

SEPARATION OF OWNERSHIP AND CONTROL

An important accompaniment of industrial growth and concentration is the tendency for the control of large corporations to become more and more concentrated in the hands of management officials who own only a small fraction of the corporation stock. Boards of directors and a few company officials often execute almost complete control over the company, sometimes to the disadvantage of the numerous heterogeneous absent stockholders. The significance of this development is that the wresting of control from the majority of owners has markedly altered the nature of private property. The purchasers of shares of stock acquire no right to use their property as they see fit, but surrender that right to company officers and directors in

Stockholders share a common vested interest in the inner workings and financial status of their company or corporation; an annual stockholders' meeting is conducted by the company to impart this and other information to its shareholders.
(United Press International)

return for receiving dividends. Although directors are theoretically elected by the stockholders, they often become a self-perpetuating clique—and the interests of management and stockholders are not completely identical.

Increasingly, actual control of corporations is in the hands of *holding companies,* separate corporations that buy up the small fraction of stock needed to control boards of directors. The producing corporation is then forced to pay large shares of its profits to the holding company rather than to its majority stockholders. Occasionally, too, the holding company, because it controls several corporations, may discourage production in one company to benefit the others. Corporation management bitterly opposes any outside regulation of corporations on the grounds that such regulation would violate the rights of private property. It fails to recognize, or finds it expedient to deny, that there has been any alteration in the *nature* of this property itself.

CONTROL OF LIFE CONDITIONS   The rise of great corporations has in another way significantly affected the conditions under which business and industry operate. After the Industrial Revolution and the appearance of the factory system, the right of free contact began to lose its original meaning. The worker's freedom of action was greatly curtailed by the course of events. As industries grew in size, employer and employee ceased to be equals in their ability to bargain. Eventually, as small cogs in a vast machine, the workers were subjected to whatever conditions industry imposed on them. Their ability to bargain as individuals disappeared along with the individual employer. Having gained this advantage over the worker, the business world has typically sought to retain it. In general, management was and is violently opposed to any measures that would give more power to labor groups.

AWAKENING OPPOSITION   Among the first signs that the validity of the free contract and private property concepts was being questioned seriously was the passage of antitrust legislation by the federal government. The Sherman and Clayton acts, in effect, served notice that other interests, operating through government, had risen to challenge the lofty position of the industrialists. Nor was this the only sign of impending change. At least since 1869, when the Knights of Labor was organized, there had been signs that working groups were actively seeking redress in the balance of power with management. In 1886 the American Federation of Labor appeared on the scene; it was joined by the Congress of Industrial Organizations after 1935. Beginning early in the 1930s, political policies traditionally sympathetic to business interests almost continually lost ground to the "common man" policies of the New Deal.

An American economist has advanced the theory that whenever a vested interest arises, certain forces that tend to foster the development of compensatory power in other segments of the population are set in motion.[4] The appearance of a *countervailing power* in the United States was manifested by the development of the labor movement. Let us now examine carefully the status of this and other newly developed interest groups.

BIG GOVERNMENT   The role of the federal government in the clash of special interests and vested interests is threefold: (1) the government, since it represents the people, supports the efforts of emerging interest groups against the established power of vested interests; (2) the government, itself a big business, has taken on the character of a vested interest; and (3) the government must make numerous administrative decisions affecting interest groups and the "public interest."

1. Government efforts to limit the power of industry by means of antitrust legislation have already been mentioned. Such efforts do not end with the passage of legislation; the prosecution of business combinations that practice restraint of trade is regularly carried on by the Department of Justice.

In a more indirect, though not necessarily less effective, fashion, the government offers aid to groups attempting to cope with business power. Government support of the rising trade-union movement is a case in point. When the Sherman and Clayton acts, originally designed to apply to business, were held by judicial interpretation to apply to labor unions also, the Norris-LaGuardia anti-injunction law of 1932 protected the growing unions against this form of restraint. The National Labor Relations Act of 1935 was even more favorable to organized labor and is often credited, by those who speak for business, at least, with having given labor a position more desirable than that of industry. In a similar fashion, the government has favored farmer and consumer groups by giving a special tax status to their cooperatives,[5] thus enabling them to compete with other business.

87

2. In addition to its role as a supporter of emerging interests, the federal government is increasingly involved in running its own business. The expansion of its self-operating activities has been accompanied by a tendency to become a self-perpetuating and self-aggrandizing agency. Since 1930 the number of civilian employees of the federal government has increased by some 500 percent, to approximately three million. It is extremely difficult to eliminate any kind of government service once it has been established. Big government has become a vested interest, and business and government are engaged in preventing one another from exercising dictatorial control over the lives of the American people.

3. The government constantly makes administrative decisions that benefit one interest at the expense of another, benefit an interest at the expense of the public, or protect the public at some cost to a vested interest. One or another government agency must rule on such questions as, How much fat may be included in hamburger and sausage? How much water may be pumped into hams? How many pounds of rodent excreta may be present in a carload of grain before it is ruled unfit for human consumption? How many test data are required before a new drug is approved for general use? Shall a merger of companies X and Y be permitted or prosecuted under the antitrust laws? What profit rates should be permitted to government-regulated monopolies, such as telephone and gas companies? On what terms should new inventions and discoveries (such as communications satellites or new drugs) financed by government research be licensed for profitable promotion by business concerns? How much should localities and industries be forced to spend to reduce air and water pollution? Should local building codes be amended to permit use of new building materials or processes?

At every government level such decisions must be made. *U.S. News and World Report* fills one page per week with a brief list of the changes in what business may or may not legally do as a result of new laws, new court decisions, or new administrative rulings. Perhaps the most important function of modern government is to provide the arena wherein the clashing interests of rival interest groups and of the public are battled out.

BIG LABOR   The past four decades have seen organized labor, with the aid of government, join the ranks of the big powers among the vested interests. The number of union members rose from 3.5 million in 1935 to 8.5 million in 1940, and then to 14 million in 1944. By 1979 the number had reached over 24 million. The Teamsters and the United Auto Workers were the largest unions with over 1½ million members each.

Although union membership has grown over the past decade, it has not grown as rapidly as the labor force itself, and the relative lack of union growth has become a source of dissension within the movement, with various factions contending for power. Both the Teamsters Union and the United Automobile Workers have been challenging the leadership of the AFL–CIO. The old stereotype of downtrodden labor hardly fits modern unionism.

Labor now claims the advantages it secured under the National Labor Relations Act of 1935 as inherent rights, while it bitterly opposes the subsequent Taft-Hartley Law as dictatorial, discriminatory, and unjust. Constantly striving to wrest a larger portion of the profits from business, organized labor is now obviously a vested interest of approximately coordinate standing with business and government. In some respects it has ceased to be a disprivileged minority group and has become a privileged group with a vested interest in the status quo.

BIG AGRICULTURE   Agriculture is not "big" in the sense that it has over 20 million farmers organized into unions, as labor has workers. Nevertheless, over the past few decades agriculture has become a potent force, demanding its share of the spoils along with business and labor. Agriculture's efforts to gain vested interest status have taken two principal directions. First, cooperative organizations have appeared for the marketing of farm products and the purchase of farm supplies and consumer goods. These cooperatives allow farmers the savings derived from large-scale operation and give them some measure of control over the supply of farm products reaching the market at any given time. The tremendously large numbers of farmers involved and the difficulty of persuading all to cooperate, however, have prevented the cooperatives from playing a major role in the development of countervailing power. It is the second development that is the major source of agriculture's power.

Though such measures were not an innovation, the program of support for farm prices and the establishment of production quotas begun in the 1930s marked the first serious government effort in the United States to help farmers establish a balance of power with industry. Beginning with the Agricultural Adjustment Act of 1933, the government has continuously kept "floors" under farm prices and has, itself, drained off excess farm products. Government subsidies and payments provide about one-half of total farm income. Many people believe that this is a temporary situation that will disappear "when the time is right." Such reasoning ignores two facts: First, the time was never judged to be "right" during the late 1960s and early 1970s, one of the most prosperous periods in American history. Second, and more important, it is now one of the functions of government to support the development and maintenance of "countervailing power" against the power of established interests. Government has aided agriculture in becoming a vested interest, and, with the aid of government, it apparently will remain a vested interest.

BIG DISTRIBUTION   Paradoxical though it may seem, certain developments within the business world itself gave rise to a new class of vested interests that further limited the power of the original business and industry groups. Contrary to general belief, the interests of all large firms are by no means identical. Specifically, there has appeared in the American economy a class of large retailers—for example, the grocery and department store chains, the mail-order houses, and the variety store chains—whose primary interest is to obtain goods as cheaply as possible from the manufacturers and then to sell them at low prices to the public. The very size of these retailers gives them great power over the manufacturers from whom they buy. By threatening to take their business elsewhere or by proposing to set up their own sources of supply, the retailers can generally force manufacturers' prices downward. This situation has resulted in great savings to the consumer, as can be demonstrated by a stroll through any chain supermarket. Curiously, the function of large retailers in limiting the power of manufacturers is not generally recognized, and much sentiment in Congress and among the general public is directed toward curtailing the buying power of such organizations. In any event, the chains are a powerful group, with which the other vested interests must reckon.

After the Industrial Revolution and into the early decades of the twentieth century, the privileged position of business and industry was firmly established. From the early 1930s onward, business power was gradually encroached upon by emerging vested interests in government, labor, distribution, and agriculture. Each acted as a source of countervailing power against the others, and the economy seemed to be held in reasonable balance. Then the power of business spread across national lines and effectively escaped the power of government to regulate it. The 1970s saw the flourishing of multinational corporations.

Multinational Corporations

Multinational corporations are not new, nor are they exclusively an American invention. Unilever, of British-Dutch ownership, and Shell, of British ownership, were among the earliest companies to go truly international. More recently Japanese and Arab multinationals have developed. But United States companies dominate the scene in numbers, in size, and in their attempts to control the world's economy.[6]

SIZE, CONCENTRATION, AND POWER

Many multinational corporations have annual sales that are larger than the gross national products of some of the countries in which they operate. General Motors, for example, has sales larger than the GNPs of Switzerland, South Africa, or Pakistan. Royal Dutch Shell is bigger than Venezuela, Turkey, and Iran. Goodyear is bigger than Saudi Arabia.[7] ITT has over 425,000 employees in 70 different countries; IBM controls over 40 percent of the world computer market.[8]

The top executives of the largest multinational corporations make decisions daily that have more effect upon economic conditions, standards of living, and lifestyles in different countries than do those of many presidents, prime ministers, or other government authorities. A prime example is to be found in the production, refining, and distribution of petroleum products, dominated by the so-called Seven Sisters (British Petroleum, Chevron, Exxon, Gulf, Mobil, Shell, and Texaco).

The United States government, through the Federal Trade Commission, in 1973 brought charges against the eight largest U.S. oil companies for monopolizing petroleum products over the previous 23 years. Specifically, it charged them with pursuing "a common course of action" such as juggling the price structure to inflate profits on the sale of crude oil, and with driving independent companies out of business by refusing to sell them petroleum products. Not only have the government's efforts at control been unsuccessful, but the companies went on during the latter months of 1973 to create a fictitious energy crisis in which gasoline prices soared and long lines of motorists waited at service stations for allegedly scarce gasoline. The companies blamed the "shortage" on environmental regulations that they claimed had made it impossible for them to develop new sources of supply, and upon a boycott by Arab oil-producing nations of countries trading with Israel. Actually, there was no shortage. In 1972 the United States was importing only about 3 percent of its oil from the Arab countries, and domestic oil stocks were actually higher at the time of the embargo than they had been a year earlier.[9] The energy crisis of 1973 was manipulated by the multinational oil companies. Even as this is being written in the summer of 1979, the scenario is being repeated. This time, the oil companies are seeking the elimination of price controls on petroleum products. The majority of the American people believe that the "shortage" of gasoline will be alleviated again as soon as prices rise high enough.

In longer perspective, the economy of the United States probably is threatened by both a shortage of refined petroleum products and constantly rising prices for those products. However, this threat, too, appears to be largely a result of multinational oil company policies and practices. The companies failed to build additional refineries because that part of their operation is not profitable enough. For decades they dominated the economies of Middle Eastern oil-producing countries, buying cheap oil and selling it in the United States at substantially higher prices. When the oil-producing countries finally organized to protect their interests, the Western oil companies were taken by surprise. Unbowed, they adjusted by simply passing along their increased costs to consumers, widening their profit margins in the process. They have little incentive either to develop new refineries or to drive hard bargains with the oil-producing countries.

Thus, in a few short years the oil companies were able to double the price of domestic gasoline, reap enormous profits, rid themselves of much unwanted competition from independent companies, sabotage environmental protection policies, and totally frustrate the efforts of the United States government to do anything about it. Only the companies, not the government, know what oil reserves the United States really has, and what their costs are for drilling, refining, and distribution. Under these circumstances not only is effective government regulation impossible, but the oil companies actually determine national policy in their area of the economy.

SUPRANATIONAL ORIENTATION

Global corporations clearly place their corporate interests above any loyalty to the countries in which they are located. They try to develop an international image, they ignore the national welfare, and they shift operations to areas of low labor costs.

INTERNATIONAL IMAGE   Because they operate in many countries, seeking a favorable political climate in each, multinational corporations try to escape identification with any one country. If they are not antinational in character, they are at least a-national, avoiding allegiance to any national government.

One of the ways in which U.S. companies are cultivating this new image is by quietly dropping the words *American* and *United States* from their corporate names. Thus, the U.S. Rubber Company has become Uniroyal, American Brake Shoe is now Abex, and American Metal Climax has become

Amax. With their new names and images, companies can be as much at home in India or Argentina as they are in the United States.

UNCONCERN WITH NATIONAL WELFARE   The global corporations are really trying to become companies without a country. The chairman of Dow Chemical Company put it bluntly: "I have long dreamed of buying an island owned by no nation and of establishing the World Headquarters of the Dow Company on the truly neutral ground of such an island, beholden to no nation or society."[10] Although this specific wish may be impractical, it conveys the attitude of corporate disregard for national problems.

The rationale for the multinationals' unconcern for the welfare of the United States is obvious enough. Much of their profit comes from operations abroad. In 1971 the pharmaceutical industry earned 22.4 percent profit abroad, compared to 15.5 percent in the United States. Similarly, the office-equipment industry earned 25.6 percent abroad, compared with 9.2 percent at home.[11]

American corporations are shifting more and more of their assets to other countries. About 75 percent of the assets of the electrical industry are now located outside the United States; 40 percent of those of the consumer-goods industry and one-third of the assets of the chemical and pharmaceutical industries have been moved abroad. A British financial analyst estimates that 90 percent of the overseas sales of U.S.-based corporations are manufactured abroad by foreign subsidiaries.[12]

An example of an American corporation's use of cheap labor in a foreign country. Liberian workers are shown here in an American-owned rubber plantation company.
(Frederick Ayer III, Photo Researchers, Inc.)

EXPLOITATION OF LOW LABOR COSTS   The exploitation of cheap labor abroad, part of the total disregard for national boundaries, threatens the U.S. economy. For example, General Electric finds it more profitable to ship components to Singapore for assembly at 30 cents per hour than to assemble in a United States plant for $3.40 per hour. Between 1957 and 1967 General Electric constructed 61 factories abroad.[13]

General Electric is far from alone. American electronics manufacturers, for example, are licensing companies in both Europe and the Far East to produce video recorders more cheaply than they can in the United States. Similarly, other U.S. companies have shifted production to low-wage Mexico, just over the border; they ship the finished products back to this country for distribution.[14]

The companies defend such practices by arguing that they pay more than the prevailing wages in other countries and thus help raise living standards around the world. That is true, as far as it goes. The modest increases for the employees of the multinationals, however, are not shared by most of their compatriots. Instead, in poor countries the divisions between the poor and the nonpoor tend to widen, and the problem of worldwide poverty is exacerbated.

In a curious way, the multinationals' policy of shifting production to underdeveloped countries is making a kind of underdeveloped country of the United States. Like traditionally underdeveloped countries, the United States is moving toward having to import many of its manufactured goods and to pay for them with exports of agricultural products and timber. This leads to food shortages at home and rampant inflation. Inflation hits hardest at the middle classes, tending to diminish the number of moderately prosperous people and widening the gap between the rich and the poor. These are classic characteristics of underdeveloped economies.

CONFLICTS WITH GOVERNMENTS

The huge global corporations not only operate in total disregard for the policies of the governments of their host countries, but they also espouse a one-world philosophy of business-created welfare that depreciates nationalism. In so doing, they advocate a very limited role for national government, and they actively subvert national policies when it is in their interest to do so.

THE BUSINESS-WELFARE PHILOSOPHY   Many top officials of the multinational corporations believe that national governments, and the policies that they have historically followed, are obsolete. Arguing that patriotic wars, antiquated geographic borders, and national pride have almost destroyed the world, business leaders envision an integrated world in which giant corporations, by pursuing their own interests, increase standards of living everywhere, create new mass markets, and forge a new sense of community based upon the pleasures of consumption. To do this, they require that governments should play a very limited role.

LIMITATIONS FOR NATIONAL GOVERNMENTS   The multinationals point out that traditional military strategies are no longer feasible for settling international conflicts. World War II helped create new alliances and antagonisms, even

93

as old ones were being defeated. Since then, in Korea, Vietnam, and the Middle East, even military victory has become elusive; certainly the political and ideological conflicts have not been solved. The experience of the United States is a case in point: it was unable to win in Korea and Vietnam, yet the government continues to follow obviously bankrupt military policies. By seeking to maintain a strong and highly visible military presence over much of the world, the United States has created a serious balance of payments problem, spending far too much overseas and fueling destructive financial inflation at home.

According to top multinational executives, governments should give up their militaristic policies and confine themselves to performing functions that will facilitate the growth of trade and industry. Government financial policy should be oriented to keeping the economy stable and interest rates level. Governments should be prepared to impose price and wage controls if necessary. In addition, they should provide the facilities that business requires: harbors, highways, communications, pure water supplies. Governments should also absorb some of the indirect costs of doing business, such as those stemming from environmental regulations and pollution controls. Governments should also bear the costs of training and retraining workers who are needed because of industry's rapid shifts in technology and the changing locations for production.[15]

SUBVERSION OF NATIONAL POLICIES   The global corporations' policies may merely remain aloof from, or they may actively subvert, those of the countries in which they operate. As long ago as World War II, for example, several U.S.-based corporations maintained cordial ties with Nazi Germany. In 1938 ITT, through a German subsidiary, bought 28 percent of the stock of Focke-Wulf, a company that produced military aircraft. During the war ITT facilities served both sides equally, and 30 years later ITT sought and received compensation from the U.S. government for damage that American bombers did to ITT's German plants.[16] More recently, U.S.-based corporations have managed to sell strategic goods to both Russia and China, despite federal regulations prohibiting such sales. During the Arab boycott of the United States, Exxon cooperated with the Arabs by refusing to sell to the U.S. Navy at Subic Bay, Philippines.

Business sometimes receives active support from some governments in its efforts to subvert the policies of other governments. The CIA and other U.S. agencies spent $20 million in Chile to defeat President Salvador Allende after Chile nationalized the Anaconda and Kennecott copper mines. Similarly, the U.S. government assisted a coup in Iran for the benefit of the Gulf and Standard Oil companies, and one in Guatemala for the United Fruit Company. Examples of U.S. pressure to open up other countries to American trade are too numerous to mention.[17]

AVOIDANCE OF PRICE COMPETITION

The multinational corporations represent themselves as delivering unprecedented quantities of goods to huge numbers of people at reasonable prices. The first two parts of the image are generally true: The multinationals are marvels of production, and they have vastly broadened their markets. Their pricing policies, however, are aimed at the maximization of profits and involve the explicit avoidance of price competition.

Many global corporations are huge conglomerates that control many companies, covering virtually every aspect of gathering raw materials, production, marketing, and distribution. The monopoly position of the major oil companies in this respect has been noted earlier. Not only do they control all aspects of the oil industry and manipulate prices almost at will, but they are now gaining control of other energy sources such as coal, shale, natural gas, and nuclear energy. As another example, banking conglomerates have acquired companies that deal in the leasing of aircraft and office equipment, travel services, insurance, commercial credit, credit cards, and mutual funds.

Such huge corporations do much of their business with themselves, one part of the conglomerate selling raw materials to another subsidiary that produces and sells them to another subsidiary, and so on and on. The situation lends itself to a system of "administered prices" in which each branch of the conglomerate presents itself as being at the mercy of other companies that in reality are part of the same large financial organization. Such conglomerates can overcharge almost at will and can shift profits among branches of the organization both to stifle competition and to avoid national taxes.

The European Economic Community has recently publicized numerous examples of price fixing and price gouging by multinational corporations. United Brands, for example, has been accused of charging twice as much for Chiquita bananas in prosperous markets such as West Germany as it charges in poorer markets such as Ireland. Kodak has been charged with price fixing, and Pittsburgh Corning with charging widely different prices in neighboring countries. An aluminum price-fixing cartel has been forced to dissolve itself, as has a sugar price-fixing arrangement. An Italian subsidiary of the New York-based Commercial Solvents Corp. has been accused of refusing to sell anti-TB drugs to an Italian company that resisted a takeover bid. There were over 100 such cases in all.[18]

CROSS-SUBSIDIZATION   Another pricing technique used by multinationals to gain near-monopoly positions in new industries is called "cross-subsidization." It involves the use of monopoly profits in one industry to subsidize sales at a loss or at abnormally low profits in the industry that the conglomerate is seeking to take over. Soft-drink bottlers, for example, can use their profits to break into the potato chip industry or the trucking industry. Once they gain control in the new industry, the prices go back up again or rise to higher levels than ever.[19] An official of United Brands admitted in public that one of its goals was to seize a "nonpre-emptable position as leader in fresh and semi-processed salad products, and then to boost the price of lettuce a hefty 70 to 90 cents per carton."[20]

Multinational corporations represent a new level of the development of business and industry as a vested interest. They have upset the existing balance of power among business, government, and labor. They have invaded agriculture and distribution to the extent that those two have become parts of business and industry rather than remaining as sources of countervailing power. Both social disorganization and value conflicts are some of the consequences.

The Social-Disorganization Approach

The social-disorganization approach traces social change through cycles of organization-disorganization-reorganization. We begin with the rules that prevailed when the United States was founded.

THE OLD RULES

There were really two sets of rules: one formal and explicit, the other somewhat informal and taken for granted. The formal rules provided that all people should be equal before the law and that representative government should preserve that equality. These premises are embodied in the Constitution, taught to school children, and repeated by adults. Yet, even as the United States was founded, a conflicting premise was assumed by those who wrote the official documents. This premise placed property at the core of society; government was conceived to occupy merely an auxiliary position. From the production of goods and services, great good was to be derived— good to be shared among all persons according to the worth of the individual's contributions. Government could best help the people by aiding the free production of goods and services. Only harm could follow from governmental action that went beyond, or failed to perform, this proper function. These assumptions, operating side by side, provided the framework within which industry and business became increasingly dominant in American life.

SOCIAL CHANGE

The period up to the beginning of the twentieth century brought an extension and consolidation of business power and influence. The economy prospered. The general prosperity was enough to forestall the development of serious value conflicts. There were some challenges to business power, of course, but these were probably more effective in alerting business to the necessity of consolidating its vested interest than in seriously attacking it. By the latter part of the nineteenth century, the position of big business appeared virtually unassailable.

During this entire period, and after it, another significant change had been occurring in politics and the economy. Collective action had been discovered by virtually every interest group in the country to be far more effective than individual action. Organized pressure groups increased in number, size, and power. The same form of organization that served business and industry efficiently was created to serve widely diverse interests. The organizational prerequisite for an effective challenge to business power was thus provided.

By the 1880s the extraordinary power of business was too obvious and too formidable to be ignored. Huge personal fortunes, ruthless use of financial power, and occasional business exposés contributed to a widespread concept of business tyranny. Then the formal rules set forth in the United States Constitution proved effective, and a period of increased regulation of business power began. The government emerged as the primary source of power in the nation, and it assisted in the development of countervailing power, particularly in labor unions and in agriculture. From the 1930s through the 1950s the powers of business, government, labor, agriculture, and distribution seemed to be in rather even balance. But just as the illusion of stability was achieved, a new cycle of social change was upsetting the balance again.

NEW RULES AND NEW CHANGE

The new rules provided that government should maintain a balance of power among all the groups and interests in the country. Moreover, it should promote "the public interest" apart from the interests of labor, agriculture, and so on. A prime example, in the pursuit of which government has vacillated, is the consumer movement that began to emerge shortly after World War II.

The movement received major impetus with the publication of two books in the 1960s: Rachel Carson's *Silent Spring,* in 1962, and Ralph Nader's *Unsafe at Any Speed,* in 1965. Carson's book was a heavily documented attack on the indiscriminate use of pesticides by agriculturalists, and the resulting harm to the environment. Nader's book alerted the public that automobile companies were ignoring safety considerations in the search for increased sales.

The whole antipollution-ecology movement, which is basically a revolt of the public against the immediate financial interests of industry and agriculture, followed upon the recognition belatedly given to Carson's book. And the large group of crusading lawyers and other young people who became known as Nader's Raiders methodically exposed the insensitivity of government, business, and industry to consumer interests. One direct result was the passage, in 1968, of consumer credit legislation that both limits interest rates and requires full disclosure of annual interest rates. The government also has become much more conscious of the problem of auto safety and is at least half-heartedly enforcing safety and pollution standards.

Finally, the prospect of a well-organized, well-financed citizens' lobby has emerged in Common Cause—a voluntary, nationwide organization founded by former HEW Secretary John Gardner. Common Cause, which has membership dues of only $15 per year, lobbies intensively in favor of efforts such as financial disclosure by office holders, the prosecution of politicians who violate the public trust, and ending the seniority system in Congress.

While these things have been happening on the domestic scene, the proliferation of huge international conglomerates has again upset the balance of vested interests. Business now wields power across national lines, while governments' powers stop at their borders. Companies shift production and manipulate profits, often to the disadvantage of their host countries. Labor unions, similarly, are mostly national unions, subject to defeat by industries that have the power to move their facilities to other continents. Big agriculture and big distribution essentially have joined the business interest, instead of contesting with it: Some of the biggest conglomerates exist to produce, process, and distribute food products.

Eventually, new sources of power will develop to contest with that of the multinational corporations. Alliances of national governments already are beginning to flex their muscles. The European Economic Community, for example, has levied fines in excess of $1 million against companies that have "abused their dominant positions" in the setting of prices, and has forced

97

them on occasion to make major price rollbacks. The EEC also maintains a staff of 40 investigators who have the power to search company files for evidence of illegal or unethical practices.

The Value-Conflict Approach

Major value conflicts between government and business have developed only recently. The potential was always there in the gap between the formal ideology that all people should receive equal protection under the law and the informal acceptance of the necessity to favor and encourage business and property. However, not until the latter part of the nineteenth century, when government began seriously to challenge business power, and a variety of interests and pressure groups had appeared, did major conflicts become numerous.

Values began to clash wherever interests competed. Possibly the greatest battle centered around increasing government regulation of the economy. The basic strife between business and the government has continued and has been augmented by conflicts between government and each new emerging interest. Basically, there appear to be two issues: "Should there be government controls?" and "If so, in whose interests?"

SHOULD THERE BE CONTROLS?

This issue is frequently stated as though it were a question either of continuing a set of thoroughly obnoxious controls or of completely freeing the economy from government interference. Such a statement implies that *all* government regulation is "bad" and that the country would have nothing to lose if all controls were ended. Even casual reflection will show that this actually is not true.

Government regulation is not new. It is almost as old as the nation itself. The postal system, free public schools, tax-supported universities, and public-utility monopolies are just a few examples of areas where government participation is firmly entrenched and substantially to the advantage of the entire nation. More recently, the regulatory activities of such bodies as the Federal Communications Commission, the Food and Drug Administration, and the Interstate Commerce Commission—all protecting the general public—have received acceptance. In social welfare, the government helps finance unemployment compensation, the United States Employment Service, Aid to the Blind and to Dependent Children, Old Age Assistance, and Old Age and Survivors' Insurance. One should not assume that opponents of government regulation oppose these and all other government aids.

The elimination of *all* government controls would destroy much of what has come to be known as the American way of life. The opponents of government control really oppose *certain types* of control that they consider harmful to their interests.

IN WHOSE INTERESTS?

Most of the opposition to government regulation of the economy is opposition to *certain types* of regulation recently instituted or threatened by the federal government. The main conflict is over which controls should be strengthened and which ones should be eliminated. The vested interests of business and industry favor one type of controls, and the vested interests of labor and agriculture, particularly, tend to favor another type of controls.

Neither side really wants a return to a laissez-faire economy. Business generally favors tariff regulations, fast tax write-offs on investments, subsidies to the maritime service, mail subsidies to airlines and railroads, and tax advantages for the holder of corporate stocks. Business is opposed to business taxation, to any tax advantages for cooperatives, to anti-injunction laws, and to the subsidy maintenance of farm prices. On the other hand, labor unions want the government to force management to bargain with the unions and to enter the conflict as mediator whenever an impasse is reached. Labor opposes any limitation on its right to strike, the outlawing of secondary boycotts and jurisdictional disputes, and the right of management to fire union employees without good cause. Farm groups, guarding their interests, look to government to protect the farmer's purchasing power by artificially maintaining parity price levels, by buying up crop surpluses, by limiting the importation of farm commodities from other countries and, at the same time, allowing them to import cheap farm labor from other countries. The basic issue is not whether to have controls, but who should benefit from them.

The current pollution controversies provide an excellent illustration of the clashing of values of opposing interest groups. Each kind of pollution exists because it is either convenient or profitable for someone. Environmental pollution cannot be reduced significantly through some simple formula or technological breakthrough. With very rare exceptions, each type

This is a scene at a Detroit Employment Security office. The auto industry, hard hit in these recessionary times, recently announced massive layoffs, and has been one of the largest contributors to this country's mounting unemployment problems.
(United Press International)

of environmental protection requires a sacrifice by someone—by virtually everyone eventually, as costs are passed on to consumers and taxpayers.

Should cities and industries be required to stop pouring sewage into our rivers? Of course, that would mean an increase in taxes and prices. Should car manufacturers be held to scheduled gas mileage standards? Already there are complaints about higher prices and sluggish automobile performance. Should more nuclear power plants be built despite the considerable environmental dangers? Or should we protect the environment and conserve energy by driving smaller cars and doing without air conditioning? Environmental protection *is* possible, but *only* at the sacrifice of other values, such as our preoccupation with speed, power, and gadgetry.

The Personal-Deviation Approach

The broad historical sweep of this chapter indicates that long-term social forces resulted in the government-business controversy, and that the "problem" was not caused by the effects of deviant personalities either in the past or in the present. Deviants have not caused this problem, and personal deviation is not as relevant to its analysis as either social disorganization or value conflicts. Personal deviation is relevant to the problem in at least two ways, however. First, within each of the major interest groups there are extremist minorities who harass their own as well as the opposing interests with their strident demands for a no-holds-barred, no-compromise struggle for complete domination. Second, as in all areas of conflict, there are seriously neurotic persons whose interests in particular outcomes in the struggle for power are secondary to the exercise of their needs to hate, to blame, to lead, and to bring drama into their frustrated lives.

EXTREMIST SUBCULTURES

Even though their prejudices may clearly favor one or another of the conflicting groups, most people recognize and accept that neither business nor labor nor any other group is apt to gain complete control of the nation's economy. Not all individuals and groups are convinced of this, however.

Using business and labor as examples, it is easy to see that adequate means exist for the perpetuation of subcultures that have their origins in an earlier period. Some people who are active in business leadership today can almost remember the period when business was completely unchallenged as a vested interest. In labor unionism the period since inception is even shorter. During this period, each group viewed the opposition as unscrupulous, unprincipled, and immoral scoundrels who must be vanquished at all cost. Gross distortion by both sides is apparent to all who examine the evidence. Not all groups, however, have access to the evidence or are willing to accept it. Some major interest groups have as little communication outside their own organization as any foreign-language–speaking ethnic group isolated within a city. The participation of like-minded people within a small group is more significant in shaping their attitudes and actions than any outside stimuli that impinge upon them.

Such labor union subcultures are apt to point to the "exploitation of the masses" and to urge labor to "fulfill its destiny." They brook no compromises with management—one must be either fanatically prolabor or a traitor to the cause. Comparable business subcultures are intent on smashing labor unions and reducing the government to the role of servant to business. They will never settle for the legitimacy of collective bargaining or government regulation; after all, one does not compromise with evil.

These extremist subcultures are generally found today on the margins of special interest group competition. Not only are they rejected by the opposition, they are often rejected by the dominant groups in the factions that they purport to represent. Responsible business and labor leaders know, whether they like it or not, that they must bargain for what they want. The tirades of extremists only stir up animosity and make it more difficult to function. The extremists, sensing their rejection and their ineffectiveness, often become adamant in their refusal to compromise. In time, these extremist subcultures may disappear, as their arguments become more and more irrelevant. Until then, they will continue to harass all organized groups.

THE NEUROTICS

Some members of the extremist subcultures described above undoubtedly are neurotics whose emotional quirks feed upon conflict. Most of these subculture members, however, have been normally socialized, but they have been indoctrinated with a different set of norms.

Just as some neurotics are found within deviant subcultures, others are found outside them. Neurotics are always more troublesome than other extremists. Extremists whose convictions are primarily a matter of background, training, and group loyalty may, in the face of continued contrary evidence, be induced to modify their positions somewhat. Extremists whose basic motivations derive from hate, fear, anxiety, or envy, however, can seldom be reasonable on any important point. New evidence does not alter their thinking but tends to force them to even more extreme measures for the defense of their positions. They have no desire to understand issues; they attack irrationally, use emotional labels, and impute questionable motives to the opposition. They play no constructive role in the solution of problems; they are usually to be found intensifying and confusing the issues.

Summary

The proliferation of groups that cater to the special interests of their members is a natural development in modern society. Common interests reflect shared values, and it is pleasant to associate with like-minded people. The interests of different groups often compete, however, and bring their members into potential conflict.

As interest groups strive with one another they often become pressure groups, seeking the power to achieve their goals. They lobby at local, state, and national levels. They try to win elections and to influence the administration of legislation. Over time, some interest groups gain advantages over others and adopt strategies intended to preserve their gains. Such groups, which seek to preserve the status quo, are called vested interest groups.

Definitions that prevailed two centuries ago, when the United States was founded, tended to encourage the development of business, and then industry, as vested interests. These definitions included the concepts of free contract, according to which workers and employers were free to bargain with one another as equals, and of private property, which encouraged people to use accumulated wealth in their best interest.

Business and industry prospered under these definitions until, by the early twentieth century, the meanings of free contract and private property had been seriously altered. Semimonopolistic conditions existed in many industries, and the development of the joint stock company created small groups of managers who owned but small fractions of the companies that they controlled. The government began to try to limit business power through antitrust legislation and through supporting the development of countervailing power in other segments of the economy.

During the early decades of this century, government itself became the chief challenger of business power. The federal bureaucracy created commissions to regulate virtually every aspect of economic life and took on the characteristics of a self-aggrandizing vested interest. In addition, it supported the growth of labor unions, passed legislation to protect farmers and ensure fair prices for their products, and encouraged the development of huge retail businesses to restrict the power of manufacturers to set prices.

If there seemed for a while to be a rough balance of power among business, government, labor, agriculture, and distribution, that balance was upset again by the development of huge international conglomerates during the 1950s and '60s. These multinational corporations, not bound by national loyalties, shift production facilities to countries offering cheap labor supplies and price their products at whatever the market will bear. They advocate a very limited role for government—that of providing support—and an environment of nonregulation for business.

According to the social-disorganization approach, business became a dominant vested interest during a period when government was not very powerful and the laissez-faire philosophy prevailed. Gradually government accumulated power, which it used not only to regulate business directly but also to support the development of countervailing power by labor unions, big agriculture, and big distribution. A workable balance of powers was maintained until big business freed itself of many constraints by going international.

Even as existing governmental controls are being shown to be inadequate, conflict persists over whether government controls should exist at all, and over what kinds of controls should be imposed. The problem is further complicated by extremists, whose motivations often derive from their personal inadequacies.

Suggested Readings

BARBER, RICHARD J., *The American Corporation: Its Power, Its Money, Its Politics* (New York: E. P. Dutton, 1970). Documents the facts of corporate growth, mergers, and market control. Reveals the alliances among business, government, and universities.

BARNET, RICHARD J., and RONALD E. MULLER, *Global Reach: The Power of the Multinational Corporations* (New York: Simon & Schuster, 1974). A primary source upon which this chapter depends. Documents how the power of global corporations is being used to disrupt the American economy.

BELL, DANIEL, *The Cultural Contradictions of Capitalism* (New York: Basic Books, 1976). A set of essays built around the theme of an inherent contradiction between the rationality of bureaucratic capitalism and the socially destructive, self-seeking character of modern society. Pleads for development of a new sense of community.

DEPARTMENT OF COMMERCE, *Annual Survey of Manufacturers, 1970: Value of Shipment Concentration Ratios* (Washington, D.C.: Government Printing Office, 1970). Official figures on the extreme degree of concentration in major U.S. industries, such as motor vehicles, cigarettes, detergents.

HIGHTOWER, JIM, *Eat Your Heart Out: How Food Profiteers Victimize the Consumer* (New York: Crown, 1975). Details how major corporations administer prices and undermine quality in the food industry.

LEKACHMAN, ROBERT, *Economists at Bay: Why the Experts Will Never Solve Your Problems* (New York: McGraw-Hill, 1976). Includes a devastating analysis of multinational corporations in the context of an argument that economics should be a moral science.

SAMPSON, ANTHONY, *The Seven Sisters: The Great Oil Companies and the World They Made* (New York: Viking, 1975). A fascinating, objective account of how the major oil companies developed their cartel status and how their policies have transformed the world economy.

Footnotes

[1] Reprinted by permission from *Time, The Weekly News Magazine,* 7 Aug. 1978, pp. 14–15; © copyright Time, Inc., 1978.

[2] Department of Commerce, *Annual Survey of Manufacturers, 1970: Value of Shipment, Concentration Ratios* (Washington, D.C.: Government Printing Office, 1972).

[3] Daniel Zwerdling, "The Food Monopolies," *The Progressive,* Jan. 1975, p. 14.

[4] John K. Galbraith, *American Capitalism: The Concept of Countervailing Power* (Boston: Houghton Mifflin, 1952).

[5] The extent of the tax advantage enjoyed by "coops" is itself highly controversial. Coops do not pay corporate income tax, but any other business could avoid this simply by returning profits to the consumer as coops do.

[6] Richard J. Barnet and Ronald E. Muller, *Global Reach: The Power of the Multinational Corporations* (New York: Simon & Schuster, 1974), p. 27. This section draws heavily from this source.

[7] Ibid., p. 15.

[8] Ibid., pp. 34, 41.

[9] William Tabb, "Peace, Power, and Petroleum," *The Progressive,* Nov. 1975, pp. 25–29.

[10] Barnet and Muller, *Global Reach,* p. 56.

[11] Ibid., p. 16.

[12] Ibid., p. 17.

[13] Ibid., p. 41.

[14] Ibid., p. 30.

[15] Ibid., p. 112.

[16] Ibid., p. 61.

[17] Ibid., p. 79.

[18] *Time,* 5 Jan. 1976, pp. 73–74.

[19] Barnet and Muller, *Global Reach,* p. 220.

[20] Zwerdling, "The Food Monopolies," p. 14.

CRIME AND DELINQUENCY: DEFINITION AND CLASSIFICATION

Youth is disintegrating. The youngsters of the land have a disrespect for their elders and a contempt for authority in every form. Vandalism is rife, and crime of all kinds is rampant among our young people. The nation is in peril.[1]

In Toledo, onetime Conscientious Objector Charles Cline, 30, who had served two years in a federal prison in Michigan for refusing to shoulder a gun, was given one to three years in Ohio Penitentiary for carrying a concealed weapon.[2]

New York police arrested fifty-five-year-old Mrs. Beatrice Kam for possession of narcotics, and then jailed her son, Herbert, 33, despite her protests. "Herbert," said his mother, "is a good son. He never brought me anything but the pure stuff."[3]

Robert Barnes of Minneapolis, the author of the book *Are You Safe from Burglars?* has been sentenced to three prison terms of up to five years each for his part in engineering—you guessed it—five burglaries.[4]

Upon being informed that his fourth-grade son had been caught stealing pencils at school, the father said, "I don't know why he stole the pencils. I bring him home plenty from the office."[5]

The Internal Revenue Service reports that farmers are among our most flagrant tax-chiselers, failing to report at least one-third the income which they are required by law to report.[6]

A recent study found that 17 percent of the students at the State University College in Plattsburg, N.Y., interviewed by psychologists Robert Gifford and Douglas Samuels, admitted that they had shoplifted within the past two years, and more than half had shoplifted at least once in their lives.[7]

At first reading, the items above may seem flippant and trivial. Yet each is significant, for each touches upon a different aspect of the crime problem. The first item shows that crime is not exactly new; the second shows how it is often the *conditions* surrounding the act, not the act itself, that determine whether one is a criminal or a hero; the third shows how value judgments define actions as good or bad; the fourth shows how knowledge can be used for acceptable or for antisocial purposes; the fifth suggests one of the many ways in which parents may encourage delinquent behavior; and the last two show how "respectable" people are a significant part of our crime problem.

Nature of the Crime Problem

DEFINITION: WHAT IS "CRIME"?

When something impresses us as being dreadful, we exclaim, "Isn't it a crime!" To call any shocking or socially injurious happening a crime reveals the popular rather than the scientific use of the term. In technical usage, *a crime is any violation of the law.* Since there are thousands of laws, there are a variety of ways to become a criminal. Some laws define harmless acts as crimes, while many acts highly injurious to society are legal. There are many legal ways to cheat people of their savings, to sell useless and harmful medicines to people who may die unless they find competent medical treatment, to destroy people's self-confidence and mental efficiency by frightening them with a host of imaginary and unlikely ailments, and to make a profit from the ignorance, gullibility, or helplessness of people.

Wise lawmaking is difficult. Aside from the fact that some lawmakers may be ignorant or venal, *there is no common agreement whether many acts are socially injurious.* Are gambling, prostitution, drug use, and homosexuality social menaces that the law should punish, or are they matters of private morality that the law should not attempt to regulate? Are holding compa-

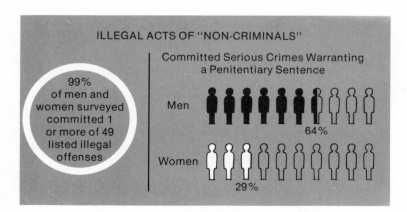

ILLEGAL ACTS OF "NON-CRIMINALS"

99% of men and women surveyed committed 1 or more of 49 listed illegal offenses

Committed Serious Crimes Warranting a Penitentiary Sentence

Men 64%

Women 29%

Figure 5–1
If all criminals were convicted, where would we put them? Has the situation changed since 1947?

Source: Based on a study reported in *Federal Probation* (Apr. 1947).

nies, high-pressure advertising, closed shops, secondary boycotts, and jurisdictional strikes socially destructive or socially beneficial? Wherever there are conflicting value judgments, each with many passionate defenders, law is relatively ineffective. Laws forbidding alcoholic beverages some decades ago proved to be unenforceable, just as laws forbidding marijuana use are proving to be unenforceable today. Law is effective and readily enforceable only when it reflects the moral consensus of the community.

Even when there is general agreement that a particular act is socially injurious, it is not always practical to try to prevent it *by law.* Overeating kills more people than all forms of crime combined, yet as long as people cherish their constitutional right to chew their way into their coffins, a law against overeating would be impractical. Furthermore, there are certain technical difficulties in lawmaking, because any law worded broadly enough to forbid the injurious act often unintentionally forbids other harmless acts or invites abuses. For example, laws designed to protect tenants from rapacious landlords have made it difficult for landlords to collect from deadbeat tenants, while laws intended to help landlords and merchants collect their debts have also permitted them to exploit tenants and customers.[8] It is exceedingly difficult to frame laws that will have only the intended effects.

A legalistic definition of crime as violation of law is not entirely satisfactory, because it labels some relatively harmless behavior as crime, while it excludes many kinds of behavior that are socially destructive. But this legalistic definition is the only one that is *usable,* for any other definition eventually results in labeling as crime anything the particular writer does not like. Consequently, the definition of crime as violation of law will be used in this discussion.

AMOUNT: HOW MUCH CRIME IS THERE IN AMERICA?

To this question the sociologist has a prompt and firm answer: *nobody knows!* Not that there is any shortage of crime statistics. Reams of crime statistics are collected by the Federal Bureau of Investigation and published annually in *Uniform Crime Reports,* listing arrests and convictions under 25 headings, ranging from homicide to suspicion, and classifying crimes by type of crime, urban–rural rates, states, size of city, age, race, and sex. This source reports that in 1977 crimes reported to the police were down slightly from 1976, the first break in a steady two-decade rise in the crime rate. Major crimes were reported at the rate of one every 3 seconds, as compared with one every 15 seconds in 1960.[9]

Crime statistics cannot give a fully accurate measure of the amount of crime[10] for several reasons. First, *much crime is never reported to the police* and never appears in crime statistics. A national Gallup Poll survey of crime victimization in 1977 found that only about 1 in 20 victims of house-breaking or attempted house-breaking, money or property theft, or vandalism reported these crimes to the police. Furthermore, the most successful crime is never detected at all—the murder that looks like accidental or natural death, the fire that looks accidental, the shoplifting by customers and pilfering by employees that is never noticed, the fraud in which the victims never realize that they have been defrauded. In other cases, although the victim realizes a crime has been committed, he may be *unwilling to prosecute.* Many sex criminals escape because their victims shrink from the notoriety of a prosecution.

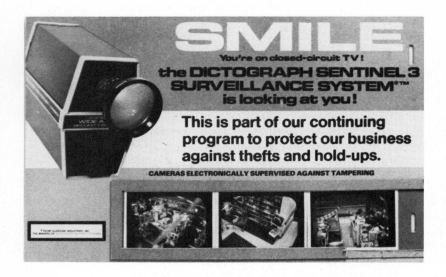

Shoplifting has become such a serious problem that more and more stores have invested in closed circuit TV cameras with accompanying warnings to discourage would-be shoplifters.
(Irene Springer)

Many embezzlements are covered up and the dishonest employee quietly discharged because the firm wishes to avoid unfavorable publicity. On-the-job stealing by employees costs business and industry far more than all the burglars, hijackers, and shoplifters combined.[11] Yet these dishonest employees are rarely caught and even more rarely prosecuted. Department stores report and prosecute an average of 5 to 10 percent of all store employees caught stealing merchandise.[12] One-third of all small-business bankruptcies are attributed to stealing by employees and customers, but according to one estimate, "only one in 1,250 shoplifters ever sees the inside of a jail."[13] Victims of robbery, theft, or embezzlement often lose interest in prosecuting once their money is returned. Victims of confidence games rarely report the crime, since they are usually swindled while trying to turn a shady dollar themselves. Graft, bribery, extortion, blackmail, and protection payments are rarely reported to the police, since secrecy is a basic feature of all of them. Much petty crime is not reported because the victims doubt that the police will be able to find the culprit or recover the property. In some areas, especially rural areas, many known crimes are not reported or officially recorded.[14]

Furthermore, *much reported crime remains unsolved.* Sometimes the police are unable to find the culprit. Figure 5–2 shows that fewer than one-fourth of the crimes reported to the police are "cleared" by the arrest of a suspect, and these figures pertain to the cities, where police are presumably better organized and more efficient than in small towns and rural areas.

Finally, *not all arrests result in convictions.* As figure 5–2 shows, these cities convict about two-thirds of those brought to trial, with wide variations among different cities. The number of arrests made in a particular city is no accurate measure of its amount of crime. A low arrest rate may indicate either a small amount of crime or an inactive police force. A high arrest rate may indicate a police force that makes arrests on slight pretext and is making a great show of combating a "crime wave." In one such battle against the underworld the Detroit police arrested over 1,500 persons, but in the end they issued only 40 warrants.[15] Wholesale arrests like this may make the local arrest rate meaningless as a measure of crime.

For the above reasons it is impossible to determine the exact amount of crime actually committed by tabulating crimes reported, arrests, or convictions. Authorities agree that criminal behavior is far more common than most people care to admit. An early study found that of 6,000 cases of delinquent behavior admitted by a representative group of youths, only 1.5 percent of these acts were followed by arrest or juvenile court hearings.[16] The same study revealed that of a representative sample of 1,968 adults, 99 percent admitted having committed one or more adult offenses, felonies carrying prison sentences of one year or more. The men in the sample admitted an average of 18 crimes, ranging from a low of 8.2 for ministers to 20.2 for laborers, while the more law-abiding women admitted an average of only 11 penal offenses! A more recent study in Flint, Michigan, found that of 2,490 legally punishable acts of delinquency admitted by 522 teenagers, only 80 offenses and 47 names appeared in police records. Thus, 97 percent of these crimes were never reported to the police.[17] A number of other studies comparing self-admitted crimes with officially recorded crimes have reached the same conclusion: *most* delinquencies are not reported to the police.[18]

REGIONAL, SEASONAL, RACIAL, AND CLASS VARIATIONS

There are some regional variations in crime rates. In 1977, some 31 percent of the households in the West reported having been victimized by some form of crime, as against 16 percent in the South, 21 percent in the East, and 23 percent in the Midwest.[19] Cities have usually reported more crime than rural areas, but it is also likely that rural crime has been less fully reported. In recent years, rural and suburban crime rates have been climbing faster than urban crime rates, reducing the rural-urban crime differential.[20]

There are *slight seasonal variations* in type of crime, with more rapes and

Figure 5–2
Offenses known, cleared by arrest, and persons held for prosecution, 1977; per 100 known offenses.
Source: *Uniform Crime Reports,* 1978, pp. 162, 214, 215.

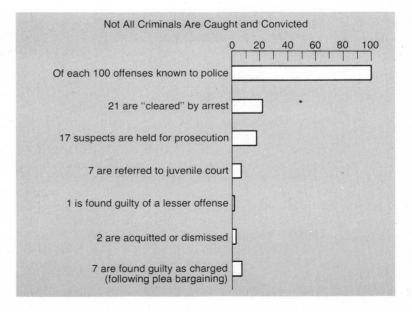

assaults in the summer months, and more thefts and larcenies in the colder months, but these variations are only moderate.

Sexual variations are striking, with males many times more often arrested and convicted than women. Female crime rates recently have shown huge percentage increases, but, as stated on p. 62, the huge percentage increases in female arrest rates, computed on a very narrow base, obscure the fact that female crime seems to be growing about as rapidly as male crime.[21] Female crime is typically nonviolent, usually confined to petty property offenses.[22] Recent increases in female crime are sometimes attributed to the feminist "emancipation" of women, but no evidence linking feminist attitudes with criminal behavior has been offered.[23]

Racial and *national variations* in crime rates are substantial but misleading. Virtually all disadvantaged minorities in the United States have arrest and conviction rates well above national averages. The Chinese minority used to be cited as an exception, but even they, too, are catching up.[24] But the high crime rates of blacks, American Indians, and other minorities are due, in part, to their clustering in the lower ages and lower socioeconomic class levels. Most American minorities have higher birth rates than other Americans; thus proportionately more of them are in the younger ages, where crime rates are higher. When racial comparisons are controlled for age, occupation, income, and family structure, the racial variation in crime rates shrinks dramatically.

It is not entirely clear whether, after controlling for such variables, ethnic crime rates are still higher. Some studies have reported *no* significant differences.[25] One study found higher black rates for officially recorded delinquency, but when delinquency was measured by self-reporting rather than police records, the black rates were no higher than white rates.[26] But some other studies find that, even after making correction for differences in age and class, black rates are still higher.[27] A possible explanation is that police and courts deal more harshly with black suspects. A number of studies using data collected before 1960 report evidence of racial discrimination in law enforcement, while more recent studies find little evidence of such discrimination.[28] A different explanation sees a higher black crime rate as a reaction against the castelike features of American life.[29] It is very likely that any racial variation in crime rates would disappear before long if all minorities shared equally in American life.

Class variations, as indicated by statistics, are spectacular. Arrests and convictions are conspicuously rare in the upper classes and frequent in the lower classes. Sheldon Glueck and Eleanor Glueck found that of 1,000 juvenile delinquents, about three-fourths were from families below the "level of comfort" (defined as having resources to survive four months of unemployment without going on relief).[30] In Chicago, Clifford Shaw and Henry McKay found a correlation of +0.89 between boy delinquency and proportion of families on relief in each square-mile area.[31] Marvin Wolfgang, Robert Figlio, and Thorsten Sellin followed a cohort of nearly 10,000 boys through their entire youth, finding that delinquencies were officially recorded against 26 percent of the higher socioeconomic status boys and against 45 percent of the lower status boys.[32]

There is considerable evidence that the lower-class delinquent is likely to be officially recorded as delinquent, while the middle- or upper-class delinquent is more often handled informally. The higher status delinquent is more likely to have a stable home to which he can be released, while the boy from a fatherless, broken, or unstable home is more likely to be sent to the juvenile home and juvenile court. When delinquency is measured by self-reporting studies, the class variation (as well as the race variation) tends to diminish if not disappear.[33] A recent survey of 35 studies of the relationship between social class and delinquency concluded that no more than a very slight association could be found.[34] One criminologist sums it up in saying that "the data provide no firm evidence that social class—no matter how it is measured—is a salient factor in generating juvenile delinquency."[35]

In the category of adult crime as well, it is uncertain whether middle- and upper-class persons are less criminal or only less often convicted. Higher status persons have many advantages—resources, connections, knowledge of their rights, public reputation, for example—that help them gain leniency. Most lower-class crime is violent crime, such as assault, burglary, or robbery, and is punished severely in criminal courts. Much middle- and upper-class crime is "white-collar crime" (discussed later), which is treated less severely, often before commissions and administrative boards instead of criminal courts. In sum, we are not certain whether law violation is

Juvenile acts of delinquency, such as rock throwing, are often merely preludes to acts of a more serious nature.
(Hugh Rogers, Monkmeyer)

more common at one class level than at another, but we do know that it is widespread at all class levels.

Discrimination against the poor and the powerless is often cited to explain why jails and prisons are filled mainly with lower-class persons. Conflict theorists especially have claimed that the socially disadvantaged are victims of unequal treatment at every point from apprehension to parole, and their views are widely shared by criminologists.[36] Is the charge true? There is good reason to be skeptical. Recent investigations have found little support for the belief that race and class bias strongly prejudice the treatment of delinquents or criminals today.[37] Several recent studies show that the poor are *not* given longer sentences than the prosperous.[38] These measure only one of the possible forms of discrimination, but they suggest that undocumented charges of unfairness in law enforcement should be questioned. A number of Supreme Court decisions in recent years have greatly aided the legal defenses of the poor. The gross miscarriages of justice of the past are no longer common.

When all factors are balanced, however, it is possible that the affluent and the powerful are less often caught and less severely punished for their crimes than are the poor. In all societies throughout history, the rich and powerful have found ways of evading or lightening their penalties. Even in communist China, as determinedly equalitarian as any country on earth, officials enjoy special privileges and immunities, while many discriminations and draconian punishments await the children and even the grandchildren of former landowners and capitalists.[39] Only in Heaven can we hope for perfect justice.

WHITE-COLLAR CRIME—THE UPPER-CLASS SPECIALTY

So-called "white-collar crime" is not merely crime committed by white-collar persons; white-collar crime is crime committed by business and professional people *in the course of their occupations*.[40] If a physician shoots his wife, forges a check, or burns his house for the insurance, he commits conventional crime; if Blue Cross or Medicare is billed for services never performed, this is white-collar crime. A business executive who systematically short-weighs a product, misbrands it, embezzles the firm's funds, manipulates a phony bankruptcy, or falsifies financial statements is engaging in white-collar crime.

There is no way of knowing the amount of white-collar crime, but all criminologists agree that it is tremendous, "probably several times as great as the cost of all the crimes which are customarily regarded as the 'crime problem.' "[41] One investigator states that employee thefts range from $3 billion to $15 billion a year, depending upon whose estimates are accepted, and notes that they are currently growing at 15 or 20 percent a year.[42] Banks lose at least five times as much to crooked employees as they lose to bank robbers.[43] One dishonest business—Equity Funding Corporation—created 64,000 fictitious insurance policies with a face value of over $2 billion, sold them to other insurance companies, and defrauded those companies of millions of dollars—just how many is not known.[44] Eight independent oil companies in Texas drilled an estimated 300 slanted oil wells and thus stole over $30 million a year of other people's oil.[45] Under Section 238 of the Housing Act of 1968, a number of dishonest FHA appraisers, bankers, and realtors unloaded thousands of crumbling old houses upon low-income buyers at outrageous prices; as a result, thousands of poor people were victimized and the federal government was defrauded of an estimated $2.4 billion.[46] The illegal "pirating" of hit records and tapes earns at least $350 million a year for the pirates, while depriving the legitimate recording companies and artists of even larger sums.[47] When government-guaranteed student loans come due, college students prove to be among the nation's leading deadbeats, with a 12 percent default rate, tempting the government to curtail the student loan program.[48] Theft by computer is the most recent innovation in white-collar crime.[49] The possibility of nuclear sabotage or diversion of materials is a frightening new opportunity.[50] The more technologically complicated our society becomes, the more opportunities for crime are created.

Arson is one of the most rapidly growing forms of crime, recently growing at a rate of 25 percent a year.[51] Not all arson is white-collar crime. Arson by emotionally disturbed "firebugs" is quite rare. Arson for vengeance is more common—by angry employees, jealous lovers, embittered enemies, or hostile neighbors. Torching one's apartment is a favorite way for welfare tenants to "relocate" quickly in a better apartment with new furniture.[52] But an estimated one-third of all building fires are set for profit, accounting for perhaps two-thirds of all fire losses.[53] Any unprofitable apartment house, office building, hotel, restaurant, or warehouse somehow becomes terribly inflammable! Yet only nine persons are arrested and two convicted for every 100 cases of known or suspected arson.[54]

Another type of white-collar crime is the violation of laws that regulate

Fires set by arsonists (such as this one in the South Bronx section of New York City) are a common occurrence in decaying urban neighborhoods.
(Susan Kuklin, Photo Researchers, Inc.)

business conduct. These laws, passed to protect consumers, workers, and competitors, are often viewed by business people as an unjustified interference in their business affairs. One young business executive complains, "It is impossible to conduct business in the United States today without breaking the law."[55] A building contractor complains that the building regulations and rules on street obstructions are so confining that "you can't build legally in New York."[56] Consequently, the bribery of inspectors, police, and other officials reportedly adds 5 percent to the cost of virtually *all* major construction projects in New York (and in many other cities).[57] Dishonest grain inspectors, by "upgrading" inferior grain shipped abroad, earned fat bribes for themselves and millions of dollars of fraudulent profits for grain exporting companies, while also damaging the reputation of American grain in world markets.[58] Dozens of other examples could be cited. One magazine some years ago described a situation that is little changed today:

Take an active, if concentrated, day in the life of a reputable New York State businessman. . . . As he walks to his downtown office after leaving his car resting snugly in a "No Parking" zone, he warmly greets the veteran cop on the beat, who thanks him for his recent annual present, a case of good blended whiskey (penalty for attempting to influence a police officer with a gift: $5,000 fine and/or 10 years in jail). After a few routine desk chores the businessman has a profitable late morning session with his personal income tax consultant, who has found a happy device for distorting repair and depreciation costs on some rental property he owns (penalty for filing a fraudulent income tax return: $10,000 fine and/or five years in jail). By this time he has worked up an appetite for a good expense-account meal, so he entertains his wife and two close friends at a lavish lunch, all on the company tab (a misdemeanor under Section 665 of the State Penal Law, subject to a $500 fine and/or one year in jail).

Back in the office, he reminds one of his assistants to "take care of" the building inspector with jurisdiction over their new plant site, thus getting as much red tape out of the way as possible (penalty for bribing a public officer: $5,000 fine and/or 10 years in jail). He then dictates a letter to an executive of a small concern with which he has just signed a contract, thanking him for *his* thoughtful gift of a new model portable TV set (penalty for secretly accepting a gift in return for corporate favors: $500 and/or one year in jail).

At a late afternoon conference he congratulates the controller on a new bookkeeping device that handily pads a few of the firm's more controversial assets (penalty for concurring in a bookkeeping fraud: $500 and/or one year in jail). He later tells the head of his company's advertising agency to disregard a recent Federal Trade Commission cease-and-desist order about misleading TV commercials, at least until the fall sales drive (this ultimately puts the company in line for an embarrassing and costly federal court action).

As the day closes, he asks his secretary to wrap up one of the new company desk sets, which will be just the thing for his den at home (penalty for appropriating company property to one's personal use: $500 fine and/or one year in jail). Safe at home, he advises his wife not to worry about the maid's social security payments because she is leaving soon anyway (penalty for willful nonpayment of employer's social security contributions: $10,000 fine and/or five years in jail). Laying aside the cares of the day, he settles down to watch the news on his souvenir TV set—and fulminates about the dishonesty of the "union racketeers" he sees on the screen.[59]

In Ohio last winter, Judge Neil W. Whitfield sentenced Robert W. Attwood, 20, who had stolen $10 worth of beer from a neighbor's garage, to four to 25 years in jail. On the same day, the same judge sentenced Mary Murray, a motor vehicle official, to five years probation for embezzling $8,000 in public funds.

Time, 20 Aug. 1979, p. 48.

ATTITUDES TOWARD WHITE-COLLAR CRIME   Public indignation at conventional crime contrasts sharply with public tolerance of white-collar crime. In the Texas community near which the slanted wells were drilled, the residents expressed no strong condemnation of the dishonest operators, only regret that they had been caught and that the local economy was suffering.[60] Most people, public and perpetrator alike, do not view many forms of white-collar crime as "real" crime. Many forms of white-collar crime are not generally considered to be actual crime, but instead are viewed merely as technical errors, or perhaps even as courageous opposition to government meddling.

The lack of strong condemnation of many forms of white-collar crime, by the public or by one's business associates, helps to account for the popularity of white-collar offenses. The attitude that white-collar crime is not real crime is further expressed in the mode of its treatment. Violators are usually dealt with not in the ordinary criminal courts, but by special quasi-judicial commissions and agencies—the Federal Trade Commission, the National Labor Relations Board, the Securities and Exchange Commission, and other agencies. Usually the violator is permitted to sign a consent decree (a promise not to break the law any more) and allowed to go free. Only since 1960 (and rarely since 1960) have any violators gone to prison for violating the antitrust laws, the labor-relations laws, or many other regulatory laws. Fines, usually nominal, are often assessed to the corporation rather than to the officers personally, meaning that if the officers break the law, the stockholders pay the fine.[61] It has been suggested that the antitrust laws be enforced by dissolving any corporation that repeatedly violates them, or punishing any corporate officer involved in repeated violations by prohibiting him from holding corporate office thereafter. Such proposals have received little support from business, the press, or the public. The rarity of severe penalties for white-collar violators of regulatory law is often excused by the doctrine that the object of these quasi-judicial agencies is not to punish the offenders, but to gain compliance with the law. This point—that law enforcement should seek to gain compliance rather than to inflict punishment—sounds reasonable and humane. Curiously enough, however, it seems to be reserved for white-collar offenders rather than extended to ordinary criminals. In recent years, penalties for some forms of white-collar crime have become more severe. Personal fines of up to $100,000, corporate fines in the millions, and even prison sentences for corporate officials, while still not common, are no longer unthinkable.[62] Yet white-collar crime remains the most costly and least often punished type of serious crime in the United States.

A Realistic Classification of Criminals

A classification of criminals according to type of crime is of little value; it tells nothing of the criminal's motives and contains no suggestions for effective treatment. A useful classification should give some insight into the purposes of the criminal and be of some practical aid in analyzing different methods of treatment. Criminals should be classified not according to type of crime, but according to personality orientation of the criminal.[63]

VICTIMLESS CRIMINALS

Victimless criminals are violators of laws forbidding certain acts that rarely injure anyone except possibly the criminal himself. These are the crimes for which the term *crimes without victims* has recently become popular.[64] The moral views of a powerful segment of the community, possibly a hundred years earlier, have written into law many regulations of matters involving private morality as well as public protection. These include laws forbidding gambling, prostitution, illegal use of liquor or narcotics, homosexuality, adultery, fornication, and certain other sex offenses. All these laws are of debatable effectiveness and probably create more problems than they solve.

Although many who engage in the illegal sale of narcotics are professional criminals, it is useless to class drug addicts as criminals. The main direct effect of narcotics is to quiet them, and if they commit a crime, it is usually in an effort to ensure their supply of drugs. They play no part in organized crime, for a drug addict is untrustworthy. There is good reason to control the sale of narcotics, but many criminologists agree that to make the use of drugs by an addict a crime only aggravates a difficult problem. Yet the higher the number of drug addicts, the more determinedly does the federal government escalate the war against the drug traffic. The main effect is to inflate the price of narcotics, and to switch users to less costly drugs.

The victimless criminals are a relatively harmless lot, aside from the secondary deviation induced by treating them as criminals. If left alone, they would wreak little injury upon society.

PSYCHOPATHIC CRIMINALS[65]

In the psychopathic class fall all criminals who are unable to control their behavior in a legally acceptable way because of a major emotional maladjustment. This includes not only the legally insane but all others with more or less permanent complexes, phobias, manias, and other instabilities or disturbances that result in criminal acts. In some cases the behavior is wildly

> The increase of crime is becoming one of the most startling notices of our daily newspapers. . . . Three, four, five, and, in one case, eight murders are announced for New York for one week. We are becoming familiar with what, twenty years ago, would have shocked the universal conscience.
>
> *Harper's Magazine*, 1853.

erratic and may result in any of a wide variety of crimes. In other cases the psychopath suffers an uncontrollable compulsion to commit a particular act which brings no enjoyment, only relief. The kleptomaniac is a compulsive thief, often specializing in a single kind of merchandise for which he or she has no use, whose stealing has symbolic meaning. In one case, a lonely unattractive girl accumulated a trunkful of costume jewelry, as the act of stealing jewelry became a substitute for gaiety and companionship. In another, a timid, ineffectual person found a temporary sense of power and accomplishment in the act of stealing. The kleptomaniac should not be confused with the ordinary shoplifter who steals for profit, nor should the arsonist who burns for profit be confused with the pyromaniac who cannot resist setting fires. The sexual psychopath is one who commits an illegal act under uncontrollable compulsion, not because it brings enjoyment, but because it brings relief. These "crimes" range from window peeping and lingerie-stealing to knifings and murderous assaults. The sexual psychopath finds sexual excitement and sexual relief through these acts rather than through normal sex activities.

Psychopathic criminals have little in common with other criminals. They seek not profit, but release from uncontrollable impulse. Punishments are probably futile, for their acts are irrational. Some may respond to treatment; others, who are dangerous, must be kept in custody for society's protection.

INSTITUTIONAL CRIMINALS

Institutional crime refers to certain criminal acts that are repeated so often that they become part of the normal behavior of a group, yet are so perfectly rationalized that these acts are not defined as crime by those committing them, or perhaps even by the community. These offenders are not professional criminals, for their crime is not a career, but is incidental to a legitimate career.

Wherever they are forbidden by law, the slot machines in American Legion halls and private clubs, and the bingo parties and raffles sponsored by certain churches, are examples of institutional crime. They are actual crimes as defined by law but are not viewed as such by those promoting them, by the law-enforcement officials, or by most of the general public. Instead, they are standard, customary practices of the groups and are likely to be testily defended with the argument that "the law is foolish," or that "the law isn't intended for this," with the implication that it is impolite to mention the matter.

Pilfering tools, office supplies, and other items from factory or office for use at home is seldom viewed as real crime. Systematic violation of weight and speed laws is nearly universal among long-distance truckers. Income tax chiseling is popular among groups that can conceal part of their income from the tax collector, such as business proprietors, doctors, dentists, farmers, gamblers, waitresses and waiters, and cabdrivers. Expense account padding is common among those with expense accounts. Few storekeepers report as personal income all the merchandise they take home for family use, as is required by income tax law. Most of these people would define their deeds not as "real" crime but as a game of wits with the government. It therefore fits the definition of institutional crime—criminal acts that are widespread but generally tolerated and not treated as actual crime either by their perpetrators or by most of the community. In fact, a public opinion poll found that income tax fraud was the least disapproved of a long list of crimes.[66] To many people, cheating big business or the government—so large, so rich, so powerful, and so impersonal—is not really crime.[67]

Institutional criminals have little in common with conventional criminals, or even with each other, for the tax evader, the pilfering longshoreman, and the wetback employer differ greatly from one another. "Treatment" would not be a conventional effort to reform criminals, since no one considers them criminals. Institutional crime is not a problem in conventional criminology, but a problem in social organization, in jurisprudence, and in public morality.

SITUATIONAL CRIMINALS

Every prison contains a number of persons who, under pressure of overpowering circumstances, have committed a criminal act entirely out of harmony with their basic life organization. A melodramatic illustration is the clerk or cashier who embezzles to pay for an operation for someone in the family.[68] Many murders are committed by husbands, wives, lovers, or in-laws caught in a domestic conflict that, in a moment of blinding anger, they resolve with a shotgun or meat axe. Many a normally law-abiding business executive, faced with ruin through adverse circumstances, will consider a profitable fire or a fraudulent bankruptcy.[69] The debts from a single gambling spree may involve a person so deeply that he tries a little larceny as a way out. Many an honest employee becomes dishonest when he acquires an expensive girl friend. A thoroughly respectable citizen may commit a serious crime while intoxicated.

Situational criminals are a substantial fraction of prison populations, for they are usually easy to locate and prosecute. Whether they should be punished is debatable. Many could be released immediately and would commit no further crimes, but we have no way accurately to identify the harmless ones.

HABITUAL CRIMINALS

There are criminals whom circumstances overpower very easily—who yield to temptation over and over. Such people repeatedly fall into financial crises from which a little larceny is needed to extract them. Or they are easily provoked to violence. Or, while they may not deliberately seek opportunities for thievery, when one arises they readily seize it. They do not view themselves as criminals and defend each lapse with a succession of excuses. Although they are chronic offenders, they have not adopted crime as a career or organized their lives around it. Therefore they are habitual, rather than professional, criminals.

Unlike the situational criminals, who are often sober and industrious, the habitual criminals include a high proportion of shiftless ne'er-do-wells. Individuals who lack vocational skills and industrious working habits or who lead the irregular life of marginal workers may be more likely to engage in many forms of petty mischief. Many habitual (not professional) criminals have a long record of petty offenses—disorderly conduct, drunkenness, traffic violations, nonpayment of bills, vagrancy, nonsupport, perhaps minor sex offenses, arrests "on suspicion," and the like. Lacking a dependable source of income, without any long-term goals, and having little "respectability" to sacrifice, the borderline between criminal and noncriminal behavior becomes faint and easily breached.

This group probably provides the major share of prison inmates. Lacking the training, skills, and connections necessary to pursue crime successfully, they are easily apprehended and convicted. They play no important role in organized crime and receive scant profit from their efforts. For them it is true that crime does not pay. Crime "pays" only those who pursue it systematically and intelligently.[70]

PROFESSIONAL CRIMINALS

Career criminals are often described as "professional criminals." This involves some misuse of the term *professional*, for a true profession implies formal, systematic training, formal procedures for admission, and systematic self-regulation of the profession. Thus the "professional" criminal is a pale reflection of a true professional; yet the term is commonly used in literature. Although there are important differences between con men and hijackers, all professional criminals have many common characteristics. They all define themselves as criminals and consciously organize their lives around a criminal career. They prize professional competence, are contemptuous of amateurs, and value their standing among their fellow professionals. They crave status and respectability and secure it through demonstrated skill in criminal behavior. Expensive clothes, jewelry, and luxury cars are prized symbols of status, just as in conventional society. To go to prison is humiliating, because it is inconvenient, because it is a confession of professional failure, because one's skills and connections grow rusty, and because possible partners lose faith if one is caught too often. To have to sell the pawn ticket to one's "hock piece" (a large diamond that can be pawned when sudden cash is needed) is a humiliating symbol of professional decline.

Professional criminals are the least likely of all criminals to be caught. Their crimes are not impulsive, but planned carefully and often skillfully. Professional criminals prefer not to undertake any criminal activity unless the "fix is in"—unless protection has been arranged by making a deal with law-enforcement officials, or a defense attorney has already been engaged. Professional criminals plan so as to receive a minimum punishment if caught; thus they never kill or resort to violence unless it is actually necessary. The professional second-story man (house robber) seldom carries a gun; he would be a fool to use it, and it increases his "rap" if he is caught with it. If convicted, the professional becomes a model prisoner and is usually paroled in the shortest possible time, with his connections sometimes applying fiscal grease to the wheels of the parole machinery. It is easy to see why professionals comprise a relatively small part of the prison population, even though many do spend some time in prison. One scholar estimates that about 1 person in 10,000 is a full-time career criminal, most of whom stay out of prison most of the time.[71]

The mental outlook of professional criminals is somewhat like that of mercenary soldiers. If they kill, they kill without passion and only when killing is useful. They take calculated risks, carefully weighed against the objectives to be gained. A set of firm beliefs justify their careers. Professional criminals believe that "only losers work" and that "everybody has a racket." They attribute their choice of career to their superior perception, not to any lack of moral sensitivity. They may use the "I'm a victim of an unjust society" of the "My parents abused me and the street was my home" arguments to seek sympathy or escape punishment, but they do not really pity themselves for being criminals—only for getting caught.[72]

This complex of attitudes and skills is not true for most criminals of other sorts, nor is it true of all career criminals. There is some evidence that true professionals, as distinct from merely career criminals, are something of a rarity today, if indeed they were ever very common.[73]

Genuine reformation among career criminals, in which the criminals truly abandon their criminal careers, aspirations, and lifestyles, and adopt law-abiding habits and aspirations, is practically unknown. They may become inactive because things are too hot or because fear of imprisonment grows as they grow older, but true reformation is exceedingly rare.[74]

POLITICAL CRIMINALS

The term *political criminal* has acquired a variety of meanings.

CLASSIC POLITICAL CRIMES   These are political acts defined and punished as crimes. Criticizing official policy, publishing an opposition newspaper, organizing an opposing political party, even speaking disrespectfully of officials will bring imprisonment or worse in much of the world. In authoritarian states, *any* political opposition, or even lack of enthusiastic support, brands one as an enemy of the people. The 1970s were a decade of widespread political dissent and repression. According to a 1974 study, imprisonment of political dissenters was routine in no fewer than 90 countries from communist to rightist dictatorships,[75] and there are no reports of recent improvements. While not very common in American history, attempts to punish political dissent with criminal penalties are not unknown, as Dr. Benjamin Spock can attest.[76]

SYMBOLIC POLITICAL CRIMES   These acts are, in themselves, relatively minor violations of law, committed for the purpose of symbolizing political dissent. Flag burnings, draft-card burnings, demonstrations (involving illegal trespass and assembly), and perhaps "trashing" (window smashing) would be examples, although when trashing becomes wholesale looting and arson, it is no longer merely symbolic. Bombings timed to avoid the loss of life also fall into the category of symbolic political crimes. Such crimes were fairly common in the 1960s, but in the 1970s, bombings intended to kill people became more common.

POLITICAL TERRORISM   This consists of major crimes committed with maximum publicity for a political purpose. Examples include political assassinations and kidnappings, and bombings or burnings for the purpose of paralyzing the government or showing its impotence. Kidnapping to force release of terrorists already imprisoned is a favorite tactic. Kidnapping for ransom is an increasingly popular way to raise funds for revolutionary activity.[77] While relatively rare in the United States, political terrorism is a common technique of revolutionists that appears to be growing in many parts of the world. Some political terrorists are undeniably psychopathic, such as the Zebra killers who shot 23 white San Franciscans as initiatory rituals for their organization in 1973–74.[78] Whether most political terrorists are irrational psychopaths or ruthless but rational revolutionists is a much-debated issue.[79]

For such questions, a new scientific journal, *Terrorism*, has recently appeared. It is undeniable, however, that all three of the above forms of political crime bear little resemblance to conventional crime, and their analysis and control lie more heavily in the field of political science than in criminology.

THE POLITICIZATION OF CONVENTIONAL CRIME This is a recent development in the United States. While in classic political crime an ordinary political act is defined as a crime, revolutionary ideology today reverses this by defining ordinary crime as a political act. According to many radicals and some black militants, most prisoners are political prisoners because they are victims of corrupt, racist, exploitative, oppressive society.[80] This follows the familiar Marxist thesis that crime is a product of capitalistic exploitation. Today's revolutionists therefore view property crimes by those who are poor, black, Puerto Rican, or Chicano as "political acts" of resistance against a corrupt and oppressive society. Some followers of the counterculture believed that it was a noble contribution to a more humane society to live by "ripping off" the establishment, and detailed instruction books in rip-off tactics circulate

Recent years have seen a proliferation in political terrorism, the leaders of such groups resort to all sorts of criminal activities, from the taking of hostages to the hijacking of commercial aircraft, in order to achieve their ends.
(United Press International)

freely.[81] Revolutionary periods have historically been periods of rampant crime of all sorts. Apparently the revolutionary attempt to direct crime selectively against the establishment does not work; instead, crime becomes general. When ripping off becomes the lifestyle, its practitioners seem to rip off anyone handy.

It is noteworthy that the politicization of ordinary crime demands the sacrifice of the prisoner to the revolution. To reform, the prisoner must accept the existing society. Convicts must accept the idea that their crimes were wrong and must not be repeated. Convicts will not reform if they see themselves as "political prisoners" and see robbery and burglary as justifiable "political acts." Very soon after their release they are likely to be either dead or back in prison. Thus the politicization of ordinary crime may promote the revolution, but it sacrifices any chances for a normal life that may remain for the convict.

Organized Crime

Professional crime varies in degree of organization. Some kinds, such as picking pockets, armed robbery, and confidence games (swindles), do not lend themselves to large-scale organization and are ordinarily handled singly or by groups of two or three. In other operations, such as gambling, narcotics peddling, and loan sharking, large-scale organization has certain advantages.

Successfully organized crime operates smoothly and quietly, rarely rating headlines, whereas unorganized and nonprofessional crime fills the front pages and gives the public an incorrect notion of its relative importance. But all authorities agree that the cost of organized crime greatly exceeds that of unorganized crime and that organized crime is largely responsible for the corruption of public officials.

A number of journalistic descriptions some years ago fairly accurately pictured the structure and functioning of organized crime,[82] and these popularizations are generally supported by sociological investigations.[83]

CONNIVANCE OF LAW-ENFORCEMENT AGENCIES

The term *organized crime* is not applied to small roving bands of robbers, pickpockets, shoplifters, confidence men, and the like. Organized crime is conducted by large, organized groups of criminals who operate in more or less clearly defined territories and maintain constant connections with law-enforcement officials. Elaborately organized crime is found in gambling, loan sharking, and narcotics. In these instances there is a large market among "respectable" people who have no interest in seeing the law enforced. This large and highly profitable market, combined with considerable public opposition to law enforcement, guarantees the development of organized crime and provides a ready-made rationalization for the law-enforcement officials who must cooperate. For *without exception, organized crime cannot exist long without the connivance of some law-enforcement officials.* When a "book" opens, the police almost invariably know about it within a short time. For it is the officers' duty to know what goes on in their precinct, and even a sudden increase in the number of cars parked before a building or in the number of people entering it calls for an investigation. As onetime gambler

Mickey Cohen remarked, "None of these operations would operate for five minutes if it wasn't for the cooperation of the powers."[84] It is safe to conclude that wherever large-scale gambling exists for long, it is with the knowledge of some public officials.

This does not mean that *all* public officials are corrupt; in fact, it would be too costly to "pay off" all of them. Only a few strategically placed officials need to be "reached" to provide effective protection. A few judges, one or two assistant district attorneys, and a few police captains are enough to guarantee that the business can operate with only occasional minor annoyances. There are many subtle ways to avoid effective prosecution while going through all the motions of determined law enforcement, and there are many points at which one corrupt public official can neutralize the integrity of a dozen honest companions and frustrate honest law enforcement. The "honest cop" soon learns who is under protection and discovers the futility (and the danger) of attempting to molest them. So the honest cop concentrates on catching traffic violators, pickpockets, and other small fry and ignores the "untouchables." It is therefore possible to have a "wide-open" town even though most of the police are honest.[85]

ROLE OF RESPECTABLE PEOPLE IN ORGANIZED CRIME

Is it possible to suppress organized gambling and prostitution when there are so many customers for these services? It is difficult to suppress organized gambling while permitting private organizations to raise funds through gambling operations, yet Adlai Stevenson, when governor of Illinois, described the opposition of many "good citizens" when he instructed his state police to remove the slot machines from veterans' posts and private clubs.[86] The widespread toleration of gambling, coupled with the powerful connection of "the syndicate," makes it extremely difficult to suppress gambling even when officials are determined to do so. Whether such laws should be repealed or enforced is a moot question.[87] Most attempts at enforcement are only temporarily successful, and the existence of these laws, forbidding what many people want and will pay for, leads directly to the corruption of law-enforcement officials.

Can labor racketeering be suppressed as long as there are many in busi-

With one book published and another under contract, I began to gaze longingly at sleek foreign sports cars. I located a beauty in a Chicago salesroom, and was about to order it when I found that I had miscalculated the price by several thousand dollars.

Seeking a graceful retreat, I remarked to the salesperson, "Well, I've just started another book and I had better wait for a while to see how it goes."

The salesperson smiled and remarked, "No worries. The cops will never bother you, not in this town."

I considered informing him that I was an author, not a bookie. But I decided that, having created a good impression, I would not spoil it.

A personal anecdote from your author's experience.

ness who would rather deal with labor racketeers than with an honest but aggressive union? In some cases the businessperson is a victim of labor racketeering, but in other cases he is a partner.[88] Organized theft and burglary could not operate without dishonest businesspeople who sell stolen merchandise through normal trade channels[89] and citizens who are happy to buy stolen merchandise at a bargain price. In this connection it is interesting to note that college students are said to be the prime market for the trade in stolen bicycles.[90] As in the days of piracy, when pirate loot (mostly merchandise) was marketed through dishonest merchants under the benevolent eye of conniving government officials,[91] organized crime is not profitable without the cooperation of supposedly honest persons.

NATIONAL OR REGIONAL ORGANIZATION

Many journalistic stories and movies have drawn the lurid picture of a national crime syndicate run by a secret brotherhood known as the Mafia or, more recently, La Cosa Nostra, complete with oaths signed in blood and other rituals of a secret society.[92] This picture is melodramatic but somewhat misleading. Since the 1890s the term *Mafia* has been attached to crime committed by Italian immigrants and their descendants, although even then, this crime was a local product, not an importation of European patterns.[93] Careful scholarly studies have shown that Mafia *is not an organization.* According to Joseph Albini, Mafia in the United States refers to "a method of executing a criminal enterprise."[94] Francis Ianni states that "Mafia is an attitude, not an organization," and a pattern of social obligations operating through a network of friendship and kinship.[95] The term is more properly used as a descriptive adjective than as a noun. To speak of "the Mafia" is as inappropriate as to speak of "the religious," "the diplomatic," or "the puritanical." The romanticized image of "the Mafia" is good theater but poor social analysis.[96]

Large-scale organized crime undoubtedly exists in the United States. The picture of a national crime syndicate with a board of directors that oversees local operations is an exaggeration, however. According to the President's Commission, an alliance of 24 criminal syndicates forms the core of organized crime in the United States, at present largely Italian in membership and in frequent communication with each other. They function not like a national board of directors, but more like a trade association of independent operators who generally agree in mapping out territories for monopolistic operation. When these agreements break down, gang warfare breaks out, but this has been rare in recent decades. Each of the 24 groups is known as a family, consisting of as few as 20 or as many as 700 members. A group of blood relations may be the core of a family, but it often includes others as well. Each family is headed by a boss, who maintains order and directs operations. Below him are several levels of management, down to the lowest-level members who conduct the day-to-day operations (a loan-shark operation, a dice game, a bookmaking operation) with a number of employees or commission agents. This hierarchical organization separates the higher-placed members by enough layers of intermediate officers so that evidence against top officials is very difficult to collect. An employee would be unable to give evidence in court against higher-ranking members even if he dared to do so. The occasional conviction of a member does not disrupt the organization; the member invariably keeps silent and does his time, while the organization proceeds as usual.[97]

The huge profits of organized crime have permitted the higher-ranking members to buy into legitimate businesses and pose as legitimate businessmen. Favorite businesses for investment include hotels, motels, restaurants, nightclubs, laundry and dry cleaning establishments, coin machines, liquor and beer distribution, real estate ownership, banking, insurance companies, and many others. Often a reputable concern is captured, milked, and then abandoned to bankruptcy. Criminals as businessmen remain criminals, enriching themselves at the expense of employees, stockholders, and the public.[98] One estimate has 60 percent of the income of organized crime coming from legitimate business activities.[99] Attempts to combat organized crime have had limited success. Few states or cities have any special units or prosecutors concentrating on organized crime.[100] The FBI under J. Edgar Hoover carefully avoided a "war" on organized crime that would be foredoomed to failure and would not enhance the FBI image. No law enforcement approach to organized crime will have more than limited success, because the main forms of organized crime are rooted in the public market for illegal goods and services. As Norval Morris and Gordon Hawkins put it:

> As long as we are determined to continue our futile efforts by means of criminal law to prevent people from obtaining goods and services which they have clearly demonstrated they do not intend to forego, criminals will supply these goods and services. . . . The way to eliminate organized crime is to remove the criminal laws which both stimulate and protect it.[101]

With low social status, strong kinship ties, and some acquaintance with Mafia attitudes and traditions, Italian immigrants were strategically situated to assume a dominant position in organized crime, largely displacing the Irish and Jews early in the present century. Today the third-generation descendants in Italian syndicate crime families are graduating from college and entering legitimate businesses or professions. In another generation, Ianni predicts that the Italians will have been replaced by blacks, Puerto Ricans, and other ethnics.[102] Thus organized crime has functioned as a mobility ladder for disadvantaged minorities.

Summary

The exact extent to which crime is a problem is not known. It probably exists in much the same degree in most areas, races, and classes in the United States, although it is mainly the lower-class violators who are caught and convicted, and the prevalence of white-collar crime has only recently become recognized.

Criminals are of several types—victimless, psychopathic, institutional, situational, habitual, professional, and political. As these types differ greatly in motivation and life organization, each poses a different problem in prevention or treatment. Organized crime is one form of professional crime. It arises from the large market for illegal goods and services and will probably persist as long as these goods and services remain illegal. The romanticized image of "the Mafia" is incorrect, for Mafia is a complex of attitudes and relationships, not an organization.

Suggested Readings

Because chapters 5 and 6 form a unit, the suggested readings for both chapters are at the end of chapter 6.

Footnotes

[1]Anonymous Egyptian priest, about 2000 B.C.

[2]*Time,* 17 Mar. 1952, p. 12.

[3]*Time,* 5 Nov. 1951, p. 26.

[4]*Playboy,* Sept. 1976, p. 19.

[5]*National Observer,* 7 Nov. 1966, p. 11.

[6]*Business Week,* 17 Apr. 1978, p. 91.

[7]*Psychology Today,* Sept. 1978, p. 79.

[8]See David Caplovitz, *The Poor Pay More* (New York: Free Press, 1967).

[9]Federal Bureau of Investigation, *Uniform Crime Reports* (Washington, D.C., 1978), p. 6.

[10]See Ronald H. Beattie, "Criminal Statistics in the United States," *Journal of Criminal Law, Criminology, and Police Science,* 51 (May–June 1960), 49–65; and Albert J. Reiss, Jr., "Assessing the Current Crime Wave," in Barbara McLennan, ed., *Crime in Urban Society* (New York: Dunellan, 1970), pp. 23–42.

[11]See Mark Lipman, *Stealing: How America's Employees Are Stealing Their Companies Blind* (New York: Harper's Magazine Press, 1973).

[12]Gerald D. Robin, "The Corporate and Judicial Disposition of Employee Thieves," *Wisconsin Law Review,* Summer 1967, pp. 685–702.

[13]*Business Week,* 15 Oct. 1979, p. 119.

[14]T. C. Esselstyn, "The Social Role of the County Sheriff," *Journal of Criminal Law and Criminology,* 44 (July–Aug. 1953), 177–84.

[15]*Annual Report,* Detroit Metropolitan Branch, American Civil Liberties Union, 1960.

[16]James S. Wallerstein and Clement J. Wyle, "Our Law-Abiding Law-Breakers," reprinted from *Federal Probation* (New York: National Probation Association, Apr. 1947).

[17]Martin Gold, *Delinquent Behavior in an American City* (Monterey, Cal.: Brooks/Cole, 1970), p. 8.

[18]Robert S. Dentler and Lawrence J. Monroe, "Early Adolescent Theft," *American Sociological Review,* 26 (Oct. 1961), 733–43; Leroy C. Gould, "Who Defines Delinquency: A Comparison of Officially-Reported Indices of Delinquency for Three Racial Groups," *Social Problems,* 16 (Winter 1969), 325–26; Ray C. Williams and Martin Gold, "From Delinquent Behavior to Official Delinquency," *Social Problems,* 20 (Fall 1972), 209–29.

[19]*Gallup Opinion Index,* 154 (May 1978), p. 28.

[20]John Herbero, "Growth in Rural Regions Brings Rapid Crime Rise," *New York Times,* 4 Nov. 1979, p. 26.

[21]Darrell J. Steffensmeier, Renee Hoffman Steffensmeier, and Alvin S. Rosenthal, "Trends in Female Violence, 1960–1975," *Sociological Focus,* 12 (Aug. 1979), 217–27.

[22]Darrell J. Steffensmeier, "Crime and Contemporary Woman: An Analysis of Changing Levels of Female Property Crime, 1960–1975," *Social Forces,* 57 (Dec. 1978), 566–84.

[23]See notes 21 and 22; also, Lee H. Bowker, *Women, Crime, and the Criminal Justice System* (Lexington, Mass.: Lexington Books, 1978).

[24]Berkeley Rice, "The New Gangs of Chinatown," *Psychology Today,* May 1977, pp. 60–69.

[25]Edward Green, "Race, Social Status, and Criminal Arrest," *American Sociological Review,* 35 (June 1970), 476–90.

[26]Gould, "Who Defines Delinquency."

[27]Richard M. Stephenson and Frank R. Scarpitti, "Negro–White Differentials and Delinquency," *Journal of Research in Crime and Delinquency,* 5 (July 1968), 122–33; Morris A. Forslund, "Standardization of Negro Crime Rates for Negro–White Differences in Age and Status," *Rocky Mountain Social Science Journal,* 7 (Apr. 1970), 151–60; Morris A. Forslund, "A Comparison of Negro and White Crime Rates," *Journal of Criminal Law, Criminology, and Police Science,* 61 (June 1970), 214–17; Ray R. Williams and Martin Gold, "From Delinquent Behavior to Official Delinquency," *Social Problems,* 20 (Fall 1972), 209–29.

[28]Michael J. Hindeland, "Equality Under the Law," *Journal of Criminal Law,*

Criminology, and Police Science, 60 (Sept. 1969), 306–13: Peter L. Burke and Austin J. Turk, "Factors Affecting Post-arrest Disposition: A Model for Analysis," *Social Problems,* 22 (Feb. 1975), 313–32.

[29]President's Commission on Law Enforcement and Administration of Justice, *The Challenge of Crime in a Free Society,* pp. 44–45; Stephenson and Scarpitti, "Negro–White Differentials and Delinquency"; Barry M. Schiller, "Racial Conflict and Delinquency: A Theoretical Approach," *Phylon,* 30 (Fall 1969), 261–71.

[30]Sheldon Glueck and Eleanor T. Glueck, *1,000 Juvenile Delinquents* (Cambridge, Mass.: Harvard University Press, 1934).

[31]Clifford Shaw and Henry D. McKay, *Juvenile Delinquency and Urban Areas* (Chicago: University of Chicago Press, 1943). See also Roland J. Chilton, "Continuity in Delinquency Area Research: A Comparison of Studies for Baltimore, Detroit, and Indianapolis," *American Sociological Review,* 29 (Feb. 1964), 71–83.

[32]Marvin E. Wolfgang, Robert M. Figlio, and Thorsten Sellin, *Delinquency in a Birth Cohort* (Chicago: University of Chicago Press, 1972), p. 245.

[33]See note 27.

[34]Charles R. Tittle, Wayne J. Villamez, and Douglas A. Smith, "The Myth of Social Class and Criminality: An Empirical Assessment of the Empirical Evidence," *American Sociological Review,* 43 (Oct. 1978), 643–56.

[35]Richard E. Johnson, "Social Class and Delinquent Behavior: A New Test," *Criminology,* 18 (May 1980), 86–93.

[36]William J. Chambliss, *Crime and Legal Process* (New York: McGraw-Hill, 1969), p. 86; T. P. Thornberry, "Race, Socioeconomic Status, and Sentencing in the Juvenile Justice System," *Journal of Criminal Law and Criminology,* 64 (Mar. 1973), 90–98.

[37]Lawrence E. Cohen and James R. Kluegel, "Determinants of Juvenile Court Dispositions: Ascriptive and Achieved Factors in Two Metropolitan Courts," *American Sociological Review,* 43 (Apr. 1978), 162–76.

[38]Burke and Turk, "Factors Affecting Post-arrest Disposition"; Theodore G. Chiricos and Gordon P. Waldo, "Socioeconomic Status and Criminal Sentencing: An Empirical Assessment of a Conflict Proposition," *American Sociological Review,* 40 (Dec. 1975), 753–72; Denice H. Willick, Gretchen Gehlker, and Anita McFarland Watts, "Social Class as a Factor Affecting Judicial Disposition," *Criminology,* 13 (May 1975), 57–77.

[39]Fox Butterfield, "Love and Sex in China," *New York Times Magazine,* 13 Jan. 1980, pp. 15ff.

[40]See John E. Conklin, *Illegal but Not Criminal: Business Crime in America* (Engelwood Cliffs, N.J.: Prentice-Hall, 1977).

[41]Edwin H. Sutherland, *White Collar Crime* (New York: Dryden Press, 1949), p. 12.

[42]Lipman, *Stealing.*

[43]*New York Times,* 1 Aug. 1976, sec. 3, p. 7.

[44]Raymond Dirks and Leonard Gross, *The Great Wall Street Scandal* (New York: McGraw-Hill, 1974).

[45]Stanley Walker, "Kilgore Has Oil, and Van Cliburn Too," *New York Times Magazine,* 23 Sept. 1962, pp. 28ff.; "Oil Slanted Larceny," *Time,* 4 June 1962, p. 78.

[46]"The Bankruptcy of Subsidized Housing," *Business Week,* 27 May 1972, pp. 42–48; Jean Carper, *Not with a Gun* (New York: Grossman, 1973).

[47]Robert D. McFadden, "Jerseyan and Concern Indicted in Pirating of Hit Records Worth Millions," *New York Times,* 28 Jan. 1979, p. 31.

[48]"Go Now, Don't Pay Later," *Time,* 26 Sept. 1977, p. 47.

[49]Donn B. Parker, "Crime by Computer" (New York: Charles Scribner's Sons, 1976); Thomas Whiteside, *Computer Capers: Tales of Electronic Thievery, Embezzlement, and Fraud* (New York: Thomas Y. Crowell, 1978).

[50]Herbert Edelhertz and Marilyn Walsh, *The White-Collar Challenge to Nuclear Safeguards* (Lexington, Mass.: D.C. Heath, 1978).

[51]*Business Week,* 21 May 1979, p. 68.

[52]Hugh A. Caulfield, "Arson: Can it be Stopped?" *U.S.A. Today,* July 1979, p. 18.

[53]*Business Week,* 21 May 1979, p. 68.

[54]Law Enforcement Assistance Administration, release of June 1978.

[55]*Fortune,* Sept. 1958, p. 116.

[56]David Shipler, "A Bribe a Day Keeps Trouble Away," *New York Times,* 13 Aug. 1972, sec. 3, p. 4.

[57]Ibid.; John Darnton, "Construction Industry: The Graft Is Built In," *New York Times,* 13 July 1975, sec. 4, p. 5.

[58]William Robbins, "Grain Scandals Hurt U.S. Sales," *New York Times,* 30 Nov. 1975, pp. 1ff.

[59]"The Crooks in White Collars," *Life,* 14 Oct. 1957, pp. 167ff.

[60]Walker, "Kilgore Has Oil."

[61]See Leo Davids, "Penology and Corporate Crime," *Journal of Criminal Law, Criminology, and Police Science,* 58 (Dec. 1967), 524–71.

[62]See "Price Fixing: Crackdown under Way," *Business Week,* 2 June 1975, pp. 42–48; Jeff Gerth, "White-Collar Criminals Feel Unaccustomed Heat," *New York Times,* 3 June 1979, sec. 4, p. 4.

[63]The classifications that follow are not commonly used by sociologists, except the three terms *situational, habitual,* and *professional.* Although the classifications used here are unconventional, we consider them practicable. There is some overlapping of categories, as is unavoidable in any typology of complex behavior.

[64]Edwin F. Schur, *Crimes without Victims: Deviant Behavior and Public Policy* (Englewood Cliffs, N.J.: Prentice-Hall, 1965); Edwin F. Schur and Hugo Adam Bedau, *Victimless Crime: Two Sides of a Controversy* (Englewood Cliffs, N.J.: Prentice-Hall, 1974).

[65]The term *psychopathic* is used broadly here as a catch-all for persons whose criminal behavior arises from mental and emotional disturbance. Since even psychologists cannot agree just what "psychopathic" means, this broad use is permissible.

[66]See "Who's Guilty? Ourselves and Crime," *New Society,* 8 (Sept. 1966), 478–80.

[67]See Erwin O. Smigel and H. Laurence Ross, *Crime against Bureaucracy* (New York: Van Nostrand Reinhold, 1970).

[68]See Gwynn Nettler, "Embezzlement without Problems," *British Journal of Criminology,* 14 (Jan. 1974), 70–77.

[69]Fred C. Shapiro, "Raking the Ashes of the Epidemic of Flame," *New York Times Magazine,* 13 July 1975, pp. 14ff.

[70]One economist concluded that ordinary thieves netted an average hourly wage of $1.55 (tax-free), including time away from work through imprisonment. See William E. Cobb, "Theft and the Two Hypotheses," in Simon Rottenberg, ed., *The Economics of Crime and Punishment* (Washington, D.C.: American Enterprise Institute for Public Policy Research, 1973), pp. 19–30. But the same economist concluded in 1971 that the skilled shoplifter averaged over $30,000 a year (over $50,000 a year at 1980 prices.) See *Business Week,* 15 Oct. 1979, p. 119.

[71]J. A. Mack, "The Able Criminal," *British Journal of Criminology,* 12 (Jan. 1972), 44–54.

[72]See Chic Conwell, *The Professional Thief,* annotated and interpreted by Edwin H. Sutherland (Chicago: University of Chicago Press, 1937); Harry King, *Box Man: A Professional Thief's Journey,* as told to and edited by Bill Chambliss (New York: Harper & Row, 1972); Bruce Jackson, *Outside the Law: A Thief's Primer* (New Brunswick, N.J.: Transaction Books, 1972); Neal Shover, "The Social Organization of Burglary," *Social Problems,* 20 (Spring 1973), 499–514; Carl B. Klockers, *The Professional Fence* (New York: The Free Press, 1974); and James A. Inciardi, *Careers in Crime* (Chicago: Rand McNally, 1975).

[73]Edwin M. Lemert, "The Behavior of the Systematic Check Forger," *Social Problems,* 6 (Fall 1958), 141–49; John Irwin and Lewis Yablonsky, "The New Criminal: A View of the Contemporary Offender," *British Journal of Criminology,* 5 (Apr. 1965), 183–90; Elmer Herbert Johnson, *Crime, Corrections, and Society* (Homewood, Ill.: Dorsey Press, 1968), p. 243.

[74]David W. Maurer, "Whiz Mob: A Correlation of the Technical Argot of Pickpockets with Their Behavior Pattern" in Donald R. Cressey and David A. Ward, eds., *Delinquency, Crime, and Social Process* (New York: Harper & Row, 1969), pp. 444–53.

[75]See Robert Shelton, "The Geography of Disgrace: A World Survey of Political Prisoners," *Saturday Review/World,* 15 June 1974, pp. 14–19.

[76]See Jessica Mitford, *The Trial of Dr. Spock, The Rev. William Sloan Coffin, Jr., Michael Ferber, Mitchell Goodman, and Marcus Raskin* (New York: Alfred A. Knopf, 1969). See also Charles Goodell, *Political Prisoners in America* (New York: Random House, 1973).

[77]See "Top Targets of Terrorists: U.S. Businessmen," *U.S. News and World Report,* 26 Nov. 1979, p. 61.

[78]Clark Howard, *Zebra* (New York: Richard Marek, 1979).

[79]Charles Mohr, "A Pride of Hesitant Scholars Investigates the Emerging Discipline of Terrorism," *New York Times,* 27 May 1979, sec. 4, p. 8.

[80]See Tad Szule, "George Jackson Radicalizes the Brothers in Soledad and San Quentin," *New York Times Magazine,* 1 Aug. 1971, pp. 10ff.; George Jackson, *Soledad Brother—The Prison Letters of George Jackson* (New York: Coward, McCann and Geoghegan, 1970); Charles A. Rea-

sons, "The Politicizing of Crime, the Criminal, and the Criminologist," *Journal of Criminal Law and Criminology,* 64 (Dec. 1973), 471–77; and Stephen Schafer, *The Political Criminal: The Problem of Morality and Crime* (New York: Free Press, 1975).

[81]Abbie Hoffman, *Steal This Book* (Pirate Editions, 1971; distributed by Grove Press, New York).

[82]Courtney Riley Cooper, *Here's to Crime* (Boston: Little, Brown, 1937); Martin Mooney, *Crime Incorporated* (New York: McGraw-Hill, 1935).

[83]President's Commission, *Challenge of Crime,* pp. 187–200; Gus Tyler, *Organized Crime in America* (Ann Arbor: University of Michigan Press, 1962); Earl Johnson, Jr., "Organized Crime: Challenge to the American Legal System," *Journal of Criminal Law, Criminology, and Police Science,* 54 (Mar. 1963), 1–29; Vernon Fox, *Introduction to Criminology* (Englewood Cliffs, N.J.: Prentice-Hall, 1976), pp. 270–72.

[84]Quoted in *Saturday Evening Post,* 11 Oct. 1958, p. 116.

[85]See Albert Deutsch, "The Plight of the Honest Cop," *Collier's,* 18 Sept. 1953, pp. 23ff., 28 May 1954, pp. 29ff., 23 July 1954, pp. 33ff.

[86]Adlai E. Stevenson, "Who Runs the Gambling Machines?" *Atlantic Monthly* (Feb. 1952), pp. 35–38.

[87]See David Weinstein and Lillian Deitch, *The Impact of Legalized Gambling: The Socioeconomic Consequences of Lotteries and Off-Track Gambling* (New York: Praeger Publishers, 1974).

[88]See *Hearings before the Select Committee on Improper Activities in the Labor and Management Field,* 85th Congress, 2nd Session (Washington, D.C.: Government Printing Office, 1958). For a popular account, see Robert F. Kennedy, *The Enemy Within* (New York: Harper & Row, 1960).

[89]See Robert Rice, *The Business of Crime* (New York: Farrar, Straus and Cudahy, 1956), for case histories of businessmen who cooperated with criminals for profit; see also Daniel Jack Chasan, *"Good Fences Make Bad Neighbors,"* New York Times Magazine, 29 Dec. 1974, pp. 12ff.

[90]Reported in *Rodale's Environmental Action Bulletin,* 19 Aug. 1972 (Emmaus, Pa.: Rodale Press), p. 5.

[91]Cyrus H. Karraker, *Piracy Was a Business* (West Ridge, N.H.: Richard R. Smith, 1953); Patrick Pringle, *Jolly Roger: The Story of the Great Age of Piracy* (New York: W. W. Norton, 1953); Hugh F. Rankin, *The Golden Age of Piracy* (New York: Holt, Rinehart and Winston, 1969).

[92]Frederick Sondern, Jr., *Brotherhood of Evil* (New York: Farrar, Straus and Cudahy, 1959); Nicholas Gage, ed., *Mafia, USA* (Chicago: Playboy Press, 1972).

[93]Robert T. Anderson, "From Mafia to Cosa Nostra," *American Journal of Sociology,* 71 (Nov. 1965), 302–10; Humbert S. Nelli, *The Business of Crime: Italians and Syndicate Crime in the United States* (New York: Oxford University Press, 1976).

[94]Joseph L. Albini, *The American Mafia: Genesis of a Legend* (New York: Appleton-Century-Crofts, 1971), p. 126.

[95]Francis A. J. Ianni, "The Mafia and the Web of Kinship," *The Public Interest,* Winter 1971, p. 83.

[96]See Dwight C. Smith, *The Mafia Mystique* (New York: Basic Books, 1975).

[97]For descriptions of organized crime in the United States, see Tyler, *Organized Crime in America;* President's Commission, *The Challenge of Crime,* pp. 187–209; Donald R. Cressey, *Organized Crime: Its Elementary Forms* (New York: Harper & Row, 1972); Denny F. Pace and Jimmie C. Styles, *Organized Crime: Concepts and Controls* (Englewood Cliffs, N.J.: Prentice-Hall, 1975); and August Bequai, *Organized Crime* (Lexington, Mass.: Lexington Books, 1979).

[98]President's Commission, *The Challenge of Crime,* pp. 187–96. For popular descriptions of what happens when organized crime moves in on legitimate business, see "The Mob," *Life,* 1 Sept. 1967, pp. 15–22ff., 8 Sept. 1967, pp. 91–106; "The Mob Muscles Into a Top-Priority Defense Plant," *Life,* 14 Feb. 1969, pp. 52–56; or Jonathan Kwitny, *Vicious Circles* (New York: W. W. Norton, 1979).

[99]Robert D. Peloquin, president of International Intelligence Corporation; reported in *New York Times,* 10 Jan. 1971, p. F2.

[100]President's Commission, *The Challenge of Crime,* pp. 197–98.

[101]Norval Morris and Gordon Hawkins, *The Honest Politician's Guide to Crime Control* (Chicago: University of Chicago Press, 1970), p. 235.

[102]Francis A. J. Ianni, *A Family Business: Kinship and Social Control in Organized Crime* (New York: Russell Sage Foundation, 1972); Francis A. J. Ianni, "New Mafia: Black, Hispanic, and Italian Styles," *Trans-Action,* Mar./Apr. 1974, pp. 26–39.

CRIME AND DELINQUENCY: CAUSES AND TREATMENT

§6

ARE MOST PEOPLE CROOKED?

"It was a heck of a sale while it lasted," police investigator David Olsen said.

About 100 motorists pumped free gasoline for themselves and pocketed packs of cigarettes at the E-Z Go service station Friday while two attendants who had been tied up by the robbers begged for help.

"I shouted, 'Help! Help! Help! We've been robbed,' " one of the attendants, Kenneth Harris, said. "They just looked and kept pumping.

"Several of them came in. One man came in with $2 to pay for his gas. He looked at me, and I said, 'Man, untie me. Get the police.' He put the money back in his pocket, grabbed a bunch of cigarettes and told me that help was on the way. Then he returned to his car, filled it with gas and drove away."

Investigator Olsen said that "With no one manning the gas pumps, angry customers began streaming into the office for service. Seeing the two attendants tied up

on the floor they laughed like hell and gassed up," he said. . . .

Police said they finally were summoned by an unidentified customer.[1]

ARE MOST PEOPLE HONEST?

A Brink's armored truck was rounding a corner in midtown Manhattan when the back door swung open and $2,000 worth of quarters—some wrapped, some loose—spilled onto the street.

People dashed off the sidewalks to scoop up the coins and, without being asked, promptly handed their fistfuls of money to the Brink's driver and two guards.

Joe Gomez, a partly blind newsstand operator, applauded. He said the incident reflected the honesty of New Yorkers.

George Semidley said he ran out of his flower shop and gathered up several hundred dollars in coins for the three Brink's men.

Brink's said all but about $10 was recovered after the incident Friday.[2]

Are most people honest? Are most people crooked? The answer to both questions is "yes." There are some situations in which nearly everyone is honest (for example, cheating the blind newspaper peddler), and other situations in which nearly everyone is dishonest (parking lot damage to another's car).[3] What causes people to act this way?

The Analysis of Causes

The classification of crime discussed in chapter 5 shows that much criminal behavior is properly a problem in jurisprudence, in public morality, or in education and social organization, rather than a problem in criminology. It is the behavior of the habitual and professional criminal, together with that of the juvenile delinquent (whose behavior may seem even more perplexing), that need to be explained in terms of crime causation.

BIOLOGICAL THEORIES

Early attempts at the scientific study of crime tried to establish physical differences that would identify the "criminal type." No distinct criminal type has been found, although some physical peculiarities are claimed. Sheldon Glueck and Eleanor Glueck compared 500 delinquent boys with 500 carefully matched nondelinquents and found that the solid, muscular boys were significantly more delinquent.[4] They do not claim that body type *causes* delinquency, but that the muscular, energetic boys seem more likely to relieve their tensions in ways that are delinquent. We have found no physical feature or biological characteristic that directly causes crime, but a physical characteristic may be socially defined and treated in ways that encourage deviant behavior. A person who is teased, taunted, ridiculed, or made to feel unworthy because of some physical characteristic is a good candidate for some kind of difficulty. But even the most exhaustive of surveys of possible biological factors in crime causation are conspicuoulsy unsuccessful in establishing any clear causal connections.[5]

PSYCHOLOGICAL THEORIES

There have been many attempts to link crime with some type of psychopathy. Although often considered the basis for criminal behavior, neuroses and psychoses are, in fact, comparatively rare among prison inmates[6] and juvenile delinquents.[7] It is claimed that delinquency often springs from emotional disturbance, and that delinquent behavior can be predicted from psychiatric observation. However, there is little agreement on which traits lead to delinquency; practically every trait is labeled predictive by one psychiatrist or another.[8] Figure 6–1 shows the difference in the amount of emotional disturbance present in lower-class delinquents and middle- and upper-class delinquents. The Gluecks found some emotional disturbance among 51 percent of their delinquents and 44 percent of their control group of nondelinquents—not a very significant difference.[9] Thus, only a limited amount of crime and delinquency can be attributed to psychological disturbances.

SOCIOLOGICAL THEORIES

The search among environmental factors for causes of delinquency seemed more promising. Many years ago Clifford Shaw found that certain slum areas maintained extremely high delinquency rates consistently over the years. Although a succession of racial or ethnic minorities might have occupied an area, the delinquency rate remained constant regardless of the group living in it.[10] Obviously, crime was not a product of the kind of people in the area but of the physical and social life of the area. Other studies show associations between juvenile delinquency and transiency, low income, large family size, parental neglect, parental criminality, school failure, parental alcoholism, and other social circumstances.[11] But these studies do not indicate *causes*, for not all children exposed to these circumstances become delinquent. Equal numbers of boys and girls are exposed to them, yet boy delinquents outnumber girl delinquents by four or five to one. Furthermore, in some cases, such as delinquency and school failure, it is difficult to determine which is cause and which is effect. After depth interviews with 240 habitual criminals by a sociologist-psychologist team, the members concluded that "we could establish no causal connection between the way the criminal thinks and acts and the circumstances of his life."[12] Instead of listing environmental factors as causes, it is more correct to list them as risk factors, since they increase the risk of coming into contact with and learning criminal behavior patterns.

Figure 6-1
Does emotional disturbance cause delinquency?
Source: Adapted from data in Walter B. Miller, "Some Characteristics of Present-day Delinquency of Relevance to Educators," paper presented at meeting of American Association of School Administrators, 18 Feb. 1959.

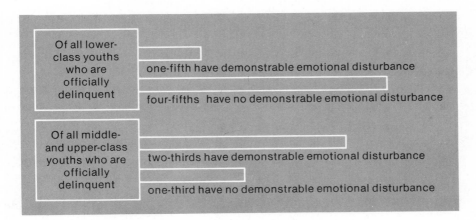

Of all lower-class youths who are officially delinquent

one-fifth have demonstrable emotional disturbance

four-fifths have no demonstrable emotional disturbance

Of all middle- and upper-class youths who are officially delinquent

two-thirds have demonstrable emotional disturbance

one-third have no demonstrable emotional disturbance

Theories of crime and delinquency are numerous, contradictory, and unsatisfactory. Perhaps "crime" covers such a broad range of behavior that no comprehensive, generic theory can possibly explain it all. The current theories can be divided into *cultural deviance theories, strain theories, conflict theories,* and *control theories.*

CULTURAL DEVIANCE THEORIES OF CRIME   Several theories note that criminal behavior, like all other social behavior, *must be learned.* This led Edwin Sutherland some years ago to formulate what has become the best-known modern theory of crime causation.

Sutherland's differential association theory   This theory states that most criminal behavior is learned through contact with criminal patterns that are present, acceptable, and rewarded in one's physical and social environment. As Sutherland says:

> The hypothesis of differential association is that criminal behavior is learned in association with those who define such behavior favorably and in isolation from those who define it unfavorably, and that a person in an appropriate situation engages in such criminal behavior if, and only if, the weight of the favorable definitions exceeds the weight of the unfavorable definitions.[13]

In a "deliquency area," where perhaps one-fourth or more of the youths are officially delinquent each year, and where most of the rest are delin-

One's environment can be a contributing factor to crime and delinquency.
(Marc Anderson)

quent without being caught,[14] it is no exaggeration to say that delinquency is normal. Although not every youth is delinquent, most are delinquent some of the time; some are delinquent most of the time; and delinquent behavior is a normal part of the area culture. Since such areas have a high adult crime rate, the juvenile graduates easily and naturally to a criminal career.

But why don't all children living in a delinquency area become delinquent, or all juvenile delinquents become adult criminals? Although criminal patterns are a normal feature of the area culture, even the delinquency area is not totally isolated from noncriminal patterns and anticriminal definitions. In many cases a stable family life, strongly integrated around the conventionally approved values, may insulate the child against the criminal patterns of the area, while an unsatisfactory home life virtually throws the child into the streets. The Gluecks, after carefully controlled studies of hundreds of delinquents, believe that the family life of the child is very nearly the all-important factor in delinquency. They believe they can predict delinquency with 90 percent accuracy from the "five highly decisive" factors in family life: father's discipline (harsh, erratic, unsympathetic); mother's supervision (indifferent, unconcerned); father's affection (lacking); mother's affection (cold, indifferent, even hostile); cohesiveness of the family (unintegrated, devoid of warm companionship). Where all five of these factors are favorable, serious delinquency is practically unknown.[15] Although the Glueck Prediction Scale has been severely criticized,[16] a number of validation studies have confirmed that it is highly predictive.[17]

In some instances the church or school may acquaint the child with noncriminal ambitions and values, but these institutions rarely affect children deeply unless supported by a constructive home environment. Life in a deteriorated area of drab, crowded housing and dubious business enterprises offers the child many contacts with criminal patterns. In a high delinquency area, several factors—unsatisfactory home life, unsolved emotional problems, and the influences of a deteriorated neighborhood—all work together to increase the child's contacts with criminal patterns, while reducing or neutralizing the child's contacts with noncriminal patterns and anticriminal values.

The pattern holds true not only for the slum delinquent but for the middle-class delinquent as well. Since middle-class and upper-class delinquents do not live in deteriorated neighborhoods, delinquent behavior is much less a normal part of their cultural world. In a certain sense, delinquency is normal for the slum child and abnormal for the middle-class child. The middle-class child has less contact with delinquent patterns and more contact with anticriminal evaluations than has the slum child. Yet the middle-class child is not isolated from contact with criminal behavior, but reads about it, sees it portrayed in movies and on television, and observes a certain amount of unreported crime. As long as there is no serious rupture of emotional life, the child's close and frequent association with anticriminal definitions is likely to keep him or her from criminal behavior. But if the child's emotional life is seriously disturbed—by parental conflicts, by social difficulties with his or her age group, or by other unsolved emotional conflicts—the child frequently grows immune to the anticriminal evaluations and becomes delinquent. Or perhaps a good deal of middle-class delinquency is merely a search for excitement by bored, aimless, pampered young people.[18]

The differential-association theory is equally applicable to white-collar crime. The discovery that many of one's associates are chiseling on their income tax, and that they view it as clever rather than shameful, is a powerful temptation to follow suit. The employee who sees the boss entertaining relatives on the company yacht, and who receives from the boss detailed instructions on how to cheat the government, may wonder what is wrong with cheating the boss now and then.

Differential association is a key concept in the new *social learning* theories, which attribute deviant behavior, like all other behavior, to the social learning process.[19] The differential-association theory does not explain all criminal behavior. It does not cover crime of impulse or passion, or those delinquencies that spring from emotional maladjustment.[20] It does not explain the original *causes* of crime, but describes a process whereby crime is transmitted and perpetuated.

Labeling theories   As we mentioned earlier, most youths commit *some* delinquencies and most adults commit *some* crimes, but only a few of these people become frequent or habitual offenders. Why? Labeling theory attaches great importance to the identification and stigmatization of the offender as a delinquent or criminal. This labeling process tends to isolate the offender from conformist associations, influences, and careers, and throws the offender into closer association with other offenders. In this way, labeling may convert the experimental or accidental deviant into a career deviant, a perfect illustration of the concept of secondary deviation. While labeling is neither a sufficient nor a necessary factor to explain all delinquency, it is a crucial milepost in many criminal careers.

Numerous studies have shown how the more contacts a juvenile has with police and court agencies, the more likely the child is to commit further delinquencies.[21] This has led many labeling theorists to conclude that police and court contacts, together with the labeling they inflict and the hostility they create, actually cause or encourage delinquents to commit repeated delinquencies. Thus, it is argued, police and court processing cause delinquency.[22] This conclusion is unwarranted, an example of assuming causation from association.[23] It is like assuming that hospitals cause illness because the more often one enters a hospital, the more likely one is to get sick again.

Research that tests labeling theory is conflicting and inconclusive.[24] One longitudinal study found that only for first offenders was there any evidence that police and court processing might increase further arrests.[25] Sometimes the effect of labeling and stigma is to encourage a return to conformity.[26] Charles Tittle, examining the empirical evidence on labeling and deterrence, concludes that under some conditions the effect of labeling is to encourage further delinquencies, while under some other conditions labeling operates as a deterrent.[27] There is also some evidence that with repeated police and court contacts, delinquents develop more positive attitudes toward police and judicial personnel, not a greater hostility, as posited by labeling theorists.[28] Thus, labeling theories are plausible but unproved.[29]

Delinquent-subculture theories   These theories note that most officially delinquent youths associated mainly with other delinquents, and that many of them become adult criminals. Several studies also show from 50 to 90 percent of official delinquents coming from homes with a record of crime in the home.[30] While 98 percent of the Glueck's persistently delinquent boys associated mainly with other delinquents, only 7 percent of the nondelinquent boys from the same area associated with delinquents.[31]

The delinquent subculture described by Albert Cohen and others[32] rejects middle-class values as expressed by teachers, ministers, police, and, perhaps, parents. Its members express masculinity by rejecting maternal influences. The *act* of stealing is more important that the object stolen. Boys outside this subculture, as well as disapproving adults, are "squares," unworthy of serious consideration. One graduate of the subculture recalls an incident:

> "Thirteen arrests." The judge shook his head over my file. "Gang-fights, shootings, burglary, stealing a car . . . I don't know what to make of you. . . Why do you do these things?"

> I shrugged. What a dumb question! Every boy I knew did these things. Maybe I just did more of them and better.[33]

Sociologists disagree over the concept of the delinquent subculture. Irving Spergel, for instance, sees not only one but three distinct criminal subcultures in urban areas: *racketsville,* a racket subculture of gambling and loan-sharking; *slumtown,* a subculture of fighting street gangs, and *haulburg,* a theft subculture, with little overlapping of either membership or area.[34] Some sociologists reject the delinquent-subculture concept and present re-

Peer pressure can be a powerful influence toward either positive or negative behavior.
(Marc Anderson)

search evidence that most delinquents have *not* adopted the deviant value system of a delinquent subculture. Instead, these sociologists say, most delinquents share the general beliefs and values of the dominant culture while failing to live up to them; that is, they hold conventional values but somehow "drift" into delinquency.[35] In a cross-cultural study, Lois DeFleur found that the delinquent-subculture concept did not apply to delinquency in Argentina, but that control theory appeared to be more readily applicable.[36] The evidence on the delinquent-subculture theory is mixed and inconclusive.

STRAIN THEORIES OF CRIME   Strain theories describe the delinquent as one who is forced into deviance in an effort to achieve legitimate desires that have been frustrated. Robert Merton some years ago theorized that when culturally inspired goals are not accompanied by institutionalized means that make these goals attainable for most people, deviation is a result.[37]

The delinquency and opportunity theory   This theory, as developed by Richard Cloward and Lloyd Ohlin, hypothesizes that delinquency arises from the frustrations of poor youths who are blocked in their wish for status in a middle-class-oriented society.[38] By trapping them in dead-end jobs (or no jobs), society creates frustrations that drive youth to delinquency. Again, confirming evidence is lacking. One study testing the Cloward-Ohlin opportunity theory failed to find any significant correlation between delinquency and occupational goal discrepancy.[39] The opportunity theory is one more plausible but unproved theory.

CONFLICT THEORIES OF CRIME   These theories see crime as a product of social conflict.

Group-conflict theories   These theories attempt to explain criminal behavior in terms of some kind of group conflict. Some theorists see delinquency as a product of the conflict between lower-class persons and middle-class institutions (school, welfare establishment, police, courts) rather than as a result of lower-class adolescents' failure to achieve middle-class aspirations.[40] Still others invoke race and ethnic conflicts as an explanation. Minority groups, defeated by discrimination and inequality, may turn to delinquency and crime in frustration and anger. To many ghetto blacks the police are the enemy and the law an instrument of oppression. They feel that they get little protection from the police, and they come into contact with the law mainly when someone is seeking to collect a bill, garnishee their wages, or repossess their property. Thus they have little respect for police or law.[41]

Many criminal acts take place in the course of other kinds of group conflict—battles between unions and management or between rival unions, contests between conservative and radical political groups, and so on. The nineteenth-century range wars between cattle ranchers and settlers are a historic example. Within each group, its vested interests are sanctified and its grievances nursed until violent reprisals seem morally justified even when they violate the law.

Group-conflict theories help explain some crimes, but not all of them. Some minorities, for instance, have high official crime rates, but the crime rates of others, such as the Chinese and Japanese, are traditionally very low.

And many individual crimes are difficult to connect with any kind of group conflict or group interest.[42]

Class-conflict theories   Some theorists view most crime as a protest against an oppressive, exploitative society, and they view laws and police as tools for the protection of privilege.[43] They claim that there is no practical way to reduce crime in an atmosphere of materialism, capitalistic exploitation, and police repression. They call for a "new criminology" in which, instead of studying and trying to change the criminal, we should study and change the society. Some of these "new criminologists" are Marxists, who see most problems as unsolvable under capitalism.

If the "new criminologists" are correct, crime should be declining in communist countries. There is very little reliable evidence on this point. Crime statistics for communist countries are seldom published and are of doubtful reliability, and differences in definitions of crime make international comparisons unsatisfactory. It is clear that a half-century after the Russian Revolution, the Soviet Union still has a serious crime problem.[44] The Kremlin invited more than 80 Western companies to demonstrate security-alarm equipment at a Moscow exhibition in 1978, without explaining why a supposedly crime-free society should need such products.[45] We have little evidence from other communist countries, but it appears that they still have well-populated jails and prisons.[46] Some criminologists suggest that traditional crime may, in fact, be relatively uncommon in communist countries.[47] It is not clear, however, whether this low crime rate exists (if it exists) because they are communist, or because they are authoritarian. It has long been noted that authoritarian dictatorships—Hitler's Germany, Franco's Spain, Batista's Cuba, Salazar's Portugal, Duvalier's Haiti—had very low rates of conventional crime.

The Marxist perspective on crime assumes a great deal that is unconfirmed.[48] Some studies find a positive association between economic inequality and crime,[49] but many others reach opposite conclusions. No dependable relationship between exploitation or hardship and crime has been demonstrated. Peter Berger describes a suburban squatter slum in Brazil where 100,000 people endure almost unbelievable poverty, unemployment, crowding, and squalor, yet have a very low crime rate.[50] Paul Spector studied 103 metropolitan areas in the United States, finding no correlation between the incidence of violent crime and either population density or unemployment.[51] Studies of developing countries find that crime increases are greatest where economic development is greatest and living standards are rising most rapidly.[52] In Sweden, a democratic socialist state often viewed as approaching Utopia, crime is now growing rapidly.[53] All these cases, however, would be dismissed by a Marxian ideologue on the grounds that they are all capitalist countries.

Since there is no firm evidence of the amount of crime in communist countries, the class-conflict theory can be neither accepted nor rejected on an evidential basis. If accepted, it must be as a profession of faith.

CONTROL THEORIES   There is some recent evidence that the deviant value systems and elaborate rationalizations for crime that the professional criminals profess are not, in fact, typical of most criminals. Instead, a number of research studies have concluded that most delinquents hold relatively conventional ideas of right and wrong, and that their delinquencies are conscious departures from their moral standards.[54] Control theories "assume that delinquent acts result when an individual's bond to society is weak or broken."[55] Many studies have found that delinquents, far more often than nondelinquents, lack effective and rewarding ties with the major social institutions.[56] Anything that weakens one's attachment to and involvement in conventional society thus promotes crime. Family and school are key points of attachment to society, and when a young person's relationship with either is unsatisfactory, delinquency is a common reaction.[57]

Control theorists describe most serious delinquents as aimless nonstrivers who work and study very little. Control theorists reject the romanticized image of delinquents as a group of capable, aspiring youths who are frustrated by an unjust social system; they see the delinquent as "relatively free of the intimate attachments, the aspirations, and the moral beliefs that bind most people to a life within the law.[58]

Friday and Hage point out that it is the *total complex* of ties to conventional institutions that discourages delinquency. No single factor—poor school adjustment, broken home, lack of job—is determining by itself. It is *all of them, taken together*, that combine to form either a control system in which it seems natural to behave conventionally or a control system in which it seems natural to become delinquent.[59]

Control theories are supported by a considerable body of research evidence.[60] It is noteworthy, for example, that Japan, a country with most of the characteristics usually associated with a high crime rate—materialistic values, rapid economic development, urbanization, high population density, class inequality—actually has less than one-fourth the American crime rate, lower even than the crime rate in Japan a quarter-century ago.[61] This is attributed to the pervasive system of informal social controls closely binding people to cohesive informal social groups, where authority is respected as legitimate and where the law, the police, and the courts hold a moral as well as a legal authority. Switzerland is another country which is capitalist, materialistic, urbanized, and with great inequality. Yet Switzerland has a low crime rate, which has shown no increase in recent years.[62] Japan and Switzerland provide substantial evidence in support of the control theories.

None of the series of theories discussed above is fully satisfactory. Each has some supporting evidence, but each is also challenged by opposing evidence, and the various theories are all in some degree contradictory. Nor is it likely that additional research and theory construction will ever give a broad, general theory that will explain crime of all kinds.[63] The basic causes of crime are unknown and probably unknowable, perhaps because they are inseparable from the same drives and motives that impel all other behavior. A search for understanding of the conditions under which criminal behavior appears and spreads has proved to be far more useful.

The Personal-Deviation Approach

The personal-deviation approach views a social problem as an outgrowth of certain individuals who, for one reason or another, fail to absorb and internalize conventional attitudes, habits, goals, and values. The criminal is viewed as a deviant person who has failed to form the normal value judgments, ambitions, and habits, and instead has developed socially disapproved ones.

A massive research report, involving thousands of hours of interviews with 240 habitual criminals, reached the conclusion that the habitual criminal is a truly deviant person who thinks differently from other persons.[64] "The habitual criminal . . . is a liar and deceiver; he has little capacity for love, friendship, or companionship; he can commit brutal acts without a twinge of conscience and yet continue to believe that he is a 'good' person."[65] But this description applies to only the habitual or professional criminals, and does not explain how they came to be such persons.

The reasons for criminal deviation are probably similar to the reasons for any other form of personal deviation. *Any factor in inheritance, environment, or social experience can become a factor either in a conventional or in a deviant personality organization.* Lack of maternal affection drives one child to the streets, another to books, still another to church. A number of biographical studies have shown how the influences of a deteriorated neighborhood interact with an unsatisfactory home life in producing many juvenile delinquents who graduate into adult criminals.[66] Yet even a "desirable" characteristic may be defined and interpreted in social experience in such a way as to contribute to a deviant personality orientation, as seen in the following case:

> School was always easy for me. By just sitting and listening to what happened I could always learn enough to pass the examinations pretty well. I never bought a textbook and never studied one single lesson throughout high school. My grades were never high but I never failed a course and my grades averaged more than satisfactory. . . . I also learned quite young that if one is smart he can outwit the ordinary suckers who are really pretty dull. Only dopes work for a living. I've never really done a day's work in my life and I don't intend to. I have always found it possible to work out some kind of a racket and you can always be sure to find some sucker who will do the work for half the gain. I live on the other half. . . . I am now 40 years old and in this scrape which will probably land me in jail. I just overstepped a little—didn't cover up too well. My lawyer tells me I won't get over four years and I may be out in two and a half for good behavior. You can bet that my behavior will be _____ good. And the guys who sent me up will be working for me yet.[67]

As this case shows, high intelligence, a pleasing personality, and a "good" home background can be incorporated into either a deviant or a conventional personality organization.

A few people may become criminally deviant through *inability* to learn conventional habits of behavior. Some crime, but relatively little, is committed by mentally deficient people who lack the mental ability to learn acceptable behavior, or perhaps to distinguish between criminal and noncriminal behavior. But such people form a small part of the crime problem.

In any society, some persons develop badly adjusted personalities or fail to internalize the conventional values and are therefore deviant; some, but not all, of these come from bad environments. Among the possible behavior outlets for deviant persons are a number that are criminal. The specific study of criminal careers in terms of personality deviation helps us understand crime but will not fully explain it. Intelligent treatment for criminals is impossible without this understanding.

The Value-Conflict Approach

The value-conflict approach analyzes the problem in terms of the conflicting values of our society. Values differ on the questions of what acts are crimes and what should be done about them. In victimless and institutional crime, the value conflict is obvious. These are widespread crimes because the value judgments of certain groups have been written into law, forbidding acts that the value judgments of other groups tolerate. Gambling and prostitution become problems purely because of such value conflicts. If *everyone disapproved* of these activities there would be no question of what to do about them, and suppression would be less difficult. Or if *everyone accepted* these activities there would be no problem, since no critical judgments would define them as situations needing correction. But wherever there is a substantial number of people whose values define as acceptable a form of behavior forbidden by law, widespread violation of the law and persistent corruption of law-enforcement officials are inevitable. John Gardiner reports a poll showing a wide tolerance for gambling, but a strong criticism of the corruption that illegal gambling necessarily entails.[68] Such value conflicts make the crime problem insoluble.

Value conflicts function in another manner as a "cause" of crime: through the corrosion of personal morality by the value conflicts inherent within the culture. At home, in church, and in school the child learns a set of moral values—truth, honesty, loyalty, and so on—and a set of copybook maxims—"honesty is the best policy," "crime does not pay," "truth wins out in the end." Eventually the child discovers that these are only half true. The child comes to realize that a considerable amount of business or professional success is based on a subtle betrayal of trust.[69] The child learns that a salesperson's job is to sell not necessarily what the customer needs but what the store has to sell. The child realizes that much advertising depends on the cautious half-truth, and on a calculated pandering to the vanities, fears, and weaknesses of the potential customers.[70] The child learns of law enforcement officials and even of presidents who violate the law; about politicians who collect graft; about physicians who split fees, collect kickbacks, and defraud Medicare; about the bribery of purchasing agents; about falsification of financial statements; about the many legal and semilegal ways of avoiding tax obligations; about padded repair bills; and about dozens of other forms of fraud. The child learns about business executives who employ prostitutes to cultivate a prospective customer.[71] One who is in business soon learns that the customers are as dishonest as business persons are, or perhaps even worse! One realizes that a customer's claim for damaged property is nearly always inflated. "We've never yet damaged an *old* piece of luggage," says an airline executive.[72] Automobile insurance companies estimate that one-fourth to one-half of all the money paid out in claims goes into secret commissions and padded charges,[73] and one claims manager even states that "every case is tainted to some degree with fraud."[74] One generally comes to accept forms of sharp practice common to one's occupation,[75] along with the rationalizations that justify them, and one is constantly reminded of the many other forms of exploitation and fraud going on everywhere. Meanwhile, according to this theory, one's moral sensitivity is blunted and one's lofty moral principles become remote, available for ritualistic repetition when needed, but carefully insulated from any controlling influence on one's personal behavior. Some criminologists consider this process to be a primary explanation of the prevalence of crime in modern society.

The indictment is in some respects an exaggeration. Although in practically every business or profession certain questionable or dishonest practices are common, it is probably true that dishonest acts are vastly outnumbered by honest acts, and false statements outnumbered by truthful ones. But it is also true that there is enough misrepresentation, exploitation of ignorance and gullibility, and deliberate fraud in the business world to make the maintenance of a strict moral conscience difficult.

Does it follow that any materialistic society with a competition-success pattern must have a high crime rate? When we encourage people to want more than most can possibly get, and to view themselves as personal failures unless they get the things they want, do we guarantee a high rate of crime?

The cases of Japan and Switzerland suggest that a materialistic and competitive society can have a low crime rate. Whether a socialist revolution or a greater push for economic equality would reduce our crime rate is a question which cannot be answered on a basis of any available evidence.

The Social-Disorganization Approach

The social-disorganization approach studies the crime problem as a product of social change. A stable, well-integrated society has very little crime. Habits and practices that are necessary and useful will have become institutionalized and thoroughly supported by the moral values of the culture. In time, an objectionable practice will be dealt with in a well-integrated culture, either by a gradual change of values so as to approve it or by suppression through the compelling system of social control found in such a society.

Social change disorganizes the existing network of arrangements and values of a society. Many old norms become inapplicable, and numerous value conflicts

Our materialistic society may encourage criminal behavior by those who want but cannot afford life's luxuries.
(Irene Springer)

appear. Children are encouraged to develop expectations that do not fit the realities they eventually find. Traditional standards seem remote and meaningless, and traditional behavior controls lose power. Western civilization has experienced such rapid and sweeping changes in the modern era that before adjustment to one set of changes is completed, new changes rush upon it.

A social-disorganization analysis of crime emphasizes how change from a rural agricultural society to an urban industrial society has revolutionized our values and disorganized our traditional social control machinery.[76] The hard-work-and-thrift value orientation of a peasant people has been replaced with live-it-up materialism. The informal controls of neighborhood and community are less effective in our anonymous urban civilization. Parental supervision of children and adolescents suffers because of modern transportation, commercialized recreation, employment of both parents, and the daily scattering of the family for work and play. For the first time in history, a society is expending great energies, through advertising and sales techniques, in deliberately encouraging people to want more than they can possibly obtain. This mass promotion of unlimited wants is a development whose impact is only beginning to become apparent. Many of the traditional values, such as thrift, simplicity of life, and pride in craftsmanship, become increasingly remote as the urge for conspicuous consumption is nurtured into full bloom.

Social change produces many new situations and practices for which the traditional mores are no clearcut guide. Although the existing mores clearly condemn murder and rape and openly support private property and marriage, they provide no positive definitions concerning the propriety of labor unions, selling watered stock, or the setback requirements for a skyscraper. To regulate such technical matters, thousands of laws not tied in with any strongly entrenched mores have been passed. There are too many such technical matters; they have developed too rapidly and are too complicated for any coherent set of moral definitions to have crystallized and preceded the passing of the law. Such laws, which are not buttressed by a strong supporting morality, are difficult to enforce. Neither the violator, the enforcement officials, nor the public view violations very seriously; they are likely to dismiss them lightly as minor administrative errors instead of criminal acts. Severe punishments for such technical violations probably would be unwise, yet it remains likely that widespread violation and lax enforcement of certain laws tend to break down the habit of obedience to law in general.

Social change also produces new interest groupings of people and alters the complexion of old ones. New occupations appear, new industries arise, new recreational groups develop, and new pressure groups of all sorts are always being organized. In the constant battle for position and power, the law is often violated. Again, the existing morality often provides no clear-cut guides. Is the wire-tapper a menace or a benefactor when he secretly (and illegally) records telephone conversations for the use of police, politicians, business competitors, or suspicious spouses? Should government officials disregard the law when they feel that "national security" is at stake? Should corporations or labor unions be permitted to make contributions to political campaign funds? Should the closed shop and industry-wide bargaining be viewed as labor rights or labor abuses? The rise of new interest groups always produces considerable new legislation and considerable confusion.

Another disorganizing feature of American life is its ethnic heterogeneity—the variety of racial and national backgrounds represented among the American people. Settled by a mixture of peoples, America has never possessed an integrated cultural tradition. Immigration during the past century brought a heavy infusion of Slavic and Latin elements into the predominantly Anglo-Saxon society, resulting in increased cultural conflict and confusion. Many of our value conflicts stem from the clash of cultural backgrounds—for example, Catholic–Protestant disagreement over gambling, abortion, contraception, divorce, or relations of church and state. In the clash of cultural backgrounds, each cultural tradition loses some of its power to control the behavior of individuals. The high crime rates among most second-generation immigrant groups reflect the assimilation problems that they confront. With parental authority undermined by the clash of cultures, the immigrant's child readily absorbs the delinquent patterns of the slum areas in which many immigrants live. We no longer have mass immigration at the level of the past century, but immigration from Mexico and Puerto Rico remains substantial, with similar results among these cultural groups.

The lack of any important role for adolescents is a prime defect in our social organization. In most societies children and adolescents have had important, productive things to do, giving them a real share in adult life and responsibility. Although often monotonous and sometimes resented, their work was important and worthwhile. In our society the task of the child and adolescent is to grow, to listen, and to wait. Adolescents have no really important *work* to do and are excluded from the important adult life of the society. They have no clearly defined role to fill, with a clearly defined set of privileges and duties for each age level, but are expected to alternate between adult responsibility and childlike dependence at the whim of adults. Just how to replace the delays, confusions, and trivialities of the present adolescent role with a more functionally significant adolescent role in our highly complex society is not clear. Perhaps delinquency and the adolescent problem are part of the price we must pay for the exclusion of adolescents from "real" life.

Of all the approaches to the crime problem, sociologists have made most use of the social-disorganization approach. It provides a very plausible explanation for much criminal behavior. The high crime rates of disorganized groups, such as second-generation immigrants and American Indians, and the increase of crime in war-devastated countries, clearly show how social disorganization is accompanied by a high crime rate. Yet no one approach gives a complete picture. The social-disorganization approach indicates the conditions under which crime may be expected to increase or decrease; the value-conflict approach reveals how people may rationalize and justify their criminal behavior, and in its Marxian version offers a highly controversial explanation for many kinds of crime; the personal-deviation approach helps explain why some people are more inclined to be criminal than others.

The Treatment of Crime

The problem of crime has probably been studied more extensively than any other social problem. After decades of effort and thousands of studies, nothing definitive about the causes of crime has been established, and no crime treatment can be confidently said to "work."[77] The many experimental treatment programs that have been tried generally appear to be theoretically sound. The initial evaluations are practically always favorable. But most treatment program experiments soon confront "the well known 'law of delinquency prevention program research': the more carefully you evaluate the program, the greater is the probability that it will show little effect. . . ."[78] When a prevention or treatment program that appears to have been experimentally successful is adopted for general use, the results are nearly always disappointing. Nothing is more clear than that we do not know much about how to prevent crime or reform criminals. Since our national expenditure for crime research is a fraction of 1 percent of our expenditure for crime control, our lack of knowledge is not surprising.

We do best at showing what does *not* work. For many centuries harsh, brutal punishments were routine. Civilized societies abandoned them when their ineffectiveness became apparent in the eighteenth and nineteenth centuries.[79] One of the arguments against mutilations was that the sight of mutilated persons had become so commonplace that it was no longer a deterrent. One of the arguments leading to the abolition of public hangings was the observation that at the very moment when the trap dropped and the viewers were presumably being impressed with the awesome fruits of crime, the pickpockets and thieves were the busiest. Public hangings may have caused more crime than they deterred.

The next "reform" was imprisonment, in every possible variation of prison design and operation. Today it is widely agreed that prisons are expensive failures. They are said to be demoralizing and dehumanizing;[80] their rehabilitation programs are mostly ineffectual;[81] and these failures are inherent in the prison system and probably will not be corrected by program innovations or the expenditure of more money.[82] Convicts who do go straight may be more likely to have "matured out" of crime than to be examples of rehabilitation success. Yet, we must be doing *something* right, because a recent national survey finds that recidivism among convicts has dropped from 31 percent in the 1960s to 23 percent in the 1970s and is still dropping.[83] Current correctional efforts are taking several directions.

LEGAL REFORMS

There is widespread support for decriminalizing most forms of victimless crime. The economic foundation of organized crime is the fact that gambling, prostitution, and many drugs are legally forbidden but widely desired. In addition to the corruption of police and law enforcement personnel inherent in such a situation, the attempt to enforce these laws occupies much of the time of the police; clogs the courts, jails, and prisons; and undermines general respect for law. Some years ago, a joint committee of the American Bar Association and the American Medical Association recommended that the drug addict no longer be treated as a criminal, but instead be permitted to buy legal narcotics under medical supervision.[84] Reducing the high cost of feeding the habit would reduce petty crimes by addicts. The National Council on Crime and Delinquency has recommended that all victimless crime be removed from the criminal code.[85]

We are moving toward decriminalization, with state marijuana laws being relaxed by stages, laws regulating voluntary adult sex behavior being relaxed or ignored, and the Supreme Court ruling to permit legal abortion.

All such moves have the effect of reducing the number of crimes and criminals, and freeing crime control facilities for concentration upon the remaining crimes.

Decriminalization, however, is no panacea. Legalized gambling has not ended illegal gambling or even decreased it. Illegal gambling persists, because the "pay-off" is higher and taxes on the winnings can usually be evaded. Decriminalization of intoxication has not reduced public intoxication.[86] Decriminalization of some forms of crime is probably a wise social policy, but unrealistic expectations should not be encouraged.

COURT REFORM

Backlogged court calendars and long delays between arrest and verdict are acknowledged defects of our court system. Long delays make conviction more difficult, are a form of punishment of suspects, and often result in the commission of further crimes by the suspect, who must eat and raise funds for his defense while out on bail. Since about two-thirds of all cases involve victimless crimes, decriminalization would greatly reduce the court glut. Our efforts to protect the rights of the accused have also increased demands on court time. Recent Supreme Court rulings that "no person may be imprisoned for any offense unless he was represented by counsel at his trial" will inevitably prolong court proceedings. Streamlining of court proceedings is widely recommended but difficult to do while still protecting the rights of the accused.

The penal institution is one of society's most serious (and drastic) penalties for criminal behavior.
(Irene Springer)

REHABILITATION PROGRAMS

A shift from rehabilitation to deterrence and prevention is the present trend in correctional thinking. There is much disillusionment with rehabilitation programs, because the results are so disappointing.[87] Nothing much seems to work, except perhaps temporarily. Hope for rehabilitation has not been abandoned, however. Rehabilitative efforts of many kinds continue.

Under *probation* the convict's sentence is suspended providing he or she stays out of trouble for a specified period of time under supervision of a probation officer. Success is measured by completing probation without revocation and without rearrest for a period of years. Success rates vary widely according to locality, type of crime, and efficiency of probation officers, and no percentage measure of success is very useful. Probation is widely used, both because it is less costly than imprisonment and because imprisonment is widely viewed as a last resort.[88]

Parole is the conditional release of a prisoner, who is supervised by a parole officer for the remainder of the term of the sentence. Most criminologists believe that unless a prisoner is to be imprisoned for life, the prisoner should be paroled at some stage, because parole permits a supervised re-entry to the community. Success is difficult to measure, and no reliable measures of parole success are available.

Community-based corrections are an attempt to avoid the inherent defects of prison and to minimize the convict's separation from the community.[89] Several states have encouraged extensive efforts to treat delinquents at local treatment centers instead of in "reform schools." As usual, early evaluative reports were encouraging and later evaluations disappointing.[90]

Community-based corrections can take other forms. *Work release* prisoners are released for paid employment outside the prison, returning for nights, weekends, or at other times as required. This program presumably reduces the prisoner's isolation and demoralization, while he earns money, pays taxes, sometimes pays restitution, and pays part of the cost of his imprisonment.[91] Some evaluations of work release are favorable,[92] others are not.[93] The *prerelease furlough* allows a prisoner to take occasional brief releases from prison as the end of his term approaches.[94] The *halfway house* is a small correctional facility intermediate between the prison and the community. With little or nothing in the way of locks and fences, small groups of convicts live together under supervision, attend school or work at private jobs, and receive counseling.[95] The halfway house is also used in the treatment of mental illness[96] and drug addiction.[97] One recently founded halfway house, the Delancey Street Foundation in San Francisco, is receiving considerable publicity and claiming spectacular success,[98] but no careful evaluation studies have been made. A number of programs using *behavior modification* techniques claim to be successful, but again there are no satisfactory evaluation studies.[99]

Why is it that rehabilitation programs that appear initially successful so often fail to fulfill their early promise? Perhaps because of the well-known "Hawthorne effect"—people respond to special attention.[100] Or perhaps the early success stems from the charisma, intuition, and dedication of the program's founder, and these qualities are not transferable to others who seek to duplicate the program's success. Or perhaps the initially favorable reports were simply based upon sloppy evaluation.

PUNISHMENT AND DETERRENCE

After decades of chanting that "punishment does not deter," criminologists are now having second thoughts.[101] Most earlier studies of punishment as a deterrent dealt only with capital punishment for murder. Violent crime is usually committed in anger and on impulse, and may be the *least* responsive to deterrence of any kind of crime. But even for murder, the possibility that capital punishment may deter is being re-examined. One economist, for example, calculates from an economic model that each execution between 1935 and 1969 "may have resulted in seven or eight fewer murders."[102] Other scholars, however, maintain that the evidence indicates that the death penalty is ineffective as a deterrent.[103] Some even report evidence that the death penalty has a brutalizing effect, which *increases* the homicide rate.[104] Thus the death penalty argument continues to be unsettled, even among the "experts."

Although estimates are difficult to evaluate, it is undeniable that many kinds of crime are highly responsive to the fear of punishment. There is very little speeding in towns where everyone knows that the speed limits are strictly enforced. In Norway, where *any* detectable alcohol odor on a driver's breath brings a certain jail sentence, the "designated driver" for each carload of party guests is conspicuously abstemious. Kidnapping for ransom is rare in the United States, where over 90 percent of kidnappers are captured, convicted, and severely sentenced.[105]

Practically all of the dozens of studies of punishment and deterrence conducted in recent years reach the same general conclusion: *Severity* of punishment is not very important for most crimes. Harsh punishments are generally no more effective than milder ones. When personal characteristics are controlled, length of term served bears no consistent relation to parole outcome.[106] Relatively short terms are as effective as longer ones, and Marshall Clinard recommends that three years be the maximum term for prisoners who are ever to be released.[107]

Certainty of punishment clearly has a deterrent effect, confirmed by numerous studies.[108] The very few studies that conflict with this conclusion deal with special groups or situations not applicable to the general, adult population.[109] Several criminologists feel that the critical level of certainty is about 30 percent—that when the probability of arrest for a single offense is believed to be less than 30 percent, the fear of arrest has little deterrent effect.[110] For most crimes, the realistic probabilities of punishment are far be-

---

Jail should be as undesirable as possible, physically, psychologically, and otherwise. . . . minimal comfort and sanitation, and food which is as unpalatable as possible while maintaining minimal nutritional standards. No TV, radios, books. . . . You get the idea.

David Clement, quoted in *Psychology Today*, April 1978, p. 35. (It should be noted that this recommendation is for short-term confinement only, used in combination with phased part-time release.)

low 30 percent. For example, one criminologist estimates the odds that a single burglary will put the burglar in prison at 1 in 400.[111] Of 29,000 people arrested for automobile theft in California in 1977, only 128 were sent to prison, making the odds 1 in 227 of being punished with imprisonment even if caught.[112] Such odds are not highly deterrent. For punishment to deter, it must be perceived as prompt and probable.[113] Some criminologists favor replacing the current "indeterminate sentence" (for example, 5 to 15 years) with fixed, uniform sentences for each crime.[114] The idea of forcing criminals to make some restitution to their victims (or suffer long imprisonment) is gaining favor.[115] Clearly, punishment is coming back into style, both among criminologists and among the public,[116] but its success will demand improvements in our procedures for apprehending and convicting criminals.

PREVENTION

Disillusionment with traditional approaches has led many people to conclude that "prevention of crime must replace punishment and rehabilitation as the goal of the criminal justice system."[117] It is noteworthy, for example, that American efforts to deter skyjacking by lethal shoot-outs were not very successful, but a switch to a prevention effort (airport searches) soon ended skyjackings within the United States.[118] Prevention efforts take two general forms.

1. *Programs intended to reduce criminal motivation.* This category includes all efforts to reduce the frustrations, anxieties, and injustices that presumably drive people to crime. Efforts range from organizing youth clubs to promoting social revolution. The idea, probably valid, is that if exploitation, poverty, unemployment, frustration, loneliness, and other forms of unhappiness could be relieved, there would be little crime. Yochelson and Samenow believe that possibly as many as 20 percent of our habitual criminals could be resocialized through an intensive program of "reality therapy."[119] Friday and Stewart call for greater efforts to integrate youth into satisfying roles within a changing society.[120] Numerous programs for prevention have been attempted, and some successes have been claimed, but programs that remain successful through repeated replications are hard to find.[121] Books on crime prevention often talk mainly in generalities, giving little specific useful information. While youth clubs, job training programs, and the reduction of poverty would be virtually universally acclaimed, there is no evidential basis for believing that they would reduce the crime rate.[122]

2. *Programs to reduce criminal opportunity.* This category includes all efforts to make the commission of crime more difficult, more hazardous, and less profitable. Dealing mainly with property crimes, this approach takes many forms. *Target hardening* involves making it more difficult to break in, to steal, and to get away.[123] Etching the owner's social security number on valuable possessions makes theft and resale more hazardous. Better door locks, better lighting, burglar alarms, television surveillance, and strategic placement of store aisles and mirrors are other examples.[124] The use of private security guards is so popular that such guards now greatly outnumber law enforcement officers.[125] Local programs teach citizens how to avoid being likely targets for burglaries, muggings, rapes, and other crimes. One

university cut violent crime on its inner-city campus nearly in half by installing emergency-call telephones throughout the campus.[126] Buildings and landscape designs are now planned for their crime prevention potential.[127]

Displacement theory suggests that if one location is made safe, the criminal merely moves to another spot. A detailed examination of the life histories of criminals shows that only a limited amount of displacement actually occurs.[128] Consequently, the effort to discourage crime by making it more difficult and less rewarding is very much in favor.

Summary

The exact extent of the crime problem is not known, but it has been growing rapidly in most parts of the world for which we have data.

A classification of criminals includes several types: victimless, psychopathic, institutional, situational, habitual, professional, and political. They differ greatly in motivation, and each poses a different problem in treatment. The causes of crime continue to be debated. *Biological* theories have failed to identify any "criminal type," and where there is any association between physical type and criminal behavior, the causes of this association seem to lie in social experience. *Psychological* theories sound plausible, but carefully controlled comparisons reveal few psychological differences between most offenders and other people. *Sociological* theories are more helpful. *Cultural deviance* theories view crime as a socially learned pattern of deviant behavior. Sutherland's *differential association* theory holds that one acts largely according to one's contact with other persons' approving or disapproving definitions of criminal behavior. *Labeling* theory sees deviation as encouraged by one's public identification as a deviant, and by one's contacts with police and court personnel. *Delinquent subculture* theories describe crime not as deviation, but as conformity to a subculture in which crime is normal. *Strain* theories hold that the delinquent resorts to deviance in an effort to achieve legitimate desires that have been frustrated. The strain theories include the *delinquency and opportunity* theory that crime arises among lower-class persons who are blocked by middle-class institutions. Conflict theories include the *group conflict* theory that crime arises from race, ethnic, and other group conflicts, and the *class conflict* theory that class exploitation is the cause of most crime, with social revolution as the cure. *Control* theories view crime not as a product of deviant value systems or of blocked opportunity, but simply as failures in social control through insufficient attachment to the basic institutions of society.

The *personal-deviation approach* views the criminal as a deviant person who has failed to develop conventional codes of behavior, or as a maladjusted person who is unable or unwilling to follow them. The *value-conflict approach* notes that many common actions are defined as crimes because of the conflicting values of different groups, and that an effective system of social control is constantly being undermined by the many value conflicts in our imperfectly integrated culture. The *social-disorganization approach* shows how social change has produced those value conflicts and has undermined the traditional morality and control system of an earlier society.

Treatment efforts take many forms. Although prisons are attacked as ineffective and alternatives have been recommended, no complete substitute has been found. Present crime control trends include (1) *legal reform,* through decriminalization of most victimless crime; (2) *court reform,* seeking more speedy and efficient trial; (3) *rehabilitation* of delinquents and adult criminals, even though results are often disappointing; (4) *punishment for deterrence*, supported by considerable evidence that swift and sure punishment is an effective deterrent; and (5) *prevention*, through efforts to defuse criminal motivation by improving the quality of life, and through efforts to use mechanical and other means of making crime more difficult and less rewarding.

Suggested Readings

BOWKER, LEE H., *Women, Crime and the Criminal Justice System* (Lexington, Mass.: Lexington Books, 1978). A survey of female criminals and treatment.

BURSTEIN, JULES QUENTIN, *Conjugal Visits in Prison: Psychological and Social Consequences* (Lexington, Mass.: Lexington Books, 1977). A brief study of the practice of permitting wives to visit imprisoned husbands in privacy.

CLIFFORD, WILLIAM, *Crime Control in Japan* (Lexington, Mass.: Lexington Books, 1976). A study of a materialistic, capitalistic country with a very low crime rate.

COHEN, LAWRENCE E., and JAMES R. KLUEGEL, "Determinants of Juvenile Court Dispositions: Ascriptive and Achieved Factors in Two Metropolitan Courts," *American Sociological Review*, 43 (Apr. 1978), 162–76. An empirical study of race and class discrimination in juvenile court treatment of delinquents.

DODGE, CALVERT R., *A Nation without Prisons: Alternatives to Incarceration* (Lexington, Mass.: D. C. Heath, 1975). A plea for replacing prisons with other kinds of treatment.

GEIS, GILBERT, ed., *White-Collar Crime: Theory and Research* (Beverly Hills, Ca.: Sage Publications, 1980). A collection of classic and recent essays on white-collar crime.

HIRSCHI, TRAVIS, *Causes of Delinquency* (Berkeley: University of California Press, 1969). A statement of the control theory of delinquency.

IANNI, FRANCIS A. J., *A Family Business: Kinship and Social Control in Organized Crime* (New York: Russell Sage Foundation, 1972); or "New Mafia: Black, Hispanic, and Italian Styles," *Trans-action*, Mar./Apr. 1974, pp. 26–39. Authoritative comment on the Mafia myth.

JEFFERY, C. RAY, *Crime Prevention through Environmental Design,* 2nd ed. (Beverly Hills, Ca.: Sage Publications, 1977). An attempt to apply systems analysis and environmental design to crime control.

JEFFERY, C. RAY, and INA A. JEFFERY, "A National Strategy for Crime Prevention and Control," *Intellect,* Sept./Oct. 1975, pp. 98–102. A brief, popularized outline for crime control.

KING, LARRY, as told to and edited by Bill Chambliss, *Box Man: A Professional Thief's Journey.* (New York: Harper & Row, 1972). A brief, anecdotal account of a thief's experiences.

KRISBERG, BARRY, *Crime and Privilege: Toward a New Criminology* (Englewood Cliffs, N.J.: Prentice-Hall, 1975). A concise statement of the Marxist view that crime arises from class exploitation.

LETKEMANN, PETER, *Crime as Work* (Englewood Cliffs, N.J.: Prentice-Hall, 1973). A readable description of how career criminals plan and carry out their crimes.

PLATTNER, MARC F., "The Rehabilitation of Punishment," *The Public Interest,* Spring 1976, pp. 104–14. A brief account of the shift from rehabilitation to punishment.

QUINNEY, RICHARD, "Crime Control in Capitalist Society: A Critical Philosophy of Legal Order," *Issues in Criminology,* 8 (Spring 1973), 75–99. A concise statement of the Marxist thesis that capitalism causes crime; more fully developed in his *Critique of Legal Order: Crime Control in Capitalist Society* (Boston: Little, Brown, 1974) and in his *Class, State and Crime* (New York: David McKay, 1977). For a critique of Quinney, see R. Serge Denisoff and Donald McQuarie, "Crime Control in Capitalist Society: A Reply to Quinney," *Issues in Criminology,* 10 (Spring 1975), 109–19.

SHAW, CLIFFORD R., *The Jack-Roller: A Delinquent Boy's Own Story* (Chicago: University of Chicago Press, 1930); or (with M. E. Moore), *Natural History of a Delinquent Career* (Chicago: University of Chicago Press, 1931); or (with H. D. McKay and J. F. McDonald), *Brothers in Crime* (Chicago: University of Chicago Press, 1938). Intensely interesting biographical accounts of delinquents, showing the interaction of social factors in producing delinquent behavior.

SUTHERLAND, EDWIN H., and DONALD R. CRESSEY, *Criminology,* 10th ed. (Philadelphia: J. B. Lippincott, 1978). An authoritative standard textbook in criminology.

TITTLE, CHARLES R., WAYNE J. VILLAMEZ, and DOUGLAS A. SMITH, "The Myth of Social Class and Criminality: An Empirical Assessment of the Empirical Evidence," *American Sociological Review*, 43 (Oct. 1978), 641–56. An assessment of 35 studies examining the relationship between social class and crime.

WILSON, JAMES Q., *Thinking about Crime* (New York: Basic Books, 1975). An eminent political scientist states the case for legal reform and the use of punishment as a deterrent.

WOLFGANG, MARVIN E., ROBERT M. FIGLIO, and THORSTEN SELLIN, *Delinquency in a Birth Cohort* (Chicago: University of Chicago Press, 1972). A longitudinal study of delinquency in a group of 10,000 youths from their tenth to eighteenth birthdays.

Footnotes

[1] Associated Press, 13 Dec. 1975.

[2] Associated Press, 4 May 1976.

[3] See discussion of situational determinants of behavior in Paul B. Horton and Chester L. Hunt, *Sociology,* 5th ed. (New York: McGraw-Hill, 1980), pp. 153–54.

[4] Sheldon Glueck and Eleanor Glueck, *Physique and Delinquency* (New York: Harper & Row, 1956); see also George B. Vold, *Theoretical Criminology* (New York: Oxford University Press, 1958), ch. 4, "Physical Type Theories"; and Juan B. Cortéz and Florence M. Gatti, *Delinquency and Crime: A Biopsychosocial Approach* (New York: Seminar Press, 1972), ch. 1, "Physique and Delinquency."

[5] S. A. Mednick and K. O. Christiansen, *Biosocial Bases of Criminal Behavior* (New York: Halstead Press, 1977).

[6] Daniel Silverman, "The Psychotic Criminals: A Study of 500 Cases," *Journal of Clinical Psychopathology,* 2 (Oct. 1946), 301–27; James C. Coleman, *Abnormal Psychology and Modern Life* (New York: Scott, Foresman, 1959), p. 349.

[7] Michael Hakeem, "A Critique of the Psychiatric Approach to the Prevention of Juvenile Delinquency," *Social Problems,* 5 (Winter 1957–58), 194–205.

[8] Ibid; also Cortéz and Gatti, *Delinquency and Crime,* pp. 182–87.

[9] Sheldon Glueck and Eleanor Glueck, *Unraveling Juvenile Delinquency* (New York:

The Commonwealth Fund, 1950), p. 239; see also Vold, *Theoretical Criminology,* pp. 109–40.

[10] Clifford R. Shaw et al., *Delinquency Areas* (Chicago: University of Chicago Press, 1929).

[11] Roland J. Chilton, "Continuity in Delinquency Area Research: A Comparison of Studies for Baltimore, Detroit, and Indianapolis," *American Sociological Review,* 29 (Feb. 1964), 71–83; D. J. West, "Are Delinquents Different?" *New Society,* 26 (22 Nov. 1973), 456–58.

[12] Samuel Yochelson and Stanton E. Samenow, *The Criminal Personality* (New York: Jason Aronson, 1976), vol. 1, p. vii.

[13] Edwin H. Sutherland, *White Collar Crime* (New York: Dryden Press, 1949), p. 234. For a more recent statement of the differential-association theory, see Edwin H. Sutherland and Donald R. Cressey, *Criminology* (Philadelphia: J. B. Lippincott, 10th ed., 1978), pp. 83–97.

[14] Robert E. Foreman, "Delinquency Rates and Opportunities for Subculture Transmission," *Journal of Criminal Law, Criminology, and Police Science,* 54 (1963), 317–21.

[15] Sheldon Glueck and Eleanor Glueck, *Predicting Juvenile Delinquency and Crime* (Cambridge, Mass.: Harvard University Press, 1959). See also Walter C. Reckless, Simon Dinitz, and Ellen Mur-

ray, "The Good Boy in a High Delinquency Area," *Journal of Criminal Law, Criminology, and Police Science,* 48 (May–June 1957), 18–25; and Eleanor Glueck, "Identification of Potential Delinquents at 2–3 Years of Age," *International Journal of Social Psychiatry,* 12 (1966), 5ff.

[16]P.F. Briggs and R. D. Wirt, "Prediction," in H. C. Quay, ed., *Juvenile Delinquency: Research and Theory* (Princeton, N.J.: Van Nostrand, 1965), pp. 170–208; Travis Hirschi and Hanan C. Selvin, *Delinquency Research: An Appraisal of Analytic Methods* (New York: Free Press, 1967), pp. 237–54.

[17]Richard A. LaBrie, "Verification of the Glueck Prediction Table by Mathematical Procedure of Discrimination Function Analysis," *Journal of Criminal Law, Criminology, and Police Science,* 61 (June 1970), 229–34; C. Downing Taft, Jr., and Emory F. Hodges, Jr., "Followup Study of Predicted Delinquents," *Crime and Delinquency,* 17 (Apr. 1971), 202–12; Cortéz and Gatti, *Delinquency and Crime,* pp. 252–57; Franco Ferracuti and Simon Dinitz, "Cross-Cultural Aspects of Delinquent and Criminal Behavior," in Marc Reidel and Terance P. Thornberry, eds., *Crime and Delinquency: Dimensions of Deviance* (New York: Praeger Publishers, 1974), ch. 3.

[18]Pamela Richards, Richard A. Berk, and Brenda Foster, *Crime as Play: Delinquency in a Middle-Class Suburb* (Cambridge, Mass.: Ballinger, 1977).

[19]Ronald L. Akers, Marvin E. Krohn, Lonn Lanza-Kaduce, and Marcia Radosevich, "Social Learning and Deviant Behavior: A Specific Test of a General Theory," *American Sociological Review,* 44 (Aug. 1979), 635–55.

[20]James F. Short, Jr., "Differential Association and Delinquency," *Social Problems,* 4 (Jan.–Feb. 1957), 233–39.

[21]For example, see Marvin E. Wolfgang, Robert M. Figlio, and Thorsten Sellin, *Delinquency in a Birth Cohort* (Chicago: University of Chicago Press, 1972).

[22]Suzanne S. Ageton and Delbert S. Elliott, "The Effect of Legal Processing on Delinquent Orientation," *Social Problems,* 22 (Oct. 1974), 87–100; Gene Kassebaum, *Delinquency and Social Policy* (Englewood Cliffs, N.J.: Prentice-Hall, 1974), p. 67.

[23]See the discussion of association and causation in chapter 3.

[24]See Walter R. Gove, ed., *The Labeling of Deviance: Evaluating a Perspective* (New York: John Wiley, 1975), for a number of nonconfirmatory studies. See also Francis J. Cullen and John B. Cullen, *Toward a Paradigm of Labeling Theory* (Lincoln: University of Nebraska Studies, 1978).

[25]Allan Horowitz and Michael Wasserman, "The Effect of Social Control on Delinquent Behavior—A Longitudinal Test," *Sociological Focus,* 12 (Jan. 1979), 53–70.

[26]Barbara Laslett and Carol A. B. Warren, "Losing Weight: The Organizational Promotion of Behavior Change," *Social Problems,* 23 (Oct. 1975), 69–80.

[27]Charles R. Tittle, "Deterrents or Labeling?" *Social Forces,* 53 (Mar. 1975), 399–410.

[28]Peggy C. Giordano, "The Sense of Injustice: An Analysis of Juveniles' Reactions to the Justice System," *Criminology,* 14 (May 1976), 93–112.

[29]Anne Rankin Mahoney, "The Effect of Labeling upon Youth in a Juvenile Justice System: A Review of the Evidence," *Law and Society Review,* 8 (Summer 1974), 583–614.

[30]Sutherland and Cressey, *Criminology,* pp. 213–14.

[31]Sheldon Glueck and Eleanor Glueck, *Delinquents in the Making* (New York: Harper & Row, 1952), p. 89.

[32]Albert K. Cohen, *Delinquent Boys: The Culture of the Gang* (New York: Free Press, 1955); Walter B. Miller, "Lower Class Culture as a Generating Milieu of Gang Delinquency," *Journal of Social Issues,* 14 (1958), 5–16; John I. Kitsuse and David C. Dietrick, "Delinquent Boys: A Critique," *American Sociological Review,* 24 (April 1959), 208–15.

[33]"A Gang Leader's Redemption," *Life,* 28 Apr. 1958, pp. 69ff.

[34]Irving Spergel, *Racketsville, Slumtown, Haulburg* (Chicago: University of Chicago Press, 1964).

[35]David Matza, *Delinquency and Drift* (New York: John Wiley, 1964). For opposing research evidence, see Michael J. Hindeland, "The Commitment of Delinquents to Their Misdeeds: Do Delinquents Drift?" *Social Problems,* 17 (Spring 1970), 502–9.

[36]Lois DeFleur, "Alternative Strategies for the Development of Delinquency Theories Applicable to Other Cultures," *Social Problems,* 17 (Summer 1969), 30–39; Lois DeFleur, *Delinquency in Argentina* (Pullman: Washington State University Press, 1970).

[37]Robert K. Merton, *Social Theory and Social Structure* (New York: Free Press, 1957), pp. 140–57.

[38]Richard A. Cloward and Lloyd E. Ohlin, *Delinquency and Opportunity* (New York: Free Press, 1960).

[39]John C. Quicker, "The Effect of Goal Discrepancy on Delinquency," *Social Problems*, 22 (Oct. 1974), 76–86.

[40]Buford Harris and Richard Brymer, "A Five Year Encounter with a Mexican-American Conflict Gang: Its Implications for Delinquency Theory," *Proceedings of the Southwestern Sociological Association*, 15 (1965), 49–55.

[41]While it is common knowledge that many ghetto blacks hate the police, see Donald H. Bouma, *Kids and Cops* (Grand Rapids, Mich.: William B. Eerdmans, 1969), for one of the very few scientific studies of youth attitudes toward police. See also Anthony Oberschall, "The Los Angeles Riot of August, 1965," *Social Problems*, 15 (Winter 1968), 322–42.

[42]Vold, *Theoretical Criminology*, ch. 11, "Group Conflict Theories as Explanation of Crime," pp. 203–19.

[43]See Barry Krisberg, *Crime and Privilege: Toward a New Criminology* (Englewood Cliffs, N.J.: Prentice-Hall, 1975); Charles E. Reasons, ed., *The Criminologist: Crime and the Criminal* (Pacific Palisades, Ca.: Goodyear, 1974); Anthony Platt, "Prospects for a Radical Criminology in the United States," *Crime and Social Justice*, 1 (1974), 2–10; Richard Quinney, *Criminology: An Analysis and Critique of Crime in America* (Boston: Little, Brown, 1975); and Richard Quinney, *Class, State and Crime* (New York: David McKay, 1977).

[44]Walter D. Connor, *Deviance in Soviet Society: Crime, Delinquency, and Alcoholism* (New York: Columbia University Press, 1969); "Ivan the Hooligan," *Time*, 2 Sept. 1974, p. 34; Peter H. Solomon, Jr., "Soviet Criminology—Its Demise and Rebirth, 1928–1963," in Roger Hood, ed., *Crime, Criminology, and Public Policy* (New York: Free Press, 1974), pp. 571–93; Peter H. Juviler, *Revolutionary Law and Order: Politics and Social Change in the U.S.S.R.* (New York: Free Press, 1976); Valery Chalidze, *Criminal Russia: A Study of Crime in the Soviet Union* (New York: Random House, 1977). Louise Shelley, "The Geography of Soviet Criminality," *American Sociological Review*, 45 (Feb. 1980), 111–22. It should be noted that Marxist scholars in the United States generally dismiss as irrelevant any evidence from the Soviet Union, on the grounds that it is not really a Marxist country.

[45]*U.S. News and World Report*, 23 Jan. 1978, p. 14.

[46]Jerome Alan Cohen, *The Criminal Process in the People's Republic of China, 1949–1963* (Cambridge, Mass.: Harvard University Press, 1968); Fox Butterfield, "Peking is Worried about Youth Crimes," *New York Times*, 11 Mar. 1979, p. 13.

[47]Johannes Andenaes, "General Prevention Revisited: Research and Policy Implications," *Journal of Criminal Law and Criminology*, 99 (Spring 1975), 363.

[48]John Hagan and Jeffrey Leon, "Rediscovering Delinquency: Social History, Political Ideology and the Sociology of Law," *American Sociological Review*, 42 (Aug. 1977), 587–98.

[49]David Jacobs, "Inequality and the Legal Order: An Ecological Test of the Conflict Model," *Social Problems*, 25 (June 1978), 515–25.

[50]Peter L. Berger, *Pyramids of Sacrifice* (New York: Basic Books, 1974), pp. 66–70.

[51]Paul E. Spector, "Population Density and Unemployment: The Effects on the Incidence of Violent Crime in the American City," *Criminology*, 12 (Feb. 1975), 399–401.

[52]Marshall B. Clinard, *Crime in Developing Countries* (Somerset, N.Y.: Wiley-Interscience, 1973).

[53]See "Something Souring in Utopia," *Time*, 19 July 1976, pp. 32–35.

[54]David Matza, *Delinquency and Drift*; M. D. Buffalo and Joseph W. Rodgers, "Behavior Norms, Moral Norms, and Attachment: Problems of Deviance and Conformity," *Social Problems*, 19 (Summer 1971), 101–13.

[55]Travis Hirschi, *Causes of Delinquency* (Berkeley: University of California Press, 1969), p. 16.

[56]James F. Short, Jr., and Fred L. Strodtbeck, *Group Process and Gang Delinquency* (Chicago: University of Chicago Press, 1965).

[57]Kenneth Polk, *Those Who Fail* (Eugene, Ore.: Lane County Youth Project, unpublished manuscript, 1965); Peter S. Venezia, "Delinquency as a Function of Intrafamily Relationships," *Journal of Re-*

search in *Crime and Delinquency*, 5 (July 1968), 148–74; Raymond J. Adamck and Edward Z. Dager, "Familial Experience, Identification, and Female Delinquency," *Sociological Focus*, 2 (Spring 1969), 37–62; Eliezer D. Jaffe, "Family Anomie and Delinquency: Development of the Concept and Some Empirical Findings," *British Journal of Criminology*, 9 (Oct. 1969), 376–88; Hirschi, *Causes of Delinquency*, chs. 6, 7.

[58]Hirschi, *Causes of Delinquency*, preface.

[59]Paul C. Friday and Jerald Hage, "Youth Crime in Postindustrial Societies: An Integrated Perspective," *Criminology*, 14 (Nov. 1976), 347–68.

[60]Hirschi, *Causes of Delinquency;* Ronald L. Akers, *Deviant Behavior: A Social Learning Approach* (Belmont, Ca.: Wadsworth, 1973); Rance D. Conger, "Social Control and Social Learning Models of Delinquent Behavior: A Synthesis," *Criminology*, 14 (May 1976), 17–40.

[61]David H. Bayley, "Learing About Crime—The Japanese Experience," *The Public Interest*, Summer 1976, pp. 55–68; William Clifford, *Crime Control in Japan* (Lexington, Mass.: Lexington Books, 1976); Japan Society, Inc., *The Police and the People: A Comparison of Japanese and American Police Behavior* (New York: Japan Society, 1977), p. 11.

[62]Marshall B. Clinard, *Cities with Little Crime: The Case of Switzerland* (New York: Cambridge University Press, 1978).

[63]Paul B. Horton, "Problems in Understanding Criminal Motives," in Simon Rottenberg, ed., *The Economics of Crime and Punishment* (Washington, D.C.: American Enterprise Institute for Public Policy Research, 1973), pp. 11–17.

[64]Yochelson and Samenow, *The Criminal Personality.*

[65]Michael S. Serrill, review of Yochelson and Samenow, *The Criminal Personality*, in *Psychology Today*, Feb. 1978, p. 86.

[66]See Clifford R. Shaw, *The Jack-Roller: A Delinquent Boy's Own Story* (Chicago: University of Chicago Press, 1930); Clifford R. Shaw and M. E. Moore, *Natural History of a Delinquent Career* (Chicago: University of Chicago Press, 1931); and Clifford R. Shaw, H. D. McKay, and J. F. McDonald, *Brothers in Crime* (Chicago: University of Chicago Press, 1938).

[67]Quoted in John F. Cuber, *Sociology*, 6th ed. (New York: Appleton-Century-Crofts, 1968), p. 221.

[68]John A. Gardiner, "Public Attitudes toward Gambling and Corruption," *The Annals of the American Academy of Political and Social Science*, 374 (Nov. 1967), 123–34.

[69]See Donald R. Cressey, *Other People's Money: A Study in the Social Psychology of Criminal Violation of Financial Trust* (New York: Free Press, 1953).

[70]See Vance Packard, *The Hidden Persuaders* (New York: David McKay, 1957); Pierre Berton, *The Big Sell: An Introduction to the Black Arts of Door-to-Door Salesmanship and Other Techniques* (New York: Alfred A. Knopf, 1963).

[71]One businessman states, "There is absolutely no doubt that prostitution *per se* does help business. This is the fastest way I know of to have an intimate relationship established with a buyer. . . . It sort of gives me a slight edge . . ." (part of a recorded anonymous statement by a businessman on a radio program, "The Business of Sex," produced 19 Jan. 1959 by the Public Affairs Department of the Columbia Broadcasting System); reprinted in Donald R. Cressey and David A. Ward, eds., *Delinquency, Crime, and Social Process* (New York: Harper & Row, 1969), pp. 973–85.

[72]Morris B. Baken, "There's Larceny in the Air," *Flying*, 64 (Mar. 1959), 56ff.

[73]*New York Times*, 1 Mar. 1959, p. 43. See also Thomas Meehan, "The Case of the Insurance Detective," *New York Times Magazine*, 6 Mar. 1960, pp. 51ff.

[74]"Insurance: The Cost of Casualties," *Time*, 2 June 1967, p. 63.

[75]For example, see "Confessions of an Appliance Salesman," *Consumer Reports*, 23 (Oct. 1958), 546–47.

[76]See Jerome Hall, *Theft, Law, and Society*, 2nd ed. (Indianapolis: Bobbs-Merrill, 1952), for a detailed analysis of how changing commercial needs and practices of the industrial revolution brought about changes in law and punishment.

[77]After a survey by Robert Martinson of 231 of the "more rigorous" evaluation studies, Stuart Adams concluded that "there is very little evidence that any mode of corrective treatment has a decisive effect on recidivism." Stuart Adams, "Measurement of Effectiveness and Efficiency in Corrections," in Daniel Glaser, ed., *Handbook of Criminology* (Chicago: Rand McNally, 1974), p. 1021.

[78]James C. Hackler, "Review of the Silverlake Experiment: Testing Delin-

quency Theory and Community Intervention," in *Contemporary Sociology: A Journal of Reviews*, 1 (July 1972), 346.

[79]See Benjamin Rush, *An Inquiry into the Effects of Public Punishments upon Criminals and upon Society* (Philadelphia, 1787).

[80]Marshall B. Clinard, "An Assessment of Prisons with Recommendations for Policy," *The Wisconsin Sociologist*, 11 (Spring–Summer 1974), 35–39.

[81]Robert Martinson, "What Works?—Questions and Answers about Prison Reform," *The Public Interest*, Spring 1974, pp. 22–54; Douglas Lipton, Robert Martinson, and Judith Wilks, *The Effectiveness of Correctional Treatment: A Survey of Evaluation Studies* (New York: Praeger Publishers, 1975); Robert Sommer, *The End of Imprisonment* (New York: Oxford University Press, 1976).

[82]Frank K. Gibson et al., "A Path Analytic Treatment of Corrections Output," *Social Science Quarterly*, 54 (Sept. 1973), 281–91; Calvert R. Dodge, *A Nation without Prisons: Alternatives to Incarceration* (Boston: D. C. Heath, 1975).

[83]Robert Martinson and Judith Wilks, preliminary report to the National Institute of Law Enforcement and Criminal Justice, reported in *New York Times*, 7 Nov. 1976, p. 61.

[84]Joint Committee of the American Bar Association and the American Medical Association on Narcotic Drugs, *Drug Addiction: Crime or Disease?* (Bloomington: Indiana University Press, 1960).

[85]National Council on Crime and Delinquency, "Crimes without Victims: A Policy Statement," *Crime and Delinquency*, 17 (Apr. 1971), 129–30. See also Gilbert Geis, *Not the Law's Business* (Washington, D.C.: National Institute of Mental Health, 1972); Edwin Schur and Hugo Adam Bedau, *Victimless Crime: Two Sides of a Controversy* (Englewood Cliffs, N.J.: Prentice-Hall, 1974).

[86]Paul C. Friday, "Issues in the Decriminalization of Public Intoxication," *Federal Probation*, 42 (Sept. 1978), 33–39.

[87]Dennis A. Romig, *Justice for Our Children: An Examination of Juvenile Delinquent Rehabilitation Programs* (Lexington, Mass.: D. C. Heath, 1978).

[88]See Sutherland and Cressey, *Criminology*, ch. 20, "Probation."

[89]Ibid., pp. 511–12.

[90]Lloyd E. Ohlin, Robert B. Coales, and Alden D. Miller, "Evaluating the Reform of Youth Corrections in Massachusetts," *Journal of Research in Crime and Delinquency*, 12 (Jan. 1975), 3–16; David F. Greenberg, "Problems in Community Corrections," *Issues in Criminology*, 10 (Spring 1975), 1–33.

[91]Stanley E. Grupp, "Work Release in the United States," *Journal of Criminal Law, Criminology, and Police Science*, 54 (Sept. 1963), 267–72.

[92]George E. Berkeley et al., *Introduction to Criminal Justice: Police, Courts, and Corrections* (Boston: Holbrook Press, 1976), p. 417.

[93]Gordon P. Waldo, Theodore G. Chiricos, and Leonard E. Dobrin, "Community Contact and Inmate Attitudes: An Experimental Assessment of Work Release," *Criminology*, 11 (Nov. 1973), 345–81.

[94]Norman Hoult, "Temporary Prison Release: California's Prerelease Furlough Program," *Crime and Delinquency*, 17 (Oct. 1971), 414–30.

[95]Oliver J. Keller, Jr., and Benedict S. Alper, *Halfway Houses: Community Centered Corrections and Treatment* (Lexington, Mass.: D. C. Heath, 1970); Calvert R. Dodge, "The Halfway House as an Alternative," in Calvert A. Dodge, ed., *A Nation without Prisons* (Lexington, Mass.: Lexington Books, 1975), ch. 10.

[96]Harold L. Raush and Charlotte Raush, *The Halfway House Movement: A Search for Sanity* (New York: Appleton-Century-Crofts, 1968).

[97]Lewis Yablonsky, *The Tunnel Back: Synanon* (Garden City, N.Y.: Doubleday, 1968).

[98]Charles Hampton-Turner, *Sane Asylum: Inside the Delancey Street Foundation* (San Francisco: San Francisco Book Co., 1976); Grover Sales, *John Maher of Delancey Street* (New York: W. W. Norton, 1976).

[99]Curtis J. Braukmann et al., "Behavioral Approaches to the Crime and Delinquency Field," *Criminology*, 13 (Nov. 1975), 299–331.

[100]The Hawthorne effect was discovered during some famous experiments at a factory in which *every* change made in certain working conditions produced a temporary rise in output. This was attributed to the extra attention the workers were given. See F. J. Roethlisberger, *Management and Morale* (Cambridge, Mass.: Harvard University Press, 1949).

[101]See Marc F. Plattner, "The Rehabilitation of Punishment," *The Public Interest*, Summer 1976, pp. 104–14.

[102]Isaac Ehrlich, "The Deterrent Effect of Capital Punishment: A Question of Life and Death," *American Economic Review*, 65 (June 1975), 397–417; Isaac Ehrlich, "Capital Punishment and Deterrence: Some Further Thoughts and Additional Evidence," *Journal of Political Economy*, 85 (Aug. 1977), 741–88.

[103]Gary Kirk, "Capital Punishment, Gun Ownership, and Homicide," *American Journal of Sociology*, 84 (Jan. 1975), 882–910.

[104]David R. King, "The Brutalization Effect: Execution Publicity and the Incidence of Homicide in South Carolina," *Social Forces*, 57 (Dec. 1978), 683–96.

[105]*New York Times Magazine*, 18 July 1976, p. 39.

[106]Dean V. Babst et al., "Assessing Length of Institutionalization in Relation to Parole Outcome," *Criminology*, 14 (May 1976), 41–54.

[107]Marshall B. Clinard, "An Assessment of Prisons with Recommendations for Policy," *The Wisconsin Sociologist*, 11 (Spring–Summer 1974), 35–39.

[108]Gordon Tullock, "Does Punishment Deter?" *The Public Interest*, Summer 1974, pp. 103–11; Jeffrey I. Chapman, "An Economic Model of Crime and Police: Some Empirical Results," *Journal of Research in Crime and Delinquency*, 13 (Jan. 1976), 48–63; Matthew Silverman, "Toward a Theory of Criminal Deterrence," *American Sociological Review*, 41 (June 1976), 442–61. There are dozens of such studies.

[109]J. Kraus, "Threat of Punishment and the Potential Offender," *Australian and New Zealand Journal of Sociology*, 10 (Feb. 1974), 61–63; William C. Bailey and Ruth P. Lott, "Crime, Punishment and Personality: An Examination of the Deterrence Question," *Journal of Criminal Law and Criminology*, 67 (Mar. 1976), 99–109.

[110]Charles R. Tittle and Alan R. Rowe, "Certainty of Arrest and Crime Rates: A Further Test of the Deterrence Hypothesis," *Social Forces*, 52 (June 1974), 455–62; Silverman, "Toward a Theory of Criminal Deterrence."

[111]Gregory Krohm, Virginia Polytechnic Institute, quoted in *Business Week*, 15 Sept. 1975, p. 92.

[112]California Highway Patrol Commissioner Glen Craig, quoted in *Motor Trend*, Sept. 1978, p. 11.

[113]Gary F. Jensen, Maynard I. Erikson, and Jack P. Gibbs, "Perceived Risk of Punishment and Self-Reported Delinquency," *Social Forces*, 57 (Sept. 1978), 757–78.

[114]Alan Dershowitz, "Let the Punishment Fit the Crime," *New York Times Magazine*, 28 Dec. 1975, pp. 7ff.

[115]Burt Galaway and Joe Hudson, *Offender Restitution in Theory and Action* (Lexington, Mass.: Heath, 1978).

[116]Ernest Van Den Haag, *Punishing Criminals* (New York: Basic Books, 1975); James Q. Wilson, *Thinking about Crime* (New York: Basic Books, 1975); "Crime: A Case for More Punishment," *Business Week*, 15 Sept. 1975, pp. 92–97.

[117]C. Ray Jeffery and Ina A. Jeffery, "A National Strategy for Crime Prevention and Control," *Intellect*, Sept./Oct. 1975, p. 102.

[118]W. William Minor, "Skyjacking: Crime Control Models," *Journal of Criminal Law and Criminology*, 66 (Mar. 1975), 94–105.

[119]Yochelson and Samenow, *The Criminal Personality*, vol. 2, ch. 13, "A Recommendation for a Rehabilitation Program."

[120]Paul C. Friday and V. Lorne Stewart, eds., *Youth Crime and Juvenile Justice: International Perspectives* (New York: Praeger Publishers, 1977).

[121]Albert S. Alissi, "Behavioral Science Influences on Legislation: The Case of Delinquency Prevention," *Journal of Sociology and Social Welfare*, 2 (Winter 1974), 227–58.

[122]Wilson, *Thinking about Crime*, p. 212.

[123]Lee R. McPheters, "Criminal Behavior and the Gains from Crime," *Criminology*, 14 (May 1976), 137–52.

[124]D. P. Walsh, *Shoplifting: Controlling a Major Crime* (New York: Holmes and Meier, 1978).

[125]Leroy E. Pagano, "Should Private Police Be Licensed?" *Intellect*, Sept./Oct. 1975, pp. 106–8; Clark Wilson, "In Guards We Trust," *New York Times Magazine*, 19 Sept. 1976, pp. 20ff.

[126]"Emergency System Credited for Crime Drop," *United Press International*, 14 Mar. 1972.

[127]Gerhard Luedtke et al., *Crime and the City Neighborhood Design Techniques for Crime Reduction* (Washington, D.C.: National Technical Information Services, U.S. Department of Commerce, 1970); Oscar Newman, *Defensible Space* (New York: Macmillan, 1972); Keith D. Har-

ries, *Georgraphy of Crime and Justice* (New York: McGraw-Hill, 1974); R. Fausto, "Public Housing Can Be Safe," *Planning,* Feb. 1975, pp. 14–15; C. Ray Jeffery, *Crime Prevention through Environmental Design* (Beverly Hills, Ca.: Sage Publications, 1977).

[128]Thomas A. Reppetto, "Crime Reduction and the Displacement Phenomena," *Crime and Delinquency,* 22 (Apr. 1976), 166–77.

Arthur Grace, Stock, Boston

FAMILY AND GENERATIONAL PROBLEMS 7

Five years ago, only 60,000 child-abuse incidents were brought to official attention in the U.S.; in 1976 the number passed the half-million mark. The National Center on Child Abuse and Neglect estimates that the reported cases represent only half of the child abuse that goes on. By the center's calculations, between 100,000 and 200,000 youngsters are regularly assaulted by their parents with cords, sticks, fists, hot irons, cigarettes and booted feet, nearly as many are sexually molested, and 700,000 are denied food, clothing or shelter necessary for their welfare. Every year, according to the center, at least 2,000 children die of abuse or neglect. "If you had a disease that affected so many children annually" says director Douglas Besharov, "you would call it an epidemic." . . .[1]

About one million teen-age girls, one in ten between the ages of 15 and 19, get pregnant every year. About 600,000 actually bear children, and childbirth often triggers consequences that cloud the rest of the mothers' lives. Teen-age mothers are much more likely than their peers to drop out of school, earn low wages, have large families, and wind up on welfare. . . .[2]

The children of divorce are suffering in greater numbers than ever before. The broken-home crisis that can spoil a toddler's life and cause untold misery for a shocked, dismayed teenager is a spreading blight. Today, new studies show that these children—whose adjustment to the crisis may be good, tolerable, or miserable, depending on what their parents do—now number 1 in 6. A study reported by the National Institute of Mental Health finds that because of the rising divorce rate, 45% of all children born this year will live in a single-parent household for some period before reaching age 18 . . .[3]

Tough new congressional restrictions have cut federal funding of abortions for low-income women by an estimated 99 percent, according to Department of Health, Education and Welfare figures. HEW Secretary Joseph A. Califano Jr. told a House subcommittee . . . that abortions for low-income women financed under the Medicaid program plummeted to 2,421 in the last 11 months of 1978 because of the funding restrictions. Before the limits went into effect, HEW estimated that the United States funded about 250,000 such abortions a year. . . .[4]

Inspectors never come at night, but night is the bad time. The old woman (it's more often a woman than a man) needs a bedpan, or needs help to get to the bathroom. She calls. Nobody comes. She must, then, lie in her body wastes, as her sores show she has often done, or struggle to make her way to the toilet unaided. She falls. That is the American way of death for countless thousands in nursing homes. . . .[5]

161

The American family is a paradox. Most people marry and stay married. Moreover, most report that their marriages are happy. On a scale from "very happy" to "very unhappy," from 60 to 85 percent describe their marriages as either very happy or happy.[6] At the same time, however, up to one-third of all women become pregnant before marriage,[7] wife beating and child abuse are common, and one-third of current marriages will end in divorce.[8] In addition, almost 20 percent of births in the United States are unwanted,[9] and a million women a year obtain abortions.[10] Finally, many old people live in poverty, spending their last months or years as victims of a totally inadequate pattern of institutional care.

Spouse and Child Abuse

Strong norms provide that husbands and wives should treat one another with affection and respect, and that parents should love and protect their children. Their importance is so great that until recently, and despite

Abortion was a hotly debated issue in the 1970s. Shown here is a pro-life demonstration held in St. Louis in July 1978.
(United Press International)

mounting evidence to the contrary, society pretended that violence within families was a rare and pathological occurrence. We know now, however, that physical abuse of husbands and wives by one another and the use of violence against children are major national problems.

SPOUSE ABUSE

At its extreme, violence results in murder; and murder occurs more often within families than in any other specific circumstance. Although national data are not available, crime reports from major U.S. cities indicate that one-fourth or more of all murders are committed upon family members, and that most of these involve wives and husbands. Many of us fear assault in the streets, but few realize that there is far more danger at home. Of course, murder is a legal problem more properly treated in a chapter on crime than in one on the family. We shall confine our attention here to the nonlethal violence that occurs between husbands and wives and that often escapes public attention.

Because it is not usually reported, no one knows how much interspousal violence actually occurs. Inferential evidence, however, indicates that it is very common. Two studies have accumulated some data on the extent of violence between spouses who were seeking divorce. The first study, which involved 150 interviews and did not ask directly about violence, found that it was mentioned spontaneously in 25 cases.[11] In the second study, of 600 Cleveland, Ohio, couples, 37 percent of the women gave physical abuse as one of the complaints that led to their divorces.[12]

The only study that has directly sought the incidence of interspousal violence used a dual sample: 40 families in which a social agency or the police reported that violence had occurred, and 40 neighbor families of the known violent families to serve as controls. Among the controls only, 40 percent reported one or more instances of violence against one of the spouses; 15 percent reported from two to five episodes of violence during the marriage; 5 percent reported violence from twice a year to once every other month; and 7.5 percent reported violence from once a month to daily.[13] Since these families were not clients of social agencies or on the police blotters for violence, the data probably under-represent the actual extent of physical violence between husbands and wives.

One study queried 385 lower-division university students concerning their awareness of physical violence between their parents during the students' senior year in high school. In 16 percent of the cases, violence was reported. Recognizing that these were intact families that had survived for at least 20 years, and that most parents probably try to conceal fighting from their teenagers, we can probably guess that the true incidence of violence in such families is at least twice as high as the study found.[14]

Data from a forthcoming national survey show that 16 of every 100 couples have at least one violent confrontation in the course of a year. In 6 of these cases, kicking, biting, punching, or using weapons is involved.[15] Violence is clearly not only common but often regular and patterned.

Most studies to date report that husbands physically abuse their wives more often than the other way around. A University of Michigan study of 20 women who were known victims of wife abuse reported that 19 of them were first beaten during the first year they were married and that, as the

163

years went by, the assaults increased both in frequency and in severity. That the beatings often followed drinking on the part of one or both spouses aroused suspicion that the alcohol triggered the release of deep rage or old frustrations. Another implication of the study was that wives who remain in such marriages probably have serious personality problems.[16]

On the other hand, Gelles's data show that often both spouses are violent. Of the 80 wives, 32 percent admitted having hit their husbands; 11 percent admitted hitting them at least six times a year. Moreover, to compensate for their lesser physical strength, wives more often hit their husbands with objects ranging from lamps to lead pipes to chairs. The only case of stabbing revealed in the interviews was of a wife who stabbed her husband.[17]

CHILD ABUSE

The physical abuse of children by their parents is at least as difficult to study as is spousal violence. For one thing, most people believe that parents have the right, and even the obligation, to spank their children in some circumstances: to deter them from harmful behavior, to teach them discipline, or when it is "for their own good."[18] The dividing line is unclear between such "normal violence" and the kind of extreme violence that virtually everyone would agree is a social problem.

The battered child syndrome, in which children are beaten so badly or otherwise mistreated that they require medical care or come to the attention of social agencies, symbolizes this part of the social problem of family violence. Even using this limited definition, we do not know how much child abuse occurs. Most of the problem remains hidden from everyone except the families involved, their neighbors who may learn of it, and public agency personnel who must deal with it.

The torture visited upon the unfortunate children is almost unbelievable. Children brought to hospitals have cigarette burns on their bodies, burns from scalding water poured on their genitals, blackened eyes, broken bones, and skull fractures. In some cases the abuse is discovered only upon investigation into the death of the child.

Unbelievable, too, is the fact that the abusers are usually the child's parents, with whom the child is living. Mothers and fathers appear to be the perpetrators in almost equal numbers, and they come from every socioeconomic level. What characteristics they share are serious problems in their own lives: marital problems, money problems, drinking problems. Unable to cope with these problems, they become socially isolated and take out their frustrations upon the children, who cannot protect themselves. All studies show, too, that many abusive parents were themselves abused and neglected as children. Failing to develop a sense of personal worth and a confidence in their ability to function as parents, they handle their parental responsibilities poorly. Baffled and frustrated by their inability to control their children, they strike out in rage. Thus, their children grow up, like themselves, to become parents of battered children as the tragic cycle is repeated.

Rape

The emergence of rape as a social problem in the United States provides an almost classic case of how social problems are socially defined. Rape is not new. Nor is there any good evidence that the frequency of rape has increased significantly in recent years. What has happened is that the women's movement, largely, has brought the issue to public attention and is demanding that something be done about it.

No one knows just how much rape occurs, because most rape victims are reluctant to report the crime to the police. Already deeply humiliated, the woman often fears that she will be blamed for the event. Traditionally, the police have been unsympathetic with rape victims, implying, often, that the woman encouraged the rapist through wearing provocative clothing or behaving seductively. Even some of the women's husbands or boyfriends blame the rape victims rather than their attackers.[19] As organized women's groups protest these situations, many police departments and hospitals are setting up rape treatment and investigation divisions staffed by women and specially trained personnel. But even if the trauma is minimized at the time of reporting the crime, it is likely to become almost overwhelming if the rapist is caught and the woman presses charges. Not only must she psychologically relive the attack in the courtroom, but she must endure the rapist's attorney's attempts to shift the blame from the man to her.

Over 50,000 cases of forcible rape are reported by local police departments to the FBI each year. Probably, these are less than one-third of the actual number of rapes. The National Crime Panel estimates that there are over 150,000 rapes in the United States each year. Although rape occurs in substantial numbers at all social levels, the most likely victims are young, poor, and black. The rapists, too, are most likely to be young, poor, and black. Most victims are of the rapist's own race. Whites tend to rape whites, and blacks tend to rape blacks.

Considerable controversy exists about the nature of rape, some interpretations tending to define it as a personal and sexual offense, others regarding it as violent crime encouraged by a sexist social structure. The traditional interpretations emphasize the role of the victim in precipitating the attack. The woman tends to be blamed for knowingly or unknowingly encouraging men by wearing revealing clothing, frequenting bars, accepting automobile rides, and so on. If concern is shown for the woman at all, it is not for the physical and psychological injury she has suffered, but for the damage done to her as the property of her husband and family. Emerging conflicting interpretations hold that rape is a violent means by which males keep females in a subordinate position. Rape can only be eliminated by giving women full equality with men.

Divorce

The United States has the highest divorce rate of any major nation. Moreover, both the number of divorces and the divorce rate have been rising at an unprecedented pace. As the figures in table 7–1 show, there were 393,000 divorces in 1960, and the divorce rate was 2.2. By 1970, there were 715,000 divorces, and the divorce rate had climbed to 3.5. The number of divorces passed one million in 1976, and the rate is still climbing. The probability that any given marriage will end in divorce is now approximately one in three.[20]

Surprisingly, the spectacular increases in divorce do not seem to reflect

TABLE 7–1   Increase in Divorces and Divorce Rates since 1960

Year	Number of divorces	Divorces per 1,000 population
1960	393,000	2.2
1970	715,000	3.5
1972	845,000	4.1
1974	977,000	4.6
1976	1,077,000	5.0
1978	1,122,000	5.1

SOURCE: U.S. Bureau of the Census, *Statistical Abstract of the United States:* 1972 (Washington, D.C.), p. 63; and National Center for Health Statistics, "Provisional Statistics, Births, Marriages, and Divorces for 1978," Mar. 15, 1979.

Although divorce rates in the United States have continued to climb, its potentially devastating emotional impact remains the same.

(Bruce Roberts, Photo Researchers, Inc.)

serious disillusionment with marriage. Most divorced persons eventually remarry. Divorce once experienced, however, appears to be somewhat contagious. The probability that second marriages will end in divorce is a whopping 59 percent.[21]

Apart from its implications for the stability of marriage and the family, divorce itself is a social problem. The divorce system in the United States creates, as well as reflects, personal unhappiness. It pits men and women against one another in a bitter contest in which both partners can only lose. Fortunately, as the nation moves toward no-fault divorce, changes are occurring that promise eventually to lessen some of the problems.

THE DESTRUCTIVE NATURE OF AMERICAN DIVORCE

Most people believe divorce to be a problem in itself. Certainly, it is evidence of marriages that have failed. An unknown amount of guilt, self-doubt, and bitterness may be the inevitable due of the people involved. Divorce also creates problems of financial support and emotional problems for the children who are present in at least 60 percent of the homes in which divorce occurs. How much these problems are inherent in the fact of divorce, however, and how much they are due to the nature of the laws that have traditionally regulated divorce in the United States is unknown. What is apparent is that most people believe divorce to be preferable to the continuance of conflict-ridden marriages, and that the law of the land is sadly out of step with contemporary attitudes and values.

The phrase "law of the land" may be misleading, because the enactment of domestic relations law in the United States is the prerogative of the individual states rather than of the federal government. There are 51 different sets of divorce laws, one for each state and the District of Columbia. Consequently, some states grant divorces on as few as four legal grounds, while others offer three or four times as many.[22] All jurisdictions have recognized divorce on grounds of adultery, 47 states desertion, 44 cruelty, 43 the commission of a felony, 40 alcoholism, 29 nonsupport, and so on.

In fact, there has been little relation between the legal grounds for divorce and the actual causes of divorce. About 52 percent of all United States divorces have been granted on grounds of cruelty, about 23 percent on grounds of desertion, some 4 percent on grounds of nonsupport, and about 1 percent on grounds of adultery. These figures do not reflect the incidence of these offenses, of course, but only indicate what are the socially most acceptable grounds for divorce. People seek divorces not so much because of cruelty, desertion, or nonsupport, but because they are unhappy with one another and no longer want to live together.

Basically, the American system of divorce law is an adversary system. It pits the spouses against one another in a contest that is hypocritical and one that produces bitterness and disillusionment. The law permits divorce suits to be heard only on the assumption that one party, the plaintiff, comes to court innocent of any offense that is ground for divorce to bring charges against the other spouse, the defendant, who has committed such offense. In truth, of course, both partners almost always are partly to blame. No good purpose is served by forcing couples into this adversary stance. Instead, even if the embattled spouses have been able to remain civil to one another up to now, the legal process soon has them fighting viciously.

The system virtually requires the spouses to have separate attorneys, who generally subscribe to a legal code of ethics that requires them to win the best possible settlement for their own clients. Nor is it irrelevant that the size of their respective fees frequently is related to the settlement achieved.

Thus begins the battle over money—property settlement and possibly alimony—and for the custody and support of any children who may be involved. Under prodding from their attorneys, the partners come to realize that each may profit only at the expense of the other. Now the woman whose pride has been injured becomes determined to make her husband pay; alimony may cost him up to one-third of his income. The children become pawns in the struggle; visiting privileges are bargained against the size of the support payments. The surprising thing is not that divorce produces some bitterness but that so many people recover from the penalties imposed upon them by a vengeful legal system.

The law operates in one other way to make liars and lawbreakers of distressed spouses. The states have residence requirements for divorce that vary from none at all (Alabama) to as long as five years for couples not married within the state (Massachusetts). Add these to widely varying legal grounds for divorce and the stage is set for couples to avoid harsh laws in their own states by securing their divorces elsewhere. There are no accurate figures on the extent of migratory divorce, but nationally it may average from 3 to 5 percent of all divorces. The figure for residents of states such as New York would be much higher, and other states such as Nevada and Idaho have profited notoriously from these temporary migrants.

Theoretically, a divorce validly granted by one state must be recognized in all other states. The "full faith and credit" clause of the United States Constitution has been so interpreted. The trouble comes in trying to determine when migration has been for the purpose of evading the laws of one state. In that event, courts may hold that the divorce is not valid because the parties are not bona fide residents of the state granting the divorce.

In practice, most migratory divorces, whether in Alabama, Nevada, Mexico, or Paris, are binding simply because both partners want the divorce and no one challenges them. Sometimes, however, injured pride or the prospect of financial advantage causes one of the partners to contest a migratory divorce, perhaps years later. Seldom are the motives involved above reproach, and the financial and social pain incurred may be very great. If the other partner has remarried, the second marriage is gravely threatened.

Some such cases have reached the United States Supreme Court, which has ruled that courts in one state have the right to review cases heard in other states for the purpose of determining whether those courts had legal jurisdiction under their own laws. The intention obviously is to discourage the establishment of phony legal residence for purposes of divorce. The practical effect has been to creat chaos. There is no assurance when a migratory divorce will be upheld or when it will be struck down. Even the Supreme Court has not been consistent in its rulings. In the meantime, in the United States there are hundreds of thousands of people whose migratory divorces have thus been thrown into legal jeopardy.

NO-FAULT DIVORCE

Recognition of the destructive effects of divorce is not new, but until recently not much was done about it. Three states—Alaska, New Mexico, and Oklahoma—permitted divorce on grounds of incompatibility, which did not imply that either spouse had committed a major offense, but the procedure remained basically adversary and not much more salutary in its effects than those of other states.

The situation began to change in 1970 when California instituted a new, no-fault procedure that did away with the term *divorce*, substituting *dissolution of marriage*. The new law also abolished all traditional grounds for divorce and provided, instead, that dissolution should be granted on the basis of "irreconcilable differences that have caused the irremediable breakdown of the marriage." The law also provided for the substantially equal division of property, and based alimony upon the length of the marriage and the earning ability of both spouses.

Following the passage of the California law, 17 other states abolished their old divorce practices and instituted no-fault systems in their place. Thirty additional states kept their traditional systems but added no-fault grounds to the existing ones. The movement toward no-fault seems destined to spread still further in the near future.

It is too early to analyze in detail the working of the new laws, but some preliminary generalizations are possible. First, they are probably not significantly increasing the total number of divorces granted, but are reducing the number of migratory divorces. More people are now divorced in the states in which they live, instead of having to travel to another state and establish phony residence to secure a divorce. Since California's law went into effect, the number of divorces granted in Nevada has dropped substantially. Second, the whole process appears to be becoming more honest, more open, and less painful. Troubled spouses, who already feel guilt and bitterness, are under less pressure to vent those feelings in court and aggravate the situation further. Third, the exorbitant costs associated with a legal contest show some signs of being lowered. Some attorneys are lowering their fees in accord with the lessened demands that no-fault divorce makes upon their time and energies. Some persons are able to represent themselves in divorce cases and eliminate attorney fees altogether.

These trends, however, are not universal. Some evidence indicates that legislators opposed to the no-fault concept are sabotaging new legislation, and some attorneys and judges are failing to observe the intent of the new laws. In Texas, for example, a law that permits divorce on grounds of "insupportability" (which means the same thing as irreconcilable differences) was enacted only after agreement was reached to retain such traditional grounds as adultery, cruelty, and abandonment. As a result, some attorneys plead cases "in the alternative," alleging adultery or cruelty in addition to insupportability in the hope that proof of fault will influence the property settlement.[23]

Some judges appear to be resisting the no-fault concept and may even be given increased power to deny divorces under the new laws. There are cases on record in which judges have required evidence of guilt under one of the old fault grounds for divorce as evidence of insupportability. Other judges continue to impose punitive property settlements on one of the spouses and continue to favor the mother in awarding custody of the children.

Attorney and law professor Robert Levy, who drafted the model statute on which many of the reform laws are patterned, points out that the use of a "breakdown" test may actually give judges the power to deny divorces if they are personally committed to the idea that people should stay married whether they are happy in their marriages or not. It would seem that under the no-fault concept judges should be required to find that a marriage has broken down whenever both parties testify to that effect; but this argument has been ineffective in some jurisdictions.

Premarital Intercourse and Illegitimacy

During the late 1940s and early 1950s, when the now legendary Kinsey Reports on American sexual behavior were published,[24] there was great public concern over the documented facts that a majority of both men and women become involved in sexual intercourse before marriage. That so many people violated the traditional formal norm prohibiting premarital intercourse, and the fear that such violations were increasing rapidly, were widely defined as social problems.

Even then there were indications that premarital intercourse was reasonably well integrated in the family structure of the society, and that fear of the situation worsening rapidly was exaggerated. Generational comparisons of sexual patterns showed, for example, that the proportion of men having premarital intercourse had not increased in over three generations. Moreover, the patronage of prostitutes had decreased, and more premarital intercourse was occurring between about-to-be-married couples.

Consistent with male sexual patterns, the Kinsey studies showed that while some 50 percent of women had intercourse before they were married, approximately half of those were involved only with their future husbands. The generational comparison did show that the incidence of premarital intercourse for women had been increasing. Many people predicted that virginity at marriage would become obsolete and that sexual relations would become increasingly promiscuous.

In the late 1950s and 1960s there was more public discussion of sexual matters, and many people became much more open about their sexual behavior. Fragmentary evidence of increased sexual behavior before marriage seemed to confirm earlier predictions. The mass media popularized the idea that America was experiencing a sexual revolution.

Over the past several years, fairly comprehensive data have become available to permit us to estimate just how much of a revolution there has been in premarital sexual behavior. Studies confirm that most men have premarital intercourse, but they fail to show consistent increases from those figures reported in earlier studies. Five separate studies showed that 48 to 70 percent of men up to 24 years of age have already had premarital intercourse. The lower percentage probably reflects the experience of men in their teens, and the higher one of men in their twenties.[25]

In addition to the five studies that report on the sexual behavior of men, three additional ones report the incidence of premarital intercourse among women. The specific percentages reported as having already had intercourse vary with the nature of the samples and the ages of the respondents, but there is convincing evidence of more premarital intercourse, beginning at younger ages. One study of 1,350 women students at Oberlin College showed that approximately 40 percent were having intercourse. The figure was as low as 21 percent for freshmen and as high as 53 percent for seniors.[26]

The most recent comprehensive study, done in 1976, was based upon interviews with 1,886 unmarried girls, ages 15 to 19, living at home. The percentage at each age level of those who had sexual intercourse was as follows: 18 percent of the 15-year-olds; 25 percent of the 16-year-olds; 41 percent of the 17-year-olds; 45 percent of the 18-year-olds; and 55 percent of the 19-year-olds.[27] There were significant differences between blacks and whites. More black girls had sexual intercourse: 38 percent by age 15 and 84 percent by age 19. Blacks, however, were less promiscuous. Some 12 percent of the white girls had had six or more partners, while only 6 percent of the black girls had done so.

The figures above confirm that a majority of American girls become involved in premarital intercourse, but the study does not support the idea that teenagers are preoccupied with sex and engage in orgiastic behavior. Instead, the portrait emerges of generally uninformed girls becoming involved in adult behavior without being adequately prepared to do so, and often suffering severe consequences.

About half of the 15- to 19-year-old girls who had been having intercourse had been involved with only one partner. Undoubtedly, many hoped that these relationships would lead to marriage. Moreover, the majority of the sexually active girls had intercourse only two times or fewer during the month that preceded their interviews. Almost half had not had intercourse at all during that month, so this is hardly a picture of promiscuous girls engaging in rampant sexuality. Instead, these appear to be somewhat troubled girls, unable to keep sex out of their lives entirely and unable to cope with it effectively.[28]

This interpretation is strengthened by the fact that most of the girls were ignorant of the processes of reproduction and made very ineffective use of contraception. Some 76 percent of the black girls and 56 percent of the white girls were not able to answer multiple-choice questions about the time of greatest pregnancy risk. More than 70 percent of the girls either never used contraceptives or used them only occasionally. The researchers estimate that 35 percent of these sexually active girls had been pregnant by age 19.[29] Although the number of these pregnancies carried to term is not available, we do know that the number of illegitimate births in the United States climbed rapidly between 1950 and the 1970s. From 89,500 illegitimate births in 1950, the number had climbed to 468,000 by 1976.[30] Moreover, illegitimacy rates have increased accordingly. From 1950 to 1973, the illegitimacy rate per 1,000 unmarried women 15 to 44 years old increased from 7.1 to 24.5.

More than half the illegitimate births now are occurring to teenagers, a shift from the pattern that prevailed just a few years ago. Legalized abortion probably accounts for this trend; older women who are sexually active but unmarried probably have more access to abortion than teenagers do. Although many pregnant teenagers manage to obtain abortions, many others do not. In 1976, 235,000 teenagers had illegitimate births. Studies of these teenagers confirm the results of the study for the Presidential Commission on Population Growth and the American Future: *By and large, these girls are not promiscuous or even especially sexually active.* They know rather little about sex and reproduction, and they are not able to use contraception effectively.

One especially enlightening study was done in 1969 and 1970, involving three groups of girls 17 years of age or younger, by Planned Parenthood in San Francisco and Oakland, California. The first group (contraception) consisted of 210 patients at Planned Parenthood Teen Centers who had never been pregnant. The second group (abortion) consisted of 100 girls seeking abortion counseling. The third group (maternity) was made up of 67 girls living in Bay Area maternity homes.

The data in table 7–2 show that the majority of girls in both pregnant groups were monogamous enough to have had only one partner in the year before they became pregnant. The girls seeking contraceptive information were somewhat less monogamous, believed by the authors to have intercourse in close relationships but to change relationships occasionally. Only 7 percent of them currently had more than one partner.

Most of the girls were poorly informed about sex in general and birth control in particular. The data in table 7–3, based upon the answers to 14 true–false questions, show that only the contraception group could answer enough of the questions correctly to attain the equivalent of a "D" grade in the classroom. Many girls believed that most teenage boys need to have sexual intercourse regularly, that no birth control methods can be trusted, and that the fertile period occurs around the time of menstruation.

Although most of the girls had used contraception at some time, about half had used no contraception since their last menstrual period, and 57 to 80 percent of the three groups had used no method at all or had used the most ineffective methods—douche and rhythm. Even of the relatively sophisticated contraception seekers, only slightly over 10 percent had access to the pill.

The facts seem inescapable that American society does a poor job of preparing teenagers to cope with their sexuality, and that many of them pay a high cost in pregnancies and illegitimate births. Some teenagers, of course, seek to solve some of their problems through abortion. Abortion in the United States is a social problem in its own right.

TABLE 7–2 Number of Sexual Partners in Past Year among Three Groups of Sexually Active Teenage Girls (in percentages)

Group	Number of partners				
	One	Two	Three to five	Five to fifteen	More than fifteen
Contraception	48	25	19	7	1
Abortion	83	11	6	0	0
Maternity	66	17	15	2	0

SOURCE: Adapted from Sadja Goldsmith, Mary D. Gabrielson, Ira Gabrielson, Vicki Mathews, and Leah Potts, "Teenagers, Sex and Contraception," *Family Planning Perspectives*, 4 (Jan. 1972), 37.

**TABLE 7–3   Sex and Birth Control Knowledge among Three Groups
of Sexually Active Teenage Girls (average percent correct answers)**

Group	General sex knowledge	Birth control knowledge
Contraception	74	70
Abortion	63	60
Maternity	68	65

SOURCE: Adapted from Sadja Goldsmith, Mary O. Gabrielson, Ira Gabrielson,
Vicki Mathews, and Leah Potts, "Teenagers, Sex and Contraception," *Family Planning Perspectives*, 4 (Jan. 1972), 33.

Abortion

Until the late 1960s legal abortions were very difficult to obtain in the United States. Before an abortion could be authorized, most state laws required that two physicians certify that continuance of the pregnancy would jeopardize the woman's life. The laws conveniently ignored that it was often the mother's mental health, rather than her physical health, that was threatened, and that the physical threats were often to the unborn fetus rather that to the mother. The Rh blood factor, for example, and maternal rubella were known to produce dead or deformed fetuses. There were occasional scandals, too, including that of the tranquilizer thalidomide, the use of which resulted in many deformed babies.

What the repressive laws and the harsh administration of them did was to drive abortion underground. No one knows how many abortions were performed illegally each year, but estimates vary between 250,000 and 1.5 million. The unfortunate medical consequences of this situation were clear enough: abortion-related puerperal mortality in the United States was tremendously higher than in European countries that permitted legal abortion. The medical profession, and psychiatrists particularly, rationalized this situation by claiming that overwhelming guilt and subsequent emotional problems were likely among women who did obtain abortions.

To some extent, a self-fulfilling prophecy operated. Society's harsh condemnation of abortion resulted in most abortions being performed by incompetent physicians, quacks, alcoholics, narcotic addicts, and others under furtive and squalid conditions. The women who underwent the operations often were condemned by the people who performed them and by everyone else who knew of the situation. Under such conditions it would not have been surprising if abortion did precipitate serious emotional problems. Surprisingly, however, the major study of abortion in the United States reported that 75 percent of the unmarried women who had them, and 82 percent of the married women, reported no unfavorable consequences whatever.[31]

During the 1960s public opinion mounted in favor of moderating harsh abortion laws. One survey of 1,484 adults, for example, showed that the majority approved of legal abortions when the woman's health was endangered, when the pregnancy resulted from rape, or when there was a strong chance of a serious defect in the baby. Most respondents disapproved, however, of abortions for low-income women who could not afford more children, for unmarried women, and for married women who did not want more children.[32]

Colorado became the first state to liberalize its abortion law, in 1967. It allowed abortion up to the sixteenth week of pregnancy if the woman's physical or mental health were endangered, if there might be a fetal abnormality, or if the pregnancy had resulted from rape or incest. Between 1967 and 1973, 16 other states liberalized their abortion laws, some of them going much further than Colorado. New York, for example, permitted abortions through the twenty-fourth week of pregnancy, and Hawaii allowed the abortion of any "nonviable" fetus.

Then, in 1973, the United States Supreme Court issued a ruling that effectively wiped out all state abortion laws, old and new. The court ruled that during the first trimester of pregnancy the matter of abortion is a private one between the woman and her physician. The only restriction permitted is that the abortion must be performed by a physician licensed by the state. During the second trimester, states can impose regulations "reasonably related to maternal health," still not limiting the grounds for abortion, but stating the qualifications of persons permitted to perform the procedure and specifying the nature of the abortion facilities, such as clinics or hospitals. Finally, after the fetus becomes viable (24 to 28 weeks), states can prohibit abortion unless it is necessary for the preservation of the mother's life or health (including mental health).

The number of abortions performed in the United States has risen rapidly since 1973. From about 900,000 abortions in 1974, the number climbed to 1,300,000 in 1977. The latter figure represents 28 percent of all pregnancies in that year.

One effect of legalized abortion has been drastically to reduce abortion-related death rates. According to a report from the federal Center for Disease Control in Atlanta, deaths related to abortion—legal, illegal, and spontaneous—dropped by more than 40 percent following the 1973 Supreme Court decision.[33] Much of this drop was associated with a sharp decline in the number of illegal abortions, but part of it was due to a trend toward legal abortions being performed earlier in the first trimester of pregnancy.

A second effect of legalized abortion has been to reduce further the number of births, both legitimate and illegitimate. So far as legitimate births are concerned, one estimate for New York City, which has had more experience with legal abortion than most of the rest of the country, places the drop at approximately 25 percent.[34] Two other studies of sample cities and states, comparing the period before 1970 with that after 1970, reported substantial drops in illegitimacy in jurisdictions with more liberal abortion laws.[35]

Evidence contradicts the claim that women who have abortions suffer afterward from overwhelming guilt feelings. The most impressive evidence is the persistence with which women all over the world as well as in the United States seek to terminate unwanted pregnancies. Apparently, they prefer abortion to having unwanted children.

Research has been done directly on the emotional consequences of abortion. In one study, 106 women who had had abortions responded to a mailed questionnaire four months later. Most of them reported some conflicting emotions about their abortions originally. Sixty percent had resolved those feelings within four months. The other 40 percent continued to be troubled.[36]

One somewhat surprising problem surrounding legalized abortion in the United States is its virtual unavailability to many women who need it, despite its apparent availability in certain major urban centers. Most hospitals still perform few if any abortions. In 1974, for example, only about one-fourth of all non-Catholic general hospitals reported even one legal abortion. Fewer than one-third of all private hospitals and fewer than one-fifth of all public hospitals reported any legal abortions. More than half of all legal abortions were performed in nonhospital clinics.

Legal abortion services are highly concentrated not only by type of medical facility but also geographically. In 1974 11 states failed to provide more than one-sixth of the estimated need for abortions, and an additional 12 states did not meet more than one-third of the estimated need. As we might guess, most of these are basically rural states. Within most states the overwhelming majority of abortions are performed in just one or two metropolitan centers. The effect of the geographical and rural–urban concentration of abortions is to make them much more available to some segments of the population than to others. Rural women often must travel long distances to abortion facilities, if they know of their existence at all. Poor women, who depend upon public hospitals and clinics, often cannot afford the fees at private abortion clinics. And pregnant teenagers often are effectively denied abortion because they lack both the knowledge and the money to permit them to use available abortion facilities. Proponents of legalized abortion argue that public hospitals should initiate abortion services on a large scale to remove these inequities.

Legalized abortion is a controversial issue in the United States. Many people are working systematically to restrict it drastically rather than to make it more widely available. The competing arguments will be presented later, within the value-conflict framework.

Problems of Aging Family Members

The number of persons in the United States aged 65 or over has increased spectacularly, from a little over 1 million in 1870 to over 22 million currently. The aged now equal the total population of our 21 smallest states. In terms of percentages, the aged were less than 3 percent of the population 100 years ago, compared with 10 percent of the population today. As figure 7–1 shows, the aged population is expected to increase by an additional 20 million within the next 40 years. Not only has the number of aged been increasing but, within the aged group, the balance has also been shifting to the older ages. In 1960, 33.6 percent of the aged were 70 years old or older; by 1970, 38 percent were of that age.

The longevity of blacks in the United States is less than that of whites. This means that there are fewer blacks numerically and proportionately

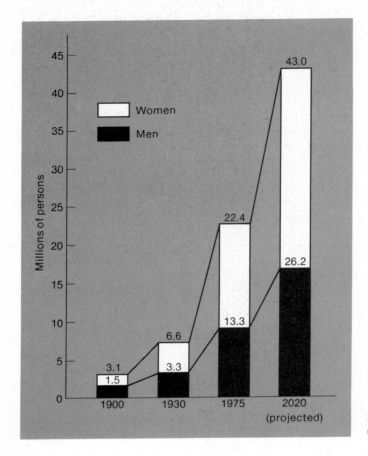

Figure 7–1
Growth of the aged population.

among the aged. There are 22.7 million blacks in the population, 11.2 percent of the total. There are only 1.7 million blacks 65 and over, however, or 7.8 percent of the total aged population.

Women outlive men. Approximately 105 to 106 males are born per 100 females and, up to age 18, boys outnumber girls. From then on, however, females are the majority with the difference becoming greater at each older age. There are 104.7 females for every 100 males during the age period 18 to 24, 109.1 women per 100 men aged 45 to 64, and 138.5 women per 100 men at age 65 and over. Moreover, as more people live to be classified as aged, the discrepancy increases. The 138.5 women per 100 men over 65 in 1970 compares to 120.7 in 1960.

MARITAL STATUS AND LIVING ARRANGEMENTS

The marital status of the aged is shown in table 7–4, broken down by sex and by race. Most older men, black and white, are married, while most older women, black and white, are widowed. Of the married men, almost 40 percent are married to women under age 65. Most of these women are destined to become widows.

Table 7–5 presents information on the living arrangements of older persons. Sixty-seven percent live in family settings. As the data on marital

**TABLE 7–4   Marital Status of Aged Persons in the United
States, 1970 (in percentages)**

Marital Status	All		Blacks	
	Male	Female	Male	Female
Single	7.8	7.7	5.6	4.1
Married, spouse present	68.4	33.7	54.5	21.5
Widowed	18.0	54.6	31.9	67.2
Divorced, separated	5.8	4.0	8.0	7.2

SOURCE: United States Administration on Aging, *Facts and Figures on Older
Americans,* No. 5 (Washington, D.C., 1972), p. 4.

status indicate, more men live with their wives, while more women live alone
as heads of households or live with other relatives. Few men or women live
with nonrelatives, and only 5 percent are institutionalized. The surprising
fact is that so many of the aged live in independent circumstances. This is
because many of the aged use increases in income, resulting largely from
social security, to enable them to avoid having to live with their children.

INCOME

Families in which the household heads are 65 and over have incomes that
average about three-fifths of the average amount received by all families:
$7,298 in 1974 compared with $12,836 for all families. These figures grossly
understate the economic deprivation faced by older people, however. Older
couples who are independent enough to live apart from their relatives,
while they are not often affluent, usually have enough income to get by. Almost half the aged population, however, live outside the married couple sit-

TABLE 7–5   Living Arrangements of Aged Persons in the United States, 1970

Living arrangements	Of every 100 older persons			Of every 100 of all ages	
	Total	Men	Women	Men	Women
In a family	67	33	34	79	59
Head of household	36	30	6	71	10
Wife of head	19	—	19	—	33
Other relative of head	12	3	9	8	16
Alone or with nonrelative	28	7	21	17	37
Head of household	26	6	20	14	35
With nonrelative	2	1	1	3	2
In an institution	5	2	3	4	4

SOURCE: United States Administration on Aging, *Facts and Figures on Older
Americans,* No. 5 (Washington, D.C., 1972), p. 6.

uation; they live with relatives, with nonrelatives, alone, or in institutions. Older couples who live with relatives are still not too strapped financially. But widows, widowers, and the never married are often in desperate financial plight. Many of them scrape by on less than $3,000 per year.

EFFECTS OF "AGE-ISM" IN AMERICA

We are beginning to become aware of a systematic pattern of discrimination against the aged in the United States. This pattern of "age-ism" is comparable in its effects to the more widely recognized patterns of racism and sexism.

The point may be illustrated by comparing the contrasting treatment of youth and age in the United States. Youth and the aged, surprisingly enough, have much in common. Both are introspective, sometimes depressed, and vulnerable to suicide. Both have bodies and personalities undergoing stress and change. Both are heavy users of drugs. When they want to marry, their families are likely to object. Both are obsessed with time; youth traces time forward from birth, while the aged figure the time until their death.

We are accustomed to thinking of a subculture of youth, but we seldom think of aging in similar terms. The youth subculture is analyzed and agonized over, and the carriers of that subculture are widely envied. The existence of a subculture of age, in contrast, is both ignored and avoided. People behave as though the aged are an alien race to which the young will never belong. The aged are largely segregated and discriminated against when they are considered at all.

Although age-ism is not a wholly new development in Western society, modern technology has greatly aggravated the situation. In other times and places adults have been sources of experience and wisdom for the young. Families have stayed together, and older family members have been cherished. In today's America, however, families are small and live apart from the grandparental generation. Social change occurs so fast that the past is regarded as largely irrelevant to the future. This makes the aged a strangely isolated group. Ironically, improvements in health care have kept the aged physically and mentally young while technology has made them obsolete.

Discrimination against the aging begins in the middle years when people suddenly find themselves unemployable. Almost 40 percent of the long-term unemployed are over 45 years of age, but only 10 percent of federal retraining programs are directed to people of that age. Gradually, older people find that it is difficult for them to obtain home mortgages, bank loans, automobile insurance, and driver's licenses. With retirement come drastic reductions in income. One out of every six older people lives in poverty, some two million of them subsisting on social security alone.

While some of the elderly have adequate incomes and are able to migrate to warmer climates upon retirement, this is not true of the overwhelming majority. Fewer than 1 percent of the aged move from their own states. Excepting Florida, the states with the highest percentages of aged are Arkansas, Iowa, Maine, Missouri, Nebraska, and South Dakota. There the aged live on farms and in small towns from which the youth have fled. One-third of the country's aged live in the deteriorated inner-city zones of large metropolitan areas, isolated from family and friends and literally in fear for their lives.

The problems of aging and the aged are financial, physical, and psychological, but they are inextricably involved in a family context. Even the aged widow, barely surviving in a nursing home, is supported financially or emotionally by her children, or suffers acutely from her isolation from former family members. As more and more people reach advanced old age, 75 and over, it is becoming common for families to have three living adult generations. Growing numbers of couples at retirement still have parents to care for, as well as children and grandchildren to consider. There is not one generation gap, but two—one between grandparents and parents, and one between parents and children. It grows increasingly difficult for the subcultures of youth and age to appreciate one another.

THE NURSING HOME SCANDAL

The basic ambivalence of American society toward the aged, and the failure of public policy to support the continued integration of older people in their families, are perhaps nowhere better illustrated than in what has come to be called the nursing-home scandal. It began in 1965 with the passage by Congress of legislation providing for Medicare, a program of subsidies for the medical care of the aged. The aim of the program, to relieve the old of concern about medical costs, was laudable. But the administration of the program has created almost unbelievable abuse.

The federal government turned Medicare over to the states, which in turn handed it over in large part to private enterprise. Medicare quickly became a big business, and one of the most lucrative possibilities was discovered to be the development of nursing homes to provide care for people too old and infirm to care for themselves, but whose medical problems do not require hospitalization. There are now some 23,000 nursing homes in the United States. They take in some $7.5 billion, over half of it from Medicare, to provide care for approximately one million patients.

Some nursing homes, chiefly those run by churches and charitable groups, provide decent care for their residents. Other homes, run by private operators, try to provide adequate care, but are forced by the economics of the situation into providing substandard care. We are concerned with neither of those groups here.

Unfortunately, the prospect of large and dependable government subsidies lured into the field a large number of promoters with little knowledge of nursing-home operation. Some such operators are simply incompetent. Others exploit their defenseless patients as systematically as possible to maximize their own profits. Several kinds of abuse are common.

Most nursing homes pay their employees poorly and consequently have unqualified help. Often the homes try to cut food costs, a major budget item, and end up providing meals that range from unappetizing to inedible. In one reported incident a nursing home was feeding each of its patients for 78 cents per day. In other cases, homes have taken over their patients' bank accounts and charged them exorbitantly high rates until all of their funds were exhausted; then the patients were carried at the lower, Medicaid rates. Over and above the basic rates, extra charges are sometimes added to the bills of those who can afford them.

Some attending physicians are venal in their practices as are the nursing-home operators. They receive favors from the operators, for example, as an incentive to keep all of the homes' beds full. In other instances physicians make hurried visits to the homes, touring all of the rooms and then billing each patient for an individual visit. Some nursing-home physicians make excessive use of sedatives because heavily sedated patients are less troublesome to the nursing-home staff.

Supervision by government regulatory agencies is supposed to prevent such abuses, but it seldom does. Many government inspectors, for example, give the nursing homes a month's warning of their arrival so that they can present as favorable an appearance as possible. Even when serious violations are discovered—such as inadequate staffing, lack of safety and sanitary procedures, or improper accounting procedures—prosecution almost never occurs. In the meantime, up to a million old people spend their last years under conditions of neglect and mistreatment.

The Status of Women

If age-ism is not yet fully defined as a social problem, it appears that women may finally be getting their point across: sexism *is* a major social problem. Discrimination against women goes back to antiquity. Things certainly have changed from the times when "bride price" was a major consideration in the arrangement of marriages, and women were sent away by patriarchs merely handing them a "bill of divorcement," but improvements in the status of women over the centuries have created a tide of rising expectations that make the remaining disabilities that women suffer a social problem today.

The current women's rights movement that grew out of the civil rights movement of the early 1960s, the student protest movement, and the new radical left is not wholly new. Nor is this the first time that feminism and civil rights have been linked together. Before the Civil War, for example, a major feminist movement grew out of the Abolitionist movement, culminating in the Women's Rights Convention at Seneca Falls, New York, in 1848. The convention demanded that women be given the vote, higher education, and equal job opportunities.

It was not to be, however. Blacks received the vote as the result of the Fourteenth Amendment to the Constitution in 1868, but not women. Some of the individual states eventually led the way, with Wyoming enfranchising women in 1890. Agitation continued, and in 1913 approximately 5,000 women staged a march in Washington that produced arrests and mistreatment of a kind similar to that encountered by antiwar protestors more than half a century later. Finally, in 1920, the Nineteenth Amendment was ratified, and women received the vote.

The 1920s and 1930s saw increasing numbers of women going to college and seeking gainful employment afterward. World War II brought a tremendous demand for labor, and women gained a major foothold in industry. By 1950, 34 percent of all adult women were in the labor force. After the war, however, there was a period of retrenchment. People sought relief from the turmoil of the depression of the 1930s and the war years of the early 1940s in a return to familistic values. While two children had been the norm before the war, couples now wanted three, four, or even five. The symbolic phrase of the day was "togetherness," and the suburban housewife became the model American woman.

Perhaps the first sign of the new militance to come was the publication of Betty Friedan's book *The Feminine Mystique* in 1963.[37] She argued that women suffered from a longstanding problem of personal identity; that "our culture does not permit women to accept or gratify their basic needs to grow and fulfill their potentialities as human beings, a need which is not solely defined by their sexual roles."[38] Friedan urged women to reject the role of housewife and to find fulfillment in the world of work. Then she and others raised outcry against the degree to which women are discriminated against, particularly in work and in public life.

One measure of that discrimination is given in table 7–6, which shows that the average earnings of employed women are only about 60 percent of those of men, and that the gap has actually been widening over the past 20 years. Other data not in the table show that the differences between the earnings of men and women are not merely a function of the fact that more women are employed in lower-status occupations. Women in professional and managerial occupations do not fare much better, in relation to the earnings of men, than do women in clerical and service work. Three out of four working women in 1970 earned less than $6,000, compared to only one out of three male workers. Similarly, college educated women in 1960 averaged only $7,400, compared to $13,000 for college educated men.[39]

Since 1964 the office of the president of the United States has been pushing for more women in government, and since 1967 the federal civil services have been reporting the numbers of women at upper civil service levels; but to little avail. In 1966, 1.6 percent of civil service jobs paying $28,000 or more were held by women; in 1970 it was only 1.5 percent. Moreover, there were 2 women in the United States Senate and 18 women in the House of Representatives in 1960. In 1975 there were no women senators and only 17 women representatives. Only 5 women have ever served in the president's Cabinet, and there has never been a woman on the Supreme Court.

In the early 1960s many women participated in the civil rights movement, protesting discrimination against blacks and other minority groups. As the radical left emerged later in the decade they participated in it, too. One factor that led directly to women's liberation becoming a separate

TABLE 7–6   Median Earnings of Full-Time Men and Women Workers, 1955–77

Year	Men	Women	Dollar difference	Percent women's income of men's income
1955	$ 4,250	$2,700	$1,550	64
1960	5,400	3,300	2,100	61
1965	6,400	3,800	2,600	60
1970	9,000	5,300	3,700	59
1975	11,800	6,800	5,000	58
1977	14,626	8,618	6,008	59

SOURCE: U.S. Department of Commerce, Bureau of the Census, and Associated Press, 8 Feb. 1976, and *U.S. News and World Report*, 15 Jan. 1979, p. 67.

movement was the crass prejudice and discrimination that women encountered even in these settings, where there was official commitment to the ideology of equality and nondiscrimination. Women in the radical movement were recruited to do typing and office work, to cook and to keep house for the men in the movement. When it came to exercising leadership, they faced resistance similar to that experienced in the larger society. That women movement members were explicitly viewed as sex objects was symbolized by a cryptic statement attributed to Stokely Carmichael: "The position of women in our movement should be prone!"

In 1966 Betty Friedan and others formed the National Organization for Women (NOW) to take action to bring women into full participation in American society and to gain for them completely equal rights with men. NOW emphasized four goals: (1) enactment of an Equal Rights Amendment to the Constitution; (2) abortion law repeal; (3) day care centers for children; and (4) equal pay for equal work.

Although NOW seemed to be a radical organization at first, it soon emerged as a fairly conservative force in the women's liberation movement. It accepted male members and did not preach that men were "the enemy." More radical groups did just that, and an array of groups sprang up to splinter the movement and to confuse the public about its goals and tactics. Two of the most radical groups were WITCH (Women's International Terrorist Conspiracy from Hell) and SCUM (Society for Cutting Up Men). Of these groups, only NOW seemed to develop a solid national organization and power base. In 1979, it was reported that there were 700 local chapters of NOW, with a membership of approximately 100,000.[40] A more recent development is the National Women's Political Caucus, which is working to put more of the levers of governmental power into women's hands.

The movement has had some success. Some of that success derived from what might be termed a legislative accident that occurred in connection with the passage of the Civil Rights Act of 1964. A Southern congressman, seeking to sabotage the provision of that law that prohibited employment discrimination on the basis of race, color, religion, or national origin, succeeded in adding the word *sex* to the list. The law passed in that form, however, and the federal government was given a powerful tool for reducing employment discrimination against women. Since 1964 there has been mounting pressure on employers to hire more women in more different kinds of jobs, and at better wages or salaries.

The most powerful tool so far in the elimination of sexual discrimination in employment has proved to be federal executive orders. Under a 1967 order, federal funds can be denied to contractors who discriminate in the hiring, pay, and promotion of women. Since most organizations of any size receive federal funds in one way or another, this affects much of the nation's economy. Ironically, the organizations brought under the most direct pressure so far appear to be the universities. Over 300 complaints against colleges and universities have been filed by women's groups, and several large universities have been threatened with the cut-off of millions of dollars in federal funds.

An event of great potential significance occurred in March 1972, when Congress approved the Equal Rights Amendment to the Constitution, considered intermittently since 1923. Three-fourths, or 38, of the state legislatures must now ratify the amendment by 1982 in order for it to take effect. It is too early to anticipate whether the amendment will be approved and all of the implications of the amendment, but the following appear to be some of them.

Relationships between men and women in marriage would be altered. A woman would not automatically take her husband's name. She might take his surname, or he might take hers; they might hyphenate both names together; or each might keep his or her own surname. In the latter event they would have to decide what surname their children would have. In the event of divorce, alimony would be available equally to both partners. The custody of any children would be decided on the basis of the children's welfare rather than being granted automatically to the mother.

Much labor legislation would have to be redrafted. Laws "protecting" women by limiting the weights they are permitted to lift and by providing for extra rest periods probably would be declared unconstitutional. Job qualifications would have to be stated strictly on the basis of the physical requirements of the job, and not in terms of any presumed differences between men and women. Special provisions would have to be made for maternity leaves and for the care of infants. Infant-care leaves would have to be granted to fathers in cases in which the couple decided that he would assume those duties.

In the area of criminal law, prostitution laws would have to punish male

The effects of the women's movement can be seen in the changing of traditional roles within the family structure. In some families today, the husband remains at home with the baby while the wife goes off to work.
(Erika, Photo Researchers, Inc.)

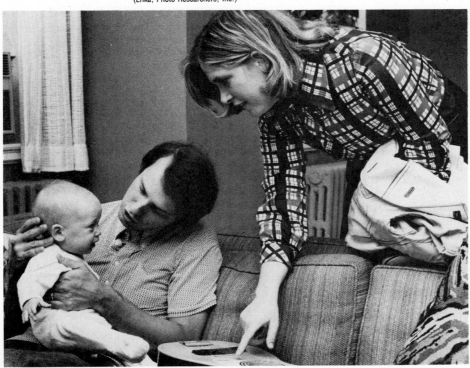

prostitutes as well as female prostitutes, and probably all such laws would be declared unconstitutional unless they provided for the punishment of the prostitutes' customers also. Statutory rape laws that set lower ages of consent for girls than for boys would also be unconstitutional.

In perhaps the most controversial area of all, women probably would become subject to military draft laws along with men. Major problems would arise in determining what roles women would physically play in the military services, but any exclusion of women from duties on the basis of sex alone would obviously be unconstitutional.

Whether the Equal Rights Amendment will be ratified by three-fourths of the state legislatures is still uncertain at this writing. It has taken 50 years to bring this idea this far, and it may take many more before genuine reform occurs. In the meantime, legislatures, regulatory bodies, and the courts will whittle away at sexual inequality, but discrimination will remain.

The Social-Disorganization Approach

THE OLD RULES

The American family that adapted to colonial and frontier life was a strong and stable organization, a rural family oriented toward agriculture. Families were large, for children were highly valued, not much additional expense, and a chief source of labor. The husband and father was the undisputed head of the household. The biblical admonition that "husbands should be the head of their wives" was interpreted literally, and children were supposed to be seen, not heard. Divorce was rare. Marriages were contracted to meet the necessity for earning a living and rearing a family. A lack of compatibility between the spouses was no reason for destroying an otherwise good marriage. The family raised most of its food; made its clothing, furniture, and other household goods; and often built its house. It was a large, patriarchal, stable group that performed numerous functions for its members.

It was not difficult for either men or women to decide what they would do in life. By and large they did what their parents had done. Boys learned to farm, to carpenter, and to assume their place as caretakers and disciplinarians for women and children. Girls learned to do all the things required of a farmer's wife, to expect marriage, and to bear large families. For neither were there any real alternatives. Farming was a family business. Men could not run their farms without the help of wives and children, and for women the only alternative to marriage was to live in the home of a relative with a status somewhere between that of a hired servant and that of a child in need of special attention. Family unity also had its positive side. Men, women, and children shared basic values in addition to the many tasks required to make a living. Each performed services for the other and each was rewarded in turn. Parents provided apprenticeships for their children and gradually turned over property and responsibility to them. As their vigor declined, the parents withdrew to part-time work without fear of economic deprivation or social isolation. The clearly defined roles for family members fit together smoothly and provided security for all.

THE TRANSITION

The Industrial Revolution had profound effects on the family. It displaced farming as the principal occupation, it brought the growth of cities, and it was accompanied by the development of a much more secular outlook on life.

Prior to the Industrial Revolution, farming was the chief occupation, and what little industry was carried on was organized under the cottage system. Small producers fabricated goods in their homes with the aid of family members and one or two hired workers. The family was an economic unit with production activities helping to build and maintain its solidarity. The appearance of the factory changed all this. No longer was work carried on in the home, and no longer did all family members participate. The husband or father was likely to be employed at some distance from his home and to be effectively removed from contact with other family members throughout most of the waking hours. Both the satisfactions and the frustrations encountered on the job came to have less and less meaning for the remaining family members, who were similarly intent on going their separate ways.

The appearance of factories required large numbers of laborers to be congregated nearby. Stores and other retail businesses sprang up to cater to the needs of the factory workers; suddenly the modern city was in the process of development. Land close to the factories became expensive and living space scarce. Families crowded into smaller quarters and spent less time in the home. Children became economic and social liabilities, expensive to raise, and troublesome in the city environment. They went out of the home to the school and church and to centers of commercialized recreation.

It was not only the material aspects of life that changed, however. Customs and traditions formerly accepted as eternal verities became the objects of rational scrutiny. Just because it had always been done that way was no reason for continuing it, if a better way could be found. People began to look for new and better ways of regulating their personal lives as well as for producing goods. Marriage assumed the character of a humanly sanctioned relationship from which the sanction could be withdrawn by divorce or separation. The requirements and expectations that formerly held families together began to give way to a new pattern.

THE NEW RULES

To compile a complete and accurate list of the new rules governing family behavior is not possible, because the transition is not yet complete. Though the large patriarchal family has largely given way, vestiges of it remain and the character of its successor is not fully established. From past changes and present trends, the following observations, at least, seem well founded.

The primary goal of marriage (and the family) is happiness—the personal happiness of each family member. The family is subordinate to its members' needs and is modified or dissolved when it does not meet individual needs. Permanence of a marriage is no longer a wholly satisfactory criterion of success, and family responsibility does not require a large number of children. Parents consider their happiness as well as that of their children and plan the size of their families to provide the maximum benefits for all concerned. More stress is placed on the quality of child care than on the number of children. Parents strive to achieve wholesome, well-adjusted personalities in their children as well as to feed, clothe, and educate them.

No longer are husbands undisputed masters, and neither women nor men know beforehand what to expect in marriage. Though women largely have gained equality with men, the nature of that equality remains vague and undefined. To some it is equality based upon the traditional division of labor between the sexes, the husband being the breadwinner, and the wife, the homemaker. To others it means that beyond bearing children the division of labor should be worked out according to the temperaments and needs of the spouses. To still others it means something intermediate between these extremes. Above all, it means confusion and dissatisfaction, because there is no one role for which persons are trained and in which they can feel comfortable. Perhaps a satisfactory set of new roles will appear, but more likely not. Rigid, unvarying roles for men and women may be incompatible with our highly individualistic, technologically advanced culture. Rather than developing any one set of satisfactory roles, we appear to be moving toward the acceptance of various role patterns. Flexibility of attitude toward roles for men and women with several possible alternatives for each may be about as much uniformity as can be achieved.

Parents, though they may continue to aid their children, are forced to let their offspring go at marriage. The marriage of children demands again the equivalent of the pre-childbearing relationship between the mother and father—and the problems of adjustment are often more difficult at 50 than they were at 20. Parents are expected to be emotionally self-sufficient and to prepare for financial independence during their old age. Modern homes are small and efficient. They assume the presence of only one set of parents and children. About the only entree into the childbearing family for grandparents is the role of babysitter or occasional visitor. The independence of the young family requires also the independence of the grandparents.

Many families have been unable to adjust to the new rules and to the urban setting in which they operate. The failure of husbands and wives to find satisfactory roles contributes to the high incidence of separation, divorce, and desertion. Parents also are puzzled about how to deal with their children and what to expect from them; and youngsters, as they grow up, are confused about their own behavior. Thus social disorganization and change in the larger society have contributed to family disorganization directly, through the resulting confusion in roles, and indirectly, through providing the setting in which extreme disorganization can develop and flourish.

Many groups bitterly oppose some or all changes in family structure. Even when the changes are not actively opposed, people are disoriented by them. They are torn between loyalty to the values of old and acceptance of new, supposedly better ways. The conflict rages between groups and within individual personalities.

The Value-Conflict Approach

PERMANENCE VERSUS ADJUSTMENT

History is replete with accounts of unsatisfactory marriages. Biblical heroes and heroines, European monarchs, and American presidents have succeeded or failed because of, or in spite of, the ambitions of their spouses. Persevering women of all countries have assumed increased stature in comparison to the incompetence and debauchery of their husbands. Outsiders have for centuries admired and pitied these (un)fortunate men and women. Only recently, and mostly in America, has anyone had the temerity to try to do anything about it. And rarely have efforts at change met such concerted opposition.

Self-sacrifice has never been the least highly regarded of virtues, and permanence of the family somehow is supposed to compensate for any sacrifices made by its members. The basic assumptions underlying this position are at least two: (1) family life itself is "sacred" and not to be trifled with; and (2) protection of the family against dissolution is necessary for the well-being of all its members. Husbands and wives who remain together, even if unhappy, reputedly are building character in themselves and will be "better men and women" for the tribulations they have undergone. Children similarly need their parents. Even though the home be strife-ridden, its continuance is presumed to be better than having the parents separate. For persons who hold these beliefs, the only solution to family problems is to seek a return to the stable family of the past. Generally they advocate stricter divorce laws or no divorce at all; clearly defined obligations for husbands, wives, and children; and punishment for those who disobey.

The "permanence" values are opposed by the emerging "happiness," or "adjustment," goals in family life. Many people deny that benefits inevitably result from preserving marriages. On the contrary, they claim that continuance of conflict-ridden marriages may be harmful to parents and children, and that such marriages had best be dissolved so that more satisfactory relationships can be formed. Presumably, unhappy parents are in no position to provide affection and security for their children. Moreover, the emotional trauma resulting from the unhappy parental relationship may be greater than that involved in divorce. In support of this position, it is true that most divorced persons remarry and that second marriages are often happy ones. Very few of these persons favor divorce; they merely regard it as less undesirable than unhappy marriages.

GENERATIONAL CONFLICTS

Overt conflict between the generations, conspicuous during the late 1960s and early 1970s, has diminished in recent years. "You can't trust anyone over 30" was the battle cry of the youth counterculture that held adults responsible for all forms of social injustice, from poverty and economic exploitation to hypocritical interpersonal relationships to war. Members of the counterculture were actually a small proportion of all youth, but because they were mostly middle-class, articulate, educated people, they wielded influence out of all proportion to their numbers. The end of the Vietnam War, a diminishing proportion of the population entering the adolescent years, and a major downturn in the economy all helped to bring the counterculture, as such, to an end.

Generational conflicts are an age-old phenomenon, however, and when one form ends another may take its place. At least 100,000 teenagers each year still show their disaffection by running away from home. They are, to say the least, a heterogeneous lot. Some are poor and have very little to run away from. Some are blacks whose running away symbolizes an effort to join the society rather than to run away from it. Some are simply not very bright and are generally unable to cope. A few are mentally ill. The most conspicuous element among them is a core of white middle-class youth whose disenchantment with their lives seems to be directly related to their family lives.

Unfortunately, little research has been done that might help us understand the relationship between family life and dropping out. One study at the University of California of a group of dropout drug-abusers did report that the chief characteristic they shared was a history of unhappy family life. In general, they were loners and losers before they dropped out.[41]

THE ABORTION CONTROVERSY

The conflict over women's right to abort their pregnancies is deeply rooted in history. Ancient Roman practices of abortion were described by the early Christians as infanticide. For some 1,800 years, church policy vacillated but generally held abortion to be an excommunicable sin. In the twelfth century, excommunication was ordered only if abortion was performed after 40 days for a male fetus and 80 days for a female. Why it took twice as long for a female fetus to acquire a soul has never been satisfactorily explained.

In the sixteenth century, abortion became an excommunicable sin from the moment of conception, according to Pope Sixtus V. Sixtus's successor, Gregory XIV, however, restored a 40-day criterion. Then, in 1869, the policy was reversed once again to hold that the soul exists from the moment of conception. The Roman Catholic church today remains the most vocal opponent of more permissive abortion laws; it decrees that abortion may not be performed even to save the life of the mother.

Many other religious groups and some civil ones oppose the Catholic stand. The National Council of Churches approves of hospital abortions where the life or health of the mother is involved. Many Jews consider the fetus part of the mother until it is born, and thus not possessed of a soul. Episcopal bishops and the Unitarian Universalist Association have taken stands in favor of more liberal abortion laws. The American Civil Liberties Union has taken the position that "a woman has a right to have an abortion—that is, a termination of pregnancy prior to the viability of the fetus—and that a licensed physician has a right to perform an abortion, without the threat of criminal sanctions. . . ."[42]

The conflict intensified after the 1973 Supreme Court ruling that made abortion during the first trimester of pregnancy a private matter between a woman and her physician. Within 21 months of the ruling, 31 state legislatures passed a total of 57 new laws on abortion, most of them aimed at circumventing the Supreme Court decision. In July 1976, however, the Supreme Court issued another ruling invalidating most of those laws: it held that states may not require a woman to have her husband's consent to secure an abortion, and that girls under the age of 18 do not need their parents' consent.

Consolidating their efforts under the banner of "Right to Life," opponents of abortion have turned to promoting three proposed amendments to the Constitution that would prevent the courts from allowing abortion. The first, the so-called Buckley amendment, states that the word *person*, as used in the Fifth and Fourteenth Amendments, applies to unborn offspring at every state of biological development. The Hogan amendment states that neither the United States nor any state shall deprive any human being, from the moment of conception, of life without due process of law. Finally, the Whitehurst amendment simply wants to turn the whole abortion question back to the individual states. The controversy promises to continue for many years.

The Personal-Deviation Approach

Moralists of a generation ago were more likely than most people today to ascribe problems in family life to the influence of deviant personalities. Divorce and sex outside marriage, for example, were widely defined as the evil actions of corrupt people.

As the data in this chapter have shown, however, these problem phenomena are exceedingly widespread and reflect basic changes in the larger society. There is no need to postulate evil or maladjustment to explain them. There is need only to specify the degree to which the problems are augmented by personal deviancy and the degree to which the problems create deviancy in persons affected by them.

Divorce rates from remarriage and marital happiness ratings in studies of remarriages present a paradox. Divorce rates from *all* remarriages are high. Most of this, however, is a function of very high divorce rates at the lowest socioeconomic levels; at middle-class levels, divorce rates from remarriages may be no higher than from first marriages. Studies of marital happiness ratings and marital adjustment scores in remarriages[43] show them to be as high as in first marriages. Such studies, of course, automatically exclude remarried couples who have divorced again, and probably also study couples who are mostly middle class. Goode verified that most remarried women in his Detroit study found their second marriages to be "much better" than their first marriages.[44] Finally, Bernard, basing her conclusion upon analysis of 2,009 cases, states that remarriages may be relatively more satisfying than first marriages.[45]

There is evidence, however, that a small proportion of divorces may reflect neurotic difficulties in the spouses, and that those same personality problems will cause them to fail in subsequent marriages. Thomas Monahan, using Iowa data, found that the risk of divorce increases with each occurrence of divorce on the part of either partner. In marriages where both spouses are being married for the first time, the risk of divorce is only 16.6 percent. Where one partner has been divorced previously, the risk jumps to 36.8 percent. Where both have been divorced twice or more, the probability reaches a staggering 79.4 percent.[46] Undoubtedly, most of these cases of serial divorce occur among basically maladjusted persons.

Divorce is also known to create temporary deviancy in some otherwise well-adjusted persons. Even though it may be anticipated for months or years, the experience of divorce frequently is traumatic. Habit patterns and personal relationships of long duration are suddenly uprooted. The person must finally face up to having failed in marriage and having been rejected by the partner. Extreme bitterness and despair often follow. To assuage the hurt and to cope with the frustrations of suddenly being unmarried again, the individual may enter a more or less promiscuous series of sex relationships. Gradually, as reorientation occurs, these symptoms of deviancy are replaced by a more conventional pattern.

When approximately four-fifths of all men and half of all women have premarital intercourse, it is fairly obvious that the fact of intercourse alone cannot be ascribed to personal deviancy. The involvement of most women, at least, appears to be directly in anticipation of marriage and to be with the future husband only. Most of these women report, after marriage, that they do not regret their premarital experience.

At the other extreme, however, there is a small group of women whose premarital involvements are linked with low self-concepts and who use sex in a pervasive pattern of self-debasement. For these women premarital sex is both the result of deviancy and the cause of further deviancy. Some of these women become pregnant and seek abortions. When they do, they are likely to number significantly among the small proportion of women for whom abortion has disastrous psychological effects.

Certainly the women's liberation movement is to be explained largely within the framework of social change. Although change in the direction of equality for women has been irregular, it has been mounting since ancient times. Perhaps in the twentieth century full equality will yet be achieved.

The leadership of the feminist movement and the membership itself appear to be motivated largely by genuine desire to right real wrongs. They have been plagued, however, by factions and members whose extremist positions threaten to discredit the whole movement. Some of the leadership of organizations, such as SCUM and WITCH, and some members of local consciousness-raising groups have preached that men are the enemy, that women can achieve freedom only by refusing to do housework or engage in child care, and that they should leave their husbands, seek lesbian relationships, and so on. Even allowing for the possible use of such tactics for simple attention-getting and other political ends, the conclusion seems inescapable that some of these extremist women are classic deviant personalities—revolutionaries, characterized by blind faith and single-hearted allegiance, people of fervent hopes, hatreds, and intolerance. Generally, these deviant personalities appear to be peripheral to the movement and seem to be losing whatever power and influence they have had. Many people, however, know of young women whose personal and marital lives have been severely disrupted by falling under the influence of such persons.

A final area in which deviant personalities appear to play a large role is that of spouse abuse and child abuse. Undoubtedly some men and women who hurt one another, and some parents who injure and maim their children, are victims of sadistic and masochistic abnormalities. Surprisingly, however, most studies report that the vast majority of physically violent people are not mentally ill. Instead, they seem overwhelmingly to be people who experienced violence as children in their own parental homes and who resort to it under conditions of emotional stress. Men who feel inadequate in their roles as husbands and providers and women who must cope with too many children in crowded living quarters appear particularly prone to child and spouse abuse. Although society formally disapproves of it, the use of violence is deeply rooted in American culture, with spouse abuse and child abuse being only slight distortions or exaggerations of behavior that occurs in many homes.

Summary

Violence between husbands and wives, and inflicted by parents on their children, is increasingly widely recognized as a major social problem. No one knows how much there is, but a variety of evidence indicates that it is widespread. Part of the uncertainty is a matter of definition: When does the normal and accepted violence of everyday life, such as spanking, become problem violence? Studies show that most physical abusers learn the use of violence as children, in their parental homes.

Both the number of divorces in the United States and the divorce rate have doubled in recent years. The chance that any individual marriage will end in divorce is now about one in three. The carnage resulting from the adversary system of divorce has become increasingly intolerable, and about half of the states have already moved in the direction of no-fault divorce. So far, the reforms do not seem to be increasing the number of divorces, but are making the process somewhat more humane.

The trend toward involvement in sexual intercourse before marriage continues, but there is little evidence of increased promiscuity. Instead, we have become aware of how ill-prepared many teenagers are to handle their emerging sexuality and the dangers of premarital pregnancy. Illegitimacy rates have increased rapidly over the past 20 years, with more than half of the illegitimate births now occurring to teenagers.

Until abortion laws began to be liberalized in the late 1960s, there was a flourishing trade in illegal abortions. High mortality rates were one consequence. The furtive nature of such procedures and the squalid conditions under which they were done encouraged guilt and remorse in the women patients, but even then most escaped without serious complications. In 1973 the United States Supreme Court ruled that abortion during the first trimester of pregnancy is a private matter to be decided between a woman and her physician. Now over one million legal abortions are performed each year. Abortion-related death rates have dropped drastically, and both legitimate and illegitimate birth rates are dropping. Nonetheless, abortions are not readily available to many rural women, poor women, and teenagers.

"Age-ism" is just beginning to be recognized as a social problem in the United States. Discrimination against the aged is revealed in the large proportion who live at or near the poverty level and in the general reluctance of society to acknowledge the social and psychological problems of the more than 20 million people who are 65 years of age or older. A recent addition to the problems faced by the aged is the burgeoning of incompetently and unscrupulously run nursing homes for the infirm aged.

Sexism is more widely recognized than age-ism as a social problem, and the women's liberation movement emerged during the 1960s to combat it. Federal legislation, beginning with the Civil Rights Act of 1964, has assisted the fight, and progress has been made. An Equal Rights Amendment to the Constitution has been approved by Congress, but it is uncertain whether it will be ratified by the necessary three-fourths of the states. If the amendment is approved, it will probably greatly alter the relationships of men and women in marriage, require the redrafting of much labor legislation, and necessitate the revision of some criminal law.

Current family problems must be seen in the context of transition from a large, stable family system oriented toward agriculture to a small, individualistically-oriented family functioning in an urban setting. The transition has disrupted traditional ways of adjusting and has produced value conflicts. Conflicts focus upon individualistic versus familistic goals and on relationships between the generations.

Most family problems do not stem directly from personal deviation. Only a small number of the people who are physically violent or who become involved in divorce, premarital sex, and abortion are basically maladjusted people.

Suggested Readings

DUNCAN, BEVERLY, and OTIS DUDLEY DUNCAN, *Sex Typing and Social Roles: A Research Report* (New York: Academic Press, 1978). Comprehensive analysis of changing sex roles in the United States.

EPSTEIN, JOSEPH, *Divorced in America: Marriage in an Age of Possibility* (New York: Penguin Books, 1974). Insightful account, by a divorced man, of the heartbreak that accompanies divorce. Deals with adjustment to families, children, and friends as divorced people reorganize their lives.

FOSTER, HENRY H., JR., *A Bill of Rights for Children* (Springfield, Ill.: Charles C Thomas, 1974). Develops principles and guidelines for fairer treatment of children under the law.

LOETHER, HERMAN J., *Problems of Aging: Sociological and Social Psychological Perspectives* (Encino, Ca.: Dickenson, 1975). Treats the various problems associated with aging, including changing family roles and widowhood.

MARTIN, DEL, *Battered Wives* (San Francisco: Glide Publications, 1976). Wife abuse is analyzed in the context of the suppression of women, the maintenance of sex-role stereotypes, and the effects of the women's movement

ROSS, HEATHER L., and ISABEL V. SAWHILL, *Time of Transition: The Growth of Families Headed by Women* (Washington, D.C.: The Urban Institute, 1975). Details the extraordinary increases in female-headed families in the United States. Relates this trend to race, divorce rates, and dependence upon public welfare.

WEISS, ROBERT S., *Marital Separation* (New York: Basic Books, 1975). Provides practical guidance for people who are contemplating or involved in divorce. Covers the process from the time of separation until the formation of new attachments.

Footnotes

[1]*Newsweek,* 10 Oct. 1977, p. 112.

[2]*New York Times,* 18 June 1978.

[3]*Business Week,* 2 Apr. 1979, p. 102.

[4]*Washington Post,* 8 Mar. 1979.

[5]John L. Hess, "The Scandal of Care for the Old," *New York Times,* 12 Jan. 1975.

[6]Susan R. Orden and Norman N. Bradburn, "Dimensions of Marriage Happiness," *American Journal of Sociology,* 73 (May 1968), 717.

[7]National Center for Health Statistics, "1964–66 National Natality Survey," as reported in *New York Times,* 8 Apr. 1970.

[8]Gerald R. Leslie and Elizabeth McLaughlin Leslie, *Marriage in a Changing World* (New York: John Wiley & Sons, 1977), ch. 1.

[9]Leslie A. Westoff and Charles F. Westoff, *From Now to Zero: Fertility, Contraception, and Abortion in America* (Boston: Little, Brown, 1968), pp. 293–94.

[10]Edward Weinstock, et al., "Abortion Needs and Services in the United States, 1974–1975," *Family Planning Perspectives,* 8 (Mar.–Apr.), 58.

[11]John E. O'Brien, "Violence in Divorce Prone Families," *Journal of Marriage and the Family,* 33 (Nov. 1971), 692–98.

[12]George Levinger, "Sources of Marital Dissatisfaction among Applicants for Divorce," *American Journal of Orthopsychiatry,* 26 (Oct. 1966), 803–7.

[13]Richard J. Gelles, *The Violent Home: A Study of Physical Aggression between Husbands and Wives* (Beverly Hills, Ca.: Sage Publications, 1972), p. 49.

[14]Murray A. Straus, "Leveling, Civility, and Violence in the Family," *Journal of Marriage and the Family,* 36 (Feb. 1974), 13–29.

[15]*Time,* 9 July 1979, p. 55.

[16]*McCall's,* June 1975, p. 37.

[17]See Nancy Wolfe, "Victim Provocation: The Battered Wife and Legal Definition of Self-Defense," *Sociological Symposium,* 25 (Winter 1979), 98–118.

[18]R. Stark and J. McEvoy, III, "Middle-Class Violence," *Psychology Today,* 4 (Nov. 1970), 52–65.

[19]Lynda Lytle Holmstrom and Ann Wolbert Burgess, "Rape: The Husband's and Boyfriend's Initial Reactions," *The Family Coordinator,* 28 (July 1979), 321–30.

[20]Paul C. Glick and Arthur J. Nor-

ton, "Perspectives on the Recent Upturn in Divorce and Remarriage," *Demography,* 10 (Aug. 1973), 301–14.

21*New York Times Magazine,* 10 Aug. 1975, p. 13.

22*The World Almanac* (New York: Newspaper Enterprise Association, 1978), p. 962.

23*Parade,* 28 Nov. 1971, pp. 14–16.

24Alfred C. Kinsey, Wardell B. Pomeroy, and Clyde E. Martin, *Sexual Behavior in the Human Male* (Philadelphia: W. B. Saunders, 1948); and Alfred C. Kinsey et al., *Sexual Behavior in the Human Female* (Philadelphia: W. B. Saunders, 1953).

25Bert N. Adams, *The American Family* (Chicago: Markham, 1971), p. 192; Harold T. Christensen and Christina F. Gregg, "Changing Sex Norms in America and Scandinavia," *Journal of Marriage and the Family,* 32 (Nov. 1970), 616–27; Eleanore B. Luckey and Gilbert D. Nass, "A Comparison of Sexual Attitudes and Behavior in an International Sample," *Journal of Marriage and the Family,* 31 (May 1969), 364–79; Peter O. Peretti, "Premarital Sexual Behavior between Females and Males of Two Middle-Sized Midwestern Cities," *Journal of Sex Research,* 5 (Aug. 1969), 218–25; Ira E. Robinson et al., "Change in Sexual Behavior and Attitudes of College Students," *The Family Coordinator,* 17 (Apr. 1968), 119–23.

26A. Wachtel and B. Taylor, "Sexual Behavior and Related Health Needs of 1,300 College Women," *Advances in Planned Parenthood,* vol. 5 (Princeton, N.J.: Excerpta Medica Foundation, 1970), p. 81.

27Melvin Zelnik and John F. Kantner, "Sexual and Contraceptive Experience of Young Unmarried Women in the United States, 1976 and 1971," *Family Planning Perspectives,* 9 (Mar.–Apr. 1977), 55–71.

28These general findings have been confirmed by other studies. See Frank Furstenberg, Jr., Leon Gordis, and Milton Markowitz, "Birth Control Knowledge and Attitudes among Unmarried Pregnant Adolescents: A Preliminary Report," *Journal of Marriage and the Family,* 31 (Feb. 1969), 34–42.

29Melvin Zelnik, Young J. Kim, and John F. Kantner, "Probabilities of Intercourse and Conception among U.S.

Teenage Women, 1971 and 1976," *Family Planning Perspectives* II (May–June 1979), 177–83.

30*U.S. News and World Report,* 26 June 1978, p. 59.

31Paul H. Gebhard et al., *Pregnancy, Birth, and Abortion* (New York: Harper & Brothers, 1958), pp. 203–11.

32Alice S. Rossi, "Abortion Laws and Their Victims," *Trans-action* (Sept.–Oct. 1966), pp. 9–10.

33Department of Health, Education and Welfare, Center for Disease Control, "Surveillances Summary: Abortion-Related Mortality, 1972 and 1973—United States," *Morbidity and Mortality Weekly Report,* 24 (1975), 22.

34Christopher Tietze, "The Effect of Legalization of Abortion on Population Growth and Public Health," *Family Planning Perspectives,* 7 (May–June 1975), 123–27.

35"Legal Abortion Reduces Out-of-Wedlock Births," *Family Planning Perspectives,* 7 (Jan.–Feb. 1975), 11–12.

36Ellen W. Freeman, "Abortion: Subjective Attitudes and Feelings," *Family Planning Perspectives,* 10 (May–June 1978), 150–55.

37(New York: W. W. Norton).

38Ibid., p. 77.

39Figures from *Congressional Quarterly,* cited in a copyrighted article by Elder Witt, "Sex Discrimination: Last Acceptable Prejudice," reported in *St. Petersburg Times,* 16 Mar. 1972.

40*Time,* 6 Aug. 1979, p. 47.

41*Time,* 7 July 1967, pp. 19–20.

42*Current,* May 1968, p. 26.

43Harvey J. Locke, *Predicting Adjustment in Marriage: A Comparison of a Divorced and a Happily Married Group* (New York: Henry Holt, 1951), pp. 302–3; and Harvey J. Locke and William J. Klausner, "Marital Adjustment of Divorced Persons in Subsequent Marriages," *Sociology and Social Research,* 33 (Nov. 1948), 97–101.

44William J. Goode, *After Divorce* (Glencoe, Ill.: Free Press, 1956).

45Jessie Bernard, *Remarriage: A Study of Marriage* (New York: Dryden Press, 1956).

46Thomas P. Monahan, "The Changing Nature and Instability of Remarriages," *Eugenics Quarterly,* 5 (June 1958), 73–85.

THE HOUSE OF GOd, The Church OF The Living God The GateS OF HeaveN

M.E. Warren, Photo Researchers, Inc.

RELIGIOUS PROBLEMS AND CONFLICTS

8

Approached by [Rev.] Moon's campus recruiters, Wendy attended a Unification weekend in Maine, where the members "radiated so much love, so much warmth" that she soon decided her search had ended. She called her mother breathlessly to ask if she had heard the "good news."

"What good news?" asked Mrs. Helander.

"That there is a new Messiah on this Earth," said Wendy.

When she came home for Christmas, her mother found her troubled. "She cried a good deal of the time, and yet she was telling me how happy she was." About this time, Wendy gave away many of her cher-

ished possessions to fellow members of what she began calling "the Family." She dropped out of college, joining the church as a full-time member.

"I never had any questions," she said later. "It all made sense." It did not make sense to her parents, and eventually they abducted her from a church center and had her "deprogrammed" by Ted Patrick, a man who specializes in such treatment, to cure her of Moon's spell. It didn't work. She left home soon after, taking only a toothbrush, and returned to the fold. "I think the poor kid was afraid," said her mother. "They had her mind all along."[1]

In early America only one person in fifteen was a church member. Today more than three in five belong to a church. Yet American religion is in a period of ferment.

The Changing Face of Religion in the United States

THE DECLINE OF MAINLINE LIBERALISM

Church membership and attendance in the United States peaked around 1960. Since then, proportionate membership has declined slightly, as shown in figure 8–1, while attendance has fallen even more, as shown in figure 8–2. But this loss has not been evenly distributed. The churches known as "mainline liberal" have suffered most. These are the major denominations that are liberal in theology and tend to support policies of moderate reform in social and political action. By contrast, the "conservative" or "fundamentalist" churches are more strict and traditional in doctrinal beliefs, and tend to emphasize spiritual evangelism rather than social action.

The liberals won most of the theological battles of the past century, maintaining control of most of the large, established ("mainline") denomi-

Figure 8–1
Church membership as percentage of population.
Source: *Yearbook of American and Canadian Churches*, 1940, 1968, 1973, 1975, 1978.

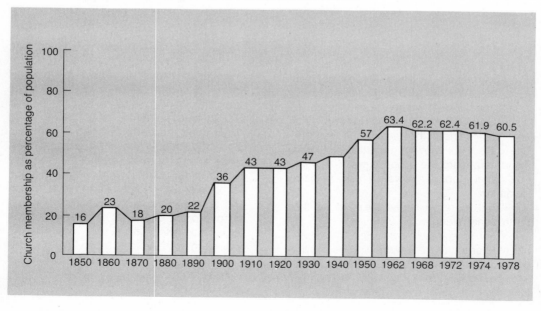

nations. Liberal theology seemed to be in tune with the direction of social change. Liberals resolved all conflicts between science and religion by modifying religious doctrines wherever they conflicted. They sought to apply the basic values of Christianity to the problems of an urban industrial society. With a population steadily growing more educated and scientific, the dominance of liberal religion seemed assured.

In recent years, however, the tide seems to have turned. The more impressive membership gains have been racked up by the conservative churches, while most of the liberal churches have even suffered an absolute loss of membership.[2] One careful research study found not only that the conservative churches are growing more rapidly but that within each church, those members who attend most faithfully and contribute most generously "are those of unwavering orthodoxy, who reject the importance of loving neighbors or doing good for others."[3] Thus, the generous supporters and zealous workers within each denomination tend to be the more conservative members, who do the work while the liberals express humane sentiments. While it may be too early to predict the eclipse of liberal religion, its future is not promising.

GROWING INTEREST IN RELIGION

Not long ago it was a fashionable idea that an increasingly educated and scientific people would have no need for religion. Such a sophisticated people, it was suggested, would find their answers in natural and social science, rather than in ancient superstitions or revealed religious dogma. Thus, as society became steadily less *sacred* and more *secular,* people's need for religion would wane. Today it is clear that this is not happening, and that some people have certain needs that only religion can fill.[4] While the established churches may be losing ground, *religion* is very much alive. Religious studies are popular on the campus and have recently become the most rapidly growing field of graduate study.[5] Recent campus surveys show an increase

Figure 8–2
Church attendance in the United States, 1955–1976.
Source: *Yearbook of American and Canadian Churches*, 1978, p. 256.

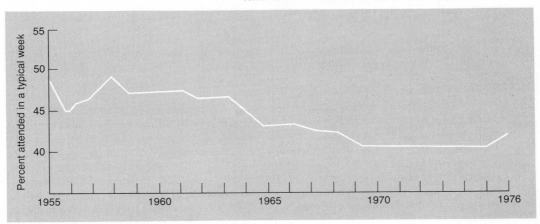

197

TABLE 8–1   Membership Changes, American Churches, 1960–76.

Denomination	1960 Membership (thousands)	Change 1960–76 (thousands)	Percent change
United Pentecostal Church	150	255	170.0
Christian and Missionary Alliance	60	150	150.0
Jehovah's Witnesses	250	577	130.8
Church of God (Cleveland, Tenn.)	170	195	114.7
Assemblies of God	509	390	76.6
Baptist General Conference	72	46	63.9
Seventh Day Adventists	318	192	60.4
Church of Jesus Christ of Latter Day Saints	1,487	905	60.1
Salvation Army	254	127	50.0
Church of the Nazarene	308	141	45.8
Southern Baptist Convention	9,732	3,186	32.7
Church of God (Anderson, Ind.)	142	32	22.6
U.S. Population	180,700	34,400	19.0
Roman Catholic Church	42,105	7,221	17.1
Lutheran Church–Missouri Synod	2,391	366	15.3
Wisconsin Evangelical Lutheran Church	348	47	13.5
Reorganized Church of Jesus Christ of Latter Day Saints	155	31	2.0
American Lutheran Church	2,242	160	7.1
American Baptist Church in the U.S.A.	1,521	73	4.8
Reformed Church in America	355	−4	−1.1
Lutheran Church in America	3,053	−78	−2.6
Presbyterian Church in the U.S.	903	−25	−2.8
United Methodist Church	10,641	−780	−7.3
Episcopal Church	3,269	−387	−11.8
United Church of Christ	2,241	−440	−19.6
United Presbyterian Church in the U.S.A.	3,259	−652	−20.0
Christian Church (Disciples of Christ)	1,801	−552	−29.0

SOURCE: Compiled from *Yearbook of American and Canadian Churches, 1978* (Nashville, Abingdon Press, 1978). (It should be noted that church membership statistics are not always comparable, due to different methods of counting "members," and are often given in round numbers, suggesting a certain amount of guesswork.)

in "religiosity" combined with a decline in traditional religious beliefs.[6] While interest in religion is high, it is taking some unorthodox directions.

CHANGING DIRECTIONS OF RELIGIOUS ACTION

THE CHARISMATIC MOVEMENT   A number of varieties of exotic and ecstatic religious experience are returning to favor. These include a renewed emphasis upon prayer and dramatic conversion experiences, interest in spiritualism, and revival of Pentecostalism, which is estimated to include at least one million Americans, including 400,000 Catholics.[7] Pentecostalism combines religious fundamentalism,[8] faith healing, and *glossalalia,* or "speaking in tongues." Pentecostals believe that a convert is "baptised with the Holy Spirit," an experience in which one enters a trancelike state and speaks or chants a stream of unintelligible syllables that resemble no known language. Although it is disdained as hysterical babbling by critics, those who have had the experience of "speaking in tongues" report it as deeply moving and spiritually fulfilling. Along with this "baptism with the Holy Spirit," Pentecostals believe that one may be given the capacity to direct God's healing power upon the sick who have faith that God will heal them.

The Pentecostal churches (Church of God, Assembly of God, Pentecostal Holiness Church, and several others) have traditionally been viewed with condescension by the mainline churches, whose members tended to equate faith healing and glossalalia with ignorance and gullibility. Pentecostals were mainly the less prosperous and poorly educated, occupying a low rung on the ladder of American denominationalism. Today the Pentecostal churches are among the most rapidly growing churches, and many converts to Pentacostal beliefs retain their existing church memberships and are usually known as "charismatics." Studies of the new Catholic charismatics show them typically to be college students or well-educated adults of middle- or upper-class status and liberal social attitudes.[9] Charismatics within mainline Protestant churches have been less carefully studied but appear to be similar in social characteristics. A recent comparison of a charismatic congregation with a mainline congregation (similar in economic and demographic characteristics) found that the charismatic congregation had stronger feelings of commitment and community and a higher sense of meaning, belonging, and cohesion.[10] Students of the charismatic movement generally interpret it as evidence of discontent with the trend toward secularism in modern society,[11] and as a search for security in a period of disquieting social change.[12]

RELIGIOUS YOUTH COMMUNES   A number of youth religious groups claim total commitment from their members, such as the Children of God, Hare Krishna, and the Unification Church of Sun Myung Moon. The flowering of youthful idealism and passion for solving social problems in the 1960s was replaced by the disillusionment of the 1970s. The New Left collapsed, campus activism withered, and student concerns shifted inward, away from society and toward the self.

The *Jesus People* include a wide variety of groups and organizations, from the relatively formal Campus Crusade for Christ to the Children of God communes. All proclaim fundamentalism and evangelism, rejecting materialism, drugs, and nonmarital sex. Members are almost entirely young, white, and middle- or upper-class in origin. Many have experienced and wearied of the drugs, sex, and mindless vacuity of the counterculture.

Although there is some variation among groups, Jesus People tend to be Pentecostal and apocalyptic (expecting an early return of Christ and the end of the present world), and to show considerable interest in occultism.[13] Lifestyles range from neatly groomed to barefoot, but cleanliness and orderliness are expected. Not all of the Jesus People opt for total commitment; some hold jobs or attend school while devoting all their spare time to worship sessions and evangelism. Others withdraw entirely into one of the religious communes operated by the Children of God or by one of its competitors. Many of these are self-supporting farm communes where members work hard and seek to live simply, as God might wish. Their "highs" come from Jesus and "Jesus rock" instead of drugs and "hard rock," and they join in the emotional ecstasy of prayer and shared religious experience, of coming forward to be "saved," and of awaiting the apocalypse.[14]

The religious communes provide a "waystation to respectability" for young people who have been alienated from the dominant culture.[15] Now that the counterculture is less prevalent, there will be fewer fugitives from the counterculture for the Children of God to recruit, but there will always be confused, discontented, rootless youths seeking the security of faith and fellowship.

The *Unification Church* of a Korean guru, the Rev. Sun Myung Moon, is either an inspiring religious movement or a highly profitable racket, according to whose evaluation is accepted. As of 1976 the church claimed 30,000 American followers and 5,000 totally committed members who devoted all their time to the movement. They operated 120 communal recruitment and fund-raising centers and sent recruiting teams to 150 college campuses.[16] Their ideology is a mixture of Pentecostal Christianity, anti-communism, Eastern mysticism, and pop psychology. Potential recruits progress through an introductory lecture, then a weekend retreat, then a week-long session of hard-sell evangelism, combining hearty fellowship with nonstop lectures based upon Moon's Divine Principle.[17] Much of this resembles brainwashing, with limited sleep, no opportunity for solitary reflection, and a constant barrage of indoctrination. Totally committed members withdraw completely from school, job, family, and friends and devote themselves to full-time recruiting and fund-raising.

A gathering of Rev. Sun Myung Moon and his devotees at Yankee Stadium in New York.
(Bettye Lane, Photo Researchers, Inc.)

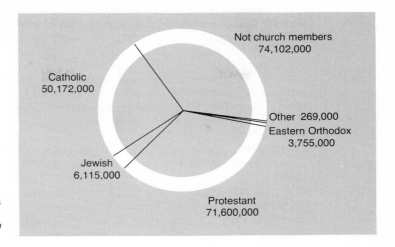

Figure 8–3
Membership in major religious faiths
in the United States, 1978.
Source: *Yearbook of American and Canadian Churches*, 1978, p. 228.

Parents often suffer bitterly, feeling that their child has been stolen from them. A brisk business (of doubtful legality) has developed in the kidnapping back and deprogramming of Children of God communards, "Moonies," and other total-commitment followers.[18] No data are available on the proportion of deprogrammed youths who return to their cult. Despite the hard-sell evangelism, their conversion is voluntary. To young people fearful of adult responsibility, the total-commitment cults offer a perpetual childhood; for lonely drifters there is warmth and companionship; for those who fear competition or failure, there is group cooperation and support; for the aimless and confused, there is certainty and purpose; to those dissatisfied with society, there is a sanctified alternative. Moon's movement—or its equivalent—will be around for a long time.

The *Hare Krishna* movement is another total-commitment movement, whose members shave their heads, wear saffron robes, and play Eastern musical instruments. They devote themselves to a life of ascetic self-denial and continuous fund-raising.[19] Maharaj Ji's *Divine Light Mission* and dozens of other lesser-known cults compete for converts.[20] Studies have shown that most converts have unhappily married parents with whom they had an unsatisfactory relationship and were basically unhappy themselves, with a history of depression, anxiety, poor heterosexual relationships, and a lack of definite goals or of success in meeting them.[21] Such people have genuine problems, and a total-commitment religious movement can bring purpose and fulfillment into their aimless, unhappy existence. Most cults demand a total submission to authority and an unquestioning acceptance of cultist "answers." Some find this intolerable and soon leave; others find it comforting. A recent study of cult members concluded that their membership arose from a "strong ideological hunger" and from a need for a "safe, structured, predictable environment which would permit a relatively conflict-free emotional affiliation with others."[22] The total-commitment movements have been criticized for their authoritarianism, anti-intellectualism, primitive theology, and neglect of responsible political action. In some cases (notably that

201

of Moon) they are accused of turning religion into a profitable racket.[23] The Hare Krishna solicitors have often roused antipathy and sometimes legal action by their fund-raising efforts.[24] This is no surprise. Most new religious movements arouse opposition and accusations of brainwashing and exploitation of members. Such charges are sometimes true, and sometimes they are unjustified.

Yet cults can be dangerous. Total submission to the authority of a charismatic leader can lead to a disaster, as it did for the nearly 1,000 followers of the Rev. Jim Jones who committed suicide (or were murdered) at his command.[25] Submission to authority has both its comforts and its dangers.

THE HUMAN-POTENTIAL MOVEMENT   Attempts at self-improvement by following a charismatic leader's formula are not new. Three-quarters of a century ago, Émile Coué traveled the world attracting a large following, whom he urged to repeat endlessly the phrase, "Every day, and in every way, I am becoming better and better." A continuous procession of self-help groups and cults have followed, ranging from the sedate speech class programs of Dale Carnegie to the pop psychology of mind control and transcendental meditation to the brutal emotional assaults of Erhard Seminar Training (est) sessions.[26] While none of these proclaims itself a religion, many are addressed to the same needs religion seeks to meet. Many are spin-offs from the encounter-group–based Esalen Institute in Big Sur, California. Most combine pop psy-

The Jonestown massacre in Guyana tragically demonstrated the dangers inherent in fanatic religious cultism.
(United Press International)

chology, rap sessions or encounter groups, and some procedure or formula for increasing feelings of self-worth, detachment from society's ills and others' troubles, and freedom from anxiety and fear.

Each of the human-potential programs "works" for some people, who undoubtedly feel better and work more effectively because of them (at least for a while; no long-term follow-up studies have yet appeared). Obviously, one will feel refreshed and relaxed after a session of closing one's eyes, relaxing one's body, and chanting one's mantra (secret word) to keep the mind unoccupied, as transcendental meditation instructs. It is very possible, however, that a good nap would do the same,[27] and that *any* word repeated over and over (Coca-Cola, Coca-Cola) would empty the mind as well as reciting one's mantra.[28] But while some people are helped, others are harmed. One carefully controlled study of encounter groups concluded that roughly one-third of the participants are damaged, one-third are helped, and one-third are unchanged.[29] Some sociologists criticize such groups for being self-centered and unconcerned with society.[30] Yet human-potential groups will continue to appear, each to flourish for a time until it is crowded aside by a newer fad. Not only are they highly profitable to their sponsors[31] but there is a large market for the kind of self-fulfillment they promise. If one fails, there is always another to try.

MYSTICISM   Nearly every variety of mysticism is gaining interested followers. *Eastern mysticism*—Zen, yoga, orthodox Buddhism, a dozen varieties of pseudo-Buddhism, and many other variants of Eastern religions—are exciting widespread interest, especially among college students. Most of these belief systems reject Western materialism and seek the attainment of peace through meditation and emotional detachment from the problems of the world.[32] *Occult mysticism* of nearly every kind has a growing audience, from the scientifically respectable explorations of extrasensory perception by the parapsychologists; through astrology, spiritualism, ouija, and divination; to witchcraft, sorcery, demonology, satanism, and exorcism. Most of these preoccupations, which educated persons only a few years ago were about to consign to the dustbin of outmoded superstitions, are popular today among solid "establishment types," not just among the nuts and kooks. Until recently, movies dealing with witchcraft, demonology, and other occult phenomena always ended with a rational explanation for the apparent supernaturalism; today many movies treat the occult as fact. Astrology is estimated to have 40 million American followers and 10 million firm believers,[33] even though every controlled experiment known has shown astrology to have no analytic or predictive value.[34]

Some scholars see the rising belief in occultism as simply one aspect of a counterculture that rejects scientific rationalism.[35] But while the counterculture has been losing steam in recent years, occultism has continued to spread, thus denying the countercultural theory. A *marginality theory* is better supported by empirical evidence. Several studies have shown that belief in astrology and other occult belief systems tends to be strongest among those who are marginal and powerless, such as the uneducated, blacks, women, and the unmarried;[36] among persons with a personal history of eccentricity and deviation;[37] and among persons who feel alienated from the conventional belief systems and who "repudiate rational cognition for an intuitive visionary gnosis."[38]

The various religious developments discussed above overlap and intertwine, with a single person or group sometimes manifesting several of them at once. They are not unrelated accidents, but movements with some common directions—away from liberal, rationalist, intellectual theology and toward emotional, nonrational, and even anti-intellectual theology; away from institutionalized leadership and toward charismatic leadership; away from denominationalism and toward noninstitutionalized religion; away from sedate, programmed, ritualized religious worship and toward spontaneous ecstatic religious experience; away from worldly concerns and toward spiritual and mystical concerns; away from concern for the state of the society and toward a self-centered preoccupation with personal spiritual and emotional experience.

What has produced these unanticipated changes? Some observers see them as a romanticized attempt to escape into a simpler and happier past. Disillusioned with modern Western civilization and with the apparent inability of the established churches to control the heedless, ruthless course of social change, people may be attempting to recapture an imagined simpler society—one that, in fact, never existed.[39] One student of modern witchcraft and paganism attributes it to "a yearning to get back to a time when people seemed more in control of their own lives, and societies . . . had a definite cultural pattern."[40]

Others see the current developments as a reaction against impersonalized, bureaucratic, ritualized religion. Efforts to replace the "artificiality" and "empty formalism" of established churches with a return to a simpler, more spontaneously emotional, and presumably more "pure" faith have been common throughout Christian history. Theologians call this effort "repristination."

A third interpretation views current religious developments as the result of disillusionment with the entire liberal society, which includes the mainline churches.[41] Stark and Bainbridge have shown that where traditional organized churches are strong (as in Utah), cults find few followers, but where traditional churches are weak and their memberships low (as in Washington or California), cults flourish.[42] Felicitas Goodman has noted, "In societies under stress, there is a strong tendency for new cults to arise.[43] Chapter 20 shows how Americans have lost confidence in established institutions and in all kinds of authority and leadership. Although the American people have greater confidence in the churches than in any other institution, confidence has wavered. Table 8–2 shows how belief in the influence of the church reached a low point about 1970 and has only partly recovered. Liberal society has failed to solve social problems; liberal religion has failed to stop wars, racism, and exploitation; neither science nor liberal religion has given clear, simple, satisfying answers to confusing and complicated questions. Fundamentalist religion provides simple, positive answers that liberals view as naive, but that many others find satisfying. Mystical and exotic cults provide an escape from a puzzling world into a satisfying inner world of private knowledge, pleasant dreams, and ecstatic emotional experience. Each of the current developments meets some needs that scientific rationalism, liberal religion, and liberal society have been unable to meet. It is too early to know

TABLE 8–2   Religion: Gaining or Losing Influence in the United States?

Year	Gaining influence	Losing influence
1957	69	14
1962	45	31
1965	33	45
1967	23	57
1968	18	67
1969	14	70
1970	14	75
1974	31	56
1975	39	51
1976	44	45

SOURCE: National Gallup Polls, reported in *Yearbook of American and Canadian Churches*, 1978, p. 257. (Percentages do not add up to 100, because "the same" and "no opinion" responses are not included.)

whether the current developments are passing fads or the beginnings of a major religious reformation.[44]

Religious Problems in American Life

The American people believe in religious liberty. As shown in table 8–3, Gallup Polls over the past quarter-century show that religious tolerance has grown dramatically in America. Yet there are several points on which religious differences or actions have become issues of sharp public controversy.

RELIGION IN THE PUBLIC SCHOOLS

The United States Constitution forbids the state from taking any action toward "the establishment of religion," or from interfering in "the free exercise thereof." The doctrine of separation of church and state—not actually stated in the Constitution—has been interpreted to mean that tax funds should not be used for the support of religious bodies or sectarian religious education. In a country of multiple religious bodies, each desiring that *its* beliefs be taught, the public schools have generally sought to avoid giving offense by refraining entirely from teaching sectarian religious doctrines.

The 1950s saw a determined and well-organized effort to get the public schools to cooperate in the teaching of religion. This was accompanied by an equally determined effort to prevent sectarian invasions of the public schools. The courts have held that any use of public funds or public school facilities for sectarian religious instruction is unconstitutional, but forms of cooperation involving no use of public funds or facilities are permissible. Under the released time plan, children may be released during school hours to receive religious instruction away from the school premises. Supporters

TABLE 8–3 Growing Religious Tolerance in the United States, 1952–79

Question: Have you or your family ever had any unpleasant experiences that might have made you dislike:

Target group:	Protestants			Catholics			Jews		
Respondent group: (percent replying "yes")	1952	1965	1979	1952	1965	1979	1952	1965	1979
Protestants				9	7	2	8	5	2
Catholics	4	4	1				6	5	2

Question: Do you think Catholics/Protestants/Jews are trying to get too much power in the United States, or not?

Respondent group: (percent replying "yes")									
Protestants				41	30	11	35	14	12
Catholics	8	5	6				33	12	13

SOURCE: Adapted from data in *Gallup Opinion Index*, # 169, Aug. 1979, pp. 30–31. (Jews are not reported as a respondent group because of the smallness of the Jewish sample.) Interpretation: In 1952, 9 percent of the Protestant informants reported unpleasant experiences with Catholics; this dropped to 7 percent in 1965 and 2 percent in 1972. (This should cue you as to how to interpret the rest of the table.)

are convinced that the benefits of such religious training far outweigh any possible inconveniences or objections. Opposition comes partly from those who doubt that such religious training is as effective as claimed. Britain since 1944 has required that in all tax-supported free schools religious instruction be given to all pupils whose parents do not object. There is no convincing evidence to show that this has made the British people any more moral or religious,[45] a point that opponents to such instruction eagerly cite. Opposition also comes from school personnel, who object to the disruption of the school schedule. To release part of the children while retaining the rest creates a dilemma for the school. If, for those children who do not elect to take the religious training, the school arranges an interesting activity, then it draws children away from the religious program; if the school does not plan an interesting activity for those remaining, a discipline problem develops. Following indifferent success, interest in released time programs waned in the 1960s.

There is no constitutional objection, however, to teaching *about* religion in public schools.[46] Despite the objections of those who argue that religion cannot be taught objectively, the number of such courses has increased rapidly.[47]

A storm of controversy arose when the Supreme Court ruled in 1962 and 1963 that public schools may not require group prayers or Bible reading. The only prayers legally permissible in public school are those a student says to himself. Many political leaders and some church leaders thundered that it was atheistic and immoral to "throw God out of our schools." A proposed constitutional amendment to legalize school prayers very nearly passed by the required two-thirds majority in the House of Representatives,

Children during recess at St. Gregory's Parochial School, New York City.
(Hugh Roger, Monkmeyer)

but interest has somewhat subsided. The proposal received some support from Catholic leaders, but most Protestant leaders supported the court's decision.[48] They argued that if the state can prescribe prayers and Bible reading in the public schools, it can also require other religious devotionals and thus impair freedom of religion.[49] It is clear that the conduct of religious devotionals in the public schools creates grave problems. If school prayers are to be said, who is to compose them? If the Bible is read, which Bible— Protestant or Catholic? How can *any* religious devotionals have any real content without offending some groups and taxing some citizens for the support of views they do not share? It has been established that children of minority faiths sometimes suffer actual emotional damage from being surrounded by a conflicting religious atmosphere.[50] There is, however, a distinction between the teaching of religious dogma and the teaching of religion as a discipline, the latter being burdened with fewer church–state dilemmas. The National Council on Religion and Public Education has promoted the teaching of religion "as a constitutionally acceptable and educationally appropriate part of secular public education."[51] It is uncertain, however, whether this idea will meet the objections of critics.

"PAROCHAID"—TAX SUPPORT FOR PRIVATE SCHOOLS?

The Catholic Church is educating as many of its children as possible in Catholic schools, which are controlled and financed by the church. Enrollment in Catholic schools grew steadily until 1965, with a peak enrollment of 5,560,000 pupils. By 1977 this had fallen to 3,300,000. Yet the effort to maintain parochial schools is a constant struggle. In an earlier period, when most students quit school early, when equipment was limited, when teachers needed little training and the supply of nuns was more adequate, the costs of a parochial school system were manageable. When the school term lengthened, as students prolonged their education, as standards of equipment and teacher training were raised, and as more lay teachers became necessary, the burden of maintaining parochial schools rose to a point that now appears unsupportable. Today the Catholics, with strong support from the Reformed church and some from Lutherans,[52] are insistently demanding tax support. They point out that their taxes support public schools so that they are doubly taxed, and that the parochial schools relieve the ordinary taxpayer of much expense. They ask for tax assistance in various forms: public support for school bus transportation and auxiliary services such as special education, literary services, and free textbooks; and a share for their schools in tax support through any of several devices, such as refunding of public school taxes to parents, and state aid grants directly to students for use in schools of their choice.[53]

Whether or not tax aid for parochial schools is constitutional has been sharply debated. A variety of services given directly *to the child,* such as bus transportation, health services, and special education, have generally been held constitutional. But a number of forms of direct or indirect tax subsidy *to the schools,* such as state payments to parents of parochial school children, or state grants to pay parochial school teachers' salaries, have been held unconstitutional by the courts.[54] The *constitutionality* of parochial school aid, however, is not the central issue. If tax aid is *desirable,* there are constitutional ways of accomplishing it;[55] or, if necessary, the Constitution can be amended.

Pressure for tax support seems to be increasing, and several state governors have publicly endorsed "parochaid." Yet opposition remains intense, with one national journal, *Church and State,* concentrating on determined opposition to any form of tax support for parochial schools.[56]

THE CONTROVERSY OVER CHURCH TAXATION

Properties owned by churches and charitable foundations are generally exempt from property taxes, and income earned by these properties and securities is exempt from income taxes. Several different estimates place the wealth of American churches at $80 to $150 billion, with the Catholic Church holding about half the total.[57] A decade-old estimate placed the value of tax exemption at $8 billion a year,[58] and today it is probably twice as great. But most of this "great wealth" is in the form of church buildings, schools, hospitals, cemeteries, and other properties that consume income rather than produce it. As this is written, the Vatican is facing serious financial problems and plans staff reductions.[59]

There is very little criticism of tax exemption for properties used for religious, educational, or charitable purposes. But some churches have substantial investments in income-producing properties and businesses. It is these *unrelated* businesses and properties whose tax exemption is under attack—office buildings, apartment houses, factories, etc.[60] Defenders of tax exemption believe that the churches put this income to worthy uses, whose benefits to the society justify the tax exemption. Critics level three criticisms: (1) tax exemption for the business properties and income of churches creates unfair competition with private, tax-paying business; (2) this exemption forces taxpayers to pay higher taxes to subsidize church operations; (3) such tax exemption, in time, may make churches so wealthy that their vested interests corrupt their "message," while their wealth invites political attack and eventual state confiscation (a situation that has developed several times in history).

A possible resolution of the issue is proposed by the Guild of St. Ives, a group of New York Episcopal lawyers and clergy. They propose that (1) properties used for religious purposes remain tax exempt; (2) properties used for charitable or educational purposes pay no more nor less in taxes than similar properties owned by similar organizations (such as public schools); (3) unrelated properties and businesses owned by churches pay all normal taxes.[61]

As with most issues, a value conflict is central to the controversy: Does society benefit from the churches' use of tax-exempt business income sufficiently to outweigh the alleged "injustices" of such tax exemption?

CHURCHES AS RACKETS

American churches have great freedom to solicit tax-free dollars and use them for practically any purpose. Churches are not required to report their use of funds to anyone (although most legitimate churches make detailed reports to their membership). Our government avoids the legal quicksand of even attempting to define a "church"; any person or group claiming to be a church is one. This opens the door to many rackets. One can escape property taxes on one's home by declaring it a "church," although to be on the safe side, some sort of "services" should be held regularly (at any hour,

Katherine Khulman, faith healer and TV preacher.
(Steve Kagan, Photo Researchers, Inc.)

with any content, and any number—or no number—of worshippers). The Universal Life Church in California openly invites people to become "ministers" in order to gain discounts and tax exemptions and currently ordains about one thousand "ministers" a week at $5.00 each.[62] Your author's little dog, Pepi (registration name, Wotan Von Alberich), is an ordained minister in the Universal Life Church.

Some radio and television preachers receive millions a year in donations, much of it in "offerings" in return for some "free" trinket, prayer towel, or other item of what is sometimes called "Jesus Junk."[63] Some of these successful media ministers live modestly and use these millions for religious purposes. Some others live like millionaires and have amassed fortunes in real estate, whose ownership may be uncertain.[64] Just where legitimate fund-raising and spending turns into personal aggrandizement and profiteering is not easy to define. Was it legitimate for Boy's Town to continue national solicitation of funds after it had built up a net worth of over $200 million with an income from investments which easily covered all its operating expenses?[65]

The Tax Reform Act of 1969 requires most tax-exempt organizations to file annual reports of their income and expenditures, but churches are exempt. An Internal Revenue Service suggestion that *church-related* organizations be asked to file reports on their tax-free expenditures has been fiercely opposed by churches.[66] No official exposure of financial profiteering by religious racketeers is practical or perhaps even constitutional. There is no real protection other than the skepticism of the donors, and that is a poor defense indeed.

CONFLICTING MORAL PRECEPTS

On many items of doctrine and moral precept, different churches are in sharp disagreement. For example, the Catholic Church forbids abortion for any reason whatsoever, forbids all "artificial" means of birth control, and does not recognize divorce. Gambling and alcoholic beverages are bitterly condemned by some Protestant churches, while the Catholic Church and some of the other Protestant churches do not view them as intrinsically wrong.

Religious differences can be tolerated as long as only the private behavior of individuals is concerned, but when religious differences create disagreements over law or public policy, toleration becomes an ineffective form of accommodation.

On such questions as divorce, contraception, and abortion, Catholic efforts to impose their views on non-Catholics by law have been bitterly resented. The Catholic justification rests upon the belief that these practices are contrary to *natural law,* and that this law is binding on all people, whether Catholic or not. Natural law is not something invented by Catholics; it is (according to Catholics and some other theologians) part of God's natural order of the universe, like the law of gravity. If one violates natural law, for instance by jumping from the rooftop, one will suffer. The basic issue, therefore, is not whether divorce or birth control are approved by the majority, but whether they are contrary to natural law. This question cannot be answered *scientifically,* since it is not a scientific question. No settlement or satisfactory compromise is possible unless one side alters its beliefs.

Protestants become indignant at Catholic efforts to impose Catholic mores on non-Catholics by force of law, yet Protestants have frequently imposed religious bans themselves. Numerous Sunday "blue laws," expressing puritanical notions of Sunday behavior, and the Eighteenth Amendment (Prohibition) were Protestant efforts to impose Protestant mores upon Catholics and others, who viewed drinking as a matter for private moderation rather than legal restraint. Protestant churches today generally support laws that forbid all forms of gambling, while the Catholic Church believes that gambling is not wrong in itself, but becomes wrong only when excessive or otherwise abused.[67] In a number of states, the question of legalizing charity bingo and certain other games of chance has provoked bitter political controversy.[68] Since differences in mores can rarely be resolved by discussion or compromise, this issue sometimes provokes extreme bitterness.

The moral disputes that divide American churches appear to be diminishing. Official Catholic opposition to legalized abortion obscures the fact that nearly as many Catholics as Protestants believe that abortions should be available to those who want them—64 percent of the Catholics and 69 percent of the Protestants[69]—while 76 percent of American Catholics would have (or approve their wives having) an abortion if the woman's health were threatened.[70] Protestants are accepting the Catholic views on gambling and alcohol; while Catholics are coming to share the dominant Protestant views on divorce, birth control, and abortion. Although the abortion issue remains particularly divisive and acrimonious,[71] the general trend is toward acceptance and consensus. In fact, the differences between Catholics and Protestants in the United States have been eroding at a rate which leads some Catholic theologians to speculate upon whether a distinctive Catholic subculture still exists.[72]

SOCIAL ACTIVISM AND THE CHURCHES

The roots of Christianity extend far back into the history of an agricultural people living in small groups within which all relations were primary group relations. Most of the Bible is written in the language of the primary group association of person with person. Little is said about impersonal group relations of the sort rare in a primitive agricultural society but important in an urban industrial society. A half-century or more ago it became increasingly apparent that many people who were moral and generous in their relations with other individuals were thoroughly ruthless and amoral in dealing with impersonal groups. A number of clerics concluded that the teachings of the Bible and the church must be reinterpreted in the language of impersonal, secondary group relations to fit the needs of modern society. This would mean that, in addition to such personal sins as murder, theft, greed, and lust, the church must also define and condemn such social sins as warfare, political oppression, economic exploitation, and racial injustice. This religious emphasis upon people's inhumanity to each other came to be called the "social gospel."[73]

Another root of the social gospel is the insights of social science. Nineteenth-century folklore held that each person consciously and freely chooses to be good or evil, Christian or pagan, lazy or ambitious, honest or deceitful. Poor people were poor because they were lazy, and the evil persons were evil because they chose to be evil. Social scientists began to cast doubt on these assumptions, showing how people may be lazy and unmotivated because they have experienced only poverty and lack of ambition in their environment, and how the "choice" between good and evil is often a response to the balance of environmental influences surrounding them.

While the traditional approach was to seek converts and assume that a better society would eventually follow, the social gospel seeks to improve the institutions and practices of society directly, in the belief that they are obstacles to Christian life. In 1910 the social gospel included support of labor's right to organize and bargain collectively, and opposition to the twelve-hour day and the seven-day week. Today the social gospel calls, for example, for opposition to war; for a determined attack on poverty, hunger, and inner-city problems; and for equal rights for minorities. The exact content of the social gospel changes along with changing social needs and issues.

The social gospel has been hotly attacked ever since its appearance. Fundamentalists charged that reforming society was no proper business of the church and betrayed the church's real purpose of saving souls. Vested interests sought to forestall clerical criticism by urging that the church confine itself to "spiritual" matters and stay out of "politics." Still others feared that the church would be torn with dissension if it became involved in social controversies. The social gospel debate accompanied the fundamentalist–modernist battle, with much the same participants and outcome. Those who are theologically liberal tend to be liberal and reformist in their social attitudes, while religious conservatives tend to be conservative in social and political attitudes.[74] The National Council of the Churches of Christ in America tends to promote the social gospel, while the much smaller American Council of Christian Churches strongly opposes the social gospel and lends tacit support to the economic status quo. Since these positions are crystallized, there is not much debate today about the social gospel within any denomination.

It is uncertain just how effectively the liberal churches are applying the social gospel approach. In some historic instances they may have turned the tide; for example, organized church efforts probably were in large part responsible for ending the twelve-hour day, seven-day week in the steel industry in 1923.[75] Most of the other social reforms of the twentieth century have been at least accompanied by some degree of church support. Yet many official resolutions on social issues produce little activity in the local congregations.[76] Protestant clergy are generally more liberal and activist than their membership, and often the result of clerical activism has been to replace the minister rather than to change the attitudes of the congregation.[77] In a number of South American countries, where segments of the Roman Catholic clergy have supported social reform, they have faced police repression, expulsion, and even torture and imprisonment.[78] It is not always safe and easy for the clergy to support social reform.

The social gospel has been reformist rather than revolutionary; it sought to make the capitalist system serve humane ends, not to overthrow it. By contrast, the radical activism of the 1960s sent shock waves of revolutionary protest through the churches. Radical theology arose in the belief that religion should be a revolutionary force in society, not a conservative force.[79] Current social activism takes several directions. One merely calls for an intensified determination to purify and civilize the liberal capitalist society. This position, for example, criticizes church investments in the securities of corporations that profit from the war system, or that do business in South Africa (thus profiting from racism). Every reformist proposal, however, arouses debate over its practicality and effectiveness. For example, it is not clear whether American corporations in South Africa are supporting or undermining the racist policies of the Union of South Africa. It is much easier to sound the clarion call for "Christian social action" or to organize a righteous demonstration than it is to know and agree on just what measures constitute effective Christian social action. The present trend among mainline churches is away from social activism and toward a somewhat more traditional emphasis upon personal evangelism.[80] Meanwhile, social activism is growing among some segments of the evangelical churches.[81]

Among the more radical activists, there is widespread support for a "liberation theology," a term which usually translates as "socialist revolution." Support for "liberation theology" is especially strong among Third World church leaders.[82]

Whether a socialist revolution is desirable is, needless to say, a major debate in itself. Whether religious radicalism would promote or retard the arrival of a more humane society can be debated. Is Christian radicalism likely to assist in promoting a radical restructuring of capitalist society? Or is it simply an exercise in radical chic that provides opportunities for heroic posturing without actually changing the social order? Could it even have a backlash effect and strengthen the status quo? The ultimate effects of radical theology cannot be predicted, but some liberal theologians fear that religious radicalism will prove to be counterproductive.[83]

The Social-Disorganization Approach

Although religious conflicts have never been absent in America, most have developed as a result of some change in the religious status quo—either the wave of immigration of a new religious group or the rise of a dissenting local group threatened the security of existing religious institutions. Insecurity breeds anxiety and distrust of the character and motives of one's rivals.

The religious problems presented here are not exceptions. Religious heterogeneity in America gives many opportunities for conflict, while the American tradition of religious liberty and tolerance has been relatively effective in containing these conflicts. With so many religious faiths, each claiming to know the absolute and exclusive truth, it is remarkable that conflict has been so limited.

Urbanization, industrialization, and secularization have had an impact on the church that it has not yet fully recognized. The Protestant churches are still largely rural institutions insecurely transplanted into an urban environment. The oft-lamented loss of influence of the churches, to the extent that it is a genuine loss, may be a result of the churches' relative isolation from many of the real problems of people in an urbanized, specialized, impersonal, secondary-group society.

The liberalizing and social action trends within American churches appear to have been accompanied by a loss of zealous commitment by church members. Whether, as some believe, the church as now constituted is doomed remains undecided. If so, *religion* will not disappear. Existing religious institutions may falter, but certain psychic needs remain, and if existing religious institutions do not meet them, new religious institutions will develop. This process is revealed in the present state of religious confusion.

In the most highly educated and most technologically and scientifically advanced nation on earth, religious mysticism and superstition are gaining in popularity. As faith in the traditional supernatural religions weakens, it is not replaced by scientific secularism, or by a stampede toward liberal, rational theology. Instead, astrology, Eastern mysticism, Pentecostalism, and a variety of mystic, occult, and pseudo-intellectual cults are flourishing, not only among the ignorant but also among the educated and presumably sophisticated. Many young people see the traditional church as one of the oppressive institutions that have prostituted technology and science to slaughter and dehumanization. The youth revolt is deeply religious, in its elevation of feeling above reason and of being above doing and in its faith that a better world will somehow emerge from its assault. Thus, the losses from one faith become the gains of another.

The Value-Conflict Approach

Religion deals with important values, and value conflicts often become religious conflicts. If all people held the same values, there would be fewer religious faiths and, therefore, fewer religious conflicts. When a religious group demands that the law and the policies of public agencies must impose its own moral judgments on the entire population, as both Catholic and Protestant churches have done in some cases, a social conflict is created. Conflicting moral judgments that divide the churches appear to be subsiding, although the current controversy over abortion promises to be conflict-producing until a new consensus is reached.

The age-old clash between spiritual and materialistic values lies at the root of the rejection of orthodox religion by many young people. Christianity originated in a rejection of Roman materialism (especially among those not privileged to share its pleasures), but any religious movement that spreads and grows must eventually come to terms with the persistent human desire to accumulate and enjoy worldly goods. Religious history is therefore dotted with cults and religious orders that rejected the prevailing materialism in favor of a simple, spartan existence (which seldom remained spartan very long). The current rash of antimaterialistic religious sentiment thus fits into a long historical tradition. Whether it will effect any more lasting changes than its predecessors remains to be seen.

Central to many recent religious developments has been the clash between two sets of incompatible values—one of them rational, scientific, intellectual, and pragmatic and the other emotional, existential, and mystical. Science and rational intellect have not ended war, racism, or oppression, so science and reason are rejected by some in favor of feeling, direct personal experience, and mystical insights. Perhaps the most exacerbating single element has been the bitter clash over the war ethic. Outraged by the seemingly endless persistence of a brutal war in Vietnam, which many Americans felt to have been clearly immoral from the outset, and outraged by the lack of forthright and unequivocal condemnation of this war by most religious leaders,[84] many young people viewed mainline religion as hopelessly compromised by hypocrisy. Many serious scholars consider the Vietnam War to have been the most disastrous experience the United States has endured since the Civil War because of its harmful effects on Americans' confidence in one another and in American institutions. Bitter religious conflicts are but one facet of the current crisis in American values and institutions. Eventually a new value consensus will emerge, but it is uncertain what form it will take.

The Personal-Deviation Approach

To what extent are deviant persons involved in religious problems? To a significant degree, in the opinion of most observers. Every minister has suffered with certain parishioners, who, with great professions of religious devotion and divine guidance, proceed to disrupt the church by stirring up trouble. Such persons are not usually hypocrites; they are simply neurotics who happen to be religious. For neurotics who belong to the church are still neurotics. They still imagine slights and insults; they define all disagreement as religious unbelief; they insist on having their own way, impugn the religious sincerity of any who block them, and finally leave to disrupt another congregation.

The number of people who are seriously mentally ill is vastly smaller than those who are in a state of neurotic adjustment. These persons are oriented to reality and are able to function in society fairly successfully, but their reactions to reality are considerably distorted by their unconscious fears, hostilities, insecurities, and unsatisfied longings. Such people are likely to be oversensitive, overcritical, jealous, aggressive, uncompromising, and very intense in their opinions and dislikes. Frequently they are prodigious workers, but their labor is often wasted because others find them so hard to work with for long. Religious activity is one of the many possible outlets for such people. Religion has certain advantages as an outlet, for the members of a religious body are required to welcome the newcomer, to refrain from sharp criticism, and to avoid ejecting even the troublesome members. Furthermore, neurotics may find through religion an effective rationalization for their motives. Where else can one sanctify selfish and petty impulses and raise them above reproach by attributing them to the will of God? The Protestant tradition of the "priesthood of the individual believer"[85] means that each person's prayerful conclusion as to the will of God must receive respectful recognition from others. Most ministers need no study of psychology to arrive at the suspicion that sometimes a member's "divine commands" arise not from the voice of God, but from the depths of the member's own unconscious compulsions and yearnings. Usually these people are intensely earnest and are deeply hurt at the suggestion that their inner motives are other than purely spiritual.

Every church is plagued with some of these maladjusted troublemakers. The Catholic Church, with its authoritarian structure, can control them with a minimum of confusion. The maladjusted troublemakers appear to be most numerous not among the major denominations but among the marginal sects and cults.[86] These groups are somewhat unconventional and therefore may attract the deviant person. They are bitterly and vocally critical of the major denominations, and provide neurotics with an approved outlet for their hostilities. Being relatively small congregations, they offer many opportunities for leadership. Aggressively evangelistic, they offer an approved opportunity to lose oneself in purposeful activity. There appears to be much more to attract and hold the interest of the deviant or the neurotic in these groups than in the sedate downtown churches. We do *not* suggest that most of the members of these bodies are neurotics, but merely that those persons who are neurotic may tend to gravitate to them.

Is the recent rash of cults, sects, and religious movements populated mainly by neurotics and maladjusted persons? There is very little solid research evidence on this question, and this evidence is mixed. Religious nonconformity is a form of deviation, and has always been so. Every mainline denomination is a descendant of a one-time group of religious deviants. Deviation from established religious norms is the way religions change and grow.

This chapter has concentrated on the Christian faith, since it is the dominant faith in the United States. The non-Christian minority faiths have not been discussed because of space limitations. Problems of Jew–Gentile relations are treated in the chapters on race relations, because these problems are not basically religious, but racial. Jews are not truly a racial group, but are socially defined and treated as one. The atheistic or Unitarian "Jew" is still defined as Jewish; his religion is irrelevant when he tries to join the country club. Anti-Semitism in the United States is to be understood within the context of race and ethnic group relations, not religious conflict.

Summary

Religious institutions in the United States are changing, perhaps more rapidly than ever before in our history. The mainline liberal churches are losing ground, while the religiously and politically conservative churches are gaining. While the established churches as a group seem to be losing in membership and attendance, *religion* itself is not dying, but attracting a growing interest from young people, among whom the Jesus Movement and other total-commitment movements are rapidly spreading. Pentecostalism and glossalalia are experiencing a revival, while astrology, Eastern mysticism, and occultism of nearly every sort have become respectable. All these changes seem to reflect some disillusionment with orthodox religion and with liberal society.

Several religious controversies have become public issues. The question of religious devotionals and instruction in the public schools seems to have been settled, but many people remain dissatisfied. Tax support for parochial schools remains a hot issue, with the eventual outcome uncertain as parochial schools continue to struggle for survival. The issue of tax exemption for church properties and income appears to be growing in public interest, with an apparently increasing sentiment favoring taxation of income-producing church properties and income from church investments and business enterprises. Our tradition of religious liberty makes it difficult to identify those who turn religion into a profitable racket, and impossible to restrain them without destroying religious liberty.

Churches differ sharply on many moral questions, and tolerance will not contain such disagreements when they include efforts to dictate law or public policy. Such moral disputes, however, seem to be subsiding as churches draw closer together in moral precepts. The social activism of the church is hotly debated, as some seek to use the church to maintain the established order, others to make the church an instrument of reform, and still others to make the church the spearpoint of revolution.

A social-disorganization approach sees all these developments and issues as products of social change. Urbanization, industrialization, and secularization have changed the world in which religion operates, and religion is changing as a consequence. The value-conflict approach notes that religious changes reflect value changes in the society, and that religious conflicts arise from value conflicts. Personal deviation is involved in many church difficulties. However the major current developments in religion cannot be attributed to individual maladjustments or deviations, but to more pervasive trends and forces.

Suggested Readings

BALSWICK, JACK, "The Jesus People Movement: A Generational Interpretation," *Journal of Social Issues,* 30 (1974), 23–42. A brief analysis of the Jesus Movement.

DOWNTON, JAMES V., JR., *Sacred Journey: The Conversion of Young Americans to Divine Light Mission* (New York: Columbia University Press, 1979). An analysis of how young people become converts to a religious cult.

ELLWOOD, ROBERT S., JR., *One Way: The Jesus Movement and Its Meaning* (Englewood Cliffs, N.J.: Prentice-Hall, 1973). A descriptive analysis of the Jesus Movement.

GREELEY, ANDREW M., *The Sociology of the Paranormal* (Beverly Hills, Ca.: Sage Publications, 1975). A brief examination of mystical experience.

HALL, JOHN R., "Apocalypse at Jonestown," *Society,* Sept. 1979, pp. 52–61; or, CAREY WINFREY, "Why 900 Died in Guyana," *New York Times Magazine,* 25 Feb. 1979, pp. 39ff. Two accounts of the mass suicide/murder of the People's Temple cultists at Jonestown in 1978.

HASTINGS, PHILIP K., and DEAN R. HOGE, "Changes in Religion among College Students, 1948–1974," *Journal for the Scientific Study of Religion,* 15 (Sept. 1975), 237–49. A survey of changing religious beliefs on the campus.

LITWAK, LEO, "Pay Attention, Turkeys!" *New York Times Magazine,* 2 May 1976, pp. 44ff. A critical appraisal of the Erhard Seminar Training program.

PATRICK, TED, with TOM DULACK, *Let Our Children Go* (New York: E. P. Dutton, 1975). A popularized account of the business of kidnapping and deprogramming members of total-commitment religious movements; also see Wayne Sage, "The War on the Cults," *Human Behavior,* Oct. 1976, pp. 40–49, for a brief appraisal of such deprogramming efforts.

QUINLEY, HAROLD E., *The Prophetic Clergy: Social Activism among Protestant Ministers* (New York: John Wiley, 1974); or HAROLD E. QUINLEY, "The Dilemma of an Activist Church: Protestant Religion in the Sixties and Seventies," *Journal for the Scientific Study of Religion,* 13 (Mar. 1974), 1–21. Examination of the difficulties of liberal clergy with conservative congregations.

RICE, BERKELEY, "The Pull of Sun Moon," *New York Times Magazine,* 30 May 1976, pp. 8ff.; and BERKELEY RICE, "Honor Thy Father Moon," *Psychology Today,* Jan. 1976, pp. 36–48. Popular description and analysis of Moon's Unification Church movement.

SCHUR, EDWIN F., *The Awareness Trap: Self-Absorption Instead of Social Change* (New York: Quadrangle/New York Times, 1976); or PETER MARTIN, "The New Narcissism," *Harper's,* 251 (Oct. 1975), 45–56. A critical look at the human potential movements and cults as escapes from social responsibility.

ZARETSKY, IRVING I., and MARK LENOE, eds., *Religious Movements in Contemporary America* (Princeton, N.J.: Princeton University Press, 1974). An authoritative and comprehensive collection of essays on recent religious movements, cults, and groups.

————, "Executive's Guide to Living with Stress," *Business Week,* 23 Aug. 1976, pp. 75–80. A brief survey advising business people of the possible benefits and dangers of TM, est, and other human-potential programs.

Footnotes

[1]Berkeley Rice, "The Pull of Sun Moon," *New York Times Magazine,* 30 May 1976, p. 8. Copyright © by the New York Times Company. Reprinted by permission.

[2]Dean Kelley, *Why Conservative Churches Are Growing: A Study in the Sociology of Religion* (New York: Harper & Row, 1972); Kenneth A. Briggs, "Shrinking Church Memberships Stirring Debate over Evangelism," *New York Times,* 11 Nov. 1979, sec. 12, pp. 1ff.

[3]Rodney Stark and Charles Y. Glock, *American Piety: The Nature of Religious Commitment* (Berkeley: University of California Press, 1968), p. 218; also Wade C. Roof, *Community and Commitment: Religious Plausibility in a Liberal Protestant Church* (New York: Elsevier, 1978).

[4]See Andrew M. Greeley, *Unsecular Man: The Persistence of Religion* (New York: Schocken Books, 1972), for a rebuttal of the secularization thesis.

[5]See "The Boom in Religion Studies," *Time,* 18 Oct. 1971, pp. 83ff.

[6]Mary M. Zaenglein, Arthur M. Vener, and Cyrus S. Stewart, "The Adolescent and His Religious Beliefs in Transition, 1970–1973," *Review of Religious Research,* 17 (Fall 1975), 51–60.

[7]*New York Times,* 16 Sept. 1975, p. 31.

[8]Fundamentalism stresses beliefs in the literal infallibility of the Bible, that Christ died for our sins, that we are naturally sinful and are saved by faith, and that heaven and hell are actual places of reward and punishment.

[9]Joseph H. Fichter, "Liberal and Conservative Catholic Pentecostals," *Social Compass,* 21 (1974), 303–10; Michael Harrison, "Sources of Recruitment to Catholic Pentecostalism," *Journal for the Scientific Study of Religion,* 13 (Mar. 1974), 49–64.

[10]Douglas B. McGraw, "Commitment and Religious Community: A Comparison of a Charismatic and a Mainline Congregation," *Journal for the Scientific Study of Religion,* 18 (June 1979), 146–63.

[11]Charles L. Harper, "Spirit-Filled Catholics: Some Biographical Comparisons," *Social Compass,* 21 (1974), 311–24.

[12]Meredith B. McQuire, "Toward a Sociological Interpretation of the 'Catholic Pentecostal' Movement," *Review of Religious Research,* 16 (Winter 1975), 94–104.

[13]Hiley H. Ward, *The Far-Out Saints of the Jesus Communes* (New York: Association Press, 1972), ch. 8.

[14]John R. Howard, *The Cutting Edge; Social Movements and Social Change in America* (Philadelphia: J. B. Lippincott, 1974), p. 208; Robert B. Simmonds, James T. Richardson, and Mary W. Harder, "Organizational Aspects of a Jesus Movement Community," *Social Compass,* 21 (1974), 269–81.

[15]Robert S. Ellwood, Jr., *One Way: The Jesus Movement and Its Meaning* (Englewood Cliffs, N.J.: Prentice-Hall, 1973), p. 12; Armand L. Mauss and Donald W. Peterson, "The 'Jesus Freaks' and the Return to Respectability," *Social Compass,* 21 (1974), 283–301.

[16]Berkeley Rice, "Honor Thy Father Moon," *Psychology Today,* Jan. 1976, pp. 36–48; also Irving Louis Horowitz, ed., *Science, Sin and Scholarship: The Politics of Reverend Moon and the Unification Church* (Cambridge: MIT Press, 1978). For a description of the Children of God, see Roy Wallis, *Salvation and Protest: Studies of Social and Religious Movements* (New York: St. Martin's Press, 1979).

[17]Sun Myung Moon, *Divine Principle* (Unification Church, 6527 Chillum Place, N.W., Washington, D.C., n.d.).

[18]See Ted Patrick with Tom Dulack, *Let Our Children Go* (New York: E. P. Dutton, 1976); Rice, "The Pull of Sun Moon;" also Carroll Stoner and JoAnne Parke, *All God's Children: Salvation or Slavery?* (Radnor, Pa.: Chilton Books, 1979; New York: Penguin Books, 1979).

[19]J. Stilson Judah, "The Hare Krishna Movement," in Irving I. Zaretsky and Mark Lenoe, eds., *Religious Movements in Contemporary America* (Princeton, N.J.: Princeton University Press, 1974), pp. 244–54.

[20]James V. Downton, *Sacred Journeys: The Conversion of Young Americans to the Divine Light Mission* (New York: Columbia University Press, 1979).

[21]Alexander Deutsch, "Observations on a Sidewalk Ashram," *Archives of General Psychiatry,* 321 (Feb. 1975), 166–74.

[22]J. Thomas Ungerleider and David K. Wellisch, "Coercive Persuasion (Brainwashing): Religious Cults and Deprogramming," *American Journal of Psychiatry,* 136 (Mar. 1979), 279–82.

[23]J. R. Manson, "Taxing the Cults," *Human Behavior,* Feb. 1979, p. 4.

[24]See "Lawsuit Aimed at Airport Soliciting," *Aviation World,* Feb. 1979, p. 25.

[25]See *Current,* Jan. 1979, pp. 7–10, for analyses of the Jonestown suicide-massacre; also Rose Laub Coser and Lewis Coser, "Jonestown as a Perverse

Utopia," *Dissent,* 26 (Spring 1979), 158–62.

[26]Joel Greenberg, "EST," *Science News,* 113 (14 Jan. 1978), 27.

[27]See *Science News,* 109 (24 Jan. 1976), p. 53; John W. White, "What's Behind TM?" *Human Behavior,* Oct. 1976, pp. 70–71.

[28]See "The TM Craze: Forty Minutes to Bliss," *Time,* 13 Oct. 1975, pp. 71–74; also, reviews of several books on TM in *Psychology Today,* Nov. 1975, pp. 90–91.

[29]Morton A. Lieberman et al., *Encounter Groups: First Facts* (New York: Basic Books, 1973).

[30]Edwin F. Schur, *The Awareness Trap: Self-Absorption Instead of Social Change* (New York: Quadrangle/New York Times Book Co., 1976). See also Peter Marin, "The New Narcissism," *Harper's,* 251 (Oct. 1975), 45–56.

[31]As of 1976, no fewer than 75,000 persons had paid $250 each for Erhard Seminar Training, with a gross income of $1 million a month anticipated. See Leo Litwak, "Pay Attention, Turkeys," *New York Times Magazine,* 2 May 1976, pp. 44ff.

[32]Jacob Needleman, *The New Religions* (Garden City, N.Y.: Doubleday, 1970); Christmas Humphreys, *The Way of Action: A Working Philosophy for Western Life* (Sante Fe, N.M.: William Gannon, 1971); Bikku Buddhadasa, *Toward the Truth* (Philadelphia: Westminster Press, 1971); Andrew M. Greeley, *The Sociology of the Paranormal* (Beverly Hills, Ca.: Sage Publications, 1975).

[33]Robert Wuthnow, "Astrology and Marginality," *Journal for the Scientific Study of Religion,* 15 (June 1976), 157–68. See also Martin Marty, "The Occult Establishment," *Social Research,* 37 (Summer 1970), 212–30; Gustav Jahoda, *The Psychology of Superstition* (Gloucester, Mass.: Peter Smith, 1971); and Marcello Truzzi, "Toward a Sociology of the Occult: Notes on Modern Witchcraft," in Zaretsky and Lenoe, eds., *Religious Movements in Contemporary America,* pp. 628–45.

[34] One of the most recent of numerous examples is a follow-up of astrologers' predictions of earthquakes, in which these predictions were less accurate than pure chance. See "The Growth of Seismic Premonitionology," *Psychology Today,* Feb. 1980, pp. 18–19.

[35]John Charles Cooper, *Religion in the Age of Aquarius* (Philadelphia: Westminster Press, 1971); Harvey Cox, "Religion in the Age of Aquarius: A Conversation with Harvey Cox and T. George Harris," in Edward F. Heenan, ed., *Mystery, Magic, and Miracle: Religion in a Post-Aquarian Age* (Englewood Cliffs, N.J.: Prentice-Hall, 1973), pp. 15–28.

[36]Wuthnow, "Astrology and Marginality."

[37]Frederick J. Scheidt, "Deviance, Power, and the Occult: A Field Study," *Journal of Psychology,* 87 (May 1974), 21–28.

[38]Nathan Adler, "Ritual Release and Orientation: Maintenance of the Self in the Antinomian Personality," in Zaretsky and Lenoe, eds., *Religious Movements in Contemporary America,* p. 286; Harvey Cox, "Why Young Americans Are Buying Oriental Religions," *Psychology Today,* July 1977, pp. 36–42; Lita Linzer Schwartz, "Cults: The Vulnerability of Sheep," *USA Today,* July 1979, pp. 22–24.

[39]Douglass McFerran, "Christianity and the Religions of the Occult," *Christian Century,* 89 (10 May 1972), 541–45.

[40]Margot Adler, *Witches, Druids, Goddess-Worshippers and Other Pagans in America Today* (New York: Viking, 1979), quoted in *New York Times Book Reviews,* 20 Jan. 1980, p. 32.

[41]Andrew M. Greeley, "Superstition, Ecstasy, and Tribal Consciousness," *Social Research,* 37 (Summer 1970), 203–11.

[42]Rodney Stark and William S. Bainbridge, cited in *Science News,* 117 (19 Jan. 1980), 40.

[43]Felicitas D. Goodman, "Prognosis: A New Religion," in Zaretsky and Lenoe, eds., *Religious Movements in Contemporary America,* p. 244.

[44]See Robert Wuthnow, *Experimentation in American Religion and the New Mysticisms and Their Implications for the Churches* (Berkeley, Ca.: University of California Press, 1978).

[45]Roy Niblett, "Religious Education in Schools: A British Viewpoint," *Christian Century,* 89 (13 Sept. 1972), 895–96.

[46]R. B. Dierenfield, "Religion in Public Schools: Its Current Status," *Religious Education,* 68 (Jan.–Feb. 1973), 96–114; James K. Uphoff et al., "Public School Religion Studies: A New Freedom through a Slow Revolution," *Intellect,* Sept./Oct. 1976, pp. 97–98.

[47]Frank L. Steeves, "State Approved Curricula in Religious Studies," *Public Education Religious Studies Newsletter,* Winter 1974, pp. 6–7; Kenneth A. Briggs, "Religion Out, Religions In at Many

Schools," *New York Times*, 2 May 1976, sec. 4, p. 16.

[48]*New York Times*, 18 June 1963, pp. 1ff.

[49]William K. Muir, *Prayer in the Public Schools: Law and Attitude Change* (Chicago: University of Chicago Press, 1968); Martin Marty, "School Prayer: Many Meanings to Many People," *New York Times*, 14 Nov. 1971, sec. 4, p. 8.

[50]Morris Rosenberg, "The Dissonant Religious Context and Emotional Disturbance," *American Journal of Sociology*, 68 (July 1962), 1–10.

[51]Edward B. Fiske, "Getting God Back into the Curriculum," *New York Times*, 3 Dec. 1972, sec. 4, p. 6. See also Kenneth M. Dolbeare and Phillip E. Hammond, *The School Prayer Decision: From Court Policy to Local Practice* (Chicago: University of Chicago Press, 1971).

[52]Catholics maintain about 90 percent of the nation's private religious elementary and secondary schools, with most of the remainder being either Reformed or Lutheran. The Reformed churches point out that their "Christian day-schools" are controlled by lay boards of control rather than by the church directly, and thus are not strictly "parochial."

[53]Neil J. McClusky, S.J., "Aid to Nonpublic Schools; Historical and Social Perspectives," *Current History*, 62 (June 1972), 302ff.

[54]See *America*, 127 (2 Oct. 1972), 304.

[55]Symposium—Constitutional Problems in Church–State Relations, "The First Amendment and Financial Aid to Religion: Limits on the Government's Conduct," *Northwestern University Law Review*, 61 (Nov.–Dec. 1966), 777–94.

[56]See any issue of *Church and State*, published by Americans United for Separation of Church and State; also, Gaston D. Cogdell, *What Price Parochaid?* (Silver Springs, Md.: Americans United for Separation of Church and State, n.d.).

[57]Guild of St. Ives, "A Report on Churches and Taxation," in Donald R. Cutler, ed., *The Religious Situation: 1968* (Boston: Beacon Press, 1968), p. 939; Martin A. Larson and C. Stanley Lowell, *The Churches: Their Riches, Revenues, and Immunities* (New York: Robert B. Luce, 1969); James Gollin, *Worldly Goods* (New York: Random House, 1971); Martin A. Larson and C. Stanley Lowell, *The Religious Empire* (Washington, D.C.: Robert B. Luce, 1976).

[58]Guild of St. Ives, "A Report on Churches," p. 943.

[59]*Time*, 11 Nov. 1979, p. 96.

[60]One minister known to this author has built up a large congregation, starting from nothing 30 years ago, and owns a large, handsome church, an apartment house, a multimillion-dollar shopping center, a plastics manufacturing plant, an electronics firm, a girdle manufacturing company, a posh restaurant, a television station, a bankrupt college campus, and various other properties (see "Should a Church Be in the Girdle Business?" *New York Times*, 2 May 1969, sec. 4, p. 7). But even with the advantage of tax exemption, he has recently run into financial difficulties.

[61]Guild of St. Ives, "A Report on Churches," pp. 946–51.

[62]Keith E. L'Hommedieu (A Director of the International Universal Life Church, Inc.), quoted in *Human Behavior*, May 1978, p. 15.

[63]Philip B. Taft, Jr., "Jesus Junk: Not for Spiritual Use," *A.D.*, (United Presbyterian), Feb. 1980, pp. 34–35.

[64]Jerry Scholes, *Give Me That Prime-Time Religion* (New York: Hawthorne, 1980); also "Stars of the Cathode Church: TV-Radio Preaching: A Controversial Billion-Dollar Industry," *Time*, 4 Feb. 1980, pp. 64–65.

[65]Carl Bakal, *Charity USA: An Investigation into the Hidden World of the Multi-Million Dollar Charity Industry* (New York: Time Books, 1979); also *Time*, 28 Jan. 1980, p. 66.

[66]See William R. Thompson, "A Shrinking Freedom," *A.D.*, Feb. 1980, pp. 21–22.

[67]Thomas N. Munson, S.J., "Gambling, A Catholic View," *Christian Century*, 69 (9 Apr. 1952), 437.

[68]See the *New York Times Index*, any issue, under the heading "Lotteries," for current citations on gambling controversies.

[69]*New York Times*, 11 Nov. 1979, p. 43.

[70]Andrew M. Greeley, *Crisis in the Church* (Chicago: Thomas More Press, 1979), p. 11.

[71]See J. C. Evans, "Abortion Debate: A Call for Civility," *Christian Century*, 96 (21 Mar. 1979), 300–01.

[72]William C. McCready and Andrew M. Greeley, "The End of American Catholicism," *America*, 127 (28 Oct. 1972), 334–38.

[73]For statements of the social gospel, see Henry F. May, *Protestant Churches and Industrial America* (New York: Harper & Row, 1949); and Robert L. Handy, ed., *The Social Gospel in America* (New York: Oxford University Press, 1966). For a

Catholic statement, see John F. Cronin, *Social Principles and Economic Life* (Milwaukee: Bruce Publishing Co., 1959). For a critique, see Paul Ramsey, *Who Speaks for the Church?* (Nashville, Tenn.: Abingdon Press, 1967).

[74]Richard J. Stellway, "The Correspondence between Religious Orientation and Socio-Political Liberalism and Conservatism," *Sociological Quarterly*, 14 (Spring 1973), 430–39; Leo Driedger, "Doctrinal Belief: A Major Factor in the Differential Perception of Social Issues," *Sociological Quarterly*, 15 (Winter 1974), 66–80.

[75]Robert Moats Miller, "American Protestantism and the Abolition of the Twelve-Hour Day in the Steel Strike," *Southwestern Social Science Quarterly*, 37 (Sept. 1956), 137–48.

[76]James B. Wood, "Authority and Controversial Policy: The Church and Civil Rights," *American Sociological Review*, 35 (Dec. 1970), 1057–69.

[77]Harold E. Quinley, "The Dilemma of an Activist Church: Protestant Religion in the Sixties and the Seventies," *Journal for the Scientific Study of Religion*, 13 (Mar. 1974), 1–21.

[78]Juan de Onis, "Juntas Move Right and the Church is Now the Left," *New York Times*, 30 Nov. 1975, sec. 4, p. 3; "The Church of the Poor," *Time*, 7 May 1979, p. 88; Daniel H. Levine (ed.), *Churches and Politics in Latin America* (Beverly Hills, Ca.: Sage Publications, 1980).

[79]John Charles Cooper, *Radical Christianity and Its Sources* (Philadelphia: Westminster Press, 1968); Paul T. Jersild and Dale A. Johnson, eds., *Moral Issues and Christian Response* (New York: Holt, Rinehart and Winston, 1971).

[80]Andrew M. Greeley, *Crisis in the Church*, p. 16.

[81]Kenneth A. Briggs, "Evangelical Christian Movement Being Reshaped by Radical Wing," *New York Times*, 16 July 1978, pp. 1ff.

[82]Gustavo Gutierrez, *A Theology of Liberation* (Maryknoll, N.Y.: Orbis Books, 1973); Ernest W. Lefever, *Amsterdam to Nairobi: The World Council of Churches and the Third World* (Washington, D.C.: Ethics and Policy Center, 1979); Alan Riding, "Latin Church in Siege," *New York Times*, 6 May 1979, pp. 32ff.; Daniel H. Levine, ed., *Churches and Politics in Latin America* (Beverly Hills, Ca.: Sage Publications, 1980).

[83]For example, see Andrew M. Greeley, *The Jesus Myth* (Garden City, N.Y.: Doubleday, 1971).

[84]Support for the Vietnam War was, in fact, more widespread among church members than among the nonreligious. See Clarence E. Tygert, "Religiosity and Universal Student Anti-Vietnam War Attitudes," *Sociological Analysis*, 32 (Summer 1971), 120–29.

[85]All Protestant churches teach that the believer may approach God directly without any intermediary priests or officials, and that God may reveal His will directly to the believer. Some Protestant bodies (for example, Jehovah's Witnesses, Friends) operate largely or entirely without a professional clergy.

[86]William R. Catton, Jr., "What Kind of People Does a Religious Cult Attract?" *American Sociological Review*, 22 (Oct. 1957), 561–66; Wuthnow, "Astrology and Marginality."

George Holton, Photo Researchers, Inc.

POPULATION PROBLEMS: NATION AND WORLD

9

There is good news and bad news from the population fronts of the world. . . .

The depressing news: In the past year, the world's population increased by 73 million to an estimated . . . total of 4,321,000,000 human beings alive on earth. The global population growth rate failed to decline appreciably. . . . According to the latest UN assessments, the growth rate of the world is projected to decline to about 1.5 percent by the year 2000. However, . . . the absolute number of people added each year is continuing to rise . . . because the world population base is continually expanding, and population growth is exponential. And this increase is happening in a world where

more than 400 million people already suffer from malnutrition. . . .

Optimistic signs: The world's birth rate did come down a notch, from the 29 births per 1,000 population estimated last year to 28 this year. . . . Significant recent fertility declines have been noted in a number of key developing countries: China, South Korea, Malaysia, Indonesia, Thailand, the Philippines, Sri Lanka, Costa Rica, and Colombia. . . . But despite these encouraging trends, . . . growth rates in the vast majority of African countries and in many countries in Asia and Latin America remain stubbornly unchanged. . . .[1]

While you read the preceding paragraph, the earth's population grew by ten people. By the time you finish reading this chapter, it will have grown by approximately 10,000 people. And by this time tomorrow there will be 190,000 more people in the world. Many people are gravely concerned about the effects of continued high birth rates and are trying to do something about it. Other people and other groups are concerned about different kinds of population problems. Organized groups are promoting new homes for refugees from Soviet dominated states, for Jews in Israel, and for Palestinians displaced from Israel. Other groups oppose the contamination of existing populations by immigration. Some groups are worried because the "less desirable elements" in the population bear the most children. All these positions suggest different population problems.

The Problems

Population problems may be divided into three categories: size, distribution, and quality.

SIZE

The world's population has grown irregularly but continuously ever since the appearance of humankind on earth. Moreover, until very recently, the rate of growth has been increasing. Whether that situation is now changing is uncertain. Some demographers think so.

Homo sapiens has been on earth for 100,000 years or so. During the first 98,000 years, or up to the time of Christ, the population grew to between 200 million and 300 million people. In the next 1650 years, the population doubled to approximately 550 million, a rate of growth almost 60 times that which existed before. In the last 330 years, world population has quintupled again—to 4.3 billion. Various estimates hold that there may be between 5.8 billion and 6.3 billion people by the year 2000.[2] The estimates vary only in the *rate* of increase predicted. Population growth in the past has been accompanied by both high birth rates and high death rates. Death rates have been dropping over much of the world, and now birth rates appear to be dropping too.

DISTRIBUTION

The approximately 4.3 billion people who populate the earth are not distributed equally over its surface. Nor are all nations or continents equally capable of supporting large populations. Differing ratios of population to resources and techniques of food production mean that population pressures are severe in some areas and practically nonexistent in others. In general, population pressures are greatest in Asia and the Near East and least in the United States, Canada, and Australia, and parts of Europe.

There are about 60 persons per square mile in the United States and approximately 584 per square mile in Great Britain. India has 415 persons, and Taiwan has 700 persons per square mile. In Japan there are 708 persons per square mile, 12 times the population density in the United States.

Within the United States, New York State has a density of 381 persons per square mile, and Rhode Island has 902. Nevada has 4.4, and Wyoming has 3.4 people per square mile. In New York City the density is 26,343 persons per square mile of land, while in some parts of rural Montana the density is less than 1 person per square mile.[3]

Bound up with these differences are problems of war and peace, famine and plenty, disease and health. Tens of millions of people have migrated from China, India, Japan, and Korea without materially reducing the size of their populations. The shrill cry for *Lebensraum* (space for living) threatens the world with future disasters.

QUALITY

Ever since Charles Darwin, the notions of struggle for survival and survival of the fittest have emphasized the idea of inequality within both animal and human species. Theoretically the fittest do survive, and the inevitable result of natural competition within the species should be to produce a constantly improving biological stock. A major difficulty with the theory, however, is that among human beings competition is not the simple biologic process that it is among lower species. Human competition is complicated by the existence of *culture*. Rarely do human beings meet in mortal combat; when they do, the meeting is not likely to be a chance occurrence. Each combatant is likely to be a chosen representative of the group, specially armed and trained for the purpose. Each is equipped with weapons designed to minimize physical advantage. Wars are fought and won through technological superiority rather than through the quality of the germ plasm. High mortality rates among infants and children generally are considered bad, and efforts are made to save the weak as well as the strong. Within human groups, *social* selection is as important as *biological* selection.

It is widely feared that human interference with the operation of biological selection means a lowering of population quality. If the inferior and incompetent are protected against extinction, will they not go on to perpetuate their kind? May they not gradually lower the quality of the entire population and, perhaps, eventually bring about its destruction? Such fears have given rise to *eugenics*, a movement that deals with influences that improve population quality. Eugenics is based on two principles: (1) discouraging reproduction of the hereditarily unfit; and (2) encouraging reproduction of the "better" biological stocks.

Population Growth

The rapid rate of world population growth has already been noted. The figures themselves are staggering. But what do they mean? If the world already holds 4 billion people, is it not capable of holding twice as many, or even more? If there are limits that may not be surpassed, what are they?

And how do they operate? A partial and classic answer to some of these questions was provided over 170 years ago by Thomas R. Malthus in his famous work, *An Essay on the Principle of Population*.[4]

THE MALTHUSIAN THEORY

According to Malthus, population tends to grow faster than the food supply can be increased. Population tends to increase in geometric fashion (1, 2, 4, 8, 16), while the food supply increases only arithmetically (1, 2, 3, 4, 5). In other words, population *multiplies* with each increase, thereby furnishing the basis for a further increase, whereas food production cannot be multiplied

Thomas Malthus.
(New York Public Library)

or endlessly increased. Consequently, at any given time, the size of a population is limited by the amount of available food. So long as they can be fed, additional children will live. Most of the world population exists at a minimum subsistence level, barely staying alive and ready to be wiped out by a variety of possible calamities.

Malthus defined the calamities that result when population size presses too closely on the food supply as *positive* and *preventive checks*. The term *pos-*

itive checks refers to those means of population limitation that operate through the taking of human life. Chief among them are war, disease, and famine. Until the time of Malthus these had been the principal forces holding down the rate of population growth. They result from the blind operation of societal forces, relatively independent of human control. The *preventive checks* reduce population size not through taking lives but through preventing additional births. They depend primarily on the exercise of human will power. To Malthus this meant chiefly that people should delay the time of marriage. The longer they waited and the older they were at the time of marriage, the fewer children would result. He did not, as is often assumed, advocate birth control in marriage. Modern contraception had not come into existence at that time, and even if it had, it is not likely that Malthus, who was also a minister, would have regarded it as desirable. He placed great emphasis on the exercise of "moral restraint" through delay in the time of marriage.

Malthus's theory was the first comprehensive one to foresee great danger to standards of living, to political freedom, and even to human survival in too rapid population growth. Drawing his illustrative material from the experience of the United States, which was growing rapidly through immigration and natural increase, Malthus postulated that under ideal conditions populations would double about every 25 years. In the absence of moral restraint, this could mean only increased dependence on the undesirable positive checks: war, disease, and starvation.

Is Malthus's theory applicable today? Instead of a real shortage of food in the United States, we more often have huge surpluses. The American problem has been one of restricting production rather than not having enough food. Here, at least, population does not seem to be pressing very hard on the means of subsistence. Important changes since Malthus's time must be taken into consideration in evaluating his theories.

England at the beginning of the nineteenth century was still very much an agricultural nation, beset by a series of ever lengthening economic recessions. It was in this atmosphere that Malthus wrote. Widespread poverty was being rendered more acute by population increases. Malthus did not live to see the tremendous changes wrought by industrialization. The Industrial Revolution in Europe and the United States transformed agricultural nations into manufacturing ones, and food production increased at an almost unbelievable rate. Unparalleled growth and expansion followed. Population increased rapidly, but the food supply increased even faster. Especially in the United States, Malthus's theory seems to have been invalidated by the course of social change. But before asserting that this is necessarily the case, let us examine more closely the current picture in the world at large and then in the United States.

THE WORLD PICTURE

Over one-half of the world's population is concentrated in Asia. China, India, Japan, Indonesia, the Philippines—all have exceedingly large populations and all are threatened with inadequate food supplies. The Industrial Revolution has left many of these areas relatively untouched. Undoubtedly, industrialization could relieve the situation somewhat. But whether even full-scale industrialization could accomplish what it has in the United States is open to serious question. The United States is blessed with a large, fertile land area and relatively low population density. The world at large is much more crowded. According to one estimate, it takes a minimum of one and one-half acres of arable land to provide a minimum adequate diet for each person. Few of the countries in Asia and the Middle East have that much land.[5]

In Asia, especially, populations are characterized by exceedingly high birth rates and are held in check only by extremely high death rates. Malthus's positive checks seem to be in full operation. Poverty, malnutrition, and even starvation are widespread. Contrary to widely held opinion, not all Asian populations have been increasing rapidly. Near saturation points were reached decades ago, and increases have been limited to the additional persons who could be supported by the slight technological advances that have occurred. Unfortunately, accurate data for most of these countries are lacking. Adequate censuses are unknown, and only estimates are available. The most reliable information comes from India, where the population has been under intensive study for a number of years. Between 1870 and 1940, the rate of population growth in India was only about one-fifth that of the United States. Yet the birth rate in India was nearly twice as high. In Asia, generally, the positive checks continued to operate with undiminished fury.

Recently, the situations in many underdeveloped nations have changed rapidly, and they are embarking on a period of explosive population growth. The death rate in India has now dropped to 16 per 1,000 population, just 2 above the worldwide average, while the birth rate remains at an extremely high 41 per 1,000 population. At this rate, India's population will double in the next 28 years.

UNITED STATES POPULATION GROWTH

Explosive worldwide growth in population contrasts with United States birth rates, which have fallen to replacement levels. The United States stands poised between the growth rates of the past, which would have produced 400 million Americans by the year 2000, and the prospect of a stable or even declining population with resulting severe dislocations in many areas of life. Let us trace the history of population growth in the United States to see how we reached this point.

TO WORLD WAR II   The United States has a history of rapid population growth. Much of this growth occurred during the last half of the nineteenth century and first quarter of the twentieth century as the combined result of falling death rates and high rates of immigration. Contrary to some popular belief, rapid population growth need not result from rising birth rates but, as in the United States and many other countries, may actually be accompanied by falling birth rates when death rates fall even faster.

Some 40 million of the United States population were gained through immigration, coming primarily from Europe. During most of the nineteenth century the United States government looked with favor upon immigration and did little to discourage it. Land was to be had almost for the taking and immigration was a means of developing and strengthening the country. Most of the immigrants came from the countries of northwestern Europe, such as England, Ireland, and Germany. Similar in cultural background to those who were already here, the immigrants adjusted easily and were quickly accepted by "Americans."

Before the turn of the century, new population policies and problems were becoming evident. Birth rates were dropping rapidly and the government began to curb immigration from the Far East. Spurred by the fear of "unfair" competition from Chinese laborers who were accustomed to very low living standards, first Chinese laborers, then all Chinese, and finally all Japanese were excluded.

Population continued to grow during the early decades of the twentieth century, though the increment added each decade was smaller than the one before. Reproduction dropped below replacement requirements, and by the 1920s immigration had virtually ceased. The prolonged depression of the 1930s depressed birth rates even further, and from 1931 to 1935 for the first time the number of persons emigrating *from* the United States exceeded the number immigrating *to* the United States. The steady decline in birth rates led demographers to predict that soon population would stop growing. That had already happened in Europe, for instance, in France and Scandinavia. Eventually, they predicted, the population would even start to decline. At first, it was believed that a stable population size would be reached by 1970 or 1975. But then World War II loomed on the horizon, the nation began to come out of the depression, and things began to happen to the birth rate.

Dining room for detained immigrants at Ellis Island, circa 1900.
(The Bettman Archive, Inc.)

SINCE WORLD WAR II   Both the number of births and the birth rate rose rapidly after World War II. In 1946, there were 3.3 million births, for a birth rate of 24.1 per 1,000 population. By 1950, there were 3.55 million births, and in 1953 there were 3.9 million. The peak was finally reached in 1957, when 4.3 million babies were born. The term "population explosion" was used to describe the situation, and the implication was that rapid population growth would continue indefinitely.

During the 1960s rapid population growth emerged as a major public issue. Suddenly, we saw too many people crowding everything from cities, highways, and skyways to the great national parks in the formerly isolated Northwest. Populous and popular states such as California and Florida actually began to toy with the idea of discouraging further in-migration of people from other states. Although most authorities recognized that far more than sheer numbers of people was involved, too many people were perceived to be a major cause of pollution and despoliation of the environment.

Zero Population Growth emerged as an effort to convince couples to limit their children to two, so that the United States population would cease to grow larger, and population stability could be achieved. This organization provides an unprecedented example of concerned citizens seeking not only to participate in the initial stage of defining a social problem but also to direct the stage of policy determination by proposing a specific solution to the problem thus defined.

Demographers and others knowledgeable about population problems have generally been sympathetic to the goals of Zero Population Growth, but have been unwilling to identify with the organization because of its drastically oversimplified approach. Demographers point out, for example, that even if the recommended two children per family average were achieved by the end of this decade, the momentum already built into the system would ensure continued population growth at least until the year 2070. If the more drastic approach of seeking zero population growth immediately were adopted, the sheer problem of management of reproduction levels and the dislocations produced in the economy would be almost overwhelming.

The idea of population growth as a social problem became widespread during the 1960s. Soon after taking office, President Richard Nixon recommended to Congress the appointment of a blue-ribbon Commission on Population Growth and American Future. That commission studied the problem for two years and delivered its final report in March 1972.[6] The comprehensive report recommended a conscious government policy to improve the quality of life by gradually slowing and eventually halting United States population growth. It advocated an eventual average two-child family obtained by voluntary means, with respect for human dignity, freedom, and individual fulfillment, and concern for social justice and social welfare. To achieve these ends, the commission called for

> The elimination of involuntary childbearing by substantially improving the access of all Americans, regardless of marital or socioeconomic status, to effective means of fertility control;
>
> Improvement in the status of women;
>
> More education about population, parenthood, sex, nutrition, environment, and heredity;

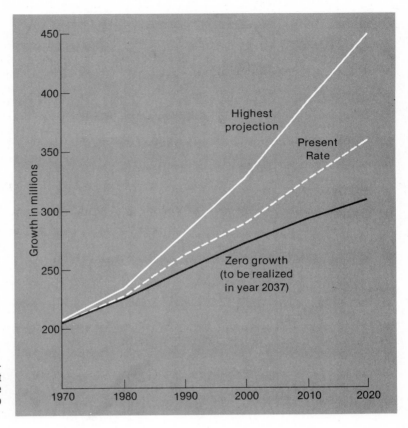

Figure 9–1
Projected United States population growth, from present rates and from the average two-child family urged by Zero Population Growth.

Maintenance of foreign immigration levels, and more national guidance of internal migration to metropolitan areas;

Increased biomedical research in human reproduction and contraceptive development;

More and better demographic research, including social and behavioral research and census reporting, and statistical reporting and evaluation of family planning services;

Organizational changes in government necessary to attain the recommended objectives.

The direct impact of the report on government policy has been minimal, but the larger significance of the report is obvious. Population growth has become a social problem worthy of attention at the highest government levels, and there is strong support for the achievement of population stability through the ideal of the two-child family. It is ironic that even as awareness of rapid United States population growth as a social problem has been emerging, there are signs that the rapid growth of the post–World War II era is over and that a whole new range of population problems is developing.

THE BABY BUST   Public awareness of population changes tends to lag behind the changes themselves and to be temporarily concealed by the fact that declining birth rates, particularly, do not immediately show their eventual impact on population growth. Thus, even while the American public was becoming aware of rapid population growth during the 1960s, the birth rate had already begun to drop.

The period of the post–World War II baby boom, as shown in figure 9–2, came to an abrupt end in 1957. The birth rate began to decline significantly, falling to 23.7 in 1960, 18.4 in 1966, and 17.5 in 1968. There was a temporary upsurge in 1969 and 1970, but in 1971 the rate fell again to 17.3, and by 1976 the rate was down to 14.7.

As early as 1967, professional demographers began to see the end of the United States population explosion.[7] More recently, scholars have suggested that the decline in birth rates is so dramatic and of such import as to merit the label of a genuine baby bust.[8] Not only did the birth rate drop rapidly,

Figure 9–2
United States fertility rates, 1909–1978
Source: George Grier, *The Baby Bust: An Agenda for the 70's, Special Report* (Washington, D.C.: The Washington Center for Metropolitan Studies, 1971), p. 28; and Monthly Vital Statistics Report, *Annual Summary for the United States 1978*, 27 (Mar. 1976).

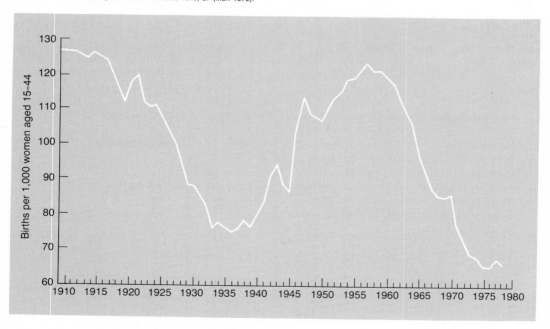

but much of the decline accompanied a record increase in the number of young adults in the most fertile age group in the population. The baby boom babies of the 1940s and 1950s began to reach age 18 in 1964 and continued to do so through 1975, setting off, according to all past experience, a new wave of births and a new surge of population growth. That has not happened, however. Instead, there has been a drop in the number of children produced, with a resulting decline in the proportion of the population under 5 years of age.

Between 1960 and 1970 there was a 15.5 percent decrease—3 million fewer children—in the preschool population. In the entire 120 years covered by appropriate United States census statistics, there is no parallel to this situation. Even in the depression years of the 1930s, the decrease in preschool children was only half that of the last decade.

What is unknown, and what there is no reliable way of determining, is what the bottom of the drop in birth rates will be, and how long the low birth rates will continue. The experts have already been confounded by this situation. Birth rates have dropped below replacement levels. Continuation of the trend for many more years will set the stage for eventual population decline. There is no assurance that the downward trend will continue, of course. Birth rates may be on their way back up even before this material appears in print. With each passing month, however, it becomes less likely that fertility will rebound significantly during the reproductive years of the baby boom generation.

A number of factors operating in the United States should help to keep birth rates low. One of these is the widespread availability of oral contraception. The introduction of the pill did not cause the drop in birth rates, because the drop started three years before the pill was commercially available. But the pill does seem to be reducing considerably the number of accidental pregnancies.

The new, liberal abortion laws also are a factor. The combination of readily available, effective contraception and abortion when desired should mean that most future babies will be wanted babies.

New lifestyles and the lack of any rush on the part of many young people to marry are a third factor. The average age at marriage is rising, keeping many people out of reproductive activity during some of their most fecund years. The average age at marriage for women increased from 20.3 years in 1960 to 21.6 years in 1977, and the proportion of 21-year-old women who are single increased from 35 percent to 47 percent. Growing numbers of people may even be opting to remain single permanently. A recent Census Bureau report says that 45 percent of all women under age 35 are single.

In the long run, the most important factor may be that changes in the status of women will dispose them to have fewer children. As more women become more highly educated and come to value occupational achievement, they may perceive less "need" for traditional rewards in the form of children.[9] This interpretation is supported by changes in the number of children that young women expect to have. The 1970 National Fertility Study showed, for example, that women in their late twenties who had married in their early twenties expected to have 2.53 children, a drop from the 1965 figure of 3.03.[10]

Distribution Problems of Migration

IMMIGRATION

For over 200 years the United States immigration policy was officially an open-door policy. The inscription on the base of the Statue of Liberty, presented to the United States by France, indicates how this policy was received abroad:

> Give me your tired, your poor,
> Your huddled masses yearning to breathe free,
> The wretched refuse of your teeming shore,
> Send these, the homeless, tempest-tossed to me:
> I lift my lamp beside the golden door.

The United States was a haven of refuge for the surplus population of Europe and, to a very slight extent, for that of Asia. America became known as the melting pot, where diverse peoples and cultures were fused into a new entity of great vigor and promise. Culturally and politically the new nation remained tied to northwestern Europe. English-speaking people outnumbered other immigrants and established their prejudices in the new land. The first restrictions barring the poverty-stricken, the insane, the disabled, and the criminal from entering the country included also the first of a series of restrictions against Orientals, who were believed to threaten the "native" population. Until after World War I, no further restrictions were imposed.

The stage for the drastically altered policies that followed World War I was set by the changed character of immigration during the last of the nineteenth and the first of the twentieth century. During this period, immigration from northwestern Europe had virtually ceased, and increasing numbers of people came from southern and eastern Europe—Italy, Greece, and the Balkans. There were language barriers to be overcome. Ethnic communities multiplied in the cities, and while the original migrants had been predominantly Protestant, the newcomers were more often Catholic.[11] The antagonism and resentment first directed against Asians were extended to the southern Europeans. The situation came to a head after 1918. There was much clamor to "keep America for Americans" and to protect Americans' jobs by halting the flood of immigration.

Laws passed in 1921 and 1924 laid down the basic policy that remained in effect until 1965. The concept of national origins underlay this legislation. Nations were allotted immigration quotas on the basis of the proportion of the United States population that was made up of persons from those nations. The 1921 law stated that immigration from any country in any one year should be limited to 3 percent of the persons of that nationality who were residents of the United States in 1910. The law of 1924 was even more drastic in that the proportion was reduced to 2 percent and the base year was moved back to 1890. The practical consequence of this immigration policy was virtually to cut off immigration to the United States.

Since the northern Europeans were the first to migrate to the United States, the national-origins system gave them very large quotas. People from central and southern Europe, who had begun to migrate in large numbers only from about 1870, had very small quotas. Moreover, unused portions of one country's quota could not be used by other countries, and unused portions could not be carried over into subsequent years. Large parts of the quotas for northern European countries remained unused, while southern Europeans who sought admittance were refused. There seems to be little question that prejudices against the Italians, Poles, Greeks, and others were instrumental in the formation of this policy. The "land of the free" was freer to northern than to southern and eastern Europeans.

Congress finally acknowledged the discriminatory nature of the national origins policy and passed the Immigration Act of 1965, which eliminated it. The new law established an annual limit of 170,000 immigrants from outside the Western Hemisphere and 120,000 from within the hemisphere. The maximum number from any one country is 20,000, plus immediate relatives of persons already residing in the United States who are not counted toward meeting the quota.

An elaborate order of preference is established to determine who actually gains entry. First preference goes to immediate relatives of United States citizens or alien residents of the United States. Next come professional persons and others with special talents or education. The third priority is allotted to skilled and unskilled laborers. Such persons, however, must obtain certification from the United States Department of Labor showing

The *Dr. Daniel,* her decks filled with 465 Cuban refugees, pulls into the docks at Key West, Florida, May 6, 1980.
(United Press International)

that there are insufficient American workers "able, willing, qualified, and available" to fill the job openings they seek. It must also be shown that their employment would not "adversely affect the wages and working conditions" of United States citizens similarly employed.

Last on the preference list are persons fleeing from communist-dominated countries or the Middle East because of persecution or fear of persecution because of race, religion, or political opinions. Persons fleeing from natural disasters also fall into this category.

The effects of the law are shown in part in table 9–1. Nine of the ten countries supplying the most immigrants in 1965 failed to make the list in 1977. With the exceptions of the United Kingdom and Canada, all the new countries in the list for 1977 are in Latin America or Asia.

The year 1975 was unique in United States immigration patterns because of the admission of 132,000 refugees from the Vietnam War. This brought the total immigration for 1975 to 493,000.

Averaging over 400,000 annually, immigration is now having greater impact upon the population of the United States than it did at the turn of the century, when there were a million or more immigrants. Of course, this is because the growth rate of the native population is declining. While immigration accounted for about 11 percent of the nation's growth in the late 1950s, it accounts for almost 20 percent currently. Moreover, a large proportion of the new immigrants are young people, whose children will raise their share of the population even higher in the future.

ILLEGAL IMMIGRATION   In addition to the 400,000 people who enter the United States legally each year, at least twice that many, and perhaps four times as many, enter the country illegally. The vast majority are Mexicans, although some are Canadians, West Indians, and Europeans. Most slip across the 6,000 miles of unguarded national borders, although some enter with visitors' visas and simply never leave.

This situation has existed for decades, with the complicity of large U.S. employers who claim that the "illegals" take back-breaking jobs that United

TABLE 9–1   Countries Sending Most Migrants to the United States in 1965 and 1977.

Country	Migrants in 1977	Country	Quota in 1965
1. West Indies	114,000	1. Great Britain	65,361
2. Cuba	69,700	2. Germany	25,814
3. Mexico	44,000	3. Ireland	17,756
4. Philippines	39,100	4. Poland	6,488
5. Korea	30,900	5. Italy	5,645
6. China	19,800	6. Sweden	3,295
7. India	18,600	7. Netherlands	3,136
8. Canada	12,700	8. France	3,069
9. United Kingdom	12,500	9. Czechoslovakia	2,859
10. Dominican Republic	11,700	10. Soviet Union	2,697

SOURCE: U.S. Bureau of the Census, *Statistical Abstract of the United States 1978* (Washington, D.C.), p. 89; and U.S. Immigration and Naturalization Service.

States citizens do not want, and who pay the migrants substandard wages. In 1975, for example, the average wage of aliens arrested near the Mexican border was only $1.74 per hour.[12] The United States Immigration and Naturalization Service, by contrast, claims that illegal aliens hold somewhere between 1 and 2 million jobs, and are a significant factor in the continuing high U.S. unemployment rate.

The authorities are virtually powerless to stem the tide of illegal immigration. Although over 1 million aliens were arrested in 1978, the INS estimates that there are 8 million more in the country, with more coming every day. The INS has only 2,000 border agents to guard the Mexican and Canadian borders, and only 900 investigators to pursue aliens within the country. Moreover, at least two groups of U.S. citizens support the aliens: those who employ numbers of them, and those who believe that the immigration of such aliens should be permitted.

INTERNAL MIGRATION

The international migration that brought some 46 million people to the United States between 1820 and 1975 was accompanied by an equally impressive pattern of migration within the country. The major flow was from east to west, as the population spread first across the Appalachians and then to the Pacific coast. The flow was also from rural areas to the cities, the population having been 95 percent rural in 1790, but 73 percent urban by 1970.

Migration patterns have historically varied by race. Blacks tended to originate in the rural South and moved first to southern cities and thence to those in the North and West. Although free blacks were concentrated in urban areas even before the Civil War, the mass rural-urban migration started, understandably, after the war. There was a surge toward the North and toward the cities from 1860 to 1870, followed by a slowdown until World War I. Over a million blacks moved north during the war. After the war the northward migration continued and spread, eventually, to the West.

Blacks moved out of the South Atlantic and East South Central states during every decade after 1870 and out of the West South Central states after 1810. This out-migration from the South reached a peak during the 1950s, leveled off during the 1960s, and may actually have been reversed during the early 1970s. Between 1970 and early 1978, as many blacks returned to the South as left it.[13] The return of some blacks to the South may reflect disillusionment with crime, ghettos, and the high cost of living in the North. It may also reflect the changing pattern of migration of Americans generally.

The total volume of movement within the country remains extremely high. Almost 20 percent of the population change their place of residence during any given year. About three-fifths of these moves occur within a single county. Approximately one-fifth, however, involve moves from one county to another within the state, and a comparable number are interstate moves.[14]

Exact causes for the high mobility rates are difficult to pinpoint. One enabling factor certainly is the ease of transportation. Cross-country moves may be made with relatively little inconvenience. Basic causes of mobility probably include economic changes in industry and agriculture; contraction within agriculture and the basic extractive industries is forcing people away from the open countryside. With international migration restricted, internal migration is required to meet the demand for labor in the major urban areas. At the higher occupational levels, geographic mobility is often an inevitable part of job advancement.

More and more Americans are choosing to live in warmer climates and adjacent to large bodies of water. By 1970 about one-half of the population lived within 50 miles of the Atlantic or Pacific Oceans, the Gulf of Mexico, or the Great Lakes. The in-migration to the South that began in the 1960s also picked up steam in the early 1970s. The so-called "sun belt," stretching across the country from Virginia and the Carolinas to Southern California, increased in population by approximately 60 percent between 1950 and 1975. Comparable increases continued at least through 1978.[15]

The same mobility that permits the United States to meet its needs for a flexible labor force and permits a growing proportion of the population to live the good life is also related to the changing nature of social problems. Problems are created in family and community life, and the whole fabric of American life, including relationships among the federal government, the states, and local communities, is being altered.

Families frequently are shaken by moves, particularly long-distance ones. Children are forced to leave their friends and their schools. They may make new friends quickly, or they may endure long periods of loneliness and being left out of school activities. Because curricula vary somewhat from location to location, there is often some loss of academic credit.

The family as a whole is torn loose from its roots in the community. The home they have labored to make attractive is suddenly gone. So are established relationships with local business and tradespeople, the church, and so on. Even when it is the means to financial advancement, a move often means temporary financial hardship. If moves are fairly frequent, roots may never be put down deeply in the new communities. There may be no network of relatives and lifelong friends to assist in times of emergency. The family may have no real interest in the welfare of the community, but only in what it can get *out of* the community. Informal networks of social controls may be conspicuous by their absence, and more reliance placed upon the inherently less adequate formal mechanisms of police, welfare agencies, and so on. High mobility rates contribute to the deterioration of community life.

As persons and families identify less with local communities, and as they move throughout the country, many social problems cease to be local problems and become nationwide in scope. Educational deficits in the lives of southern rural blacks are a problem not just for the South, but also for the northern and western cities in which many of them eventually will live. Welfare laws that traditionally have required a period of residence for eligibility leave growing numbers of persons without aid. The states of New York and Florida operate a joint program of research and aid to the migrant laborers who winter in one state and summer in the other.

Too often, cities and states either do not care to or cannot cope with the problems created by population mobility. Local officials, who have insufficient revenue and who are responsible to local voters, find it easy to disclaim responsibility for those who are only recently or temporarily in their area. This leaves a vacuum in which needs are great and into which the federal government is forced to move. Federal tax monies are allocated to state and local governments, with guidelines to make sure that the funds are used for their intended purposes. The guidelines, and the federal control that they represent, are as inevitable as the provision of federal funds.

Although many persons and groups at all levels are opposed to the expansion of federal aid and federal control, all are powerless to stop it. The same conditions that move the population over the landscape, and steadily transform regional cultures into a national culture, are creating national social problems with which only national resources can hope to cope.

Quality

THE DIFFERENTIAL BIRTH RATE

A society's birth rate is an average of the higher birth rates of some groups and the lower rates of others. The higher-birth-rate groups account for a larger proportion of succeeding generations than do the lower-birth-rate groups. To paraphrase a beatitude, the high-birth-rate groups shall inherit the earth. People have long speculated on the meaning of such differential birth rates. Any special characteristics of the high-birth-rate groups would appear more and more frequently in future generations. If these characteristics are desirable, the quality of the population would be improved; if they are undesirable, quality would be lowered. Eugenics, founded on these premises, attempts to encourage reproduction of the hereditarily fit and to discourage reproduction of the hereditarily inferior.

Within the United States two instances of birth-rate differences have received considerable attention. Rural birth rates are higher than urban ones, and birth rates vary inversely with socioeconomic status.[16] Rarely is it contended that the rural population is either markedly superior to, or inferior to, the urban. The rural–urban difference generally is considered to be of primarily social significance. Therefore, it will be treated in the chapter on urban and rural problems rather than here. Birth-rate differences according to socioeconomic status, on the other hand, are frequently conceived to have social *and* biological significance.

Economically disprivileged people tend to have large families, while white-collar, business, and professional groups are more likely to limit the number of children to one or two. The inference is not that lower economic groups are biologically more capable of having children, but that the upper economic groups marry later and make more use of birth control. Typically, the higher the income, the more respected the occupation, the higher the educational level, and the lower the birth rate. The college-educated population has never had enough children to replace itself, while groups with little or no formal education overreproduce themselves.

How does this affect population quality? The arguments advanced stress biological factors, social factors, or both.

BIOLOGICAL FACTORS   Francis Galton, the English biologist, was among the first to recognize and systematically explore the possible consequences of birth-rate differences. Galton assumed that the biological struggle for survival and natural selection results in persons with greater innate ability or superior genetic endowment rising to the top of the social ladder, while the less talented remain on the lower rungs. Hence, the upper classes of society should be the superior biological stocks. That these groups do not adequately reproduce themselves presupposes that the quality of the population is reduced accordingly. The human race thus might be breeding itself into mediocrity, perhaps eventually out of existence.

To many, these conclusions represent unquestioned fact. Though it would be an error to assert that eugenicists have uncritically accepted them, many eugenics proposals do, in fact, rest on them. What is called "negative" eugenics calls for the sterilization of certain classes of people *believed* to have defective heredity. Since 1907, over two-thirds of the states have passed laws permitting or requiring the sterilization of certain groups. Most commonly, the laws call for sterilization of the feeble-minded, but some laws include the psychotic, the epileptic, certain criminal classifications, and persons with certain types of hereditary malformation. The goal, of course, is to prevent the multiplication of hereditarily inferior types. However desirable the goal, the laws fall far short of achieving it.

The error in this approach is in its original assumptions, namely, that feeble-mindedness, psychosis, epilepsy, and criminality are completely hereditary and that they can be eliminated or markedly reduced through sterilization. The difficulties are twofold. First, the role of hereditary factors in causing these difficulties has been overestimated. Probably not more than half of feeble-mindedness is strictly hereditary, the other half being the product of adverse environmental conditions, birth injuries, disease, and still other factors.[17] Adverse social conditions, as well as genetic factors, can produce feeble-mindedness in generation after generation, with whole families being affected. Similarly, only a part of all epileptic cases are hereditary, and even fewer cases of mental illness are entirely genetic. With regard to criminality, hereditary factors now are regarded as negligible. Social scientists believe that wholesale sterilization of such groups would result in sterilizing large numbers of people who are not organically defective and would do little to reduce the number of defectives in the next generation.

As many as 70,000 mental patients in 30 states may have been involuntarily sterilized over several decades, many of them by doctors who believed such operations would help rid society of human maladjustment. . . .

. . . Many of the patients at state mental hospitals were never told of the operations or were operated on for no other reasons than convenience. . . . authorities in the mental health field add that the national figures do not include thousands of sterilizations performed on mentally retarded people who have never been institutionalized. . . . The study was prompted by recent disclosures that an estimated 8,300 sterilizations had been performed in Virginia mental institutions.

Figures collected from the Social Welfare History Archives at the University of Minnesota and other sources show almost 64,000 sterilizations had been performed on patients at state mental hospitals in 30 states by 1964. . . . National totals apparently were not kept after that year, but figures compiled from individual states indicate the total may have reached 70,000 by now, it said.

The American Civil Liberties Union is considering filing legal action against Virginia to get the state to notify those who were sterilized. . . .

Associated Press, March 24, 1980.

The second difficulty is that most defective organisms are produced not by defectives but by the so-called normal population. At least some of the genes that cause conditions such as organic feeble-mindedness are carried recessively; they may be present even when there are no observable symptoms in the individual. They may remain hidden for several generations, only to reappear. According to a reliable estimate, ten times as many normal persons as morons carry a simple recessive gene for mental deficiency. Most of the carriers of recessive harmful genes cannot be identified; but if they could be, and sterilization were recommended, *Almost every one of us would have to be sterilized!*[18]

SOCIAL FACTORS   Galton and his followers generally failed to recognize the role of *social selection* in determining the placement of individuals within the socioeconomic structure. They assumed, but could not demonstrate, that superior innate ability accounts for the movement of people upward in the class system. It is probable, however, that such nongenetic factors as motivation, shrewdness, and ruthlessness play a role in determining who gets to the top. Moreover, the class system itself exerts a major selective influence. A given class status, once attained, becomes somewhat hereditary. The upper classes may contain many persons of decidedly inferior ability who are able to stay there simply because of the competitive advantages that upper-class status provides them. Similarly, there is believed to be a vast reservoir of potential ability among lower socioeconomic groups that is not tapped because of unfavorable social environment. On these assumptions, a somewhat more realistic eugenics program has been developing.

Poverty-stricken adults beset by malnutrition and illness and living in ignorance, whether or not they are organically inferior, are not the best fitted to bear and raise young. The upper economic groups, however, with their higher standards of housing, nutrition, medical care, education, and awareness of personal and social responsibility, have traditionally had few children. Beyond the question of biologic capacities, large numbers of children have had the cards stacked against them *socially*. Consequently, eugenicists advocate larger families among the upper economic groups and lower birth rates among the economically disprivileged. The expansion of planned-parenthood facilities including adequate and inexpensive birth-control information is basic to the latter.

Although the efforts of eugenicists to alter the differential birth rate appear to have had little effect, there is growing evidence that the general course of social change may be tending to eliminate the problem. A disproportionate part of the baby boom after World War II occurred not among lower-income people but among middle- and upper-income groups. During the 1960s, the birth rate among lower-income women fell more rapidly than for the general population. A difference still exists, but it is diminishing. Some demographers now predict that the time will come when higher-income families will have more children than lower-income families.[19]

AN AGING POPULATION

Ordinarily we think of "population" as including persons of all ages—we seldom stop to think that some populations may be "younger" or "older" than other populations. Expanding populations with high birth rates tend to be "young" because of the large proportion of infants and children in them.

241

Stable or decreasing populations tend to be "older" because of their low birth rates and smaller numbers of children. Traditionally the United States has had a young population, but more recently there has been a rapidly increasing proportion of older persons.

During its early history the average age of the United States population was kept down by high birth and immigration rates. The effect of high birth rates has already been mentioned, and immigrants are primarily young adults. Married immigrants also tend to have high birth rates. But birth rates have dropped steadily, at least since 1790, and immigration from Europe dropped after 1920. In 1800 the median age was 16 years; in 1920 it was approximately 25 years; in 1977 it was 29.4 years. The average life expectancy increased from 49.2 years in 1900 to 67.5 years in 1950, and has now reached 73 years. In 1900 there were only 3 million people in the United States over 65 years of age. The number had increased to 12 million in 1950, and is more than 23.5 million now. This great increase in the number of aged persons will have extensive repercussions on the population at large.

The effects on the nation of increasing numbers of old people depend not only on the absolute number of aged but also on their proportion of the total population. Until 1940 the increased proportion of older persons was accompanied by steadily decreasing proportions of younger persons. With fewer persons being born, the potential burden of support posed by growing numbers of elders loomed very large.

After World War II, the baby boom greatly increased the proportion of

Senior citizens frequently retire to warmer climates, such as here, at St. Petersburg, Florida.
(Bonnie Freer, Photo Researchers, Inc.)

younger persons and reduced the potential proportion of elders. Now that birth rates are lower again, the aged are becoming a larger proportion of the population. At present, persons over 65 make up slightly over 10 percent of the United States population.

The presence of a large number of older people poses a variety of problems. In many industries, 65 is the usual retirement age. Persons beyond this age are largely a dependent population—dependent for even the barest living on their children and other younger adults. With rare foresight, the federal government anticipated this situation during the 1930s and instituted the social security program to help care for the increasing numbers of aged. Labor unions and, increasingly, business, are emphasizing retirement and annuity programs as one way to help meet the needs of the aged. The next 20 or 30 years will probably see considerable expansion of such efforts. It is questionable, however, whether the country can afford an arbitrary retirement philosophy, no matter how great its old-age assistance efforts. When the number of aged persons was very small, their retirement did not materially reduce the size of the effective labor force. But when the number of persons over 65 exceeds 10 percent of the total population, their enforced retirement might mean lower standards of living for the entire nation. Certainly per capita production would suffer. Many persons of 65 years and more are still capable of performing their jobs efficiently, and many physically undemanding tasks now performed by younger people might well be done by older persons. In managerial and executive positions the value of increased maturity and experience has long been recognized. These same traits should be useful in many lesser jobs.

Beyond its employment significance, the changing age structure of the population will have other consequences for the economy. The bright young person of today who desires a rosy financial future should not overlook the expanding market for hearing aids, bifocals, wheelchairs, canes, crutches, and other products in demand among older persons. Clothing manufacturers will need to devote more attention to the subdued styles and colors. Contractors will likely find increased demand for single-story houses with no stairs. Geriatrics (care of the aged) may be the coming medical specialty. Attorneys specializing in probate matters (wills and estates) will be in demand.

The Social-Disorganization Approach

During most of human existence, populations were small, techniques of food production were crude, and large populations were not possible. Though Malthus did not write until the beginning of the nineteenth century, the principles that he expounded probably had been operating through the millenniums—population growth up to the maximum permitted by the level of technology, then relative stability until some new technological advance permitted growth to be resumed. As growth continued, the rate of growth accelerated. The greatest of all stimuli to population growth—the industrial and agricultural revolutions—ushered in a period of change that provides a classic example of social organization yielding to disorganization. And the prospect of reorganization in terms of new norms looms on the horizon.

The relatively slow growth of population up to the Industrial Revolution resulted from a particular balance between birth rates and death rates. Birth rates were high and the average number of children born to married couples was relatively large. Population did not grow rapidly, however, for death rates also were high. In fact, the high death rate actually required a high birth rate, for the average size of the *surviving* family was small. This situation persisted until after the Industrial Revolution.

The Industrial Revolution lowered the death rate by providing modern sanitation and improved medical care, and it also resulted in greatly increased food supplies. With the death rate down and no increase in the birth rate, population began to grow by leaps and bounds. In our sentimental fondness for the large families of our grandparents' time, we have been slow to realize that large *surviving* families actually were rare. And we have not yet fully recognized that the birth-rate levels that were functional before the Industrial Revolution have been turned into a major cause of population problems by changes in the death rate.

In a well-organized society birth and death rates are adjusted to each other. If population growth outstrips production, or if population shrinks, the traditional social arrangements of the society are disrupted. Throughout most of the world and for most of the time since the Industrial Revolution, disorganization has been produced by the explosive population growth resulting from falling death rates. Now in the United States there is the prospect of new forms of disorganization, as the decline in birth rates has persisted through the 1970s. If anything like zero population growth is achieved, the American economy, which relies on steady expansion, will have to undergo severe readjustment. Everything from schooling to medical care will cost more. There will be less money available to fight urban congestion and pollution, and the burden imposed by the aged will be greater. Ultimately, birth rates and death rates must come to some stable balance.

The Value-Conflict Approach

Although it is overshadowed recently by the abortion controversy described in chapter 7, there is still severe conflict over limiting population growth through contraception. The conflict involves the private decisions of couples to limit their families, religious control of those decisions, and the promulgation of birth control by local and national governments.

The evidence is unmistakable that the overwhelming majority of Americans espouse both the principle and the practice of family planning. A national survey of a probability sample of 1,708 men and women almost ten years ago found that almost nine out of ten Americans believe not only in birth control but also that information about contraception should be made available by the government.[20]

The term *contraception* includes oral and mechanical contraceptives, along with the use of the rhythm method. Since the Roman Catholic Church has appeared to give tacit consent to the use of rhythm, while explicitly forbidding all other means of birth control, statistics on contraceptive use frequently have distinguished between the use of rhythm and the use of all other methods, and between their use by Catholics and by non-Catholics.

Research during the 1970s showed that growing numbers of Catholics were disobeying church teachings on contraception and that differences between Catholics and non-Catholics in the use of contraceptive methods had virtually disappeared. Nationwide, by 1975, fewer than 3 percent of married women were using the rhythm method, and the prediction was made that by 1980 that method would be of historical interest only.[21]

General knowledge of the extent and trend of contraceptive use among Catholics is widespread. In the wake of the ecumenical movement and Vatican II, many people believed that Pope Paul VI would officially soften the Church's position. In a 1968 encyclical, *Humanae Vitae*, however, he reaffirmed the Church's opposition and appeared even to forbid the use of rhythm in most circumstances. The wave of hostile reaction that followed indicated how deep the split within the Church had become. Beyond the almost universal criticism of the Pope's stand in the press, priests and lay people alike challenged the enforceability of the Pope's ruling. One-third of the congregation walked out of a mass where a cardinal read a letter requiring compliance with the edict. Many of those who remained showed the depth of their feelings by standing and applauding when the cardinal had finished reading the letter. The strict position of the hierarchy in the United States is further weakened by the fact that many European cardinals have taken a more equivocal stance, recognizing that a large segment of Catholics will practice contraception, regardless of what the Church dictates.

By the mid-1970s, controversy over population growth and family planning had become worldwide. The industrialized nations which by and large have slowed their rates of population growth, are urging the Third World (less-developed countries) to embark upon large-scale birth control programs to stimulate their economic development. The poor nations retort, angrily, that the problem is not their high birth rates, but the neocolonialist and exploitative policies of the wealthy nations. The poor nations demand that the rich nations sacrifice some of their high living standards and share their wealth with less fortunate countries.

The conflict is being pursued in various international forums. At a United Nations Conference in Bucharest in 1974, the battle lines were drawn and the positions hardened. In the United Nations General Assembly, the less-developed countries have formed a solid voting bloc on economic issues that regularly defeats the industrialized nations. Each side accuses the other of playing power politics and of acting out of self-interest. The United States has hinted that it might restrict its financial support of the UN if bloc voting by the Third-World nations continues. Those nations, in turn, are determined to increase their shares of the world's wealth.

The Personal-Deviation Approach

THE GENETICALLY INFERIOR

One of the most difficult problems facing biological and social scientists is to define the role played by heredity and environment in the production of defective, deficient, and deviant organisms. The problem is difficult because in many instances it is not heredity *or* environment but heredity *and* environment that bring the undesirable condition into being. Frequently, a hereditary potential or tendency will not appear unless the environmental conditions are adverse, and adverse environmental conditions will not bring the condition about unless there is some hereditary tendency present. To be hereditary, the condition must definitely be tied to the operation of one or more genes. The genetic composition is determined at the moment of conception and normally cannot be changed by anything that happens during the lifetime of the individual. But the presence of unfavorable genes does not always produce a deviant organism. Geneticists estimate that practically all persons carry some unfavorable genes. Because it generally takes two or more such unfavorable genes to produce a trait, the deviancy does not appear unless unfavorable genes from the father match with similar genes from the mother. Thus, the deviancy may appear several generations apart, in seemingly unpredictable fashion, and still be hereditary. In other instances, the condition may repeat itself in successive generations. Certain recurrent physical abnormalities—for example, the presence of additional or fewer than the usual number of fingers and toes—are known to be hereditary. Blindness, deafness, gross physical deformities, and mental deficiency are *often* hereditary. It is further believed that some family lines carry greater than ordinary susceptibility to certain diseases such as tuberculosis and schizophrenia. The difficulty as we move down this list is that environmental factors come to play larger and larger roles. Between those conditions that are purely hereditary and those that are purely social lie an intermediate group of constitutional deviancies.

THE CONSTITUTIONALLY INFERIOR

Not all conditions that are present at birth are hereditary. Some of these "congenital" conditions are produced by the intrauterine environment and some are contracted during birth. In hemolytic disease, for instance, the genetic combination of an Rh-negative mother and Rh-positive fetus permits development of the disease *when and if* there is sufficient transmission of antigens and antibodies between mother and child. Hereditary factors alone will not produce the condition, yet when found, it is present at birth. Syphilis is a good example of a disease frequently believed to be hereditary. Syphilis cannot be inherited, but it may be transmitted to the child during birth by a syphilitic mother. Birth injuries, particularly to the head and to the central nervous system, occasionally produce defective and deficient persons for whom little can be done. Such conditions are *congenital* and organic, yet they are not hereditary. In still other cases there may be no abnormality present at birth but there may be a proneness toward diabetes, tuberculosis, epilepsy, and other conditions. The genetic structure may be such that the individual is constitutionally weak in one or more regards, not having inherited any specific diseases but being especially susceptible to them. At the present state of knowledge, however, it has not been definitely proved which constitutional susceptibilities can be inherited.

THE SOCIALLY INFERIOR

Research tends to ascribe continually increasing importance to social-environmental factors in the production of deviants. Many conditions that were once thought to be hereditary are found instead to be socially transmitted. It is now recognized that merely because a condition tends to run in certain families is not sufficient reason to label it as biological. Many of the ills associated with lower population quality can be reduced through bettering environmental conditions. Slum conditions, poverty, malnutrition, and filth are capable of producing as much havoc in *physical* functioning of human beings as are genetic factors. Among the diseases, tuberculosis is an excellent illustration. In 1900 tuberculosis resulted in more deaths in the United States than any other disease. Now, thanks largely to improved sanitary conditions, the tuberculosis death rate is only about one-sixth what it was then. To illustrate further: blacks are widely *believed* to be more susceptible to tuberculosis than whites. True, black death rates from tuberculosis are generally far higher than white tuberculosis death rates. *But* blacks generally live under conditions far inferior to those of whites. Examination of the situation in Milwaukee in 1940 revealed that

> The tuberculosis mortality rate among Negroes living in a slum area was 15 times as high as for whites of the city. But a generation before (in 1915), the rate among whites, mostly foreign-born, who lived in the same depressed environment *had been almost exactly the same as it was among the Negroes who succeeded them there.* And among descendants of those same whites, now living elsewhere and under much better conditions than their forebears, *the tuberculosis mortality rate had dropped to one-fifteenth*—to the same rate current for other whites in the city.[22]

Not all diseases result so directly from environmental conditions as does tuberculosis, of course, but much of the deviancy in any population is less closely tied to physical factors than is true in the case of physical disease. Adverse environmental conditions play an even larger part in the development of mental and emotional malfunctioning.

Summary

Population problems are chiefly those associated with size, distribution, and quality.

The tremendous size of modern populations is a relatively recent development. The world's population has more than quintupled in the past 300 years. Throughout history, however, operation of the Malthusian principle—that population size tends to press upon the available means of subsistence—has been applicable. Most of the world today has too many people in proportion to the available resources. The United States and part of Europe have escaped the struggle, temporarily at least, through the tremendous production advances that followed the industrial and agricultural revolutions.

The United States has shown continuous growth ever since its founding. Though both birth and death rates have dropped steadily, immigration sustained the pattern of growth until approximately 1920. The period beginning about 1940 saw a reversal in the birth rate with a trend toward larger families. The birth rate remained high until 1957, when it started downward again. It has continued downward for the last two decades.

After about 45 years of discriminatory immigration policy, Congress in 1965 eliminated the national origins system. The 1965 law permits 170,000 immigrants annually from outside the Western Hemisphere and 120,000 from within it. More immigrants now are coming from Latin America, southern Europe, and Asia, while the flow from northern Europe has declined.

The United States also has a large flow of internal migration. About 20 percent of the population changes residence annually with the prevailing direction of the flow being north and west. During the past decade, a movement toward warmer sections of the country developed. Migration flows reflect the expansion and contraction of different industries and meet the need for labor in the large urban areas. Migration also tends to be disruptive of involvement in community life, to create adjustment problems for families, and to transform local social problems into national ones.

The quality of the United States population has been affected by the tendency for lower economic groups to have the highest birth rates, and by the gradual aging of the population. While the lower economic groups may not be biologically inferior, the upper economic groups probably are best fitted to care for large families. If recent shifts in birth rates continue, the upper economic groups may eventually have the largest families.

The number of persons over 65 in the population is increasing rapidly. How much of a burden the growing numbers of aged will present depends, in part, upon the birth rate, that is, on how many younger people there will be to support them. The changing age structure of the population also will alter the production of goods and services.

Rapidly growing populations disrupt the entire social organization. High birth rates are functional when death rates also are high. When death rates fall, birth rates must be brought into balance with them. The control of birth rates through family planning raises bitter controversy. There are religious and racial overtones to this conflict, as well as debates over national and international policy.

Among the deviant persons in any population may be distinguished the genetically inferior, the constitutionally inferior, and the socially inferior. The socially inferior are probably the largest of these three groups and offer the quickest and surest route to improvement of population quality.

Suggested Readings

BROWN, LESTER R., PATRICIA L. McGRATH, and BRUCE STOKES, *Twenty-Two Dimensions of the Population Problem* (Washington, D.C.: Worldwatch Institute, 1976). A brief but informed account of the impact of rapid population growth on societal qualities ranging from pollution and hunger to individual freedom.

COMMISSION ON POPULATION GROWTH AND THE AMERICAN FUTURE, *Population and the American Future* (New York: New American Library, 1972). The full report of the presidential commission, assessing the impact of continued population growth on the United States.

ENDRES, MICHAEL E., *On Defusing the Population Bomb* (Cambridge, Mass.: Schenkman, 1975). A sophisticated but readable effort to develop a comprehensive national population policy.

HERNANDEZ, JOSÉ, *People, Power, and Policy: A New View on Population* (Palo Alto, Ca.: National Press Books, 1974). An introductory analysis that explicitly assumes the point of view of the poor people of the Third World.

NAM, CHARLES B., and SUSAN O. GUSTAVUS, *Population: The Dynamics of Demographic Change* (Boston: Houghton Mifflin, 1976). A readable introductory textbook that emphasizes the social aspects of demography.

REID, SUE TITUS, and DAVID L. LYON, eds., *Population Crisis: An Interdisciplinary Perspective* (Glenview, Ill.: Scott, Foresman, 1972). Collaboration between a biologist and a sociologist has produced a broad set of readings on the many facets of the population problem.

WESTOFF, CHARLES F., ed., *Toward the End of Growth: Population in America* (Englewood Cliffs, N.J.: Prentice-Hall, 1973). A collection of readings that assume that the United States has experienced a period of rapid growth and is now moving toward a stable population.

[1]*INTERCOM*, the International Population News Magazine of the Population Reference Bureau, 7 (Apr. 1979), pp. 1, 4.

[2]Amy Ong Tsui and Donald J. Bogue, "Declining World Fertility: Trends, Causes, Implications," *Population Bulletin*, 33 (Oct. 1978), 6.

[3]U.S. Bureau of the Census, *Statistical Abstract of the United States* (Washington, D.C., 1978), pp. 13, 25.

[4]*First Essay on Population*, 1798 (New York: Macmillan, 1926).

[5]I. W. Moomaw, *To Hunger No More* (New York: Friendship Press, 1963), p. 33.

[6]*Population and the American Future* (New York: New American Library, 1972).

[7]Donald J. Bogue, "The End of the Population Explosion," *The Public Interest*, 7 (Spring 1967), 11–20.

[8]See George Grier, *The Baby Bust: An Agenda for the 70's Special Report* (Washington D.C.: The Washington Center for Metropolitan Studies, 1971); and "Is U.S. Baby Boom Going Bust?" *Family Planning Perspectives*, 3 (Oct. 1971), 4–5.

[9]See John Scanzoni and Martha McMurry, "Continuities in the Explanation of Fertility Control," *Journal of Marriage and the Family*, 34 (May 1972), 315–22.

[10]*New York Times*, 17 Nov. 1971.

[11]The United States never was a true melting pot, uniformly assimilating immigrants, regardless of religious and national backgrounds. One study has shown three distinct melting pots—one for Catholics, one for Protestants, and one for Jews—in one American city. There is considerable intermarriage between persons of the same religion but different nationality backgrounds, but relatively less marriage across religious lines. See Ruby Jo Reeves Kennedy, "Single or Triple Melting Pot? Intermarriage Trends in New Haven, 1870-1940," *American Journal of Sociology*, 39 (Jan. 1944), 331–39.

A subsequent careful analysis concluded that similar forces operate in all of American life. See Milton M. Gordon, *Assimilation in American Life: The Role of Race, Religion, and National Origins* (New York: Oxford University Press, 1964). Other evidence shows increased willingness of persons to marry across religious lines. See Gerald R. Leslie and Elizabeth McLaughlin Leslie, *Marriage in a Changing World* (New York: John Wiley & Sons, 1980), ch. 6.

Comprehensive data from the Current Population Survey conducted by the Bureau of the Census show a moderate tendency toward intermarriage for Protestants and Roman Catholics, but only a very slight tendency for Jews. See Hugh Carter and Paul Glick, *Marriage and Divorce: A Social and Economic Study* (Cambridge, Mass.: Harvard University Press, 1976), pp. 138–42.

[12]*U.S. News and World Report*, 26 Jan. 1976, p. 85.

[13]U.S. Bureau of the Census, "Geographical Mobility: March 1975 to March 1978," *Current Population Reports*, Series P-20, no. 331 (Nov. 1978), Table 7.

[14]U.S. Bureau of the Census, *Statistical Abstract of the United States: 1971* (Washington, D.C.), p. 34.

[15]Jeanne C. Biggar, "The Sunning of America: Migration to the Sunbelt," *Population Bulletin*, 34 (Mar. 1979), 11–12.

[16]Ronald R. Rindfuss and James A. Sweet, "Rural Fertility Trends and Differentials," *Family Planning Perspectives*, 7 (Nov.–Dec. 1975), 264–69.

[17]For a balanced, readable account of the role of heredity in mental deficiency and mental illness, see Amram Scheinfeld, *Your Heredity and Environment* (Philadelphia: J. B. Lippincott, 1965).

[18]Ibid., p. 549. Italics in the original.

[19]Population Reference Bureau, "Boom Babies Come of Age: The American Family at the Crossroads," *Population Bulletin*, 22 (Aug. 1966).

[20]Gerald Lipson and Diane Wolman, "Polling Americans on Birth Control and Population," *Family Planning Perspectives*, 4 (Jan. 1972), 39.

[21]Charles F. Westoff and Elise F. Jones, "The Secularization of U.S. Catholic Birth Control Practices," *Family Planning Perspectives*, 9 (Sept.–Oct. 1977), 203–07.

[22]Scheinfeld, *The New You and Heredity* (Philadelphia: J.B. Lippincott, 1950), p. 172. Italics in original.

EDUCATION IN AN AGE OF CHANGE

10

I tell you we don't educate our children in school; we stultify them and then send them out into the world half-baked. And why? Because we keep them utterly ignorant of real life. The common experience is something they never see or hear. All they know is pirates trooping up the beaches in chains, tyrants scribbling edicts, oracles condemning three virgins to be slaughtered to stop some plague. Action or language, it's all the same; great sticky honeyballs of phrases, every sentence looking as though it has been plopped and rolled in poppy-seed and sesame.[1]

. . . Let every child be the planner, director, and assessor of his own educa-tion. . . . Allow and encourage him, with the inspiration and guidance of more experi-enced and expert people, and as much help as he asks for, to decide what he is to learn, when he is to learn it, how he is to learn it, and how well he is learning it.[2]

Have you felt, as I have, that the impli-cation in many books and articles dealing with the failure of American education is that no one knows how to teach except the au-thor of the article and a few of his friends? All these great teachers are always traipsing down to Cuernavaca to discuss teaching while the rest of us plodders are back here on the job.[3]

From Socrates's trial to last night's PTA meeting, schools have been attacked and defended, teachers have been blessed and damned. At no time in history have we all agreed upon what the schools should be and should do. Today is no exception.

The Changing Task of Education

Schools were invented several thousand years ago to prepare a select few for leadership. A century or more ago, public schools were created to teach the three Rs to the masses. Today we may be nearing the close of a third educational revolution that has sought a college education for practically everyone. In 1977 the median number of years of schooling completed by Americans over 25 was 12.4 and half of all young civilians of college age were in a college of some sort. It appeared that the curve of rising educational levels would continue indefinitely. But college enrollments have suddenly fallen off a bit, as grave questions are being asked about the desirability of universal college education.

Rising levels of education have undoubtedly been due, at least in part, to the changing nature of work in modern societies. Between 1910 and 1980 the proportion of all workers who were employed as professionals quadrupled; meanwhile, the proportion of all workers employed as unskilled laborers declined in almost exactly the same proportion. Such changes as are shown in figure 10–1 may be expected to continue. But it is by no means certain that rising job requirements are the main cause for rising levels of education. In many cases the educational qualifications for a position are irrelevant to the work that is to be performed.[4] Often these educational requirements seem to have been established for the purpose of reducing job competition, thereby giving a degree of monopoly protection to the children of those who have already "made it."[5] Aside from its cash value, education confers status upon the "educated," and competition for status may be one explanation for rising levels of education.[6] Thus the role of education in modern society has become a matter of debate. It is beyond question that our society will continue to need a high level—possibly a steadily rising level—of education and training. Exactly how and in what areas education can be most beneficial is less certain.

Problem Areas in American Education

THE COST BIND

About two out of seven persons in the United States are attending some kind of school this year. In 1978 we spent $142 billion on schools of all kinds and levels: $92 billion for elementary and secondary education and $50 billion for higher education. These costs have been skyrocketing in recent years. The share of our gross national product devoted to education rose from 3.1 percent in 1930 to 5.1 percent in 1960, and has remained a little over 7 percent since 1972.[7] Why these changes?

One explanation is the high birth rate in the years following World War II. Another factor has been the lengthening educational span, with communities adding kindergartens at one end and community colleges at the other. A third factor is the rising popularity of a college education. But beyond these, the average cost per pupil at every level has been rising faster than either the price level or the gross national product. This is due in part to a national drive to improve education, with the customary prescription being a generous infusion of money. It is also due in part to the rising economic status of teachers, whose incomes have been rising about twice as fast as the general wage rates in the past two decades.[8] Teachers' salaries rose in

Figure 10–1
Rapid growth of professional, technical and service occupations. Percentage change, 1960–78.
Source: *Statistical Abstract of the United States*, 1978, pp. 418, 419.

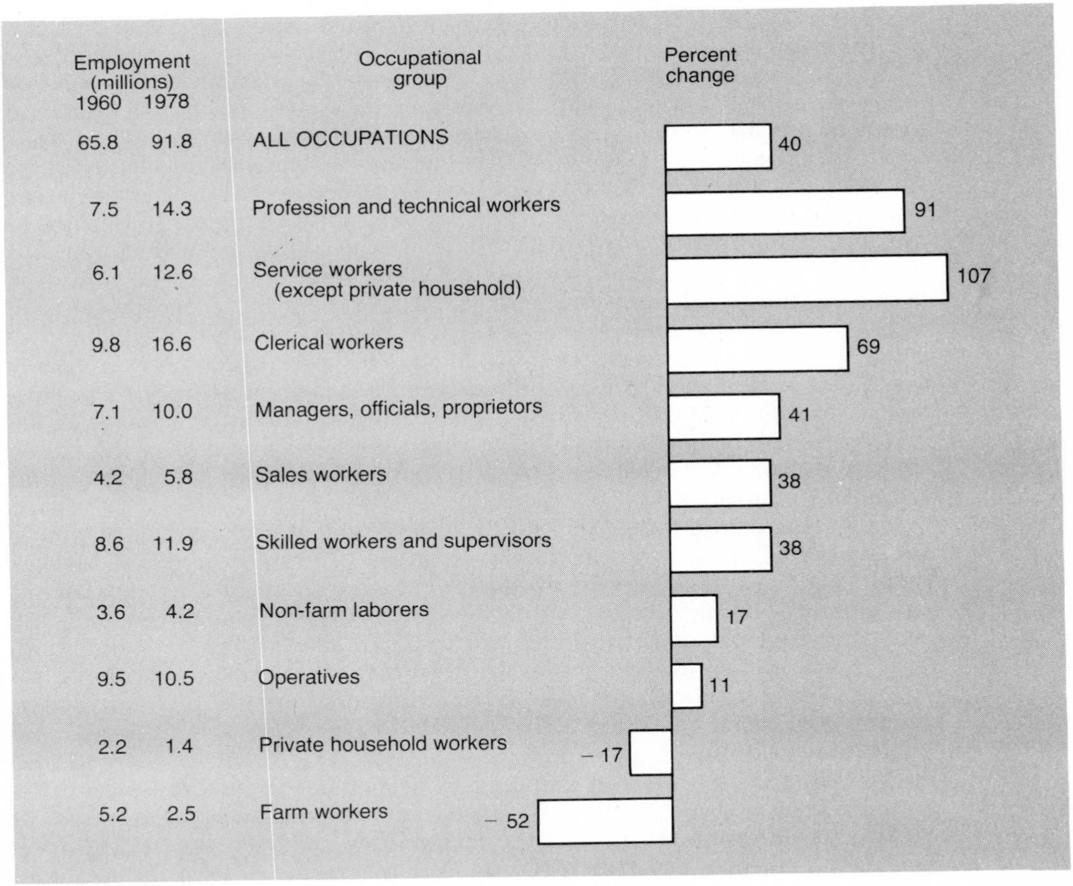

Employment (millions) 1960	1978	Occupational group	Percent change
65.8	91.8	ALL OCCUPATIONS	40
7.5	14.3	Profession and technical workers	91
6.1	12.6	Service workers (except private household)	107
9.8	16.6	Clerical workers	69
7.1	10.0	Managers, officials, proprietors	41
4.2	5.8	Sales workers	38
8.6	11.9	Skilled workers and supervisors	38
3.6	4.2	Non-farm laborers	17
9.5	10.5	Operatives	11
2.2	1.4	Private household workers	– 17
5.2	2.5	Farm workers	– 52

response to the teacher shortage, together with collective bargaining and union representation, backed by a growing willingness to strike.[9]

Today the situation is changing. Schools and colleges now face a shortage of students, not teachers.[10] The post-World War II "baby boom" has worked its way into adulthood, and enrollments at all levels have been falling. This has created an acute job shortage for new teachers and has given communities the politically sensitive task of deciding which schools to close. By 1985, however, a modest baby boom is expected to resume, starting another wave of school expansion.[11] In higher education, private colleges are hit with rising costs and falling enrollments, and many are expected to close within the next decade.[12] Rising enrollments call for costly expansion; falling enrollments increase costs per pupil. No matter what happens, there is a cost problem.

EQUALITY OF EDUCATIONAL OPPORTUNITY—PROSPECT OR PIPEDREAM?

Equality of opportunity has for some decades been firmly enshrined in the hierarchy of American ideals. Although thoughtful observers might note that *absolute* equality of opportunity is unattainable, the acclaim of *equality of educational opportunity* as a minimum goal has been so unanimous that few have questioned its possibility, and even fewer its desirability. This faith has been buttressed by a serene confidence that even our imperfectly "equal" education has, in fact, for some generations been providing a mobility ladder for poor but ambitious youth.

All these complacent faiths have recently been questioned. A group of *revisionist* critics maintain that our educational system has *not* operated to promote upward mobility for low-status persons and groups. Instead, they claim that the educational system has operated to perpetuate inequality by socializing children for status roles based on race and class.[13] Colin Greer points out that for three-quarters of a century, an unchanging 40 percent of the pupils, mostly poor or from ethnic minorities, have been dropping out of school before reaching the expected grade level.[14] Instead of education being the means whereby the immigrant poor achieved economic success, Greer suggests that the reverse was true—that economic success has preceded educational success, for only those who were already economically successful were able to get much from attending school. Most of these revisionist critics are Marxists who maintain that the schools not only had the *effect* of perpetuating inequality, but that they were *intended* by the ruling class to protect themselves and block the upward mobility of the poor and the ethnic minorities.

This last charge—that the educational system was *designed* to preserve privilege and block upward mobility—can be dismissed as typical Marxist polemics. The critics present no documentary *evidence* of any such intent; they merely assume that, as the lackeys of a corrupt capitalist system, the educational reformers of the past century *must have had* such an intention. The documentary evidence indicates, however, that these educational reformers passionately hoped to equalize educational opportunity and shared a naive confidence that their reforms would do so.[15]

The revisionists' main arguments—that social class is the main determinant of school progress and that schools perpetuate inequality—are worthy of more serious consideration. These charges are now attracting two lines of rebuttal. One group argues that the schools have relatively little effect upon the class structure, in either direction.[16] If they were *intended* to block mobility and perpetuate inequality, they have failed. Another line of rebuttal argues that the revisionist critique is simply groundless.[17] A recent study of the effect of New York City's turn-of-the-century schools finds that these schools, however imperfect, *did* operate as a mobility ladder for immigrant children.[18] A number of studies conducted several decades ago concluded that social class background was the strongest determinant of school progress, but many recent studies have found that, at least today, social class is less important than some other variables, especially individual ability.[19] Sewell and Hauser, for example, attribute to social class background only 16 percent of the variance in educational attainment and 12 percent of the variance in occupational status.[20] Hauser and Featherman conclude that the importance of class background on educational attainment has declined in recent years.[21] As one bit of evidence supporting Hauser and Featherman's conclusion, the spread between college attendance rates of youth from poor and affluent families has been shrinking, as shown in Table 10–1.

While socioeconomic background is a *significant* factor in school progress, and examples of class favoritism are easy to find, recent evidence clearly shows that the Marxist/revisionist image of the school as an instrument of class oppression is a grotesque caricature of reality. There is considerable agreement that equality of educational opportunity has never been fully attained, and probably never will be. Even socialist countries that have sought equality of opportunity are finding that in the "classless society," family and class influence have reappeared and make the goal of absolute equality more and more remote.[22] It is inevitable, *under any social system,* that highly successful persons will eventually find ways of giving special assistance and advantages to their children. Thus a new upper class evolves, even in socialist countries.[23] The passion for absolute equality that characterized the Soviet Union in the 1920s and China in the 1960s is a transitional stage, leading not to a "classless society" but to a new system of socialist stratification.

Suppose that absolute equality of educational and social opportunity were attained. What would be the probable consequence? Not equality, but a *meritocracy,* in which native ability and degree of effort would determine who came out on top. To whatever extent native ability is inherited—and this is a debated point—a meritocracy would become hereditary. There is

TABLE 10–1	Parental Family Income and College Attendance, 1967–77	
	Percent of children attending college	
Year	Family income $5,000 or less	Family income $15,000 or more
1967	20.0	68.3
1977	22.6	59.8

SOURCE: *Statistical Abstract of the United States,* 1978, p. 164. (Income is given in 1967 dollars; for 1977, the figures should be $9,000 or less, and $27,000 or more.)

some evidence that our society has been moving in the direction of a meritocracy.[24] Possibly a meritocracy would be preferable to our present stratification system, although even this can be debated. The only certainty is that inequality of opportunity and reward will persist, but the degrees and kinds of inequality are somewhat subject to our control.

EDUCATIONAL GOALS—STABILITY OR CHANGE?

Conservatives berate the schools for failing to teach traditional moral values; radicals complain that the schools perpetuate an oppressive status quo. Thus the critics of education are divided between those who want the schools to do a better job of what they have been doing and those who want the schools to promote revolutionary change.

Minority studies are one arena in which the clash between accommodation and change is sharply drawn. There is no general agreement on what "black studies" should be and do. Should black studies be one of the humanities, in which black history, art, literature, and music simply take their place beside classical history and Elizabethan drama? Should black studies be an academic social science, studying black culture, personality, behavior, and problems within a neutral or liberal integrationist frame of reference? Or should black studies be a device for arousing black militance and cultivating revolutionary black nationalism? Should improvement of black self-esteem be a

Some students add some decorations to the Peace Statue at The University of Pennsylvania in Philadelphia as they prepare for an anti-draft rally. Some 500 people attended this demonstration.
(United Press International)

major goal of black studies? (If so, they are failing to achieve this goal).[25] Should black studies be a cafeteria, with something for everyone? Should classes be restricted to blacks, or should they admit whites? While there is no complete agreement on these questions, most early programs rejected integrationist goals and chose to encourage black nationalism and militant leadership.[26] Here again, no agreements on curriculum can be reached without a decision on goals. If integrationist goals are sought, then black studies may be largely a waste of time, or even counterproductive.[27] But if separatist and nationalist goals are to be sought, then black studies are probably a useful instrument.[28]

Interest in black studies peaked about 1970, with 37 articles indexed in Vol. 20 of the *Education Index,* falling to only 4 articles indexed in Vol. 28 (1977–1978), while black studies courses have been losing popularity on the campus.[29]

Should the schools try to promote radical change in society? Your answer to this question will probably depend on your view of whether radical change is necessary.

Can the schools promote radical change? Earlier educational philosophers such as Horace Mann, John Dewey, and George S. Counts envisioned the school as the key instrument for the attainment of a steadily more democratic and egalitarian society. Their hopes have not been fulfilled. The idealized image of an autonomous educational system, free to educate and indoctrinate in total disregard for the power system, is a romantic dream. Why, for example, have the land grant colleges consistently followed policies of teaching and research that have greatly aided the commercial farmers and the food processing companies, but have largely ignored and indirectly harmed the small, marginal farmers? Possibly because the food processing companies provide scholarships and research grants, and the large commercial farmers are well organized to provide articulate support for the colleges' budget requests in the state legislatures, while the struggling marginal farmers are a steadily shrinking group without effective organization or political influence.[30] Educational systems are responsive to the power centers within the society. In the name of academic freedom, educators have established *some* degree of freedom to teach, conduct research, and publish without unwelcome outside interference, but this freedom is limited. Some degree of social criticism from the campus may be tolerated, but it is sheer romanticism to imagine that schools would be permitted to promote goals and values that conflict sharply with those approved by the dominant power groups in this (or any other) society.

EDUCATIONAL TECHNIQUES—DOES ANYTHING WORK?

It is widely accepted that American schools are terrible. A host of critics have charged that the schools stifle creativity, extinguish the child's natural love of learning, bury the poor and the ethnic-group children under layers of indifference and middle-class snobbery, and impose on the children a deadly subservience to an oppressive social system.[31] A veritable flood of books proposing cures for the schools' failures seem to begin by assuming that the failure of today's schools is so evident that the schools' self-appointed saviors can forget about investigating the problems and get on with the overhaul.[32] It is undeniable that a substantial fraction of children—

at least one-third—learn very little at school, and that these are disproportionately the poor and minority-group children. Apparently this has always
been true in the United States,[33] and it is generally true throughout the
world.[34] In any worldwide comparison, America's schools are among the
more advanced and innovative,[35] but to the critics of American education,
this is merely to quibble about relative degrees of incompetence.

It is ironic that criticism of schools for their failure to create an egalitarian democracy should coincide with a growing body of research that suggests that such a goal is inherently beyond the capacity of the school to
achieve. Evidence is accumulating that variation in individual ability is the
most important single determinant of individual school achievement, with
variations in family commitment to education probably second in importance.[36] Variations in socioeconomic background are important, although recent research is assigning less importance to this factor than formerly. Although children with good teachers learn somewhat more than children
with poor teachers,[37] the quality of the school and staff may not be one of
the most important factors. One carefully controlled national study found
that

> after much effort spent measuring and analyzing school differences and re-
> lating them to changes in young people's achievement, socialization, and
> personal growth, the resulting data failed to show that any of the character-
> istics of the schools seemed to make an appreciable difference for students.
> "There are differences between schools in the outcomes of their students,
> to be sure," report investigators Lloyd Johnson and Jerald Bachman, who
> have summarized their findings in a chapter in [*Understanding Adolescence,*
> second edition (Boston: Allyn & Bacon, 1973)]. "But when we ask what pro-
> duces these differences, we find almost invariably that they can be attributed
> to individual differences in backgrounds and basic abilities. In other words,
> the different outcomes are most convincingly explained by the differences
> in the types of students who go to those high schools in the first place."[38]

A study team headed by Jencks reached the same conclusion: that

> the character of a school's output depends largely upon a single input, the
> characteristics of the entering children. Everything else—the school budget,
> its policies, the characteristics of the teachers—is either secondary or com-
> pletely irrelevant, at least as long as the range of variation among schools is
> as narrow as it seems to be in America.[39]

These conclusions are reinforced by the disappointing results of the
many expensive educational innovations of the 1960s and 1970s. For example, in one unprecedented experiment a school system was provided *unlimited* funds to provide every educational resource and service money could
buy. The conclusion: "all that was done to make a difference made *no* difference."[40] Billions were spent on *compensatory education, Head Start, performance contracting, bilingual education,* and other innovations, with very few
learning gains that could be documented. Year by year, children's SAT
scores and other standard test scores declined.[41] Of all these programs, only
for Head Start is there—after several years of disappointing findings—some
evidence that the program may be working.[42]

Why has all this innovation brought so little success? The example of
bilingual education is instructive. The U.S. Supreme Court ruled in 1974

that all school districts receiving federal funds (virtually *all* public school systems) *must* provide bilingual instruction to all non-English-speaking children. The sensible way to proceed would have been to develop a number of small experimental programs and learn from this experience. But this was not politically feasible. Any public school board that did not immediately authorize a bilingual program faced certain denunciation as "racist." Thus thousands of programs were hastily initiated and funded with no clear knowledge of what to do or how to do it. Of the $500 million of federal funds expended for bilingual education through 1977, only one-half of 1 percent was spent for research.[43] The results were disappointing. A U.S. Office of Education report in 1978 announced that the Spanish-English programs were not very effective.[44] Very little evaluative research on bilingual education has been done, and the few completed studies show that, at best, the good programs help while the poor programs retard learning and "provide children who are illiterate in two languages."[45] A study of bilingual education in Ireland found that students in the bilingual program did not speak and write English as well as those who were not in the program.[46] Even the goals of bilingual education are in dispute.[47] Is the program *assim-*

With the influx of increasing numbers of immigrants (especially those whose native language is Spanish), there has been a rapid implementation of bilingual classes in American schools, such as this seventh and eighth grade class in New Jersey.
(Sybil Shelton, Monkmeyer)

ilative, designed to get non-English-speaking children into English facility and English instruction as soon as practical? Or is the goal *cultural pluralism,* with a permanent bilingual program to perpetuate a non-English language and culture? With no agreement on goals, and little solid knowledge of effective techniques, we have spent vast sums on a program without knowing whether it would do more good than harm. This is a prime example of how *not* to treat a social problem. The U.S. Department of Education has now demanded program evaluation, and we may soon learn whether bilingual education is a help or a hindrance to learning.

ALTERNATIVE SCHOOLS, FREE SCHOOLS, AND OPEN SCHOOLS

These three terms are often used interchangeably, with no exact definitions or distinctions. Each has been applied to a wide variety of school types and programs. In general, all of them began with the assumption that the public schools were simply terrible—stultifying creativity, stifling the child's natural love of learning, and oppressing children as outlined by Herndon, Holt, Kohl, Kozol, and others.[48] All operated on the assumptions that children know what they need to learn and will do so if permitted, and that children would rather discipline themselves and learn than to waste time. Consequently such schools had a permissive atmosphere, with plenty of open space, but no formal lectures, no structured sequence of "lessons," no formal discipline, and no formal grading. Children did whatever they wished, with teachers making suggestions but issuing no commands.[49] An estimated 600 such schools were operating in 1972, at the height of the movement.[50] Most participants in these schools were supremely confident of their superiority over conventional schools, but notably disinterested in empirical studies that would measure their effectiveness. In view of the characteristics of most free schools—a core of passionately dedicated teachers, with one teacher for each five to ten pupils, and pupils drawn largely from educated, liberal families[51]—these pupils *should* rank far above national norms in learning achievement, no matter what teaching methods were used. Yet evaluation studies found that learning gains were no greater, and were often less, under informal than under structured programs.[52] The most common reason reported for the closing of free schools is that the parents withdraw the children because they don't learn to read.[53] School systems that tried wholesale conversion to the "open classroom" have generally pronounced it a failure, although some of the open classroom techniques may be continued.[54] Some of the workable techniques joyously announced by free school practitioners, often drawing upon only a year or two of teaching experience, turn out to be the same techniques that *good* teachers have been using for generations. Educational historians report that the fundamental idea—that children will study whatever they need to know in an unstructured learning situation—is far from new, but has been tried repeatedly and discarded as ineffectual.[55] Most of the free schools have either closed or adopted more structured and conventional procedures.

THE PROBLEM OF CONTROL

Who should control the educational establishment? The control of school boards and administrators has been shriveling as federal and state laws, federal courts, government administrative agency rulings, parent groups, faculty unions, and even the students themselves have disputed the control of the schools. Governing the schools is growing steadily more difficult and deserving of "combat pay."[56]

THE STUDENT REVOLT   All over the world, students went on a rampage in the 1960s[57]—not that student disorders are entirely new. To cite only a few instances, students at Plato's Academy rioted through Athens in 387 B.C.; thirteenth-century Paris students rioted over wine prices, with many casualties; fourteenth-century Oxford students had a three-day battle with townspeople, with over 58 fatalities; Harvard in 1655 felt it necessary to forbid students to "weare Long haire, Locks or foretops";[58] Princeton has no complete records on student behavior, because students twice burned down Nassau Hall, which housed the archives.

While grievances varied, the student revolt in the United States operated at two levels. One was a revolutionary attack upon the entire social system, including the university as part of a corrupt establishment. The second level was a critique of the university itself. Students demanded—and soon received—freedom of student life. Most of the rules governing student life were relaxed or revoked. Students now generally live where, how, and with whom they wish.

Student participation in academic governance was demanded—and granted. In most colleges and universities, students now publish uncensored school papers, use "student activity fees" to buy Rock rather than Rachmaninoff, and hold student membership on most of the administrative committees. Timorous professors and administrators who feared that the Halls of Ivy would crumble if students shared the boredom of committee meetings need not have worried.[59] The period of student revolt has now passed, bringing unquestioned gains and perhaps some losses.

> Typically, a school was imagined to be a place of obtuse, malignant adults who were dedicated to oppressing pure-hearted, liberty-seeking, instinctively humane children. With such cartoon imagery as this, it is no wonder so little was accomplished or that it ended so soon.
>
> Neil Postman, *Teaching as a Conserving Activity* (New York: Delacorte Press, 1979), p. 9.

ACCOUNTABILITY—TO WHOM AND FOR WHAT?   One of the marks of a profession has traditionally been its control over its members through sets of professional ethics, with discipline through professional associations. Thus it was assumed that physicians, lawyers, professors, and (to a lesser degree) school teachers could be trusted to act in the interest of their patients, clients, or pupils with very little external supervision or regulation. Recently, however, the term *accountability* has appeared, suggesting that professionals should be held to account by their clients as well as by their colleagues. Educational accountability[60] includes such ideas as measuring teacher performance by student evaluations or by class learning gains as demonstrated on standardized tests, and holding a school accountable for the pupils' average showing on national norms.[61] Some "educational malpractice" suits have been filed by parents or by former students, claiming damages from the school for their (or their children's) failure to learn. To date, such suits have won no cash judgments.[62] Schools are also being held accountable for the physical safety and study conditions of students. Several lawsuits have been filed by parents of students who suffered physical assault at school, or who blame academic failure on the school's failure to keep the dormitories quiet and studious.[63] This gives university administrators the puzzling task of keeping dormitories safe and quiet without infringing on student freedom.

The movement for educational accountability is too new to have developed any established guidelines. The word *accountability* answers nothing. Who is to be held accountable to whom, for what, measured in what manner?[64] Just how the responsibility for pupil learning should be divided among the school, native pupil abilities, pupil effort, and family background is still being studied. Any comparison of pupil learning under two different teachers or schools must control a number of other variables. The drive for accountability is probably more than a passing fad, and nearly all states now have some sort of statewide accountability law.[65] Carefully controlled evaluative reports are few, and most are unfavorable.[66]

COMMUNITY CONTROL   For several decades we have been closing one-room schools and consolidating school districts. In the major cities this has created vast, impersonal, cumbersome bureaucracies. The inner city schools are heavily populated with poor children—some white, many black, and in some regions Hispanic. Partly as an expression of "black power," and partly as a reaction to huge, impersonal educational bureaucracies, the demand for community control of neighborhood schools arose in major cities. This means that most of the policy-making responsibilities (curriculum, staff selection, and the like) for at least a part of the schools in an area are turned over to a neighborhood school board. Over one-fourth of our largest cities decentralized their schools in this manner.[67] Operating smoothly in some instances, community control brought massive teacher strikes and bitter parent-teacher confrontations in New York City,[68] and most experiments in community control have been surrounded by controversy since their beginning.[69] Community control conflicts with busing for racial balance, and even more sharply with cross-district busing.[70] The busing controversy (discussed in chapter 12) appears to have somewhat eclipsed interest in community control.

CRIME IN THE SCHOOLS   Recent opinion polls have listed "discipline" as the most serious school problem. Classroom order has eroded, while actual crime has grown rapidly.[71] In a typical month, 2.4 million, or 11 percent of all the nation's secondary school students, are robbed, while 282,000 (1.3 percent) are physically assaulted at school, with both victim and attacker usually of the same race and sex.[72] What explains this "crime wave" in the schools?

The crime increase in the schools parallels the increase in juvenile crime throughout the society, but there may be other factors as well. Critics picturing teachers and administrators as oppressive louts may have helped undermine respect for and authority of teachers. The idea of children's rights to "due process" in disciplinary cases may have prevented some injustices, but may also have made it so complicated to apply disciplinary measures that many school staff simply quit trying. School crime is widely believed to have accelerated the flight to the suburbs and the private schools.

THE VOUCHER PLAN FOR ALTERNATIVE SCHOOLS   One possible solution to a number of school problems is the voucher plan. This would permit any number of competing school systems to operate, with parents receiving a voucher that they might cash for their child's attendance at the school of their choice.[73] This would encourage experimentation and variety, but would also increase transportation problems, separatism, provincialism, possibly segregation, and probably over-all costs through duplication. Whether it is desirable to splinter and fragment the public school system can be debated. Our past experience with multiple school systems is not encouraging, but interest in the voucher plan continues.[74]

> . . . the single most important difference between safe schools and violent schools was found to be a strong, dedicated principal who served as a role model for both students and teachers, and who instituted a firm, fair, and consistent system of discipline.
>
> National Institute of Education, *Violent Schools—Safe Schools* (Washington, D.C.: Department of Health, Education and Welfare, 1977), vol. 1, p. iv.

DOES ANYTHING REALLY WORK?   Have the experiments, innovations, and failures of the past two decades taught us anything about how schools must operate if children are to learn?

Yes, we have learned some things. Much of the experimentation and innovation of the 1960s and 1970s was either unproductive or counterproductive, and most of that is being discarded. Some signs of improvement can be found, with a number of school systems reporting 1979 achievement levels above 1978 levels.[75] Possibly the long decline in learning is ending. Ironically, many of the "new" methods given the credit are a return to older methods, which had become unfashionable during the 1960s. When we examine the schools that show the highest achievement averages, we find that they are schools with a strong emphasis upon academic learning, where real learning effort is demanded and rewarded, with teachers who assign homework and parents who insist that it be done—schools with firm discipline, orderly classrooms, and safe halls and toilets. Even an inner-city school, filled with children who are mostly poor and black, can show high achievement levels if the above conditions are met.[76] Even dress codes are coming back into style. Competency tests, as a promotion and graduation requirement, are spreading.[77] School improvement is possible, and we may be making progress toward it.

THE DESCHOOLING MOVEMENT

For a century or more, a worldwide trend toward more and more formal schooling for practically everybody has been matched by the faith that more and more education is just what everybody needs. Today that faith is called into question with the beginning of a reverse trend, away from the endless pyramiding of academic credits. Under the rather clumsy term *deschooling,* this critique of formal education takes several forms.

CREDENTIALS—LADDER OR BARRIER?   A century ago one could perform major surgery, design a bridge, or pilot a locomotive without any kind of license, degree, diploma, or certificate. Many tombstones, collapsed bridges, and compacted railroad trains gave mute testimony to the consequences of incompetence. Today there are very few responsible positions for which one can even make application without presenting the proper credentials. Credentialism provides some assurance of minimum competence, but many critics allege that this assurance of competence is highly unreliable. Instead, the one truly reliable consequence of credentialism, they allege, is to protect the monopoly position of the "ins" and block the upward mobility of the "outs."[78] A number of studies have found instances in which the formal educational requirements proved irrelevant to successful job performance.[79] Educational requirements for a particular job have often been raised without any clear evidence that this will improve job performance. Often it does not; in fact, job performance and job satisfaction often suffer when people are overeducated for the job.[80] The overeducated worker is more often restless or frustrated, changes jobs more frequently, and actually produces less for the employer.

Credentialism is being attacked in the courts, which have held that any credentials requirements that cannot be shown to bear a functional relationship to job performance are in violation of the Equal Employment Opportunities Act. The period of uncritical acceptance of credentials appears to be over, replaced by a more careful assessment of the actual learnings and skills needed for good job performance.

THE OVEREDUCATED SOCIETY—TOO MUCH FOR TOO MANY?   For several decades the shift from unskilled labor to skilled, technical, and professional employment appeared to have created an inexhaustible demand for education. But by the 1970s higher education caught up with demand, and competent college graduates in many fields were disconsolately scanning the want ads. This job crisis is likely to grow more severe in the near future. For example, in 1965 there were two teaching vacancies for each new Ph.D.; in 1972 graduates and vacancies were about equal; today, new Ph.D.'s in nearly all fields are begging for jobs. The blunt truth is that the job market will not absorb all the college graduates our system of higher education is now geared to produce, at the kinds of jobs that college graduates expect.[81]

What are the alternatives? One is to cut back on college admissions. This is politically very difficult. If admissions are to be cut, which applicants are to be rejected? To reverse the recent trend toward more open admissions for poor youths and ethnics would be politically explosive, aside from all ethical considerations. Any real cuts in admissions from the middle and upper classes would be vetoed or circumvented by these powerful segments of society, and probably could not be accomplished without a social revolution. Furthermore, enrollment cuts would injure the short-run vested interests of everyone now engaged in the educational process: students already in the pipeline who wish to graduate, beginning instructors whose jobs are vulnerable to an enrollment decline, tenured professors who want graduate assistants, and administrators with empires to build. It might be sensible to adjust college admissions to the job market, as is done in communist countries. In Prague, for example, 1 in 5 applicants is admitted to law school, and 1 in 12 who wishes to study psychology is permitted to do so.[82] Universities in the People's Republic of China admitted 278,000 students from 5.2 million applicants in 1979—1 in 19.[83] It is doubtful whether any democracy could be so restrictive.

A second possibility is to continue a policy of relatively open admissions but ensure high attrition by strict grading. This counters all present trends in grading. In recent years grades have been drifting upward. Apparently one professorial response to student protest has been lenient grading. Aside from these political considerations, it would be a dangerous social policy to admit and then fail large numbers of young people. It is difficult to imagine a policy more productive of social discontent.

A final proposal is that the society should *find* jobs for all the graduates who need them.[84] In view of the current tax revolt, this proposal is unlikely to be followed. No society in the world—and certainly no Marxist society—recognizes a social obligation to provide for everyone the *kind* or *level* of job he or she desires.

What will happen? All the apparent possibilities are politically impractical. It is possible, however, that some cutback in college enrollment may come through voluntary action. College enrollment slowed its rapid expansion in the 1970s and is likely either to remain stable or decline slightly in the 1980s, after which a modest expansion is expected. Meanwhile, some critics have questioned whether a college education is worth its cost. Caroline Bird argues that a college education does not pay off financially and doubts that the other "benefits" of a college education are very significant.[85] One survey of 30,000 workers finds that each year of additional education gave a greater economic gain in 1973 than in 1962;[86] while another study claims that the "pay-off" for college education has been declining in recent years (except for blacks).[87] Which of these two views predominates may determine whether graduations and job openings are in balance.

A rise in social discontent and conflict would be a predictable result of a persistent job crisis. An unemployed army of highly educated young people forms an explosive political force. They might veer to the radical left, as many radicals hope, or to the fascist right, as they did in Hitler's Germany.[88] But it is unlikely that they would silently suffer.

DESCHOOLING EDUCATION   Another sacred cow—compulsory school attendance—is also being gored today. Some educators are concluding that forcing teenagers to remain in schools that they find boring and pointless probably does them more harm than good. Schools are not the only place where learning can take place, and not always the best place. While some kinds of learning—for example, learning to read—can perhaps be most efficiently learned in a classroom situation, some others—such as learning a vocational skill—are often learned inefficiently and badly in the highly artificial work situation of the classroom. This leads to the suggestion that those areas of teaching that the school does not handle well (for at least some pupils) should be moved outside the school and pursued elsewhere.[89] *Compulsory school attendance* beyond a certain age (possibly 12 or 14) might be replaced by a *compulsory educational program.* For some pupils, this would proceed at school; for others, it might use a variety of programs—split work-study programs, on-the-job training, work training programs operated by business and industry, home-study courses, and evening school are a few possibilities. Such programs are far from new. Many European countries have been using them extensively, and a great expansion of them in the United States is an imminent possibility.

> If we want school to *feel* like a special place, there is no better way to begin than by requiring students to dress in a manner befitting the seriousness of the enterprise and the institution. I should add, teachers as well. I know of one high school in which the principal has put forward a dress code of sorts for the teachers. (He has not, apparently, had the courage to propose one for the students.) For males the requirement is merely a jacket and tie. One of his teachers bitterly complained to me that such a regulation infringed upon his civil rights. And yet, this teacher will accept without complaint the same regulation when it is enforced by an elegant restaurant. His complaint and his acquiescence tell a great deal about how he values schools and how he values restaurants. Apparently, owners of elegant restaurants know more about how to create an atmosphere in a social situation than do many school principals who appear indifferent to the symbolic meaning of dress.
>
> Neil Postman, *Teaching as a Conserving Activity* (New York: Delacorte Press, 1979), pp. 206–07.

AND OTHER PROBLEMS

No one chapter can discuss all the problems of education without becoming impossibly long. Several other problems, possibly of equal importance, can only be mentioned.

Sex education in the schools continues to be hotly disputed. Some argue that explicit sex education beginning in the upper elementary grades will encourage more responsible sexual behavior; while others fear that it will excite more sex irresponsibility. *Sexual harassment* on the campus, especially of female graduate students by senior professors, is commanding increasing attention.[90] *Sex discrimination* remains a problem in such areas as faculty hiring, promotion, and compensation; in granting of scholarships and assistantships; and in allocation of athletic funds.

Testing for college, graduate school, and professional school admission and for professional certification is under fire.[91] The state of New York now requires that all such test answers be published after one use, a move which testers claim will make tests less reliable and more costly. *Diploma mills* continue to sell academic degrees.[92] *Athletic scandals* erupt regularly, with colleges finding ways to "pay" athletes in violation of National Collegiate Athletic Association regulations and falsifying grades to keep athletes eligible.[93]

Mainstreaming children with physical handicaps or emotional disturbances is required under the Education for All Handicapped Children Act, which took effect in 1977. Proponents argue that most levels of handicap are better handled in regular classrooms than in "special education" classes, where children are isolated from the real world in which they must eventually live.[94] Critics question the benefits for handicapped children of such mainstreaming, and charge that classes are often so disrupted that the learning of other children suffers.

Drugs have become a serious school problem. Whatever the effects of long-term alcohol or marijuana use (see chapter 16), the immediate effect is to impair memory and learning capacity.[95] Pupils who come to school stoned or who take a snort or a joint between classes will learn nothing much that day. Any school where the toilets regularly smell of marijuana is a school where average achievement levels will be predictably low.

These and other problems could easily fill another chapter—or another book.

The Social-Disorganization Approach

The swift changes in the definition of educational "problems" illustrates how problems grow from social change. A few years ago, the main educational "problems" were the shortage of teachers and school facilities, the issue of federal aid to education, and the controversy over "communism in the schools."[96] Today none of these topics is widely perceived as a major issue.

Our century-long drive to give more and more education to everybody

Efforts have been growing to mainstream the handicapped student into the traditional classroom, as in this high school math class.
(Sybil Shelton, Monkmeyer)

is wavering as the suspicions of overeducation form. Our faith that money solves most educational deficiencies is disproven by recent evidence. A generation of young people are emphatically rejecting the notion that their elders know what is best for them, and are vociferously demanding greater control over their learning process. Parent and neighborhood groups clamor for control. Teachers' unions are flexing their muscles at all levels from kindergarten to the university. If the planned merger of the American Federation of Teachers and the National Education Association is accomplished, they will form the nation's largest union.

Will our educational institutions digest these changes and emerge from the present state of disorganized confusion into a new, stable equilibrium? Probably not, for social change is too continuous and rapid. Campus turmoil has receded from the late 1960s peak, but most of the basic issues remain unsettled. School desegregation and busing (treated in the chapter on race relations) remain unsettled. The current trend toward making higher education more accessible to the poor and the nonwhites is on a collision course with the need to restrict college enrollments. No resolution of basic issues in a new equilibrium seems likely. An indefinite period of continuing tumultuous adjustment seems to be the most likely prospect.

The Value-Conflict Approach

A conflict of values is basic to each educational problem. What should be the goals of education? To preserve or to transform the society? To maintain or to undermine the class system? To educate for adjustment to our existing society or to promote the recruitment and training of change agents? To indoctrinate the young in which set of values?

Should the schools try to promote equality of opportunity or equality of reward? We have already decided that each adult citizen shall have an equal vote. Does democracy also require that each person should also have an equal income? Thus, the unsettled value conflicts of the society become the problems of the school, since the members of the society cannot agree on what the school should be and do. Not only differences over *means*, but also differences over *ends* are involved. People who disagree about the kind of society they want must also disagree upon how children should be trained to live in society. As long as such value conflicts persist—and they will persist at least as long as our society continues to change—educational controversies are inevitable.

The Personal-Deviation Approach

Educational problems are ones in which deviant persons are incidental rather than major factors. If there were no value conflicts involved, deviant persons would be unable to transmute their private grudges into social issues. Since there *are* important value conflicts, plus many misinformed people, it is possible for deviant persons to play a major role in mobilizing people for school battles. Close observers of local school battles have been impressed by the large number of hostile, aggressive, resentful, hate-filled persons who appear at mass meetings. Many persons who, throughout an adult lifetime, have shown no particular interest in the school suddenly become bitter participants in a school battle. Sometimes these are maladjusted people who have displaced their inner emotional conflicts upon the school or upon some group of school people. The occasional eruption of local battles over sex education, in the face of the overwhelmingly popular support of sex education in the schools, shows the power of a dedicated handful of fanatics to promote a local controversy.

Not all who criticize the school, of course, are neurotics. Some are cynical opportunists, planning to cut school costs or to capture the school as an instrument for their propaganda. Some are honest critics, calling attention to the genuine failures and dubious aspects of the school's operation. And not all the neurotics are found among the attackers. Educators and teachers have their share of eccentric and maladjusted personalities, apparently in about the same proportion as in other professions. Although neurotics and fanatics appear more likely to join the free-swinging attackers, they may also turn up among the school's defenders.

Nor should deviance be equated with neuroticism. One does not need to be a neurotic or a fanatic to feel that something needs changing in our schools. While some of the schools' critics and innovators have been arrogant, polemical fanatics, many others have been well-balanced, dedicated educators seeking new answers to old problems. The basic causes of most educational problems are found, not in the failings of individuals, but in the value conflicts of a changing (disorganized) society.

Future Prospects

Since educational problems are rooted in the value conflicts that a changing society inevitably produces, no complete or final solutions are possible. Even if final solutions for educational problems were possible, further social change would soon produce new problems. All major educational problems—curriculum, teaching methods, finances, controls—are *permanent problems,* in that social changes will continue to excite debate and call for readjustment. The prospect is for a continuing process of *accommodation* through which conflicting wishes and pressures of a democratic society can be compromised. Wherever ultimate solutions are unavailable, accommodation provides democracy's alternative to chaos, and nowhere is this more true than in education. This is a far from gloomy prospect, since most of us consider the argumentative and wordy compromises of democracy far preferable to the orderly discipline of monolithic authority.

Summary

American education transmits the culture, prepares people for work, confers status, and possibly excludes others from choice positions.

Costs are a growing problem, with taxpayers in rebellion at rising taxes, and many private schools and colleges are probably doomed to close. Equality of educational opportunity is a goal that can never be perfectly attained. Revisionist critics charge that schools were planned to perpetuate inequality and privilege and to block mobility, but most of the evidence indicates otherwise. While class background is an important factor in school progress, individual abilities and efforts and family encouragement of learning are more important factors.

Considerable expensive experimentation and innovation in recent decades has been largely unproductive. Schools are now reviving some older procedures, which are shown to produce higher levels of achievement. Alternative or free schools were a fad whose high hopes proved largely illusory.

School control remains an important issue, with administrators under many pressures which limit their decision-making functions. Community control, briefly a key issue, is now largely buried under the busing issue. School crime has become a major problem. Other issues revolve around credentials and testing, the question of overeducation, the issue of bilingual instruction, and still other unsolved matters. Present trends include a move back toward firm discipline and structured education.

Suggested Readings

BIRD, CAROLINE, *The Case against College* (New York: David McKay, 1975, excerpted as "College Is a Waste of Money," *Psychology Today,* May 1975, pp. 28ff.). A controversial attack upon the value of college education. For a critical reply, see Fred M. Hechinger, "Murder in Academe: The Demise of Education," *Saturday Review,* 20 Mar. 1976, pp. 11–18.

BOWLES, SAMUEL and HERBERT GINTIS, *Schooling in Capitalist America: Educational Reforms and the Contradictions of Economic Life* (New York: Basic Books, 1976). A radical critique of American education.

BRUCK, CONNIE, "Battle Lines in the Ritalin War," *Human Behavior,* Aug. 1976, pp. 25–33. An account of the controversy over the use of ritalin upon "hyperactive" children.

COLEMAN, JAMES S., et al., *Equality of Educational Opportunity* (Washington, D.C.: U.S. Department of Health, Education and Welfare, 1966). A monumental study of the quality and the inequality of American schools.

FINCHER, JACK, "Depriving the Best and the Brightest," *Human Behavior,* Apr. 1976, pp. 17–20. A brief lament over our national inattention to the educational needs of gifted children.

HASSETT, JOSEPH D., and ARLINE WEISBERG, *Open Education: Alternatives within Our Tradition* (Englewood Cliffs, N.J.: Prentice-Hall, 1972). A brief, balanced discussion of open education.

HOLT, JOHN, *Instead of Education: Ways to Help People Do Things Better* (New York: E. P. Dutton, 1976). A popular critic presents a mixed bag of proposals, some promising and some long since tried and discarded.

JENCKS, CHRISTOPHER, et al., *Inequality: A Reassessment of the Effect of Family and Schooling in America* (New York: Basic Books, 1972). Concludes that schools have not, and probably cannot, greatly affect the distribution of income and status. Summarized briefly in Mary Jo Bane and Christopher Jencks, "Schools and Equal Opportunity," *Saturday Review of Education,* 16 Sept. 1972, pp. 37–42.

KASUN, JACQUELINE, "Turning Children Into Sex Experts," *The Public Interest,* Spring 1979, pp. 3–14; PAUL V. CROSBIE, "Sex Education: Another Look," *The Public Interest,* Winter 1980, pp. 120–29; JACQUELINE KASUN, "More on the New Sex Education," *The Public Interest,* Winter 1980, pp. 129–37. Three short articles in which Kasun criticizes and Crosbie supports sex education in the public schools.

POSTMAN, NEIL, *Teaching as a Conserving Activity* (New York: Delacorte Press, 1979). A readable book by one who used to be viewed as an education radical, but who now favors an orderly, disciplined, structured school experience.

RAVITCH, DIANE, *The Revisionists Revised: A Critique of the Radical Attack on the*

Schools (New York: Basic Books, 1977). An evidence-based reply to radical critics.

REHBERG, RICHARD A., and EVELYN R. ROSENTHAL, *Class and Merit in the American High School: An Assessment of the Revisionist and Meritocratic Arguments* (New York: Longmans, 1978). A research study concluding that merit rather than social class is the strongest determinant of school achievement.

SEWELL, WILLIAM H., ROBERT M. HAUSER, et al., *Education, Occupation, and Earnings in the Early Career* (New York: Academic Press, 1975). A research study of male college graduates, finding that IQ and college grades correlated more highly with earnings than did socioeconomic background.

SOWELL, THOMAS, "Patterns of Black Excellence," *The Public Interest* (Spring 1976), pp. 26–58. An examination of high-achieving black schools.

TOBY, JACKSON, "Crime in American Public Schools," *The Public Interest* (Winter 1980), pp. 18–43. A readable analysis of violence and disorder in public schools.

ZAJONC, ROBERT B., "Birth Order and Intelligence: Dumber by the Dozen," *Psychology Today*, Jan. 1975, pp. 37–43; or, Carol Tavris, "The End of the I.Q. Slump," *Psychology Today*, Apr. 1976, pp. 69–74. Claims that recent declines in achievement test scores are due to increased family size after World War II.

Footnotes

[1]Gaius Petronius, *The Satyricon*, A.D., First Century.

[2]John Holt, *The Underachieving School* (New York: Pitman, 1969), p. ix.

[3]Barret J. Mandell, "The Absurd Calling: or, I Know Someone Who Knows John Holt . . . ," *AAUP Bulletin*, 57 (Autumn 1971), 334–40.

[4]Ivan Berg, *Education and Jobs: The Great Training Robbery* (New York: Praeger, 1970).

[5]Randall Collins, "Functional and Conflict Theories of Educational Stratification," *American Sociological Review*, 36 (Dec. 1971), 1002–19.

[6]Ibid.

[7]*Statistical Abstract of the United States*, 1979, p. 136.

[8]Daniel P. Moynihan, "Equalizing Education—In Whose Benefit?" *The Public Interest*, Fall 1972, pp. 68–89.

[9]It is possible that the teacher shortage was the major factor and that collective bargaining and union representation were relatively unimportant, according to Hirschel Kasper, "The Effects of Collective Bargaining on Public School Teachers' Salaries," *Industrial Labor Relations Review*, 24 (Oct. 1970), 56–72. See also Sam P. Santelle, *Teacher Militancy, Negotiations, and Strikes* (Washington, D.C.: Dept. of Health, Education and Welfare, 1972).

[10]John A. Centra, *College Enrollment in the 1980s: Projections and Possibilities* (New York: The College Board, 1978); excerpted in *Academe*, 66 (Feb. 1980), 16–18; Edward A. Fiske, "A New Kind of Shortage: Students," *New York Times*, 11 Nov. 1979, sec. 12, pp. 1ff.

[11]Sally Reed, "Another Baby Boom in Sight for Schools," *New York Times*, 11 Nov. 1979, sec. 12, p. 21.

[12]David W. Breneman and Chester E. Finn, Jr., *Public Policy and Private Higher Education* (Washington, D.C.: The Brookings Institution, 1978).

[13]Michael B. Katz, *Class, Bureaucracy and Schools: The Illusion of Educational Change in America* (New York: Praeger, 1971); Colin Greer, *The Great School Legend* (New York: Basic Books, 1972); Martin Carnoy, *Education as Cultural Imperialism* (New York: David McKay, 1975); Walter Feinberg, *Reason and Rhetoric: The Intellectual Foundations of Twentieth-Century Educational Policy* (New York: Wiley, 1975); Jonathan Kozol, *The Night is Dark, and I Am Far from Home* (Boston: Houghton Mifflin, 1975); Joel Spring, *A Primer of Liberation Education* (New York: Free Life Editions, 1975); Samuel Bowles and Herbert Gintis, *Schooling in Capitalist America: Educational Reform and the Contradictions of Economic Life* (New York: Basic Books, 1976); Michael W. Apple, *Ideology and Curriculum* (Boston: Routledge and Kegan Paul, 1979).

[14]Greer, *The Great School Legend*.

[15]Ravitch, Diane, *The Revisionists Revised* (New York: Basic Books, 1978), ch. 7, "A Critique of Radical Criticism."

[16]Murray Milner, Jr., *The Illusion of Equality* (San Francisco: Jossey-Bass, 1972); Christopher Jencks et al., *Inequality: A Reassessment of the Effects of Family and Schooling in America* (New York: Basic Books, 1972).

[17]Ravitch, *The Revisionists Revised;* Richard A. Rehberg and Evelyn R. Rosenthal, *Class and Merit in the American High School: An Assessment of the Revisionist and Meritocratic Arguments* (New York: Longmans, 1978).

[18]Thomas Kessner, *The Golden Door: Italian and Immigrant Mobility in New York City, 1880–1915* (New York: Oxford University Press, 1977).

[19]Rehberg and Rosenthal, *Class and Merit in the American High School;* Michael Rutter et al., *Fifteen Thousand Hours* (Cambridge: Harvard University Press, 1979), p. 180.

[20]William H. Sewell and Robert M. Hauser, *Education, Occupation and Earnings: Achievement in the Early Career* (New York: Academic Press, 1975), p. 184.

[21]Robert M. Hauser and David L. Featherman, "Equality of Access to Schooling: Trends and Prospects," *Center for Demography and Ecology, Working Paper 75–17* (Madison: University of Wisconsin, 1975), pp. 20–21.

[22]Mervyn Matthews, "Class Bias in Russian Education," *New Society,* 12 (19 Dec. 1968), 911–13; Seymour Martin Lipset, "La mobilité social et les objectifs socialistes," *Sociologie et Sociétés,* 4 (Nov. 1972), 193–224; Joseleyne Slade Tien, "Percy Bysshe Shelley and the Cultural Revolution at Wuhan University," *Harvard Educational Review,* 45 (May 1975), 211–23.

[23]See Milovan Djilas, *The New Class* (New York: Praeger, 1957), for an account of the rapid development of the new upper class in the "classless" society of Yugoslavia. For accounts of similar developments in other socialist countries, see David K. Shipler, "Making It in Russian Style," *New York Times Magazine,* 11 Feb. 1979, pp. 38ff.; Seymour Topping, "China's Long March into the Future," *New York Times Magazine,* 3 Feb. 1980, pp. 28ff.

[24]David L. Featherman and Robert M. Hauser, "Sexual Inequality and Socioeconomic Achievement," *American Sociological Review,* 41 (June 1976), 481.

[25]Philip Carey and Donald Allen, "Black Studies: Expectation and Impact on Self-Esteem and Academic Performance," *Social Science Quarterly,* 57 (Mar. 1977), 811–20.

[26]Arnold L. Robinson et al., *Black Studies in the University: A Symposium* (New Haven, Conn.: Yale University Press, 1969); Bayard Rustin, ed., *Black Studies: Myths and Realities* (New York: A Philip Randolph Educational Fund, 1969); Walter G. Daniel, "Black Studies in American Education," *Journal of Negro Education,* 39 (Summer 1970), 189–91.

[27]Bayard Rustin, *Black Studies;* Clement E. Vontress, "Black Studies—Boon or Bane?" *Journal of Negro Education,* 39 (Summer 1970), 192–201.

[28]William David Smith, "Black Studies: Recommendations for Organization and National Consideration," *Journal of Negro Education,* 44 (Spring 1975), 170–76; Nick Aaron Ford, *Black Studies: Threat or Challenge?* (Port Washington, N.Y.: Kennikat Press, 1973). For a severe indictment of black studies, see Thomas Sowell, *Black Education: Myths and Tragedies* (New York: David McKay, 1972).

[29]St. Clair Drake, "What Happened to Black Studies," *Educational Quarterly,* 10 (Sept. 1979), 9–16.

[30]Jim Hightower, *Hard Tomatoes, Hard Times: Failure of the Land-Grant College Complex* (New York: Schenkman, 1973).

[31]See John Holt, *How Children Fail* (New York: Pitman, 1965); Herbert Kohl, *36 Children* (New York: New American Library, 1967); Jonathan Kozol, *Death at an Early Age* (Boston: Houghton Mifflin, 1967); Joseph Katz, *No Time for Youth* (San Francisco: Jossey-Bass, 1968); James Herndon, *The Way Its Spozed to Be* (New York: Simon & Schuster, 1968); also Greer, *The Great School Legend;* Carnoy, *Education as Cultural Imperialism;* Kozol, *The Night Is Dark;* and Bowles and Gintis, *Schooling in Capitalist America.*

[32]Ibid.

[33]Greer, *The Great School Legend.*

[34]See "Global Report Card," *Time,* 9 Oct. 1972, pp. 46–47.

[35]Ibid.

[36]Rehberg and Rosenthal, *Class and Merit in the American High School,* pp. 252–62; Rutter et al, *Fifteen Thousand Hours,* p. 178.

[37]Rutter et al., *Fifteen Thousand Hours,* pp. 179–80.

[38]Quoted from *Institute for Social Research Newsletter* (Ann Arbor: University of Michigan, Autumn 1972), p. 6. A similar study by the International Association for the Evaluation of Educational Achievement, covering 20 countries, also concluded that differences in individual abilities and home atmosphere are the most important variables in pupil learning. See *Science News,* 103 (9 June 1973), 372.

[39]Mary Jo Bane and Christopher Jencks, "Schools and Equal Opportunity," excerpt from "Inequality: A Reassessment of the Effect of Family and Schooling in America," *Saturday Review of Education*, 16 Sept. 1972, pp. 37–42.

[40]John H. Martin and Charles H. Harrison, *Free to Learn: Unlocking and Ungrading American Education* (Englewood Cliffs, N.J.: Prentice-Hall, 1972), p. 2.

[41]Frank E. Armbruster, "The More We Spend, the Less Children Learn," *New York Times Magazine*, 28 Aug. 1977, pp. 9ff., excerpted as "Why American Education is Failing," *Reader's Digest*, Jan. 1978, pp. 106–09; "On Further Examination: The SAT Score Decline," *Science News*, 112 (3 Sept. 1977), 148–49; Paul Copperman, *The Literacy Hoax: The Decline of Reading, Writing, and Learning in the Public Schools and What We Can Do about It* (New York: William Morrow, 1978).

[42]Edward Ziegler and Jeanette Valentine, *Project Head Start: A Legacy of the War on Poverty* (New York: Free Press, 1979); Nancy Rubin, "Headstart Efforts Prove Their Value," *New York Times*, 6 Feb. 1980, sec. 13, p. 13.

[43]Rudolph Troike, "Bilingual Education in the United States," *International Review of Education*, 24 (no. 3, 1978), 401–05.

[44]*New York Times*, 9 Mar. 1978, p. 26.

[45]Christina Bratt Paulston, "Research," in *Bilingual Education: Current Perspectives—Linguistics* (Arlington, Va.: Center for Applied Linguistics, 1977), pp. 1–63.

[46]John MacNamara, *Bilingualism in Primary Education: A Study of Irish Experience* (Edinburgh: University of Edinburgh Press, 1966).

[47]Rolf Kuoseth, "Bilingual Education in the United States: For Assimilation or Pluralism?" in Bernard Spolsky, ed., *The Language Education of Minority Children* (Rowley, Mass.: Newbury House, 1977), pp. 94–121.

[48]See footnote 31.

[49]See Anne Brewer and John Brewer, *Open Education* (New York: Holt, Rinehart and Winston, 1972); and Joseph D. Hassett and Arline Weisberg, *Open Education: Alternatives within Our Tradition* (Englewood Cliffs, N.J.: Prentice-Hall, 1972).

[50]Allen Graubard, "The Free School Movement," *Harvard Educational Review*, 42 (Aug. 1972), 351–73.

[51]Ibid.

[52]Mary Jo Bane, "Essay Review: Open Education," *Harvard Educational Review*, 42 (May 1972), 273–81; Marilyn Kourilsky and Eva L. Baker, "An Empirical Comparison of Open and Nonopen Structured Classrooms," *California Journal of Educational Research*, 26 (Nov. 1975), 238–81; David E. Denton, "Open Education: Search for a New Myth," *Educational Theory*, 25 (Fall 1975), 397–406.

[53]Jonathan Kozol, "Free Schools Fail Because They Don't TEACH," *Psychology Today*, Apr. 1972, pp. 30ff.

[54]See "Students Protest Teaching Method," *New York Times*, 29 Feb. 1976, p. 54.

[55]Bane, *Essay Review*, p. 74.

[56]See William Lowe Boyd, "The Changing Politics of Curriculum Policy-Making for American Schools," *Review of Educational Research*, 48 (Fall 1978), 577–628; Ewald B. Nyquist, "So You Think Schools Make the Curriculum," *New York Times*, 11 Nov. 1979, sec. 12, p. 28.

[57]Joseph A. Califano, Jr., *The Student Revolution: A Global Confrontation* (New York: W. W. Norton, 1970); Raymond Boudon, "Sources of Student Protest in France," *The Annals of the American Academy of Political and Social Science*, 395 (May 1971), 139–49; William John Hanna, "Student Protest in Independent Black Africa," *The Annals of the American Academy of Political and Social Science*, 395 (May 1971), 171–83; Fritz Stern, "Reflections on the International Student Movement," *American Scholar*, 40 (Winter 1970–71), 123–37.

[58]Bill Severn, *Five Thousand Years of Fun and Fury over Hair* (New York: David McKay, 1971).

[59]The main difficulty with student committee members has been nonattendance (at least in the experience of your author).

[60]Leon M. Lessinger and Ralph W. Tyler, eds., *Accountability in Education* (Belmont, Ca.: Wadsworth, 1971); Sheila Huff, "Accounting for Education," *Society*, Jan. 1976, pp. 44–52.

[61]Gene I. Maeroff, "Schools Now Are Taking Account of Accountability," *New York Times*, 10 Oct. 1976, sec. 4, p. 8.

[62]"Litigous Parents Lose on Schools," *New York Times*, 23 Dec. 1979, sec. 4, p. 7.

[63]Editorial, *Southern Sociologist*, Jan. 1972, pp. 1ff.

[64]Edward Wynne, "Accountability for Whom?" *Society*, Jan./Feb. 1976, pp. 30–37.

[65]Allan C. Ornstein, "The Politics of Accountability," *Clearing House,* 49 (Sept. 1975), 5–10.

[66]Ernest R. House et al., "An Assessment of the Michigan Accountability System," *Phi Delta Kappan,* 55 (June 1974), 663–69.

[67]George R. LaNove and Bruce L. R. Smith, "The Political Evolution of School Decentralization," *American Behavioral Scientist,* 15 (Sept.–Oct. 1971), 73–93.

[68]"Crisis in Education: A Power Struggle Overwhelms New York's Schools," *New York Times,* 15 Sept. 1968, sec. 4, p. 11; Albert Shanker, "Decentralization: Politics or Education," *New York Times,* 28 Nov. 1976, sec. 4, p. 9.

[69]See "Turmoil over Local Control," *New York Times,* 3 Dec. 1972, sec. 4, p. 7; Herbert Kohl, "Community Control: Failed or Undermined," *Phi Delta Kappan,* 57 (Feb. 1976), 370ff.

[70]See chapter 12, "Race Discrimination in American Life," for a discussion of busing for racial balance.

[71]National Institute of Education, *Violent Schools–Safe Schools* (Washington, D.C.: Department of Health, Education, and Welfare, 1977); James M. McPartland and Edward L. McDill, *Violence in the Schools: Perspectives, Programs, and Positions* (Lexington, Mass.: Lexington Books, 1977).

[72]*Violent Schools–Safe Schools,* vol. 1, pp. iii, 113.

[73]Mario Fanfani, *Public Schools of Choice* (New York: Simon and Schuster, 1973).

[74]See "Radical Change in the Schools: Two Views of the Voucher Plan" (by John E. Coons and Albert Shanker), *New York Times,* 30 Dec. 1979, sec. 13, p. 16.

[75]Gene I. Maeroff, "Inner City Schools Show Signs of Progress," *New York Times,* 6 Jan. 1980, sec. 13, p. 1.

[76]J. S. Fuerst, "Report from Chicago: A Program That Works," *The Public Interest,* Spring 1976, pp. 59–69; Thomas Sowell, "Patterns of Black Excellence," *The Public Interest,* Spring 1976, pp. 26–58.

[77]National Council for the Social Studies, "Graduation Competency Testing in the Social Studies: A Position Statement," *Social Education,* 43 (May 1979), 367–72; Ralph D. Turlington, "Good News from Florida: Our Competency Program Is Working," *Phi Delta Kappan,* 60 (May 1979), 649–51; Arthur Wise, "Why Minimum Competency Testing Will Not Improve Education," *Educational Leadership,* 36 (May 1979), 546–49; discussion, 549–52ff.

[78]Ronald Dore, *The Diploma Disease: Education, Qualification, and Development* (Berkeley, University of California Press, 1976); Randall Collins, *The Credential Society: An Historical Sociology of Education and Stratification* (Charlottesville: University of Virginia Press, 1979).

[79]Berg, *Education and Jobs,* chs. 7–9; also Blanche D. Blank, "Degrees: Who Needs Them?" *AAUP Bulletin,* 58 (Autumn 1972), 261–66.

[80]Berg, *Education and Jobs,* chs. 5–7; Robert P. Quinn and Martha S. Baldi de Mandilovitch, *Education and Job Satisfaction: A Questionable Payoff* (Ann Arbor: Survey Research Center, University of Michigan, 1975).

[81]Richard B. Freeman, *The Over-Educated American* (New York: Academic Press, 1976).

[82]Associated Press, 19 Aug. 1976.

[83]*New York Times Magazine,* 3 Feb. 1980, p. 48.

[84]When labor unions do this, it is called featherbedding, a practice which comfortable academics used to criticize. To practice it, academics will have to find another name for it.

[85]Caroline Bird, *The Case against College* (New York: David McKay, 1975); excerpt reprinted as "College Is a Waste of Money," *Psychology Today,* May 1975, pp. 28ff.

[86]Featherman and Hauser, "Sexual Inequality and Socioeconomic Achievement."

[87]Freeman, *The Over-Educated American,* ch. 1.

[88]See Calvin B. Hoover, *Germany Enters the Third Reich* (New York: Macmillan, 1933).

[89]Ivan Illich, *Deschooling Society* (New York: Harper & Row, 1971); James S. Coleman, "The Children Have Outgrown the Schools," *Psychology Today,* Feb. 1972, pp. 72–82; Peter Marin et al., eds., *The Limits of Schooling* (Englewood Cliffs, N.J.: Prentice-Hall, 1975).

[90]"Fighting Lechery on the Campus," *Time,* 4 Feb. 1980, p. 84.

[91]Edward B. Fiske, "Finding Fault with the Testers," *New York Times Magazine,* 18 Nov. 1979, pp. 152ff.

[92]Your author's little dog, Pepi, mentioned in an earlier chapter as a minister ordained by the Universal Life Church, also holds a Ph.D. degree from a diploma mill calling itself the University of Eastern Florida.

[93]"Behind Scandals in Big-Time

College Sports," *U.S. News and World Report,* 11 Feb. 1980, pp. 61–63.

[94]James Barron, "How Mainstreaming Works . . ." (and) Penny Rogg, ". . . And How Parents Can Help," *New York Times,* 11 Nov. 1979, p. 13.

[95]Elizabeth Loftus, "Alcohol, Marijuana, and Memory," *Psychology Today,* Mar. 1980, pp. 42ff.

[96]See this chapter in the first two editions of this textbook (1955, 1960), from which scarcely a line is retained in this edition.

POVERTY

Some 15 years after having been officially declared, America's war on poverty is still bogged down in the trenches, little closer to victory than when it began. . . . Despite all the innovative programs and the hundreds of billions of dollars spent, the number of people classed as poor remains essentially unchanged from what it was a decade ago. In fact, experts today cannot even agree on what poverty is, let alone how to eliminate it.

Some authorities argue that the government's own statistics prove that poverty programs have been an unmitigated failure and should be scrapped. Others contend that their studies show the exact opposite—that, for all practical purposes, real deprivation no longer exists in this country and victory over poverty should be declared. . . .[1]

Poverty offers excellent justification of our definition of social problems. Poverty has probably always affected large numbers of people, but has not always been regarded as bad, and there has not always been agreement that something should be done about poverty through collective social action.

Fifty years ago, the Great Depression of the 1930s plunged millions of formerly financially comfortable people into poverty, and thus it was defined as a social problem. With the end of the depression, however, they recovered, and poverty no longer received great public notice. In fact, in the prosperity of the 1940s and 1950s, stereotypes of the poor that blamed them for their own problems became popular. The poor were portrayed as lazy, shiftless, unwilling to work, immoral, and anxious to live on the public dole. Not until the early 1960s did the accumulation of data by the federal government cause scholars and policy makers to recognize that the costs of poverty were huge, and that the popular stereotypes were far off the mark.

The Size and Cost of the Problem

In 1962 the Conference on Economic Progress reported that one-fifth of the American population lived in actual poverty and that another fifth lived just above the poverty line but still in deprivation. It found substantial amounts of poverty in every section of the country, in almost every occupational category, in the cities and in the country, families and among single people, among whites, blacks, and virtually all ethnic groups, among children and among old people.[2]

Between 1962 and 1970, under the impact of a federal antipoverty program and also because of general prosperity, the fraction of the United States population defined officially as living in poverty dropped to one-eighth, or some 25.5 million people. Poverty seemed on the way to elimination.

By 1970, however, the poverty program had run into serious trouble, the Vietnam War was draining away a large share of federal resources, and the economy took a major turn for the worse. Between 1970 and 1974 the official poor declined by only 1.2 million people, from 25.5 million to 24.3 million. From 1973 to 1975 the poor actually increased to 25.9 million because of an economic recession. Future prospects for the economy are not uniformly bright, and it may be that the trend of the past twenty years or so, in which improvements in the economy reduced the number of poor, is over. If poverty is to be reduced further, it may have to be as a direct result of new federal programs.

The total cost of the poverty problem is unknown and, perhaps unknowable. Currently, some 12 percent of the population is officially defined as poor.

Feeding the hungry marchers in Washington, D.C. during the Great Depression.
(United Press International)

Undoubtedly, the indirect costs of poverty are great. One of those costs is the underdevelopment and underuse of human resources. The standard of living for the entire society is dragged down by the need to support the poor, and the ugliness and unhealthiness of poverty affects us all. The United States Department of Labor estimates that 25 to 50 percent of the labor force in poverty areas of eight large cities is employed at below capacity.

Poverty is linked to many forms of social pathology. A study of tuberculosis in New Orleans, for example, revealed that 44 percent of all cases were concentrated in slum sections covering only about one-fourth of the residential areas of the city. A similar study in Newark revealed the incidence of tuberculosis and infant mortality to be two and two-thirds times as high in slum areas as in public housing areas. The incidence of communicable disease among children under five years of age was two and one-half times as high in the slum areas. Additional studies in Philadelphia, Cleveland, and other cities showed juvenile delinquency rates several times higher in poor housing areas than in other areas.[3]

This is the general magnitude of poverty in the United States, along with some of its costs. The problem of specifying costs is directly linked to definitions of poverty. Satisfactory definitions of such a seemingly obvious phenomenon as poverty are, upon close examination, remarkably complex.

Definitions of Poverty

Most of us are so accustomed to reading newspaper reports to the effect that such and such numbers of people fall below the poverty line that it never occurs to us to question whether there really is a "poverty line," how that poverty line was arrived at, or whether some alternative method of establishing the poverty line might not be more appropriate.

There are at least three different ways to define poverty, each starting from a separate set of assumptions and leading to its own conclusions about the extent of poverty and the degree to which it is being lessened. The first way is to set the poverty line arbitrarily in terms of some absolute income needed to maintain a minimum standard of living. This is the approach followed by the federal government, and we will return to it later.

A second way to define poverty uses a relative standard rather than an absolute one. The poverty level is designated as some fraction (say 25, 33, or 50 percent) of mean or median income. When the poor are identified in this way, they are simply those who have fallen behind the standards of the society.

Still a third way is to define poverty in terms of the share of the total national income that is received by some fraction of the population. Although some other convention might be used, over the years it has become customary to look at the share of the national income received by the bottom one-fifth of the population.

The implications of these three ways of defining poverty are suggested in the figures presented in table 11–1. The table presents data covering the 25-year period from 1950 to 1975. The implications of the absolute standard approach are suggested by column 2. If the poverty line is set at $3,000, 16 percent of the population was poor in 1950, but only 4.5 percent were still poor in 1975. Using this conception of poverty, it is obvious how the extent of poverty might be reduced further. Welfare programs might be increased, a negative income tax might be instituted, or a guaranteed annual income might be provided. Each of these would raise additional numbers of people above the poverty line.

The implications of the second, or relative standard, approach can be seen in column 3 of table 11–1. The figures show that the proportion of the population whose incomes remained at less than one-half of the median income remained relatively unchanged from 1950 through 1975. Although the dollar incomes of many people rose during that time, some one-fifth of the population remained, relatively speaking, as far behind as ever. The meaning of this approach for national policy also is striking. The only way that poverty could be reduced would be through measures designed to decrease differences in income. Welfare and income measures for the poor would help, but sharply progressive income taxes also would be required.

Finally, the "share" approach to defining poverty is shown in columns 5 and 6 of table 11–1. These figures show virtually no change over the 25-year-period. The bottom 20 percent of the population had less than 5 percent of the income in 1950, while the top 20 percent had almost 43 percent of the income. In 1975, the bottom fifth was receiving only slightly over 5

TABLE 11–1   Family Income in the United States, 1950–75 (standardized 1975 dollars)

Year	Percent of families with incomes				Percent family income received by	
	Over $25,000	Under $3,000	Less than half the median	Median income dollars	Wealthiest one-fifth	Poorest one-fifth
1950	2.0*	16.1	20.0	$ 7,422	42.8	4.5
1955	2.8	12.6	20.0	8,881	41.8	4.8
1960	5.0	10.2	20.3	10,214	42.7	4.9
1965	8.2	7.4	20.0	11,867	41.3	5.3
1970	12.6	5.3	19.6	13,676	41.6	5.5
1975	14.1	4.5	19.7	13,719	41.1	5.4

*Precise figures not available; these are our interpolations.
SOURCE: Gerald R. Leslie, Richard F. Larson, and Benjamin L. Gorman, *Introductory Sociology: Order and Change* (New York: Oxford University Press, 1980), p. 368.

percent, while the top fifth was still getting 41 percent. According to the assumptions underlying this approach, poverty cannot be eliminated by drawing the poor above either an absolute or a relative line. The only thing that would help would be to reduce inequalities in income. To the array of measures described in connection with the first two approaches, one might add the imposition of ceilings on wages, salaries, and profits.

Until the 1960s definitions of poverty were important to scholars only, and not even to many of them. Then, suddenly, poverty became a public issue and various groups began trying to define and measure it. The first "official" estimates were made by the President's Council of Economic Advisers in 1964. Arbitrarily, they chose $3,000 total annual family income as the dividing line and analyzed 1959 income data on that basis; 34.5 million people were classified as poor.

The deficiencies in such an arbitrary definition were obvious enough, and efforts were undertaken to find an objective basis for measuring poverty. The Department of Agriculture, the Social Security Administration, the Office of Economic Opportunity, and other agencies became involved. The standard that came to be used was based on a food budget estimated as an "economy food plan for emergency use." The poverty level was set at three times the amount of that food budget.

Obviously, food budgets vary by size of family and by where the family lives, so allowances were made for number of people in the family and separate estimates were made for farm and nonfarm groups. No allowances have yet been made for regional variations or for the higher prices encountered in central city areas.

The 1960s and 1970s were a period of substantial inflation; finally, in 1968, changes in the Consumer Price Index began to be taken into account. Since the price level has increased each year, the so-called poverty line has also been raised. In 1969 the poverty line for a nonfarm family of four was $3,553. In 1971 it was $4,137, and in 1979 it was $6,700. These increases represent no raising of standards but only increases in the cost of living.

The Trend of Poverty

The trend of poverty in the United States, using the official definition of poverty, is shown in figure 11–1. The upper chart shows the number of people defined as poor, and the lower chart shows the percentage of the population defined as poor. Both charts slope steadily downward. From 40 million poor in 1960, the figure dropped to 24.7 million in 1979; and while 22.2 percent of the population were poor in 1960, only 11.6 percent were poor in 1979.

At first glance, these figures seem to indicate considerable success in dealing with the poverty problem. A closer look at the situation, however, gives less cause for optimism. Virtually all of the apparent progress was made prior to 1968, when, for the first time, increases in the cost of living were taken into account in setting the poverty line. Without changes in price levels having been considered from 1960 to 1968, there is a strong possibility that the purchasing power of formerly "poor" families did not increase significantly as they were lifted above an artificial and increasingly unrealistic poverty line.

That the apparent progress in conquering poverty is more apparent than real is also suggested by what has happened since 1968 when cost of living differences have been taken into account. There was no drop in the number of poor from 1968 to 1970, a slight increase from 1970 to 1975, and another slight decrease from 1975 to 1979. The percentage of the pop-

Figure 11–1
Decline in the number and percentage of poor since 1960.
Source: Department of Commerce, Bureau of the Census.

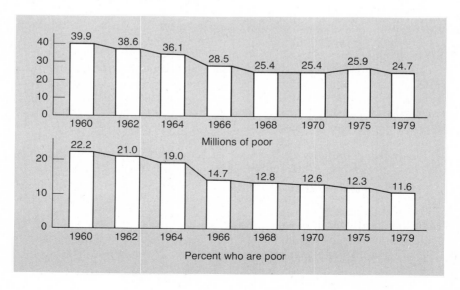

TABLE 11–2   United States Poverty Income Guidelines, 1979
(except Alaska and Hawaii)

Family Size	Nonfarm	Farm
1 person	$ 3,400.	$ 2,910.
2 people	4,500.	3,840.
3 people	5,600.	4,770.
4 people	6,700.	5,700.
5 people	7,800.	6,630.
6 people*	8,900.	7,560.

*For families of more than 6 people, add $1,100 for each additional member in non-farm families and $930 in farm families.

ulation classified as poor dropped from 12.8 to 12.6 from 1968 to 1970, and to 11.6 in 1979. Now that the effects of inflation have been ruled out, it does not appear that we are making much progress in the war on poverty.

The Distribution of Poverty

Poverty tends to be concentrated among certain groups of especially vulnerable people. By identifying such groups and the problems they face, we get at some of the immediate, if not the ultimate, causes of poverty in the United States. The following categories are somewhat arbitrary and not mutually exclusive. Taken together and analyzed, they provide the basis for considering what may be done to alleviate the problem.

THE UNSKILLED AND UNEDUCATED

In an age when approximately one-third of all young people attend college and with a bachelor's degree promising soon to become the norm for American society, the heads of more than half of all poor families did not attend school beyond the eighth grade.[4] These school dropouts are common both in urban slums and in economically depressed rural areas. Unlike the stereotype of the ambitious child from the poor family who drops out of school to make it possible for all the brothers and sisters to continue, most of these people drop out because they do poorly in school and have little motivation to continue. Instead of finding jobs where they can work their way up, they have difficulty finding any work at all. By and large, they are illiterate and capable of doing only the most menial work. There have always been large numbers of such persons in the population, but the number of jobs available for them is shrinking steadily. Automation, with all its ramifications, is drastically lessening the demand for such unskilled persons and is widening the income gap between them and the technologically sophisticated. The plight of such persons promises to worsen as time goes on.

APPALACHIA AND THE SOUTH

Almost half of the poor live in the South.[5] Poverty in the South is complicated by at least two factors. First, a large portion of the southern population is rural, and farming today is closely linked with poverty. Second, the South contains a disproportionate share of blacks, whom prejudice, discrimination, and lack of education combine to concentrate among the ranks of the poor. The farming economy of Appalachia has suffered also in its inability to compete with the efficiency of other farm areas. The geographical inaccessibility of the region, complicated by a very poor highway system, makes it difficult for new industry to enter the area. The outlook for Appalachia is so unencouraging that much of the federal government's poverty program has been aimed directly at this area.[6]

MARGINAL FARM OPERATORS AND LABORERS

It is estimated that 1 million families, containing a total of 4 million people, live on marginal farms with cash incomes under $4,497 per year.[7] In addition, approximately one-quarter of all nonfarm rural people, some 10 million, live in poverty.[8] All of the federal government's price support and subsidy programs for agriculture have failed to lessen substantially the plight of small farmers working marginal land. As farms become larger and more mechanized, the competitive position of the small farmer worsens. Poverty will most likely continue to exist on small farms until many of these people are driven off the land altogether.

Rural poverty is equally as devastating as its more publicized urban counterpart.
(CARE)

About half of the 2 million farm laborers in the United States are migrant workers who follow the harvests over the country. About two-thirds of these migrant workers are United States citizens. Most of the others are Mexicans who enter the United States to work under treaty agreements between the two countries. The average migratory farm worker earns less than $3,000 a year from all sources combined.[9] The Federal Unemployment Compensation law does not apply to migrants. Social security applies to them only if they work 20 or more days on an hourly rate for one employer or earn at least $150 from one employer. Since many of the migrants work at piece-rate wages for very short periods of time for many different employers, most of them are not covered. Typically, the migrant family travels in John Steinbeck's *Grapes of Wrath* fashion, in a dilapidated car crowded with children and all of the family's belongings. Often they have no housing at all, sleeping outside in good weather and in the car in bad weather. In some areas housing is provided by farmers, but more often than not it is substandard. The housing problem is avoided altogether if the migrant workers are brought to the fields daily by labor contractors.

MINORITIES AND DISCRIMINATION

The toll of prejudice and discrimination is high, with just one of its effects being poverty among much of the nonwhite population. We can state these effects in two ways: in terms of the proportion of the minority group that is poor, and of the proportion of the poor who belong to the minority group. Among blacks, who are the largest of the racial and ethnic groups, 34 percent were poor in 1974. Among black children under the age of 14, the figure was 40 percent. Turning the figure around, over 30 percent of all the poor were black.

In a report released late in 1971, the Census Bureau for the first time gave data on the proportions of various ethnic groups that are poor. Twenty-four percent of all people of Spanish-speaking origin are poor. Then the percentages drop rapidly. Ten and one-half percent of those of Irish origin are poor, 9.3 percent of those of French origin, 8.6 percent of those of British and German origin, 6.1 percent of those of Italian origin, 5.3 percent of those of Polish origin, 4.5 percent of those of Russian origin.[10]

Poverty among American Indians is a special case both because of its extent and severity and because of the role of the federal government in both perpetuating it and reducing it. The Bureau of Indian Affairs administers programs for Indian, Eskimo, and Aleut populations, among whom some 452,000 people are eligible for assistance. The extreme poverty of Indians living on reservations is indicated by the fact that their median family income is about one-half of the federal poverty level. More than half of the Indians on reservations live in one- or two-room dwellings, mostly self-built of indigenous materials. An average of 5.4 persons live in each of these dwellings, and more than 80 percent haul their water and have inadequate waste disposal facilities. The federal government has provided a minimum of services to the Indian population for a century, without ever coming to grips with the real problems. Appropriations for these programs recently have been raised considerably, but it is too early to tell whether they will be of much help.[11]

Poverty among the nation's minorities is self-perpetuating. Job discrimination combines with lack of education and motivation to produce generation after generation of poverty.

THE AGED

Approximately 16 percent of all families in which the household head was 65 years of age or older lived in poverty in 1970. The 4.7 million people involved represent a drop of 1.3 million from the number of aged poor in 1959. While this shows some progress, the number of poor people under 65 years of age fell even faster, so that the aged today are a larger proportion of the poor than they were a decade ago; from being 15 percent of the poor in 1959, they were 20 percent of the poor in 1970.[12]

The proportions of aged poor vary drastically by race and living arrangement. While 16 percent of all aged families live in poverty, only 14 percent of those with white males as heads do. In contrast, 46 percent of the families with black females as heads are poor. Among the aged who do not live in families, 47 percent are poor—36 percent of white males and 79 percent of black females.[13]

By far the most significant reason for poverty among the aged is the inadequacy of the welfare and social security programs on which they depend for most of their income. These benefits have been increasing somewhat, and as they continue to rise, the elderly may prove to be the easiest of the poverty groups to eliminate.

FATHERLESS FAMILIES

Families headed by women are more than twice as likely to be poor, and stay poor, as those headed by men—28 percent compared to 12 percent.[14] Moreover, there are more poor women today than there were 20 years ago. Much of this poverty is a consequence of divorce and, ironically, of increased welfare benefits for divorced women. Many women who formerly would have been forced to return to the homes of their parents are today living alone with their children. They maintain separate homes but, often, at very low income levels.[15]

Women who are heads of families often have many handicaps when it comes to securing an adequate living. The presence of minor children in the home may make it difficult for them to work and may also require them to take less remunerative jobs that will not interfere so much with their parental responsibilities. Even if child support is paid by the absent father, it is often in token amounts that do not permit a decent standard of living for either mother or children. Ordinarily, too, women have less job training than men, and swell the ranks of unskilled workers. Part of their distress is also due to discrimination against women in hiring practices.

UNEMPLOYMENT

The facts about poverty and unemployment present a paradox. Most of the unemployed are not poor, and most of the poor are not unemployed. At first glance this is startling: How can unemployed people fail to be poor? The answer is that most unemployed people are not *permanently* unemployed. In the United States, unemployment averages about 15 weeks per worker. Moreover, about half the people who are unemployed are eligible for unemployment benefits that supplement the income that they get when they are working. Finally, there is often more than one wage earner in the family. While one family member is unemployed, another may be working.

It is also surprising that the segment of the unemployed who actually are poor constitute one of the easiest of many poverty-stricken groups in the United States to rehabilitate. Most of these unemployed poor live in the cities where jobs and training for jobs are at least somewhat available. They can often read and write passably, have worked with tools, and have histories of fairly steady work. They know that it is possible to live better and they have some motivation to improve their lot.

Yet, there is a sizable group of hard-core unemployed whose poverty tends to persist generation after generation. Often they are unemployable because of lack of skill or family or health reasons. Some are people, often urban black males, who have given up hope of employment, and all effort to find employment, and consequently are not even counted among the "officially" unemployed. Some are tenant farmers who are employed in such unproductive ways that they cannot possibly be paid a living wage. While migration and retraining offer some hope to some of them, most of this generation will remain permanently poor. The best hope for them appears to be that their children will obtain enough formal education to permit them to become productive workers.

There is much overlap in these categories. They must be considered not as discrete groups, but as some of the intricately interrelated causes and con-

Teaching English to Spanish-speaking farm workers.
(United Press International)

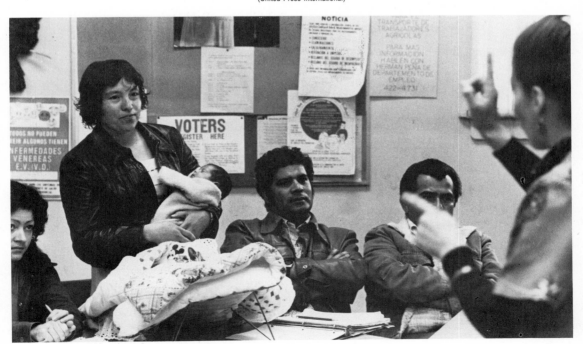

sequences of American poverty. Implied in the discussion of some categories are trends working in American society to alleviate at least some kinds of poverty. Let us turn now to a systematic examination of those trends.

Trends Tending to Alleviate Poverty

The nature of American poverty has changed drastically since the depression years of the 1930s and has changed even over the past decade. Most studies show that poverty was reduced rapidly after the depression. As we have seen, the apparent reduction of poverty during the 1960s was complicated by the canceling-out effects of inflation. What are the present trends in American society that tend to reduce poverty?

INCREASING EDUCATIONAL ATTAINMENT

The most pervasive cause of poverty in the United States appears to be the lack of a high-school education. But educational standards are being raised and a larger proportion of each generation manages to gain the basic literacy that stems from a high-school education. Over the past generation, the proportion of children graduating from high school has doubled from 33 to 66 percent. How great the increase will be over the next generation is impossible to say, but it is likely to be substantial. Much of the future increase may come among minority groups, whose lack of education up to now has reinforced the prejudice against them. In New York City at the present time, for example, blacks average nine and one-half years of schooling, only about one year less than the average for whites.

Ultimately, all but about 3 percent of the population can be educated at least through high school. For the approximately 3 percent of the population who are mentally retarded, it will not help to have education universally available. In a fully competitive system, this disadvantaged minority would remain predominantly poor for a very long time to come.

THE IMPROVING STATUS OF MINORITIES

Some groups of blacks made impressive gains during the 1960s and 1970s. The average gains for all blacks were less spectacular, and some groups of blacks made no progress at all. On balance, however, the trend is substantially upward.

Income differences between black and white husband-wife families under 35 years of age and living outside the South have virtually disappeared. One factor in this change is the larger percentage of the black wives who work outside the home, 62.7 percent compared to 54.1 percent of white wives. When the comparison is made between only black and white families in which the wives work, however, the progress is still evident. The earnings of the black couples in 1976 were slightly higher than those of the white couples. When black and white couples under thirty-five years of age and living in the North and West were compared, the black families had almost the same income as the whites—$16,715 for blacks to $16,691 for whites.[16]

As an indicator of progress, a study by The Conference Board, an independent business research organization, showed that the number of black families earning more than $10,000 per year doubled between 1965 and 1970. The number of whites earning over $10,000 increased by only one-third during the same period. Twenty-eight percent of black families compared to 52 percent of white families, earned over $10,000 in 1970.[17]

Less progress is apparent when we consider changes in the income picture nationally, but there has been progress. While in 1960 the income of black families was 55 percent of that of white families, it had risen to 62 percent by 1974. The dollar figures in 1974 were $13,356 for whites and $8,265 for blacks.

Still other comparisons show little or no progress. The 1.5 million black families with no father present failed to register any gains at all. Moreover, the number of female-headed families has been increasing, to 36 percent in 1977. Two other factors should not be overlooked. First, black families outside the South are more likely to be urban than white families are, and because wages are higher in urban areas, the over-all comparisons between white and black incomes may not be appropriate. Second, fully half of the black population still lives in the South, where incomes are lowest.

In summary, the status of blacks, as blacks, has been improving. As more blacks move to urban areas, and as they receive more formal education, more of them will rise above poverty.

GROWTH OF THE SOUTHERN ECONOMY

Much of American poverty is concentrated in the South and in Appalachia, but in much of the South, economic levels have been rising. As a matter of fact, the growth rate of the South since 1929 has been greater than that of any other region of the country.[18] With the federal government's assistance in highway construction in Appalachia, its isolation has become less pronounced and its growth rate has increased. Part of the South's poverty problem, of course, is that so much of the South is rural. Changes in the rural sector are vital to the southern economy.

THE CLOSING OF MARGINAL FAMILY FARMS

Great nostalgia is attached to the widespread stereotype of the self-sufficient family farm. Many of these marginal farms are closing, and many people bitterly resist the fact that many such farms are uneconomical and doom their inhabitants to deprivation and poverty. The number of families in the United States operating farms declined from 6.5 million in 1947 to just under 3 million in 1970. This decrease has not dropped the proportion of farm-operator families living below the poverty line, but it has considerably reduced the number of farm families living in poverty, and will continue to do so.

EXPANDING PROGRAMS FOR THE AGED

The aged make up a large share of the American poor, and both the number and proportion of aged in the society will continue to increase. Much of the poverty of the aged has been linked to the failure of social security to cover many of them. This situation is changing rapidly; currently, more than 90 percent of the labor force is covered. This means that the number and proportion of aged receiving social security payments in the future will climb steadily. In the meantime, social security benefits are gradually being raised. The average payment over the past 25 years has increased by two-thirds and is likely to increase more in the future.

Paradoxically, the increasing income of the aged has tended temporarily to increase the number of aged classified as poor. A generation ago, when aged parents lived with their children, they were not counted as separate families and often were not numbered among the poor. But as more older people have sought to maintain their own homes, which they could do only because of social security benefits, they became classified as poor. Even though financially they were better off than before, the income per family showed a decline.

Some Countertrends

Not all the changes in American society work in the direction of decreasing poverty. Some of them appear to approximate countertrends, increasing the number and proportion of the poor.

STABILITY OF INCOME DISTRIBUTION

For several decades, the poor were helped by the general leveling of incomes in the society. However, that leveling appears virtually to have stopped. The share of the nation's income received by the poorest one-fifth of the population has not increased significantly since World War II. The poorest 20 percent of the population receive about 5 percent of the nation's total family income. There has been no major redistribution of income over the past 20 years. Even the middle-income groups, who formerly were thought to have been increasing their share of the national income, have not really gained. It does not appear likely that the poor will benefit very much in the near future from any further leveling of incomes.[19]

BENEFITS RECEIVED BY THE POOR IN 1976	
Program	
Social Security, railroad retirement	$ 44.8 bil.
Education	$ 18.3 bil.
Public assistance, Supplemental Security Income	$ 14.9 bil.
Medicaid	$ 11.2 bil.
Medicare	$ 10.5 bil.
Public–employee pensions	$ 9.9 bil.
Food stamps	$ 4.7 bil.
Unemployment insurance	$ 4.4 bil.
Veterans' programs	$ 4.1 bil.
Workers' compensation, temporary disability insurance	$ 3.3 bil.
Public housing	$ 1.1 bil.
Other medical programs	$ 6.9 bil.
Other housing, social services	$ 8.7 bil.
Total	$142.8 bil.

Source: Reprinted from *U.S. News and World Report*, 22 Jan. 1979, p. 21. Copyright 1979 U.S. News and World Report, Inc.

THE DECLINING PROPORTION OF UNSKILLED JOBS

The proportion of unskilled jobs in the American economy is dropping with increasing rapidity. This drop leaves an increasing number of uneducated persons in the ranks of the permanently unemployable. Although the long-term trend toward more education should eventually solve most of this problem, it may worsen before it improves. The present generation of young adults who lack a high-school education may face a declining job market for the next 40 years.

IMPACT OF AUTOMATION ON SKILLED WORK

We do not really know what all the effects of increasing automation will be on the economy. We do know that some skilled jobs are already being eliminated in some industries. We also know that production is becoming more efficient. One line of thought is that fewer workers will be needed to maintain an ever-higher standard of living for much of the population, with increasing permanent unemployment in prospect for another segment of the population. Unless both production and consumption rise fast enough to require permanent full employment, substantial hard-core poverty is likely to result.

ECONOMIC SLOWDOWN

From the close of World War II through the 1960s, substantial growth in the economy contributed greatly to reduce poverty. The 1970s, however, brought signs that such growth might not continue. Rampant inflation combined with escalating unemployment lowered living standards for all but the truly affluent. A negative balance of payments situation, fueled by decades of exorbitant war expenditures, led to devaluation of the dollar. Finally, energy crises signaled both rapidly increasing costs for fuel and the necessity to alter styles of living. The details of the economic situation will change, but the larger picture probably will not. Economic growth will continue at a slower pace, and living standards in general probably will ease downward.

Some years in the 1970s actually saw increases in the number of people living below the poverty line. Blacks and people living in fatherless families appeared to be hit the hardest. Other, less visible minorities probably suffered equally, however. The aggravation of poverty in urban areas probably will slow the closing of marginal farms. Without jobs available in the cities, not only will poor rural people remain on their farms, but a reverse migration to substandard farms may actually develop.

Programs for Alleviating Poverty

Poverty became a major public issue in the early 1960s. From the beginning most people assumed that the resources of the federal government would have to be used to solve the problem; in 1963 the Kennedy administration launched a "war on poverty." The end of that war was never officially declared, but by the early 1970s it was over for all practical purposes. In the past few years, efforts to deal with poverty have focused upon the welfare system and upon some form of guaranteed annual income.

THE WAR ON POVERTY

President John F. Kennedy proposed the war on poverty shortly before his untimely death, and the passage of the Economic Opportunity Act of 1964 was the first major legislative achievement of the Johnson administration. The act established 11 major programs to aid the poor. Six of them were low profile programs that provided direct assistance to poor persons and families. Included were the Neighborhood Youth Corps, giving part-time work to teenagers who were dropouts or who needed money to stay in school; the College Work Study Program, which did the same thing for college students from poor families; an Adult Basic Education Program; a Small Business Loan Program; a Rural Loan Program; and a Work Experience Program, which assisted unemployed heads of families to gain on-the-job experience and prepare for regular employment.

These programs did not attract a great deal of public attention, and they received little systematic evaluation. They directly assisted many poor persons and families, but they were often poorly administered and uncoordi-

A VISTA volunteer in Indiana, whose job it is to work with community organizations to find people whose homes are in need of repair.
(VISTA/Conklin)

nated, and they appeared to benefit the government agencies involved more directly than they did the poor.

The other five major programs in the war on poverty gained much more visibility and became the subjects of varying degrees of controversy. The Job Corps, for example, established residential training centers for youths from 14 to 22, where school dropouts could complete their education and learn a trade. Many of the centers, however, were established in remote rural areas, where the imported youths clashed with the local population. Disciplinary problems were common, and the costs of running the program soared to an incredible $8,000 per enrollee. Congress put budgetary limits on the program. Finally, President Richard Nixon transferred it from the Office of Economic Opportunity to the Department of Labor, where it still operates, training some 45,000 youth per year.[20]

The most successful of the programs was Head Start, a preschool program designed to prepare "culturally disadvantaged" children to be successful in school and to meet their medical and nutritional, as well as educational, needs. When preliminary evaluations of this program showed that many Head Start children did well in the primary grades but then gradually fell behind again, a Follow Through program was established to continue the educational innovation in the primary grades. Upward Bound continued the sequence by providing precollege tutoring for minority students.

The VISTA program (Volunteers in Service to America) was a sort of domestic Peace Corps, enlisting volunteers to work with migrant laborers, on Indian reservations, and in slum areas, schools, hospitals, and institutions for the mentally ill and retarded. Some VISTA representatives sought to wield political power and to help the poor to do so directly, leading to alarm on the part of local authorities, who accused VISTA of agitation and of fomenting revolution.

The largest and most controversial of the antipoverty programs was the Community Action Program. It provided financial support, through the Office of Economic Opportunity, for programs including child development, remedial education, literacy courses, legal aid, day care, consumer education, birth control, services to the aged, and more. Controversy developed as a result of the requirement that there be "maximum feasible participation" by the poor themselves in the planning and execution of the programs. The poor did organize in many cases, with the assistance of young lawyers and VISTA personnel, and they pressed for policies and programs that would benefit them directly, even at the expense of the larger community. They took aim at local merchants, slumlords, and even mayors. The legal services program brought suits against state agencies and against large agricultural interests. Naturally, this upset public officials, who were accustomed to deciding for themselves what was in the public interest and to wielding the power that having control of public funds bestows. Congress yielded to the pressure, and permitted local governments to take charge of the Community Action Programs.

The war on poverty began with high hopes and met with some early successes. By 1965 the OEO had a budget of $1.5 billion and Community Action Programs were functioning in more than 1,000 communities. Early in 1966 OEO developed a four-year plan that called for outlays to grow by $6.4 billion the first year and $3 billion a year thereafter. Two-thirds of the

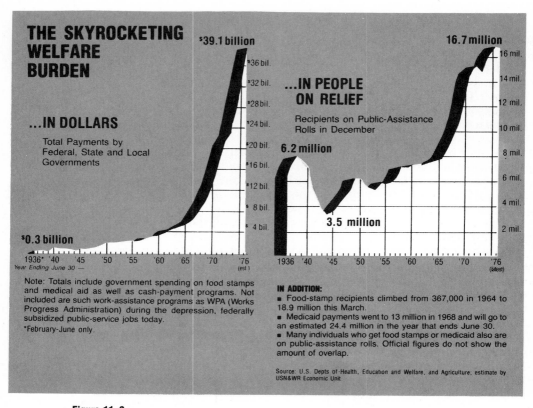

THE SKYROCKETING WELFARE BURDEN

...IN DOLLARS

Total Payments by Federal, State and Local Governments

$39.1 billion

$36 bil.
$32 bil.
$28 bil.
$24 bil.
$20 bil.
$16 bil.
$12 bil.
$8 bil.
$4 bil.

$0.3 billion

1936* '40 '45 '50 '55 '60 '65 '70 '76
Year Ending June 30 — (est.)

...IN PEOPLE ON RELIEF

Recipients on Public-Assistance Rolls in December

6.2 million

16.7 million
16 mil.
14 mil.
12 mil.
10 mil.
8 mil.
6 mil.
4 mil.
3.5 million
2 mil.

1936 '40 '45 '50 '55 '60 '65 '70 '76
(latest)

Note: Totals include government spending on food stamps and medical aid as well as cash-payment programs. Not included are such work-assistance programs as WPA (Works Progress Administration) during the depression, federally subsidized public-service jobs today.
*February-June only.

IN ADDITION:
■ Food-stamp recipients climbed from 367,000 in 1964 to 18.9 million this March.
■ Medicaid payments went to 13 million in 1968 and will go to an estimated 24.4 million in the year that ends June 30.
■ Many individuals who get food stamps or medicaid also are on public-assistance rolls. Official figures do not show the amount of overlap.

Source: U.S. Depts. of Health, Education and Welfare, and Agriculture, estimate by USN&WR Economic Unit

Figure 11–2
The skyrocketing welfare burden.
Source: Reprinted from *U.S. News & World Report*, 7 June 1976. Copyright 1976 U.S. News & World Report, Inc.

36 million poor were to be lifted out of poverty by 1972, the remainder by 1976. These grandiose aspirations were not to be realized, however.[21]

The controversy that surrounded several of the programs caused Congress to back away from their support, and by the late 1960s the Vietnam War was draining away revenues that might have been used to fight poverty. Moreover, the Nixon administration was far less supportive than the previous two administrations had been. Influenced by Daniel Patrick Moynihan, Nixon proposed a Family Assistance Plan that would have removed the need for continuing other antipoverty programs. The FAP, which would have established the principle of a guaranteed annual income (although at the low level of $1,600 a year for a family of four), failed to gain approval in Congress.

President Nixon moved to dismantle the OEO. His 1973 budget funded the agency at the 1969 level, and his 1974 budget contained no funds at all for OEO. The Head Start program was transferred to the Department of Health, Education and Welfare. The Job Corps was moved to the Department of Labor. In January 1975, the Community Services Administration was created to replace the Office of Economic Opportunity. Intended to be an advocate for the poor within the federal government, the new agency administers about $300 million in grants to over 900 local community action agencies.[22]

A major new program was created in 1973 with the passage of the Comprehensive Employment and Training Act (CETA). CETA was intended to distribute federal funds to state and local governments so that they could create jobs in the public sector for hard-core unemployed people. In its first five years, the program was funded at an average of over $5 billion per year.

Local governments are supposed to use the money to hire more workers than they would otherwise have hired. Some 725,000 workers are now being paid by the program. Two problems have plagued the program from the beginning, however. First, hard-pressed local governments have often used CETA funds to pay for existing jobs that formerly had been paid for out of tax funds. Second, the people hired, instead of being chronically poor, have often been middle-class professional people. The situation got so bad in 1978 that the Department of Labor hired a staff of 200 investigators to look into charges of fraud and mismanagement in the program.[23] CETA has spent lots of money, but has had little effect upon poverty.

Overall, the war on poverty was lost. It was never adequately funded and it ran afoul of the political process. Yet it did have an impact on the society: it introduced new techniques for coping with neglected problems, such as neighborhood health and legal services; it altered the concept of community responsibility for educating citizens; it stimulated the use of paraprofessionals; and it encouraged the idea of self-help in the slums. Community action probably is with us to stay. Society will never be the same again.

THE PROBLEM OF PUBLIC WELFARE

Almost everyone who reads newspapers or magazines is aware that the public welfare system in the United States is widely defined as a social problem.

Figure 11–3
State inequities in AFDC payments.
Source: Domestic Council, Executive Office of the President, *Highlights of Welfare Reform: Reform/Renewal for the '70's* (Washington, D.C., 1971), p. 9.

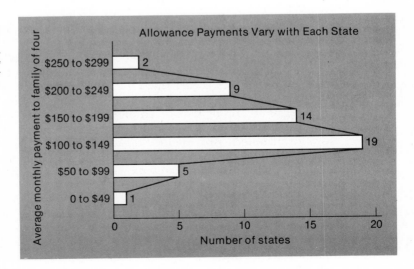

Allowance Payments Vary with Each State

Average monthly payment to family of four

	Number of states
$250 to $299	2
$200 to $249	9
$150 to $199	14
$100 to $149	19
$50 to $99	5
0 to $49	1

Phrases such as "the welfare mess" and "welfare cheaters" are symptoms thereof. Let us examine the situation.

No less an authority than a report of the Senate-House Joint Economic Committee describes federal assistance programs as an intricate maze of overlapping and often conflicting programs that often achieve the exact opposite of what is intended.[24] The study reports that some 119 million people—more than half the nation's population—receive nearly 100 billion dollars in welfare and social insurance benefits combined. Since many people benefit from more than one program—for example, Medicaid, food stamps, and school lunch programs—there may be only about 60 million individuals involved. Of those, approximately 25 to 30 million are receiving some form of public welfare.

The largest of the public welfare programs, accounting for about two-thirds of the welfare recipients identified regularly in government statistics, is Aid to Families of Dependent Children (AFDC). There are 10.9 million persons receiving AFDC out of a total of more than 15 million identified public welfare recipients.[25]

AFDC was established several decades ago to aid widows and orphans, but during the depression of the 1930s it was extended to help separated, divorced, and unmarried mothers. The case load at that time was under one-half million, and public concern about the program was minimal. After World War II, however, the rolls began to grow rapidly and the 1960s saw the emergence of great political and public concern. From about 2 million recipients in 1956, the figure climbed to almost 4 million in 1963, to more than 8 million in 1970, and about 11 million currently.

As the accompanying costs soared, public hostility to the program mounted and a stereotype of welfare recipients became popular that labeled them as mostly black, shiftless, promiscuous, and prone to produce illegitimate children to increase their welfare benefits. Several features of the stereotype are simply inaccurate, and others are produced by the structure of welfare itself.

A study of AFDC showed, for example, that the largest percentage of recipients, 48.3 percent, are white. Some 43 percent are black, a high proportion in relation to the 11 percent of the population that is black, but not so high in relation to the 30 percent of the poor who are black or the 40 percent of poor children who are black.[26] Moreover, a much larger proportion of blacks live in female-headed families.

A second element in the stereotype holds that welfare recipients are lazy people who prefer to live on government handouts than to work for a living. Several studies refute that charge. One study of 275 chronically unemployed men in a New England city found that their commitment to work was just as strong as that of employed blue- and white-collar workers, and that work was important to the maintenance of their self-concept as well as for the income it provided.[27] Still another study of an Office of Economic Opportunity experiment, which pays a negative income tax to poor families, found that they are not content with their government payments, but increased their other incomes also.[28]

Part of the image of welfare recipients as shiftless loafers actually derives from the nature of the welfare program itself, which sometimes penalizes people for doing productive work. The study by the Joint Economic Committee reported that families whose incomes rise above the cutoff point may be worse off than they were on welfare, because they lose their eligibility for school lunches, surplus food, and Medicaid programs.

Another complication is that federal welfare benefits are supplemented by state payments that vary drastically. In New York City, for example, a welfare mother can earn $2,000 and still collect up to $3,386 in AFDC payments. At the other extreme, Mississippi pays only $8.50 per month for each eligible family member.[29] In the states with poorer benefits, and this is the vast majority of them, there is no way that people can live decently, to say nothing of extravagantly, on welfare payments.

In a few of the more prosperous states, there have been growing numbers of cases in recent years in which people have been hesitant to accept low-paid jobs that they know cannot support their families and are far less dependable than welfare benefits. The President's Council of Economic Advisers reported in 1976, for example, that a study of 100 counties showed that a welfare mother with three children could receive benefits equivalent

Figure 11–4
The structure of AFDC encourages family break-up. In all states there is no federally financed assistance to poor families with a full-time father. In more than half the states there is no aid to poor families with an unemployed father at home. Result: the system encourages men to leave home so their families can qualify.
*Where father is incapacitated and hence eligible for AFDC or covered by unemployed father provisions of AFDC.
Source: The Domestic Council, Executive Office of the President, *Highlights of Welfare Reform/Renewal for the 70's* (Washington, D.C., 1971), p. 7.

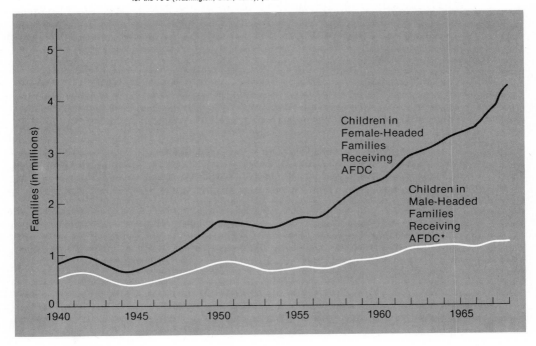

to $5,815 in taxable income, not counting household subsidies. The Council also reported that these benefits have made it easier in recent years for such women to form and remain in their own households.[30]

Another characteristic of the welfare program, and one that encourages the stereotype of poor men as irresponsible and poor women as promiscuous breeders of illegitimate children, is the widespread provision that families in which an able-bodied man is present are ineligible for AFDC benefits. That the accusation of widespread illegitimacy among welfare mothers is false is indicated by government figures showing that fewer than one-third of AFDC children are illegitimate. What really happens is that men who know that they cannot support their families adequately are encouraged not to live with their families, so that the mother and children will be eligible for AFDC. Having probably more than their share of problems to begin with, many of the families break up, and other, informal unions that must be hidden from welfare officials are established; then when the woman becomes pregnant she does not have the access to abortion that more prosperous women have.

THE FOOD STAMP PROGRAM

Although technically part of the welfare system, the food stamp program is a sufficiently recent development, sufficiently significant in its implications, and sufficiently controversial to merit separate discussion. The program developed in two stages.

Originally established in 1964, the food stamp program was designed more for the disposal of agricultural surpluses than as a welfare program for the poor. It is administered by the Department of Agriculture, rather than by the Department of Health, Education and Welfare. It was also a relatively low-cost program. In 1965, for example, citizens in only 110 counties were eligible, 424,000 people participated, and the cost was $36 million.[31]

The food stamp program in its present form became law in 1969. It operates nationwide and is intended to ensure that all of the needy have a nutritionally adequate diet. Approximately 45 percent of the recipients are on welfare, 15 to 20 percent are defined as working poor, and 10 percent receive Supplemental Security Income benefits from the Social Security Administration. The remainder are elderly, unemployed, or students. Some 87 percent of the households have annual incomes of less than $6,000.

The real growth of the program occurred after 1972, when Russian grain purchases helped put an end to the problem of farm surpluses. The surpluses were replaced by shortages, the economy turned downward, and the unemployment rate rose. With every increase of one percentage point in the unemployment rate, an estimated 750,000 people signed up for food stamps. In 1979 more than 19 million people received stamps, and the annual cost of the program rose to $6.9 billion.

By mid-1974 the program was under concerted attack for its high costs, for eligibility requirements that permit some of the nonpoor to participate, and for alleged fraud and mismanagement. Stories spread in almost every community of people standing in supermarket checkout lines behind college students who purchased gourmet foods with food stamps and then loaded their groceries into shiny new automobiles. In fact, college students are only about 5 percent of food stamp recipients—but they are a very conspicuous 5 percent.

Eligibility for food stamps is figured through use of a complex formula, and that is one of the problems. In brief, the Department of Agriculture figures what it costs a family to have a special "economy" diet plan. When that cost exceeds 30 percent of the family's income, they become eligible for food stamps. The net income figures used involve the computation of rent, child-care costs, and taxes. The opportunities both for error and for fraud are large.

There is evidence of widespread cheating and mismanagement. An official survey, for example, reported that 17 percent of the recipients investigated were ineligible to participate. An additional 26 percent were receiving either more or less than they were entitled to, through a combination of administrative bungling and cheating. Another study, in Pennsylvania, showed that half the abuses originate within the system: 35 percent of the errors occurred at the county level, and 8 percent at the state level. In 23 percent of the cases the recipients had made false statements in their applications, and in another 34 percent they had failed to report all relevant facts.[32]

The long-term significance of the food stamp program goes beyond eligibility requirements, fraud, mismanagement, and even total costs. The food stamp program works, without most people being aware of it, like a negative income tax or a guaranteed annual income. It is designed to assist all of the needy, including those who are on welfare or social security. The value of the stamps received by a family of four with virtually no other income is almost $2,000 per year, well above that proposed by the Nixon administration in its abortive Family Assistance Plan. That form of guaranteed annual income had a floor of only $1,600. With the food stamp program, the country has taken a big step in the direction of some form of income maintenance program.

A GUARANTEED ANNUAL INCOME

The United States has been moving, irregularly and reluctantly, toward some form of guaranteed minimum income for all families. In the late 1960s, the mechanism that was used was the minimum wage law. The Fair Labor Standards Act of 1968 set the minimum hourly wage at $1.60 and raised many families' income at least to the general vicinity of the poverty line. Since then, the legal minimum wage has risen to $3.10.

The first official proposal for a guaranteed annual income, the Family Assistance Plan, failed to win approval by Congress. As we have just seen, however, the food stamp program continues to move the country in that direction. Experiments with income maintenance plans have also been going on quietly in various areas of the United States under the sponsorship of the Office of Economic Opportunity. These experiments have been directed to learning what the costs and effects of a national program would be. Six such guaranteed income experiments have been conducted over the past decade or so. Early reports from them were encouraging. There was little evidence of withdrawal from the labor market, although there was a slight reduction in the number of hours that people worked.

The final results of these experiments, however, were discomfiting. They showed that a guaranteed annual income, combined with a high effective tax rate on earned income, caused many low-income workers to reduce substantially the number of hours they worked. In some cases, they stopped working altogether. Moreover, there was a startling number of divorces among couples receiving the income guarantees. The divorce rate apparently increased as much as 70 percent.[33]

It is too soon for the effects of these experiments on national policy to be assessed fully. But it does appear that efforts to provide a guaranteed annual income have received a major setback. More effort is likely to be invested in the near future in trying to improve the existing welfare system.

The Social-Disorganization Approach

There is no question that there was more poverty in the past than there is today and that absolute deprivation was greater then than now. In 1909, for example, the Bureau of Labor Statistics computed a minimum standard of living for a cotton mill worker's family that figures out to about $1,000 a year at today's prices. By 1923 the Bureau decided that a five-person family was poor only if it had an income below $1,900 per year. Today the poverty line is over 100 percent higher than it was forty years ago. Poverty has always been with us; only with the absolute lessening of poverty has it come to be widely recognized as a social problem.

The emergence of poverty as a social problem has been encouraged by a larger and larger proportion of the society living in relative affluence. When most people lived close to the minimum subsistence level, there was not a great deal of apparent difference between them and the poor. Now, however, differences between the living standards of the poor and the middle class are startling. If only by contrast with middle-class standards of living, poverty is more obvious than it used to be.

We also live in an age in which government wealth and power are coming to be accepted instruments for bringing about social change. The mammoth foreign-aid program to underdeveloped countries is a case in point. If the United States can help to raise living standards in all of South America and in such far-away places as Jordan and Afghanistan, the reasoning goes that it should be able to raise the living standards of the American poor.

Change also disorganizes and reorganizes some aspects of the society that appeared to function less problematically before. In the 1920s and 1930s, soft coal was the chief source of fuel in the United States. Although the lives of miners and their families were very hard, and many of them lived in real poverty, they did have jobs. The decline of the soft coal industry almost by itself made a tremendous poverty pocket of most of Appalachia. Now, with the energy crisis, soft coal is in demand again and much of Appalachia is benefiting. Changes in the agricultural sector of the economy have had a similar effect. Though many farmers were poor, the country used to depend on the production of a myriad of small farmers. With the mechanization of agriculture, small farmers and those working marginal land simply could not compete successfully any more. The relatively growing poverty of rural America is linked partly to large numbers of families still trying to farm the way they have always farmed.

Now, automation in virtually all areas of the economy is bringing about tremendous changes that will eliminate some kinds of jobs and throw many people out of work. That automation will require new skills and create new jobs does not change the fact that it will help either to plunge some groups into poverty or to keep them there. Poverty has always been with us, but social change constantly alters its character.

The utopia in which no one is poor will probably never be reached, partly because society constantly upgrades its definition of poverty as living standards improve. But, increasingly, poverty is seen as a problem that can be solved. According to a spokesperson for the United States Census Bureau, we now seem to have within our means the ability to eliminate it completely.

The Value-Conflict Approach

Inherent in the proposals that have been made to ameliorate or eliminate poverty are many value conflicts, some of which were analyzed in the foregoing discussion of programs for the alleviation of poverty. There is, in addition, an overarching conflict over the nature of poverty and what should be done to relieve it. The central issue is reflected in the ancient question, "Am I my brother's keeper?" Stated bluntly, the issue is, "How much should self-supporting citizens contribute to the poor?" It is generally agreed that a democratic society cannot allow its poor to starve to death. At what level, above sheer physical survival, should the poor be subsidized by the rest of us? Some people consider it a national scandal that millions of citizens should live in squalor, but many others grumble bitterly about present welfare costs, and rebel at the thought of any further increase in the subsidy to

Poverty has always been with us, but social change constantly alters its character.
(Bonnie Freer, Photo Researchers, Inc.)

the poor. Our economy is producing enough to abolish poverty entirely, but many refuse to accept the personal sacrifices entailed in doing so.

There is also a conflict—rooted partly in divergent perceptions of the facts and partly in conflicting values—between those who see poverty as a self-perpetuating cultural system and those who see poverty as a product of the structure of the contemporary economic system. It has been noted that many of the poor *work very hard,* but at low-paying jobs. Our economic system clearly does not, if indeed it ever did, have enough decent jobs to go around. When the economy falls 10, 20 or 30 percent short of enough jobs to employ everybody at a "living wage," then poverty is *structurally mandated.* This makes the study of the characteristics and personal inadequacies of the poor an interesting academic parlor sport, but contributes nothing to the solution of the problem. To the extent that poverty is structurally mandated, it can be removed only by basic changes in the economic and political system that carry some guarantee of jobs and a minimum income for all.

A somewhat different (although not necessarily opposing) view sees much poverty as an expression of a self-perpetuating cultural system that has come to be called the "culture of poverty." This concept comes most directly from the studies of Oscar Lewis, in his *La Vida: A Puerto Rican Family in the Culture of Poverty*[34] and other volumes, although similar ideas had been expressed by earlier writers.[35] According to this view, the stable, orderly life amid peasant poverty, in which most of the world has always lived, now becomes replaced by a culture of poverty in the modern urbanized world whose poor are surrounded by affluence. Under such conditions, today's poor have developed a set of patterns that are *functionally useful* for survival. To endure hunger, illness, squalor, and insecurity without losing one's mind, it is useful to have the ability to accept and tolerate squalor, to live each day as it comes, and to seize and enjoy whatever immediate gratifications one can without worrying about tomorrow. Ambitions and long-term goals would only increase the frustrations of those whose opportunities are so few. People whose grasp on food and shelter is short-term are unlikely to form long-term goals or to practice the "deferred gratification pattern." Nor are long-term plans and ambitions pursued by people who have no feeling of control over their destiny. A strong sense of marital and filial duty is unlikely to arise among men who see little realistic prospect that they will ever be able to support a family decently, no matter how monumental their efforts. Where men are at best undependable providers, a woman may weaken her control over her household if she marries the man she is living with, and thus lose her ability to throw him out if he mistreats her. Consequently, there are many casual and temporary unions, with the woman as the central figure in the family and the "husbands" only marginally involved. Divorce, nonsupport, desertion, sexual promiscuity, and illegitimacy are common, are not strongly disapproved, and are functionally useful in meeting certain needs of the people involved.[36]

While these patterns may have survival value for the poor, they also lock the poor into permanent poverty by incapacitating them for using any mobility opportunities that may appear. Consequently, relatively few of the children attend school regularly and study conscientiously, many vacancies in current job training programs remain unfilled, and many who enroll soon disappear. Thus, the lifestyle of the culture of poverty that facilitates their survival also tends to be self-perpetuating.

The culture of poverty idea has been eagerly embraced by those who love to blame the poor for their misery, and has been angrily rejected by those who wish to perceive the poor as the helpless, innocent victims of a rapacious, oppressive society. Both miss the point, for "blame" is, after all, a theological concept, not a scientific concept. The central point is that poverty encourages a lifestyle that, in turn, tends to perpetuate poverty. Those who use the "culture of poverty" to justify their unconcern for the poor fail to see that the lifestyle is a *rational, functionally necessary product* of poverty. Those who see the poor as purely helpless victims, and see the "culture of poverty" concept as a cruel canard, simply refuse to recognize that this lifestyle *is* a barrier to mobility for the poor.

Just how much poverty persists because of the "culture of poverty," and how much is structurally mandated, is an unsettled question.[37] Both the structural view and the "culture of poverty" view see the special characteristics of the poor as arising from the fact that they are poor. They both view the poor as dealing rationally with joblessness, low incomes, discrimination, and frustration. The poor want much the same things as the affluent. They do not want their spouses to become heroin addicts or to be mugged on the streets, or their children to be sick and malnourished. Those who emphasize the structural view of poverty see the solution as one of guaranteeing people the jobs and incomes to remove these harmful influences from their lives. Those who emphasize the "culture of poverty" are divided into two camps: those who search for ways to interrupt the self-perpetuating cycle of the poverty lifestyle, many of whom agree that simply giving them more income might be the best way to do this; and those who attribute the "culture of poverty" to some genetic defect or innate perversity of the poor, and thus feel that we should do as little as possible for them.[38]

The Personal-Deviation Approach

The culture of poverty concept implies that, collectively, the poor are a deviant group. "The poor," says Michael Harrington, "are not like everyone else. They are a different kind of people. They think and feel differently; they look upon a different America."[39]

The situation of the Appalachian poor provides an example.[40] Some younger mountain people, when they lose their jobs or after a long period of not being able to find jobs, go away to seek employment in the cities of the North and West. Their disappointment there, compounded by frequent unemployment and high living costs, leads them to return to the mountains, because they love the mountains and because they can live more cheaply there on unemployment checks than in the cities.[41] They have little to do but sit around the stove, or in good weather on the front porch, and wait for their relief checks. Outwardly, at least, they are lazy, and inwardly this is true of some of them also. Students can construct other examples in other settings: in urban slums, in ghettos, and in isolated rural areas. Each case gives some credence to the stereotype of the poor: lazy, shiftless people who will take all handouts without ever making an effort to improve their situations.

This is not surprising. What is surprising is that so many of the poor resist conforming to the stereotype. Although 45 percent of all families receiving AFDC have experienced a marital breakup, the surprising thing is the number of families that remain stable in the face of unemployment, disability, or the death of a husband. Although one-third of AFDC children are illegitimate, two-thirds are not.

Most of the poor want to work, try to keep decent homes, and suffer from the stigma that society attaches to them. How much of the apparent deviance of the poor is primary deviance, and how much is secondary deviance resulting from being labeled as inferior and unworthy, cannot be said with certainty. Careful studies find that the poor are fully comparable to the middle class in their *desire* for jobs, in their willingness to work, in their wish to improve their status, and in their appreciation of the importance of education. Yet the poor nonetheless fail to make the necessary effort to attain these goals by attending school regularly and studying faithfully, by completing job training programs, and by developing dependable work habits.[42] Leonard Goodwin attributes this to a lack of self-confidence among many of the poor, who have already failed so regularly and have been made to feel inadequate and worthless so often that they are literally crippled in their capacity to respond to an available opportunity. Thus, while most poor parents and children affirm the importance of education, few of the children work very hard at school. If this analysis is correct, then the alleviation of poverty is far more complicated than the simplistic solutions often advanced. Among the requisites for a solution would be a national value consensus that poverty should be eliminated, not just contained at minimum cost; a willingness to provide a living income to all who are unable to work; enough decent jobs for all who can work; realistic education and job training for all who need it; and, finally, some procedures for enhancing the self-image, confidence, and sense of personal worth of those too psychologically crippled to use their capacities to good advantage.

Summary

Approximately one of every eight Americans live in poverty, although poverty is very unevenly distributed over the population. The South has more than its share, and a disproportionate number are blacks and members of various ethnic groups. Many poverty families are headed by women.

Whether one feels that progress in eliminating poverty is being made depends partly on how one defines poverty. If it is defined in terms of some fraction of average income or in terms of the share of the national income received by a fraction of the population, then little progress has been made for at least two decades. If an absolute standard—a defined minimum level of living—is used, however, then some progress has apparently been made since 1960. When inflation is taken into account, however, even that progress may be more apparent than real.

Almost half of the poor live in the South, including the economically depressed area of Appalachia. Many of the poor are unskilled and uneducated, many are marginal farm operators and laborers, many are victims of prejudice and discrimination, and many are aged. Surprisingly, not all of the poor are unemployed, and not all of the unemployed are poor. Unsteady work at low wages is a major factor in poverty.

Certain trends in American society are working to alleviate poverty. These include increasing educational attainments, especially for blacks, and the improving economic status of blacks generally. Other factors include the growth of the southern economy, the closing of marginal family farms, and expanding programs for the aged. Some social changes work in the direction of increasing the amount of poverty. These include the stability of the distribution of income over the population, the declining proportion of unskilled jobs available, and the impact of automation on employment.

Current federal efforts to eliminate poverty were initiated in the mid-1960s. The so-called war on poverty embraced 11 major programs, none of which was ever adequately funded, most of which were poorly managed, and a few of which became openly controversial. The result has been a gradual federal retreat from this effort.

The public welfare program in the United States is both an effort to reduce poverty and a social problem in its own right. With 15 million people receiving welfare and with the regulations governing welfare tending to perpetuate dependency, the program has become a national scandal. The food stamp program may be viewed either as a part of the welfare program or, more properly, as an unwitting step toward the establishment of a guaranteed annual income. Problems involving eligibility standards, mismanagement, and fraud plague the program. Meanwhile, income maintenance experiments in various sections of the country cast doubt on the political and economic feasibility of programs to provide a guaranteed annual income.

Social disorganization analysis shows that the definition of poverty as a major social problem actually accompanied the decline of poverty in America. Some changes have increased poverty among some groups and reduced it among others. The long-term trend is toward the reduction of poverty, but the end is not yet in sight.

A major value conflict exists over whether there is a special culture of poverty, and whether the poor are substantially to blame for their plight. The authors of this book incline to view that poverty is a complex problem that does not lend itself to a simple solution. Most of the poor share the achievement values of the larger society, but many have also been caught up in a culture of poverty that involves them in self-defeating behavior.

Suggested Readings

GALBRAITH, JOHN KENNETH, *The Nature of Mass Poverty* (Cambridge, Mass.: Harvard University Press, 1978). An unusual book by a noted economist and statesman, who analyzes worldwide poverty patterns in social psychological terms.

HAVEMAN, ROBERT H., ed., *A Decade of Federal Antipoverty Programs: Achievements, Failures, and Lessons* (Madison, Wisc.: Institute for Research on Poverty, 1977). A series of papers from a major conference held in 1975.

HUBER, JOAN, and H. PAUL CHALFANT, eds., *The Sociology of American Poverty* (Cambridge, Mass.: Schenkman, 1974). A comprehensive collection of essays covering the various dimensions of the poverty problem in the United States.

LAWRENCE, WILLIAM J., and STEPHEN LEEDS, *An Inventory of Federal Income Transfer Programs, Fiscal Year 1977* (White Plains, N.Y.: The Institute for Socioeconomic Studies, 1978). A succinct summary of all of the income transfer programs of the federal government. Dramatizes the comprehensiveness and the complexity of the effort.

ROSS, HEATHER L., and ISABEL V. SAWHILL, *Time of Transition: The Growth of Families by Women* (Washington, D.C.: The Urban Institute, 1975). Analyzes the role of public policy in the increase in female-headed families and their links with the system of public welfare.

STREET, DAVID, GEORGE T. MARTIN, JR., and LAURA KRAMER GORDON, *The Welfare Industry: Functionaries and Recipients in Public Aid* (Beverly Hills: Sage,

1979). An autopsy on the body of the war on poverty. Focuses on the AFDC program.

TURNER, JONATHAN H., and CHARLES E. STARNES, *Inequality: Privilege and Poverty in America* (Pacific Palisades, Ca.: Goodyear, 1976). Places poverty in the context of the historical pattern of social inequality in America. Shows how the system perpetuates itself.

WILLIAMSON, JOHN B., et al., *Strategies against Poverty in America* (Cambridge, Mass.: Schenkman, 1975). Systematic evaluation of the various efforts to eliminate poverty in the United States. Calls for new policies and programs.

Footnotes

[1]*U.S. News and World Report,* 22 Jan. 1979, p. 20.

[2]Conference on Economic Progress, *Poverty and Deprivation in the United States: The Plight of Two-Fifths of a Nation* (Washington, D.C., April 1962).

[3]Ibid.

[4]Sar A. Levitan, *Programs in Aid of the Poor for the 1970's* (Baltimore: Johns Hopkins Press, 1969), p. 54.

[5]*U.S. News and World Report,* 8 Nov. 1976, p. 58.

[6]Jon Nordheimer, "America's Rural Poor: The Picture Is Changing," *New York Times,* 17 Aug. 1975.

[7]President's Commission on Income Maintenance Programs, *Background Papers* (Washington, D.C.: Government Printing Office, 1969), p. 285.

[8]President's Advisory Commission on Rural Poverty, "The People Left Behind," *Employment Service Review,* April 1968, pp. 17–19.

[9]*New York Times,* 20 Feb. 1977.

[10]*New York Times,* 14 Nov. 1971.

[11]President's Commission on Income Maintenance Programs, *Background Papers,* pp. 295–97.

[12]United States Administration on Aging, "Measuring Adequacy of Income," *Facts and Figures on Older Americans* (Washington, D.C.: Government Printing Office, March 1971), p. 3.

[13]United States Administration on Aging, "An Overview for the Delegates to the White House Conference on Aging," *Facts and Figures on Older Americans* (Washington, D.C.: Government Printing Office, 1971), p. 8.

[14]*U.S. News and World Report,* 8 Nov. 1976, p. 58.

[15]Elliott Currie, "The New Face of Poverty," *The Progressive,* Jan. 1979, pp. 38–40.

[16]Associated Press, 19 June 1979.

[17]Associated Press, 21 Aug. 1972.

[18]Oscar Ornati, "The South's Regional Disadvantage," in Robert E. Will and Harold G. Vatter, eds., *Poverty in Affluence: The Social, Political, and Economic Dimensions of Poverty in the United States* (New York: Harcourt, Brace & World, 1970), p. 70.

[19]Irving Kristol, "Taxes, Poverty, and Equality," *The Public Interest,* 37 (Fall 1974), 3–28.

[20]*U.S. News and World Report,* 7 June 1976.

[21]Mark R. Arnold, "The Good War That Might Have Been," *New York Times Magazine,* 29 Sept. 1974, pp. 56–73.

[22]Associated Press, 25 Jan. 1976.

[23]*Newsweek,* 24 Apr. 1978, p. 83.

[24]As reported in *U.S. News and World Report,* 24 Apr. 1972, p. 80.

[25]U.S. Department of Health, Education and Welfare, as reported by Associated Press, 31 July 1972.

[26]Social and Rehabilitation Service, U.S. Department of Health, Education and Welfare, *Findings of the 1971 AFDC Study: Part I. Demographic and Program Characteristics,* 22 Dec. 1971, p. 3.

[27]H. Roy Kaplan and Curt Tausky, "Work and the Welfare Cadillac: The Function of and Commitment to Work among the Hard-Core Unemployed," *Social Problems,* 19 (Spring 1972), 469–83. Another recent study showed that welfare mothers define being on welfare as failure and that they are likely to develop symptoms of illness as a means of rationalizing their failure. See Stephen Cole and Robert Lejeune, "Illness and the Legitimization of Failure," *American Sociological Review,* 37 (June 1972), 347–56.

[28]Sonia Wright, "Work Responses to Income Maintenance: Economic, Sociological, and Cultural Perspectives," *Social Forces,* 53 (June 1975), 553–62.

[29]John R. Price, "Recent Proposals to Reform Welfare Programs," *Agricultural Policy Review,* 10 (Spring 1970), 8.

[30]Lee M. Cohn, "Welfare Report Is Critical," *Washington Star* News Service, 26 Jan. 1976.

[31]*New York Times,* 18 Apr. 1976.

[32]*U.S. News and World Report,* 3 Nov. 1975, p. 26.

[33]Martin Anderson, "Wealth of Truth about Radical Welfare Reform," *New York Times,* 31 Dec. 1978.

[34]New York: Random House, 1966.

[35]For example, see Allison Davis, "The Motivation of the Underprivileged Worker," in William F. Whyte, Jr., ed., *Industry and Society* (New York: McGraw-Hill, 1946), pp. 84–106.

[36]This is the interpretation that was widely placed on the controversial report by Daniel P. Moynihan, *The Negro Family: The Case for National Action* (Washington, D.C.: U.S. Department of Labor, 1965).

[37]Dwight Billings, "Culture and Poverty in Appalachia: A Theoretical Discussion and Empirical Analysis," *Social Forces,* 53 (Dec. 1974), 315–23; Barbara E. Coward, Joe R. Feagin, and J. Allen Williams, Jr., "The Culture of Poverty Debate: Some Additional Data," *Social Problems,* 21 (June 1974), 621–34; Chandler Davidson and Charles M. Gaitz, "Are the Poor Different? A Comparison of Work Behavior and Attitudes among the Urban Poor and Nonpoor," *Social Problems,* 22 (Dec. 1974), 229–45; L. Richard Della Fave, "The Culture of Poverty Revisited: A Strategy for Research," *Social Problems,* 21 (June 1974), 609–21.

[38]See Edward C. Banfield, *The Unheavenly City* (Boston: Little, Brown, 1970).

[39]Michael Harrington, *The Other America: Poverty in the United States* (New York: Macmillan, 1962), p. 138.

[40]Harry M. Caudill, *Night Comes to the Cumberlands: A Biography of a Depressed Area* (Boston: Little Brown, 1962).

[41]See John Fetterman, *Stinking Creek: A Portrait of a Small Community in Appalachia* (New York: E. P. Dutton, 1970).

[42]Leonard Goodwin, *Do the Poor Want to Work? Studies in the Work Orientation of the Poor* (Washington, D.C.: Brookings Institution, 1972).

RACE DISCRIMINATION IN AMERICAN LIFE

LONDON— . . . The second Notting Hill riot in less than 20 years came and went like a summer thunderstorm. But though it lasted only a few hours, last week's clash between white policemen and black youngsters in West London—the worst racial disturbance here in recent memory—left deep scars and raised broad questions.[1]

In the autumn of 1972 Mrs. Oza and thousands of other Asians who had settled in Uganda scrambled aboard planes at Entebbe's airport, leaving behind them bank savings, homes, possessions and a once-secure status as middle-class businessmen, shopkeepers, government clerks and skilled workmen. The abrupt expulsion order by President Idi Amin accused the Asians, who were largely of Indian descent, of "sabotaging" Uganda's economy. . . . Nearly 50,000 Asians were expelled by President Amin.[2]

The Malaysian government, worried that indigenous Malays are not sharing in the country's economic growth, is moving to ex-ert stronger control over foreign operations. In addition, it is pressing the foreigners to give Malays, as distinct from local Chinese or Indians, a larger share of both jobs and equity in foreign subsidiaries.[3]

There are people in Israel so prejudiced against the Sephardic Jews that they think we are all members of the underworld. One even told me, "Until you Moroccans came here, we had no prostitutes, pimps or gangsters in Israel!" This, of course, is a complete absurdity, but it reveals the extent of prejudice on the part of some Ashkenazi Jews. And it would have made not a particle of difference for me to point out that I was not from Morocco, but from Tunisia. For people like that, all Sephardic Jews are from Morocco, whether they come from Tunisia, Algeria, Chile, Spain, Mexico, Cuba, Greece, Turkey or Iraq. As long as they are Sephardic Jews, they are Moroccans. And if they are Moroccans, it doesn't even pay to talk to them. They are automatically prostitutes, pimps or gangsters.[4]

All over the world, racial, national, and ethnic minorities are suffering persecution. It is impossible to identify the most brutal offenders or the most wretched victims—there are too many qualified contestants for each title. One recent survey found that no fewer than 34 countries had "subordinate" minorities of more than a million persons.[5] The United States is not included in this number, which suggests that no fewer than 34 countries have sizable minorities that are treated worse than are minorities in the United States. Since it is not possible to describe all the world's minority problems in a single chapter, this chapter will concentrate upon race and ethnic relations within the United States.

Some Problems of Definition

What is a race? The term is variously used to refer to everyone (the "human race"), to a nationality (the "German race"), to a highly mixed group that is socially designated as different (the "Jewish race"), and to a group with some common physical characteristics (the "white race"). Since biological characteristics overlap, exact classifications are difficult. An acceptable definition might be, "A race is a category of people differing somewhat from others in a number of inherited physical characteristics, but race is also substantially determined by social definition."[6] To simplify, a race is any group of people who are viewed and treated as a race.

For a half century or more, *Negro* was the respectful and dignified term used for dark-skinned people of non-Caucasian African ancestry. Today many American Negroes prefer *black* or *Afro-American* and apply *Negro* only to blacks who grovel and kowtow to whites. To some black spokespersons, "black" is not a color, but a way of thinking about oneself and one's group identity. In substituting "black" for "Negro," they are symbolically rejecting white people's right to assign a status to blacks, or to exercise any control over black life and thought.[7] Since "Negro" is only the Spanish word for "black," the difference may appear trivial to whites, but symbolic differences are important to every group. Yet not all black people reject "Negro," and it is now common for both terms to be used interchangeably.

The term *genocide* is appearing as a descriptive term for many situations and policies that are perceived as aggressions against the black people. Genocide is defined in the dictionary as "deliberate, systematic measures toward the extermination of a racial, political, or cultural group." Historic examples include the attempt of the early Hebrews to exterminate the Canaanites, the massacre of the American Indians, the Turkish massacre of over a million Armenians in 1917–19,[8] Hitler's cremation of 6 million Jews,[9] a number of recent tribal massacres in the newly-independent African states,[10] and the death of at least one-half the Cambodian people through a combination of communist massacre and neglect.[11]

If white Americans are intent on exterminating black people, they have been spectacularly inefficient, since the black population has remained at a constant 10 or 11 percent for many decades, and the rate of black population growth in the United States is now about three times as high as for whites. Since 1900, black life expectancy in the United States has more than doubled, rising from 69 percent of white life expectancy in 1900 to 93 percent in 1976. Even the most ardent white bigot is seldom in favor of exterminating blacks; to exploit them is far more attractive.

Some extremists have extended the term *genocide* to include all sorts of *damaging consequences* to blacks, regardless of white motives or intentions. Higher black death rates among both civilians and military personnel, lower levels of welfare payments in southern states, birth control, substandard housing, and many others are denounced as "genocide."[12] *Coercive, involuntary* birth control, imposed upon blacks as a widespread governmental program, would clearly be a form of genocide, but *equal access* to *voluntary* birth control does not fit the definition,[13] for this would only give poor women of both races the same right to control their childbearing that more affluent women now enjoy.

The terms *racism* and *racist* have lost all precise meaning. In the past, the terms carried one of two related meanings: (1) a belief in inherited race differences that explained differences in racial behavior, or (2) support of segregation, discrimination, or unequal treatment of the races, often accompanied by strong prejudices and intense hostilities. Today the terms are freely applied to any person or policy that black people resent.

Obviously, if all whites are racists then the term is only a synonym for "white" and loses all useful meaning. We shall retain the historic usages given above, which correctly apply, in varying degrees, to some members of all or nearly all races. The racist response can be seen today in the strictures of some black militants in the United States, in the British reaction to nonwhite immigration,[14] in the expulsion of Asians from Uganda,[15] in the massacre of the Hutu tribe by the Tutsis in Burundi,[16] in the treatment of "foreign workers" in Western Europe,[17] the massacre of the Cambodians by the Vietnamese,[18] and in many other situations. Every major race in the world appears as a practitioner of racism in some times or places and as victims of racism in others.[19] Racism knows few boundaries of faith, color, time, or place.

The term *institutional racism* has recently appeared in the literature.[20] It refers to policies and practices that result in racial inequalities, even though there may be no discrimination based directly on race itself. A selection procedure which gives more choice positions to whites than to blacks will be called institutional racism, regardless of the basis of selection. The United States Supreme Court recently ruled that a policy that has a disproportionately adverse effect upon a racial group is not unconstitutional unless it can be shown that discrimination was the intent of the policy.[21] Thus, much institutional racism, while perhaps unfair, is not illegal. Meanwhile, there is no doubt that institutional racism often operates even in the absence of racist intentions. For example, access (to an apprenticeship, a scholarship, a position, a club membership) often depends on personal recommendations. If practically everyone who has the rank and status to make a highly influential recommendation happens to be white, it may be difficult for blacks even to be considered. The extraordinarily gifted black (or poor youth of any race), by working hard and following the mobility rules, can usually gain the attention and favorable recommendation of influential persons. But the black or poor youth who is competent but not outstanding has difficulty cracking this barrier. The informal networks of information, nomination, and recommendation are extremely important, especially for higher-level positions and for beginning positions with high career potential (such as law clerk to a Supreme Court justice). This is only one of the many ways in which established traditions and procedures discriminate against all who are "on the outside." This has been true throughout history, and probably always will be.

The Scientific Facts About Race Differences

The belief that one and one's group are basically different from and better than others has long been a comfort to practically every people. By the decade of the 1950s, however, the scientific world had reached a substantial consensus on race differences. Most scientists, both physical and social, believed that *in biological inheritance, all races are alike in everything that really makes any difference.* There are differences in coloration and slight differences in facial features and bodily proportion but, according to all evidence available, these differences have no effect on learning or behavior. With the exception of several very small, isolated, inbred primitive tribes, *all racial groups seem to show the same distribution of every kind of ability.* All races learn in

Research has shown that the Indian IQ average is the same as the white man's. The higher he advances gradewise, however, the farther behind in achievement he falls. The reason for this is obvious—the subject matter taught is in direct contradiction to the cultural inheritance of the Indian. He is being taught the values of the white man's world, which are often in direct conflict with his heritage.

This dismal state of affairs has resulted in a widespread belief that the Indian is incapable of competing in a white society. This is grossly untrue, as was proven emphatically in the early nineteenth century when the powerful Cherokee nation, numbering nearly 20,000, successfully adapted itself to living at peace with the white man, while still occupying 7 million acres of their own land, mostly in northwest Georgia. Here they far surpassed their white neighbors' accomplishments. By 1826, the Cherokees had, among other accomplishments, accrued thousands of cattle, swine, sheep, and horses. They also had 10 sawmills, 62 blacksmith shops, 31 grist mills, and 18 public schools. Many lived in fine city-style houses or on large plantations, and their children were often sent to boarding schools for the finest education. They read British and American newspapers, along with their own paper, *The Phoenix,* which was printed in both English and Cherokee. They ascribed to a written constitution and established a unicameral legislature. From this, it is clear that the Indian can compete when he is not forced to forsake all of his own tradition and values.

From W. Red Sky Schuchman, "Three Puffs of Smoke," *Mankind Magazine.* Reprinted by permission.

the same way, and most scientists believe that if all the circumstances were the same, all races would learn at the same average speed. Most scientists believe that *all important race differences in personality, behavior, and achievement are purely a result of environmental factors.* Such differences (for example, ignorance and shiftlessness among some blacks) are cited by the majority group to justify its discrimination, which in turn perpetuates those very differences. Thus a vicious circle is completed, and an illusion of innate race differences is preserved.

There is no *conclusive* proof either that the races are equal or that they are unequal in inherited abilities. To define "inherited ability" satisfactorily and measure it exactly is not yet possible, and may never be possible. But the evidence *for* inherited race differences is not very convincing to most scientists.[22] In its absence, most scientists are prepared to *assume* that all races are equal in native abilities until proven otherwise.

A few scientists believe that some average difference in inherited ability levels can be shown by IQ scores.[23] Hans Eysenck, for example, attributes 20 percent of the differences between individual IQ scores to environment and 80 percent to heredity, while Arthur Jensen estimates that an average IQ difference of 15 points between whites and blacks is hereditary.[24] Most scientists, however, criticize virtually all IQ studies as fatally flawed and inconclusive. No test measures native ability directly; a test can only infer native ability from some kind of tested performance. Thus, a variety of social and cultural factors are also being measured—educational background, health, diet, family background, test situation, and many others. Many studies seem to indicate a greater environmental influence than the 20 percent factor conceded by Eysenck. For example, a study of children in Israeli kibbutzim found that while children in Europe normally average about 105 and children in the Middle East average about 85 in IQ, kibbutz children from both places average about 115 in IQ.[25]

The question of innate racial differences thus remains unsettled. *Neither the existence of significant inherited racial differences nor the innate equality of races in ability has been definitely established.* While the preponderance of evidence seems to favor the idea of equality in inherited abilities, this cannot be positively proven, and research on the question continues in an atmosphere that is sometimes more polemical than scientific. Eysenck, Jensen, Richard Herrnstein, and William Shockley have been treated not as scientists raising scientific objections, but as heretics who have strayed from the faith. At times they have even been prevented from speaking by angry critics who claim to be guided by science but who desert the scientist's passion for truth when their own beliefs are challenged.[26]

WHAT DIFFERENCE DOES IT MAKE WHETHER ALL RACES ARE EQUAL IN AVERAGE ABILITIES? Whether this is a vital issue or merely an academic exercise depends on the social policy choices that are made.

1. A difference in *average* native abilities could not justify segregation or discrimination because of *overlap.* Even if it should be proven true, as Jensen suggests, that there is a genetically-based black–white difference of 15 IQ points, there is still a great deal of overlap that no study has calculated at less than 10 percent. This would mean that the top 10 percent of the blacks were superior to one-half of the whites. It would be difficult to

find any moral basis for denying superior blacks the opportunities and rewards offered to inferior whites. Only if *all* blacks were inferior to *all* whites could a castelike discrimination be justified.

2. Under conditions of *equal opportunity*, the "equal ability" argument becomes unimportant. Under equal opportunity, each person of any color would achieve a status and reward according to his or her abilities and efforts (and possibly luck). The more closely a society approaches conditions of equal opportunity, the more irrelevant the "equal abilities" argument becomes.

3. Under conditions of *proportionate distribution*, the "equal abilities" question is crucial. If each race is to be assigned a quota of the desired positions proportionate to its size, this implies that each race has the same proportion of persons who are qualified to fill these positions. Since proportionate distribution in desired positions is today being demanded by racial and ethnic minorities, the question of innate comparative abilities becomes highly important. The burden of proof, however, remains on the affirmative—on those who claim that innate racial ability differences *do* exist. Until this has been conclusively demonstrated, a democratic society must act on the assumption that all racial and ethnic groups possess the same range and level of abilities.

Theories of the Causes of Prejudice and Discrimination

Prejudice is not the same as discrimination. Prejudice refers to one's *judgments* of others, while discrimination refers to one's *actions* toward others. Race discrimination is a treatment given to a person, consciously or unconsciously, because of that person's race rather than because of his or her individual characteristics. A prejudice is, literally, a *prejudgment*, a judgment arrived at before having really examined any evidence about the case or person involved. *A racial prejudice is any judgment of a person based on race rather than on the true characteristics of the individual.* Both the teacher who expects the black child to be dull in algebra and the teacher who expects the black child to be gifted in music are showing their race prejudices, for both impute qualities to the child because it is black instead of discovering this person's individual qualities. A prejudice is a stereotyped image, favorable or unfavorable, that one "sees" in place of the actual individual.

The causes of prejudice are hard to evaluate, for there appear to be several causes, often operating in combination with one another. The following are the principal theories of the causes of prejudice and discrimination.[27]

ECONOMIC THEORIES

THE ECONOMIC-COMPETITION THEORY   This theory assumes that when groups compete, hostilities and prejudices often arise. If the competing groups differ in race or religion, the prejudice takes the form of race or religious prejudice. The more highly identifiable a group is (or is imagined to be), the more easily such prejudice can be focused on the differences that identify it—race, religion, or nationality. Thus, prejudice against the Irish, once intense, largely disappeared as Irish immigrants became assimilated, while prejudice against the easily recognized Japanese remained.

There is considerable evidence to support this theory. Both in Hawaii and on the West Coast, little prejudice against the Japanese developed until Japanese immigrants began to enter types of work that competed with white occupations. Medieval anti-Semitism in Europe increased greatly when banking and finance, previously left to the Jews, grew profitable enough to be attractive to gentiles. Emory Bogardus, comparing race attitudes in different regions, concluded that prejudice is least where there is little social or economic competition between ethnic groups that are in contact with one another.[28] Immigration by a different racial or ethnic group often brings competition for housing, jobs, or land, and is followed by increasing prejudice and hostility. This is seen in the rapid development of race hostility and racist legislation in England following an influx of blacks from the West Indies and Asians from Africa (after the Asians were expelled from Africa in an outbreak of black racism).[29] Many of the newly independent Third World states soon began to discriminate against prosperous racial or ethnic minorities whose success aroused local envy and resentment—Indians in Uganda,[30] Chinese in Malaysia,[31] the Ibo tribe in Nigeria.[32] A particularly interesting case is the island of St. Croix, whose history of racial harmony has been shattered by recent economic development and immigration. St. Croix now has four main groups: (1) immigrant American continentals, who condescend to everyone; (2) Puerto Ricans, who identify themselves as white and are enviously resentful of the continental Americans and disdainful of the blacks; (3) native blacks, who resent all the newcomers and particularly despise the (4) alien blacks from "down island" (the nearby Antilles), who do the dirty work for the lowest wages.[33] Yet, although one can cite many in-

Segregated drinking fountain—street car terminal in Oklahoma City, July 1939.
(Library of Congress)

stances of prejudice following competition,[34] it is unlikely that competition is the sole factor in prejudice. The intensity of prejudice is not exactly proportionate to the strength of competition or the strength of the competing minority. Furthermore, as Gunnar Myrdal pointed out, the economic ambitions of the blacks in the United States met much less white verbal opposition than did the blacks' social and political aspirations.[35]

THE ECONOMIC-EXPLOITATION THEORY   This theory maintains that prejudice is helpful in maintaining economic privilege. It is much easier to keep black wages low if blacks are believed inferior. As Margaret Halsey wrote in her "Memorandum to Junior Hostesses" serving in a nondiscriminatory servicemen's canteen during World War II,

> The real reason back of the refusal of some of you to mingle with Negroes at the canteen isn't nearly so romantic and dramatic as you think it is. The real reason has nothing to do with rape, seduction, or risings in the night. The real reason can be summed up in two extremely unromantic little words: cheap labor. As long as you treat Negroes as subhumans, you don't have to pay them so much. When you refuse to dance with Negro servicemen at the canteen, you are neither protecting your honor nor making sure that white Southerners won't have their homes burned down around their ears. All you are doing is making it possible for employers all over the country to get Negroes to work for them for less money than those employers would have to pay you.[36]

Considerable evidence supports the exploitation theory. Modern race theories first appeared when European nations established colonial empires and needed a theory to sanction their exploitation of the native peoples. Prejudice against the Japanese-Americans appears to have arisen, at least in part, as a result of agitation by vested interests.[37] The use of white supremacy as a political issue in the South long served to keep poor blacks and poor whites in hate and fear of each other, and prevented them from discovering their common interest in modifying an economic status quo that impoverished them both.

The classical Marxist analysis of racism follows this economic exploitation theory in seeing racial conflict as an expression of class conflict, appearing as a result of economic exploitation, and incurable except by ending class exploitation. This analysis overlooks the fact that prejudice and racial conflict sometimes appear between groups where there is no exploitation.[38] Jews in the Soviet Union today would hardly agree that Marxism carries any guarantee of racial justice,[39] nor is racism absent from Fidel Castro's Cuba.[40] As mentioned earlier, the most spectacular acts of genocide under way as this is written are in Cambodia, whose people are victims of a racist war between two communist governments, Vietnam and Cambodia. Wilson argues that class-based theories of race discrimination are now outdated, since class rather than race is now the main basis for inequality in the United States.[41] We may reasonably conclude that economic exploitation is an important source—but not the only source—of racism.

SYMBOLIC THEORIES

A great many theories, some of them fantastic, claim that prejudice arises because we see in another group certain traits that become symbols of what we hate, fear, or envy. For example, whites hate blacks because their (supposedly) uninhibited sex life symbolizes a freedom whites envy; or whites see in blacks' allegedly lazy, easygoing life a symbol of a wish that whites' ambitions force them to renounce. The symbolic theories have most often been applied to anti-Semitism. The Jew is seen as a symbol of urbanism and of the impersonality and sophistication that rustic folk envy and distrust. Other theories see the Jew as a symbol of internationalism, of capitalism, of communism, or of nonconformity, and accordingly the Jews are hated by the nationalists, the communists, the capitalists, and the worshippers of conformity.[42] Such symbolic theories, although difficult to prove or to disprove, find some acceptance among students of prejudice.

PSYCHOLOGICAL THEORIES

THE SCAPEGOAT THEORY   Nearly 2,000 years ago Tertullian wrote in Rome, "If the Tiber rose to the walls of the city, if the heavens did not send rain, if an earthquake occurred, if famine threatened, if pestilence raged, the cry resounded, 'Throw the Christians to the lions.' " After the Christians became the majority, Jews took their place as scapegoats. During the great plague of the fourteenth century, some 350 Jewish communities were exterminated within a two-year period on the charge that they had already poisoned, or might poison, the water supply and spread the plague.[43]

People have always sought to blame something or someone else for their troubles. The ancient Hebrews each year loaded their sins onto a goat and chased him into the wilderness.[44] This goat, allowed to escape, came to be known as a scapegoat, and the term came to be applied to anyone forced to bear blame for others' misfortunes. Most minority groups have at some time or other served as convenient scapegoats. According to one analysis,[45] a suitable scapegoat should be (1) easily recognizable, either physically or through some trait of dress or behavior; (2) too weak to fight back; (3) near at hand; (4) already unpopular; (5) a symbol of something that is hated and despised.

The scapegoat theory helps to explain German anti-Semitism under Hitler, as the Jews were blamed for the loss of World War I and for postwar difficulties. Hitler actively cultivated the scapegoating tendency, for without the Jews to fill the role of devil, the Nazi movement might have failed.[46] Today the urban crisis, disorder in the schools, the "welfare mess," and "crime in the streets" are all too conveniently blamed on black people.

THE FRUSTRATION-AGGRESSION THEORY   There is some experimental evidence that aggressive impulses arise when one is frustrated.[47] All persons, both children and adults, are often unable to do the things they wish to do, and their frustration produces aggressive impulses that can find a socially approved outlet through race prejudices and hatreds. The abuse and mistreatment of a minority drains off the irrational, latent hostilities produced by the frustrations of social living. Thus the poor whites, prevented by custom and by the power system from any attack on the landlord or the industrialist, vent their hostilities on blacks. The business executive, struggling to survive in a competitive system but enjoined from hating a competitor and fellow Rotarian, hates the Jew instead. Incompetent, unsuccessful persons would be particularly tempted to find in racial prejudice a compensation for their own failures.

This theory is not easy to prove or disprove. There is some evidence that unsuccessful people show greater than average amounts of prejudice. One study found that veterans who were downwardly mobile expressed more aggressive attitudes than those who were moving into better jobs and improved status.[48] The same study reported that those who believed they had received a bad break in the army were inclined to be anti-Semitic. The spectacular growth of organized anti-Semitism during the New Deal era, mainly among groups bitterly opposed to New Deal policies, suggests that many who were frustrated by "that man in the White House" may have found an outlet for their anger in anti-Semitic hostilities.[49] These studies, however, do not show that loss of status is always associated with higher levels of prejudice, for research reveals many exceptions.[50] What the studies do show is that discontent of any kind may find outlet in prejudice and hostility. For example, one study found that "whites who are dissatisfied with their local community services and with their city government are more given to hostility toward Negroes than white people who describe themselves as satisfied."[51] The frustration-aggression theory thus receives considerable support; yet it is an incomplete explanation, because aggression is only one of the several possible consequences of frustration (including identification, conversion, repression, retreat into fantasy, and others), and aggressions need not be directed at a minority group. Nor does the theory explain why one group rather than another becomes an object of abuse.

THE SOCIAL-NEUROSIS THEORY   There are several versions of the social-neurosis theory, which views race prejudice as a *symptom of a maladjusted, neurotic personality*. According to this theory, people who are insecure, troubled, and discontented find refuge in prejudice. As Ben Hecht says, "Prejudice is our method of transferring our own sickness to others. It is our ruse for disliking others rather than ourselves. . . . Prejudice is a raft onto which the shipwrecked mind clambers and paddles to safety."[52]

Beginning over 30 years ago, a number of scholars sought to find whether certain personalities were predisposed toward tolerance and others toward prejudice.[53] This concept of the prejudiced personality inspired scores of studies that generally agree in finding the prejudiced personality to be anxious and insecure, highly active, preoccupied with strength and toughness, nonstudious, self-centered, domineering, immature, somewhat puritanical, critical of others, ethnocentric, superficial in interests, and cliché-bound in thinking; while the unprejudiced personality is seen as more studious and serious, cooperative rather than domineering, tolerant of others, benevolent and humanitarian, and relatively free of stereotypes and rigid categories of thought. But these studies also show that prejudice involves other factors beyond those stated in the authoritarian personality thesis.[54]

It seems probable that tolerance and prejudice are functions of both the total personality and one's individual experience. It is known that prejudiced people generally show similar prejudices against many groups, irrespective of their knowledge of or contact with them, but there are many exceptions—prejudiced persons who are tolerant toward certain groups, and tolerant persons who are prejudiced about certain groups. It is also true that many widespread prejudices are simply learned as supposed facts (for example, "Jews have an instinct for making money," "blacks are naturally musical"). Such "facts" may have no particular impact on the personality, merely being filed away as part of one's store of information. It is probable that the social-neurosis theory applies only to the extremes of the prejudice continuum, with the central group of mildly or moderately prejudiced persons explained by some other theory. It is clear beyond all question, however, that *we find the explanation of prejudice in the personality and experience of the person holding the prejudice, not in the character of the group against whom the prejudice is directed.* The utter irrelevance of the true characteristics of the victims of prejudice has been demonstrated again and again! The precise manner in which the degree to which prejudice and tolerance identify different kinds of basic personalities can be learned only through much further research.

These are the principal theories of the origin of race prejudices, although there are several others of lesser import.[55] The principal theories are more than idle speculation; each is supported by a respectable body of research. No one of them explains *all* prejudice, for prejudices are of many kinds and degrees and may have as many origins. Each helps to explain certain kinds of prejudice. Taken together, they provide a good deal of insight, and place the techniques of controlling prejudice somewhere between a science and an art.

Minority Adjustments to Prejudice and Discrimination

Of all the popular nonsense about race, perhaps none exceeds the nonsense of attributing racial behavior to instinct rather than to experience. People note what they see, or think they see, in a particular race or group and attribute it to "racial nature." They fail to realize that all group behavior is a product of group experience, and all racial behavior is a product of the conditions under which that race has lived. In a noted rabbi's remark, "I have been a Jew for a thousand years," we see that many generations of experience—of working, of struggling, of fleeing in the night, and of traditions and legends told and retold—enter into the making of the so-called racial nature of a group.

A minority that endures discrimination and inequality in a society that professes democracy and equality of opportunity is doubly affected by this experience. The *fact* of discrimination and inequality promotes certain behavior in the minority, while the cultural *ideal* of democracy and equality of opportunity promotes different behavior. Consequently, there is no single racial personality for any minority in America, but a variety of personality outcomes, all of which represent minority adjustments to the conditions under which they live.

ACCEPTANCE

The stereotype of the contented, easygoing black is not entirely untrue, although it is less true today than in the past. A considerable number of blacks, especially in the South, accepted the doctrine of innate black inferiority and white domination. These were probably the most successfully "adjusted" blacks of all, since they escaped most of the frustrations and resentments that bedeviled other blacks. These blacks also gained the approval of those whites who described the black who was obedient, docile, and deferential as a "good nigger." This white stereotype also defines the "good nigger" as hard-working but unambitious. In attempting to limit black ambitions to simple and childish goals that in no way jeopardized white status or income, whites also deprived blacks of their main reason for working, and guaranteed that some blacks would be "lazy." But if blacks will not work hard unless motivated by ambition, many whites would prefer that blacks be lazy, for, while the lazy black is an irritation, the ambitious black is a threat. Many whites may be unaware of making such a choice, but the effects of their choice remain. *For some blacks, laziness and lack of ambition have been an intelligent and functionally useful adjustment to their lack of opportunity.*

ACCOMMODATION

Some blacks resented white domination but made expedient compromises with it to advance themselves. Fearful of attacking white people's prejudices, they sought to manipulate these prejudices to their own advantage. This involved the studied use of flattery, cajolery, and humble petition. It involved observing racial etiquette and making no challenge to the racial status quo. It entailed acting the way whites expected blacks to act, and required the use of many subterfuges to avoid disturbing any white illusions about blacks. By preserving an outward appearance of acceptance of white domination, many blacks achieved a tolerable existence and even some advancement. Today this "Uncle Tom" pattern is passé; in today's accommodation pattern the whites are less patronizing and the blacks less servile than in earlier decades.

The accommodation pattern often includes *avoidance,* an effort by the minority to minimize contacts with the majority. The clannishness of a minority is an avoidance technique. The medieval ghetto originated as a voluntary clustering of Jews for common protection and escape from insult; only later did it become compulsory. The self-segregation pattern of many black students on the campus today is an example of avoidance.

AGGRESSION

Not all who resent discrimination are able or willing to accommodate themselves successfully. Some find outlet for their frustrations in some form of aggression against someone—the majority, another minority, or even each other. The many forms of aggression range from revolts, riots, and street fights to such subtle provocation as loud talk or intentional incivility. C. S. Johnson described numerous subtle methods that blacks have long used to vent their hostility upon whites: "talking back," quitting jobs without notice, spreading gossip, paying exaggerated courtesies, committing acts of petty sabotage, and so on.[56]

Certain members of the minority develop what has been called the *oppression psychosis,* an oversensitivity to discrimination that leads them to imagine discrimination where it is absent. Some black students who receive low grades because of poor work are quick to accuse the teacher of unfairness. A prominent black explained the oppression psychosis as follows:

> When I was a barefoot boy in Franklin County, Virginia, sometimes I stubbed my toe in the spring and it would not heal until the fall. It seemed that everything in nature, including the leaves, wind and grass, conspired to

hit that toe. The children, dogs, flies, and cats always deliberately selected that toe to brush against or to trample upon. My suffering, I admit, was more psychological than physiological, for I was always expecting somebody or something to pick on that sensitive toe.

The Negro has been stubbed and snubbed so constantly by prejudice, that he not only reacts to the slightest rebuff in word or act, but he often reacts when there has been no intended action.[57]

A person with the oppression psychosis blames all disappointments and failures on discrimination and is likely to be highly aggressive in venting his hostilities. Such persons irritate and alienate the majority group and embarrass their own group, whose complaints they exaggerate and caricature.

There was a spectacular escalation in black aggression in the later 1960s. Urban riots, widespread during the summers, were unorganized, usually beginning with a police incident and spreading, with considerable burning and looting. Unlike the historic race riots in the United States, these were battles not between whites and blacks, but between blacks and police, and they were most likely to occur in cities with a large black population.[58] The typical riot participant in the past was a young, unmarried, unemployed male, but these riots involved much larger proportions of mature persons, women, and employed persons than traditional riots have included. Studies still showed an inverse correlation between riot participation and age, marital status, education, income, social contacts with whites and a positive correlation with feelings of alienation, powerlessness, racial dissatisfaction, and isolation from the white community. Although the most deprived segments of the black community participated the most actively,[59] these riots had a far greater degree of approval from the "responsibles" in the black community than has been traditional. There was a widespread feeling that rioting, looting, and burning were the only way "to make whitey listen."[60] But the riots accomplished little and were soon perceived by blacks as counterproductive, since their main effect was to destroy the sectors of the city inhabited by blacks. They now appear to have been a passing rather than an enduring tactic.[61]

ORGANIZED PROTEST

While aggression is primarily a way to vent one's hostile feelings, organized protest is a calculated campaign for change. Organized protest often uses aggressive devices, but only as part of a carefully organized plan. Organized protest goes beyond the humble petitions of a Booker T. Washington to include an insistent demand that the promises of the Constitution be fulfilled. The National Association for the Advancement of Colored People (NAACP) is perhaps the most effective organization in the country fighting for black rights. It vigorously demands enforcement of existing laws and enactment of additional laws to ensure equal police protection, and to reduce occupational, educational, and social discrimination against blacks. It has successfully pressed many legal actions resulting in court rulings that have weakened and reduced many kinds of discrimination. The National Urban League is primarily concerned with increasing economic opportunities for blacks. Using mainly negotiation and conciliation, it seeks to increase job opportunities and job training, and to promote housing and welfare services. Both of these organizations are relatively conservative. They are committed to integration as a goal, and to legal means as tactics.

A number of more aggressive organizations, including the Congress of Racial Equality (CORE) and the Student Non-Violent Coordinating Committee (SNCC) were active in the 1960s, but have now disappeared. The Black Panthers were the most radical of all, urging blacks to arm for battle with police officers.[62] But by 1975, the Black Panthers had dropped aggressive tactics and become a black service organization, still revolutionary in goals but moderate in tactics.[63]

Organized protest is the minorities' most effective weapon. For lack of effectively organized protest (among other reasons), blacks made no important gains during World War I. In World War II, however, well organized plans for a march on Washington to dramatize failure to employ blacks in the defense industry—an incident that would be highly embarrassing to a nation fighting a war against fascism—resulted in President Franklin Roosevelt's establishment of the Fair Employment Practices Committee. During 1963 there were at least 930 protest demonstrations in 115 communities in 11 states. Although more than 20,000 demonstrators were arrested, they won sweeping concessions in public accommodations.[64]

Organized protest can be effective when it is directed to a specific goal and when a specific person, group, or authority can grant that goal.[65] For integrating public accommodations, organized protest was effective; but it has proved to be almost totally ineffective in opening residential neighborhoods to black residents. By the late 1960s black patience was exhausted, and nonviolent protest was increasingly replaced by violent action. But the obvious limitations of violence as a tactic led to the decline of violence in the early 1970s, leaving black leadership divided and uncertain as to proper strategy.[66]

The Social-Disorganization Approach

Race problems can be viewed as products of social disorganization. Some factor—migration, population growth, technological change—disturbs an existing equilibrium between races, or between groups that are defined as races. In America most blacks were slaves, whose status was clearly defined by law. This system ended with the Civil War. After the war, the North ruled the South with the help of the blacks, to whom they gave the vote and whom they placed in political office.[67] After a decade the North abandoned the blacks to the tender mercies of an embittered South, who promptly dis-

One activist recalls an argument he had with her [Patricia Roberts Harris, Secretary of the Department of Housing and Urban Development] about black protests. "You can accomplish a lot more in an IBM board meeting," she told him, "than demonstrating in the streets."

"You wouldn't be on the board of IBM," he answered, "if it weren't for the people in the streets."

Robert Shrum, "Carter and the Blacks," *New Times*, 21 Jan. 1977, p. 25.

enfranchised the blacks, removed them from political office, and set about returning them to servitude.[68] An elaborate etiquette developed to regulate all contacts between whites and blacks[69] (for example, blacks were never addressed as "Mr." or "Mrs."; white and black children might play together only while young; blacks never sat down in the presence of adult whites). This etiquette sought to permit close and intimate contacts but to prevent any suggestion of equality; therefore, black servants might live on the same block or in the same house with whites; prepare their food and even nurse white babies at their breasts, yet they could not eat with whites or wear hats in their presence.

Before the Civil War many of the skilled workers in nearly all occupations except the professions were black slaves. After the war, a popular classification of all jobs as either "white man's work" or "nigger's work" developed, and each postwar census showed a decline in the proportion of skilled workers among blacks. Within a generation, blacks were largely excluded from all but the most menial jobs.

In this way a new equilibrium developed to replace the prewar slave-oriented society of the South. Although there were many local variations and minor uncertainties, this new equilibrium did tell people, white and black, where they stood and what they might do. This equilibrium persisted without great change for over half a century. Meanwhile, blacks made some

A wood engraving after A.R. Waud of blacks escaping from slavery.
(Library of Congress)

gains in education and in ownership of farms and businesses, but they made few gains and suffered net losses in their bid for political and occupational equality. But the northward migration of blacks, the accumulated findings of natural and social science, and the development of industrial unionism after 1933 all eventually undermined this post-Civil War equilibrium. During the 1930s the CIO organized many industrial unions, which include all the workers in a particular *industry* rather than those in a given *trade* or skill (as in the AFL trade unions). The industrial union cannot exclude blacks without weakening itself, nor can it allow race animosities to disrupt union affairs. Although discrimination against blacks (and everybody else) has been the rule in trade unions, enlightened self-interest led most industrial unions to admit blacks, and the national office of the CIO and some locals have waged an energetic campaign to reduce prejudice and discrimination.[70]

The outbreak of World War II found traditional race patterns beginning to weaken, and it greatly accelerated their decay. The war produced a serious labor shortage together with an emphasis on the values of democracy and equality. Blacks and sympathetic whites took full advantage of this unique opportunity to press for minority rights. The effect of such changes is further to disorganize and eventually to complete the destruction of the traditional pattern of race relations all over the country. The old equilibrium is irretrievably gone and a new equilibrium has not yet crystallized.

The old equilibrium owed much of its stability to the fact that the status of the blacks was fully consistent with the beliefs of the period. Since nearly all Americans, including even the blacks, believed that blacks were innately different from and inferior to whites, it seemed perfectly sensible to treat them as inferiors. "All men are created equal" did not apply to blacks, since they were "property," not people. Theories of a biblical Hamitic curse,[71] of

All [French restauranteurs in New York City] agree that one of the most impressive of recent changes in professional French kitchens is the attitude about race. Ten years ago, the French chefs who ruled the kitchens of the principal luxury restaurants, particularly in Manhattan, insisted they would be ruined if they had to hire a cook or chef who was not born and raised in France.

Today, Lutece, for example, has four Dominicans on the staff. One started 16 years ago as a dishwasher. "Now," said Soltner, "he is very, very good in all his food preparation—he bones meat as well and as fast as any French cook, and he makes an excellent mousse au chocolat."

The principal chef at the Coach House is Puerto Rican. The previous chef was black. The No. 2 cook in the kitchen is a talented young American woman who studied cooking in France.

Similarly, the kitchen in La Caravelle is staffed not only with French cooks but with one Puerto Rican, one Ecuadorian and a young American. Of his Puerto Rican *poissonnier* or fish cook, Fessaguet says, "I wouldn't trade him for a French chef"—quite a revolutionary thought for a Lyonnais whose eyes light up when he hears *"La Marseillaise."*

From Craig Claiborne with Pierre Franey, "Pique behind the Kitchen Door," *New York Times Magazine*, 25 Nov. 1979, p. 31. Copyright © by *The New York Times Company*. Reprinted by permission.

incomplete or separate evolution, of geographic determinism, and of intelligence test evidence were successively employed to justify inferior treatment of blacks. As long as such notions were believed—and most people did believe them—there was no inconsistency in professing democratic ideals while practicing race discrimination.

But as natural and social science destroyed the intellectual respectability of such beliefs, the inconsistencies between democratic ideals and racial practice became increasingly apparent. A society that professes democracy and equality of opportunity yet practices race discrimination is to this degree disorganized. This disorganization gives whites a bad conscience and drives blacks into frustrated confusion. Only through the full participation of all minorities in American life can we achieve a stable new equilibrium as a democratic society.

The Value-Conflict Approach

As we have repeatedly implied in this chapter, the race problem is basically a moral problem—a choice of values. The existence of race discrimination is a problem only to one whose values define race discrimination as abhorrent. Although practically everyone agrees that there is a race problem, some define the problem as the task of eliminating prejudice and discrimination, others as one of putting the blacks back in "their place." What some hail as progress in race relations, others view with alarm and dismay. If all, or even most, Americans could agree on what kind of solution to the race problem they wished, such a solution might not be long in coming. We have enough knowledge to "solve" the problem if we shared a consensus on objectives. But there can be no agreement between those who want blacks to be ambitious citizens and those who want them to be servile inferiors.

Even sympathetic whites must make difficult value choices. Should they seek the prevention of race conflict, the reduction of discrimination, or the reduction of prejudice? In at least the short run, these objectives may conflict. Techniques of reducing discrimination may produce at least a temporary increase in conflict and prejudice, as the school desegregation controversy reveals. While over the long run it is likely that conflict, prejudice, and discrimination move together, some short-run sacrifices may be unavoidable.

The Personal-Deviation Approach

Those who fail to internalize and reflect the conventional attitudes and prejudices of their society are deviant, while the conventionally prejudiced person is "normal." Thus, both the racist bigot and the dedicated racial equalitarian are deviants who create race problems by undermining conventional ideas and prejudices that support a discriminatory racial equilibrium.

The extremist, whether a racist bigot or a fanatic devotee of equality or reverse discrimination, is likely to be a maladjusted person finding an outlet for personal frustrations and inadequacies. Whether such extremists do more good than harm to their cause can be debated. Some of the militant black leadership appears to be irrational. In many cases, however, what whites perceive as irrational irresponsibility may be no more than the intentional use of the same organizational and agitational techniques that the leaders of social movements have always used. These leaders may be culturally deviant, in that they are rejecting and attacking the established social system, but they are not necessarily psychologically deviant. There are also some, mainly at the local level, who are so consumed by bitterness that they are virtually psychotic. Yet, without deep wells of widespread black bitterness and resentment to tap, even the irrational psychotics would be ineffective. Thus, the deviant person may make race relations more explosive, but is not the cause of the problem. To blame race troubles on agitators alone is to evade the problem.

The totally unprejudiced person is also a deviant, in not having absorbed the normal prejudices, racial stereotypes, and institutionalized racism of others. Racial equality, or even reverse discrimination, may become a cause to which one is fanatically dedicated. In this as in most other problems, the extremists at both ends of the continuum are likely to be deviant persons.

Techniques of Reducing Prejudice and Discrimination

EDUCATION

Many studies have shown that the better educated are more often tolerant, and that ignorance and prejudice are common bedfellows. It is not clear, however, that education is the *cause* of the more tolerant attitudes, for other variables of class and personality selectivity are involved.[72] It is naive to expect either church or school to educate people toward beliefs and values very different from those already held by the community. Both church and school depend on the community for financial support and are staffed and directed by persons who share most of the views and prejudices of the community. Certain church bodies, especially the National Council of Churches, have been active in issuing liberal racial pronouncements and supporting minority rights. Although these pronouncements may have helped promote a national atmosphere more favorable to minority rights, not much of this interest in race problems has filtered down to the local congregational level. Several studies suggest that conventionally religious persons are *more* likely to be racially prejudiced,[73] although the least prejudiced persons are often highly religious, but not conventional or orthodox in their religion.[74] There is certainly no basis for assuming that conventional or traditional religion reduces prejudice. All major denominations have adopted national policies of integrating church congregations, but few congregations are significantly biracial.

EXHORTATION AND PROPAGANDA

Exhortation and propaganda form a double-edged weapon. Exhortation at the level of platitudes and generalities, like the posters, radio plugs, and sermons saying "All people are brothers and sisters," "Prejudice is un-American" are ineffective. Prejudiced persons apply them to other people, since they are unaware of their own prejudice. Their prejudices are so fully rationalized as to be immune to such slogans. In fact, such exhortation may have a negative effect, since it allows the prejudiced person to feel self-righteous, while it gives the liberal the illusion of "doing something" about race problems and thus substitutes for more effective action.

More specific propaganda also has its dangers. Publicizing the achievement of minority members may arouse jealousy rather than respect. Publicizing recent black gains may inspire jealousy and insecurity among less prosperous whites, while describing black poverty and handicaps may confirm prejudices instead of arousing sympathy. Attempts to answer false rumors and racial accusations may even spread the falsehood more widely. Propaganda must be used skillfully or it will defeat its purposes. Propaganda is seriously limited because (1) it fails to reach the right audience, since many prejudiced persons read and watch little that is of serious content, and (2) prejudiced persons interpret propaganda in such a way that their prejudice remains undisturbed, or is even strengthened.[75] The television series "All in the Family" was enjoyed by liberals, who perceived it as a devastating satire upon bigotry, and also by bigots, who perceived Archie "telling it like it is."[76] All in all, it is doubtful that propaganda has much effect in reducing prejudice or discrimination.

CONTACT

Contact between peoples produces a variety of attitudes, depending on the *kind of contact*. A mere "getting together" of whites and blacks or of gentiles and Jews does not automatically reduce prejudices; it may even increase them. One study of an interracial boys' camp found that the boys with the most interracial contacts also offered the most spontaneous unfavorable comments (correlation of $+.83$ for whites and $+.67$ for blacks), and that those whose prejudices diminished were matched by an equal number whose prejudices were intensified.[77]

Certain kinds of contact, however, generally reduce prejudice and hostility. A number of studies over the past three decades have researched the effects of integration of blacks and whites in the military services, in employment, in housing, and in schools. In most cases the dire predictions of trouble have not been fulfilled, while significant attitude and behavior changes have followed. Morton Deutsch and Mary Evans Collins studied two integrated housing projects in which blacks and whites were scattered indiscriminately, and two segregated projects in which blacks and whites occupied separate sections of the project. They found that in the integrated projects, agreeable relations between whites and blacks were ten times more common and bad relations only one-fourth as frequent as in the segregated projects.[78]

A number of other surveys support the conclusion that certain kinds of contact are likely to reduce prejudice. Richard Morris and Vincent Jeffries, studying white reactions to the Watts riot of 1965, found that white persons without intimate social contact with blacks ranked high in antagonism toward them.[79] Edward Ransford found this equally true of the black participants; those most prone to violence were those without intimate social contacts with whites, especially when their racial isolation was combined with feelings of powerlessness and acute dissatisfaction.[80] Jerry Robinson and James Preston summarize the numerous studies of the contact theory with the following generalizations:

> First, interracial contact is most likely to yield favorable results (i.e., reduce prejudice) when participants are: (a) of equal status; (b) majority group members interacting with high-status representatives of the minority groups; (c) in a voluntary contact situation; and (d) engaged in intimate interaction, pursuing common goals in a cooperative relationship with institutional supports. Second, interracial contact is most likely to yield unfavorable results (i.e., intensify prejudices and stereotypes) when participants are: (a) of unequal status; (b) majority group members interacting with low-status representatives of the minority group; (c) in involuntary contact situations; (d) engaged in casual interaction, competing; and (e) in conflict for goals which cannot be shared.[81]

The sharp increase in race conflict in the 1960s and early 1970s may seem to contradict this contact theory. In the armed services, for example, racial conflicts multiplied and at times paralyzed some military units.[82] A Pentagon survey in 1973 found some feelings among both black and white recruits that the other race was receiving favored treatment, and these feelings increased greatly as recruits progressed through basic training.[83] Such incidents show that the armed services cannot insulate themselves from the rest of society, in which there was a sharp polarization of race attitudes during the later 1960s. While equal status cooperative contacts between blacks and whites increased during the 1900s, there was probably an even greater increase in competitive tension-laden contacts, as old barriers were painfully demolished. Thus the contact theory was confirmed, not disproved by the race conflicts of the later 1960s, and by the decline in race conflicts in the mid-1970s.

SOCIAL REVOLUTION

All of the preceding approaches involve attempts to alter race relations within the context of the present capitalist society. But some scholars feel that it is impossible to purge a capitalist society of its racism. Following the Marxist analysis, which sees racism as an aspect of class exploitation, they conclude that racism can be ended only in a social revolution that abolishes all privileges of birth, class, or race in a common surge toward human equality.[84]

As we indicated earlier, economic exploitation is undoubtedly a factor in racism, but not the sole factor. Race discrimination exists between groups that are not in a competitive or exploitative relationship to one another. Racial discrimination has not disappeared from any of the presently Marxist societies. While it is true that the Soviet Union is far less racist today than Czarist Russia at the turn of the century, this is also true of capitalist United States. A great deal of change in the direction of racial equality has transpired under America's capitalist democracy; meanwhile, in a number of countries—some capitalist and some avowedly socialist—racism has increased in recent years. Clearly, the origin of racism—and its extinction—is far too complex to be circumscribed by simplistic Marxian analyses. A social revolution might bring a great reduction in racism; but there is no guarantee that it would not bring an ugly new form of racial stratification. Revolutions rarely develop the way they are expected to by their promoters.

Current Trends in Race Relations in America

DECLINE OF REGIONAL VARIATIONS IN RACE ATTITUDES

Regional variations of all sorts—rural–urban, agrarian–industrial, East–West, and North–South—are rapidly fading. Mass communication, migration, and decentralization of industry are fast dissolving the quaint provincialism of region, hamlet, and mesa. Georgia blacks and Georgia whites not only work at the same bench and belong to the same union in Detroit; they are doing so in Georgia as well. The noble pose of moral superiority that Northerners are wont to strike has lost whatever validity it may have possessed. The barriers to blacks voting in the South have crumbled, with registered black voters in the South rising from 1,463,000 in 1960 to 4,150,000 in 1976, a gain of 184 percent.[85] This is profoundly altering the political structure of the South. While considerable school desegregation has been achieved in the South, both school and residential segregation have in-

---

TABLE 12–1   Black Political Gains in the United States

White and black voter registration in 11 southern states, 1960–76

	1960	1976
Percent of whites registered to vote	61.1	67.9
Percent of blacks registered to vote	29.1	63.1

Black elected officials in the United States, 1970 and 1979

	Offices held by blacks 1970	Offices held by blacks 1979	Percent increase 1970–79	Number of such offices in U.S.*	Percent held by blacks, 1979
Total elected black officials	1,472	4,584	211	—	—
U.S. and state legislatures	182	315	73	8,017	3.9
City and county officials	715	2,647	270	196,939	1.3
Law enforcement officials (judges, magistrates, sheriffs)	213	486	128	n.a.*	n.a.
Education (college boards, school boards)	362	1,136	214	87,062	1.3

*Not available.
SOURCE: *Statistical Abstract of the United States*, 1979, p. 512.

creased in the North. In nearly all respects, regional variations are diminishing.

SHIFT FROM ATTACK ON PREJUDICE TO ATTACK ON SEGREGATION AND DISCRIMINATION

Social scientists long accepted the popular assumption that segregation was necessary to prevent race conflict in a prejudice-ridden society. Only after prejudice had declined, it was believed, could segregation be relaxed and equality achieved; meanwhile, the races might enjoy "separate but equal" facilities and opportunities. People interested in minority rights were urged to tolerate and work within segregation—to seek to reduce prejudice first, after which discrimination and segregation would disappear.

One of the significant discoveries of recent decades is that attempts to reduce prejudice while retaining segregation and discrimination were ineffective. For segregation prevented the sorts of contact that reduce prejudice, instead channeling the races into the kinds of contact that create and reinforce prejudice. To seek to reduce prejudice by exhortation and propaganda was largely futile when segregation was so busily creating it. Segregation even failed in its primary objective of preventing conflict, at least in a society in which democratic values made segregation frustrating to blacks and embarrassing to whites. Action in recent years has been directed at ending discrimination. Prejudices cease to be important after discrimination is ended.

SHIFT FROM EDUCATION AND CONCILIATION TO LEGAL AND ADMINISTRATIVE ACTION

In the days of Booker T. Washington, conciliation was perhaps the only practical approach open to blacks. To *demand* anything from whites would only infuriate them; but to *petition* whites—to appeal to their sympathy, generosity, and vanity—was sometimes effective in obtaining schools, hospitals, and other benefits that did not seriously disturb the status quo. But today a better educated and more restive black group faces a less self-satisfied white group that has been repeating the slogans of democracy so long that it almost believes them. In recent years minority leaders, aided by many members of the dominant group, have made a determined legal attack upon every form of discrimination. Although blacks are the main beneficiaries of this movement, Jews, American Indians, Americans of Mexican or Oriental ancestry, and other minorities share in the gains made. The legal approach involves (a) enforcing existing laws; (b) seeking court interpretations that extend the coverage of existing laws; and (c) passing additional laws.

ENFORCING EXISTING LAWS   Many rights legally guaranteed to blacks (and other minorities) have in fact been unavailable. The rights to vote, to use public facilities, and to equal protection of the law were long denied. Violence and threats of violence often deterred minority members from claiming their legal privileges. Blacks seeking service in hotels and restaurants were often met by a bland refusal of proprietors to obey the law, or else by evasion, inattention, and humiliation. Law enforcement officials were likely to stall when legal action was sought. Such situations have changed. The NAACP, the American Civil Liberties Union, and other organizations often prod local law enforcement officials into action when necessary. Hundreds of legal actions have been pressed for the sole purpose of demonstrating that noncompliance with the law will not be accepted without complaint. While not entirely successful, the effort to gain enforcement of existing laws has produced a great many changes.

EXTENDING INTERPRETATIONS OF EXISTING LAWS AND CONSTITUTIONAL PROVISIONS Civil rights organizations, mainly the NAACP, have pressed many court cases seeking legal ruling that a particular practice is contrary to law, or violates some guarantee of the Fourteenth Amendment. One decision held that Jim Crow segregation on interstate trains and buses was unconstitutional; another had the effect of requiring the admission of blacks to tax-supported university, graduate, and professional schools of most Southern states; another ruled that restrictive racial covenants (preventing resale of real estate to blacks or other "undesirables") are unenforceable; another ruled that hotels, restaurants, and other places of public accommodation could not legally discriminate if they engaged in interstate commerce—and nearly all of them do. This approach has been successful in destroying segregation in public accommodations. In housing and public schools, however, the numerous court victories have not reversed the trend toward increasing segregation.

NEW LAWS AGAINST DISCRIMINATION   The early 1900s brought a flood of state laws and local ordinances *requiring* the segregation of parks, streetcars, and many other facilities. A half-century later, law began to demolish the barriers those laws had erected. The first federal civil rights legislation of this century was passed in 1957, empowering the attorney general to aid any person who is denied his voting rights, and establishing a federal Civil Rights Commission to investigate voting abuses and make recommendations to Congress. The Civil Rights Act of 1960 sought further to strengthen voting rights. The Civil Rights Act of 1964 is the most sweeping civil rights act ever passed. It (1) forbids racial discrimination in most places of public accommodation, (2) authorizes the attorney general to intervene in school desegregation and other discrimination cases, (3) forbids discrimination by employers and unions, (4) permits halting of federal funds for programs in which race discrimination exists, (5) prohibits election registrars from applying voting requirements unequally, and (6) permits federal registrars to register voters where local officials refuse to register voters equally.[86]

The Civil Rights Act of 1968, after meeting defeat in 1967, was passed in the aftermath of the assassination of Dr. Martin Luther King.[87] It set up a timetable so that by 1970 discrimination was forbidden in all multiple-unit housing except owner-occupied developments with four or fewer units; it barred discrimination in all housing sales handled by real estate brokers; and it simplified prosecution procedures. Strictly private sales of homes are exempted; thus the frequent complaint that the government has "destroyed your right to sell to whom you wish" is totally untrue. All the law requires is that *if you engage a realtor* to sell your house, or advertise it to the public for sale, you must sell without race discrimination.

Over half the states now have Fair Employment Practices acts, forbidding discrimination in employment, while the federal Civil Rights Act of

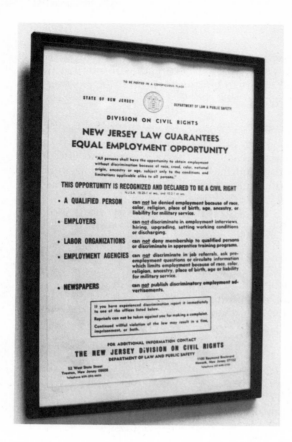

Equal Opportunity Legislation guarantees our rights against job discrimination.
(Irene Springer)

1964 forbids employment discrimination by all employers and unions engaged in interstate commerce. Today that includes nearly all businesses and industries. Such laws were long bitterly opposed by employers, who feared government interference with their operations and worried that the law would stir up trouble in the plant. But in operation these laws proved to be no great nuisance to business. The expected trouble rarely developed.[88]

Today the Equal Employment Opportunity Commission has several hundred inspectors engaged in prodding employers to obey the law in their hiring and promotion practices. It may be debated whether legislation or other forces were the primary factor in the improvement of the economic status of blacks, but the improvement is undeniable. Between 1947 and 1974, median family income of black families increased from 51 to 65 percent of average white family income.[89] But this figure understates the actual improvement in black earnings. The sharp rise in the proportion of female-headed black families (up from 17.5 percent in 1960 to 33.9 percent in 1977, compared with 8.5 percent and 10.9 percent for whites)[90] holds down the average family income for blacks more than whites. Divide a population into a larger number of families and the average family income is less. Furthermore, black families have fewer workers per family than white families. But between 1969 and 1978, while the proportion of white families with two or more wage earners rose from 54 to 57 percent, the proportion of black families with two or more wage earners fell from 56 to 47 percent.[91]

A more accurate measure of income inequality is the average earnings per worker. Average black male earnings were 78 percent of average white earnings in 1977, up from 58 percent in 1959; for black female workers, the increase was from 64 percent to 1959 to 95 percent in 1977.[92] Thus the lag of black family income behind white family income is due in part to black choice of living arrangements.[93] While blacks still lag behind whites in most income categories, the impressive occupational gains made by blacks in recent years are shown in figure 12–1.

Figure 12–1
Blacks made job gains, 1960–1978. Changes in percentage employed in selected occupations.

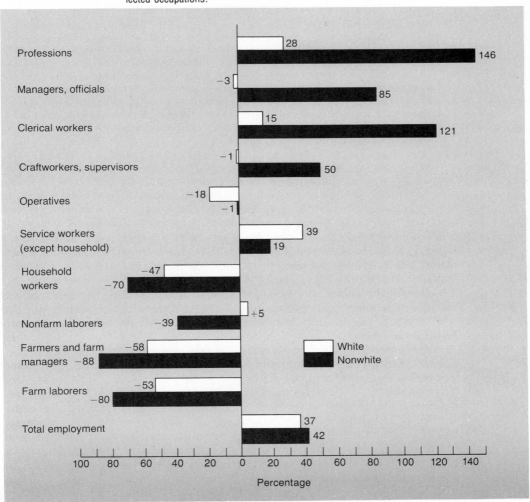

Black gains are impressive, yet great inequalities remain. Black unemployment remains more than twice as high as white unemployment, and has recently grown while white unemployment was falling; meanwhile, inequality *within* the black race has grown as the gains have been heavily concentrated at the top, leaving the poor blacks relatively worse off than before.[94] The extent to which this is due to discrimination or to other factors is debated. What "other factors" depress black income levels?

1. The rising proportion of female-headed black families, mentioned earlier, is a major factor. Female-headed families, white or black, are far below intact families in average income.

2. Black workers are less likely than whites to have the education or training needed for higher-paid jobs. Blacks still lag about two years behind whites in years of school completed, and considerably behind whites in average learning achievements at each grade level. As compared with whites, blacks are less than half as likely to be college graduates, although black youth today are almost as likely to be in college as white youth.

3. Blacks, especially older blacks, are concentrated in the lower-paid occupations. The widely quoted statement that "black college graduates earn less than white high school graduates" is true for older, college-educated blacks who are locked into low-paid professions (teaching, social work, the ministry) and are too old to change easily to higher-paid professions such as medicine, accountancy, or civil engineering. For young educated or trained blacks, the entry-level job market is equal to or possibly better than the job market for equally qualified whites. While recessions slowed black gains in the 1970s, educated blacks continued to progress faster than comparably educated whites.[95]

Some dissenting scholars claim that persisting job discrimination accounts for most of the black–white income difference,[96] but often their own data do not support this conclusion. For example, Robert Althauser and Sidney Spivak find that black college graduates earn less than white college graduates who are equal in education completed, quality of college attended, and grade point average. Their data, however, also show that of those graduating between 1931 and 1948 (and now over 50 years old), blacks averaged only 68 percent of white earnings; but of those graduating between 1960 and 1964, blacks averaged 96 percent of white earnings.[97] This small difference may be attributed to the continuing concentration of blacks in the lower-paid professions. Thus, it is *past* discrimination, not present discrimination, that explains most or all of the persisting income differences.

We may conclude that except for a few remaining pockets of discrimination, such as the building trades, job discrimination against young black workers is no longer a major factor in income inequality, and in some places it is countered by preferential hiring. For example, white professors have become more numerous in black colleges, which cannot afford the higher salaries black professors now command.[98] Today, lower average incomes of blacks can be attributed largely to family structure, to lower average levels of education and training, and to the concentration of blacks in low-paid occupations.[99] Job discrimination against blacks is no longer widespread, but the legacy of past discriminations lingers.

AFFIRMATIVE ACTION PROGRAMS   An impressive body of state and federal law now forbids discrimination in employment in interstate commerce and in businesses supplying government contracts. In practice, this covers virtually all large businesses and most smaller ones. Until recently these employers could satisfy demands for nondiscrimination by proclaiming their willingness to employ qualified members of minorities on an equal merit basis. Today, this *passive nondiscrimination* is insufficient. Courts have repeatedly held that *affirmative action* is necessary to comply with the law. Affirmative action operates at several levels: (1) active efforts to locate and recruit qualified minority workers; (2) positive action to increase the pool of qualified applicants through training programs and other measures; (3) preferential hiring, with a systematic favoring of even marginally qualified minority applicants; and (4) hard quotas, under which specific numbers of minority members must be hired, regardless of qualifications.[100] While the level of compliance demanded has varied, determined pressure for affirmative action has come from private organizations and from the Department of Labor. The effectiveness of affirmative action programs is difficult to measure, as it is impossible to separate the effect of affirmative action from other forces. A Rand Corporation study concluded that the economic gains of blacks have been more largely due to improved education than to affirmative action.[101] Yet a 1977 federal law requiring that 10 percent of all federal construction grants to local communities be given to minority-controlled construction firms was followed by such firms getting, not 10 percent, but 19 percent of the $4 billion in federal public works grants in 1978.[102]

The affirmative action program involves an extremely important strategic shift of responsibility. Under earlier enforcement procedures, it was necessary for the complainant to prove that the offender was guilty of discrimination, and this was sometimes difficult. Now the burden of proof is shifted upon the employer (or union) to prove itself *not* guilty of discrimination. And even this is not enough. It must also prove, according to a detailed checklist of positive measures, that it is making a determined, comprehensive effort to increase the pool of black employees at each level of employment. The result is a mixed employment picture. Blacks and other minorities are still the victims of discrimination in some employment areas but the beneficiaries of preferential treatment in others.

Unsettled Issues in Race Relations

Numerous opinion polls show that today a clear majority of Americans, black and white, agree that minority citizens should have equal access to public accommodations, equal opportunity for education and jobs, equal pay for equal work, and equal rights to vote and hold office. Within the past decade harmonious interracial contacts and friendships have become more numerous, and support for racial equality has increased, especially in the South.[103] While many whites may balk at fully implementing these goals, at least they give them verbal acceptance. But there are a number of vital issues on which there is no consensus, and there is recent evidence of an increase in white resistance.[104]

SCHOOL DESEGREGATION

In the most important decision in decades affecting blacks, the Supreme Court in 1954 declared segregation in public schools to be unconstitutional. In a unanimous decision written by Chief Justice Earl Warren, the Court declared that even though physical facilities and other tangible factors may be equal, segregated black schools are "inherently" unequal. The Court did not order the *immediate* end of school segregation, but ruled that the states must end compulsory racial segregation in the public schools "with all deliberate speed."

The speed was deliberate indeed. Ten years later only 1.18 percent of Southern black children attended desegregated schools, although in the "border" South the figure reached 54.8 percent.[106] After 20 years the percentage of black children attending schools that were 90 percent or more black ranged from 23 percent in the South to 63 percent in the Midwest, with a national average of 41 percent.[107]

The successes have been mainly in smaller cities that could desegregate by redrawing attendance boundaries without extensive busing of children. In larger cities, racial balance can be attained only by busing. In many cases the white flight to the suburbs and white shifts to private schools have left the central city with so few white children in public schools that no racial balance is possible without cross-district busing, in which children of two or more school systems are exchanged. The suburbs have strenuously resisted cross-district busing, the results of court action have been inconclusive, and no significant cross-district busing has occurred. Considerable busing within single school districts has been accomplished, with considerable controversy and resistance, but with only a few instances of prolonged violence, as in Boston.[108] The U.S. Supreme Court has ruled against cross-district busing, although one justice (Potter Stewart) suggested that cross-district busing might be appropriate where school district boundaries had been set or changed for the purpose of keeping the races in separate schools.[109]

Parents whose children have been bused *within* a single school district report no intense dissatisfaction, as shown in figure 12–2. But cross-district busing was opposed by a 79 to 21 percent majority in 1978, with opposition down only slightly from the 89 to 11 percent figure in 1970.[110] As this is written, two small communities in Michigan, Eau Claire and Coloma, are appealing a Federal District Court order to cross-bus their children with predominantly black Benton Harbor, ten miles distant.

Have school integration and busing paid off in greater learning gains? To control all other variables and to isolate and measure the effects of school integration or busing is an enormously complicated research problem. It is not surprising, therefore, that research findings are inconclusive. The first black children to be integrated into white schools were those of highly motivated parents who ranked high in knowledge and school expectations.[111] Not surprisingly, the first evaluation studies showed significant black learning gains following school integration. In later studies, covering a more representative sample of black children, the expected learning gains failed to materialize. After reviewing dozens of studies, Nancy St. John concludes that while integration has not produced learning losses for either race, neither has it produced any consistent learning gains.[112] Other reviews of research studies reach conflicting conclusions. Weinberg concludes that "overall, desegregation does have a positive effect on minority achievement levels."[113] By contrast, Bradley and Bradley review 29 of the more recent studies and agree with St. John that the findings are inconsistent and inconclusive.[114] Nor can any significant reduction of prejudice or other discrimination be attributed to school desegregation. Even within "integrated" schools, a high degree of racial separation results from tracking and other administrative procedures, while voluntary self-segregation keeps the races apart in most school activities.[115] Thus, the contact theory is not really tested, since equal-status cooperative contacts between black and white children are uncommon even in "integrated" schools.

Is school desegregation a success? This is now being debated. Since early evidence showed learning gains from desegregation,[116] and since to oppose desegregation aligned one with the racist bigots, all race liberals supported desegregation. But as time passes with no consistent evidence of learning gains, some serious scholars are having doubts. While no responsible person today advocates a return to forced school segregation, some do question whether concentration upon racial balance may be a misplaced emphasis. For example, Bradley and Bradley conclude their review of studies of black achievement under desegregation by suggesting that "such massive transfers

Court-ordered busing as a means of public school integration has evoked highly emotional reactions and much violent opposition.
(United Press International)

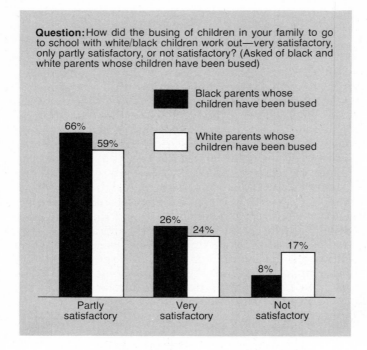

Question: How did the busing of children in your family to go to school with white/black children work out—very satisfactory, only partly satisfactory, or not satisfactory? (Asked of black and white parents whose children have been bused)

■ Black parents whose children have been bused

□ White parents whose children have been bused

66% 59%

26% 24%

8% 17%

Partly satisfactory

Very satisfactory

Not satisfactory

Figure 12–2
Parents report on busing
Quoted by permission from *Public Opinion* Dec./Jan., 1980, p. 38.

of students within our school systems may not be the best way of improving black student achievement."[117] Paul Adams, a black principal in the Chicago ghetto, states, "It's not necessary to be bused 20 miles and sit beside someone of a different color. Quality education is the key. If a school is operating properly, a child can get a good education."[118] A recent study of the "racial climate" of high schools finds that "racial composition (measured in terms of racial balance, seems to have little or no predictable effect."[119] Thus the question of learning gains remains unsettled. Perhaps a longer period of trial is needed for learning gains to become evident.

Yet there are some losses. Some previously excellent all-black schools have become mediocre,[120] black pupils in black schools have greater opportunities for leadership than black pupils in desegregated schools,[121] and the black school once functioned as a center of the black community in ways which the desegregated school cannot duplicate.[122] Busing for racial balance is costly in money, energy use, and students' time, and further isolates the school from parents and the community. In the opinion of some scholars, busing has intensified the white flight to the suburbs,[123] leading these scholars to advocate a retreat from busing for racial balance. Other scholars deny that busing has produced any significant white flight, but hold that the exodus of whites from the central city merely continued its established pattern.[124] All of these studies, however, report on migration only through the early 1970s (since there is considerable time lag in collecting migration data). Thus they do not measure the impact of court-ordered busing, leaving the question of white flight unsettled.

Does the burden of evidence support or reject busing for racial balance? It is unsatisfying to answer with a question mark, but no other answer can yet be justified.

THE HOUSING DILEMMA

One scholar, doubtful that busing will ever produce integrated schools, calls for residential desegregation as the only practical answer.[125] Yet two decades of marches, protests, demonstrations, and housing legislation today find black citizens more segregated than ever. Although black people's right to buy or rent housing wherever they can afford it is now fully protected by law, they must often run a gauntlet of evasion and resistance. The growing number of prosperous blacks who can afford quality housing now find the barriers considerably relaxed, if not destroyed, and most middle-class neighborhoods today have a very thin sprinkling of black residents. But most of the substantially mixed neighborhoods have meanwhile become all-black, as white residents who moved were replaced by blacks.

The heavy concentration of blacks (and other minorities) in the inner city is based partly on poverty but even more heavily on discrimination.[126] The recent economic gains of blacks have not produced a comparable black exodus from the inner city.[127] Despite the move of some prosperous blacks into white areas, residential segregation of blacks has been increasing in recent years[128] and seems likely to continue in the near future.[129]

Existing housing programs have generally encouraged housing segregation rather than reduced it. Urban renewal programs have usually destroyed more black housing than they created.[130] Federally subsidized housing generally becomes segregated housing because of local resistance to the placing of projects where they would bring black residents into white residential areas. Also, local black politicians have no enthusiasm for dispersing their constituents and diluting their political base; therefore, they favor placing housing for blacks right where those black voters already live.[131] Whites who have fled the central city in search of physical security now fear that housing for blacks would bring the high crime rates they sought to escape.[132] Furthermore, middle-class residents do not want subsidized housing to bring lower-class people into their neighborhood, black or white. In fact, middle-class blacks who have escaped the ghetto are as eager as middle-class whites to block the entrance of lower-class blacks into their neighborhood.[133] Most black movement to the suburbs has been into deteriorating suburbs with a heavily black population, so that little residential integration takes place.[134]

Meanwhile, housing has improved for all Americans. Between 1960 and 1970 the proportion of all housing listed by the census as substandard (either dilapidated or lacking plumbing fixtures) fell by one-half for both races, from 45.4 percent to 23.0 percent for blacks and 13.6 percent to 6.7 percent for whites.[135] Again we find significant progress for blacks, together with a wide gap separating them from whites.

REVERSE DISCRIMINATION

For several decades, race liberals sought to gain *equality* of treatment for racial minorities whose members suffered many exclusions because of race, regardless of their characteristics as individuals. Thus the illiterate white tenant farmer might vote, but the black university professor could not. In this situation, to disregard race and simply treat persons strictly according to their characteristics as individuals would be a great victory. This drive for equal treatment of equally qualified individuals culminated in the passing of the civil rights legislation of the 1960s, forbidding most kinds of formal discrimination on a basis of race.

Soon, however, it became apparent that under this "color blind" approach, most blacks would remain near the bottom of the heap. As the legacy of past discrimination, relatively few blacks could pass the necessary qualifying tests even when they were fairly administered. In many places "equal treatment" results in unequal ethnic distribution of rewards. In Israel, the Third World Jews of Middle Eastern and North African backgrounds compete poorly with the better educated, urbanized European Jews and have organized a bitter protest group called the Black Panthers.[136] In Hawaii, ambitious, studious, hard-working Japanese score high on civil service exams and obtain a disproportionate share of the civil service positions. These include the Honolulu office of the United States Employment Service, where the Japanese are then accused of discriminating against native Hawaiians and mainland whites.[137] And Japan has its own oppressed minority, the *burakumin,* racially identical but stigmatized by centuries of castelike isolation and now organizing for protest.[138]

What does an ethnic group do when equal treatment works to its disadvantage? One response is to attack the qualifications and the examinations, charging that they have a middle-class bias that effectively discriminates against the poor, especially the minority poor. This has led to several court decisions that qualifying tests for admission to schools or jobs must be limited to material that is functionally related to successful performance. This is no more than a further refinement of "equal treatment," which still leaves blacks disproportionately clustered at the bottom.

A different course of action departs from equal treatment by demanding some form of *preferential treatment,* sometimes called *reverse discrimination.* Its supporters claim that centuries of inequality have been so crippling in their effects that equal treatment is still unjust—that preferential treatment should be given to help blacks overcome this handicap.

Reverse discrimination takes several forms. One is the provision of special aids, such as remedial classes and special tutoring for students, special training courses for workers, special loans and business consultation services for black businesspeople. This level of reverse discrimination has met with little opposition and some success.

Another level of reverse discrimination involves lowering the qualifications for blacks so that more can qualify. Many colleges and universities have lowered admission standards for blacks and other minority students, and formal job requirements have sometimes been lowered for black applicants. The *quota* is a variant in which the applicant need meet no set standards at all. Under a quota system black applicants do not compete with whites, but only with each other, for the designated number of positions. Historically, quotas were used to hold down the number of minority admissions and were thus an instrument of race discrimination. But today, when proposed as a means of increasing minority representation, they are referred to as "benign quotas."

Affirmative action has often become reverse discrimination. The Civil Rights Act of 1964 prohibits discrimination against any race—white or black—and reverse discrimination is clearly contrary to a literal reading of the law. A number of legal actions have been filed by white males against universities that admitted minority applicants (usually to medical or law school) who ranked lower in grades and admission test scores than the whites who were rejected. Government agency orders have sometimes been inconsistent and contradictory. One day, a university is ordered to set affirmative action goals which cannot be met without reverse discrimination; then the next day, the same university is reminded not to engage in reverse discrimination. When about 1 percent of the nation's Ph.D.s are black and a university is cited by the Department of Health, Education and Welfare for a "deficiency" because only 3 percent of its faculty and 5 percent of its new appointees are black, it is obvious that affirmative action goals can be met only by wholesale discrimination against whites.[139] Courts have not been eager to rule upon such cases, but have recently delivered a number of decisions generally upholding minority quotas.

The effects of generations of discrimination cannot be overcome in a year or a decade. The most highly qualified candidates for admission to law school, appointment to a faculty, or executive promotion are likely to be those who have not only the requisite abilities and training but also a family background that gives them poise, general knowledge, and superior language skills. Even under ideal conditions, it will be another generation or

WHO IS RIGHT? ARE BOTH RIGHT?

They swarmed over the construction site like a people's crusade, black and Puerto Rican men, women, and children with posters waving, their hands clawing down cement forms and setting them aflame. . . . The posters told the demonstrators' story: *"Pare La Obra,"* they read, "Stop The Work," "End Construction Industry Discrimination."

To make certain the message got across to the predominantly white work force, the invaders who came from the surrounding community told individual workmen to lay down their tools. "If we don't work here," they said, "you don't work here."

A white laborer wheeling a load of mortar objected. "I ain't gonna stop," he said. "I got a family to support."

"We got families, too," replied a black youth as he tipped over the wheelbarrows.

Some workmen waved shovels in defiance. The demonstrators picked up rocks and pipes. Police arrived. A few arrests were made, and work . . . stopped.

A few weeks later, the scene was duplicated in Spanish Harlem. . . . Again, nearly everyone working on the site was white, nearly everyone protesting was not. But this time, police and demonstrators fought, and there were injuries on both sides. Two stumpy Irish-American workmen, brothers, watched and when a foreman announced work was suspended, one said bitterly, "Those black bastards. My brother here had to wait 12 years to get into the union. We worked like hell for everything we got. And now these bastards want it all handed to them."

Paul Good, "The Bricks and Mortar of Racism," *New York Times Magazine,* 21 May 1972, p. 2. Copyright © 1972 by the New York Times Company. Reprinted by permission.

two before the proportions of highly qualified blacks and whites are equal. Meanwhile, should young white applicants today be discriminated against to compensate for discriminations against blacks one, two, or several generations ago?

This is not an easy question to answer. Supporters of reverse discrimination maintain that it is morally necessary as redress for past injustices, that it is functionally necessary to overcome the handicaps incurred through past injustices, and that it is politically necessary to prevent whites from continuing to discriminate while pretending equal treatment. Opponents of reverse discrimination argue that it makes an invidious assumption of black inferiority (that standards must be lowered because blacks cannot meet them), that white beliefs in black inferiority are confirmed when unqualified blacks are admitted and then perform poorly, that it undermines the principle of equal treatment of equals that in the long run is the minority's best protection, that it arouses white blacklash when whites with superior qualifications are passed over in favor of less qualified blacks.

Commie clerks and longhairs and school teachers and Johnsonites— t'ey don't know shit. But t'at don't keep 'em from buttin' in. "Here, now," t'ey say. "Take t'is poor black bastard into your union, and let him get some of t'at wonderful money you're makin'. He's starvin' to deat' and runnin' up t'e welfare rolls." So you say, "Why don't you take him into your business? Let him be a big banker, or a school principal, or somet'in."

"Oh, well," t'ey say, "we couldn't do t'at. He's uneducated, you see, so he wouldn't fit in wit' our kind. But you guys are all dumbhead dropouts anyhow, and he'll fit in wit' *you* just fine. Besides, you *know* you're way overpaid for just plain old manual labor, and you ought to share the pie."

From Mike Cherry, *On High Steel: The Education of an Ironworker* (New York: Ballantine, 1974), p. 68.

This arouses considerable white resentment, especially among blue-collar whites. Many working-class whites feel that they are paying for black gains, which are ordered by a prosperous and secure white elite leadership.[140] Race violence in Boston came when busing coincided with a decline in the number of jobs available in the area, and blacks became the scapegoat for white frustration.[141] While figure 12–3 shows that there is no general "white backlash" against black gains, some white groups feel that they have been victimized.

In any event, affirmative action and reverse discrimination are short-range policies. If we get a more proportionate distribution of our minorities through the economic system, these policies will become unnecessary and will be abandoned.

BLACK SELF-HELP

To "blame the victim" is a popular cop-out for evading social problems. If "it's their own fault," then the rest of us need not bother ourselves about the plight of the unfortunate.

American blacks are descended from slaves who were torn from African societies where family ties were strong and where people were proud and energetic. Whatever habits American blacks have developed, they developed

342

BLACK PROGRESS ABOUT RIGHT

Question: (Asked of whites) Do you feel blacks in this country have tried to move too fast, too slow, or at about the right pace?

Note: In a survey conducted by the Survey Research Center, University of Michigan by Angus Campbell and Howard Schuman in 1968, 65% of blacks felt there had been a lot of progress in getting rid of racial discrimination in the last 10-15 years. In 1978, CBS News/*New York Times* asked the same question and found that only 47% of blacks felt this way.

Source: Surveys by Louis Harris and Associates, conducted for *Newsweek*, 1963 and 1966; Louis Harris and Associates, 1977; Louis Harris and Associates, conducted for the National Conference of Christians and Jews, October 6-November 8, 1978.

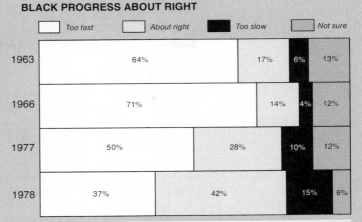

	Too fast	About right	Too slow	Not sure
1963	64%	17%	6%	13%
1966	71%	14%	4%	12%
1977	50%	28%	10%	12%
1978	37%	42%	15%	6%

. . . AND IN THE NEIGHBORHOOD

Question: Which of these statements would you agree with: first, white people have a right to keep blacks out of their neighborhoods if they want to, or second, blacks have a right to live wherever they can afford to, just like white people. (Sample equals whites only)

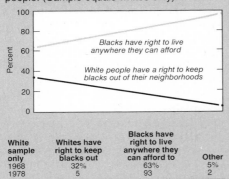

Blacks have right to live anywhere they can afford

White people have a right to keep blacks out of their neighborhoods

White sample only	Whites have right to keep blacks out	Blacks have right to live anywhere they can afford to	Other
1968	32%	63%	5%
1978	5	93	2

Note: The 1968 study was funded by the Kerner Commission. The sample included 5,393 black and white respondents from large northern cities. The 1978 sample included 932 whites, blacks, and other nonwhites from large eastern and midwestern cities.

Source: Survey by Survey Research Center, University of Michigan, under the specific direction of Professors Angus Campbell and Howard Schuman 1968; CBS News/*New York Times*, February 16-19, 1978.

AND IT DOESN'T UPSET ME

Question: Would it upset you personally a lot, some but not a lot, only a little, or not at all if blacks moved into this neighborhood?

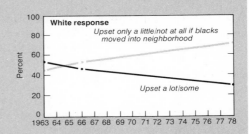

White response

Upset only a little/not at all if blacks moved into neighborhood

Upset a lot/some

1963 64 65 66 67 68 69 70 71 72 73 74 75 76 77 78

White response	Upset a lot/some	Upset only a little/not at all
1963	53%	47%
1966	50	50
1978	30	70

Note: For comparison purposes, the response "already in neighborhood (vol.)", which only appeared in 1978, was calculated out.

Source: Surveys by Louis Harris and Associates, conducted for *Newsweek*, 1963 and 1966; Louis Harris and Associates, conducted for the National Council of Christians and Jews, October 6-November 8, 1978.

Figure 12–3
Is there a "white backlash" against blacks in the United States?
Quoted by permission from *Public Opinion*, Dec.–Jan., 1980, p. 38.

while living in American society. Our ancestors *wanted* blacks to be uneducated, unambitious, docile, obedient, nonassertive, and dependent. Then we scolded them for being what we wanted and had trained them to be.

Today, much has changed. A little over a century ago, some Southern states had laws making it a crime to teach a Negro to read. Northern states allowed blacks to get diplomas, but excluded them from jobs where diplomas made any difference. Today, education brings greater economic gains to blacks than to comparably educated whites.[142]

Not all blacks, however, take advantage of their new opportunities. Of blacks aged 18 to 24 in 1976, only 26 percent exercized their right to vote, compared to 45 percent for whites of the same ages.[143] In your author's home town of Kalamazoo, the black absence rate from high school was exactly twice the white rate in 1978. Many blacks eagerly seize their opportunities, while many others do not.

The Rev. Jesse Jackson is one of many black leaders now preaching a message of black self-help. While urging blacks to continue to demand every right and opportunity, he also urges them to *use* their opportunities. His Project EXCEL, operating in 21 major city schools in 1978 and rapidly spreading, makes demands upon both parents and children:

> We get parents to pledge four things: to meet with the child's teacher and exchange telephone numbers, to pick up report cards four times a year, to pick up test scores, and to make sure that their children study two hours a night without radio or television.[144]

For American blacks to continue their march toward equality in America will require two things: a white willingness to accept, promote, and finance such change, and a black determination to take full advantage of every opportunity. Without both, the prospect is bleak indeed.

This chapter has concentrated upon black-white relations in the United States. Other American minorities—Puerto Rican, American Indian, Mexican–American—have problems and complaints that in many respects are similar to those of black Americans. For example, a study of employed Navajo workers a few years ago found that they rated somewhat above Anglo workers in job performance, but were paid an average of 50 cents an hour less.[145] Hispanics are the fastest growing minority in the United States, and may soon be the largest.[146] But space limitations made it seem wiser to discuss one racial minority in some detail and direct students to pursue their own interest in the other minorities.

Summary

Scientists assume that all races are alike in innate learning capacities, although this can neither be proven nor disproven. The question of whether there are race differences in innate abilities is not important unless proportionate quotas are assigned.

Theories of the origin of prejudice and discrimination include economic competition theories, economic exploitation theories, symbolic theories, the frustration-aggression theory, and the social neurosis theory. Minority adjustments include acceptance, accommodation, aggression, and organized protest.

The social-disorganization approach sees race problems as growing from the breakdown of a stable set of racial arrangements through social change. The value-conflict approach notes that the "problem" arises from different ideas of how the races should interact. The personal-deviation approach sees extremes of racism as forms of personality disorder.

Education, as well as exhortation and propaganda are ineffective means of changing race relations. Cooperative, equal-status contacts improve race attitudes, while competitive, unequal-status contacts arouse hostilities. Social revolution is often followed by new persecutions, rather than by new acceptances.

Current trends in the United States include a decline in regional variations, a shift from attacking prejudice to attacking discrimination, and a shift from education and propaganda to legal and administrative action against discrimination. Blacks have made great gains in recent decades, but inequality among blacks has increased, and a considerable black-white employment and income gap remains. School desegregation has not yet brought clearly demonstrable learning gains, and busing for racial balance remains a debatable policy.

Affirmative action programs set quotas for minorities, often calling for some degree of reverse discrimination. These are temporary policies, which are likely to be abandoned when jobs and statuses are more equally distributed.

Suggested Readings

BENEDICT, RUTH, and GENE WELTFISH, *The Races of Mankind,* Public Affairs Pamphlet No. 85 (New York: Public Affairs Committee, 1943). Still the finest brief summary of the scientific facts about race, interestingly written in nontechnical language.

BRADLEY, LAWRENCE A., and GIFFORD W. BRADLEY, "The Academic Achievement of Black Students in Desegregated Schools: A Critical Review," *Review of Educational Research,* 47 (Summer 1977), 399–449. A review of research on desegregation outcomes.

BROMLEY, DAVID G. and CHARLES F. LONGINO, JR., *White Racism and Black America* (Cambridge, Mass.: Schenkman, 1972). An extensive collection of essays and research on black–white relations.

FEAGIN, JOE R., and HARLAN HAHN, *Ghetto Revolts: The Politics of Violence in American Cities* (New York: Macmillan, 1973). An analysis of the causes and effects of ghetto riots.

FISHER, CHARLES W., *Minorities, Civil Rights, and Protest* (Encino, Ca.: Dickenson, 1977). A concise paperback covering a number of fields of discrimination and civil rights activity.

FULLINWIDER, S. P., *The Mind and Mood of Black America* (Homewood, Ill.: Dorsey Press, 1969). A historical account of black thought, as revealed by black scholars and writers, from the Civil War to the present.

GROSS, BARRY R., ed., *Reverse Discrimination* (Buffalo, N.Y.: Prometheus Books, 1977). A collection of papers giving the pros and cons of affirmative action.

HUNT, CHESTER L., and LEWIS WALKER, *Ethnic Dynamics: Patterns of Intergroup Relations in Various Societies* (Holmes Beach, Fla.: Learning Publications, 1979). A description and analysis of the race relations scene in a number of societies.

HUSOCK, HOWARD, "Boston: The Problem That Won't Go Away," *New York Times Magazine,* 25 Nov. 1979, pp. 32ff. A report on the problems underlying a city's racial tensions.

KING, MARTIN LUTHER, *Stride toward Freedom: The Montgomery Story* (New York: Harper & Row, 1958). A moving account of how blacks organized a successful boycott against segregated bus seating in Montgomery, Alabama, and launched nonviolent resistance as a technique for changing race relations in the United States.

RIST, RAY C., ed., *Desegregated Schools: Appraisals of an American Experiment* (New York: Praeger, 1978). Accounts of the desegregation experiences of several American communities.

ST. JOHN, NANCY, *School Desegregation: Outcomes for Children* (New York: John Wiley, 1975). A summary and analysis of numerous research studies of the effects of school desegregation.

VIDMAN, NEIL, and MILTON ROKEACH, "Archie Bunker's Bigotry: A Study in Selective Perception and Exposure," *Journal of Communication,* 24 (Winter 1974), 36–47. A research study of how the television show, "All in The Family," was perceived by different viewers.

WILSON, WILLIAM J., *The Declining Significance of Race* (Chicago: University of Chicago Press, 1978). Argues that class, rather than race, is the primary basis of inequality in the United States.

Interesting well-written books dealing with other minorities in the United States include Brewton Berry, *Almost White* [black–white–Indian mixed] (New York: Macmillan, 1963); Vernon M. Briggs, *The Chicano Worker* (Austin: University of Texas Press, 1977); Samuel Carter II, *Cherokee Sunset* (Garden City, N.Y.: Doubleday, 1976); Vine Deloria, Jr., *Custer Died for Your Sins: An American Indian Manifesto* (New York: Macmillan, 1970); Anthony Gary Dworkin and Rosalind J. Dworkin, *The Minority Report: Race, Ethnic and Gender Relations* (New York: Praeger, 1976); Joseph P. Fitzpatrick, *Puerto Rican Americans: The Meaning of Migration to the Mainland* (Englewood Cliffs, N.J.: Prentice-Hall, 1971); Dorothy E. Harth and Lewis M. Baldwin, *Voices of Aztlan: Chicano Literature of Today* (New York: New American Library, 1974); Judith R. Kramer and Sidney Levantman, *Children of the Gilded Ghetto: Conflict Resolutions of Three Generations of American Jews* (New Haven, Conn.: Yale University Press, 1961); Sar A. Levitan and Barbara Hetrick, *Big Brother's Indian Programs—With Reservations* (New York: McGraw-Hill, 1972); Gus Tyler, ed., *Mexican-Americans in America's Tomorrow: Educational and Economic Perspectives* (Albuquerque: University of New Mexico Press, 1975).

Footnotes

[1] Robert B. Semple, Jr., "Racism and the Former Colonial Empires," *New York Times,* 5 Sept. 1976, sec. 4, p. 2.

[2] Bernard Weintraub, "Uganda Exiles—In Britain, I Miss . . ." *New York Times,* 14 Mar. 1975, p. 24.

[3] "Malaysia: A Get-Tough Policy on Foreign Control," *Business Week,* 7 July 1975, p. 32.

[4] Harold Feender, *Problem: Race* (New York: Washington Square Press, 1973), p. 113.

[5] John Deedy, "There Are Many Forms of Minority," *New York Times,* 9 Feb. 1975, sec. 4, p. 3.

[6] See Paul B. Horton and Chester L. Hunt, *Sociology* (New York: McGraw-Hill, 1980), p. 352, for a more extended discussion of the concept of race.

[7] See H. Rap Brown, *Die Nigger Die* (New York: Dial Press, 1969).

[8] Wahakn N. Dadrian, "Factors of Anger and Aggression in Genocide," *Journal of Human Relations,* 19 (1971), 394–417.

[9] Lucy S. Davidowicz, *The War against the Jews: 1933–1945* (New York: Holt, Rinehart and Winston, 1975).

[10] Leo Kuper, *The Pity of It All: Polarization of Racial and Ethnic Relations* (Minneapolis: University of Minnesota Press, 1977).

[11] *U.S. News and World Report,* 26 Nov. 1979, pp. 62–64.

[12] William A. Darity et al., "Race Consciousness and Fears of Black Genocide as Barriers to Family Planning," *Population Reference Bureau,* Selection #37, June 1971, pp. 5–12; Roy Innis, "The Zero Population Game," *Ebony,* Nov. 1974, p. 110.

[13] Robert Weisbord, *Genocide? Birth Control and the Black American* (Westport, Conn.: Greenwood Press, 1975).

[14] Anthony Lester and Geoffrey Bindman, *Race and Law in Great Britain*

(Cambridge, Mass.: Harvard University Press, 1973); Robert B. Semple, Jr., "Race Still Issue to British Public," *New York Times*, 13 June 1976, p. 9.

[15]See Weintraub, "Uganda Exiles."

[16]See "God Help the People," *Time*, 25 Sept. 1972, pp. 32–33; and "Bloodbath in Burundi," *Time*, 23 July 1973, pp. 40–41.

[17]See Ray C. Rist, *Guestworkers in Germany: The Prospects for Pluralism* (New York: Praeger, 1978).

[18]See note 11.

[19]See Ben Whitaker, ed., *The Fourth World* (New York: Schocken, 1973), for accounts of oppressed minorities around the world.

[20]Louis L. Knowles and Kenneth Prewitt, *Institutional Racism in America* (Englewood Cliffs, N.J.: Prentice-Hall, 1970); Charles H. Bullock III and Harrell R. Rodgers, Jr., "Institutional Racism: Prerequisites, Freezing and Mapping," *Phylon*, 37 (Sept. 1976), 212–23.

[21]*New York Times*, 8 June 1976, p. 1; 16 Jan. 1977, sec. 4, p. 2.

[22]Ken Richardson and David Spears, eds., *Race and Intelligence* (Baltimore: Penguin Books, 1972); Ashley Montagu, *Man's Most Dangerous Myth: The Fallacy of Race* (New York: Oxford University Press, 1974).

[23]For example, see Audrey M. Shuey, *The Testing of Negro Intelligence* (Lynchburg, Va.: J. P. Bell, 1958); Arthur E. Jensen, "How Much Can We Boost IQ and Scholastic Achievement?" *Harvard Educational Review*, 39 (Winter 1969), 1–123; also, "Discussion," 39 (Spring 1969), 273–356; Hans J. Eysenck, *The IQ Argument: Race, Intelligence, and Education* (New York: Library Press, 1971); Arthur E. Jensen, *Bias in Mental Testing* (New York: Free Press, 1979).

[24]Eysenck, *The IQ Argument*, p. 60; Jensen, "How Much Can We Boost IQ?" See also Kevin Marjoriebanks, "Ethnic and Environmental Influence on Mental Abilities," *American Journal of Sociology*, 78 (Sept. 1972), 323–37, for evidence of race differences in mental abilities that the author cannot attribute to environmental influences.

[25]Benjamin Bloom, letter, *Harvard Educational Review*, 39 (Spring 1969), 419–21, citing research by M. Smilansky.

[26]For accounts of the persecution of scientists who challenged the scientific establishment view of race, see "Views Linking Race and IQ Called Unfit to Discuss," *New York Times*, 18 Nov. 1973,

p. 20L; Berkeley Rice, "Race, Intelligence, and Genetics: The High Cost of Thinking the Unthinkable," *Psychology Today*, Dec. 1973, pp. 89–93.

[27]As outlined in Brewton Berry and Henry L. Tischler, *Race and Ethnic Relations*, 4th ed. (New York: Houghton Mifflin, 1978), pp. 239–46.

[28]Emory S. Bogardus, "Racial Reactions by Regions," *Sociology and Social Research*, 43 (Mar.–Apr. 1959), 286–90.

[29]Daniel Lawrence, *Black Migrants, White Natives: A Study of Race Relations in Nottingham* (New York: Cambridge University Press, 1974).

[30]See Weintraub, "Uganda Exiles."

[31]See "Malaysia: A Get-Tough Policy."

[32]Chester L. Hunt and Lewis Walker, *Ethnic Dynamics: Patterns of Intergroup Relations in Various Societies* (Holmes Beach, Fla.: Learning Publications, 1979), ch. 9.

[33]Edward O'Neill, "Paradise Lost," *Environmental Quality Magazine*, June 1973, pp. 37ff.

[34]For example, see Margaret Peil, "Ghana's Aliens," *International Migration Review*, 8 (Fall 1974), 367–81.

[35]Gunnar Myrdal, *An American Dilemma* (New York: Harper & Row, 1944), pp. 60ff.

[36]Margaret Halsey, *Color Blind* (New York: Simon & Schuster, 1946), pp. 56–57.

[37]See Carey McWilliams, *Japanese-Americans: Symbol of Racial Intolerance* (Boston: Little, Brown, 1944).

[38]Leo Kuper, "Theories of Revolution and Race Relations," *Comparative Studies in Society and History*, 13 (Jan. 1971), 87–107.

[39]See advertisement, "Don't Fail Us Now," sponsored by Greater New York Conference on Soviet Jewry, and published in *New York Times*, 29 Apr. 1973, sec. 4, p. 5; William Korey, *The Soviet Cage: Anti-Semitism in Russia* (New York: Viking Press, 1973); Hunt and Walker, *Ethnic Dynamics*, ch. 3.

[40]John Clytus, with Jane Ryker, *Black Man in Red Cuba* (Miami: University of Miami Press, 1970).

[41]William J. Wilson, *The Declining Significance of Race* (Chicago: University of Chicago Press, 1978), p. 152.

[42]See Arnold Rose and Caroline Rose, *America Divided* (New York: Alfred A. Knopf, 1948), pp. 285–92.

[43]Isaque Graebner and S. H. Britt, eds., *Jews in a Gentile World* (New York: Macmillan, 1942), p. 95.

347

[44]Lev. 16:5–26.

[45]Gordon W. Allport, *ABC's of Scapegoating* (New York: Anti-Defamation League of B'nai B'rith, 1948), pp. 42–43.

[46]When asked whether the Jew should be destroyed, Hitler replied, "No . . . we should then have to invent him. It is essential to have a tangible enemy, not merely an abstract one." (Herman Rauschning, *Hitler Speaks* [New York: G. P. Putnam's Sons, 1940], p. 234.)

[47]John Dollard et al., *Frustration and Aggression* (New Haven, Conn.: Yale University Press, 1939), especially pp. 151–56.

[48]Bruno Bettelheim and Morris Janowitz, *Dynamics of Prejudice, A Psychological and Sociological Study of Veterans* (New York: Harper & Row, 1950), p. 59.

[49]Donald S. Strong, *Organized Anti-Semitism in the United States* (American Council on Public Affairs, 1941), records 5 anti-Semitic organizations founded between 1915 and 1932, 9 in 1933, and 105 between 1934 and 1939.

[50]George E. Simpson and J. Milton Yinger, *Racial and Cultural Minorities: An Analysis of Prejudice and Discrimination*, 4th ed. (New York: Harper & Row, 1972).

[51]Angus Campbell, *White Attitudes toward Black People* (Ann Arbor: Institute for Social Research, The University of Michigan, 1971), p. 116.

[52]Ben Hecht, *A Guide for the Bedeviled* (New York: Charles Scribner's Sons, 1944), p. 31.

[53]Else Frenkel-Brunswick and R. Nevitt Sanford, "Some Personality Factors in Anti-Semitism," *Journal of Psychology*, 20 (Oct. 1945), 271–91; Eugene Hartley, *Problems of Prejudice* (New York: King's Crown Press, 1946); T. W. Adorno et al., *The Authoritarian Personality* (New York: Harper & Row, 1950).

[54]Simpson and Yinger, *Racial and Cultural Minorities*, pp. 84–100.

[55]See footnote 27.

[56]C. S. Johnson, *Patterns of Negro Segregation* (New York: Harper & Row, 1943), pp. 267–93.

[57]Adam Clayton Powell, *Riots and Ruins* (New York: Richard R. Smith, 1945), p. 28.

[58]Seymour Spilerman, "The Causes of Racial Disturbance: Tests of an Explanation," *American Sociological Review*, 36 (June 1971), 427–42; R. M. Jiobu, "City Characteristics, Differential Stratification, and the Occurrence of Interracial Violence," *Social Science Quarterly*, 52 (Dec. 1971), 508–20.

[59]Joe R. Feagin and Harlan Hahn, *Ghetto Revolts: The Politics of Violence in American Cities* (New York: Macmillan, 1973).

[60]Jeffery M. Paige, "Political Orientation and Riot Participation," *American Sociological Review*, 36 (Oct. 1971), 810–20; Joseph S. Himes, "A Theory of Racial Conflict," *Social Forces*, 50 (Sept. 1971), 53–60.

[61]Robert L. Crain and Carol Sachs Weisman, *Discrimination, Personality, and Achievement: A Survey of Northern Blacks* (New York: Seminar Press, 1972), p. 180.

[62]Philip S. Foner, ed., *The Black Panthers Speak* (Philadelphia: J. B. Lippincott, 1970); "Old Panther Speaks with a New Purr," *Newsweek*, 17 Mar. 1975, p. 40.

[63]G. Louis Heath, ed., *The Black Panther Leaders Speak* (Metuchen, N.Y.: Scarecrow Press, 1976).

[64]See *Between the Lines*, The Wells Newsletter (Box 143, Princeton, N.J.), 1 Mar. 1964.

[65]James Q. Wilson, "The Strategy of Protest: Problems of Negro Civic Action," *Journal of Conflict Resolution*, 5 (Sept. 1961), 291–303.

[66]This partial list of minority reactions, largely taken from Berry, *Race and Ethnic Relations*, pp. 479–508, is not the only such listing. M. R. Davie finds seven black responses: acceptance, resentment, avoidance, overcompensation, race pride, hostility and aggression, and protest (M. R. Davie, *Negroes in American Society* [New York: McGraw-Hill, 1940], pp. 434–55). Johnson sees four black reactions: acceptance, avoidance, direct hostility and aggression, and indirect or deflected hostility (Johnson, *Patterns of Negro Segregation*, pp. 244–315).

[67]See H. Donald Henderson, *The Negro Freedman: Life Conditions of the American Negro in the Early Years After Emancipation* (New York: Henry Schuman, 1952).

[68]For a brief history of blacks in America during the past century, see Herbert Hill and Jack Greenberg, *Citizen's Guide to Desegregation* (Boston: Beacon Press, 1955), ch. 2, "The Negro's Changing Social and Economic Status: From Reconstruction to Desegregation"; Charles Silberman, *Crisis in Black and White* (New York: Random House, 1964), chs. 2–4.

[69]See Charles S. Johnson, *Growing Up in the Black Belt* (Washington, D.C.: American Council of Education, 1941), pp. 277–80; also Bertram Doyle, *The Etiquette of Race Relations in the South* (Chicago: University of Chicago Press, 1937).

[70]F. Ray Marshall, *The Negro and Or-*

ganized Labor (New York: Random House, 1965); F. Ray Marshall and Vernon M. Briggs, Jr., *The Negro and Apprenticeship* (Baltimore: Johns Hopkins University Press, 1967).

[71]The curse wherein the "sons of Ham" are eternally to be "hewers of wood and drawers of water" is a favorite of those seeking a divine sanction for segregation or discrimination. The biblical account (Genesis, ch. 9) tells how Ham made fun of his drunken, naked father, Noah, who then angrily pronounced the curse (not upon the sons of Ham, but upon the sons of Canaan, Ham's youngest son). The "curse of Ham" now becomes a bit inconvenient, since according to biblical historians most of the descendants of Ham settled in the Middle East, not Africa, and are thus Caucasian, not Negroid. Also, while the Bible reports Noah's curse, nowhere does the Bible state that God accepted and enforced a curse pronounced by a man who was apparently too drunk to realize whom he laid the curse upon.

Some also claim that God forbade racial intermarriage; yet while the Bible contains many strictures against intermarriage with *unbelievers*, there are no references to *racial* intermarriage. In fact, "race" in its modern sense is not even mentioned in the Bible. For discussion of the lack of any biblical basis for racial segregation, see James O. Buswell III, *Slavery, Segregation, and Scripture* (Grand Rapids, Mich.: Wm. B. Eerdmans, 1964); Herbert C. Oliver, *No Flesh Shall Glory* (Nutley, N.J.: Presbyterian and Reformed, 1959).

[72]Simpson and Yinger, *Racial and Cultural Minorities*, pp. 81–82, 283–84.

[73]Rodney Stark et al., *Wayward Shepherds: Prejudice and the Protestant Clergy* (New York: Harper & Row, 1971); Richard L. Gorsuch and Daniel Aleshire, "Christian Faith and Ethnic Prejudice: A Review and Interpretation of Research," *Journal for the Scientific Study of Religion,* 13 (Sept. 1974), 281–307.

[74]Simpson and Yinger, *Racial and Cultural Minorities*, pp. 526–31.

[75]Patricia Kendall and Katherine Wolf, in Paul Lazarsfeld and Frank Stanton, eds., *Communications Research 1948–49* (New York: Harper & Row, 1949), p. 158; Eunice Cooper and Helen Dinerman, "Analysis of the Film, 'Don't Be a Sucker': A Study in Communication," *Public Opinion Quarterly*, 15 (Summer 1951), 243–64.

[76]Neil Vidman and Milton Rokeach, "Archie Bunker's Bigotry: A Study in Selective Perception and Exposure," *Journal of Communication*, 24 (Winter 1974), 36–47.

[77]Irwin Katz, *Conflict and Harmony in an Adolescent Interracial Group* (New York: New York University Press, 1955).

[78]Morton Deutsch and Mary Evans Collins, "Intergroup Relations and Interracial Housing," *Journal of Housing* (Apr. 1950), pp. 127–29ff., reprinted in Arnold Rose, ed., *Race Prejudice and Discrimination* (New York: Alfred A. Knopf, 1951), p. 556.

[79]Richard T. Morris and Vincent Jeffries, "Violence Next Door," *Social Forces*, 46 (Mar. 1968), 352–58.

[80]H. Edward Ransford, "Isolation, Powerlessness and Violence: A Study of Attitudes and Participation in the Watts Riot," *American Journal of Sociology*, 73 (Mar. 1968), 581–91.

[81]Jerry W. Robinson, Jr., and James D. Preston, "Equal-Status Contact and Modification of Racial Prejudice: A Reexamination of the Contact Hypothesis," *Social Forces*, 54 (June 1976), 912.

[82]B. Drummond Ayres, Jr., "Army Is Shaken by Crisis in Morale and Discipline," *New York Times*, 5 Sept. 1971, pp. 1ff.

[83]See "Black, White GI's See Other Side Favored," UPI, 20 Feb. 1973.

[84]E. L. Nitoburg, "Natsionalny Aspekt Negrityanskogo Voprosa v SSHA (The National Aspect of the Negro Question in the USA)," *Voporosy istorii*, 48 (Apr. 1973), 59–75.

[85]*Statistical Abstract of the United States, 1978*, p. 519.

[86]"Civil Rights Act," *New York Times*, 5 July 1964, sec. 4, p. 1.

[87]"Civil Rights Bill Wins Final Vote," *New York Times*, 11 Apr. 1968, pp. 1ff.

[88]"Does State FEPC Hamper You?" *Business Week*, 5 Feb. 1950, pp. 114–17; "N.I.C.B. Study Finds Work Force Integration Is a Lot Smoother than Expected," *Business Week*, 11 June 1966, p 86.

[89]*Statistical Abstract of the United States, 1978*, p. 452.

[90]Ibid., p. 46.

[91]Robert B. Hill, "Black Families in the 1970s," in James D. Williams, ed., *The State of Black America, 1980* (New York: National Urban League, 1980), p. 39.

[92]*Statistical Abstract of the United States, 1978*, p. 423.

[93]The Aid to Families with Dependent Children (AFDC) program makes it easier for widowed, divorced, separated, or unmarried mothers (white and black) to maintain separate households, instead of sharing their households with other relatives, as most did in earlier years. Thus a program which actually *increases* the financial resources of low-income black families, by also helping to increase the proportion of female-headed black families, increases the illusion of a widening income gap between black and white families.

[94]Wayne J. Villemex and Candace Hinson Wise᷄ ell, "The Impact of Diminishing Discrimination upon the Internal Size Discrimination of Black Income," *Social Forces,* 56 (June 1978), 1019–1034; Edward Schumacher, "Joblessness Worsens among Blacks Despite Gains by City," *New York Times,* 10 Feb. 1980, p. 341.

[95]Wilson, *Declining Significance of Race,* p. 153.

[96]Robert P. Althauser and Sidney S. Spivak, *The Unequal Elites* (New York: John Wiley, 1975); Stanley H. Masters, *Black–White Income Differentials: Empirical Studies and Policy Implications* (New York: Academic Press, 1975).

[97]Althauser and Spivak, *The Unequal Elites,* p. 34.

[98]Daniel C. Thompson, *Private Black Colleges at the Crossroads* (Westport, Conn.: Greenwood Press, 1973).

[99]There are other difficulties. Blacks have difficulty gaining craft apprenticeships, because craft unions discriminate against anyone who lacks friends or relatives already in the union. Seniority rules slow merit-based promotions. Minimum wage laws disemploy workers who are marginally productive, who are disproportionately black. Thus some features of our economy are especially restrictive upon blacks.

[100]Daniel Seligman, "How Equal Opportunity Turned into Employment Quotas," *Fortune Magazine,* Mar. 1973, pp. 160ff.

[101]See "Better Schooled Blacks Catching up to White Wages," *New York Times,* 14 May 1978, sec. 4, p. 20.

[102]*Time,* 10 Dec. 1979, p. 79.

[103]Angus Campbell, University of Michigan, Institute for Social Research, interview summarized in *Human Behavior,* Mar. 1976, p. 19.

[104]"Whites Evince Increasing Resistance to Accept Steps to Achieve Integration," *New York Times,* 2 Dec. 1979, pp. 1ff.

[105]The terms, "desegregation" and "integration" are sometimes used interchangeably. This is incorrect. *Desegregation* means only that whites and blacks are in the same schools. *Integration* requires positive intergroup interaction and joint participation in school activities. Exceedingly few schools are integrated.

[106]"School Desegregation," *Southern School News,* 17 May 1964, p. 1.

[107]Center for National Policy Review, *Trends in Black School Segregation,* (Washington, D.C.: School of Law, Catholic University, 1977).

[108]See Howard Husock, "Boston: The Problem That Won't Go Away," *New York Times Magazine,* 25 Nov. 1979, pp. 32ff.

[109]Milliken vs. Bradley, S. Ct. 73–434, 1974.

[110]Surveys by the Gallup Organization, 1970; National Opinion Research Center, *General Social Surveys,* 1978.

[111]Murray B. Binderman, "The Failure of Freedom of Choice: Decision-Making in a Southern Community," *Social Forces,* 50 (June 1972), 487–98.

[112]Nancy St. John, *School Desegregation: Outcomes for Children* (New York: John Wiley, 1975); also, James Schellenberg and John Halteman, "Busing and Academic Achievement: A Two-Year Follow-Up," *Urban Education,* 10 (Jan. 1976), 357–65.

[113]Meyer Weinberg, "The Relationship between School Desegregation and Academic Achievement: A Review of the Research," *Law and Contemporary Problems,* 39 (Spring 1975), 368.

[114]Lawrence A. Bradley and Gifford W. Bradley, "The Academic Achievement of Black Students in Desegregated Schools: A Critical Review," *Review of Educational Research,* 47 (Summer 1977), 399–449.

[115]Charles H. Bullock, III, "Defiance of the Law: School Discrimination before and after Desegregation," *Urban Education,* 11 (Oct. 1976), 239–62; Ray C. Rist, ed., *Desegregated Schools: Appraisals of an American Experiment* (New York: Academic Press, 1979), pp. 113, 237.

[116]James S. Coleman et al., *Equality of Educational Opportunity* (Washington, D.C.: Department of Health, Education, and Welfare, 1966).

[117]Bradley and Bradley, "The Academic Achievement of Black Students," p. 445.

[118]Quoted in *Kalamazoo Gazette,* 16 July 1969, p. B–8.

[119]James D. Davidson, Gerhard Hoffman, and William R. Brown, "Measuring and Explaining High School Inter-

racial Climates," *Social Problems*, 26 (Oct. 1978), 50.

[120]Thomas Sowell, "Patterns of Black Excellence," *The Public Interest*, Spring 1976, pp. 26–58.

[121]Frederick A. Rodgers, *The Black High School and Its Community* (Lexington, Mass.: D.C. Heath, 1975).

[122]Ibid.

[123]David J. Armor, "The Evidence on Busing," *The Public Interest*, Summer 1972, pp. 90–126; James S. Coleman, "Racial Segregation in the Schools: New Research with New Policy Implications," *Phi Delta Kappan*, 57 (Oct. 1975), 75–78; Clarence Wurdock, "Public School Resegregation After Desegregation: Some Preliminary Findings," *Sociological Focus*, 12 (June 1979), 271.

[124]Reynolds Farley, "Racial Integration in the Public Schools, 1967 to 1972: Assessing the Effect of Government Policies," *Sociological Focus*, 8 (Jan. 1975), 3–26; Thomas F. Pettigrew and Robert L. Green, "School Desegregation in Large Cities: A Critique of the Coleman 'White Flight' Thesis," *Harvard Educational Review*, 46 (Feb. 1976), 1–53; James J. Bosco and Stanley J. Robin, "White Flight from Busing: A Second, Longer Look," *Urban Education*, 11 (Oct. 1976), 263–74; David F. Sly and Louis G. Pol, "The Demographic Content of School Segregation and Desegregation," *Social Forces*, 56 (June 1978), 1072–86; Harvey Marshall, "White Movement to the Suburbs: A Comparison of Explanations," *American Sociological Review*, 44 (Dec. 1979), 975–94.

[125]Ray C. Rist, *The Invisible Children: School Integration in American Society*, (Cambridge, Mass.: Harvard University Press, 1978), pp. 275–78.

[126]Karl E. Taeuber, "Racial Segregation: The Persisting Dilemma," *Annals of the American Academy of Political and Social Science*, 422 (Nov. 1975), 87–96; Rist, *The Invisible Children*, pp. 275–78.

[127]Harvey Marshall and Robert Jiobu, "Residential Segregation in United States Cities: A Causal Analysis," *Social Forces*, 53 (Mar. 1975), 449–60; Wade Clark Roof, Thomas L. van Valey and Daphne Spain, "Residential Segregation in Southern Cities, 1970," *Social Forces*, 55 (Sept. 1976), 59–71.

[128]Taeuber, "Racial Segregation."

[129]Avery M. Quest and James A. Weed, "Ethnic Residential Segregation: Patterns of Change," *American Journal of Sociology*, 81 (Mar. 1976), 1088–1111.

[130]Simpson and Yinger, *Racial and Cultural Minorities*, pp. 438–39.

[131]James Q. Wilson, *Negro Politics* (New York: Free Press, 1960), pp. 202–3.

[132]Nathan Glazer, "When the Melting Pot Doesn't Melt," *New York Times Magazine*, 2 Jan. 1972, pp. 12ff.

[133]Jonathan Kandel, "Opposition to Smaller-Site Housing Transcends Racial and Economic Lines," *New York Times*, 6 Feb. 1972, p. 60; Paul Delaney, "Black Middle Class Joining the Exodus to Suburbia," *New York Times*, 4 Jan. 1976, pp. 1ff.

[134]Phillip L. Clay, "The Process of Suburbanization," *Urban Affairs Quarterly*, 14 (June 1979), 405–24.

[135]*Statistical Abstract of the United States, 1975*, p. 720.

[136]Mark Iris and Abraham Shama, "Black Panthers: The Movement," *Society*, May 1972, pp. 37–44; Sammy Smooha, "Black Panthers: The Ethnic Dilemma," *Society*, May 1972, pp. 31–36.

[137]Observed by the writer in various visits to Hawaii.

[138]See "Japan: The Invisible Race," *Time*, 8 Jan. 1973, p. 31.

[139]Malcolm J. Sherman, "Affirmative Action and the AAUP," *AAUP Bulletin*, 61 (Dec. 1975), 293–303; Sheila K. Jackson, "It's Action, But Is It Affirmative?" *New York Times Magazine*, 11 May 1975, pp. 18ff.

[140]See Arthur B. Shostak, *Blue-Collar Stress* (Reading, Mass.: Addison-Wesley, 1980), pp. 55–57.

[141]Husock, "Boston: The Problem That Won't Go Away."

[142]Wilson, *Declining Significance of Race*, p. 153.

[143]*Time*, 3 Sept. 1979, p. 66.

[144]Quoted in *Time*, 10 July 1978, p. 45.

[145]Robert S. Weppner, "Socioeconomic Barriers to Assimilation of Navajo Migrants," *Human Organization*, 31 (Feb. 1972), 303–13.

[146]"It's Your Turn in the Sun," *Time*, 16 Oct. 1978, pp. 48–61; "Hispanic Minority Fastest-Growing in United States," *New York Times*, 18 Feb. 1979, pp. 1ff.

Marc Anderson.

SOME OTHER DISCRIMINATIONS 13

Big Dave Masiak was once described as one of the strongest men at Baker, but the plant closing has left him practically totally disabled. His blood pressure is much too high; his headaches are bad, so is his arthritis, his diabetes and obesity, and he is getting worse each day.

At Baker there was a place for him; he functioned there. His health and concern about his health [have] become Masiak's job, his way of life, his functioning. When he is not talking about his health, he is usually asleep.[1]

Last night I told Jim: "I been working in the same factory as you 10 years now. We go in at the same time, come out at the same time. But I do all the shopping, get the dinner, wash the dishes and on Sunday break my back down on the kitchen floor. I'm real tired of doin' all that. I want some help from you." Well, he just laughed at me, see? Like he done every time I mentioned this before. But last night I wouldn't let up. I mean, I really *meant* it this time. And you know? I thought he was gonna let me have it. Looked mighty like he was gettin' ready to belt me one. But you know? I just didn't care! I wasn't gonna back down, come hell or high water. You'll just never believe it, he'd kill me if he knew I was tellin' you, he washed the dishes. First time in his entire life."[2]

The first of these two items reveals the personal disorganization and physical deterioration of a person who loses a job at 50 and cannot find another. That is one of the forms of discrimination presented in this chapter: discrimination on the basis of sex, age, handicap, appearance, and sexual preference.

Sex Discrimination

The Bible says that God created woman as an afterthought, to be a helper to man,[3] but this subordinate role is one that growing numbers of women today reject. The status of women has varied considerably over time. As measured by power and by participation in the social and intellectual life of the society, women's status was very low in ancient Greece and Rome, much higher in the later Roman Empire, then greatly lower after the spread of Christianity.[4] In hunting societies men were the principal food providers, and the status of women was generally low; in agricultural societies based on

An 1868 Currier and Ives cartoon emphasizing the prevailing attitude that giving the vote to women was as ridiculous as men's taking over the household duties.
(Library of Congress)

hoe-cultivation, women generally did the cultivation and their status was somewhat higher. Throughout history work roles have been assigned through sexual ascription, with women generally given the work tasks that harmonize with child care—work that is interruptible, repetitive, and not dangerous and that does not require intense concentration.[5] Most of the exciting and adventurous work has been done by men, and most of the monotonous drudgery by women.

A veritable flood of literature, ranging from the dispassionately scholarly to the fiercely polemical, has challenged the traditional subordination of women.[6] Yet not all women share the feminist perspective, as is shown by the popularity of Marabel Morgan's *The Total Woman*[7] which tells women how to be sensual, submissive housewives, and by the market success of two sets of courses teaching the joys of nonliberation.[8] American women today are sharply divided upon what they want.

THE CONTENT OF SEX EQUALITY

Many people favor the idea of sex equality but disagree over just what constitutes sex equality. Men and women are not equal in their ability to reach high shelves, lift anvils, nurse babies, or perform delicate finger manipulations. Women and men differ in their needs for toilet space and toilet paper, mashed potatoes, and football helmets. Simply to treat the sexes exactly alike is not always practical, since they are not exactly alike.

Men and women have different life expectancies; consequently, women pay lower premiums for life insurance. But in the case of retirement pensions an equal pay-in will buy a woman a smaller monthly pension, since women on the average live many more months to draw their pensions. An equal *monthly* pension would result in higher *total* pension payments to women, while equal total pension payments would mean smaller monthly pension payments for women.[9] Which pattern does equal treatment require? Would sex equality require men and women to pay the same life insurance premiums and receive the same monthly pension payments?[10] Should sick leave plans cover pregnancy leave, even though pregnancy is not an illness but usually results from a voluntary choice between alternative life satisfactions?[11] Clearly, the content of sex equality is undefined.

Alice Rossi suggests three models of sex equality: (1) a pluralistic model, in which sex divisions of labor persist, but categories of work performed by both sexes are equally prestigious and rewarded; (2) an assimilationist model, in which women participate in the occupational and political roles of the society equally with men; and (3) an androgynous model, in which all sex role differences in work, personality, and behavior are cut to the irreducible minimum.[12] Of these, the pluralistic model is probably unattainable, while supporters of sex equality are divided between the assimilationist and the androgynous models.

SEX ROLE SOCIALIZATION

All known societies have used sex as one of the bases of role ascription. Although the particular attributes defined as masculine and feminine differ considerably from society to society, every known society has ascribed some tasks and behaviors to men and others to women, while leaving still others that may be appropriately performed by either sex. In American society boys have been rewarded for being aggressive, competitive, and forthright; girls have been rewarded for being gentle, perceptive, and manipulative. Men have been expected to exercise power through authority and command; women have been expected to cultivate power through influence, sought through sex appeal, coquetry, flattery, and pandering to male egoism.[13] When frustrated, men have been expected to shout and swear and women to pout and cry. While this contrast contains some exaggerations, average sex differences of these sorts are easily established.

Sex-role socialization began very early, as boys were given tools and trains and were asked, "What will you be when you grow up?" while girls were given dolls and toy stoves and asked, "Where did you get that pretty dress?" Boys were trained to be strong, dependable breadwinners, women to be dutiful housewives and mothers.

Although there is *some* association between innate sex differences and work ascription, this is largely limited to nursing babies and to heavy manual labor, which have grown steadily less important in modern societies. Most scientists agree that *most* work tasks today can be equally well performed by either sex, while most work-role ascription is based on tradition, not upon innate sex differences (although fictitious sex differences or culturally acquired sex differences may be cited as justification for a particular work-role ascription). The fact that even today the majority of women prefer relatively traditional roles (marriage and parenthood plus a "feminine" type of employment) is due to socialization, not to biology. Those who wish to change this are critical of sexist children's gifts, textbooks, mass media entertainment, and anything else that encourages females to form traditionally "feminine" goals and aspirations.

FORMS OF SEX DISCRIMINATION IN AMERICAN LIFE

Discrimination is usually defined as the unequal treatment of equals. When persons are treated unequally as a rationally justified recognition of genuine differences—for example, in denying employment as a bookkeeper to some-

These pictures graphically illustrate the opening up of traditionally sex-stereotyped jobs to both men and women in today's society.
(A.T.&T. Co. Phone Center)

one who cannot add—there is no discrimination. When people who are equal in capacities, needs, or training are treated unequally, this is discrimination.

A national magazine describes a family with the words, "Their son Joe is a lawyer in Houston; their daughters Joanie and Claire are both married." The sexism of this description becomes apparent if we turn it around to read, "Their daughter Joanie raises horses and their daughter Claire is a church worker; their son Joe is married."

Adapted from *Time*, 8 Apr. 1974, p. 5.

LEGAL RIGHTS   The laws of most of the United States followed the English common law in viewing women as perpetual children. Most women spent their entire lives under the domination of men—first father, then husband, and finally son, brother, or other male relative. Although adult single women had many of the legal rights of males, married women had virtually no legal rights but were legally one with their husbands, who had the right and duty to decide for and care for them. In most states, married women could not hold or dispose of property, receive and control personal income, or make legal contracts. Their status was much like that of a minor child.

Women have legal rights in most states today but are not always able to claim them. They can buy real estate, provided they can find a lending institution to give them a mortgage without a male cosigner. Married women may have a legal right to hold, buy, and sell property but found it much easier with their husbands' signatures on every document. Married or single, women have often had difficulty obtaining credit or opening independent charge accounts. Business and professional women have often been required by their employers to assume their husbands' surnames, thus sacrificing the recognition value of their birth names. Thus, the earlier published work of women in academic life or scientific research is virtually "lost." While there have been many recent legal changes, women still suffer many handicaps in claiming their legal rights.

There have been some compensations in the form of legal protections. Women have been exempt from military service; wives can claim economic support from their husbands, and have community property and dower inheritance rights which husbands lack; women have social security widows' rights denied to widowers; and there are many laws intended to protect women from harmful working conditions. The Equal Rights Amendment to the Constitution, now under consideration by the states, would presumably abolish these special protections, along with any remaining disabilities.

RIGHTS OF CHOICE   Women are legally free to marry or to remain single, to remain married or to seek a divorce, to be housewives or employed wives if they are married, and to seek any kind of work they can obtain (with a very few exceptions). In actual practice, however, these choices may be more illusory than real. In the past, women were under great social pressure to marry, have children, and absorb themselves contentedly in homemaking.

357

Today this is greatly changed, and it is sometimes the housewife who is placed on the defensive.

Women's rights of occupational choice have expanded enormously in recent years. There is virtually no occupation today from which women are categorically excluded. The "male" and "female" listings in help-wanted columns are forbidden. Employers may list performance criteria among job qualifications only if they are relevant to the work tasks. Thus, a minimum weight-lifting test is acceptable for loading-dock workers but not for accountants.

In practice, however, efforts to enter "inappropriate" work roles meet various kinds of obstruction and harassment. Women seeking to enter schools of law or business administration, or men entering elementary education, meet relatively little opposition today—and even encouragement—but women seeking to be truck drivers, firefighters, airline pilots, or members of the clergy meet strong opposition. Male applicants for traditionally female jobs have even greater difficulty getting past the first phone call than do females seeking "male" jobs.[14] In an experiment with "sexually inappropriate" job applicants, however, another form of discrimination appeared. Males applying for "inappropriate" jobs were invited to apply for a higher-status job and women for a lower-status job than the job about which they had inquired.[15] It is clear that the choices open to the sexes have greatly broadened in recent years, but freedom of occupational choice is still incomplete.

EMPLOYMENT DISCRIMINATION   Women have suffered employment discrimination of many kinds. First, the typically "female" occupations are relatively poorly paid for the level of training and skill they require. To cite a few examples, Denver County (in 1979) paid staff nurses a starting salary of $1,064 a month, but the (mostly male) tree trimmers started at $1,164 and painters at $1,191.[16] The University of Washington (in 1979) assigned different kinds of jobs a "point-count" based on the skill, responsibility, and effort needed. It rated the (mostly female) food service workers at 93 points and started them at $646 a month; it rated traffic guides (mostly men, who sat in entrance booths and issued passes to visitors) at 89 points and started them at $806 a month.[17] How did such obviously unfair pay scales develop?

The "female" occupations are a displacement from the home of certain historically "female" tasks—care of children and the sick, cooking, cleaning, sewing, weaving, and assisting men. Thus, the predominantly female occupations are teaching, nursing, social work, domestic service, textile manufacturing, and clerical and secretarial work. Some formerly "male" occupations, such as teaching, became "female" occupations when large numbers of cheap workers were required. For once an occupation became identified as a "female" occupation, workers could be hired cheaply, since women had so few choices.

Second, in the "female" occupations the higher-level administrative positions were reserved for men, blocking female avenues of promotion. School superintendents, hospital directors, office managers—the higher the level, the fewer the women. When a woman replaced a man at the supervisory or executive level, she was usually given a new title and a lower salary than the man; the reverse followed when a woman was replaced by a man.

Third, even when women did the same work as men, they were often paid less. Numerous studies made in the late 1960s, before the present drive for sex equality gained effect, showed substantial income disparities in every occupation studied. Not all of this average income difference was caused by overt sex discrimination. As Villamez has noted, "not all discrimination against women derives from sexism; females in the labor force, after all, do have characteristics other than gender."[18] Some other factors are involved in male-female income differences. What are these other factors?

Changes in the composition of the labor force   Between 1950 and 1978 the percentage of all women who were in the labor force rose from 34 to 49 percent, while the percentage of men in the labor force showed little change. As a result, as compared with men the female labor force is top-heavy with beginning workers at entry-level wages. This distorted the comparison of "average" male and female earnings. The oft-quoted data showing a widening gap between male and female average earnings[19] can be partly explained by this change in the composition of the labor force.

The interruptibility of women's work   Prolonged departure from work, most often for childbearing or for home care of aged relatives, is a handicap. A single, uninterrupted work career usually pays better than a succession of two or three short-lived careers. Furthermore, women in the civilian labor force average only about two-thirds as many hours at work as men average.[20]

Geographic mobility   The husband has usually been viewed as the principal breadwinner, with the wife's earnings viewed as supplementary. Thus, the husband's career has been the principal career, with the wife's career opportunities sacrificed to his whenever they clashed. If the husband's career is advanced by a move to another location, the wife has been expected to sacrifice her seniority, her contacts, and her present career advantages. When a wife's geographical job market is determined by her husband's career opportunities, her career and her income usually suffer.

Motivation   Motivation for career advancement is difficult to measure, and rash generalization is dangerous. Yet there are good reasons to suspect that intense career ambitions have been less common among women than among men. Beginning in early socialization, most girls have been trained to please and to charm others; boys have been trained to impress and outdistance others. Boys have been trained to dominate and lead, girls to submit and follow. Boys have been taught to make demands upon others; girls learn to serve others' needs. As adults, men in our society have been evaluated primarily according to their career success ("Meet my son, the doctor"), while women have been evaluated primarily according to their skill in human relationships ("She has a handsome husband and three darling children"). Husbands who neglected their families to pursue career advancement (moonlighting, night school, weekends working at the office) were praised for their ambition, while wives who allowed their careers to interfere with family life were scolded. A woman's spectacular success might alienate men, and much has been written about the avoidance-of-success syndrome in women.[21] This all contributes to a lower level of career expectation among women than men, for which there is solid research evidence.[22] Whether men and women *should* have equal career aspirations and make equal sacrifices can be argued. There is some evidence that the happiest women are those with husband, children, and a job to which they are only moderately committed.[23] Young women today are becoming more like men in their career expectations,[24] which will demand major adjustments from both sexes.

THE RESIDUE OF OVERT DISCRIMINATION

After making allowances for all the factors discussed above, how much of the income difference between men and women remains to be attributed to overt discrimination? Several studies have attempted to compute this, comparing men's and women's earnings when occupation, education, seniority, work history, productivity, and other factors are controlled. These studies conclude that after allowing for such factors, women earn about two-thirds as much as comparable men.[25] One such study concludes that 85 percent of the earnings difference in 1962 and 84 percent in 1973 were attributable to discrimination.[26] Such research, however, studied the 1960s or early 1970s, before the current drive for equal pay had borne much fruit. Thus, the conclusions cannot be applied to the present situation, and it will be some years before the effects of more recent changes can be measured. Furthermore, some factors such as motivation cannot be measured. While the studies clearly establish the *fact* of overt discrimination, their *measures* may be questioned.

Other evidence of discrimination is found in the granting of postdoctoral fellowships in science, where women receive fewer and less prestigious fellowships than comparably qualified men.[27] Still another study finds that among college faculties, married men are paid more than single men, while single women are paid more than married women, suggesting that each sex is being paid on a basis of presumed financial need instead of productivity.[28] Many other illustrations of overt discrimination could doubtless be found if other occupations were studied with equal care.

Many subtle forms of sex discrimination persist. Despite considerable "desexing" of the vocabulary and illustrative content of textbooks, most students still think in terms of sexual stereotypes.[29] A mid-1970s study of business administration students sought to measure sex stereotyping among management trainees. A description of a management situation was presented with alternate male and female names attached. The students' evaluation of management skill dropped markedly whenever the manager was identified as female.[30] There have been many experiments of this kind, involving identical term papers, creative writing examples, artistic productions, or descriptive accounts, with alternate male and female attributions. Such studies, if made before 1970, amost always show that identical work was downgraded when attributed to a woman. More recent studies are finding no such sex bias in evaluations (except when evaluating achievements in a "sexually inappropriate" or nontraditional field).[31] Sex bias in evaluating achievements no longer appears to be a major barrier to women.

PRESENT TRENDS IN SEX ROLES

THE FEMINIST MOVEMENT   Nineteenth-century feminism died with the achievement of voting rights. Employment of women grew steadily, but mainly within the feminine occupations. In the early twentieth century, women began to smoke, drink, and drive, but little else changed. Meanwhile, however, natural and social science steadily demolished the ideas of innate sex differences that sanctioned the subordination of women. When the new feminism arose in the 1960s, the intellectual atmosphere was much more receptive.

The new feminism emerged from the general spirit of protest that spawned the civil rights and New Left movements of the 1960s. One of the sparks was the demeaning treatment given women by the New Left. One woman writes, "Suddenly women found themselves *serving*, as secretary, mother and concubine, while men did all the speaking, writing, and negotiating—and these were men who professed to reject the 'oppressive' ritual machinery of their society."[32] In 1966 the National Organization for Women (NOW) was formed with Betty Friedan as its first president. Its goals included "a sex-role revolution for men and women which will restructure all our institutions: child rearing, education, marriage, the family, medicine, work, politics, the economy, religion, psychological theory, human sexuality, morality, and the very evolution of the race."[33] While the goals of NOW may sound radical, they are moderate in comparison to those of the man-hating, marriage-rejecting, radical splinter groups such as WITCH (Women's International Terrorist Conspiracy from Hell) and SCUM (Society for Cutting Up Men).[34] The various feminist organizations attracted wide attention, claiming a national membership of 70,000 to 80,000 by 1973.[35] A few studies of activist feminists have found that they tend to be young, white, educated, middle- or upper-middle-class, atheist or agnostic, and radical in politics and sex mores.[36] Sex-role attitudes have become notably more egalitarian in recent years, but it can be debated whether the feminist movement helped *cause* the changes, or is itself a *result* of the attitude changes.[37]

LEGISLATION AND LITIGATION   Effective social movements usually bring legislative changes that, in turn, give further impetus to the social movement. The Equal Pay Act of 1963 and many similar state laws now require equal pay for equal work. The Civil Rights Act of 1964, which outlaws discrimination on the basis of race, color, religion, or sex, has been a most useful tool in expanding sex equality. Executive Order 11246, as amended by Executive Order 11375 of October 13, 1967, bars discrimination by federal contractors and suppliers and provides machinery for enforcement. Numerous court decisions have clearly established the illegality of sex-based discrimination in hiring, rates of pay, and promotion. Several landmark decisions required employers to pay women employees millions of dollars to compensate for past wage discrimination.[38] The Equal Credit Opportunity Act of 1974 forbids discrimination on the basis of sex or marital status in credit operations, but women may not obtain these rights unless they are aggressive in claiming them.[39] Even now, as one observer notes, "the biggest obstacle women entrepreneurs face is dealing with a 99 percent male banking and financial community."[40]

AFFIRMATIVE ACTION   Guidelines provided by government departments to government contractors and suppliers, recipients of government funds, and businesses engaged in interstate commerce require that affirmative action goals be established and pursued. As in the case of race discrimination (see chapter 12), affirmative action goals have sometimes been unattainable without reverse discrimination because too few qualified women were instantly

361

available to fill the quotas. The issue of reverse discrimination against men is very similar to the issue of reverse discrimination against whites: should today's young men be required to atone for yesterday's discriminations against women? In any event, reverse discrimination is likely to be a temporary expedient.

The Equal Rights Amendment (ERA) was passed by both houses of Congress in 1972, after a half-century of temporizing. It states that "equality under the law shall not be denied or abridged by the United States or by any state on account of sex." It was quickly ratified by 30 states, but ratification now appears to be stalled a few states short of the required 38 that must ratify it by May 22, 1982. If the amendment is ratified, it will remain for the courts to decide exactly what ERA requires, but it seems likely that it would do the following: (1) prohibit all sex-based discrimination in employment and pay rates (already prohibited for all but strictly local businesses); (2) end automatic male responsibility for economic support of wives, and make parents equally liable for alimony, spouse support, and child support; (3) make both sexes subject to military conscription (although their tasks within the armed forces need not be identical); (4) forbid all kinds of sex discrimination in education and use of any other tax-supported activity or public service. There has been some weird nonsense circulated about unisex toilets, locker rooms, and football teams, but the ERA would not forbid "separate": it would only forbid "unequal."[41] Beyond this, the implications remain to be determined.[42]

Opposition to ERA comes from many who take a traditional view of sex roles, but some who favor sex equality also question the ERA route. They fear that many existing protections for women would be sacrificed and claim that the goals of ERA could be better achieved by specific issue-by-issue legislation.

OTHER ACTIONS   Issue by issue, decision by decision, the remaining bastions of male privilege are falling. None of the nation's largest businesses has a woman president or chairman of the board,[43] but women directors of *Fortune Magazine*'s list of 500 largest business concerns have grown from a handful in 1970 to 400 in 1976.[44] This is still very few, but 25 years ago scarcely any women attended graduate schools of business administration. They are attending now, and 25 years hence we may anticipate a much larger feminine representation in the board room. A federally-funded American Woman's Economic Development Corporation (AWED) in New York City is now running a pilot program for training women as business entrepreneurs. Of the first 332 alumni, only 2 had gone bankrupt at time of writing (compared with a national 50 percent rate of failure for new busi-

WHO SHOULD PAY FOR PAST DISCRIMINATION?

My parents and grandparents were discriminated against because they were wops and micks. Am I now to be discriminated against because stereotypes of inequality insist that I and others like me are the privileged heirs to centuries of racial and sexual discrimination?

Richard H. Alba, *ASA Footnotes*, Dec. 1975, p. 3.

nesses within two years).[45] Even that epitome of male WASP exclusiveness—the men's club—is opening its doors.[46] Although they are professed to be entirely social, such clubs function as places to make contacts, entertain prospects, and close deals. Business and professional women are at a competitive disadvantage if they are excluded. Clubs that bar women may soon find that their tax-exempt status is canceled and that members' dues are no longer tax-deductible.[47] Without these tax concessions, few men's clubs could survive. Like it or not, most male retreats are doomed.

SEXUAL HARASSMENT   This has recently become recognized as a form of sex discrimination. Defined as "repeated and unwanted sexual advances,"[48] women are the usual victims. Men are rarely the object of unwanted female advances, and sexual harassment is uncommon among homosexuals of either sex.

Sexual harassment is an ancient practice. Attractive female slaves were routinely bought as sex playthings, and domestic servants were often exploited. If the Victorian housemaid denied her bed to a lecherous master, he dismissed her; if she admitted him, she soon became pregnant and disgraced, and his wife dismissed her. Either way, she lost!

Sexual harassment can be found anywhere, but is likely to be a problem only where men have supervisory or gatekeeper power over women. The "casting couch" is a well-known feature of show business, and women in many occupations can escape unwelcome attentions only by quitting their jobs, often at a sacrifice. Sexual harassment on the campus has surfaced, with many female graduate students claiming that senior professors claimed sexual privileges as the price for grades, degrees, and recommendations.[49]

In a landmark case in 1978, a federal court defined sexual harassment as a violation of Title VII of the Civil Rights Act.[50] A Working Woman's Institute, funded mainly by corporate contributions, now operates in New York City to counsel and aid victims of sexual harassment, and other sources of counsel and support are available.[51] Yet even a successful protest

---

WHAT IS SEXUAL HARASSMENT?

Molly works in a factory and wears an apron filled with bolts for the assembly line. Her supervisor "checks" the bolts by reaching into the apron and feeling around. He does not "check" the aprons of the male workers. He also waits until Molly is alone in the cloakroom and backs her up against the wall. When Molly protests, he says he's being "friendly" and she shouldn't be "uncooperative" or she'll lose her job.

Susan works in an insurance office and has to travel to other cities with her boss. He wants to share a hotel room "to save some money." When Susan refuses he tells her to "smarten up" or he'll give her a poor rating on her next job review and demote her back to a clerical job. In the meantime, he doubles Susan's workload and complains that she "can't keep up."

From leaflet, Sexual Harassment on the Job, distributed by Michigan Task Force on Sexual Harassment in the Workplace, in cooperation with WJBK—TV2, Detroit.

leaves the victim the loser. She must endure the unpleasantness of pursuing the complaint, must confront the suspicion that she invited the advances, and may need a new job as the old workplace becomes uncomfortable. Here, as elsewhere, those who seek to change things often do so at a personal sacrifice.

ANDROGYNY: POSSIBLE? DESIRABLE?

Is androgyny possible? Except for a few activities directly connected with reproduction, can most sex differences in work, personality, and behavior be eliminated? If sex roles became androgynous, would they *remain* androgynous, or would sex-role differentiation and male dominance return?

Since no known society has ever been androgynous, we have no positive answer. It is significant, however, that there have been a number of determined attempts to establish androgynous sex roles, and none have yet succeeded.

Marxist efforts at sex equality follow from the Marxist belief that sex discrimination is simply another aspect of class exploitation, and can be ended only by socialist revolution.[52] Marxist theoreticians reject the Women's Liberation Movement as futile in a capitalist society and as a capitalist trick to recruit cheap labor.[53] Yet Marxist societies are far from achieving sex equality. A recent study of work in the Soviet Union finds no change in work roles between 1923 and 1966.[54] A recent study of pay rates finds that in the Soviet Union, as in the U.S., the prevailing wage is highest in occupations with few women; as the proportion of women in a job category rises, the wage rates fall.[55] Another study of male-female earnings concluded that Soviet women averaged 65 percent of male hourly wage rates; when compared with wage differentials in eight Western capitalist countries, Soviet women were higher (more nearly equal) in two of 13 measures of income equality, and lower in eleven.[56] One of your authors has observed in travels in other communist countries that the person driving the tractor is predictably male, while the one with the hoe or pulling weeds is predictably female.

Communist countries recite a rhetoric of sex equality while practicing sex discrimination.[57] "Sex equality" in communist countries has "freed" women to fill two jobs, for men do very little of the shopping or housework,[58] making women possibly the most exploited "class" in communist countries. It is possible that the real goal of communist policy is not sex equality, but enlarging the labor force.[59]

The class exploitation theory of the origin of sexism is clearly contradicted by the experience of the Hutterites, a communal religious sect among whom there is complete economic equality and no class exploitation, yet among whom male dominance is total and complete.[60] The kibbutz experience in Israel further contradicts the class exploitation thesis. With a socialist ideology and a strong commitment to both economic and sexual equality, kibbutzim sought to minimize all difference in sex roles. The result was economic equality without sex equality: The trend over the years has not been toward the progressive elimination of remaining sex-role differences; instead, the trend has been away from an initially egalitarian system and toward an *increasing* sex-role differentiation.[61] Evidence linking sexism to capitalism or class exploitation is unconvincing.

The experiences reported above give little comfort to those who believe that androgynous sex roles can be attained and maintained. Some scholars

364

believe that male dominance is biologically based and inevitable.[62] Thus, the question of whether androgynous sex roles are possible remains unanswered.

Are androgynous sex roles desirable? Some scholars argue that the attempt to eliminate sex-role differences would be harmful to both sexes and destructive to the society.[63] It can be argued that ascription of household and child care responsibilities by sex is efficient, since role performance is most successful when role preparation begins early in life. But it can also be argued that an equal sharing of income producing, of household work, and of child care will afford greater fulfillment for all members of the family.[64] One researcher reports evidence that men who are strongly "masculine" and women who are strongly "feminine" in personality are less happy than persons of both sexes who fall near the midpoint on a masculinity–femininity continuum.[65] Leo Srole, repeating a 1954 mental health study in New York City in 1976, found a surprising gain in the mental health level of women (with no change in male levels), and attributes this to the feminist movement, saying: "Women . . . had a greater freedom to live their lives as they chose, rather than having them determined largely by men. And, demonstrably, fulfillment is an important component of good mental health."[66] Ultimately, the question of the desirability of androgyny is a choice between values: What kind of men, women, and families do we want?

Age Discrimination

All known societies practice role ascription according to age. All societies ascribe different duties and privileges to the young, the mature, and the aged. It is clearly impractical to expect the very old to carry a full adult work load, and it would be unwise to allow a small boy to sign a legal contract committing him to crushing lifelong payments.

Just what constitutes sensible protection and what constitutes unjust discrimination is not easy to determine. A few years ago, responding to the argument that "a man who is old enough to carry a gun for his country is old enough to buy a beer," a number of states lowered the legal drinking age from 21 to 18 years. Automobile accidents involving drinking drivers under 21 nearly doubled,[67] and drunkenness in schools skyrocketed.[68] By 1979, nine states had raised the legal drinking age, some to 19 and some back to 21.[69] It is often noted that about half of the "juvenile delinquents" have committed acts that are entirely legal for adults. This is not necessarily an unjust discrimination, for a 14-year-old staying out all night or running away is a prime candidate for trouble of some kind. Drawing the line between wise protection of and unjust discrimination against the young is a perplexing task.

Discrimination against the aged is somewhat easier to define. The denial of any of the rights of adult citizenship on the basis of age alone is unjust age discrimination.

EMPLOYMENT DISCRIMINATION

It is no secret that employers prefer relatively young job applicants. People over 40 have difficulty finding any but undesirable jobs. There are several explanations for this:

1. Recruiting, training, and "breaking in" new employees is expensive. Most employers hope for lifelong employees, and older people have fewer years left to work.
2. Older employees cost more for health insurance, life insurance, and possibly sick leave.
3. Employers fear, often without foundation, that older workers will be less trainable, less productive, and more illness- and accident-prone.

For all these reasons employability declines sharply with age, not only among factory workers but at practically all levels of employment. In addition, years of seniority are seldom transferable, so the older job-hunter must usually start a new job at a starting salary.

There is some legal protection for the aged. The Age Discrimination Act of 1967 protects most workers between the ages of 40 and 65, and was amended in 1978 to forbid enforced retirement before the age of 70 (except for college teachers, who may be retired at 65).

> In a pioneer country the old were useless; in a culture based on the rejection of dynastic tradition they were obsolete; in a culture commercially and philosophically bent on the constant pursuit of the new and the better, they were in the way. Worst of all, from 1900 on they became increasingly numerous.
>
> Alex Comfort, *New York Times Book Reivew*, 17 April 1977, p. 30.

Compulsory retirement at a specified age, usually 65 or 70, is convenient for employers. It offers a simple, impersonal way of trimming the deadwood without the unpleasantness of accusing older workers of having lost their effectiveness. Yet is also means that many workers who are still highly productive are nonetheless cast aside like empty soda bottles. Some retired but energetic employees start second careers, but the odds are heavily against them.

The trend is definitely toward a longer working life, reversing the recent trends toward early retirement.[70] Due to the aging of our population, a declining ratio of workers to retirees threatens to bankrupt pension programs. It is likely that minimum retirement ages for Social Security benefits will soon be raised and other changes made to encourage (force?) people to work longer. In this respect, as in so many others, we are only starting to consider the consequences of an aging society.[71]

SOCIAL DISCRIMINATION

In many ways we tell our old people that they are irrelevant and useless. Many societies have honored and revered their old people as sources of knowledge, wisdom, and guidance. But in a rapidly changing society where knowledge becomes quickly out of date, old people can seem to be a nuisance rather than an asset.

Discrimination takes many forms. Commercial television largely ignores the aged audience; old people do not buy enough to interest sponsors. Youth either ignores the aged as irrelevant or resents the aged as an obstacle. Our accent on youth is painful to the aged. Youth is identified with beauty, glamour, and adventure; the old may sit quietly and listen to their arteries harden. Many people who are highly permissive toward the sexual needs of the young are disgusted at the idea that sexual desire persists into old age. Most nursing homes operate on the assumption that all sexual interests vanish among the aged.[72]

Possibly the most cruel discrimination of all combines age and sex discrimination. This is the double standard of declining sex desirability. While both sexes gradually lose their desirability as sex objects, women's desirability is seen to decline more rapidly than that of men. The man who escorts or marries a woman half his age meets a mixture of mild disapproval and envy; the older woman who takes a young lover or husband is almost universally ridiculed or condemned. Numerous advertisements show older men surrounded by admiring, nubile young women; advertisements showing older women surrounded by panting young men are conspicuously lacking.

While employment discrimination against the aged can be attacked by legislation, social discrimination against the aged is immune to legal attack. Firmly rooted in our traditions and values, social discrimination against the aged can be changed only if and when values change. The aged form a growing fraction of our population and should gain increased political power. Whether this is accompanied by a decline in social discrimination against them is doubtful.

It should also be noted that the aged enjoy some positive discrimination. They receive many discounts and some special services not enjoyed by younger people. Yet on balance, ours is not a particularly happy society in which to grow old.

Still Other Forms of Discrimination

THE HANDICAPPED

Our largest minority are the physically and mentally handicapped, numbering from 40 to 68 million, depending upon whose estimate is accepted. The Rehabilitation Act of 1973 prohibits any federally-funded agency from excluding the handicapped from any programs or facilities on the basis of handicap alone, "regardless of the nature or severity of the handicap."[73] Once again, Congress gave us an example of how *not* to solve a social problem. This was a "sleeper" provision, a floor amendment to another bill and voted without committee hearings or floor debate. Consequently, it is vague as to whom is covered and what services shall be provided, and it is open-ended as to costs. To remove *every* barrier for *every* handicapped person would be enormously expensive and sometimes wasteful. For example, to replace all buses with new buses which admit wheelchair passengers will serve only 7 percent of the handicapped at a cost estimated by the Congressional Budget Office at $38 per ride. Door-to-door taxi service could serve 26 percent of the handicapped at a cost estimated at $8 per ride.[74] Obviously, the question of how best to meet the needs of the handicapped calls for more careful analysis than a "sleeper" amendment whooped absent-mindedly through Congress.

The present trend is to help the handicapped to be more active and independent. Some organizations such as the Disabled in Action and the National Federation for the Blind accuse helping agencies such as the March of Dimes of encouraging paternalism and dependency, instead of promoting rehabilitation and supporting attacks on discrimination.[75] Employ-the-handicapped campaigns would be unnecessary if the handicapped did not suffer severe employment discrimination.

Numerous studies have shown that many of the handicapped, with proper vocational guidance and training, can equal or exceed other workers in productivity and dependability, yet they have great difficulty finding employment. Many people simply do not like to be around handicapped people, who often are not very pretty and are an uncomfortable reminder of one's own vulnerability to misfortune. The handicapped person's chances for promotion to executive or managerial positions are poor, for promotion increases the number of a worker's contacts and multiplies the number of persons who may feel uncomfortable.

THE UNATTRACTIVE

A number of research studies have shown that beautiful people "get the breaks." Other things being equal, most employers prefer pretty secretaries to homely ones. Research shows that people evaluate pretty women and handsome men higher than homely people in ability, personality, kindness, and professional success.[76] Attractive children get significantly higher grades and score somewhat higher on achievement tests than unattractive children.[77] Attractive interviewers get better cooperation from interviewees than homely interviewers, suggesting another reason why employers prefer attractive persons as salespersons or counselors.[78] Attractiveness appears to be the most important single factor in dating preferences, with the handsome dating the beautiful while the uglies date each other, if they date at all.[79] Glamour even rubs off. In one experiment a group of student judges rated a man higher in ability and personality when he was paired with a beautiful woman than when the same man was paired with a homely woman.[80] People are also judged to be more moral and upright if they are good-looking. In a study of this phenomenon, written accounts of child misconduct were presented to a group of subjects for evaluation. Each account was presented to one group of judges with a picture of an attractive child attached, and to another group of judges with a picture of a homely child. Most judges excused or minimized the conduct when it was attributed to an attractive child, but severely condemned it when it was attributed to a homely child.[81] Two studies even found that physically attractive persons are less likely to become mentally ill, and that they recover more quickly, than unattractive persons.[82] Many similar experiments and surveys show how an attractive appearance opens doors, excuses shortcomings, and gains advantages. Once again, this is a form of discrimination that no law can diminish. As far as we know, all societies have always distinguished beautiful people (however defined) from the homelies and have continued to treat them differently.

THE OBESE

The obese are categorically excluded from some jobs and are most likely to be placed in jobs where they can be hidden from the public. They are the butt of much cruel humor, to which they are expected to react with jolly tolerance. Their choice of courtship partners is limited. They are made uncomfortable in many situations where facilities (for example, chair spacing) are not designed for persons of their bulk.

The overweight are blamed for their blubber on the assumption that they are merely the victims of unbridled self-indulgence. Recent research casts doubt on this assumption, for it begins to appear that obesity often follows from organic factors not entirely under individual control.[83] A lifelong tendency toward obesity also arises from the excess number of fat cells produced by overfeeding in infancy and early childhood. Thus, when both par-

In addition to the more blatant prejudices, our society fosters many more subtle forms of discrimination that may not at first glance be apparent.
(United Press International)

ents are obese, there is an 80 percent probability that the child will be obese.[84] There is universal agreement that obesity is physically unhealthful and personally inconvenient, but simply to blame the obese is too facile an interpretation. Today the National Association to Aid Fat People seeks to promote a more sympathetic acceptance of obesity, but its members are fighting an uphill battle.

THE SHORT

Tall, well-built men are admired; short men usually find that they are often downgraded, underestimated, and not taken seriously. Even our vocabulary equates shortness with undesirability: for example, *short-sighted, short-changed, short-circuited,* and the denigrating synonyms for *short,* such as *runt, shrimp,* and *shorty.*[85] Several studies have found that leaders tend to be taller than average.[86] There is no empirical evidence that Mr. Shoulders is wiser than Mr. Pipsqueak, but a towering build seems to inspire confidence. One study of business graduates found that tall men (over 6′2″) received a starting salary 12 percent higher than graduates under 6′ tall.[87]

Men are the disadvantaged sex with respect to height. Shortness (unless it is extreme) is often desired in women but generally a handicap to men. The courtship limitations of tall women and short men are too well known to require documentation. For some physical tasks shortness is an inherent handicap, but most of the penalties inflicted upon short men are based upon social attitudes, not upon performance capacities.

HOMOSEXUALS AND SINGLES

Not all singles are homosexuals, of course, but mature singles, especially male singles, are likely to be suspected of being homosexual, and thus to be on the receiving end of some of the hostile attitudes toward homosexuals.

The persecution of homosexuals has declined markedly in recent years. Not long ago a single homosexual act could bring imprisonment, career ruin, and social ostracism. Today the penalties are less severe, and many homosexuals have come out of the closet to admit their sexual orientation.[88] (For a more complete discussion of homosexuality, see chapter 16; in this chapter we shall deal only with discrimination against homosexuals.)

The notion that homosexuals are sick or mentally ill has been effectively demolished by recent research. A number of studies have found that aside from sexual preference, no personality characteristics or maladjustments distinguish homosexuals from heterosexuals.[89] For some jobs, such as teaching or the ministry, there may be a basis for excluding homosexuals, although this is debated. Most child molesters are heterosexuals, not homosexuals,[90] and it may be argued where and with whom the child is most safe from harm. In most kinds of work, the instant dismissal of the homosexual is clearly punishment, not social protection. The Gay Liberation Movement seeks to aid homosexuals to dispel negative self-images, to end all legal and social discrimination against homosexuals, and to gain acceptance of homosexuality as a valid alternative lifestyle, different from but not inferior to the heterosexual lifestyle. Gays are having considerable success with the first of these goals, some success with the second, but little with the third.[91]

The list of victims of discrimination could be extended at length, progressing from the serious to the minor to the trivial. The mentally retarded are often victimized; exconvicts have difficulty finding employment; hippies are often treated discourteously and harassed by the police; smokers complain about being confined to the rear of the plane. There will always be some forms of discrimination, some of which are proclaimed as justified protections, others as expressions of widely held values. Often such justifications are merely rationalizations for prejudice and personal discomforts. However, people *do* have a right to withhold personal response from those who offend them, for whatever reason.

The Social-Disorganization Approach

In a perfectly integrated culture there would be no discrimination. There might be great inequalities, but these would be so rationalized and sanctioned by the society's value system that no one would feel deprived of his or her rights.

Change undermines established systems of rights and sanctions. The earlier stages of capitalist industrialization destroyed the relatively independent economic and individual status women had enjoyed and increased their subordination to men.[92] In the recent stages of capitalist industrialization, women are again gaining status. Technological change has reduced the proportion of jobs in which muscle is important. Change in the form of increased knowledge about inherent sex differences has undermined the justification for female subordination. The democratic ideology also places advocates of female subordination on the defensive.

Industrialization has had the opposite effect upon age statuses. The entry of the young into adult roles has been postponed as they acquire more complicated learnings. The *adolescent* stage of extended semichildhood is a product of modern society. The aged have been dethroned from the position of respect they held in most agricultural societies. Rapid social change has transformed the image of aged from wise oracles into fussy scolds whose "wisdom" is dismissed as irrelevant. Urbanization and industrialization prevent most of the aged from retiring gradually on the farm, while still performing useful work tasks according to their energies. It is no wonder that so many of the aged die quickly in retirement.

The other forms of discrimination discussed in this chapter do not neatly fit into the framework of social disorganization. Such forms of discrimination, found in many societies, do not appear to be closely linked to the social or economic structure of the society.

The Value-Conflict Approach

All of the forms of discrimination discussed in this chapter are deeply rooted in value conflicts. The women's liberation movement, the gay liberation movement, and the organizations seeking to change treatment of the aged, the handicapped, the obese, or the unattractive are all attempting to change people's values. Legislation may reduce discrimination in employment and pay scales, but many forms of social discrimination are not responsive to legislation and can be changed only through value change.

To some extent values *have* changed, but the direction of future value change is unknown. We can only guess, for example, whether children raised by partly liberated parents will proceed toward greater sex equality or will revert to more traditional sex roles as adults.

The Personal-Deviation Approach

Like racial bigots, the extremists in cases such as those in this chapter are likely to be unhappy, resentful people. The classic male chauvinist is an insecure man who fears and dislikes women; some of the most ardent feminists are women who dislike men, which is detectable in the more passionate feminist literature. This should be no surprise, for most social movements are led by angry fanatics.

The proposals of feminists, gay liberationists, and others who wish to change things are, of course, deviations from the traditional order. Women who enter "masculine" occupations and men who accept equal responsibility for housework and child care are deviants. All changes in sex roles first appear as deviations; if widely copied, these deviations eventually become new norms.

Age discrimination does not easily fit the framework of personal deviation. The remaining forms of discrimination are illustrations of the social abuse most societies visit upon those who deviate from the norm or the ideal in either physical or behavioral traits. Few societies are kind to deviants; our society is more tolerant than many, and more tolerant than it was in the recent past.

Summary and Prospects

Possible solutions for the various forms of discrimination have been indicated throughout this chapter rather than being presented in a single section. The feminist and gay liberation movements have been accompanied by highly significant changes in their respective areas of discrimination. The extent to which these movements *caused* the changes can be debated. Sex was included among the bases for discrimination forbidden by the Civil Rights Act of 1964 as the result of a legislative accident, not of any massive groundswell of popular demand. In an effort to embarrass the supporters of the Civil Rights Act, a southern legislator offered an amendment adding "sex" to the categories; it was approved with little discussion and apparently with little awareness of its eventual importance. This law provides a powerful lever for feminist groups seeking change. The social atmosphere of the late 1960s was highly receptive to attacks upon any form of discrimination. Sexist vocabulary and practices that had been unquestioned a few years earlier suddenly became chauvinist. The success of the feminist movement is an example of how small activist groups can achieve (or receive credit for achieving) significant and rapid change when they operate in a favorable cultural climate and are aided by some strategic legislation. As this is written the cultural climate is less favorable than it was a few years ago. After rapid ratification by 30 states in the early 1970s, the drive to ratify the ERA appears to be stalled 3 states short of ratification. The long-run prospects for sex equality look favorable because of recently acquired knowledge about innate sex differences and because of the nature of work in modern societies. But the rapid gains of recent years seem unlikely to be matched in the next decade.

The prospects for the aged are more promising, as the aged form a steadily growing sector of the voting population. There is little basis for forecasting action to curb the remaining forms of discrimination. Sociologists who attempt to predict value changes are treading on dangerous ground.

Suggested Readings

CARDEN, MAREN LOCKWOOD, *The New Feminist Movement* (New York: Russell Sage, 1974). A history and analysis of the women's liberation movement.

COMFORT, ALEX, *A Good Age* (New York: Crown, 1976). An optimistic popular account that dispels many myths about the aged.

FISCHER, DAVID HACKETT, "Putting Our Heads to the 'Problem' of Old Age," *New York Times,* 10 May 1977, p. 33; abstracted in *Current,* July/Aug. 1977, pp. 45–48. A brief comment on age as a social problem.

GILDER, GEORGE F., *Sexual Suicide* (New York: Quadrangle/New York Times, 1973; Bantam Books, 1975). A popular but scholarly argument that feminism will destroy society.

GLAZER-MALBIN, NONA, and HELEN YOUNGELSON WAEHRER, eds., *Woman in a Man-Made World* (Chicago: Rand McNally, 1972). A collection on women's status and role in modern society.

GOLDBERG, STEPHEN, *The Inevitability of Patriarchy* (New York: William Morrow, 1973). A sociologist argues that biological differences predispose toward male domination.

HOLMSTROM, LYNDA LYTLE, *The Two-Career Family* (Cambridge, Mass.: Schenkman, 1973). An analysis of the adjustments needed when both partners work.

MEDNICK, MARTHA TAMARA SHUCH, et al., eds., *Women and Achievement: Social and Motivational Analyses* (Washington, D.C.: Hemisphere, 1975). A collection of research on sex roles, motivation, and achievement of women.

MONTAGU, ASHLEY, *The Natural Superiority of Women* (New York: Collier, 1970); and WALLACE REYBURN, *The Inferior Sex* (Englewood Cliffs, N.J.: Prentice-Hall, 1972). Two opposing views of which is the superior sex.

MORGAN, MIRIAM MARABEL, *The Total Woman* (Old Tappan, N.J.: Fleming Revell, 1973). A popular defense of the traditional concept of feminine sex roles.

SAGARIN, EDWARD, ed., *The Other Minorities* (Waltham, Mass.: Ginn, 1971). A readable collection dealing with a number of nonracial and nonethnic minorities, such as the handicapped, the clumsy, ex-convicts, and others.

SCHWARTZ, JANET S., "Women under Socialism: Role Definitions of Soviet Women," *Social Forces,* 58 (Sept. 1979), 67–88; and, MICHAEL SWAFFORD, "Sex Differences in Soviet Earnings," *American Sociological Review,* 43 (Oct. 1978), 657–73. Two research articles on the status of women in Soviet society.

Footnotes

[1]Institute for Social Research, University of Michigan, *Newsletter,* Winter 1970, p. 6.

[2]Quoted from Vivian Gornick, "Consciousness," *New York Times Magazine,* 10 Jan. 1971, p. 22. Copyright © 1971 by The New York Times Company. Reprinted by permission.

[3]Genesis 2:18–23.

[4]Gerald R. Leslie, *The Family in Social Context* (New York: Oxford University Press, 1976), ch. 6.

[5]Judith K. Brown, "A Note on the Division of Labor by Sex," *American Anthropologist,* 72 (Oct. 1970), 1073–78.

[6]Betty Friedan, *The Feminine Mystique* (New York: W. W. Norton, 1963); Kate Millett, *Sexual Politics* (New York: Random House, 1970); Barbara K. Moran and Vivian Gornick, eds., *Women in Sexist Society* (New York: Basic Books, 1971); Alice Rossi, ed., *The Feminist Papers: From Adams to de Beauvoir* (New York: Columbia University Press, 1973); Jo Freeman, *Women: A Feminist Perspective* (Palo Alto, Ca.: Mayfield, 1975).

[7]Miriam Marabel Morgan, *The Total Woman* (Old Tappan, N.J.: Fleming Revell, 1973). For other books in a similar vein, see Helen Andelin, *Fascinating Womanhood* (New York: Bantam, 1975); Oleda Baker, *Be a Woman!* (New York: Ballantine, 1975); and Arianna Stassinopoulos, *The Female Woman* (New York: Dell, 1975).

[8]*Time*, 10 Mar. 1975, p. 77.

[9]See "On Equal Monthly Retirement Benefits for Men and Women Faculty," *AAUP Bulletin*, 61 (Winter 1975), 316–22.

[10]Courts have recently upheld women's claim to equal monthly pensions, but feminists have not asked for the right to pay equal life insurance premiums.

[11]The United States Supreme Court ruled in 1977 that employers may exclude pregnancy from worker disability programs.

[12]Alice Rossi, "Sex Equality: The Beginning of Ideology," in Betty Roszak and Theodore Roszak, eds., *Masculine/Feminine* (New York: Harper & Row, 1970), pp. 173–86.

[13]See Paula B. Johnson and Jacqueline D. Goodchilds, "How Women Get Their Way," *Psychology Today*, Oct. 1976, pp. 69–70.

[14]Richard M. Levinson, "Sex Discrimination and Employment Practices: An Experiment with Unconventional Job Inquiries," *Social Problems*, 22 (Apr. 1975), 533–43.

[15]Ibid. See also Al Szymanski, "The Socialization of Women's Oppression: A Marxist Theory of the Changing Position of Women in Advanced Capitalist Society," *The Insurgent Sociologist*, 76 (Winter 1976), 31–58.

[16]Carol Krucoff, in the *Washington Post*, quoted in the *Kalamazoo Gazette*, 25 Nov. 1979, p. C–16.

[17]Ibid.

[18]Wayne J. Villamez, "Male Economic Gain from Female Subordination: A Caveat and Reanalysis," *Social Forces*, 56 (Dec. 1977), p. 626.

[19]For example, see Dean K. Knudsen, "The Declining Status of Women: Popular Myths and the Failure of Functionalist Thought," *Social Forces*, 48 (Dec. 1969), 183–93.

[20]David L. Featherman and Robert M. Hauser, "Sexual Inequalities and Socioeconomic Achievement in the United States, 1962–1973," *American Sociological Review*, 41 (June 1976), 462–83.

[21]Peter J. Weston and Martha T. Shuch Mednick, "Race, Social Class, and the Motive to Avoid Success in Women," *Journal of Cross-Cultural Psychology*, 1 (Sept. 1970), 283–91; Matina S. Horner, "Toward an Understanding of Achievement-Related Conflicts in Women," *Journal of Social Issues*, 28, no. 2 (1972), 157–75; Lois Wladis Hoffman, "Fear of Success in Males and Females," *Journal of Consulting and Clinical Psychology*, 42 (Apr. 1974), 353–58.

[22]Irene Hanson Frieze, "Women's Expectations for and Causal Attributions of Success and Failure," in Martha T. S. Mednick et al., eds., *Women and Achievement* (Washington, D.C.: Hemisphere, 1975), pp. 158–71.

[23]Angus Campbell, "The American Way of Mating," *Psychology Today*, May 1975, pp. 37–43; Philip Shaver and Jonathan Friedman, "Your Pursuit of Happiness," *Psychology Today*, Aug. 1976, pp. 26–32.

[24]Gerard A. Brandmeyer, "Effects of Role Modeling: An Experimental Program to Alter Career Patterns among Women," paper presented at the 41st annual meeting of the Southern Sociological Association, New Orleans, April 1978.

[25]Larry E. Suter and Herman P. Miller, "Incomes of Men and Career Women," *American Journal of Sociology*, 78 (Jan. 1973), 962–74; Donald J. Treiman and Kermit Terrell, "Sex and the Process of Status Attainment: A Comparison of Working Women and Men," *American Sociological Review*, 40 (Apr. 1976), 174–200; Featherman and Hauser, "Income Inequalities and Socioeconomic Achievement."

[26]Featherman and Hauser, "Income Inequalities and Socioeconomic Achievement."

[27]Barbara F. Reskin, "Sex Differences in Status Attainment in Science: The Case of the Postdoctoral Fellowship," *American Sociological Review*, 41 (Aug. 1976), 597–612.

[28]Marianne A. Ferber and Jane W. Loeb, "Performance, Rewards and Perception of Sex Discrimination among Male and Female Faculty," *American Journal of Sociology*, 78 (Jan. 1973), 995–1002.

[29]Beta Lamda Pi Chapter, Pi Lambda Theta, University of Akron, "You've Come a Long Way, Baby! A Report on Sex Bias in Textbooks," *Educational Horizons*, 54 (Winter 1975–76), 94–98.

[30]Kathryn M. Bartol and D. Anthony Butterfield, "Sex Effects in Evaluating Leaders," *Journal of Applied Psychology*, 61 (Aug. 1976), 446–54.

[31]Alice Ross Gold, "Re-examining Barriers to Women's Career Develop-

ment," *American Journal of Orthopsychiatry,* 48 (Oct. 1978), 690–702.

[32]Annie Gottlieb, "Feeble Human Beings," *New York Times Book Review,* 21 Feb. 1971, sec. 2, pp. 1ff.

[33]Betty Friedan, "Up from the Kitchen Floor," *New York Times Magazine,* 4 Mar. 1973, p. 30.

[34]See Valerie Solanis, "Excerpts from the SCUM Manifesto," in Robin Morgan, *Sisterhood Is Powerful* (New York: Random House, 1970), pp. 514–19.

[35]Maren Lockwood Carden, *The New Feminist Movement* (New York: Russell Sage, 1974).

[36]Ibid., ch. 2; J. A. Dempewolff, "Some Correlates of Feminism," *Psychological Reports,* 34 (Apr. 1974), 671–76; Edwin W. McClain, "Religious Orientation, the Key to Psychodynamic Differences between Feminists and Nonfeminists," *Journal for the Scientific Study of Religion,* 18 (Mar. 1979), 40–45.

[37]Karen Oppenheim Mason, John L. Czajka, and Sara Arber, "Changes in U.S. Women's Sex-Role Attitudes, 1964–1974," *American Sociological Review,* 41 (Aug. 1976), 573–96.

[38]See "$2 Million Settlement Is Reported in Women's Bias Suit against NBC," *New York Times,* 13 Feb. 1977, pp. 1ff.

[39]Martha L. Garrison, "Credit-Ability for Women," *The Family Coordinator,* 25 (July 1976), 241–48.

[40]Joseph R. Mancuso, Center for Entrepreneurial Management, Inc., quoted in *Business Week,* 25 Feb. 1980, p. 85.

[41]The U.S. Supreme Court based its rejection of "separate but equal" schools on the grounds that "segregated schools are inherently unequal." It may be assumed that under the ERA, separate activities would be rejected only where shown to be unequal.

[42]Barbara Brown et al., *Women's Rights and the Law* (New York: Praeger Publishers, 1977).

[43]Frederick L. Sturdivant and Roy D. Adler, "Executive Origins: Still a Gray Flannel World," *Harvard Business Review,* 54 (Nov./Dec. 1976), 125–32.

[44]"The Corporate Woman," *Business Week,* 10 Jan. 1977, pp. 49–50.

[45]"Women Rise as Entrepreneurs," *Business Week,* 25 Feb. 1980, pp. 85–91.

[46]Stephen Birmingham, "The Clubs Griffin Bell Had to Quit," *New York Times Magazine,* 6 Feb. 1977, pp. 20ff.

[47]"Twilight Comes to the All-Male Business Club," *Business Week,* 20 Dec. 1976, p. 65.

[48]Karen Sauvigne and Susan Meyer, quoted in the *New York Times,* 23 Dec. 1979, sec. 3, p. 7.

[49]Adrienne Munich, "Seduction in Academe," *Psychology Today,* Feb. 1978, pp. 82–84ff.

[50]Lawrence Stessin, "Two against Harassment," *New York Times,* 23 Dec. 1976, sec. 3, p. 65.

[51]Ibid.

[52]Juliet Mitchell, "Women: The Longest Revolution," *New Left Review,* 40 (Nov./Dec. 1966), 11–37; Margaret Benson, "The Political Ideology of Women's Liberation," *Monthly Review,* 21 (Sept. 1969), 13–25; Rayna R. Reiter, ed., *Toward an Anthropology of Women* (New York: Monthly Review Press, 1975).

[53]Peggy Powell Dobbins, "Toward a Theory of the Women's Liberation Movement," *The Insurgent Sociologist,* 7 (Summer 1977), 53–62.

[54]Michael Paul Sacks, "Unchanging Times: A Comparison of Everyday Life of Soviet Working Women between 1923 and 1966," paper presented at 71st Annual Meeting of the American Sociological Association, 1975.

[55]Janet S. Schwartz, "Women under Socialism: Role Definitions of Soviet Women," *Social Forces,* 58 (Sept. 1979), 67–88.

[56]Michael Swafford, "Sex Differences in Soviet Earnings," *American Sociological Review,* 43 (Oct. 1978), 657–73. (This study also shows American women at the bottom, receiving 61 percent of male hourly wages in 1976.)

[57]H. Hunt Geiger, *The Family in Soviet Russia* (Cambridge, Mass.: Harvard University Press, 1968).

[58]Leonid A. Gordon and Eduard V. Klopov, *Man after Work,* tr. by John Bushmess and Kristine Bushmess (Moscow: Progress Publishers, 1975).

[59]Michael Paul Sacks, *Women's Work in the Soviet Union* (New York: Praeger, 1976).

[60]John A. Hostettler, *Hutterite Society* (Baltimore: Johns Hopkins Press, 1974).

[61]Martha T. Shuch Mednick, "Social Change and Sex-Role Inertia: The Case of the Kibbutz," in Mednick et al., eds., *Women and Achievement,* pp. 85–103; Lionel Tiger and Joseph Shepher, *Women in the Kibbutz* (New York: Harcourt Brace Jovanovich, 1975).

[62]Stephen Goldberg, *The Inevitability of Patriarchy* (New York: William Mor-

row, 1973; Pierre L. Van den Berge, *Man in Society: A Biosocial View* (New York: Elsevier, 1975).

63Midge Dector, *The New Chastity and Other Arguments against Women's Liberation* (New York: Coward, McCann and Geoghegan, 1972); George F. Gilder, *Sexual Suicide* (New York: Quadrangle/New York Times, 1973).

64Connie Bruck, "Professing Androgyny," *Human Behavior*, Oct. 1977, pp. 21–31.

65Sandra Lipsitz Bem, "Androgyny vs. the Tight Little Lives of Fluffy Women and Chesty Men," *Psychology Today*, Sept. 1975, pp. 58–62.

66Leo Srole, quoted in the *New York Times Magazine*, 16 Dec. 1979, p. 138. The study mentioned is Leo Srole and Anita H. Fischer, eds., *Mental Health in the Metropolis* (New York: McGraw-Hill, 1977).

67UPI, 2 Oct. 1974; "Dramatic Rise Found in Young Drinkers' Accident Rates," *Kalamazoo* (Michigan) *Gazette*, 19 July 1976, p. A–12; and Jerry Cheske, "The Young Driver: Michigan's #1 Traffic and Insurance Problem," *Motor News* (Automobile Club of Michigan), Apr. 1977, pp. 14ff.

68See "School-Age Drunks: A Fresh Worry," *U.S. News and World Report*, 14 Apr. 1975, p. 40; "Teen-Aged Alcoholism: It Makes for a Horrifying Story," *American School Board Journal*, 163 (Mar. 1976), 41–42.

69*New York Times*, 25 Nov. 1979, sec. 4, p. 6.

70See "When Retirement Doesn't Happen," *Business Week*, 19 June 1978, pp. 72–89.

71M. Powell Lawton, ed., *Community Planning for an Aging Society* (Stroudsburg, Pa.: Dowdon, Hutchinson and Ross, 1976).

72See Claire Townsend, *Old Age: The Last Segregation* (New York: Grossman, 1972), for an account of mistreatment and neglect in nursing homes.

73Terri Schultz, "The Handicapped, a Minority Demanding Its Rights," *New York Times*, 13 Feb. 1977, sec. 4, p. 8.

74Editorial, *New York Times*, 18 Nov. 1979, sec. 4, p. 18.

75Terri Schultz, "The Handicapped."

76Arthur G. Neal, "Role of Physical Attractiveness in Impression Formation," *Psychonomic Science*, 19 (25 May 1970), 241–43; Karen Dion et al., "What's Beautiful Is Good," *Journal of Personality and Social Psychology*, 24 (Dec. 1972), 285–90; David Bar-Tel and Leonard Saxe, "Perceptions of Similarly and Dissimilarly Attractive Couples and Individuals," *Journal of Personality and Social Psychology*, 33 (June 1976), 772–81; Sharon D. Peters and N. Theodore Greenstein, "Physical Attractiveness as a Diffuse Status Characteristic? An Expectation-Status Approach," paper read at Annual Meeting of the North Central Sociological Association, Cincinnati, 1978.

77John Salvia et al., "Attractiveness and School Achievement," *Journal of School Psychology*, 15 (Spring 1977), 60–67.

78Robert J. Pellegrini et al., "Physical Attractiveness and Self-Disclosure in Mixed-Sex Dyads," *Psychological Record*, 28 (Fall 1978), 509–16.

79Ellen Berscheid and Elaine Walster, "Physical Attractiveness," in Leonard Berkowitz, ed., *Advances in Experimental Social Psychology* (New York: Academic Press, 1974), vol. 7, pp. 158–215; Eugene W. Mathes, "Effects of Physical Attractiveness and Anxiety in Heterosexual Attraction over a Series of Five Encounters," *Journal of Marriage and the Family*, 37 (Nov. 1975), 769–73.

80Kary Lee Meiners and John P. Sheposh, "Beauty or Brains: Which Image for Your Mate?" paper presented at American Psychological Association, Washington, D.C., Sept. 1976.

81Karen Dion, "Physical Attractiveness and Evaluations of Children's Transgressions," *Journal of Personality and Social Psychology*, 24 (Nov. 1972), 207–13. The only experiment in which attractiveness was not always an asset was in rating applicants for managerial positions, among whom attractiveness was judged to be an asset to men but a handicap to women. (See *New York Times*, 22 June 1980, sec. 3, p. 16.)

82Amerigo Farnia et al., "Physical Attractiveness and Mental Illness," *Journal of Abnormal Psychology*, 86 (Oct. 1977), 510–17.

83Jean Mayer, "Genetic, Traumatic and Environmental Factors in the Etiology of Obesity," *Psychological Review*, 33 (Apr. 1953), 472–508; Richard E. Keesey and Terry L. Powley, "Hypothalamic Regulation of Body Weight," *American Scientist*, 63 (Sept./Oct. 1975), 558–65; Michael F. Lakat, "In Pursuit of Hunger: Physiological Considerations," *Intellect*, Feb. 1977, pp. 261–62.

84Janet Chase, "Obese in the Land of Milk and Honey," *Human Behavior*, June 1975, pp. 56–63; also, Evan Charles et al., "Childhood Antecedents of Adult Obesity: Do Chubby Infants Become Obese Adults?" *New England Journal of Medicine*, 275 (1 July 1976), 6–9.

85Saul D. Feldman, "The Presentation of Shortness in Everyday Life—Height and Heightism in American Society: Toward a Sociology of Stature," in Saul D. Feldman and Gerald W. Thielbar, eds., *Life Styles: Diversity in American Society* (Boston: Little, Brown, 1976), pp. 437–43.

86Cecil A. Gibb, "Leadership," in Gardner Lindzey, ed., *Handbook in Social Psychology* (Reading, Mass.: Addison-Wesley, 1954), vol. 2, pp. 884–89.

87Leland Deck, "Short Workers of the World Unite," *Psychology Today*, Aug. 1971, p. 102.

88Robert G. Meyer, "Legal and Social Ambivalence regarding Homosexuality," *Journal of Homosexuality*, 2 (Spring 1977), 281–87.

89Thomas R. Clark, "Homosexuality as a Criterion Predictor of Psychopathology in Non-Patient Males," and Andrea Kincses Oberstone and Harriet Sukoneck, "Psychological Adjustment and Style of Life of Single Lesbians and Single Heterosexual People," papers presented at the Annual Meeting of the Western Psychological Association, Sacramento, April 1975.

90David E. Newton, "Homosexual Behavior and Child Molestation: A Review of Evidence," *Adolescence*, 13 (Spring 1978), 29–43.

91Laud Humphries, "Exodus and Identity: The Emerging Gay Culture," in Martin P. Levine, ed., *Gay Culture: The Sociology of Male Homosexuality* (New York: Harper & Row, 1979), pp. 134–47.

92Judith Blake, "The Changing Status of Women in Developed Countries," *Scientific American*, 23 (Sept. 1976), 137–47.

Marc Anderson.

URBAN AND RURAL PROBLEMS 14

With one more major company—Union Carbide Corp.—close to leaving New York City and moving to an office campus near Danbury, Conn., and another—Time Inc.—thinking about moving, it is clearly time for business to consider carefully the long-run effects of its flight from the cities. . . .

The nation, and especially its business leaders, have not examined whether it makes sense to go on spending resources to transfer the economically viable activities remaining in existing cities to the suburbs, rather than using those resources to try to save and restore the cities.

Cities, no longer primary manufacturing centers, wholesale-retail marketplaces, or preferred residences for the middle class, are now losing those very activities that . . . have always seemed to belong downtown: the headquarters, "nerve center" functions. . . .

This process cannot continue without destroying major cities as significant forces in the country's economic and social life. The U.S., some urban experts believe, may become the world's first industrialized urbanized country without important cities. . . .[1]

Not far from the luxurious hotels and sparkling beaches of southern Florida, where the affluent loll in the sun, lie sandy snake-infested fields where stoop laborers toil under the sun. Each is just another pair of hands in the army of migrant workers who harvest the winter vegetable crop.

On some of the great corporate farms, he earns barely enough to pay for three tasteless meals, a filthy mattress to sleep on and a bottle of wine to dull his backache. Unable to pick vegetables fast enough to keep up with the charges that are deducted from his paycheck, he lives in virtual bondage. . . .[2]

379

Over 80 million people in the United States live in areas of over a million people each. The traditional forms of social organization were never designed to manage such complexes. Such things as county commissioners, neighborhood planning, zoning, and civic spirit apply readily to cities of 25,000 people, or even 250,000 people, but become almost meaningless in a city of 10 million. And even as urban living has changed, living in the country has changed also. The self-sufficient family farm, probably the rural equivalent to the small city in urban society, is becoming less typical of rural living. Corporation management, research specialists, and automation seem natural enough in the city, but strange indeed on the farm. Moreover, important changes in either urban or rural areas upset the relations between them. Throughout these changing ways of life, familiar symptoms of social problems appear.

The Tremendous Growth of Cities

The city itself is not new, for ancient history revolves around such cities as Rome, Athens, Jerusalem, and Constantinople. What *is* new is (1) the great size of modern cities; (2) the tremendous number of cities; and (3) the rapidly increasing proportion of the population that lives in cities.

GREAT SIZE

Ancient and medieval cities were not very large by modern standards. London in 1400, with only about 35,000 inhabitants, was the largest city in Europe. Modern cities by contrast are behemoths. If we consider only that portion of the city population living within the corporate limits, the United States has six urban centers each with more than a million people. New York, Chicago, Detroit, Los Angeles, Philadelphia, and Houston together contain more than 17 million people. To define as urban, however, only the population living inside the corporation limits is grossly unrealistic. Many of the people who are functionally a part of large cities actually live outside the city limits. New York City contains approximately 8 million people, but greater New York contains over 11.5 million. In 1950 the United States census for the first time reported "urbanized areas," including as "urban" all of the people who are part of urban life. There were 12 Standard Metropolitan Statistical Areas[3] in the United States, *each with over a million population* in 1950; the 1960 census added 12 more; and by 1977 the number had climbed to 37.[4]

THE NUMBER OF CITIES

There is a tendency to equate urban life with life in New York or Chicago, but there are 7,062 "urban" places in the United States.[5] Most of these are incorporated places of 2,500 or more population, but also included are some smaller incorporated places and some unincorporated areas, around cities, that are definitely urban in character. The United States is not organized primarily around any one city, any five cities, or any hundred cities. Certain industries and certain products may be identified with a particular urban center (for example, automobiles with Detroit and garment-making with Philadelphia and New York), but there are at least several hundred cities serving as primary sources for employment, commerce and trade, public utility services, newspaper publication, and many other goods and services that are an essential part of modern life. The early part of the present century saw unparalleled growth and centralization in the largest cities, and more recent decades have brought increases in the numbers of smaller cities. The present 7,062 urban places represent a gain of 2,321 over 1950 and a gain of 3,598 over 1930.

ULATION IN CITIES

In 1790 only 5 percent of the United States population was urban. New York had fewer than 60,000 people. By 1970, 74 percent of the population was defined as urban, as figure 14–1 shows. The urban portion of the population ranges from about half in the South to almost four-fifths in the Northeast. In 10 separate states more than four out of five inhabitants live in urban areas, and in 42 states half or more of the population live in urban areas. Some 139 million people live in Standard Metropolitan Statistical Areas delimited by the United States Census. The United States has become predominantly an urbanized nation. Large central cities and extensive metropolitan areas are a fundamental part of modern life. The development of such urban centers has created a whole series of new social problems.

Figure 14–1
Distribution of the United States population, 1970.
Source: Department of Commerce, Bureau of the Census.

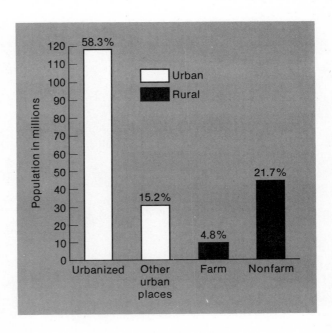

The Problems of Cities

The census usually defines places as urban if they are incorporated or have over 2,500 people. This definition is not adequate for all purposes. Even the census has moved toward a *social* definition of city, a definition that recognizes the peculiar qualities of urban life as well as the number of people included. The classic sociological definition of a city is "a relatively large, dense, and permanent settlement of socially heterogeneous individuals."[6] Many of the special problems of cities result from large numbers of unlike persons living very close together.

Cities typically are inhabited by large numbers of people who were not born there. Although birth rates vary widely from one area of the city to another, for the city as a whole they have been low. Since cities have been growing rapidly, this means that large numbers of city residents have migrated there from rural areas.

During the early part of the present century, there were two principal streams of migration to the cities. One stream was composed of ethnic and racial minorities. Until the 1920s, various European groups—Italians, Greeks, Poles, Germans, Russians, and others—brought their families and settled in the deteriorating central areas of the cities near the factories and other places where they worked. They created the "Little Italys," the "Germantowns," and so on, remnants of which can be found in many cities today.

Mulberry Street in New York City's Little Italy. Such neighborhoods are remnants of the turn-of-the-century migration to the cities of various European groups.
(Yan Lukas, Photo Researchers, Inc.)

TABLE 14–1   Forty Largest SMSAs in 1980 and Projected to 1990

	SMSA	1980 Population	1990 Population	Percent Change
1.	New York	9,173,000	8,437,000	− 8.0
2.	Chicago	7,032,000	7,087,000	+ .8
3.	Los Angeles–Long Beach	7,027,000	7,012,000	− .2
4.	Philadelphia	4,782,000	4,741,000	− .9
5.	Detroit	4,346,000	4,258,000	− 2.0
6.	Boston	3,917,000	3,986,000	+ 1.8
7.	Houston	2,740,000	3,754,000	+37.0
8.	San Francisco–Oakland	3,210,000	3,314,000	+ 3.2
9.	Dallas–Fort Worth	2,795,000	3,285,000	+17.5
10.	Washington, D.C.	3,074,000	3,247,000	+ 5.6
11.	Nassau–Suffolk, N.Y.	2,740,000	2,937,000	+ 7.2
12.	Anaheim–Santa Ana–Garden Grove, Ca.	1,970,000	2,731,000	+38.6
13.	San Diego	1,826,000	2,455,000	+34.4
14.	Atlanta	1,930,000	2,334,000	+20.9
15.	St. Louis	2,368,000	2,326,000	− 1.8
16.	Baltimore	2,176,000	2,287,000	+ 5.1
17.	Minneapolis–St. Paul	2,065,000	2,170,000	+ 5.1
18.	Pittsburgh	2,255,000	2,118,000	− 6.1
19.	Tampa–St. Petersburg	1,511,000	2,097,000	+38.8
20.	Phoenix	1,381,000	1,964,000	+42.2
21.	Denver–Boulder	1,560,000	1,963,000	+25.8
22.	Newark	1,937,000	1,823,000	− 5.9
23.	Miami	1,513,000	1,806,000	+19.4
24.	Cleveland	1,908,000	1,764,000	− 7.5
25.	Riverside–San Bernardino–Ontario, Ca.	1,375,000	1,659,000	+20.7
26.	Ft. Lauderdale–Hollywood, Fla.	980,000	1,550,000	+58.2
27.	San Jose	1,280,000	1,539,000	+20.2
28.	Milwaukee	1,435,000	1,467,000	+ 2.2
29.	Seattle	1,428,000	1,432,000	+ .3
30.	Cincinnati	1,371,000	1,355,000	− 1.2
31.	Portland, Oregon	1,168,000	1,355,000	+16.0
32.	Kansas City	1,301,000	1,328,000	+ 2.1
33.	San Antonio	1,082,000	1,318,000	+21.8
34.	New Orleans	1,168,000	1,303,000	+11.6
35.	Buffalo	1,300,000	1,252,000	− 3.7
36.	Columbus, Ohio	1,114,000	1,220,000	+ 9.5
37.	Indianapolis	1,156,000	1,203,000	+ 4.1
38.	Sacramento	982,000	1,200,000	+22.2
39.	Hartford–New Britain–Bristol, Conn.	1,058,000	1,082,000	+ 2.3
40.	Salt Lake City–Ogden	871,000	1,076,000	+23.5

SOURCE: Reprinted from *U.S. News and World Report*, 15 Oct. 1979, p. 69. Copyright 1979 U.S. News and World Report, Inc.

In the midst of World War I, there also developed a large-scale migration of blacks from the rural South to the urban North. With this movement residential segregation of blacks developed, and the Harlems and "black belts" made their appearances.

The second major rural-to-urban stream of migration was composed of lower- and middle-class farm people, whites whose families had come from northern and western Europe a few generations before. These were predominantly young people without families who, being less subject to discrimination and better assimilated to American culture, were more successful in the competition for jobs and status.

Cities became segregated early, and the various groups lived in different areas of them. The very center of the city tended to be devoted to business and commercial use with few, if any, people actually living there. Immediately adjacent were areas of deteriorating buildings owned by people who hoped to sell their land at great profit for expanding business use. Into these areas poured the lower-class immigrants and blacks. Male dropouts from middle-class white society also settled in these areas, which bore such labels as the Bowery or Skid Row.

Beyond the deteriorated zone were middle-class residential areas where slums and tenements were replaced by single houses with lawns and other amenities. There was something of an inverse correlation between income level and distance from the city center, with the wealthiest families living on the urban fringes that came gradually to be called suburbs.[7]

Not until the 1930s did a major suburban movement begin. The automobile and the highway system made it possible; the steadily worsening conditions of city living made it desirable to many people. The movement was slow until after World War II, when cities almost literally exploded into the surrounding countryside. Many urban problems are linked to the original pattern of urban settlement and to the changes wrought by the shifting patterns of migration. Included among them are (1) the racial and ethnic composition of cities; (2) slums and housing problems; (3) economic and political problems; (4) pollution and congestion; and (5) suburban sprawl.

RACIAL AND ETHNIC COMPOSITION

The racial composition of cities changed drastically after World War II. Many of the white residents who had formerly inhabited most of the middle-class residential areas fled to the suburbs, leaving a vacuum that was filled by immigrating blacks.

Between 1940 and 1960 the black populations of New York and Philadelphia doubled, those of Detroit and Chicago tripled, and that of Los Angeles multiplied five times. During the 1960s blacks became the majority in 14 cities of over 25,000 population. Washington, D.C., with 71.1 percent blacks, has the largest number of blacks among cities with black majorities; among cities of over 200,000 people, Newark and Atlanta have a majority of blacks. Compton, California; East St. Louis, Illinois; Gary, Indiana; and East Orange, New Jersey, are cities of over 50,000 that are mostly black. Finally, Bessemer, Alabama; Willowbrook, California; Westmont, California; East Cleveland, Ohio; Florence-Graham, California; Highland Park, Michigan; Petersburg, Virginia; Greenville, Mississippi; and Prichard, Alabama, have black majorities.

Still far ahead in the total number of blacks living there are New York and Chicago. New York has 1,666,636 blacks, or 21.2 percent of the total population; Chicago has 1,102,620 blacks, 32.7 percent of its total.

The significance of these changes lies in what they signify for the future. What problems are created when a minority group in 20 years' time is able to replace 50 percent of the population of our major cities?

A pattern was established when the first waves of black migration north were forced into already overcrowded residential areas. Most were able to secure only menial work. Succeeding waves encountered the same conditions. White realtors employed "blockbusting" techniques, threatening whites who lived adjacent to black areas with loss of property values as the first blacks moved in. When the whites panicked and sold, the realtors rented the properties to blacks at vastly inflated prices.

The violent conditions of urban life today are not wholly new. For example, more than a dozen black homes in transitional neighborhoods in Chicago were bombed from 1917 to 1919. A bloody five-day riot occurred in July 1919, in which 38 people were killed and more than 500 injured.[8]

This was a prelude to the urban riots of the 1960s. They started in Birmingham, Alabama, in the spring of 1963 and quickly spread to New York, Rochester, Chicago, and Philadelphia—then to dozens of other cities. In 1967 there were 233 riots in 168 cities, causing 82 deaths, and 3,400 injuries and resulting in 18,800 arrests. Following the assassination of Dr. Martin Luther King, in 1968, there were 202 riots in 172 cities, causing 43 deaths and 3,500 injuries and resulting in 27,000 arrests.

Though the government is officially committed to desegregation and the elimination of black urban ghettos and poverty, there are dominant counter-forces in the urban scene. As whites move out, blacks move in and the central city becomes a black enclave in which joblessness, poverty, and despair are the order of the day. During the 1960s central cities gained 3.2 million black residents, but lost 600,000 white residents.

It should not be overlooked, however, that there are substantial ethnic groups in the cities other than blacks. At bottom, the problem is not a racial problem but simply one of socioeconomic status compounded by discrimination. The groups to whom cities are least hospitable are those who lack the education, the skills, and in some cases the motivation, to rise out of poverty and dependence.

Since the end of World War II, the United States has had a large influx of people from Puerto Rico. By 1950 there were some 300,000 United States residents of Puerto Rican origin. In 1960 there were 888,000 and in 1973 there were over 1.5 million.[9] They are heavily concentrated in the urban Northeast, with about 70 percent living in New York City. Their native tongue is Spanish.

Most Puerto Rican migrants find jobs at what appear to them to be relatively high wages. But the cost of living is also high, and the temptations to buy unwisely are formidable. The migrants cannot protest effectively when they are gouged by unfeeling landlords, because their frequent lack of schooling and language difficulties make them easy prey. If they try to settle personally with their persecutors, as would be permissible in their former homes, they run afoul of the law—a law that always appears to be loaded against them. Irresponsible merchants, who promise payments of only a few pennies a day, urge naïve migrants to purchase automobiles, television sets, furniture, and a host of other items that they would dearly love to have but cannot afford. When these items must be repossessed, the merchants' stereotypes of the untrustworthiness of Puerto Ricans are confirmed, and the migrants have one more bit of evidence of the hostility and unfairness of the world around them.

The great importance assigned to skin color in the United States results in the subjection of most Puerto Ricans, some of whom are very dark in color, to economic and residential segregation, a type of discrimination many of them have never experienced before. The one way by which an other-than-white Puerto Rican can demonstrate to those around him that he is not an American black is through his use of the Spanish language. Consequently, the same process of speaking another language that holds him back occupationally, and complicates his life in countless other ways, becomes functional to him in this area. Studies have shown a marked correlation between darkness of skin color and reluctance to give up Spanish for English.[10]

The family lives of Puerto Ricans also suffer. Many of them come from the lower socioeconomic level with its tradition of family instability. Whatever stabilizing influence the family had in Puerto Rico becomes lost in the anonymity of the American city. Relatively high wages, loneliness, racial discrimination, and bewilderment combine to encourage the formation of casual associations between men and women, although families both on the continent and in Puerto Rico try to protect their members against them.

At least one other group of rural–urban migrants who suffer from the same lack of education and skill as blacks and Puerto Ricans is of white, Anglo-Saxon stock. Since the 1930s, there has been an increasing migration of whites from the economically depressed mountain areas of the upper South to northern and midwestern cities.[11] So-called hillbillies from West Virginia, Kentucky, Missouri, and Tennessee have fled their worn-out farms and worked-out mines for the rumored high wages in the cities.

According to American folklore, the hillbilly migrants should have been desirable additions to the cities. Municipal authorities, landlords, employers, social workers, and ministers, however, have found these migrant whites almost impossible to cope with. They congregate in slum areas as thickly as any racially segregated group. Their disregard for, and suspicion of, law and order is reinforced by a social code that encourages casual sex contacts, hard drinking, and the settling of disputes by resort to fists, knives, and guns. Employers often find them unreliable, creditors find them evasive, and landlords run the risk of losing their furnishings along with the rent that is often overdue.

For one thing, many hillbilly migrants maintain primary allegiance to their communities in the South rather than to their new homes in the cities. When they get into a scrape or lose their jobs or fall behind in the rent, they sometimes just quietly pack up and return home until the whole thing blows over. Needless to say, this is disconcerting to law enforcement officers, landlords, and creditors.

Moreover, the migrants find the cities as hard on them as they are on the cities. With their typically large families, they usually are unable to find housing that they can afford outside of slum districts. Because of this, many landlords exploit them unmercifully and use the law to coerce payment. Merchants encourage them, as they do all minorities, to use credit in ways that they have no experience with, and then repossess the merchandise when it cannot be paid for. The city appears to these minorities to be a hostile place where they can expect fair and predictable treatment only from their own kind.

SLUMS AND HOUSING PROBLEMS

The segregation of minorities in cities and problems of inadequate housing are closely linked. Both are tied, of course, to inadequate incomes. An estimated 10 percent of the nation's occupied housing is classified as dilapidated or deteriorating or lacks adequate plumbing facilities.[12] For whites the figure is 8 percent, but for nonwhites it is 29 percent. The figures also show that relatively few whites have poor housing in the cities and suburbs, and that both white and nonwhite housing is worse in small towns and rural areas than it is in larger cities. More will be said about this later.

The cities' housing problems are concentrated in nonwhite areas. This trend will continue to be true, because the principal route to the improvement of housing is for middle- and upper-income families to construct new housing. Such new construction would make the housing that is vacated available to those lower-income families who are able to compete for it. These are mainly white families.

That race discrimination is an even more powerful determinant of inadequate housing than is income is shown by the fact that even blacks with high incomes tend to live in poverty areas. Within the segregated poverty areas, blacks frequently have to pay more for comparable housing than do whites. Table 14–2 presents data on the relative cost of housing in mainly black neighborhoods compared with mainly white neighborhoods with the same percentages of "sound" and "dilapidated" housing. Of the seven urban

TABLE 14–2   Rents Paid by Blacks and Whites for Comparable Housing

City	Average Monthly Rent in Median Black Census Tract	Average Monthly Rent in White Census Tract with Comparable Housing	Black Rent Minus White Rent for Comparable Housing
Atlanta	$37	$38	$ − 1
Baltimore	66	55	11
Detroit	61	60	1
Los Angeles	58	56	2
New York			
Manhattan	59	61	− 2
Brooklyn	60	51	9
Philadelphia	49	40	9

SOURCE: Estimates provided by Barbara Bergmann, Department of Economics, University of Maryland, as reported in U.S. Department of Health, Education and Welfare, *Toward a Social Report* (Washington, D.C., 1969), p. 38.

areas, three showed blacks paying much higher rents. In the other four there was no significant difference in rental costs to whites and blacks.

The United States has been attempting to improve housing conditions for the urban poor since the 1930s, with meager results. One effort has been the construction of public housing. Over the last 40 years some 1.4 million low-rent, federally-administered housing units were constructed.[13] Numerically this is a drop in the bucket. The program never really got off the ground because, from the very beginning, powerful real estate and business interests opposed it. Moreover, the public housing that was constructed tended to segregate its inhabitants even more rigidly than in the city at large. Residents of public housing often became objects of scorn even to the poor people who lived in surrounding areas.

Beginning in 1949 urban renewal programs began to renew deteriorated central city areas and to provide decent housing in those areas. The plan was simply to permit local urban renewal agencies to buy up slum properties, demolish them, and sell the properties to private developers, who would then build low- to moderate-priced housing. If the aim was to provide low-cost housing for the people who were displaced from the slums, Herbert Gans has shown how ill-conceived the program was. "Suppose," he said, "that the government decided that jalopies were a menace," and took them away from their owners. Suppose, also, that the government gave to each former owner a hundred dollars to buy a good used car. Then, suppose it made large grants to the automobile manufacturers to lower the cost—although not necessarily the price—of Cadillacs by a few hundred dollars. It does not take much insight to see that the auto manufacturers would benefit tremendously and the jalopy owners little if at all.[14]

This has been the case with urban renewal. From 1949 through fiscal 1967, urban renewal provided only 107,000 new and 75,000 rehabilitated housing units. It had actually demolished more housing units (383,000) than it had completed! The time required for urban renewal projects to be completed has been estimated at six to nine years.[15]

Urban renewal actually increased the housing problem of the urban poor. No provision ordinarily was made for the people who were displaced from slums scheduled for razing. They were simply crowded into adjacent slums, making them even more uninhabitable. When new housing finally was completed on the original site, it was likely to be so costly as to be available only to middle- and upper-class people. Many blacks refer to urban renewal contemptuously as "Negro removal."

Another federal government effort to upgrade housing for the urban poor began in 1968, when Congress authorized the Federal Housing Administration to guarantee mortgages for poor people seeking to buy houses in so-called high-risk areas. The FHA initiated the program with enthusiasm, and large numbers of mortgages were thus financed. By the middle of 1972, however, the program had become a national scandal of unprecedented proportions. Undeniable evidence appeared that real estate dealers, lending institutions, lawyers, FHA officials, and even the prestigious credit rating firm of Dun & Bradstreet had conspired on a large scale to defeat the purposes of the program, to enrich themselves, and once again to exploit the poor.

Details of the situation varied from city to city, but the basic pattern was the same. Real estate speculators would buy old houses and make some superficial repairs on them. They would then arrange to sell the houses with very small down-payments to low-income families, promising them that their monthly payments would also be low. Corrupt FHA appraisers would then appraise the properties at wildly inflated values, and mortgages based on those values would then be arranged. Buyers would also be encouraged and assisted to inflate their ability to pay. After the unsuspecting buyers moved in, they often found that either the houses needed major repairs that they could not afford, or the payments were much higher than promised, or both. Faced with a desperate situation, they often did the only thing they could: they simply moved out, abandoning the properties and forfeiting their down-payments. The properties then reverted to the FHA, which had guaranteed the mortgages. No accurate figures are available, but one estimate is that almost 250,000 units were involved.[16]

The latest federal effort to assist the poor to secure adequate housing is a rent subsidy program established by the Housing and Community Development Act of 1974. This measure provides for the government to help pay rent for families whose income is less than 80 percent of the median income in their communities. A major advantage of the program is that, unlike other approaches to public housing, it allows poor families to disperse over the entire urban area. Unfortunately, during the first two years of operation of the program, only 33,000 families were helped by it.[17] Obviously, the nation is still far from finding solutions to the problem of securing adequate housing for the urban poor.

ECONOMIC AND POLITICAL PROBLEMS

The cities' economic and political problems are tied intimately to the flight of whites to the suburbs, leaving the central city to impoverished minorities. For decades, cities have been confronted with problems of increasingly inadequate revenues. Even before the suburban exodus, cities were having problems building and maintaining streets; providing police, fire, and sanitation services; and offering quality education to their children. Real estate taxes, which had traditionally carried the burden, were raised until they threatened to become confiscatory. Sales taxes were enacted, city income taxes inaugurated, city automobile taxes imposed, personal property levels raised, and so on. Each increase spurred the flight to the suburbs by those who could best afford the taxes and left the central cities inhabited by those who were least able to pay and most in need of its services.

Many people were somewhat aware of the financial plight of the cities, but few were prepared for the threatened bankruptcy of New York City in 1975. The New York situation is not typical: no other city maintains a city hospital system that costs $870 million a year, or a university system that costs $550 million. New York also pays its huge force of municipal employees unusually well, and provides them with a generous retirement system. Partly coerced by New York State, but partly on its own initiative, the city also provides among the most generous welfare benefits in the nation. For the time being New York seems to have averted the threat of bankruptcy, but its fiscal crisis is far from over. Moreover, while the New York situation is the most dramatic, many major cities are not much better off. City taxes cannot be raised much more, and city services, already cut severely, cannot be reduced much further. Sooner or later state and federal intervention will be required.

The cities' ability both to finance and govern themselves has been complicated by the rings of suburbs that surround most of them. For example, the control of illicit businesses such as gambling, prostitution, and after-hours liquor sales is almost impossible when all they have to do is to move across the corporate limits into a more hospitable suburb or into the open countryside.

As cities have become metropolises, any apparent relationship between the urban population and the government for that population has disappeared. A single metropolitan area may have several dozen local governments within it. These governments squabble about jurisdiction and find themselves unable either to provide adequate services or to enforce the law.

The 1970 census showed that relationships between the central cities and the suburbs are changing, and that the advantageous economic positions of many suburbs are quickly being eliminated. The process, generally, is one in which the old pattern of high population density in the inner city and low population density in the suburbs is being replaced by relatively more even population density over the whole urban area. In 1950, for example, the average population density in all "urbanized areas" in the United States was 5,408 per square mile. In 1960 it was only 3,752, and in 1970 it was down to 3,376.[18]

During the 1960s all central cities in the nation added only 700,000 persons within their 1960 corporate limits—less than 4 percent of the total increase in metropolitan population. Moreover, small central cities (under 100,000) actually suffered a loss of population of 0.6 percent within their 1960 boundaries. It probably comes as no surprise that such cities as Baltimore, Boston, Chicago, Detroit, Philadelphia, Pittsburgh, and St. Louis have begun to decline in population. What is surprising is that the same thing is happening to some established suburbs.

Most urban population growth has always occurred at the fringes of urbanized areas, and cities have grown by annexing such areas. As suburbs incorporated during the 1950s and 1960s, they blocked the efforts of central cities to expand, and central-city growth slowed appreciably. Now the same thing is happening to the growth of established suburban communities that are being surrounded by other suburban cities, such as Brookfield, Illinois; Burbank, California; Chevy Chase, Maryland; Dearborn, Michigan; and University City, Missouri.[19]

One growing reaction to the economic and political problems of proliferating municipalities has been to create regional governments based on counties and combining several city governments. Nashville, Tennessee, became the first city in the United States to consolidate, in 1963, when it combined with Davidson County and grew immediately from an area of 73 square miles and 175,000 people to an area of 533 square miles and 399,000 people. Since then, city-county consolidation has occurred in Jacksonville–Duval County, Florida; Indianapolis–Marion County, Indiana; and the city and borough of Juneau, Alaska. The National Association of Counties reported recently that city-county consolidation studies are underway in 70 other locations.[20]

A modification of this approach is a "two tier" system that has been initiated in Toronto and, in a different form, in Miami–Dade County, Florida. This approach retains and even permits the expansion of political power in the central city while "metropolitanizing" functions that both the central city and the suburbs are willing to delegate to an area government. A recent survey of urban counties reported that 114 of them were responsible for planning, and 82 had zoning authority. Most were also administering building and housing codes, and parks and recreation.

Most of these experiments are too new for detailed evaluation. In the meantime, although it is obvious that city problems are not solved simply by the act of combining government services, preliminary results are encouraging. In Nashville, for example, the city has added 51,000 people since consolidation, the downtown section shows signs of rejuvenation, more efficient sewer and water service is being provided, dual school systems have been eliminated, and law-enforcement agencies have been combined. At least as important, old city–county conflicts have been eliminated because the government no longer has to fear losing taxpaying businesses to surrounding communities. Taxes have continued to climb, but more slowly, officials believe, than would have been the case under the old system.

POLLUTION AND CONGESTION

When cities were smaller and scattered among vast open spaces, the possibility that such natural resources as land, air, and water might be threatened was scarcely considered. The early decades of the twentieth century, however, brought unmistakable signs of serious trouble. Cities became huge, heavy industries proliferated, and automobiles appeared by the millions.

Over Donora, Pennsylvania, in October 1948, a heavy, polluted fog settled, causing 20 deaths and making 6,000 persons ill. Then in December 1952, a similar smog over London produced 4,000 deaths while the fog held, and 8,000 more died from respiratory illnesses over the following two months. London was hit again in 1956 and 1962, causing the loss of 1,300 more lives. In New York City, temperature inversions in 1953, 1963, and 1966 produced smogs that killed 200, 400, and 80 people, respectively. Scientists now suspect that thousands of deaths every year, in cities all over the world, are caused by air pollution.

Research into the causes and cures of air pollution is relatively new, but two tentative sets of air quality goals have already been set up: short-range and long-range goals. The short-range goals aim at elimination of most of the presently recognized undesirable effects. The long-range goals set higher standards, because it is thought that all the effects of air pollution are not yet known.

An index of air pollution, based on the short-range goals, has been constructed for six American cities. The results are shown in table 14–3. None of the cities meets even the tentative short-range standards. On the basis of less detailed data, the National Center for Air Pollution Control has ranked 65 metropolitan areas in terms of the severity of their air pollution problems.[21] The ten worst cities are:

1. New York
2. Chicago
3. Philadelphia
4. Los Angeles—Long Beach
5. Cleveland
6. Pittsburgh
7. Boston
8. Newark
9. Detroit
10. St. Louis

As evidenced by increased media coverage, pollution has become the most widespread and serious environmental problem facing us today.
(Irene Springer)

The NCAPC estimates that 60 percent of the major air pollutants and 90 percent of the carbon monoxide come from automobiles and other vehicles. Industrial sources create 18 percent of pollutants, and utilities create another 21 percent. Emission control measures in industry and among the public utilities are beginning to help, and could help greatly in the future. A government report estimates that particulate matter coming from electric power generation could be reduced 80 percent by the year 2000 at a cost of only $11 million per year.[22]

Any major reduction in overall air pollution will require that something be done about the use of automobiles. Either the use of autos will have to be restricted drastically, or some new form of propulsion, such as steam or electricity, will have to be perfected. Automobiles are also a major source of urban congestion.

The twin problem to the pollution of the natural environment is congestion. As cities continue to spread outward, people live farther and farther from their places of work. Early in the morning, they pour through highways and streets into the city centers. There they merge with the heavy flow of commercial traffic, which keeps business and industry operating, and in the evening they fight their way back out again. Until recently, the system worked fairly well. The same streets that once accommodated horse and

TABLE 14–3   Air Pollution Indexes for Six Cities

City	Index*
Chicago	2.7
Los Angeles	2.2
Philadelphia	2.2
Washington	1.6
Cincinnati	1.6
San Francisco	1.1

*An index of 1.0 indicates barely adequate air. The higher the number, the greater the pollution.

SOURCE: U.S. Department of Health, Education and Welfare, *Toward a Social Report* (Washington, D.C.: Government Printing Office, 1969), p. 30.

buggy movement handled automobile traffic, and great superhighways were constructed to move traffic quickly from one city to another. But the city itself has proved the bottleneck. Central city streets fronted by ten-story buildings cannot easily be widened. It is no longer merely a joke that pedestrians move more rapidly than automobiles.

The number of automobiles in the United States has tripled since the end of World War II. Moreover, the 134 million automobiles, trucks, and buses are increasing eight times more rapidly than is the human population.[23] In recent years, the federal government doled out more than $4 billion per year for freeway construction. Each of those freeway miles ate up 40 acres of land, removing them from the tax rolls. Every freeway interchange consumed an additional 80 acres or so. Yet the problem grows worse.

The only answer appears to be in the development of adequate public transportation. With airports being pushed farther and farther from cities, attention is turning again to railroads as a possible solution. While one lane of a freeway can move only 2,400 people per hour, a train can move more than 20,000.

Pleas for mass transit systems in the United States, however, have so far gone virtually unheeded. In 1961 a federal law did require that mass transportation be considered as an essential part of city planning, and a program of loans and grants for experiments in the improvement of public transportation was established. Then in 1966, Congress took a significant step in favor of mass transit and against further highway development when it wrote into the law establishing the federal Department of Transportation a provision making it national policy to "preserve the natural beauty of the countryside." Finally, the Urban Mass Transportation Assistance Act of 1970 and a similar bill passed in 1974 promise to bring federal funding in this area up to one-fourth to one-half of that allocated to highway construction. San Francisco's Bay Area Rapid Transit (BART) is now open, new systems are being built in Washington, D.C., New York, and Atlanta, and one has been commissioned for Baltimore.

SUBURBAN PROBLEMS

The image that the term *suburb* suggests to many Americans is still that of the 1950s—a prosperous, comfortable "bedroom" community without in-

Urban renewal projects, such as "Project Pride," shown here, are an attempt to renovate slum housing and to provide decent housing for the urban poor. (HUD)

dustry or large businesses, and inhabited largely by white middle-class people, rearing their families in comfortable isolation from urban congestion, pollution, crime, and racial conflicts. Such communities were numerous then, and they still exist. Under the surface, however, many such communities appear far less than idyllic, and the 1970 census showed that they are far from representative of suburbia.

During the 1960s suburban living changed rapidly, but the ideal of attractive, homogeneous, residential suburbs held on. Disturbed homeowners found their tax rates soaring, crime rates rising, schools deteriorating, and pollution and congestion increasing. Even the sought-after cultural homogeneity turned out to be as much a curse as a blessing. More and more suburban residents came to disapprove of this violation of the American tradition of cultural pluralism, and began to experience a peculiarly suburban cultural dehydration. The original rationale had been that suburban living would be good for children, but increases in vandalism, larceny, and drug use by suburban youth indicated that they had not escaped the general malaise.

If any doubt remained that the suburbs had been transformed and were as much a problem as a solution, data from the 1970 census should have removed that doubt. While suburbs held about one person in five in 1940, and contained 19 million fewer people than the central cities, the 1970 census reported that 40 percent of Americans, some 76 million of them, were suburban residents. Suburbia now held 12 million more residents than the cities that spawned them. Figure 14–2 shows the tremendous growth of the suburbs compared to the growth of the central cities over the last 50 years.

Suburbia had become a gigantic, centerless development stretching in huge bands across the country. The bedroom communities had been swallowed up in urban complexes containing industrial plants, corporation headquarters, luxury hotels, and big league stadiums. Instead of the old pattern of commuting to the central city, half or more of suburban residents also worked in suburbs. A standard suburban cliché became, "Why, I haven't been downtown in months—or years!" These suburbanites are almost totally dependent on their automobiles—living in one town, working in a second, and shopping routinely in three or four others. The scattered nature of industries, businesses, shopping, and schools and the lack of major traffic patterns make mass transit impractical and complicate the problems.

What many people moved to the suburbs to recapture—a firm sense of identity with the community—becomes increasingly evasive in the sprawling, seemingly endless suburbs. Instead of a sense of community, there is a pervasive feeling of rootlessness. The suburbs have become the city all over again, but without the stability and tradition for which the central city stands. As this happens, all the characteristic urban pathologies—crime, racial and ethnic conflicts, vandalism, drug abuse—become increasingly common.

Figure 14–2
Growth of central cities and suburbs since 1920.

Source: *New York Times*, 30 May 1971. Reprinted by permission of The New York Times Company.

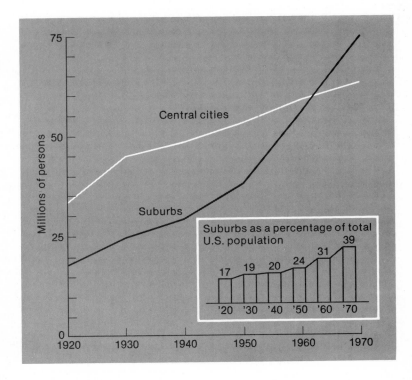

Rural Problems

For many people the illusion persists that while the city is a polyglot mixture of variant social and personal types, the rural environment is homogeneous. The facts do not support this belief. The rural environment includes 50,000-acre cattle ranches in Texas, 1,000-acre wheat farms in Kansas, and 10-acre turkey farms in Ohio; it includes mining camps in Colorado, logging operations in Washington, oil fields in Oklahoma, shantytowns in all regions, housing for migratory labor, trailer parks, and many other kinds of living.

At one time the rural population and the farm population were virtually synonymous. From 1790, when the first census was taken, to 1920, however, the nonfarm population grew to 39 percent of the rural population. Since 1920, while the national population has been growing rapidly, the rural nonfarm population has also grown, but the number of farmers has declined greatly.

Between 1940 and 1950 the losses in farm population offset the growth of the nonfarm population and the total rural population failed to grow. About 11 million people gave up farming during that one decade alone. By 1960 the farm population had declined to 15.6 million people. By 1970 it had dropped to 9.7 million, and it was down to 7.8 million by 1977.

Many factors contribute to the flight of people from the farms. The mechanization of agriculture, declining farm income, the expansion of industry into rural areas, and the economic opportunities available in the cities all play a part. From almost any viewpoint, the traditional rural way of life suffers by comparison with the alternatives.

LOW LIVING STANDARDS

The price paid for rural residence can be measured in many ways, for almost any index of material living standards shows up the inferior position of rural, farm-based residents. The median income of farm families, for example, is only about two-thirds that of urban families. Fewer farm families have modern plumbing and appliances in their homes, electricity, inside bathrooms, television, and other amenities that most city-dwellers consider necessities.

Many people reply to such comparisons by saying that life in the country is healthier for living and for rearing children. The intangibles of living are, of course, hard to measure. Moreover, not everyone would agree on what is desirable as a way of life. There is considerable evidence, however, that the nostalgia that many people feel for rural living is a matter of stereotype and of prior conditioning as much as of rational choice.

In the matter of health facilities, there are approximately three times as many physicians per 100,000 population in the most urban areas of the country as there are in the most rural areas. There are over 28,000 physicians in greater New York City, but hundreds of square miles of rural territory in other areas without even one. There are 71 dentists per 100,000 in the most urban areas, but only 27 in the most rural areas. Similar differences exist in the numbers of nurses and pharmacists in urban and rural areas.

The farm and rural populations also suffer in the area of educational attainment. Proportionately more rural children are below their age levels in school, and proportionately more drop out of school before graduation. Needless to say, proportionately fewer attend college.

UNFAVORABLE AGE STRUCTURE

One of the most pervasive of rural problems is born of the customary pattern of migration from rural to urban areas. Rural birth rates, particularly farm birth rates, are well above replacement requirements, whereas urban centers fall short of reproducing themselves by approximately 25 percent. Moreover, productivity per worker-hour on the farm is steadily increasing, requiring consistently fewer farmers to feed the same urban population. As a consequence, there is a steady stream of migration from rural to urban areas. Predominantly, the migrants are young adults. Children ordinarily are unable to migrate alone, but once they are of age or have completed school, they trek into the cities to find employment.

The problem is not migration per se, but its heavy concentration among the young adult age groups. The high rural birth rate means a relatively large dependent population that must be fed, clothed, housed, and educated. The burden of supporting this large number of children falls upon the productive adults whose ranks are seriously depleted via urban (or suburban) migration. Not only are the rural areas poorer to begin with, but they bear a disproportionate amount of the cost of raising future urban adults. Each young woman or man who migrates represents a lost investment to the country and financial gain to the city. Thus, rural areas inadvertently subsidize urban life.

MIGRATORY FARM WORKERS

Although living standards in rural areas are generally lower than those in the cities, American agriculture is plagued with one set of conditions that is particularly productive of human misery. These conditions result from seasonal demands for labor in the harvesting of perishable crops, particularly fruits, vegetables, cotton, and sugarbeets.

Approximately 540,000 farm workers, with up to 1,000,000 additional members of their families, travel three major routes in search of work. Each migratory stream begins in the South and follows the harvests north. The largest stream flows north and west from Texas, beginning in the spring and ending about December. A somewhat smaller stream originates in the southeastern states and moves north through the Atlantic states to New England. The third stream starts in southern California and moves north along the Pacific coast.

The poverty and degradation under which migrant workers live remains hidden from most Americans. Because they are not permanent members of any community, their presence can be ignored for a short period each year. Housing is usually provided for them by farm employers or by grower associations, removing them from most direct contact with other members of the community. They live in shacks and hovels; in hotels and rooming houses; in cars, trailers, and tents; or on the ground.

There are few trustworthy data on migrant workers' incomes, but by any standards they are abysmally low. In a fairly common pattern, recruiters of migrant laborers pick them up near the Texas border, transport them to the area of the current harvest, and charge them $1,000 for the service. Deductions are made from each day's pay until the $1,000 is paid. After this deduction the worker may be left with $4, $5, or $6 a day plus meals. In some instances the workers actually receive as little as $2 a day.[24] Another source reports that one corporate grower charges workers $42 or more per week for meals, or over half their wages. In addition, the grower sells wine to the workers nightly at three times the usual retail price. By payday the accumulated charges have literally wiped out the workers' earnings.[25]

The children of migratory workers have fewer educational opportunities and lower educational achievement than any other group of Americans. Because they are on the road from early spring until late fall, their school attendance is irregular. Even if their parents are interested in educating them, they may have to keep them out of school to work. Local school authorities often are reluctant to enforce compulsory school attendance laws where migrants are concerned.

About 140,000 children under 14 years of age travel with their migrant parents. Another 119,000 migrant workers are between 14 and 17 years of age. Thus, up to a quarter of a million youth may be being denied the opportunity to climb out of poverty by getting a minimum formal education.

This Maryland migrant farm worker's camp highlights the extremely poor living conditions these people have endured.

(Lew Merrim, Monkmeyer)

The force that promises to alter migrant labor patterns most significantly is that of technological displacement. It appears very likely that most of the harvesting now done by hand will soon be done by machines. Machines to pick tomatoes, asparagus, beans, lettuce, cucumbers, fruits, and berries are now in advanced stages of development. Perhaps within a decade, 90 percent of the present migrant agricultural labor will disappear. The unschooled and unskilled people, however, will still be with us. Their most likely destinations appear to be the slums of the cities.

AGRIBUSINESS AND THE DILEMMA OF PRICE SUPPORTS

Since the early 1930s the United States government has been committed to a program of price supports for farm products. The details of the program and the methods of its administration have varied, but the goal has been to maintain an equitable relationship between farm and nonfarm prices.

In the 1930s, farms by and large were family farms. Farming was a way of life instead of just a way of earning a living. It was a way of life that was widely admired and just as widely recognized as fraught with financial hazard. Cash income generally was low, and any income at all often was contingent on a favorable combination of weather and market conditions with abundant hard work. Children learned to be farmers by serving apprenticeships with experienced parents and neighbors whose folk skills and folk wisdom had accumulated for generations and were usually adequate in a society where farm families were almost as numerous as city families.

Urban conditions were changing, however. Industrialization brought undreamed-of efficiency. Living standards climbed. More and more people were drawn to the city. Considerable control was gained over market conditions. In the country the process was slower. Some farmers increased their efficiency more rapidly than others and did well financially.

Gradually, modern technology was applied to farm production, and the nature of farming changed drastically. Farm production became increasingly concentrated in the hands of large producers, who used more machinery and advanced farming techniques. These large producers no more tolerated the inefficiency of the old family farm than would a modern factory tolerate handloom methods. Farm production today is planned on the basis of market forecasts and makes maximum use of machine methods and automation.

The farm price support system has remained much the same through it all—only bigger and more complicated. The Department of Agriculture uses so-called crop loans to support the prices of staple crops such as wheat, cotton, rice, tobacco, peanuts, corn, oats, rye, and barley. In an attempt to limit production, it imposes acreage controls that restrict the number of acres that each farmer can plant of each crop; but because farm production continues to increase, this method of price support becomes more and more riddled with inequities.

Late in 1968 the President's Commission on Rural Poverty released a report entitled *The People Left Behind*, which made it very clear that price support and related programs do very little for small family farmers. Instead, price support programs have become a favorite way for a minority of members of Congress to enrich themselves and other large farmers, while the needs of small farmers continue to be ignored.

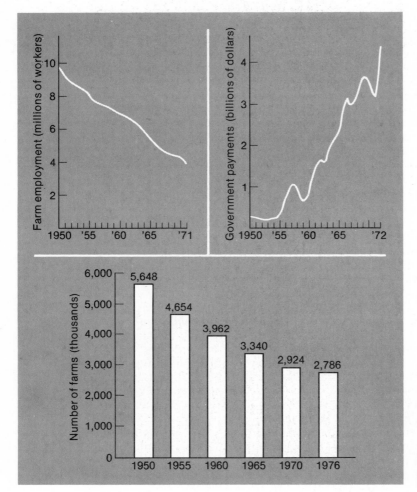

Figure 14–3
Farm subsidy payments rise as the number of farmers declines.

Source: *Time,* 24 Apr. 1972, p. 25. Reprinted by permission from *Time,* The Weekly Newsmagazine; copyright Time Inc., 1972. 1976 data from Associated Press, 2 Jan. 1976.

Crop support programs in Congress have received special attention from the southern senators and members of Congress who dominate the agriculture committees in both houses. It is perhaps no accident that cotton appears to receive especially preferential treatment. Some of that special preferential treatment benefits some members of Congress directly. Otherwise, it benefits relatively few large growers.

One former senator, an outspoken foe of federal spending, consistently voted for cotton subsidies that happened to benefit his 5,200-acre plantation. In 1967 the corporation that operated his plantation collected almost $168,000 in government subsidies. Then, in response to public outcry against huge subsidies being paid to the wealthy, Congress imposed a ceiling of $55,000 on the payments to any one farmer. This enterprising senator simply created eight new business entities to farm his plantation, and in 1973 he again received subsidies of approximately $170,000.[26]

A Hollywood actor who holds extensive cotton allotments in Arizona similarly reorganized his landholdings to avoid the new federal limits. Before the new law was passed, he collected $810,000 in subsidy payments. Afterward he collected $218,000. The government also paid more than $500,000, however, to others who had leased some of the actor's allotments from him.[27]

These attempts to limit subsidy payments were short-lived. A revision of the law in 1977 raised maximum subsidies to $40,000 per commodity for the year 1978, $45,000 for 1979, and $50,000 for 1980 and 1981. There is no limit on the number of commodities for which subsidies can be received.

The farm price support program was, and is, predicated upon the assumption that the United States is a nation of family farms. But the role of the family farm in agriculture declines steadily. Price supports have become special subsidies to agricultural business.

The Social-Disorganization Approach

RURAL DISORGANIZATION

The United States is becoming more and more urbanized, and the proportion of persons living in rural areas and engaged in farming has been steadily dropping. Until recently, however, most rural areas actually have been gaining population. The whole population has been growing so rapidly that rural areas could gain millions of people in a decade and still decline in proportion to the urban increases. So long as the rural–urban difference was purely a matter of *relative growth*, there was little general rural disorganization. Evidence of disorganization appeared as the rate of rural growth declined and some rural areas actually began to lose population.

To pinpoint any one date as the point when depopulation became disruptive of rural social organization would be artificially to break a long-term process. Nevertheless, it seems clear that the 1930s both aggravated and served as a further causal factor in the rural decline. The Great Depression actually reversed the usual flow of migration, sending many persons scurrying back to the farms where they could at least grow food. But at the same time the depression dealt a serious blow to the prestige and security of farming as an occupation. Foreclosures were frequent, and tenancy increased. When economic conditions finally bettered, the appeal of immediate high wages in the city often seemed more attractive than years of struggle to build up a farm again, perhaps only to have it destroyed in the next crisis. The 1930s also saw several years of severe drought, especially in the Middle West. Parts of several states became a vast dust bowl where sun and wind destroyed the land. The mass migrations to California and elsewhere were part of the first large-scale decreases in local rural populations. Then the increased mechanization of farming in most areas from the 1940s to the 1960s led to fewer but larger farms, with more rural depopulation. The introduction of modern technology changed the conditions of rural living faster than rural people and rural institutions could adapt.

Community institutions by and large must be supported by the local population. Schools and churches, the Granges, police and fire protection, medical and legal services, mills, elevators, feed stores, groceries, clothing stores, and all the rest must be paid for. In a growing community this is relatively easy, for in a sense the population can mortgage its future inhabitants. Services of all sorts are attracted to the community because of the promise of the future. But when growth stops, the burden shifts. Each existing family unit must bear a larger share of the costs. The mortgage for a contemplated new church, or even the minister's salary, becomes a much more serious problem. When the population actually begins to decline, the maintenance of *existing* services becomes difficult. Churches may have to double up and share a single minister's salary. Physicians drift away in search of patients, and the local grain elevator merges with one 30 miles away. Meanwhile, good roads and automobiles have drained away the economic lifeblood of smaller rural trading centers wherever larger towns are nearby. The decline renders the community a less attractive place in which to live and thus compounds itself. An increasing number of rural communities probably will face this kind of decline in the near future. Eventually, if large-scale corporate farming becomes the norm, it appears likely that the traditional rural institutions may disappear altogether. As rural society becomes increasingly urbanized, its institutions will approximate an urban or regional character.

URBAN DISORGANIZATION

Urban disorganization stems from growth rather than depopulation and from shifts in population and institutions within the city. Disorganization appears (1) in the physical conditions of life; (2) in city government and administration; (3) in the changing character of the urban population; and (4) in increasing congestion, especially in large cities.

THE PHYSICAL CONDITIONS OF LIFE   In addition to urban pollution and congestion, there are other symptoms of urban breakdown. Just outside the city's central business district there generally lies an area of utmost dilapidation. It has the misfortune to be cast between the high land values of the business district and the lower values of residential districts, and between the land use of a former day and that of the future. It has been largely deserted by its wealthy former residents and has been eagerly seized upon by businesses that cannot afford the high-rent district. Landlords hope that the high-rent district will expand outward and that, consequently, their properties will multiply in value. It is a short-run venture that has a way of seeming to become permanent. In the meantime the smellier, dirtier, noisier businesses, knowing full well that the area will go to ruin, move in, in anticipation of one day selling the land at a large profit. When, and *if,* that day arrives, the existing buildings will have to be torn down anyway to make room for more modern structures. Therefore, why bother to maintain them? Besides, taxes will be lowered as the buildings deteriorate, and since it is primarily the location that tenants are paying for, rents will not suffer.

Not all of this area is converted to business use. People also live in it. The processes are the same. The smells and dirt accumulate. Disgust, resentment, and antisocial tendencies are fostered. There are tenements, warehouses, and the symptoms of blight. The processes involved are as normal as those that create the new suburbs. The old patterns of land use have broken down and new ones have not yet appeared, unless, of course, the present patterns become permanent. When new patterns do appear, the blighted areas probably will move a little farther out.

CONDITIONS IN CITY GOVERNMENT AND ADMINISTRATION   About 75 years ago in *Shame of the Cities*,[28] Lincoln Steffens described the graft, corruption, and maladministration typical of large United States cities. So these are not new. Showing the sagacity that made him famous, Steffens drew upon the Old Testament, saying in effect, "The cause of sin was not Adam nor Eve, *but the apple!*" Had he been more social scientist than journalist he might have gone on to explain. The factors that keep people honest (including, among others, the unavailability of anything worth stealing, the high probability of being caught, and the searching eyes and souls of moralistic primary groups) are frequently absent in the city's governing circles. Television crime shows to the contrary, this kind of corruption often does pay—and handsomely. And, as Steffens concluded, as long as it pays it will exist.

Yet conditions already may have changed enough to make such corruption less blatant. The modern city boss appears to rely more on having decent government and less upon doing favors for the poor and the distribution of patronage. Moreover, the spotlight of public observation that was directed toward city administrations a few decades ago has more recently revealed a similar corruption in so-called clean rural areas.

CHANGING CHARACTER OF THE URBAN POPULATION   One of the major problems facing larger American cities is the continued creation of a stable middle class. Cities have always done this, the raw material being the immigrants first from northwestern and then from southeastern Europe. Now, however, that stable middle class is fleeing to the suburbs and being replaced by newcomers with whom the city is not dealing successfully. These new arrivals come not from Ireland or Italy but from places like Dothan, Alabama, and McComb, Mississippi. The newcomers by and large are black.

In their efforts to rehabilitate large cities, city officials have followed policies that have generally damaged rather than aided the ethnic minorities. Urban renewal programs have had the effect of creating middle-class neighborhoods by driving lower-class black residents out and attempting to bring white middle-class residents back from the suburbs. Driving the black migrants out of one area after another simply creates new and larger slums in other areas of the city.

This is not a new pattern in American history: only the race of the migrants differs. As early as the 1840s, for instance, the section of New York in which George Washington lived when he was inaugurated president had become a slum so violent that police did not dare to enter except in groups of six or more. And by the 1870s New York officials were much concerned about the exodus of middle-class people to surrounding towns. A journalist of that day commented, "New York has drifted from bad to worse and become the prey of professional thieves, ruffians, and political jugglers."

It is much harder for blacks today to bear their poverty and lack of status than it was for the European immigrants who entered a society in which most people were poor. Much of urban America today has high living standards and blacks share the nation's rising expectations for higher living standards. Their impatience is turning into bitterness, anger, and hatred. Not only do many blacks feel permanently alienated from American society, but they have recently turned to large-scale violence. In the deep hostility that prevails between the races, communication has largely broken down and life in the city is threatening to turn into armed warfare.

Nor is there any easy solution to the problem. Even as the dominant white society attempts to remove discrimination, it is confronted with the lack of formal education and technical training among blacks. Employers willing to hire blacks are unable to find qualified people to hire. Colleges willing to admit blacks cannot find enough qualified applicants.

The problem is not the responsibility just of the black community, of course. Its solution will require at least a generation and drastically revised policies by a host of official agencies. The greatest hope probably lies in the public schools, which have for generations been the principal means by which newcomers to the city have been able to qualify themselves for higher social and economic status. If the problem is to be solved in the near future, cities must come to practice discrimination in reverse, in favor of blacks instead of against them. Only in that way is a new, urban, black middle class likely to develop soon.

INCREASING CONGESTION   Many large cities are threatening to strangle upon their traffic problems. Frank Lloyd Wright's prophecy that cities will die and grass grow in the streets seems a remote possibility indeed, but while grass

Every city dweller is all too familiar with the problems of traffic congestion. (Marc Anderson)

may never grow in the streets, it may someday grow on the roofs of the cars caught in the daily five o'clock traffic jam.

Arithmetic explains the problem. Since 1930, automobiles have multiplied five times as rapidly as the nation's population, and currently they are increasing eight times as fast. As the use of private passenger cars increases, mass transportation is dwindling rapidly. The subways and commuter railroads are dwindling, the interurban bus has become a limited carrier, and the trolley car has almost disappeared.

Automobiles are the most convenient and the least efficient form of transportation. A single traffic lane in one hour can move 2,400 people in automobiles, 9,000 people in buses, 40,000 in subway trains, and 60,000 in express subway trains. Bewildered public officials are striving to determine how they can make mass transportation attractive enough to win back the motorist. It is a formidable undertaking. The tax laws generally favor the use of private automobiles. So-called highway-use taxes generally are collected as gasoline and excise taxes and fees, and only about 5 percent as direct tolls. On the other hand, public carriers generally pay high taxes on their right-of-way as well as on their equipment. In addition, they are subject to detailed public regulation, sometimes for frankly political purposes.

Commuting trains have real disadvantages. Their tracks often go to the wrong places, and their terminals are often poorly located. Moreover, unless trains can be used a fair proportion of the time, overhead and capital costs more than offset their potentially high output per traffic lane. Because commuter lines have lost most of their business during weekends and the middle of the day, they are forced to run at maximum speed for about 20 hours a week and to lie nearly idle most of the time.

The decentralization of the large city makes the problem even more difficult. No longer do cities simply spread outward along the main commuting and streetcar lines, and no longer is the traffic pattern simply from the outlying areas to the central business district. When people travel around the city in more nearly random fashion, public transportation becomes even more difficult to develop and maintain.

The foreseeable future will bring no rapid solution. Automobile use will become increasingly expensive and inconvenient. Cities will struggle to renovate and develop new mass transportation at increasing costs and with decreased efficiency. And cities are apt to develop increasingly bad reputations as places to live.

The Value-Conflict Approach

RURAL

In the beginning, virtually all farmers were enthusiastically behind the idea of price supports. Many of them still are. Other powerful groups, however, bitterly oppose controls and call for a return to what they call a free market. The Department of Agriculture has become a powerful advocate of price supports and controls. Joined with it in this effort are the Farmer's Union, the National Grange, and several other smaller farmers' organizations. The most articulate group in opposition to the government programs is probably the National Farm Bureau Federation. Recently the Committee for Economic Development, a respected organization of top businesspeople and educators, has joined the contest, arguing that the basic problem is that the United States has too many farmers and that the problems will not be solved until many marginal farmers have turned to some other activity.

The opponents of price support programs attack them as giving undue favoritism to farmers and label them as "socialism." To place floors under farm prices, they argue, is to give unfair protection to one segment of the economy, to nullify the operation of supply and demand, and to encourage overproduction.

The advocates of price supports reply that the above arguments involve gross distortions of fact, that farm production and industrial production are not comparable, that industry does not operate in a free economy, and that industrialists are seeking only to preserve their special advantages. First, they point out, industrial production is frequently concentrated in the hands of relatively few producers who arbitrarily restrict output either to maintain or to raise prices. On the other hand, there are millions of farmers and no few farmers control even a small fraction of the market. Farmers must produce and sell in a market over which they have no control. Farm produce cannot be held from the market indefinitely until prices rise. Without price supports, individual farmers chance ruin with each small adjustment in the market. Furthermore, they claim, industry has long enjoyed protection through tariff barriers, and more recently in the form of fast tax write-offs and rapid depreciation allowances on plants and machinery. The "free" economy advocated by business interests, they assert, is one in which industry would be free to profit and farmers would be free to go bankrupt.

Up to now, all efforts to get the government out of the farm price subsidy business have failed miserably. The program continues to increase in size and scope. With each passing year, however, the battle lines become more clearly drawn and the conflict grows sharper.

URBAN

The conflict between the advocates of the automobile and the advocates of mass transit grows increasingly bitter. Until now the proponents of highways and automobiles clearly have had the upper hand. Detroit is turning out automobiles at the rate of 22,000 per day, and the total number of autos, trucks, and buses is expected to reach 170 million by 1991. More than 32,000 miles of Interstate Highway System are completed, with the remaining 10,500 miles scheduled for completion soon. The Highway Trust Fund, which collects the revenue from a four-cent tax on each gallon of gasoline, has more than $5 billion per year earmarked for highway construction.

The backers of automobiles and highways point out that the Interstate Highway System has greatly reduced both the time and the cost required for travel. Motorists soon will be able to cross the country in 48 hours of driving without encountering a traffic light. The Federal Highway Administration reports that the Interstate system will have saved the public $107 billion by the time it is completed. This total results from savings in vehicle operating costs, reductions in travel time, and striking decreases in rates of death, injury, and property loss from accidents. They estimate that one life is saved for every five miles of Interstate completed.[29]

Since the mid-1960s, however, effective opposition to highway construction in general, and to the Interstate system in particular, has been mounting. Construction of urban segments of the system has been brought to a halt by lawsuits or administrative action in 15 separate cities. Loose coalitions of city interests have been joined by suburbanites fearing proposed new loops and radials to serve the new outer suburbs, and by mayors, governors, and environmentalists who oppose further despoilation of the countryside. Even some members of Congress have joined the opposition. Arrayed against them are the American Automobile Association, the American Trucking Association, the Automobile Manufacturers' Association, the American Road Builders Association, the Highway Users Federation for Safety and Mobility, and many other organizations estimated to spend $100 million per year on their Washington offices.[30]

The conflict is just beginning. The sudden public awareness of the energy shortage, including gasoline and diesel fuel, has raised the possibility that use of the highway system will have to be drastically curtailed, and that improved mass transit will become a necessity. The issue will be raised again, and in other forms.

The Personal-Deviation Approach

The terms *urban* and *rural* cannot begin to convey the full complexity of the phenomena to which they apply, for there is not one integrated urban culture, and there is not one integrated rural culture. Both urban and rural cultures are composites of a vast array of subcultures.

RURAL

Within the overall rural culture, for example, are Amish settlements, Ozark mountain cultural patterns, and snake-worshiping religious cults. The Amish refusal to bear arms in time of war, their insistence that formal education cease with the completion of the eighth grade, and their rebellious adolescents who secretly acquire jalopies pose the very least of the police's problems. Mountain-cultivated patterns of distilling moonshine; the exacting of personal vengeance for actual or alleged wrongs; and religious frenzies accompanied by floggings, self-mutilation, and even death make headlines in urban newspapers, reflect urgent preoccupations of the people involved, and forecast the clash of cultures. These practices all represent variability in group norms and the contribution of such variability to problem situations.

One of the most striking characteristics of rural culture is its ability to suppress deviation *within* the group. Rural communities are generally small, particularly in terms of the number of people involved; ties to the land tend to give them a highly permanent and stable population; and relations between country families are informal and personal rather than formal and impersonal. The group typically is homogeneous in religious and economic background; in attitudes, feelings, and beliefs; and in definitions of right and wrong. Constant pressure is brought to bear upon individuals to conform to the expectations of the group. Conform they must, for there is nowhere to go and no one to whom to turn to escape the social pressure. Rebellion is impractical for it is quickly discovered and easily punished.

Complete conformity to group expectations cannot be secured, of course, but no group sanctions can be expected to support deviant behavior and every effort is made to minimize its effect on the community as a whole.

Statistics on such matters generally show deviant behaviors—crime and mental illness, for example—to be relatively infrequent in rural areas. There are fewer recorded arrests, fewer trials, fewer jail sentences, and fewer admissions to mental hospitals. Burglaries and larcenies *are* fewer in number, precisely because of the closer regulation of individual behavior. But the means of handling violations that do occur make them seem to happen even less frequently than they actually do. Teenagers apprehended in a minor violation are likely to be turned over to their parents for "correction" rather than to be booked and to appear before a judge. The community is law-enforcement officer, judge, and penal agency all in one—and an effective one at that. Whether mental illness is less prevalent in rural areas is open to serious question. In the country, there *is* more likely to be an extra room for the not-quite-right relative, and the distances involved prevent him from bothering neighbors and other people. Besides, rural families are supposed to take care of their members. The whole of rural culture is oriented toward the discouragement of deviant personal behavior and, failing that, toward the elimination of its disruptive effects.

URBAN

Variability among group norms is at least as common in urban as in rural areas—probably more so. Large urban centers are the characteristic locations of many ethnic and racial groups. The Puerto Rican communities, the Mexican communities, the Harlems—all signify diverse cultural patterns. Americanization battles among the first, second, and third generations of immigrant families, the encroachment of one group upon another's territory, restrictive convenants, and the like, are all parts of typical intergroup conflict.

The anonymity and impersonality of the city are the keys to its attraction as a haven for deviancy. Urban residents are perhaps no more tolerant of deviancy *within their groups* than are rural residents. But in the city, one's face-to-face primary-group associations are limited to a very small proportion of the total population. There is no one set of mores or other accepted definitions, and each small group is unconcerned with the other's activities unless directly and seriously threatened by them. In a small rural area any deviant behavior is likely to bring censure, for "most everyone knows" and "most everyone cares." In the metropolis, on the other hand, it is not too difficult to find other persons who share one's problems and to congregate with them in areas unmolested save by curiosity-ridden tourists and the law. Most large cities embrace local counterparts of the Bowery and Greenwich Village. Though these names identify actual places in New York City, they have come to identify patterns of deviant behavior that extend far beyond their geographical boundaries.

The inner city is generally thought to be highly productive of anomie. Slums abound there, incomes and educational attainments are low, and symptoms of almost every sort of human pathology (mental illness, physical illness, drug abuse, alcoholism, sexual deviation, and so on) are high. The conditions of life are hard, and primary deviation is common.

Labeling also plays a role. When drug users, for example, are labeled as junkies, are treated as junkies, and begin to think of themselves as junkies, secondary deviation occurs and a whole lifestyle based upon those self-conceptions emerges. Similar examples based on alcoholism, homosexuality, mental illness, and other forms of deviance could be given. In time, deviant subcultures and contracultures may take shape. In perhaps no other context can all three of the sociological theories of deviance—cultural supports theory, labeling theory, and anomie theory—be seen operating so clearly.

Future Prospects

Inexorable time already has drastically altered the relation between city and country. The very terms *city* and *country* are no longer adequate to connote housing conditions, standards of living, occupations, political attitudes, or recreational patterns. Farmers now include trips to the grocery among their chores, and many city people have large gardens. The rural residents who can be identified on the street by their dusty and dilapidated automobiles, by the uncomfortable Sunday-dress appearance of their clothes, and by their twangy or drawling speech are a small minority. The labels "rube" and "city-slicker" are hardly applicable any longer. One can drive for miles along many highways and never be sure whether one is in the city or the country; it would take this entire page to describe all the types of settlements the census now defines as urban.

High-speed transportation and transmissible electric power have done much to urbanize the entire nation. Together they reduced the need for cities to be concentrated around a single center and stimulated suburbanization. They made it possible for urban residents to move outward and for rural people to have daily contacts inside the city. The rate of growth of the largest cities has slowed appreciably, while satellite cities around the central ones are growing at a furious rate. Urbanized areas are expanding, and the number of farmers required to feed a given urban population steadily declines. There is every reason to believe that these trends will continue—at least for the near future.

The central city will probably be one of the big problems of the next few decades. As its buildings and streets deteriorate, the unwillingness to pour large amounts of capital into reconstruction will foster slum conditions. The suburban movement narrows the tax base but increases the tax load, which somehow must be redistributed. Soot and grime will become greater enemies, and vehicular traffic may have to be banned from the city's center.

Traffic problems in general threaten to grow worse before they grow better. Much of the nation's street and highway system is in need of improvement or replacement, and even the most adequately planned thoroughfares are overcrowded almost from the time of completion. Again, large capital outlays will be required. How these improvements are to be financed already is a matter of bitter conflict among trucking interests; railroads; city, state, and federal governments; and automobile drivers.

A multiplicity of overlapping political and economic units can be expected. Many small communities, incorporated and unincorporated, rural and urban in varying degree, and with varying dependence upon larger communities, are coming to be the rule. As people dwell in one area, work in a second, and seek recreation in still a third, residence-based communities become more difficult to maintain. Police, financial, and administrative problems are not coextensive with community boundaries. Action taken by one administrative or police body directly affects neighboring ones and interferes with the efficiency of both. Adequate representation of interested parties becomes almost impossible.

These are but some of the existing undesirable conditions that we are gradually becoming aware of; however, no wholly satisfactory techniques have yet been invented for the solution of these problems.

Suggested Readings

DUNBAR, ANTHONY, and LINDA KRAVITZ, *Hard Travelling: Migrant Farm Workers in America* (Cambridge, Mass.: Ballinger, 1976). A perceptive and informal account of a problem that has plagued the country for decades.

FISCHER, JOHN, *Vital Signs, U.S.A.* (New York: Harper & Row, 1975). An optimistic analysis of some recent developments on the urban scene. Includes the establishment of consolidated governments and new towns.

GREER, SCOTT, *The Urbane View: Life and Politics in Metropolitan America* (New York: Oxford University Press, 1972). A collection of essays on the social and political behavior of urban residents. Considers efforts to reform cities and to establish new goals for them.

PALEN, JOHN J., *The Urban World* (New York: McGraw-Hill, 1975). An analysis of the development of cities, the various lifestyles they encourage, and urban planning and redevelopment.

RINDFUSS, RONALD, and JAMES A. SWEET, *Postwar Fertility Trends and Differentials in the United States* (New York: Academic Press, 1977). Traces fertility patterns since 1945. Contains a section on rural fertility trends and differentials.

RUSHING, WILLIAM A., *Community, Physicians, and Inequality: A Sociological Study of the Maldistribution of Physicians* (Lexington, Mass.: Lexington Books, 1975). Confirms the disadvantages, described in this chapter, that are characteristic of urban life.

WAGENHEIM, KAL, *A Survey of Puerto Ricans on the U.S. Mainland in the 1970s.* (New York: Praeger, 1975). A fully documented account of the demographic and economic situations of one of the nation's most significant urban minorities.

Footnotes

[1] *Business Week,* 2 Feb. 1976, p. 66.

[2] Jack Anderson with Les Whitten, "No Paradise for Farmhands," syndicated column, 10 Mar. 1976.

[3] Standard Metropolitan Statistical Areas contain at least one, and sometimes more than one, city of at least 50,000 population plus an adjacent county or counties meeting specified criteria of urban character.

[4] *U.S. News and World Report,* 14 May 1979, p. 47.

[5] *Statistical Abstract of the United States, 1978,* p. 23.

[6] Louis Wirth, "Urbanism as a Way of Life," *American Journal of Sociology,* 44 (July 1938), 8.

[7] For a more detailed and technical account of these processes, consult Walter Firey, *Land Use in Central Boston* (Cambridge, Mass.: Harvard University Press, 1947); Homer Hoyt, *One Hundred Years of Land Values in Chicago* (Chicago: University of Chicago Press, 1933); and Robert E. Park, Ernest W. Burgess, and Roderick D. McKenzie, *The City* (Chicago: University of Chicago Press, 1933).

[8] Stokely Carmichael and Charles Hamilton, "Dynamite: Black Ghettos," *Atlantic Monthly,* Oct. 1967, p. 99.

[9] U.S. Bureau of the Census, *Statistical Abstract of the United States: 1975* (Washington, D.C.), p. 34.

[10] Clarence Senior, "Research on the Puerto Rican Family in the United States," *Marriage and Family Living,* 19 (Feb. 1957), 36.

[11] Todd Gitlin and Nanci Hollander, *Uptown: Poor Whites in Chicago* (New York: Harper & Row, 1970).

[12] U.S. Department of Health, Education and Welfare, *Toward a Social Report* (Washington, D.C.: Government Printing Office, 1969), p. 35.

[13] *U.S. News and World Report,* 3 May 1976, p. 70.

[14]Herbert J. Gans, "The Failure of Urban Renewal: A Critique and Some Proposals," *Commentary,* Apr. 1965, p. 29.

[15]HEW, *Toward a Social Report,* p. 36.

[16]William Chapman, "The Housing Hustlers," *The Progressive,* May 1974, pp. 29–32.

[17]Ernest Holsendolph, "Rent Subsidy's Achievement Lags," The New York Times Service, 12 Aug. 1976.

[18]*Report on National Growth, 1972* (Washington, D.C.: Government Printing Office, 1972), p. 19.

[19]Ibid., p. 22.

[20]Ibid., p. 51.

[21]Ibid., p. 30.

[22]Ibid., p. 31.

[23]*U.S. News and World Report,* 16 Aug. 1976, p. 48.

[24]"Grapefruit of Wrath," *Gainesville (Florida) Sun,* 14 Mar. 1975.

[25]Jack Anderson with Les Whitten, "No Paradise for Farmhands."

[26]Charlotte Hays, "Mississippi's Eastland: Elusive as He Is Powerful," Washington Post Service, 16 Jan. 1974.

[27]Associated Press, 5 July 1971.

[28]New York: P. Smith, 1904.

[29]Juan Cameron, "How the Interstate Changed the Face of the Nation," *Fortune,* July 1971, p. 78.

[30]Ibid., pp. 124–25.

RCA.

COMMUNICATION PROBLEMS IN MASS SOCIETY

15

On September 3, 1919, President Woodrow Wilson climbed into his dark-blue private railroad car and set out on a campaign to convert the American people to the country's participation in the League of Nations. Most Senators opposed the League, but Wilson had faith that the citizens themselves would support it if he could but present his case to them. In the next twenty-two days, he traveled more than 8,000 miles in 17 states and made 40 formal speeches. Hugh Baillie, who covered the tour for the United Press, remarked thirty years later in his memoirs, *High Tension:* "If he'd had radio and television to carry his message and personality to millions instead of thousands, the history of the world might have been dif-ferent. With television, I am convinced, Wilson would have carried the country for the League."[1]

"Casettes are the new weapon of the twentieth century," says an Egyptian magazine.

The gadget is becoming an instrument of politics, more subtle even than the transistor, which spread the nationalist revolutions of a generation ago. The press, radio and television in the Middle East are all firmly controlled by governments; thus recordings provide a kind of underground press, easily copied and distributed behind the censors' backs.[2]

Communication makes human social life possible. The nature and quality of our communication processes mold the character of our social life. What kind of social life, and what kind of individual attitudes and responses, are modern communications media developing in us?

Structure of the Mass Media

THE PRESS

From the publication of the first daily newspaper in 1783, the number of daily English-language newspapers in America rose to a peak of 2,600 in 1909 and has settled to a present figure of about 1,750. Daily circulation totals about 62 million—a little less than one newspaper for each household in the United States.[3] Once a medium devoted to news and opinion, the modern newspaper is primarily a medium for advertising and entertainment. Advertising occupies much of the space and supplies two-thirds of the income. Although the modern newspaper prints more news more accurately than its predecessors, newspaper circulation campaigns stress features—syndicated columns, comics, sports sections, style shows, lovelorn columns, and the like—more than news coverage, and many news stories are selected for oddity in human interest rather than for social significance. Opinion, once scattered through the news stories, is now (theoretically) limited to the editorial page and to the signed columns of the commentators.

About 9,700 periodicals are now published, ranging from mass magazines like the *Reader's Digest* (circulation 18,300,000) to many tiny, obscure journals. Eleven hundred book publishers currently print over 35,000 new books each year, while unknown numbers of booklets, pamphlets, tracts, leaflets, and handbills appear in constant succession.

The press includes daily, weekly, and semiweekly newspapers, the foreign language press, the labor press and the black press, trade journals, house organs (prestige, good will, and employee morale publications of business corporations), the underground (countercultural) press, and magazines aimed at every age level, occupation, class, region, and interest group.

THE MOTION PICTURE

The motion picture, born about the turn of the century, reached its peak of popularity during World War II. Since the advent of television, movie attendance has fallen by over half, to less than once a month for the average American. Moviegoers are youthful, but older people see many old movies on television. Movie studios now produce about 175 theater films a year plus several thousand shorter films for television showing. Thus, for several hours each week the average American is exposed to this medium, which is tremendously effective in shaping attitudes and conditioned responses.[4] The resurrection of old movies on television also has the effect of disinterring the prejudices and biases of two or three decades ago; racial stereotypes and wartime caricatures of the enemy, avoided by current movies, are perpetuated for the television audience.

The motion picture medium also includes the educational film, whose use in schools, colleges, adult education groups, and most recently on television by the Public Broadcasting Service is steadily expanding; and the promotional film, loaned out by vested interests—corporations, trade associations, labor organizations—and containing a mixture of education and propaganda.

RADIO BROADCASTING

In a little over half a century radio has developed from a novel toy into an industry with 4,500 AM broadcast stations, 3,900 FM stations, over 1,500,000 special-purpose radio stations (aeronautical, marine, public safety, industrial, experimental, disaster communications), 325,000 amateur stations and operators, and at least twelve million citizens' band transmitters in 1977. No other communications medium reaches as many people as does radio, which enters 99.9 percent of all homes (with over two sets per home) and is found in 96.6 percent of all automobiles. With the advent of television, radio listening declined; then it rebounded with the appearance of the cheap, compact, battery-powered transistor radio. Today *attentive* listening is less than before television, while *marginal* listening (radio on while one is working, reading, or otherwise occupied) is higher than ever before.

Network radio, with local stations carrying network programs, has virtually disappeared as television has taken over mass entertainment. Local radio stations, aside from network newscasts, broadcast mainly records and local material interspersed with commercials.

Since losing the mass entertainment audience to television, radio broadcasting has become characterized by *audience segmentation*. One local station (usually FM) concentrates on classical music, another on "light" music, and another on pop or rock music. Any sizable ethnic minority will have one or more local stations catering to its tastes.

TELEVISION

Television has grown even more rapidly than radio, now reaching 99.9 percent of all homes in the nation. In 1977, 725 commercial and 260 educational television stations were on the air. Television has affected all the other media. As we mentioned earlier, attendance at movie theaters has declined since the advent of television, while movie-viewing has increased. Reading has shown some decline: fiction and entertainment reading has fallen off greatly, and newspaper reading has shown a slight decrease. However, reading for information and intellectual stimulation shows no drop. Highbrow magazines have doubled in circulation, middlebrow magazines have grown by about half, while the lowbrows (pulps, confessions, Westerns) have shown no growth during this period of growing population and rising income. Most of the famous old general-interest magazines (*American, Colliers, Saturday Evening Post, Look, Life*) have disappeared, while the greatest growth has been among the how-to-do-it and special interest magazines (*Popular Photography, Boats and Boating, Motor Trend*) and, recently, new magazines aimed at working women.[5] It appears that people seeking entertainment and escape have turned to television, while others are reading more than ever.

The *communications revolution* is the combination of all the ways in which the media have altered people's lives and feelings. The average American now spends more time watching television than in any other activity except working and sleeping,[6] while television has reduced the time spent by the average American in every other activity except working.[7] In the average American household, television is on nearly seven hours a day and is clearly the major news source for most people, with viewing slightly higher for the less educated; considerably higher for children, old people, blacks, and women; and highest among those who read least.[8]

By the age of 18, the average American child has spent 11,000 hours in school and 15,000 hours watching television.[9] A century ago the average person's free time was probably spent, in declining order, in (1) conversation; (2) games and participation sports; (3) spectator sports and organized or commercialized "entertainment"; (4) mass communication. Today this order has been approximately reversed. Robert M. Hutchins has even suggested that conversation may become a lost art, as television may convert us into "a high order of plant life."

Problems of Mass Media

As each new medium appeared and grew, it raised both hopes and fears—hopes that it would checkmate tyranny and arm justice, and that it would unify the masses and bring them the benefits of learning and culture; fears that it would become an instrument of tyranny, and that it would adulterate learning, degrade culture, and promote social unrest. Each medium has been an object of social concern and controversy almost from its inception. Among the topics of concern are monopoly or concentration of control, bias and responsibility, and content, or culture versus commerce.

CONCENTRATION OF CONTROL

The development of the mass media illustrates both the ideal of vigorous competition and the tendency toward noncompetitive practice that pervades our economic system. As in all forms of modern business and political organization, the pressing problem is, what degree of centralized organization and management is in the public interest?

THE PRESS   The doctrine of freedom of the press, protected by the First Amendment, implies that books, magazines, and newspapers may be published and distributed by anyone, without official permission or censorship. This freedom to publish was considered the indispensable bulwark of democracy. Through the free press, tyranny would be challenged, corruption exposed, and a marketplace provided for the free competition of ideas, in which truth would finally prevail. This passionate faith in the eventual triumph of truth lies behind Thomas Jefferson's statement, "Were it left to me to decide whether we should have a government without newspapers or newspapers without a government, I should not hesitate to prefer the latter."

The free competition of ideas is complete only when the publication of conflicting opinions is politically and economically possible. In the days of the hand-operated press, a paper could be established cheaply, and a large paper had little competitive advantage over its smaller competitor. Today, newspaper publishing is big business. Changing technology and the advantages of large-scale operation have steadily reduced the number of daily newspapers from the 1909 figure of about 2,600, serving a population of 90 million, to the present 1,744 dailies (down 39 from 1978) for a population of 220 million. By 1945 daily newspaper competition had disappeared from all but 117 American cities. By 1954 this number had fallen to 74; by 1959 to 42; by 1969 to 33; by 1976 to 27, and by 1979 to 24, while the remaining cities were either one-newspaper towns or had two newspapers under a single management. By 1979 there were 31 states in which no city had competing daily papers. In a large part of America, local newspaper competition has disappeared.[10]

Effective newspaper competition is further reduced by chain ownership. The eight largest newspaper chains account for nearly half of all daily newspaper circulation and over 60 percent of all newspapers, up from 50 percent only a few years ago.[11] It should be noted, however, that newspapers are less monopolized in the United States than elsewhere in the world. Among the 15 major developed countries of the world, the United States has the least concentration of newspaper ownership.[12]

Except for purely local news, most news that reaches print passes through one of the two major newsgathering services—the Associated Press, a cooperative to which most papers belong; and the United Press International, affiliated with the Scripps-Howard and Hearst chains. Most newspapers rely on syndicated features both for entertainment—comic strips, lovelorn columns, fashion features, and the like—and for their columns of news interpretations and opinion (Jack Anderson, Mary McGrory, James Reston, and others). Even the editorials are sometimes "canned"—supplied by the chain owner or some other nonlocal source.

While it is commercially impossible to establish a new metropolitan daily newspaper, the development of offset printing makes it possible for anyone with a few hundred dollars to publish a "little" paper. Hundreds of such papers (seldom dailies) are included in the underground press, the neighborhood or suburban shopping guides, and other ventures aimed at some

In book publishing, freedom of the press is widely upheld, with instances of owner sensorship relatively rare.
(Irene Springer)

> The press's institutional bias when it acts as a social critic is to expose individual malefactors rather than to attack social arrangements. Nevertheless, the American daily press has a constant potential for social subversion. Its institutional bias as a merchant of the novel and the unexpected makes it an instrument for popularizing new attitudes, opinions, and behaviors. If these deviant ways of thinking and acting are taken up by sizable segments of the mass-media audience, the consequences are institutional change, revised social values, the restructuring of newsmen's frame of reference, and the redefinition of what and who is newsworthy.
>
> Bernard Roshco, *Newsmaking* (Chicago: University of Chicago Press, 1975), p. 125.

specific audience. They supplement rather than compete with the daily newspaper.

In magazine publishing, although 9,719 periodicals (up 137 from 1978) are published by 2,500 publishers, the top four publishers account for about one-fourth of the total circulation (down from one-third in 1947). While magazine publishing is fiercely competitive, the need for a large circulation makes it hazardous and expensive to launch a new magazine.

Of the more than 1,100 book publishers, the top 20 publish over half the 35,000 books published each year. Yet book publishing is intensely competitive, and publishers are eager to print anything that will sell. With very few exceptions, any book worth printing (and many not worth printing) will find a publisher. However, the recent trend toward acquisition of book publishers by other corporate interests threatens the freedom of book publishing. As an example, *Reader's Digest,* which purchased Funk & Wagnall's in 1965, ordered it to cancel publication of a book that was critical of the advertising business.[13] Fortunately for free competition of ideas in book publishing, instances of owner censorship are rare.

The total picture of the press is far from freely competitive in the traditional sense, yet it is far from a complete monopoly. The degree of concentration in the industry vests a relatively small number of persons with great power to determine what shall reach the presses. If most of them should chance to think alike on some issue—and sometimes they do—other points of view may have difficulty being printed and widely distributed.

MOTION PICTURES   Although the major production studios dominate the industry, smaller studios and independent producers are highly active, and movie-making is highly competitive. Although the risk is high, an independent producer and a gifted director can shoot a picture on a shoestring and make millions on it.

RADIO AND TELEVISION   Since their infancy, radio and television have been subject to some governmental regulation, arising from the need to assign frequencies in a spectrum that has room for only a limited number of stations. Since the limitations on the number of stations that can operate are technical rather than economic, broadcasting is viewed not as a strictly free enterprise, but as a sort of public utility. The law creating the Federal Communications Commission (FCC) establishes the principle that the air waves belong to the public, that a station operator may own the studio equipment but not the frequency on which he broadcasts, and that licenses to operate a station are to be granted only "in the public interest, convenience, or necessity." Established practice, however, has made a joke of these principles. In theory a station's license renewal each three years is dependent upon how it has served the public. In practice, renewal is practically automatic. In 38 years of operation (1939–77), the FCC has revoked or denied renewal to 39 licensees, only two of these because of program content.[14] While a station owner does not legally own the license, stations normally sell for many times the value of their tangible assets, showing that it is really the license that is being sold. Established for the declared purpose of regulating the broadcast industry "in the public interest," the FCC has usually functioned to regulate the industry in the industry's interest—that is, in whatever way the industry can make the most money. Its occasional efforts to enforce rulings not profitable to the industry are usually defeated.[15] Thus, as often has happened with regulatory agencies intended to protect the public from the industry, the agency protects the industry from the public.[16] As former FCC Commissioner Nicholas Johnson has stated, "The FCC suffers from the virtual domination of its day-to-day activities by the very industry it is supposed to regulate."[17]

Some recent technological developments threaten the established position of the present broadcast industry. Pay-TV attaches a coin box or a com-

Cable TV broadcast of a Tri-State Town Meeting.

puterized billing service connection to the viewer's television set, along with an "unscrambler" to limit the signal to the paying receivers, but so far it has had little success.[18] Cable-TV connects individual receivers to a central reception tower and permits viewers to choose among a great many channels, including any material the local operator wishes to add. Cable-TV undermines the monopoly of local broadcasters, while pay-TV offers potential competition to the locals, the networks, and the movie theaters. These vested interests have reacted predictably, trying to suppress the competitive threats arising from new technology. The FCC, protecting the industry rather than the public, has resisted both innovations.[19] Yet Cable-TV has grown steadily, mostly in smaller towns and cities, where few channels can be received without it, growing to 4,000 systems serving 13 million homes in 1978.[20] Many Cable-TV systems include a "home box office" option, another form of Pay-TV. For an added monthly fee, one channel is "unscrambled" so that the subscriber can receive programs (usually recent movies or current sports events) not available to other subscribers. The videocasette now permits home viewing of commercially-recorded TV programs, as well as home recording and replay of TV programs.

FCC rules allow one person or company to own no more than 7 television stations, 7 FM stations, and 7 AM stations, and no more than one newspaper and one broadcast outlet in a single market area. Concentration in broadcasting, therefore, rests less upon station ownership than upon network affiliation and program sponsorship. Most TV and AM stations and many FM stations belong to one of the four national or several regional networks. One corporate giant, American Broadcasting Company, owns 399 theaters in 34 states, 6 AM and 6 FM stations, 5 TV stations, one of the three TV networks, and one of the four radio networks; while the other networks, NBC and CBS, are comparable in size.[21] The drift toward media concentrations continues as more mergers are completed. The FCC's efforts to promote the one-to-a-customer doctrine—that each owner have only one media outlet in any one market—recedes farther and farther from attainability.

Most local stations give little time to locally originated programs, especially during prime listening hours, and most of the broadcast material consists of network shows or of phonograph records separated by commercials. Practically all network broadcasts are sponsored by advertisers, and it is often stated that advertisers control broadcasting. To a degree this is true, since no program that fails to attract sponsors is likely to last very long. But sponsor power is not unlimited. Networks will not permit a weak program in their prime evening schedule, even though an advertiser may be eager to sponsor it. Sponsor control has probably declined in recent years, since television programs have become so costly that few sponsors will buy an entire program; instead, sponsors today buy minutes of commercial time distributed over many shows. It would probably be correct to say that the networks and sponsors share control of broadcasting.

In the early days of broadcasting many stations were affiliated with newspapers. As late as 1970 there were 90 cities in which a single newspaper-radio-television joint ownership had an absolute local monopoly of local news.[22] Yet newspaper ownership of broadcasting has been declining, with no more than 5 percent of all radio stations and 24 percent of all television stations newspaper-owned.[23]

HOW MUCH HAS CHANGED SINCE THIS STATEMENT WAS MADE IN 1961?

When television is good, nothing—not the theater, not the magazines, or newspapers—is better. But when television is bad, nothing is worse. I invite you to sit down in front of your television set when your station goes on the air . . . keep your eyes glued to that set until the station goes off. I can assure you that you will observe a vast wasteland. You will see a procession of game shows, violence, audience participation shows, formula comedies about totally unbelievable families, blood and thunder, mayhem, violence, sadism, murder, Western bad men, Western good men, private eyes, gangsters, more violence, and cartoons. And, endlessly, commercials—many screaming, cajoling, and offensive. And most of all, boredom. You will see a few things you will enjoy. But they will be very, very few.

Children spend as much time watching television as they do in the schoolroom. If parents, teachers, and ministers conducted their responsibilities by following the ratings, children would have a steady diet of ice cream, school holidays, and no Sunday School. . . . What about your responsibilities? Is there no room on television to teach, to inform, to uplift, to stretch, to enlarge the capacities of our children?

Newton Minow, former chairman, Federal Communications Commission, speaking before the National Association of Broadcasters; reported in the *New York Times*, 10 May 1961, pp. 1ff.

SIGNIFICANCE OF CONCENTRATION   Concern over concentration is nothing new. Of the great trading towns, Jefferson complained that "though not one-twenty-fifth of the nation, they command three-fourths of its public papers." Nearly every serious study of ways of improving the mass media includes recommendations for reducing concentration. In a society in which the mass media have replaced the town meeting and the soapbox, it is argued, freedom of speech has little meaning unless it is easily possible for each group to get its ideas into print and on the air. This freedom, many critics feel, is gravely weakened by the highly centralized managements of a motion-picture industry dedicated to the pursuit of maximum profits, a broadcast industry seeking to offend nobody, and a press largely devoid of local competition. Critics also complain that centralized control imposes upon the media a dead level of mediocrity, squeezing out the next-to-last-drop of diversity, originality, and imagination. Newspaper chain owners usually claim that each paper has editorial independence, but a careful study of chain newspapers found that the different papers of a chain are remarkably like one another.[24]

No doubt centralization does pose a certain threat to freedom and to diversity, but the effects of centralization are not entirely pernicious. Yellow journalism was a product of the circulation wars of a half-century ago. William Randolph Hearst's circulation battle with Joseph Pulitzer probably caused the Spanish-American War,[25] and his circulation battle with Joseph McCormick is widely thought to have helped establish Chicago gangdom.[26] As one liberal journal comments editorially, "Too much competition can sometimes reduce all publishers to the lowest common denominator of sensationalism; whereas monopoly can sometimes encourage independence, letting a publisher feel that he can afford to put out a good paper."[27] Two studies found little difference between competing newspapers and those without local competition; they were equally good—or bad—regardless of competition.[28] Another study arrived at the same conclusion, finding that when a paper came under chain ownership, the content remained unchanged, but the prices went up.[29] The large broadcast networks bring us many artistic productions and perceptive documentaries that no local studio can produce. Whether partial centralization of control of the mass media has done more harm than good remains debatable; meanwhile, any attempt to alter greatly the present pattern of control would probably be economically difficult and politically impossible.

BIAS AND RESPONSIBILITY

THE MEDIA—FREE TO INFORM AND MISINFORM   The problem of bias appears only in free societies. In much of the world the concept of media objectivity is totally absent. According to one observer, no more than 20 countries in the world have a relatively free press; elsewhere, the media are vehicles for official propaganda, and any dissenter is quickly silenced.[30] Even in many democratic countries, most newspapers and magazines are the self-confessed voice of a particular party or interest group and recognize no obligation even to try to be objective.

This was equally true of American newspapers and magazines in the nineteenth century, when even a small city would support a Republican paper, a Democratic paper, and possibly several others. But the economies of large-scale operation ended local newspaper competition in most American cities. This was accompanied by a growing feeling among publishers that the publisher of the *only* newspaper in the area had a responsibility to present a complete and balanced news: the paper's news columns should be objective and unbiased, and opinion should be confirmed to the editorials and to the signed columns of commentators who should reflect a variety of biases, thus preserving the overall balance of viewpoints. Most newspaper publishers and most broadcasters seem to take seriously these obligations for balance and fairness.

Do they reach this goal? For some years, repeated polls and surveys found that the public considered television newscasters to be the most reliable sources of information, with 47 percent of a national sample reporting TV news to be "more objective than biased," while 34 percent considered it "more biased than objective."[31] But the latest Gallup Poll shows greater public confidence in newspapers than in television by a margin of 51 to 38 percent.[32] Yet accusations of bias fill the air. Conservatives accuse the media of a liberal bias, of being antibusiness and prosocialistic big government;[33] while liberals and radicals accuse the media of acting as the paid voice of the conservative establishment.

Objectivity can be defined in many ways and is not easily measured.[34] Most efforts to measure bias empirically have been content analyses of political news reporting. One such study concluded that publishers' political biases were definitely reflected in political news reporting.[35] Another study of the 1968 presidential campaign found that newscasters' comments were balanced (62 percent neutral, 19 percent pro-Nixon, 19 percent anti-Nixon).[36] A content analysis of 1969–70 television news coverage of the Vietnam War concluded that bias either was nonexistent or slightly favored the Nixon administration.[37] Two content analyses in 1972 suggested that bias may be issue-connected rather than party-connected. One studied television news coverage of the Vietnam War, concluding that coverage was overwhelmingly unfavorable to the Nixon administration; the other studied the 1972 presidential campaign, finding no bias toward either party.[38] A study of network coverage of the 1976 New Hampshire primary concluded that both parties received equal coverage.[39] A study of newspaper coverage of Vice-President Agnew's speeches found no evidence to support Agnew's claim that the papers distorted them.[40] The evidence for a clear or consistent media bias is not very convincing.[41]

However, that conclusion does not fully solve the problem. One study calculates that a newspaper's support of a candidate gives that candidate a 6 percent edge in votes over the opponent among that paper's readers.[42] Most voters have access to only one paper, and many local elections are won by less than a 6 percent margin, making local press support a tremendous advantage. A study of presidential access to national television concludes that an incumbent president has a tremendous advantage over any challenger or critic.[43] Where media independence and criticism are silenced and the media become press-agents for a ruling administration, it becomes very difficult to change rulers. The Nixon-Agnew administration made a determined attempt to intimidate the media, with some momentary success,[44] but the collapse of that administration into national disgrace prevented a clear test of its long-term success in destroying the independence of the media.

THE DILEMMA OF BIAS AND OBJECTIVITY   Bias is inherent in human communication; all persons and groups have beliefs to defend and interests to promote. Since our perception and recall are highly selective, each of us "sees" the facts in a way that supports our views. Thus, what one person sees as a balanced, objective presentation, another sees as outrageously biased. Perfect objectivity may be impossible to attain, and even if attained, it would not stop accusations of bias. Very often the accusation reflects the bias of the accuser. Thus, an accurate, neutral account of a race incident may arouse angry accusations of bias from both Black Panthers and Ku Klux Klanners, and for opposite reasons. Just what is objectivity in reporting? Does it mean according equal respect for all points of view? Should a patent falsehood be reported neutrally, with no corrective comments? Should a documentary about an undeniably oppressed group, such as Mexican wetback laborers, give equal weight to the cry of the oppressed and the rationalizations of their oppressors? As Edward R. Murrow once remarked, not all arguments are equal. A CBS news president commented on a 1958 documentary on statehood for Alaska and Hawaii:

> In an effort to be fair to both sides, we almost made it appear that for every point made for statehood there was an equal argument against it, when the facts clearly indicated that an overwhelming majority of the leaders of both parties, including all living presidents, the press and public opinion, would indicate admission of the two territories.[45]

The statement above suggests that there may be some issues upon which a responsible treatment will necessarily be somewhat one-sided. For example, a content analysis study concludes that CBS news coverage of the Vietnam War in 1972 was 62 percent critical of the United States military policy,

30 percent neutral, and only 8 percent favorable.[46] Does this mean that CBS was highly biased, or that CBS was accurately reporting facts that most Americans eventually came to accept as having been true all along?

There are no easy or formula answers for the problems of objectivity, fairness, and responsibility. It is arguable whether absolute objectivity always gives a truthful overall picture. For example, simply by reporting accurately the daily accusations of disloyalty made by the late Senator Joseph McCarthy, the press contributed to his malevolent political power, even though the press faithfully printed all the replies of the people falsely accused.[47] With neutrally objective reporting and equal time or space for all sides, extremists and demagogues usually win the argument, while moderates lose. In one experiment, "an hour-long debate between three of the Chicago Seven [radical activists] and three liberals produced large shifts toward the New Left positions among college students of all persuasions from left to conservative."[48] Extremists usually win debates by a simple technique: they make a rapid series of sweeping claims and dramatic accusations; if the moderates ignore the accusations, this looks like an admission; if the moderates try to refute the accusations, they quickly bog down in boring detail. An accusation takes one sentence to hurl, but usually hundreds or thousands of words to answer. Meanwhile the audience has lost interest, while the extremist has moved onto another series of accusations. This is why scientists rarely win television arguments with sensationalists. Commenting upon talk-show debates between diet-fad promoters and scientific critics, one broadcast critic notes,

> There is never enough opportunity for rebuttal on a TV show. What usually happens is that the scientific spokesman ends up sounding like a close-minded establishment bore who wants to suppress bright new ideas. I've hardly ever seen a confrontation in which the scientific man came out ahead or even fought to a draw.[49]

One critic claims that distortion in TV news arises, not so much from the biases of the news personnel, but from the scheduling demands of TV, which must have a simplified, interesting, dramatic news show for each time slot.[50] This is what makes television news coverage open to manipulation by activists.[51] Violence is telegenic; lack of violence is not newsworthy. It is likely that television coverage of terrorists in action encourages terrorism. Terrorists wish maximum publicity, and television plays into their hands.[52]

There are many examples of distortion by focusing on the colorful and dramatic. The Tellico Dam project, under severe fire as a wasteful boondoggle, was stalled when nearly completed by discovery that the small snail darter fish would lose its only habitat. Media coverage, however, concentrated on the fish story instead of the dry statistics of cost-benefit ratios. It is likely that most people remember the controversy as a 2-billion-dollar-dam-vs.-a-three-inch-fish story.[53] What is newsworthy is often not significant, and what is significant is often not newsworthy.

One answer to the problem of distortion through literal objectivity is to ignore or downplay events or statements that are relatively insignificant in themselves but are potentially inflammatory. For example, after World War II the press downplayed the actions of the American Nazi Party lest reporting them inflame racial tensions.[54] Many local racial clashes have been buried for the same reason. But should the publisher be entrusted with decid-

An exchange with a taxi driver, reported by Reuven Frank, president of NBC News, was amusing and disheartening at the same time.

"That George Wallace is right," he said.
"Right about what?" I asked.
"He said the media never tell what he says. They keep him away from the people. They don't report his speeches."
"When did he say that?" I asked.
"Last night."
Since I had not known Governor Wallace was in the New York area that week, I asked, "Were you there?"
"No," he said. "I saw the speech on Huntley-Brinkley."

From *Survey of Broadcast Journalism, 1969–1970* (New York: Grosset & Dunlap, 1970), p. 38.

ing what it is not good for the public to hear? Will his assessment of the public interest be correct or will he mistake his biases for the public interest? These are disturbing questions.

Another answer to the distorting effects of literal objectivity is the technique of reporting in depth. This involves providing background information, additional facts, and analytical comment to put the event or statement into a proper perspective. But this process brings fresh accusations of bias.

Advocacy journalism consciously abandons objective reporting or neutrality for a deliberate manipulation of news reporting so as to support certain causes or values. Media owners are predominantly conservative, while the "working press"—news reporters, analysts, commentators, editors—tend to be liberal. If advocacy journalism were to become the norm, one wonders which bias would prevail.

MEDIA DIFFERENCES   The problem of bias affects each medium differently. In book publishing bias is no great problem because the industry is fiercely competitive and any book that seems likely to sell will be published. The national newsmagazines *(Time, Newsweek, U.S. News and World Report)* recognize some obligation to be objective, while journals of opinion are frankly the biased voices for particular points of view, from the right-wing *American Opinion* and *National Review,* through the moderate-liberal *Harpers* and *Atlantic,* to the left-wing *International Socialist Review* and *Social Policy.* There is no important interest group or segment of American thought that is not represented by some magazine.

Freedom of the press is theoretically guaranteed by the freedom for anyone to publish a newspaper. In practice this freedom is limited by the economic reality that only in the largest cities can more than one daily newspaper be profitable. Thus the newspaper publisher generally recognizes a responsibility different from that of book and magazine publishers.

Since the air waves have room for only a limited number of broadcasters, the FCC imposes upon radio and television a special obligation to be impartial. Most station operators appear to make an honest attempt to give equal time to most groups and viewpoints, but as we showed earlier, this is not always a satisfactory answer. Consequently, the fairness doctrine, under which broadcasters are required to offer equal time to all contestants, is under serious attack.[55] Some critics fear that forcing broadcasters to offer free time for reply will give governments and special interest groups a club with which to intimidate broadcasters into carrying no independent thought or social criticism.[56] As one surveys these opposing arguments, it is easy to see why the question of bias and responsibility has no fully satisfactory answer.

CONTENT—CULTURE VERSUS COMMERCE

Who has the right to say what the press shall print, movies shall show, and radio and TV shall broadcast—the owners, the public, the government? According to surveys over the years, the public overwhelmingly favors leaving primary control of the mass media where it is—with the private owners.[57] But to the critics this merely proves the truth of George Bernard Shaw's dictum, "if we do not get what we like, we shall grow to like what we get."

What do we get? In general, newspapers give us news, comment, editorial opinion, and a variety of features that are entertaining and sometimes mildly informational. Books and magazines give us a great choice, with ample opportunity to gratify any taste. Movies are devoted almost entirely to entertainment—either light, frothy entertainment or rootless melodrama that exploits serious issues for shock rather than insight. Various studies of television programming show a fairly constant distribution of about 80 percent of broadcast time devoted to light entertainment, 10 percent to informational and public affairs programs, 5 percent to news broadcasts, and 5 percent to "heavy" entertainment (serious drama, opera, classical music).[58] Even in the Soviet Union television operates mainly as an entertainment medium. Although government-operated television carries a great deal of "educational" and propagandistic material, the Russian people largely ignore it and twirl to the entertainment.[59]

Obviously, entertainment is what most people want. A 1960 survey found three out of five people well satisfied with television program content, with only one in four critical; a repeat survey in 1970 found these proportions virtually unchanged.[60] The more highly educated people are the more critical. They watch and listen less, and are more interested in classical music and discussions of public issues. But the viewers' stated preferences cannot always be taken at face value. For example, one survey found the more highly educated viewers asking for more informational shows; yet when these viewers were choosing between "Marcus Welby" (a medical melodrama) and CBS's informational "60 Minutes," the set monitors showed that they chose entertainment over information in about the same proportions as the less educated viewers.[61] Persons who are critical of one of the mass media are far more likely to be critical of the others, showing that a significant minority is clearly dissatisfied with the mass media in general.[62] Just what do they dislike about them?

CRITICISMS OF MEDIA CONTENT   Critics indict the mass media on three main counts: that much of the content is either *trashy, harmful,* or *so limited in variety* that the public has little choice but to learn to like trash.

Trash—where and why?   The charge of trashiness involves a value judgment: by whose values is trash defined? This charge is rooted in the fact that most media content is scaled to mass tastes, to the dismay of those who view mass tastes as vulgar. Each of the media (excepting books and specialized magazines) seeks to attract as large an audience as possible for each issue, show, or broadcast. This means *scaling the content to the least common denominator of audience acceptability*. Since one-fourth of U.S. adults never entered high school, and nearly half never completed it, a local newspaper can gain circulation by containing little that cannot be read and understood by a 15-year-old child. Since nearly everyone likes human interest stories while few will read a column about foreign trade, the serious but undramatic news must make room for lurid scandal and sentimental trivia. When Old Bob, the coon dog, was lost in a cave near Bedford, Indiana, he was on or near the front page of several papers for a full week—at a time when the country was involved in a hasty mobilization, an unpopular war, price inflation, a political crisis, and a basic reorientation of foreign policy. In the search for excitement newspapers tend to emphasize the bizarre, the exceptional, and the illicit, while sober but serious news developments are buried in the back pages. At times newspaper treatment of crime may make impossible a fair trial of the accused, a situation that occasionally leads to judicial rebuke of the press.[63]

The least-common-denominator approach is revealed most clearly in movie and broadcast content. The crime-sex-adventure trio of themes accounts for most movie plots because movie makers are under no illusions as to which kinds of pictures make money. The president of MGM complains that "the introduction of social issues in films was followed by a drop at the box office."[64] Despite occasional exceptions, serious drama and genuinely artistic films rarely make money, and no producer can afford to make many films like *The Treasure of Sierra Madre,* widely acclaimed as an artistic triumph, but a box-office failure (no sex!). Films involving social criticism and intellectual challenge are both commercially doubtful and politically dangerous. Skin flicks, horse operas, and whodunits are both safer and more profitable.

A similar situation is found in radio and television. One television producer observes, "Whenever you raise the quality and make your show more educational, you lose audience. Of course you gain support from civic groups. Community leaders tell us what a high-quality show we have: no violence, no cartoons—and no ratings."[65]

Although some educational and artistic values may occasionally emerge from this diet of entertainment, it is unrealistic to expect the sponsor to cater to minority tastes. Commercial sponsorship must scale the program to mass tastes if the sponsor is to sell his product and earn dividends for his stockholders. The result is to penalize artistic creativity and social relevance and to reward mediocrity, monotonous imitation, and triviality. The blame—or praise, according to one's view—rests not with the sponsor for acting as sponsors must, but with the system wherein the pursuit of profit determines program content.

Another explanation for the mediocrity of much movie and television drama lies in their fantastic appetite for story material. All the Pulitzer Prize novels and plays ever written would not fill broadcast schedules for more than a few days. A vaudeville routine, once usable for years, is now gone in a few minutes. The insatiable appetite of modern media makes it inevitable that as long as the emphasis is on *newness and entertainment of the mass audience,* the average quality of output will be mediocre.

Still another explanation is that pallid fare is less dangerous. The television documentary is unsurpassed as a means of public enlightenment, but any good documentary is certain to offend some group or vested interest. Documentaries delight intellectuals but arouse interest group anger and sponsors' anxieties.[66] For example, a 1975 CBS documentary, "The Guns of Autumn," mercilessly displayed the brutal aspects of hunting. Although most television stations carry programs glorifying hunting and fishing at least once a week,[67] this single critical documentary aroused a storm of protest from gun clubs and sporting groups, followed by the withdrawal of six of the seven scheduled sponsors and the filing of $300 million damage suit against CBS.[68]

These are among the reasons why controversial documentaries have become increasingly rare.[69] CBS's popular "60 Minutes" courageously exposes small-time "con" operations and critically examines unpopular government bureaus such as the Internal Revenue Service, but seldom tackles any powerful vested interests or topics that might outrage very many people. Many suitable topics—the bombing, burning, and vandalizing of entirely legal abortion clinics by antiabortionists; the scandalously wasteful dam and flood control projects which benefit local landowners at national taxpayer expense—these are unlikely to be aired on "60 Minutes" or any other documentary. Nor are they likely to be aired on Public Broadcasting, where political pressure remains a compelling argument for avoiding controversy.

Media content—harmless or vicious?   The second criticism—that much of the content is actively harmful—is easy to hurl but difficult to test. Since their appearance the movies have flickered in the baleful glare of those who distrusted their influence. Many studies, especially the early Payne Fund studies,[70] established that movies had great influence upon viewers, without clearly establishing whether that influence was good or bad. As each new medium spreads, critical attention shifts to it; at present television is the prime suspect.

During the early days of television, when broadcast time was cheap and the industry was seeking acceptance, many highly regarded children's programs were developed. As the industry became established and time became salable at good prices, children's programs waned; children's drama, for example, dropped in New York from 30.4 percent of total television time in 1951 to 6.7 percent in 1953,[71] and virtually to zero by 1970.[72] Even a high audience rating does not save a children's program, since children are not a very profitable market. Virtually the only current children's programs that rise above the cartoon level are Public Broadcasting System's "Sesame Street" and "The Electric Company."

Children clearly enjoy violence, and there is evidence that most parents have little influence upon their children's viewing choices.[73] The British Broadcasting Corporation lost two-thirds of its juvenile audience when a new, competing system of commercial television brought violence to the screen.[74] The National Association for Better Broadcasting estimates that the average American child sees 13,000 violent deaths on television between the ages of 5 and 15.[75] How does all this violence affect behavior?

There is substantial evidence that delinquents and criminals copy the criminal *techniques* they see on television.[76] But does television violence increase the *frequency* of real-life violence? Some research studies find no association between television violence and violent behavior.[77] The preponderance of research evidence, however, points to the conclusion that violence on the screen *does* encourage violence in society, although the relationship is relatively weak.[78] This is the carefully qualified conclusion of the most exhaustive research investigation, reached by the Surgeon General's Scientific Advisory Committee on Television and Social Behavior[79]—a committee "stacked" in favor of the broadcast industry.[80] Direct cause-and-effect relationships are difficult to prove, but there is convincing evidence that heavy viewers of television "see the world as more dangerous and frightening than those who watch very little. Heavy viewers are less trustful of their fellow citizens, and more fearful of the real world."[81] These studies "provide strong evidence that television violence is teaching children to accept aggression as a way of life."[82] The burden of evidence thus supports the fear that violence on tube and screen is helping to create a more violent world.

Limited choice—the triumph of monotony   A third criticism is the charge that the media—mainly radio and television—fail to offer the public the wide range of choice that is supposed to be a special virtue of free enterprise. Each sponsor, with occasional exceptions, tries to draw the same mass audience and to keep it from switching stations; therefore, each sponsor tends to offer at a particular hour a program of the same type as is scheduled on competing stations. This means that at a particular hour, the listener may have very little choice as to *type* of program.

Is the public dissatisfied? A 1979 survey found more people (33 percent) reporting that television programming is getting *worse* than think it is getting better (22 percent).[83] Yet a study of the UHF stations established in recent years finds that those which are the most successful are those broadcasting the same kinds of programming as their rivals.[84] Obviously, there is no agreement as to what is "good" programming.

The minority audience is neglected most of the time. There are a number of small minority audiences whose tastes may run to classical music, to pure jazz, to literary readings, to book reviews, to leisurely dramatizations of the classics, and so on. For these people, the commercial broadcast industry offers very little.

In theory, stations are expected to offer something for everybody by carrying sustaining (nonsponsored) programs during some prime listening hours, since sponsors obviously cannot afford to cater to minority tastes. In this way program balance can be achieved. In practice, much of the industry has failed to do this. Although the networks and some individual stations have developed some sustaining programs of high quality and great popularity, these programs have rarely been offered during prime listening hours, have often been shifted around whenever a sponsor wanted the hour involved, or have been unaccountably dropped. Network-sustaining programs are often not carried by local stations. It would appear that sustaining programs are used mainly to fill any leftover time that no sponsor wants at that moment.

Attempts to secure a more balanced offering run into a fundamental obstacle—sustaining programs are not profitable. In applying for a license or a license renewal, the applicant must state how he will divide his broadcast time, achieve program balance, and serve the public interest. Once the license is granted these promises are almost universally disregarded. The FCC described the situation some years ago:

> The most immediately profitable way to run a station may be to procure a network affiliation, plug into the network line in the morning, and broadcast network programs throughout the day—interrupting the network only to insert commercial spot announcements, and to substitute spot announcements and phonograph records for outstanding network programs. . . . Some stations are approaching perilously close to this extreme.[85]

Efforts of the FCC to secure greater diversity and balance in programming have been generally ineffective, and have been sharply denounced by the industry and by much of the press as a government attack on freedom of speech and free enterprise. The development of FM radio raised hopes of increased experimentation and variety of offerings, but many commercial FM stations are jointly owned and operated with AM stations and broadcast the same programs. Cable-TV carries the potential for greatly expanded program variety, which is beginning to be realized.[86] In an effort to promote greater program variety, the FCC ruled in 1970 that local stations could broadcast no more than three hours of network programs between prime time hours of 7:00 and 11:00 P.M., with the remaining hour devoted to local programming. The principal result was to cut the network documentaries and public affairs programs, replacing them with dull local talk shows.[87]

As we mentioned earlier, audience segmentation has increased somewhat the variety of radio fare, but hopes for program variety and enrichment in commercial television remain largely unrealized.

The Social-Disorganization Approach

Without the technological revolution in communication, the social problems concerning communication would be few and simple. As long as books were few, expensive, and owned by only the wealthy, rulers saw little need for censorship. When printing made books and handbills so cheap that they could be widely circulated among the common people, who had less stake in the status quo, rulers began to fear books and demand censorship of printed matter. When newspaper publishing was small-scale, minority views could easily find expression; when the publisher must necessarily be wealthy, conflicting views reach a wide audience only by his grace. When the primary means of communication was face-to-face conversation and the town meeting or country store was the main forum, freedom of speech was secure if the government kept hands off. Today, the press, radio, and television have become the main public forum, and effective freedom of speech—the chance for all groups to share in a discussion of all vital issues—is neither greater nor less than their controllers decree. Under these conditions, *the protection of freedom of speech sometimes requires the intervention, rather than the abstention, of government.*

Yet each governmental attempt to protect the freedom actively—an antitrust suit to keep a newspaper from throttling a competitor, a senatorial proposal to reserve part of the radio frequencies for noncommercial stations, or a proposal that the industry pay something for its use of the air waves—is denounced by the industry as an attack upon freedom. A widespread confusion as to what freedom of speech means and how it functions lies at the root of many current controversies.

The technological revolution is not over. Cable-TV has reached maturity, videocasettes and electronic games are in a period of rapid growth, and many other innovations—home computers, facsimile newspapers, optical fiber transmission, direct satellite transmission, electronic shopping, electronic money transfer—may soon make newspapers, checkbooks, money, letter-writing, and shopping excursions obsolete.[88] And it is certain that each innovation will bring new problems in the continuous process of adjusting to technological change.

The Value-Conflict Approach

The value conflicts of society are the cause of arguments over the mass media. Each group wishes to use the media to propagandize its values, and often seeks to deny use of the media to its opponents. Radicals berate the media for failing to promote the revolution; liberals wish the media to give more discussion to social problems and social reforms; conservatives wish the media to support the status quo. Highbrows deplore the vulgar taste of

The COMSTAR D-3 high capacity satellite for U.S. domestic telephone communications, launched in June 1978 at the Kennedy Space Center. Direct satellite transmission is one of many communication innovations that will soon make more traditional methods obsolete. (NASA)

the masses, while the masses snort at the highbrows. As long as values differ so widely, as they must in a changing, highly differentiated society, it is difficult to please everybody.

Perhaps the most fundamental value clash concerns the basic question, what are the media for? Should the mass medium be primarily a profitmaking business enterprise, a means of mass entertainment, an instrument of mass improvement, or a something-for-everyone cultural cafeteria? In what proportions should these different objectives be blended? The media owners favor the first, the masses prefer the second, while educators and highbrows prefer (or claim to prefer) the third and fourth. Beneath most criticisms of the media are such value judgments as these.

The Personal-Deviation Approach

The personal-deviation approach contributes relatively little to an understanding of communications problems. There are deviant persons who are somewhat of a nuisance—those who write crank letters to the editor, and who pester radio stations with unreasonable complaints and demands—but they pose no serious problem. At times a deviant person may secure leadership of a respectable local or national organization—a veterans' organization, labor union, chamber of commerce, DAR chapter—and use the power of this position in an effort to intimidate the media into airing only his or her neurotic viewpoints; but such persons cannot long be effective unless they also express the character and viewpoint of the other members of the organization. Occasionally a deviant person secures control of a newspaper or radio station and seeks to use it to promote his or her intemperate views. In broadcasting, such behavior may soon lead to trouble with the FCC. In the newspaper world, the extremism of an owner is seldom very profitable. The underground press offers the most clear examples of deviant persons in the media. Whether the editors and writers are regarded as maladjusted neurotics or as the courageous vanguard of social change (or as both), they are undeniably deviant. Their journalistic irresponsibility and their infatuations with four-letter words, erotica, and excrement offend many people. Yet they unquestionably add to the variety of newspaper fare and give expression to a significant body of critical opinion.

Even if all editors, writers, newscasters, and private citizens were perfectly adjusted personalities, communications problems would remain very much the same. Social change always disorganizes, and values differ even among well-adjusted persons. Deviant persons may complicate communications problems, but they do not cause them.

Improving The Mass Media

Although the owners and operators of the mass media have generally argued that they should be permitted to run their affairs like any other business enterprise, some critics contend that the mass media owe a special obligation to the public, differing from the obligations of other business enterprises. For private citizens are forced by circumstances to support the mass media, whether or not they wish to do so. Of each dollar they spend, a few cents go for advertising, which provides two-thirds of the income of magazines and newspapers and nearly all the income of radio and television. Each radio and television station is a partial monopoly; since the air waves have room for only a limited number of stations, each licensee is protected from unlimited competition. As a result, the industry has had monopoly profits. Commercial television showed profits of $1,250 million in 1977, for a profit rate of 24 percent on sales and 153 percent on depreciated investment.[89] Commercial radio is less profitable, earning $179 million in 1977, for a profit rate of 9 percent on sales and 27 percent on depreciated investment.[90]

Such profit rates, far higher than those earned by most competitive businesses, are possible only because the public grants to a limited number of operators the free use of the air waves. Far from receiving the products of modern communication free, the public pays the entire cost in one way or another, often in ways over which they have no individual control. In citing these facts *we do not necessarily imply that this situation is "bad."* It may be (and probably is) in the public interest to subsidize the media in various ways, for the public's subsidies to the press, and the gift of air waves that have earned such handsome profits for broadcasting, have greatly aided in their development and expansion. Furthermore, they lay the basis for viewing communications as a public utility, answerable to the public for their standards of performance. Many proposals for improvement have been offered, most of them falling into the categories that follow.

ANTIMONOPOLY ACTION

Practically every set of proposals includes measures designed to preserve and increase competition or infuse new blood into the media. Specific proposals include vigorous application and prosecution of the antitrust laws, government encouragement to new ventures in communications, sponsorship of new ventures by philanthropic foundations, encouragement of noncommercial radio and television stations, control of radio program content by stations rather than advertisers, and many others.

To find the most widely acceptable balance between the efficiency of large-scale operation and the presumed benefits of competition is not easy. Any decision involves a value judgment and rearranges an array of vested interests. At present, the trend toward concentration of control appears to be continuing. Whether it is either desirable or politically possible to reverse it is debatable.

CENSORSHIP

Almost every important book ever written, from the *Holy Bible* to *Lady Chatterley's Lover,* has been banned at some time or in some place.[91] That such efforts are unending is revealed in any issue of the American Library Association's *Newsletter of Intellectual Freedom,* which is studded with attempts to strip certain books or magazines from the bookstores and library shelves. A new *Index on Censorship* is now being circulated every other month by Random House (publishers), carrying reports and articles about censorship all around the world. The greatest censorship activity in the United States is probably in the schools, where books are quietly removed from textbook and reading lists or library shelves when a protest is received.[92] There probably have always been and always will be some persons who are confident

While the controversy over censorship of pornography continues to rage, it remains a profitable enterprise. (Irene Springer)

that they know just what words, ideas, or pictures will be harmful for other people to see or hear. But systematic censorship did not appear until the invention of the printing press created the first of the mass media.

Censorship may be *political,* forbidding or punishing the publication of any facts or ideas offensive to the ruling powers. Most of the world's people live in countries where no author, editor, playwright, or public figure dares criticize the society's rulers, or even repeat undeniable facts in a manner that implies criticism. While relatively rare in American history, political censorship, intimidation, and harassment are not unknown.

National security censorship in time of war is practiced by all nations, but in peacetime as well, all governments, including that of the United States, use the national security screen to conceal politically embarrassing information.

In the United States, censorship issues have often involved questions of *obscenity and pornography.*[93] Bawdy songs, tales, and plays have a long tradition, as a glance at Ovid, Chaucer, or Elizabethan drama will illustrate. But laws defining and punishing obscenity were rare until the mid-nineteenth to early twentieth centuries, when many were passed in the United States.[94] In the 1950s the Supreme Court began striking down such laws, culminating in the *Roth* decision, which set the test of obscenity to be "whether to the average person, applying contemporary community standards, the dominant theme taken as a whole appeals to prurient interest.[95] To be obscene, the material had to be "*utterly* without redeeming social value." Under this test it became virtually impossible to obtain a conviction for obscenity, for even the most shallow and vapid series of explicit sexual episodes can be claimed to teach some lessons about life, and an occasional moralizing or philosophizing phrase ("I made a real mess of my life") will enable a work to pass the "utterly without redeeming social value" test. Following these court decisions, pornography came out of hiding. Adult bookstores and "art" theaters multiplied, carrying material that literally left nothing to the imagination, while nudity and occasional sexual intercourse began to be seen on the family theater screens.

In 1973 a changed Supreme Court made obscenity prosecutions less difficult. It ruled that "contemporary community standards" referred to the local community, and changed "utterly without redeeming social value" to "do not have serious literary, artistic, political or scientific value"—a test that practically no hard-core pornography could pass. Under this decision, some successful prosecutions were completed, but were not upheld on appeal. Efforts to punish pornography distributors continue to sputter along without accomplishing much.

Censorship has several basic limitations. (1) It is purely negative. Although it may eliminate "bad" content, it cannot produce "good" content. To censor obscenity does not produce noble drama; instead, it is more likely to produce a studious playing at the fringes of the obscenity code. (2) There may be a boomerang effect. Nothing stimulates the sale of a book like being banned in Boston. A considerable number of third-rate books and shows have been rescued from commercial oblivion by the censors.[96] There is also some experimental evidence that the mere attempt at censorship makes people more receptive to the censored material.[97] It is possible that a flood of local obscenity prosecutions may provide the pornographers with a great deal of priceless advertising. While the Supreme Court's idea of providing for local variations in tolerance level may be plausible, its practical consequence may be to stimulate the sale of pornography by advertising it while making a separate conviction in each locality necessary for suppression. (3) To be fully effective, censorship must be imposed before publication or production. To prosecute the publisher or distributor after appearance of the work will rarely prevent the work's eventual distribution, and often greatly increases its popularity. (4) No satisfactory definition of obscenity has yet been reached, as is shown by the Supreme Court's struggles. Every possible definition involves a subjective judgment, eventually becoming, "If I think it's obscene, then it's obscene." Absolute nudity is less provocative than gossamer covering. Innocent dialogue may become suggestive through gesture or inflection.[98] Pornography in music may be easy to recognize but difficult to put into a useful legal definition.[99] To define obscenity so as to prevent the cheap exploitation of sex without also preventing literary realism and artistic integrity seems impossible. To define subversion so as to prevent the deliberate undermining of the social system yet permit mature social criticism is also impossible. In fact, many attempts to censor subversion are basically attempts to prevent the expression of any social criticism. (5) It is hard to place limits upon censorship. The power to censor indecency also includes the power to censor *ideas* personally offensive to the censors—and sooner or later, this usually happens. For these reasons, scholars and intellectuals seem generally to feel that censorship represents a treatment more dangerous than the disease,[100] although there are some scholarly voices raised in defense of obscenity censorship.[101]

Pornography is opposed by both those who view it as harmful and those who find it personally offensive. Feminists oppose pornography because of its male chauvinism[102] and because it exploits and degrades women.[103] Supporters of censorship and antismut campaigns are confident that bad literature promotes bad behavior. Opposed to this is the opinion of some behavioral scientists that pornography fulfills a safety-valve function for sex deviants and potential sex offenders.[104] Until recently there was exceedingly little real evidence on the question. Most existing evidence was inferential. For example, none of the scientific studies of crime, delinquency, or sexual deviation has pointed out reading or viewing material as a factor in their development. One study asked a sample of women college students what stimuli aroused them sexually; they reported that reading material and pictures were unimportant, while the main stimulus was man—who, though he may deserve censure, is difficult to suppress.[105]

In 1967 Congress provided for a President's Commission on Obscenity and Pornography, whose research teams conducted and collected the first substantial body of research evidence on the effects of obscenity on behavior. Published in 1970, the report gave no evidence that pornography harms people.[106] The commission reported that delinquent and nondelinquent youth have had a similar exposure to pornography,[107] and that while viewing explicit sexual materials is followed by some increase in sex activity, this takes place within the person's established pattern of sex behavior.[108] In other words, it appears that a pornographic book or film causes one to do more of whatever one is in the habit of doing, but does not lead one to do something one is not in the habit of doing. The commission concluded,

> Extensive empirical investigation, both by the Commission and by others, provides no evidence that exposure to or use of explicit sexual materials plays a significant role in the causation of social or individual harms such as crime delinquency, sexual or nonsexual deviancy, or severe emotional disturbance.[109]

The commission also cites the experience of Denmark, where the end of obscenity censorship and the increased availability of pornography was followed by a sharp decline in the sale of pornography and in the frequency of sex crimes.[110] The decrease, however, was not in violent sex crimes but in minor offenses (exhibitionism, voyeurism, homosexuality), and it may have been due to less complete reporting.[111] In the United States, unlike Denmark, relaxation of pornography censorship was followed by a tremendous expansion of the porno market, which shows no signs of declining.

The pornography commission failed to settle the pornography issue. Although it concluded that pornography appears to be harmless and recommended that laws against pornography be repealed, not all people accept this judgment.[112] One critic notes that the evidence for harmful consequences of pornography and for harmful consequences of media violence is very similar, and suggests that wishful thinking may have led to the conclusion that television violence is harmful while pornography is harmless.[113] Another observer attributes the conflicting research conclusions on the effects of pornography and the effects of violence to the machismo of the researchers.[114]

> The inherent flaw in the ability of commercial broadcasting to serve the public interest adequately is that the broadcasters make money by serving advertisers necessarily; make money by serving the public only incidentally, if at all; often lose money by serving the public well and often can make more money by serving the public ill.
>
> Robert J. Blakely, *The People's Instrument: A Philosophy of Programming for Public Television* (Washington, D.C.: Public Affairs Press, 1971), p. 15.

Present public policy toward pornography is in a state of confusion. Sporadic prosecutions are seldom effective, and pornography is freely available nearly everywhere. There is some experimentation with pornography zoning. In *concentration zoning*, porno houses and other commercial sex businesses are confined to a small area, such as Boston's so-called combat zone. But high levels of prostitution, mugging, and other crimes are reported results, and wherever the porno zone is placed, immediately adjacent areas become blighted.[115] More widely favored is *dispersal zoning*, such as that in Detroit, where a minimum distance of 1,000 feet between sex businesses is required, with consent of over half the residents or businesses located within 500 feet of the operation.[116] Whether such restrictions are constitutional has not yet been tested.[117]

DEVELOPMENT OF NONCOMMERCIAL MEDIA

It is unrealistic to expect commercial broadcasting to be concerned primarily with anything except making money. As one television executive remarks, "Because television can make so much money doing its worst, it cannot often afford to do its best."[118] If broadcasting is to offer much besides popular entertainment at the least-common-denominator level, this variety must come from noncommercial broadcasting.

The history of educational radio and television is largely one of hopes unfulfilled. By 1977 over 900 educational radio and 260 educational television stations were in operation—some for only a few hours a day. The National Association of Educational Broadcasters and National Educational Television serve as clearinghouses for the exchange of tapes and programs. Considering the funds expended, the achievements are impressive. But many educational stations have yearly budgets of less than that of a single episode of a major commercial show such as "Hawaii Five-O."

In 1968 Congress established a Corporation for Public Broadcasting (CPB) to receive annual federal appropriations and private contributions to finance a noncommercial network. The CPB, directed by ten presidential appointees, contracts with National Educational Television and other producers to produce the programs. These are then distributed through the Public Broadcasting Service (PBS) to local noncommercial television stations, and through National Public Radio (NPR) to noncommercial radio stations. Most of these noncommercial stations are operated by universities or school systems.

This organizational structure is unsatisfactory. It is vulnerable to presidential politics, as President Nixon's near-destruction of it illustrates.[119] Its

437

divided authority insures feuding between CPB and PBS, with duplication of efforts and waste of funds.[120] A Carnegie Commission report in 1979 called for a reorganization to remove divided authority, along with a great increase in funding, paid largely by a tax on commercial broadcasters for use of the air waves.[121] It is most unlikely that this tax will be enacted.

REGULATION

Self-regulation of some sort is proclaimed by all of the media, each of which has some sort of voluntary code of ethics that is piously praised and widely disregarded. Experience seems to indicate that self-regulation is effective only when an industry feels the public breath hot upon its collective neck. Whether purely voluntary codes without machinery for enforcement accomplish anything is debatable. They may persuade an industry toward a greater sense of social responsibility, or they may retard this development by lending an implied sanction to certain dubious but widespread practices within the industry. The rating code of the Motion Picture Association of America, (G, GP, R, and X) has not noticeably "cleaned up" the movies; instead they have been growing more erotic. Its main effect—and possibly an important one—has been to enable patrons to select movies unlikely to offend them, and thus to reduce criticism of the industry.[122] The National Association of Broadcasters since 1948 has had a voluntary code limiting the part of each hour that may be devoted to commercials, but it is widely ignored.[123] When the FCC threatened to enforce the industry's own code upon it, the industry sought passage of the law to prevent the FCC from regulating time given to commercials.[124] The most recent industry exercise in self-regulation is the 1975 "family viewing time" rule, under which the sex-and-violence shows were moved to 9:00 P.M. or later (on the dubious assumption that children were in bed by 9:00). While a majority of the public approved, most people reported no change in their viewing habits. In a national survey in 1979, "too much violence" and "too much sex" were the two most common complaints.[125] It is unrealistic to expect that self-regulation will stop any practice that is profitable to the industry, or that it will elevate standards of performance above the level of bare public tolerance.

Government regulation is found only in broadcasting, arising from the fact that some system of licensed wave-lengths is necessary to avoid chaos. There are some who believe that the FCC has the capacity to improve broadcast content but has been spineless and negligent in not doing so. Typical of many criticisms is the observation that "the behavior of the regulators generally was shown to be largely verbal posturing accompanied by acquiescence to industry practices in the area of programming."[126]

There is some debate over whether the FCC should attempt to influence program content, or should merely regulate technical operations and leave program content to the discretion of the station owner. One group argues that (1) the air waves belong to the public; (2) since technology limits the number of broadcast channels, the protected monopoly position of the broadcast licensee should be subject to government regulation in the public interest; and (3) competition will not provide balanced program content.[127] An opposing group contends that (1) recent technology has greatly enlarged the number of channels, so that (2) broadcasting is today less a monopoly than the press, and (3) broadcasting should have the same freedom of expression enjoyed by the press.[128] The current trend seems to be in the direction of reducing FCC regulatory efforts to influence program content.[129]

Since an estimated one-third of all members of Congress have a financial interest in broadcasting, Congress is not likely to require the FCC to do anything that would reduce profits, and any such proposals are generally defeated as invasions of freedom of speech.[130]

Citizens' media councils are a possible means of exerting public pressure for media self-improvement. A number of local media councils have attempted to influence local newspaper content but appear to have been ineffective.[131] Citizens' groups such as Action for Children's Television and the National Citizens Committee on Broadcasting have had some influence upon broadcasters and in some instances have challenged license renewals before the FCC.[132] The National Federation for Decency claims credit for pressuring some advertisers to drop sponsorship of some violent shows.[133] Possibly because of citizen pressures, television violence has declined slightly since 1975, to be replaced by an increasing emphasis upon sex.[134]

It is questionable, however, whether widespread changes in media performance will come from any deliberate attempts at improvement, through either government regulation or citizen group pressure. Changes in media performance, for better or worse, are more likely to come as incidental by-products of changing technology or changing profit opportunities. The support of noncommercial media may offer the greatest opportunities for improvement of media programs.

Summary

Changes in the technology and business organization of communication have revolutionized the interchange of ideas and the formation of the public opinion by which democracy operates. To many responsible critics, the performance of the media and the vitality of democracy are threatened (1) by tendencies toward monopoly and concentration of control of the media, (2) by their biases and occasional irresponsibility, and (3) by the limited variety and low cultural level of content. Critics also feel that the public, due to its indirect investments in and subsidies to the media, has a legitimate right to a voice in shaping their policies. The numerous suggestions include (1) action to reduce the degree of concentration of control, (2) censorship, (3) development of noncommercial facilities to supplement commercial media, and (4) regulation.

Critics of the media concede some improvement. The press is greatly more accurate, impartial, and responsible than it was in earlier decades. Movies have become in general more artistically produced, but remain mostly trivial and often offensive. Noncommercial radio and television are helping to provide greater diversity than ever before. The mass media have helped to elevate the level of popular taste, so that as early as 1951 we were buying more admissions to symphony concerts than to baseball games.

There is a tendency throughout the media to avoid controversial issues and curtail minority viewpoints. Whether this tendency continues will depend upon what happens to the general intellectual atmosphere of our society. If this atmosphere grows steadily more repressive and authoritarian, all discussions of press freedom will become purely academic. But if such curbs are avoided, there is some prospect that the performance of the media will grow more steadily satisfactory to public and critics alike.

Suggested Readings

AUDISON, F. SCOTT, "TV Violence and Viewer Aggression: A Compilation of Study Results," *Public Opinion Quarterly*, 41 (Fall 1977), 314–31. A brief summary of research findings on television violence and aggression.

BAGDIKIAN, BEN H., *The Effete Conspiracy and Other Crimes of the Press* (New York: Harper & Row, 1972). An interestingly written, popular critique of the press. See especially ch. 5, "Alas, the Small Town Press," which tells how special interest groups used canned editorials and press releases to advance their interests.

BAIRD, JOHN E., JR., "Television Programming: The 'Boob Tube' Takes a Bum Rap," *Intellect*, 104 (May–June 1976), 590–93. A brief defense of network television.

BERKOWITZ, LEONARD, "Sex and Violence: We Can't Have It Both Ways," *Psychology Today*, Dec. 1971, pp. 14ff. An argument that social scientists have followed similar evidence to opposite conclusions respecting the harmful effects of pornography and violence.

CHRISTENSON, REO M., "Censorship of Pornography? No," *The Progressive*, Sept. 1970, pp. 24–27; also A. S. Engel, "Censorship of Pornography? Yes," *The Progressive*, Sept. 1970, pp. 28–30; both reprinted in *Current*, Nov. 1970, pp. 31–43. A rational debate of the censorship issue.

COMSTOCK, GEORGE M., et al., *Television and Human Behavior* (New York: Columbia University Press, 1978). A thorough review of the question of the total effects of television upon behavior.

ALFRED I. DuPONT FOUNDATION and COLUMBIA UNIVERSITY GRADUATE SCHOOL OF JOURNALISM, *Survey of Broadcast Journalism* (New York: Grosset & Dunlap). An annual survey of the developments and issues in broadcast journalism.

FRIENDLY, FRED W., "The Campaign to Politicize Broadcasting," *Columbia Journalism Review*, Mar.–Apr. 1972, pp. 9–18; reprinted in *Current*, May 1973, pp. 19–31. A documented accusation that the Nixon administration sought to intimidate the media into adopting a more favorable bias. See also rejoinder by William F. Buckley, Jr., "Broadcasting Dilemma," *New York Post*, 8 Mar. 1973; reprinted in *Current*, May 1973, p. 32.

HARWOOD, MICHAEL, "America with Its Ears On," *New York Times Magazine*, 15 Apr. 1976, pp. 28ff. A popular description of the explosion of, uses of, and problems created by citizens' band radio.

MARTINO, JOSEPH P., "Telecommunications in the Year 2000," *The Futurist*, Apr. 1979; reprinted in *Current*, June 1979, pp. 25–34. An effort to forecast the development and consequences of technological change in telecommunications.

RIST, RAY C., ed., *The Pornography Controversy* (New Brunswick, N.J.: Transaction Books, 1975). A collection on the issue of pornography.

ROBINSON, MICHAEL J., "Television and American Politics, 1956–1976," *The Public Interest*, Summer 1977, pp. 3–39. An analysis of political bias in television.

TUCHMAN, GAYE, *The TV Establishment: Programming for Power and Profit* (Englewood Cliffs, N.J.: Prentice-Hall, 1974). A critical analysis of the television industry.

WEAVER, PAUL H., "The New Journalism and the Old: Thoughts after Watergate," *The Public Interest*, Spring 1974, pp. 67–88. A discussion of liberal versus adversary journalism.

WYNN, MARIE, *The Plug-In Drug* (New York, Viking, 1977). Argues, with considerable evidence, that television is turning us into a nation of mindless, spineless zombies.

ZURCHER, LOUIS A., JR., and GEORGE KIRKPATRICK, *Citizens for Decency: Antipornography Crusades as Status Defense* (Austin: University of Texas Press, 1976). A research study of antipornography crusaders and their motivation.

Footnotes

[1] William L. Rivers et al., *The Mass Media and Modern Society* (San Francisco: Rinehart Press, 1971), p. 277.

[2] Flora Lewis, "Language a Key to the Spirit of an Islamic Revival," *New York Times*, 30 Dec. 1979, p. 1.

[3] *'79 Ayer Directory of Publications* (Philadelphia, Ayer Press, 1979). Many

statistics in this chapter are given in round numbers. They are not exact and not always comparable, for the data are constantly changing, and different sources compile and classify data differently.

[4]Several studies have established that motion pictures can produce striking changes in attitudes and beliefs. See Solomon P. Rosenberg, "Change of Socioeconomic Attitudes under Radical Motion Picture Propaganda," *Archives of Psychology*, no. 166 (New York: Columbia University Press, 1934); L. L. Thurstone, "Influence of Movies on Children's Attitudes," *Journal of Social Psychology*, 2 (Aug. 1931), 291–305; Herbert Blumer, "Molding Mass Behavior through Motion Pictures," *Publications of the American Sociology Society*, 29 (1934), 115–17; see also the 28 volumes of the Payne Fund studies (*Motion Pictures and Youth*, various authors, Macmillan, 1933; Arno Press, 1970). So conclusive were these earlier studies that little recent research in this area has been published.

[5]"Magazines Targeted at the Working Woman," *Business Week*, 18 Feb. 1980, pp. 150–52.

[6]Robert C. Bower, quoted in *TV Guide*, 14 July 1973, p. 5.

[7]George Comstock et al., *Television and Human Behavior* (New York: Columbia University Press, 1978), p. 154.

[8]Ibid., pp. 88, 89, 92, 125.

[9]Ellen Torgerson, in *TV Guide*, 23 Apr. 1977, p. 4.

[10]Data from *'79 Ayer Directory of Publications*.

[11]"The Big Money Hunts for Independent Newspapers," *Business Week*, 21 Feb. 1977, pp. 56–62; John Hohenberg, *A Crisis for the American Press* (New York: Columbia University Press, 1978), p. 35.

[12]Raymond B. Nixon and Tae-Youl Hahn, "Concentration of Press Ownership: A Comparison of 32 Countries," *Journalism Quarterly*, 48 (Sept. 1971), 5–16.

[13]Henry Raymont, *"Reader's Digest Suppresses Book," New York Times*, 2 June 1968, p. 88.

[14]Federal Communications Commission, *43rd Annual Report, Fiscal 1977* (Washington, D.C., 1978), p. 132.

[15]See "The Tuned-out, Turned-off FCC," *Consumer Reports*, 33 (Oct. 1968), 532–36; Frank Wolff, *Television Programming for News and Public Affairs: A Quantitative Analysis of Networks and Stations* (New York: Praeger, 1972), p. 61.

[16]See Grant McConnell, *Private Power and American Democracy* (New York: Alfred A. Knopf, 1966), for a discussion of "regulation by the regulated for the regulated." See also Manuel F. Cohen and George F. Stigler, *Can Regulatory Agencies Protect Consumers?* (Washington, D.C.: American Enterprise Institute for Public Policy Research, 1971).

[17]Nicholas Johnson, on CBS "Face the Nation," 14 Sept. 1969.

[18]"Still Pitching for Pay-TV," *Business Week*, 11 Apr. 1977, pp. 111–14.

[19]"The Networks Shrug Off New Competition," *Business Week*, 27 Mar. 1971, pp. 90–96; Benno C. Schmidt, Jr., in Glen O. Robinson, ed., *Communications for Tomorrow: Policy Perspectives for the 1980s* (New York: Praeger, 1978), p. 210.

[20]*Statistical Abstract of the United States, 1979*, p. 585.

[21]Pam Eversole, "Concentration of Ownership in the Communication Industry," *Journalism Quarterly*, 42 (Summer 1971), 251–60.

[22]Eversole, "Concentration of Ownership."

[23]Gerald L. Grotta, "Consolidation of Newspapers: What Happens to the Consumer?" *Journalism Quarterly*, 48 (Summer 1971), 245–50.

[24]Daniel B. Wackman et al., "Chain Newspaper Autonomy as Reflected in Presidential Campaign Endorsements," *Journalism Quarterly*, 52 (Autumn 1975), 411–20.

[25]Frank Luther Mott, *American Journalism* (New York: Macmillan, 1950), ch. 31.

[26]Ferdinand Lundberg, *Imperial Hearst* (New York: Equinox Co-operative Press, 1936), pp. 151–73.

[27]*The Reporter*, 17 Aug. 1954, p. 5.

[28]Raymond B. Nixon and Robert Jones, "The Content of Noncompetitive vs. Competitive Newspapers," *Journalism Quarterly*, 33 (Summer 1956), 299–314; John C. Schweitzer and Elaine Goldman, "Does Newspaper Competition Make a Difference to Readers?" *Journalism Quarterly*, 52 (Winter 1975), 706–10.

[29]Gerald L. Grotta, "Consolidation of Newspapers: What Happens to the Consumer?" *Journalism Quarterly*, 48 (Summer 1971), 245–50.

[30]Hohenberg, p. 372.

[31]Comstock, pp. 133–34, 137.

[32]*Gallup Opinion Index, Report No. 166*, May 1979, p. 1.

[33]Edith Efron, *The News Twisters* (Los Angeles: Nash, 1971); Joseph Kelley, *The Left-Leaning Antenna: Political Bias in Tele-*

vision (New Rochelle, N.Y.: Arlington House, 1971); see also Edith Efron's frequent "News Watch" columns in *TV Guide*.

[34]Bernard Roshco, *Newsmaking* (Chicago: University of Chicago Press, 1975), p. 38.

[35]Philip J. Coffey, "A Quantitative Measure of Bias in Reporting Political News," *Journalism Quarterly*, 52 (Autumn 1975), 551–53.

[36]Study conducted by International Research Associates for CBS, summarized in Appendix C in Edith Efron, *How CBS Tried to Kill a Book* (Los Angeles: Nash, 1972).

[37]Frank D. Russo, "A Study of Bias in TV Coverage of the Vietnam War: 1969 and 1970," *Public Opinion Quarterly*, 35 (Winter 1971–72), 536–43.

[38]Ernest W. Lefever, *TV and National Defense: An Analysis of CBS News, 1972–73* (Boston, Va.: Institute for American Strategies Press, 1974); C. Richard Hofstetter, *Bias in the News: Network Television Coverage of the 1972 Election Campaign* (Columbus: Ohio State University Press, 1976).

[39]Michael J. Robinson and Karen A. McPherson, "Television News Coverage before the 1976 New Hampshire Primary: The Focus of Network Journalism," *Journal of Broadcasting*, 21 (Spring 1977), 177–86.

[40]Jerry K. Frye, "American Newspapers vs. Agnew's 1970 Political Campaign," *Journal of Applied Communications Research*, 4 (Apr. 1976), 25–39.

[41]Michael J. Robinson, "Television and American Politics: 1956–1976," *The Public Interest*, Summer 1977, pp. 3–39.

[42]John B. Robinson, "Perceived Media Bias and the 1968 Vote: Can the Media Affect Behavior After All?" *Journalism Quarterly*, 49 (Summer 1972), 239–46.

[42]Newton H. Minow et al., *Presidential Television* (New York: Basic Books, 1973).

[44]Fred W. Friendly, "The Campaign to Politicize Broadcasting," *Columbia Journalism Review*, Mar.–Apr. 1973, pp. 9–18; Ben H. Bagdikian, *The Effete Conspiracy and Other Crimes by the Press* (New York: Harper & Row, 1974), ch. 15; Marvin Barrett, ed., *Moments of Truth: The Fifth Alfred I. DuPont–Columbia University Survey of Broadcast Journalism* (New York: Thomas Y. Crowell, 1975), pp. 170–73.

[45]Fred W. Friendly, *Due to Circumstances beyond Our Control* (New York: Random House, 1967), p. 90.

[46]Lefever, *TV and National Defense*.

[47]Robert Stein, *Media Power* (Boston: Houghton Mifflin, 1972), pp. 216–17.

[48]Roger Seasonwein and Leonard R. Sussman, "Can Extremists Using TV Move an Audience?" *Journalism Quarterly*, 49 (Spring 1972), 61–64.

[49]Max Gunther, "The Worst Diet Advice," *TV Guide*, 11 Jan. 1975, pp. 5–6.

[50]David L. Altheide, *Creating Reality: How TV News Distorts Reality* (Beverly Hills, Ca.: Sage Publications, 1976).

[51]Stephen E. Rada, "Manipulating the Media: A Case Study of a Chicano Strike in Texas," *Journalism Quarterly*, 54 (Apr. 1977), 109–13.

[52]Patrick Buchanan, "Television: Patsy and Promoter for Terrorists," *TV Guide*, 26 Mar. 1977, pp. 5–6.

[53]David Sleeper, "Media Coverage of the Environment: The News May Not Be the Truth," *USA Today*, Jan. 1980, pp. 49–51.

[54]Ben H. Bagdikian, *The Effete Conspiracy*, ch. 4.

[55]Chris Welles, "The Fairness Doctrine," *TV Guide*, 30 Aug. 1975, pp. 4–9.

[56]Fred W. Friendly, *The Good Guys, the Bad Guys, and the First Amendment* (New York: Random House, 1976).

[57]Gary A. Steiner, *The People Look at Television* (New York: Alfred A. Knopf, 1963); Robert T. Bower, *Television and the Public* (New York: Holt, Rinehart and Winston, 1973).

[58]Bower, *Television and the Public*.

[59]David E. Powell, "Television in the U.S.S.R.," *Public Opinion Quarterly*, 39 (Fall 1975), 287–300.

[60]Steiner, *People Look at Television*; Bower, *Television and the Public*.

[61]Bower, *Television and the Public*.

[62]Steiner, *People Look at Television*, p. 38; Bower, *Television and the Public*.

[63]Dan Rottenberg, "Do News Reports Bias Jurors?" *Columbia Journalism Review*, May–June 1976, pp. 16–18.

[64]James Aubrey, quoted in *Business Week*, 23 June 1973, p. 117.

[65]Bill Everett, quoted in *TV Guide*, 2 June 1973, p. 7.

[66]See John Cuchane, "Where TV Documentaries Don't Dare to Tread," *New York Times*, 20 Feb. 1977, sec. 2, pp. 1ff.

[67]Melvin Durslag, "They Preach the Gospel of the Great Outdoors," *TV Guide*, 25 Oct. 1975, pp. 12–15.

[68]Editorial, "How 'The Guns of Autumn' Backfired," *American Rifleman*, Nov. 1975, pp. 21–24; Editorial, "The 'Guns of Autumn' Aims Low," *Columbia Jour-*

nalism Review, Nov.–Dec. 1975, p. 4; Irv Drasin, "'The Guns of Autumn': The Producer Replies," *Columbia Journalism Review*, Jan.–Feb. 1976, pp. 48–49. (The $3-million-dollar damage suit was dismissed in 1980.)

[69]Douglas Bauer, "Are Those Powerful Documentaries Gone Forever?" *TV Guide*, 28 July 1979, pp. 2–7.

[70]*Motion Pictures and Youth*, 28 vols. by various authors (New York: Macmillan, 1933; reissued by Arno Press, 1970).

[71]Diane Shipler, "Murder for Moppets," *The Progressive*, Mar. 1953, pp. 28–29.

[72]Neil Hickey, "Skipper Chuck and Buckskin Bill are Not Feeling Very Jolly," *TV Guide*, 2 June 1973, pp. 3–9.

[73]George Comstock, "The Evidence So Far," *Journal of Communication*, 25 (Autumn 1975), 25–34.

[74]Burton Paulu, *British Broadcasting in Transition* (Minneapolis: University of Minnesota Press, 1961), p. 194.

[75]*Time*, 7 June 1976, p. 63.

[76]Grant H. Hendrick, "When Television Is a School for Criminals," *TV Guide*, 29 Jan. 1977, pp. 4–10.

[77]Seymour Feshback and Robert D. Singer, *Television and Aggression* (San Francisco: Jossey-Bass, 1971); Timothy Hartnagel, James J. Teenan, Jr., and Jennie J. McIntyre, "Television Violence and Violent Behavior," *Social Forces*, 54 (Dec. 1975), 341–51; Dennis Howitt and Guy Cumberbacht, *Mass Media, Violence and Society* (New York: John Wiley, 1975).

[78]F. Scott Audison, "TV Violence and Viewer Aggression: A Cumulation of Study Results," *Public Opinion Quarterly*, 41 (Fall 1977), 314–31.

[79]Surgeon General's Advisory Committee on Television and Social Behavior, *Television and Growing Up: The Impact of Televised Violence* (Washington, D.C.: U.S. Public Health Service, 1972), pp. 5, 7, 11, 177, 178; Robert M. Liebert et al., *The Early Window: Effects of Television on Children and Youth* (New York: Pergamon, 1973); Douglass Cater and Stephen Strickland, *TV Violence and the Child: The Evolution and Role of the Surgeon General's Report* (New York: Russell Sage, 1975).

[80]The broadcast industry was permitted a veto over appointments, and it blackballed nominees unfavorable to industry views. See Rose K. Golden, "Review Essay: Alice in Wonderland," *Society*, May–June 1973, pp. 64–66.

[81]George Gerbner and Larry Gross, "The Scary World of TV's Heavy Viewer," *Psychology Today*, Apr. 1976, pp. 41ff.

[82]Ronald S. Drabman and Margaret Hanratty Thomas, "Does TV Violence Breed Indifference?" *Journal of Communication*, Autumn 1975, pp. 86–89.

[83]Myles Callum, "What Viewers Love/Hate about Television," *TV Guide*, 12 May 1979, pp. 6–12.

[84]Michael Alan Stroller, "The Economics of UHF Television: Effects of a Government Policy," reviewed in *TV Guide*, 19 Aug. 1978, p. A-4.

[85]Federal Communications Commission, *Public Service Responsibility of Broadcast Licensees* (Washington, D.C., 1946), p. 39.

[86]"Cable TV: The Lure of Diversity," *Time*, 7 Mar. 1979, pp. 82–86.

[87]See Les Brown, *Television: The Business behind the Box* (New York: Harcourt Brace Jovanovich, 1971), ch. 15; also, "The Networks Fight to Regain a Half Hour," *Business Week*, 8 Apr. 1972, pp. 76–77; "Perfect Boomerang," *Time*, 5 Feb. 1973, p. 55.

[88]Walter Baer, "Telecommunications in the 1980s," in Glen O. Robinson, ed., *Communications for Tomorrow*, ch. 2.

[89]FCC, *43rd Annual Report*, pp. 133, 146.

[90]Ibid., pp. 127, 133.

[91]Anne Lyon Haight and Chandler B. Grannis, *Banned Books, 387 B.C. to 1978 A.D.* (New York: R. R. Bowker, 1978).

[92]*New York Times Book Review*, 30 Jan. 1977, p. 33; "Was Robin Just a Hood?" *Time*, 31 Dec. 1979, p. 76.

[93]Strictly defined, *pornography* refers to offensive sexual material, while *obscenity* refers to *any* kind of offensive material. The two terms are commonly used interchangeably.

[94]Thomas I. Emerson, *The System of Freedom of Expression* (New York: Random House, 1970), ch. 13.

[95]*Roth vs. United States*, 354 U.S. 476 (1957); *Memoirs vs. Massachusetts*, 303 U.S. 413–419 (1966).

[96]See Dick Meister, "How 'Howl' Became a Best Seller," *The Progressive*, Feb. 1958, pp. 36–37.

[97]Stephen Worchel and Susan E. Arnold, "The Effects of Censorship and Attractiveness of the Censor on Attitude Change," *Journal of Experimental Social Psychology*, 9 (1973), 365–77.

[98]Stan Freberg's recording, "John and Marsha" contained only two words

John and *Marsha,* repeated over and over with various inflections and hesitations. It was banned from the airwaves as too suggestive. See Daniel Dixon, "Laughing at Madison Avenue for Fun and Profit," *Esquire,* Feb. 1959, pp. 55ff.

[99]David Devoss, "Aural Sex: The Rise of Porn Rock," *Human Behavior,* July 1976, pp. 65–68.

[100]Morris L. Ernst and Alan U. Schwartz, *Censorship: The Search for the Obscene* (New York: Macmillan, 1964); W. Cody Wilson, "Why Should We Worry about Pornography?" *Annals of the American Academy of Political and Social Science,* 397 (Sept. 1971), 105–17.

[101]Harry M. Clor, *Obscenity and Public Morality: Censorship in a Liberal Society* (Chicago: University of Chicago Press, 1969); Irving Kristol, "Pornography, Obscenity, and the Case for Censorship," *New York Times Magazine,* 28 Mar. 1971, pp. 24ff. Bernard L. Bonniwell, "Social Control of Pornography and Sexual Behavior," *Annals of the American Academy of Political and Social Science,* 397 (Sept. 1971), 97–104.

[102]Don R. Smith, "The Social Content of Pornography," *Journal of Communications,* 26 (Winter 1976), 16–24.

[103]"Women's War on Porn," *Time,* 27 Aug. 1979, p. 64.

[104]Eberhard Kronhausen and Phyllis Kronhausen, *Pornography and the Law* (New York: Ballantine, 1959), pp. 261–89.

[105]Benjamin Karpman, quoted in *Censorship Bulletin* (New York: American Book Publishers' Council, Aug. 1958), p. 3.

[106]*Report of President's Commission on Pornography and Obscenity* (Washington, D.C., 1970); also Michael J. Goldstein and Harold Sanfort Kant, *Pornography and Sexual Deviance: A Report of the Legal and Behavioral Institute* (Berkeley, Ca.: University of California Press, 1973).

[107]Ibid., p. 26.

[108]Ibid., p. 25.

[109]Ibid., p. 52.

[110]Ibid., p. 27.

[111]Leonard Berkowitz, "Sex and Violence: We Can't Have It Both Ways," *Psychology Today,* Dec. 1971, pp. 14ff.

[112]Victor B. Cline, "The Scientists vs. Pornography: An Untold Story," *Intellect,* 105 (May–June 1976), 574–76.

[113]Berkowitz, "Sex and Violence."

[114]Thelma McCormack, "Machismo in Media Research: A Critical Review of Research on Violence and Pornography," *Social Problems,* 25 (June 1978), 544–55.

[115]Robert Lindsey, "Drive by Cities on Pornography Spurred by Detroit Zoning Case," *New York Times,* 28 Nov. 1976, pp. 1ff.

[116]Ibid.

[117]Tom Goldstein, "Will Porno Zoning Stand Up in Court?" *New York Times,* 30 Jan. 1977, sec. 4, p. 7.

[118]Friendly, *Due to Circumstances beyond Our Control,* p. xii.

[119]Friendly, "The Campaign to Politicize Broadcasting"; Editorial, *Columbia Journalism Review,* July–Aug. 1973, pp. 3–4; "A Blow to Public TV," *Time,* 22 Jan. 1973; "Call from the White House," *New York Times,* 29 Apr. 1973, p. 1.

[120]Neil Hickey, "Public TV in Turmoil," *TV Guide,* 23 July 1977, pp. 2–9.

[121]"New Blueprint for Public TV," *New York Times,* 28 Jan. 1979, sec. 4, p. 18; "Recasting the Public System," *Time,* 12 Feb. 1979, p. 93; Les Brown, "The 'New' PBS—More Than a Facelift," *New York Times,* 23 Dec. 1979, sec. 2, pp. 33–34.

[122]Stephen Farber, *The Movie Rating Game* (Washington, D.C.: Public Affairs Press, 1972).

[123]FCC *Hearings,* pp. 5526–27; David H. McGannon, "Is the TV Code a Fraud?" *TV Guide,* 22 Jan. 1977, pp. 11–13.

[124]R. L. Shayon, "Forty-three Cheers," *Saturday Review,* 47 (18 Apr. 1964), 30.

[125]Callum, "What Viewers Love/Hate about Television."

[126]Frank Wolff, quoted in *Columbia Journalism Review,* Mar.–Apr. 1973, p. 61.

[127]Johnson, *How to Talk Back to Your Television Set;* Kenneth A. Cox, "The FCC's Role in Television Programming for News and Public Affairs," *Villanova Law Review,* 14 (Summer 1969), 590–601.

[128]Edmund A. Barker, "The FCC's Role in TV Programming Regulation," *Villanova Law Review,* 14 (Summer 1969), 623–28; Ben C. Fisher, "Program Control and the Federal Communications Commission: A Limited Role," *Villanova Law Review,* 14 (Summer 1969), 602–18.

[129]Benno C. Schmidt, Jr., "Pluralistic Programming and Regulation of Mass Communications Media," in Johnson, ed., *Communications for Tomorrow,* ch. 5.

[130]Estimate by Edmund C. Bunker, president of the Radio Advertising Bureau, quoted in *Time,* 84 (18 Sept. 1964), 102.

[131]L. Erwin Atwood and Kenneth Stark, "Effects of Community Press Councils: Real and Imagined," *Journalism Quarterly,* 49 (Summer 1972), 230–38.

[132]Donald L. Guimary, *Citizens' Groups*

and Broadcasting (New York: Praeger, 1975); Leonard Gross, "Television under Pressure," *TV Guide,* 22 Feb. 1975, pp. 4–7.

[133]Harry F. Waters, "The Rev. Donald Wildman's Crusade against 'Sexploitation'," *Family Weekly,* 27 Jan. 1980, p. 18.

[134]Ron Powers, "Pressure Groups Are Forcing Mayhem off TV—But They May Not Like What Replaces It," *TV Guide,* 5 Aug. 1978, pp. 2–8.

SOCIAL DEVIANCE 16

[Kenneth] Donaldson was committed to [The Florida State Hospital] in 1957. He was a college dropout and a divorced father of three; though he had had regular jobs, he had begun complaining that he was being harassed by unknown people. Since Donaldson was given virtually no psychiatric treatment, he repeatedly sued for his freedom. . . .

Last week, at 67 Donaldson joined the ranks of those whose cases have prompted major Supreme Court decisions. The court unanimously ruled that every mental patient . . . who is held involuntarily has the right to be either treated or released. . . .[1]

There are no reliable estimates on the number of alcoholic women—there may be anywhere from 900,000 to 4.5 million. Past estimates said one in five alcoholics in this country are women; more recent estimates say one in three alcoholics is a woman. . . .

When men drink excessively, they often get into trouble on the job or with the law. When a woman drinks excessively, it may be years before anyone outside her immediate family recognizes she is an alcoholic. . . .[2]

Peter B. Bensinger, new head of the federal Drug Enforcement Administration, says that while he is going to enforce all the laws against narcotics, his lowest priority is marijuana—just above aspirin.[3]

A child custody suit involving a 38-year-old nurse who is a self-described lesbian may become a landmark case in the area of homosexual rights. . . . The nurse admitted in court testimony that her love for a 30-year-old divorcee with whom she lives . . . does not interfere with her ability to raise her 9-year-old son. . . .[4]

The quotations above suggest a few dimensions of forms of deviance that are widely regarded as social problems: mental illness, alcoholism, drug abuse, and sexual deviation. With the exception of mental illness, government has attempted unsuccessfully to stamp them out by making them illegal; they are often referred to as "crimes without victims," because ordinarily no one is hurt by these crimes except the deviants themselves.[5] We treat them together in this chapter because they lend themselves to combined analysis in terms of the three sociological approaches.

Mental Illness

HISTORY OF THE PROBLEM

Mental illness has been defined as a social problem for perhaps as long as humankind has been on earth; the Ebers Papyrus of 1550 B.C. stated, ". . . his mind raves through something entering from above," which is assumed to mean that primitive people attributed mental illness to evil spirits. Even after the dawn of civilization, holes were cut in the skulls of mentally ill people to let the evil spirits out, and attempts were made to exorcise the spirits through religious rites.

In the fifteenth century asylums (hospitals) for the insane appeared. The popular name of one of these, Bedlam, subsequently came to connote the conditions that existed there. Violent patients in chains were exhibited to the public, while the harmless were sent into the streets to beg. At first there were no mental hospitals in the United States, and the mentally ill were often locked up in attics or cellars. If they were poor and could not be isolated, they might be driven out of town so that the town would not have to support them. The first mental hospital in this country opened in 1773.

In the mid-nineteenth century Dorothea Dix campaigned for the humane treatment of the mentally ill. She is often given credit for establishing state mental hospitals. New York in 1890 became the first to require the state government to provide hospitals and care for the legally insane. Massive hospitals were built and hordes of people for whom there was no effective treatment were crammed into them. Ignorance of how to treat mental illness combined with grossly inadequate hospital funding to create unspeakably bad conditions. The hospitals were crowded beyond capacity; patients were quartered in the corridors, sat on the floor for lack of furniture, and sometimes even lacked clothing. Psychosurgery, which destroys areas of the brain; electric shock treatment; and hydrotherapy were widely used to calm violent patients. By the end of World War II conditions in the state hospitals were becoming a national scandal.[6]

448

The Madhouse (Bedlam) by William Hogarth. Engraving from the Rake's Progress.
(The Bettman Archive, Inc.)

The greatest change in the treatment of mental illness resulted from the development of psychoactive drugs—tranquilizers and antidepressants—during the mid-1950s. While they did not cure mental illness in any specific sense, these drugs became increasingly widely used to enable the mentally ill to continue functioning in the community. Fewer people were sent to hospitals, and many who were already there were released (see figure 16–1).

In 1963 Congress passed the Community Mental Health Centers Act, which authorized federal funding for the construction and staffing of community centers offering inpatient care; outpatient clinics; partial hospitalization for those needing only day, night, or weekend care; emergency care; and consultation and education. Several hundred such community centers have been established, providing close-to-home service for a growing proportion of the population. Long-term hospitalization is rapidly becoming a last resort.[7]

SIZE AND COST OF THE PROBLEM

The total cost of mental illness to the society is unknown and probably unknowable. Perhaps the best informed estimate is that of the National Insti-

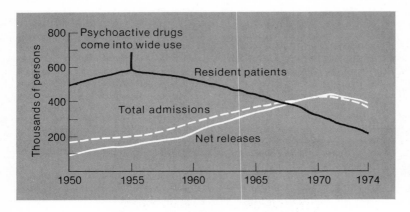

Figure 16–1
Admissions, resident patients, and net releases, state and county mental hospitals, 1950–1974.

Source: National Institute of Mental Health, Biometry Branch.

tute of Mental Health (NIMH), which figures the cost of medical bills for mental treatment and lost productivity at more than $36 billion per year.[8] There are several other ways to estimate the size and cost of the problem. We might consider the number of people in mental institutions, the number of people being treated outside institutions, and estimates of the number of people in the population who are afflicted with mental illness.

As we have already indicated, the number of people in mental hospitals increased until the mid-1950s and then began to decline. From under 300,000 in the early 1920s, the number of hospitalized mental patients increased to over 400,000 in the mid-1930s and 632,000 in 1955. By 1967 the figure was back down to 426,000, and in 1977 it was only 171,000. Obviously, these figures tell us more about facilities for and modes of treatment of mental illness than they do about the *amount* of mental illness. While mental patients occupied approximately one-half of all hospital beds a decade ago, today they occupy some 37 percent. There are 501 mental hospitals in the United States: 312 state and county hospitals, 39 VA neuropsychiatric hospitals, and 150 private hospitals. In addition, some 1,300 general hospitals report that they have psychiatric treatment facilities.

The number of people receiving outpatient treatment for mental illness has increased even more markedly than the number of hospital patients has declined. One writer, working with NIMH data, estimates that from about 1.5 million people being treated 15 years ago, the figure has now climbed to 3 million, all but 600,000 being treated outside of hospitals. The number of outpatient clinics has increased from 1,300 to more than 2,100 during the same 15-year period.[9] If as many as 3 million people in the United States receive mental treatment in any one year, careful studies show that the number of people troubled by mental illness must be still larger.

Large-scale studies of the incidence of mental illness have been carried out in New York City,[10] Baltimore,[11] Florida,[12] and a Canadian seacoast province.[13] These studies yielded estimates of significant emotional impairment in the population, ranging from approximately 10 to more than 40 percent. Most researchers agree that a major difficulty in measuring the prevalence of mental illness stems from lack of agreement on the criteria to be used. Normality shades into illness almost imperceptibly. By any standard, however, the amount of mental illness is very large, and the associated costs to the nation are great. Not all the costs are financial; some have to do with the victim's dignity and freedom and have stimulated great controversy over the nature of mental illness and how it should be treated.

CONTROVERSY OVER THE NATURE OF THE PROBLEM

The diagnosis and treatment of mental illness has long been the prerogative of the branch of medicine called psychiatry, and organized psychiatry has come to have a major vested interest in perpetuating that situation. Psychiatrists define two major types of mental illness: *neurosis* and *psychosis*. Neurotic behavior ordinarily is the less disabling of the two, covering a range from almost normal to that which is sufficiently serious to warrant institutionalization. The most "normal" of us occasionally checks two or three times to make sure that the gas is turned off, for example; or that a door is locked. Similarly, wondering if people are talking about us, feeling excluded, and compulsively following certain routines are behaviors that are at least borderline neurotic. The vast majority of neurotics function well enough most of the time so that, while they may be regarded as peculiar, they do not have to seek professional help. When they do need help, they are likely to obtain it as outpatients from a mental health clinic, social agency, or private counselor.

Psychotic behavior generally is more serious than neurosis, involving a severe break with reality. Psychotics may have delusions and believe themselves to be someone else; they may believe that they have a sacred mission to perform, or that they are being persecuted. They may suffer hallucinations in which they hear voices or see visions, or they may withdraw from relationships with other people to the point where they become as helpless as an infant.

Psychotics may be declared by courts of law to be insane, insanity being a legal status and not a type of illness. Once declared insane, an individual may be forcibly committed to a mental institution. Not all psychotics are declared insane, of course; some function well enough most of the time to stay out of serious trouble. Some psychotics also realize that they are ill, consciously seek help, and sometimes commit themselves voluntarily for hospital treatment. But other psychotics who do not want help may have it forced on them, and some people who may not even be psychotic are declared insane and forced into treatment. Some psychiatrists and sociologists see this situation as a major social problem in itself.

MENTAL ILLNESS AS A MYTH   Over the past 20 years or so, Dr. Thomas Szasz has emerged as a major controversial figure in psychiatry. A physician of impeccable credentials, Szasz is both a psychiatrist and a qualified psychoanalyst, and is professor of psychiatry at the State University of New York at Syracuse. From this entrenched position he attacks accepted psychiatric concepts as unsound and psychiatric procedures as medieval and barbarous.

According to Szasz, psychiatry is not really a healing science, but a means of social control that permits some people forcibly to incarcerate others whose behavior offends them. The people who are incarcerated are disproportionately the old and the poor. Psychiatrists, for their part, become "jailers" inflicting punishment on the "inmates" in the form of electric shock treatments, psychosurgery, and tranquilizing injections. These treatments, according to Szasz, are no better than the pyre and the rack of the Inquisition.

Szasz believes that the traditional concept of mental illness is a myth.[14] Minds can be sick, he says, only in a metaphorical sense that jokes are "sick," or that the economy is "sick." He likens psychiatry instead to a form of religion in which an essentially theological view has been substituted for a medical one: "If you talk to God," he says, "you are praying. If God talks to you, you have schizophrenia." Psychiatry thus becomes a belief system in which "salvation" is offered to true believers, and "heretics" must permit the "evil spirits" that possess them to be exorcised.[15]

According to Szasz, the distinction between voluntary and involuntary treatment is of utmost importance. Voluntary treatment, of which he approves, he compares to attending the church of one's choice. He likens involuntary treatment to forced religious conversion. In those cases in which the disease has a known organic cause, he favors hospital treatment, but on the same voluntary basis as it is afforded to people with other organic diseases.

Szasz opposes the process of labeling persons who have committed serious crimes as insane and committing them to mental institutions. This is no better, he says, than saying that they are possessed of the devil. Moreover, to commit people who are labeled as insane often is to sentence them to lifelong incarceration without trial. Missing from the psychiatric lexicon, says Szasz, are the all-important concepts of *freedom* and *individual responsibility*. The proper business of psychiatry, he states, is dealing with human conflicts rather than with medical diseases. Psychiatry should not coerce conformity to social norms under the guise of promoting "mental health"; it should encourage self-determination and responsible liberty.

COMMITMENT AS A SOCIAL PROCESS   Perhaps taking their lead from Szasz, sociologists have been conducting research into the procedures by which people are committed to mental hospitals. A solid base of data has been accumulated that shows that when procedures for determining mental illness have been initiated, a pervasive momentum almost irresistibly leads to commitment, while the alleged legal safeguards actually do little to protect the rights of those who are charged with being mentally ill.

Bias toward commitment has been shown by several studies. Scheff, for example, found that 86 of 116 judicial hearings regarding commitment proceedings in a midwestern state failed to establish that the persons were mentally ill. Yet not one of these patients was recommended for release.[16] Similarly, Mechanic, studying two large mental hospitals in California, reported that all persons who appeared at the hospitals were admitted regardless of their ability to function outside the hospital. Not once did a psychiatrist advise a person that he did not need treatment.[17] Miller and Schwartz, observing 58 individual hearings of a county lunacy commission, found that the hearings were routine rituals averaging only four minutes each.[18] Finally, Kutner, describing comparably superficial hearing procedures in Chicago, reports that the physicians recommended commitment in 77 percent of the cases, presuming the allegedly mentally ill persons to be insane and placing the burden of proof on them rather than on their accusers.[19]

The failure of legal procedures to provide safeguards for persons accused of being mentally ill is illustrated amply by Sara Fein and Kent Miller in a study of the records in one Florida county over a five-year period. According to the law, the court must notify alleged incompetents that proceedings have been initiated against them and that a hearing is to be held. Legal notice is delivered, however, if anyone over the age of 14 in the household signs for it. In 64 percent of the 756 cases, the person who signed the notice was the same person who had filed the commitment petition. To make the situation even more absurd, the person who signs the notice may also waive the alleged incompetent's right to a legal hearing. In 82 percent of the cases studied, the right to a legal hearing was waived. In all, only two hearings were actually held over the five-year period.[20]

COMMITMENT AS INCARCERATION   The degrading physical conditions that characterized state mental hospitals earlier in this century were mentioned earlier. Mental health professionals are quick to point out that these conditions have improved, both as public pressure has forced improvement and as the general drop in the hospital census has lowered patient–staff ratios. That the situation remains unsatisfactory, however, is indicated by charges such as that made recently by a qualified psychiatrist who is a former staff member of NIMH,[21] and by the defensive response of NIMH to this criticism and others.[22]

Szasz and others have deplored the dehumanization in mental institutions, and have described the ways in which hospital routines systematically strip patients of all dignity. Sociologist Erving Goffman describes vividly how patients, upon entering the hospital, are likely to seek anonymity and to hide from former acquaintances to protect their previous identities. He describes how hospital personnel systematically attack that anonymity and force the patient to accept their humiliating evaluation of him and his situation.[23] Elsewhere, Goffman reports that mental hospital case records are completely one-sided accounts of the patient's behavior, chronicling in detail incidents that might have "symptomatic significance" and ignoring the many occasions when the patient copes adequately with other people and his surroundings. He concludes that while the incidents in the case records are true, almost anyone's behavior could yield enough derogatory facts to justify commitment to an institution.[24]

BIOLOGICAL FACTORS IN MENTAL ILLNESS

The etiology of mental illness is a mystery. For decades physicians and scientists have been attempting to discover a biological basis for it, and to establish that the term *disease* should be used to refer to it. So far their efforts have been to little avail. They have succeeded in determining only that many different behavior patterns are labeled mental illness, and that these do not have a common origin. They keep trying, however, and as knowledge of chemistry and genetics becomes more sophisticated, they may succeed.

Two lines of recent research are worthy of mention here. One focuses on manic-depressive psychosis, and attempts to link this condition with factors transmitted on the X chromosome and associated with color blindness. The second involves testing a body chemical, Alpha-2 globulin, for its influence in causing chronic schizophrenia. The therapeutic implications of this research are obvious. If this suspected connection can be established, and if the chemical abnormality is found to be causative and not derivative, then chemical treatment could be used either to prevent the development of the disease or to cure it. Even if genetic or chemical bases for certain very limited forms of mental illness can be established, however, it will leave the vast bulk of mental illness unexplained. Even biological scientists acknowledge that the role of social factors in mental illness looms very large.[25]

SOCIAL FACTORS IN MENTAL ILLNESS

SOCIAL FACTORS ASSOCIATED WITH HOSPITALIZATION   Research on social factors in mental illness has been underway since the mid-1930s. For almost two decades the research was based primarily on mental hospital admissions and therefore revealed less about who was mentally ill than about who was likely to be committed for mental illness. It was discovered that men were more likely to be committed than women, single people more likely than married people, city dwellers more than rural people, and blacks and foreign-born more than native whites. Within cities, rates of commitment decreased with the distance from the city's center.[26]

Two general hypotheses were formulated to explain these patterns. One was that mental illness is likely to be found in persons living under conditions of stress. Presumably men, in having to earn a living, generally encounter more stress than women; single persons generally have less satisfactory living conditions than married people; and poor people, minority group members, and people living in the inner city all encounter special stress. The other hypothesis was that mental illness is more likely to be *diagnosed* in these groups living under stress even if they do not suffer more mental illness. Because of the social contacts required by their occupations, mental illness may become more obvious in men than in women. Because they do not have spouses to protect them, mental illness in single people may become more troublesome, and along with the other inequities suffered by the economically disprivileged and minority groups, they may be more quickly committed to mental hospitals.

There has been a good deal of speculation concerning the reasons for the drop in hospital commitment rates with increased distance from the inner city. One theory has it that unstable people tend to move frequently and drift into the socially disorganized inner city. They live there in relative anonymity until they become troublesome enough to be committed. If this drift theory is correct, then living conditions in the inner city do not necessarily cause more mental illness than do conditions of life elsewhere.

Another theory holds that the inner city actually produces mental illness. One study of catatonic schizophrenics showed that they were self-conscious, timid persons unable to cope with harsh, individualistic, and competitive conditions of life in crowded areas.[27] There may be merit in each of these positions; disorganized areas may both produce and attract deviants.

SOCIAL CLASS AND MENTAL ILLNESS   Studies of the treatment of mental illness in the general population, in contrast to studies of hospitalized patients, began in the 1950s. The first of these, which emphasized the role of social class in the likelihood of people being in treatment and in the kind of treatment they receive, was a study of all persons in the urbanized area of New Haven, Connecticut, who were receiving psychiatric treatment.[28]

The study produced two major sets of findings. First, it confirmed the evidence from earlier studies of hospital admissions that there is an inverse relationship between social class and the probability of being under treatment. Proportionately fewer high-status persons and proportionately more low-status persons were psychiatric patients. Second, it showed that patients' social class positions affect *where, how,* and *how long* they are treated.

Using a system of five social classes in which Class I is composed of the highest-status persons and Class V contains the lowest-status persons, the researchers found that persons from the top three classes are treated primarily by psychiatrists, persons from Class IV are treated in about equal numbers in private and public agencies, and persons from Class V go primarily to public agencies. In chronic cases, only Class I persons make continued use of private hospitals; Class II and III persons gradually shift from private to public hospitals; and Class V persons are completely dependent on public agencies from the onset of their illness.

The treatment for neurotics also varies with social class. The highly regarded psychotherapies are used almost universally with Class I and II patients, but with only 59 percent of Class V patients. The less widely approved organic and shock therapies are used more commonly with lower-class patients. Lower-class patients in psychotherapy receive less of the psychiatrist's time and are treated for a shorter period. Ninety-four percent of Class I patients saw their therapists for a 50-minute hour, while only 45 percent of Class V patients received that much time, and 36 percent of them had interviews lasting less than 30 minutes. Also, 40 percent of Class I and II patients had been in continuous treatment for more than three years, while not one Class V patient had received any form of treatment for as long as two years.

Much additional evidence could be introduced to document the relationship between class status and treatment for mental illness, but the pattern is clear.[29] Many factors in the social class backgrounds of both patients and psychiatrists combine to influence the amount and kind of treatment received. Persons from higher class backgrounds not only can afford prolonged and expensive treatment, but because of their attitudes and habits of dealing with their problems verbally, they are probably better candidates for psychotherapy. Lower-class persons are more likely to receive abbreviated, inferior treatment. The therapists themselves frequently are middle-class, upwardly mobile persons whose professional judgments may be unwittingly influenced by their social class backgrounds.

SEX ROLES AND MENTAL ILLNESS   Early studies of hospitalization for mental illness indicated that men are more likely to be committed than women, and that unmarried people are more likely to be committed than married people. From these scanty data investigators leaped to broad conclusions about the relationship between mental illness and sexual and marital roles. Being married, they concluded, is associated with good mental health either because married life is less stressful or because many of the maladjusted do not marry. They reasoned, further, that men, single or married, are subject to more stress than women. Subsequent research, however, has shown that while the facts uncovered by the early research were correct, the interpretations of the influence of marital and sex roles on mental health were misleading. Extensive data indicate that serious mental health hazards are associated with the role of the married woman.

Table 16–1 compares rates of mental illness among married men and married women, from 16 separate studies conducted in several countries. Every study found mental illness more common among married women than among married men. When single men are compared with single women the evidence is less conclusive, but it suggests that single men probably have higher illness rates. When comparisons are made among the divorced and the widowed, the same pattern appears: men show higher rates of illness than women do. Because of the systematic variations by marital status, all other possible explanations are ruled out. There is something in the role of married women that is at least statistically associated with mental illness.[30]

Walter Gove, who did the analyses described above, has also analyzed five factors in married women's roles that may cause high rates of mental illness. First, the status of most married women is more precarious than that of married men because many women have only one major role—housewife—to sustain them, while most men have two—breadwinner and household head. When men encounter difficulty in one role, they can sometimes adjust by concentrating on the other. Most women do not have that alternative. When they encounter difficulty with the role of housewife, they have no equally available major alternative source of gratification.

Second, the role of housewife often carries little prestige ("I'm just a housewife") and requires a low level of training and skill. Many housewives who have had extensive education are locked into a role that is endlessly frustrating. Third, the private nature of the role of housewife denies to women the supports that men typically have on their jobs. No matter how inclined to introspection and dwelling on their own problems, most men are required to maintain a supervised level of performance on the job. Their co-workers also provide them reassurance and emotional support. Housewives, by contrast, are not directly supervised and may not have daily contact with other people who support them. If they let their housekeeping duties slide, there is no one to correct them and to keep their poor performance from becoming an additional factor in their problems.

Fourth, those women who are employed outside the home also confront special problems. They often are ineligible for the better jobs and they are discriminated against by employers and co-workers. Their job commitments are regarded as subordinate to their family obligations, and their concepts of themselves as workers suffer accordingly. On top of everything else, they are expected to put in a full day on the job and then to perform most household duties in the evening, while their husbands are relaxing from their labors. Finally, role expectations for women are diffuse and unclear. Because

TABLE 16–1   Studies Showing Comparative Rates of Mental Disorder among Married Men and Women (persons per 100,000)

Researchers*	Men	Women	Ratio: Women/Men
1. Tauss	18,000	35,100	1.95
2. Srole et al.	19,300	19,900	1.03
3. Hagnell	900	2,500	2.78
4. Cooper	17,400	29,000	1.67
5. Shepherd et al.	8,934	16,154	1.81
6. Miles et al.	788	926	1.18
7. Susser	465	706	1.52
8. Hollingshead and Redlich	504	566	1.12
9. Innes and Sharp	495	651	1.32
10. Kramer (n.d.)	83	96	1.16
11. Jaco	62	92	1.48
12. Thomas and Locke (New York)	68	92	1.35
13. Thomas and Locke (Ohio)	65	66	1.02
14. Gregory	45	59	1.31
15. Kramer (1967)	16	29	1.81
16. Frumkin	4.2	10.7	2.55

*B. Cooper, "Psychiatric Disorder in Hospitals and General Practice," *Social Psychiatry,* 1 (1966), 7–10; R. Frumkin, "Social Factors in Schizophrenia," *Sociology and Social Research,* 38 (July–Aug. 1954), 383–86; J. Gregory, "Factors Influencing First Admission Rates to Canadian Mental Hospitals, III: An Analysis by Education, Marital Status, Country of Birth, Religion and Rural-Urban Residence," *Canadian Psychiatric Association Journal,* 4 (Apr. 1959), 133–51; Olle Hagnell, *A Prospective Study of the Incidence of Mental Disorder* (Sweden: Barlingska Boktryckeriet, 1966); A. Hollingshead and F. Redlich, *Social Class and Mental Illness* (New York: John Wiley, 1958); G. Innes and G. Sharp, "A Study of Psychiatric Patients in North-East Scotland," *Journal of Mental Science,* 108 (July 1962), 447–56; E. G. Jaco, *The Social Epidemiology of Mental Disorders* (New York: Russell Sage Foundation, 1960); M. Kramer, "Epidemiology, Biostatistics, and Mental Health Planning," in R. Monroe et al., *Psychiatric Epidemiology and Mental Health Planning* (Washington, D.C.: American Psychiatric Association, 1967); M. Kramer, *Some Implications of Trends in the Usage of Psychiatric Facilities for Community Mental Health Programs and Related Research,* Public Health Service Publication No. 1434 (Washington, D.C.: Government Printing Office, n.d.); H. E. Miles et al., "Accumulative Survey of All Psychiatric Experience in Monroe County, N.Y.," *Psychiatric Quarterly,* 38 (July 1964), 458–87; M. Shepherd et al., *Psychiatric Illness in General Practice* (London: Oxford University Press, 1966); L. Srole et al., *Mental Health in the Metropolis* (New York: McGraw-Hill, 1962); M. Susser, *Community Psychiatry* (New York: Random House, 1968); W. Tauss, "A Note on the Prevalence of Mental Disturbance," *Australian Journal of Psychology,* 19 (Aug. 1967), 121–23; and D. Thomas and B. Locke, "Marital Status, Education and Occupational Differentials in Mental Hospitals," *Milbank Memorial Fund Quarterly,* 41 (Apr. 1963), 145–60.

SOURCE: Reprinted from *Social Forces,* 51 (Sept. 1972), 34–44, "The Relationship Between Sex Roles, Marital Status, and Mental Illness" by Walter R. Gove. Copyright © The University of North Carolina Press.

of the subordination of their needs to those of their husbands and families, women have far less control of their destinies than men do.

The problem of mental illness is characterized by professional uncertainties about both causes and treatment, with gross inequalities in access to professional help, and with serious and unresolved issues of the personal and civil rights of those diagnosed as mentally ill.

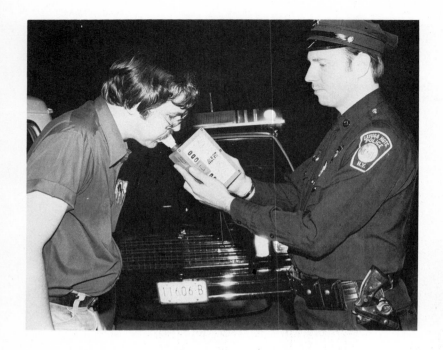

Motorist submits to Breathalyzer examination by law enforcement officer—one of the most commonly used law enforcement tools in combating the drunk driver problem.
(United Press International)

Alcoholism

SIZE AND COST OF THE PROBLEM

Slightly over two-thirds of all American adults drink alcoholic beverages—some 145 million people. Most of these are social drinkers who drink according to the norms of the groups to which they belong. Such norms vary widely in terms of what they drink, where, when, and in what quantities. Beer, wine, whiskey, bourbon, scotch, and brandy have different appeals at different social levels. In some groups men drink with other men; in some groups men and women drink together; and in still other situations women drink together—or alone. In one situation the goal is to become rapidly and boisterously drunk; in another, drinking is measured and sedate.

Research indicates that between 1 in 13 and 1 in 16 drinkers eventually become alcoholics. Although the line between serious problem drinking and alcoholism is not clearly drawn, the figure of 10 million alcoholics in the United States is frequently cited. Directly or indirectly, some 36 million families, friends, and close associates of these persons also are involved.

The direct economic costs of drinking are huge, some $8 billion per year. The total costs, including indirect costs, amount to $15 billion each year.[31] In addition, alcohol use contributes directly to 85,000 deaths in the United States each year, including half of the people killed annually in automobile accidents. Two and one-half million people each year are arrested and charged with drunkenness or disorderly conduct, several times the number charged with gambling, drug use, and prostitution combined. To these costs must also be added immeasurable costs in human suffering—broken homes, deserted families, and emotional and physical problems.

HISTORY OF THE PROBLEM

Alcoholic beverages are probably as old as agriculture itself. Indeed, early people's storage of wild grapes may have resulted in fermentation even before the development of agriculture. Even the modern distillation of spirits is some two thousand years old.

A great clash began in the 1830s between those who sought prohibition of the manufacture and sale of alcohol and those who argued for its free production and use. The prohibitionists, or "drys," first tried persuasion and then turned to legislative action. From about 1890 the prohibitionists directed their efforts to securing federal prohibition, and partly because the opposition was not well organized they succeeded in securing passage of the Eighteenth Amendment to the Constitution in 1917.

Ironically, the Volstead Act, which sought to enforce the amendment, forbade the wholesale manufacture, transportation, and sale of liquor but did not prohibit buying, using, or making it for private use. Not only was there widespread home production, but bootlegging became a major industry whose control became a primary goal of organized crime. Prohibition proved to be virtually unenforceable. Many people, including some religious and ethnic groups, believed that prohibition was absurd and that violation was morally blameless. The failure of enforcement, corruption of the police, effective organization of the "wets," and the argument that legalization would help cure the depression together brought about repeal in 1933.

CONTROVERSY OVER THE NATURE OF ALCOHOLISM

During the great struggle between prohibitionists and advocates of the free use of alcohol during the nineteenth and early twentieth centuries, the prohibitionists made drinking a moral issue and popularized the image of mother and children in tattered clothes huddling in the cold outside the saloon wailing, "Father, dear father, come home with me now." The message was clear: drinking leads to drunkenness, and drunkenness leads to loss of job, home, and family. The prohibitionists were joined by many, but not all, church groups, with ministers as their spokesmen, and soon drinking became a religious as well as a moral issue. Drunkenness became a sin.

This image persisted well into the present century, lasting through the prohibition imposed by the Eighteenth Amendment. During prohibition especially, bootlegging and ties with organized crime encouraged the definition of drinking as a police problem also, with punishment for violation of the law. Even after the repeal of prohibition these definitions persisted. But rejection of the moralism of the prohibitionists by the country at large and the ineffectiveness of police action in dealing with drinking led to efforts to define alcohol problems in therapeutic terms. The conception emerged that alcoholism is an illness, and groups as varied as organized medicine and Alcoholics Anonymous emerged to try to cure it. From roughly 1940 to the present, the medical view of alcoholism has prevailed.

The American Medical Association defines alcoholism as a form of drug dependence characterized by preoccupation with alcohol and loss of control over its consumption, usually leading to intoxication. Its victims, who tend to relapse, suffer physically, emotionally, occupationally, and socially. For the most part the AMA believes alcoholics to be treatable patients; but as in other chronic diseases, it believes that control is more feasible than cure. Efforts to find a physiological basis for alcoholism have been unsuccessful, but recent findings suggest that it may be biochemically similar to narcotic addiction.

The federal government has accepted the illness definition of alcoholism and is urging the states to adopt a Uniform Alcoholism and Intoxication Treatment Act, which its backers describe as a bill of rights for alcoholics. According to Dr. Morris Chafetz, "It removes the crime of public intoxication and the illness of alcoholism from the criminal codes and places them in the public health area where they belong."[32] Where the law is adopted, drunks picked up by the police are taken to special treatment centers for emergency medical treatment. They also receive counseling and social services.

Most physicians, public health authorities, and public officials believe that the medical view of alcoholism and the removal of drunkenness as a criminal offense represent major steps in coping with the problem. They are confused and disappointed in the growing number of social scientists who oppose labeling alcoholics as being sick because they believe that such a definition obscures the basically sociological and psychological nature of the problem. The most explicit and systematic analysis of the problem from a social science perspective was done by psychiatrist Tomas Szasz.

According to Szasz, alcoholism is not a disease but a bad habit. Illnesses have specific physiological bases, and alcoholism does not. As a believer in individual freedom and responsibility, Szasz particularly opposes the provision of the Uniform Alcoholism and Intoxication Treatment Act that "guarantees in those few instances where the civil commitment [of alcoholics] is necessary, a right to treatment which is likely to be beneficial."[33] Such power, he maintains, would give physicians the power to imprison alcoholics without trial. Moreover, it would effectively absolve alcoholics of responsibility for crimes that they commit while drunk. As in the case of mental illness, Szasz believes that those who wish to help alcoholics should be free to offer their services, but alcoholics should have the right to accept or reject those services. Szasz fears the power of medicine and government to compel people to accept treatment more than he fears alcoholism itself.

Lest it be concluded that Szasz's position is simply that of one eccentric psychiatrist, we emphasize that his arguments are supported by a growing number of social scientists. Claude Steiner, a psychologist, states that alcoholism is not an illness and that dealing with it is not the proper business of physicians. The responsibility for drinking belong to alcoholics themselves, who should not be afforded the dignity that goes along with being "sick."[34] Other social scientists believe that many alcoholics are not consumed by a physiological craving for alcohol and that they can learn to drink socially instead of compulsively. A Rand Corporation study of 1,340 alcoholics found that up to one-third of them had learned to drink normally.[35]

The controversy over the nature of alcoholism is not simply academic; nor does it hinge on questions of freedom and responsibility alone. It also has practical implications for programs to treat alcoholics. A recent proposal in New York City, for example, requested $10 million to use medical means to try to wean 9,000 alcoholics from drinking. The proposal was attacked for its high cost (which ballooned to $25 million) and because similar treatment programs had shown little success. Opponents of the program cited figures from a national survey of 1,359 drinking and 1,359 nondrinking Americans showing that 6 percent of the heavy drinkers quit drinking heavily over a three-year period.[36] The study suggested that problem drinking may be prevented by changing public attitudes toward drinking. Instead of viewing drinking as virile, fun, or a solution to psychological problems, society should consider it bad for health, bad for the mind, and socially abhorrent.[37]

SOCIAL FACTORS IN ALCOHOLISM

Alcoholism has been widely studied in the United States and elsewhere, yet no wholly satisfactory explanation of variations in drinking patterns has emerged. In the United States, where alcoholism is a serious problem, Jews have a very low alcoholism rate.[38] However, only 13 percent of Jews as compared to 21 percent of Roman Catholics and 41 percent of Protestants are teetotalers. Moreover, Jews drink more regularly than members of either of the other two religious groups. But judging from admissions to hospitals for alcoholism, Jews are almost completely nonalcoholic. Mormons in the United States ban alcoholic beverages altogether and experience almost no alcoholism. Apparently, more Canadians than Americans drink, but the alcoholism rate is twice as high in the United States as in Canada. France has an extremely high alcoholism rate, but in Italy, despite almost universal drinking, the alcoholism rate is very low. Among the Aleut Indians, heavy and extended drinking appears to result in no true alcoholism, and there are practically no guilt feelings associated with drinking or drunkenness.[39] Both the pattern of alcohol use and the incidence of alcoholism vary widely over the world.

Clues to the reasons for this variability can be found in the ways in which drinking patterns fit into overall cultural patterns. Where drinking is associated with virility—as among the Irish and the French, and in the United States—alcoholism is common. Jews and Mormons, on the other hand, have strong taboos against excess—and have little alcoholism. Among Italians, drinking fits into the nutritional pattern; unlike the French, Italians do not often drink except at meals. It has also been suggested that alcoholism is more common in countries with a strong Puritan ethic. Thus, "where the social group withdraws its approval from drinking, it becomes either a solitary vice or a wickedness covertly shared with a few boon companions."[40] The alcoholism rates of Sweden and the United States, where prohibition has been tried, are among the world's highest.

DRINKING AMONG COLLEGE STUDENTS   Partly because alcohol research has been carried out on college campuses and partly because of their traditionally elite position, special attention has been paid to the drinking patterns of college students. A classic study of the drinking habits of over 15,000 college students indicated that 80 percent of the men and approximately 60 percent

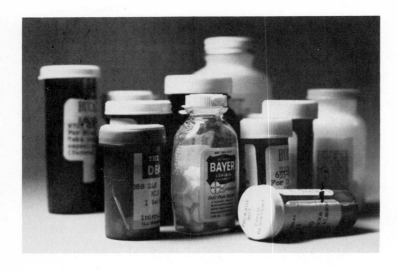

The impulse to reach for a pill as a solution to a problem, mental or physical, has contributed to this country's widespread drug abuse.
(Irene Springer)

of the women engage in some kind of drinking. Moreover, the study revealed that knowledge of the students' backgrounds and their present social situation provides some basis for predicting how many of them drink, what they drink, how much, and how often they drink. The probability of drinking is greater among people who attend nonsectarian colleges, those who do not belong to the Mormon church, those whose families have substantial income, those whose parents drink, and those whose friends drink. Moreover, most student drinkers begin drinking before they enter college, taking their first drinks in their homes.[41]

If anything, college student drinking is becoming more of a problem over time. A 1978 survey of 7,000 students at 34 colleges in New England reported that 95 percent of the students drink at least occasionally. Some 29 percent of the male students and 11 percent of the female students were classified as heavy drinkers. Many of the colleges have set up alcohol abuse centers and programs to combat the problem.[42]

SOCIAL CLASS AND ALCOHOLISM   A widespread stereotype of alcoholics that emerged from the prohibition struggles early in this century portrayed them as skid-row bums living in utter degradation and drinking themselves daily into a stupor on cheap wine. It is now estimated, however, that no more than 3 percent of all alcoholics are skid-row bums, and that no more than 15 percent of those living on the nation's skid rows are alcoholics.[43]

We now know that alcoholism has no respect for social status. As a matter of fact, the more educated Americans are, the more urban they are, and the higher their salaries, the more they drink. The statistically average American alcoholic is a man between 35 and 50 years of age, employed at the same place for at least seven years, married, owning his home, and having two or more children. In recent years, large corporations have become especially concerned about alcohol problems among their top executives.[44]

One study of the treatment of alcoholics showed that social class factors intrude into treatment. Of 402 patients at the Toronto Addiction Research

Foundation clinic, 11 percent were placed into Class I, 54 percent in Class II, and 35 percent in Class III. Different treatment began with diagnosis. Physical disorders were more often part of the diagnosis for Class I patients, personality disorders were more commonly "found" among Class II patients, and alcoholic psychoses were more frequently diagnosed among Class III patients. The manner in which professionals related to patients was a function of both the social class position of the patient and that of the therapist. Class I patients, who were similar to the therapists, were described in terms of their feelings—guilty, discontented, outgoing, and so on; Class III patients were described in terms of their behavior—nervous, tense, fearful, and so on. More Class I patients were treated by psychiatrists, more Class II patients received medication, and Class III patients received fewer antidepressant medicines and fewer sedatives.[45]

Drug Abuse

HISTORY OF THE PROBLEM

Although the ultimate roots of the drug problem are lost in prehistory, it appears likely that the earliest people discovered the exhilarating and depressing effects of certain plant substances. References to drugs and drug problems are found throughout history, but not until modern times and the development of comprehensive government records could the major dimensions of the problem be specified. In the United States such records began to accumulate early in the present century.

A federal survey estimated that in 1913 there were a quarter of a million narcotic addicts out of approximately 100 million people in the United States, an addiction rate that approximately equals today's. Narcotics, however, were not illegal then, and most patent medicines contained them, stimulating sales with promises ranging from curing rheumatism and cancer to restoring lost virility.[46]

With the passage of the Harrison Act in 1914, addiction became a crime. After that, and until recently, the only useful national figures were of arrests, prosecutions, convictions, and commitments, and these were far from complete. Moreover, there is suspicion that the Federal Bureau of Narcotics used the figures as much to solicit support for its attempts to eliminate drugs through hard law enforcement as to report accurately to the American people. Nevertheless, the Bureau reported, and evidence from draft rejection figures for addiction during World Wars I and II supports the fact, that addiction rates dropped in the United States until after 1945.[47]

The Bureau of Narcotics figures almost certainly exaggerate the decrease in addiction from 1914 to 1945. For one thing, the statistics fail to take into account the changing treatment of narcotics offenders. Before 1930 narcotics violations were handled almost entirely on the federal level. After 1930, however, more and more came to be handled by local police. While the Bureau's figures showed narcotic addiction to be on the decline, it may actually have been on the increase.

As long as the drug involved was chiefly heroin and the problem remained confined largely to black ghettos, the public outcry against drug abuse was minimal. But after World War II the problem changed. Marijuana began to appear in quantity and to have allure at varied social levels. During the 1950s tranquilizers became popular; as one author put it, "much of the adult society looked for peace in a pill."[48] The hallucinogenic drugs were joined by amphetamines and barbiturates. There seemed to be a virtual explosion of drug use at all social levels, becoming most conspicuous among college-age youth and then working its way down into the high schools, junior high schools, and even the grade schools.

Public and official attention to the drug problem expanded apace. So many federal and state laws were passed that it would be hopelessly confusing even to summarize them here. Suffice it to say that the laws frequently failed to distinguish between addictive and nonaddictive drugs, and that they provided severe penalties for drug use. In 1951, for example, federal law introduced mandatory minimum sentences for all narcotic and marijuana offenses: two years for the first offense, five years for the second offense, and ten years for the third and subsequent offenses. In 1956 the length of the mandatory sentences was increased and suspension of sentence and probation were prohibited for all but the first offense of unlawful possession.

Public concern about the drug traffic and drug abuse intensified during the 1960s. The Federal Bureau of Narcotics, renamed the Bureau of Narcotics and Dangerous Drugs, was joined by new agencies and supported in others by increased attention to drug matters. The Bureau of Narcotics and Dangerous Drugs, with approximately 1,600 agents, helped seize $1.5 billion worth of illicit narcotics over one year. The new federal Drug Enforcement Administration, during its first 18 months, seized 7,235 pounds of heroin or morphine base and made 25,000 arrests. The Internal Revenue Service, with a special antinarcotics unit, obtained taxes and penalties of more than $54 million from persons linked with narcotics rackets. Finally, the U.S. Customs Bureau stepped up its efforts, seizing 11,000 pounds of hard narcotics and 100 tons of marijuana over a one-year period.[49]

SIZE AND COST OF THE PROBLEM

The monetary costs of the drug traffic are phenomenal. Consider the cost of one kilogram of morphine base as it moves from its origin in Turkey, through processing in France, to the streets of New York. Originally worth $350, it costs $3,500 after being refined to heroin in France. At the docks in New York, it is worth $18,000. The pure heroin is then cut into one-ounce lots of 25 percent heroin that cost the street pusher $500 each. He cuts them into packets of 3 to 5 percent heroin and retails the so-called nickel bags for $5. The first user often splits the nickel bags, using some and selling some to help maintain his habit. All told, the original investment of $350 nets $225,000 for suppliers, traffickers, pushers, and peddlers.

A second approach to the problem of costs is through estimates of the money required to support the habits of addicts. There are an estimated 450,000 narcotics addicts in the United States, by far the largest number in any nation for which data are available.[50] On the average, and conservatively, each of these addicts spends $8,000 per year to support the habit. If even half of these addicts must steal to support their habits, they must steal some $5 dollars worth of property for every dollar they net. Altogether, the habits of these 450,000 addicts probably cost between $14 and $15 billion.

The cost of drug addiction must also be measured in human lives. In 1977 there were at least 2,800 drug-related deaths in the United States.[51] Heroin and cocaine addicts also are suicide prone. A study in Washington, D.C., showed that one out of five of the addicts studied had made at least one effort to kill himself.[52]

Other statistics also indicate the size of the problem. The international drug trade has a $5 billion heroin market in the United States. The cost of the Special Action Office of Drug Abuse Prevention will be $331 million. President Nixon in 1973 requested $2.2 million for research and development of techniques for detection of illegal drug traffic, $2 million for research and development of herbicides to destroy narcotics-producing plants, and $26.6 million for the Treasury Department to intensify customs controls. An additional $10 million has been requested for improved drug education and training. A complete list of the costs of drug abuse in the United States would probably be impossible to compile.

THE MARIJUANA CONTROVERSY

The rapid spread of marijuana use in the mid-1960s caught the country by surprise and drastically altered the nature of the drug problem. An unprecedented proportion of the population became users of illegal drugs, confusion developed over the nature of marijuana and its alleged harmfulness, and controversy erupted over how to cope with the problem.

THE EXTENT OF USE   The surprise engendered by widespread marijuana use and the rapid growth in the number of users have made it difficult to assemble reliable statistics on the current extent and nature of its use. Studies in local high schools produced rates that varied from as low as 5 percent of the students having tried the drug at some time to a high of 90 percent having done so.[53]

A Gallup Poll, late in 1979, reported that 41 percent of teenagers have tried marijuana,[54] and that 39 percent had smoked it within the last month.[55] Another Gallup Poll in 1977 reported that 24 percent of adult Americans have also smoked marijuana at least once.[56]

Some data also are available on the sociodemographic characteristics of marijuana users. Generally, they tend to be young, male, single, and middle or upper-middle class. Most do not participate in organized religion. The sex ratio of users appears to be dropping, with at least one study showing as many female users as male users. A study in one Houston, Texas, high school showed that whites were the most frequent users, Chicanos second, and blacks the least frequent users.[57]

Personnel in the armed forces are a special case. It is estimated that more than half of lower-grade enlisted men in Vietnam used marijuana, and one study found that 68 percent of a group of airborne soldiers have tried it. Studies also show that few officers and higher-ranked enlisted men use pot. About half of the lower-ranked enlisted men who try it continue to use it.[58]

THE EFFECTS OF MARIJUANA   Until fairly recently little serious attempt was made to determine the effects of marijuana use on physical and behavioral functioning. The policy of the Federal Bureau of Narcotics was to lump marijuana together with narcotics, leading to the widespread belief that marijuana is both physically and psychologically addictive, leads to the use of heroin and other drugs, and that most users experience severe personality disorganization. Consistent with this view, wide publicity was given to studies done in the 1930s that showed that some marijuana users developed toxic psychoses. Marijuana, which had occupied a respected place in therapeutic medicine until then, was outlawed in 1937.

In the late 1960s several studies supported the belief that marijuana smoking was harmful. One research group showed that the chemically active ingredient in marijuana could cause psychotic reactions in human beings,[59] and other studies showed less extreme psychological effects.[60] Still other studies showed effects of marijuana on animals including stimulation and excitement, followed by depression.[61] More recently, two psychiatrists reported severe psychological effects of marijuana smoking on 38 of their patients.[62] Unfortunately, studies of the effects of marijuana's active ingredient on either animals or human beings do not tell us very much about the effects of marijuana smoking, and studies of psychiatric patients do not tell us very much about the experiences of a general population.

In the late 1960s the federal government decided to permit marijuana research on human beings; currently it is funding such research in the amount of $4 million per year. Research results are just beginning to come in, but they are not at all supportive of the view that marijuana is especially harmful. In one of the most thorough studies, for example, but one involving only a few subjects, a Boston University research group compared the effects of marijuana smoking on nine experienced users with its effects on nine "naive" subjects who smoked cigarettes but had not used marijuana before. The research design included the use of placebo hemp plant cigarettes, some cigarettes containing moderate amounts of marijuana, and some containing large amounts of marijuana. The laboratory was sprayed with a scent to mask the telltale odor, and neither experimenters nor subjects knew who was smoking what. For three hours after the smoking began, the experimenters measured the subjects' heart and respiratory rates, pupils and blood glucose, and gave them a series of psychological tests.[63]

All of the experienced users became high on the heavy dose cigarettes while only one naive subject did so, despite careful instruction by the experimenters to all subjects on how to smoke the cigarettes for maximum effect. This finding, frequently reported by marijuana users and confirmed in other studies, is puzzling, because experience with other drugs has shown that tolerance develops with use, requiring steadily increased amounts of drugs to achieve the same effects. There are both psychological and physiological processes that might explain the reverse phenomenon with marijuana. Marijuana smoking generally is learned in a group situation, and suggestibility may play some role in inducing the high. Researchers are also working on a physiological explanation.

Somewhat surprisingly, virtually no significant physical changes were induced by the drug. There was evidence of slightly increased heart rates, and there was dilation of the blood vessels in the conjunctivae of the eyes. The researchers concluded that this "red eye" syndrome is the best test of marijuana intoxication.

On three separate mental and muscular coordination tests another interesting pattern emerged. The naive subjects had their performance impaired on two of the three tests, but the experienced subjects actually did better on two of the three tests when they were stoned. Again, there are at least two possibilities: first, a marijuana high may be much more manageable than an alcoholic high, as many drug users claim; or second, these results may reflect special motivation on the part of the user subjects to prove that the drug is not harmful.

Large-scale cultural and clinical studies of marijuana use began in the early 1970s. Studies of long-term users were conducted in Jamaica, Greece, and Costa Rica. Although the details of the findings vary, the three studies generally failed to find significant harmful effects of marijuana use, but did report favorable reactions to marijuana by the users who believed that it increased their motivation and their ability to do a hard day's work.[64]

The debate over the alleged harmfulness of marijuana is far from over. Possible long-term effects may not become evident for another generation. In the meantime, bitter controversy has erupted over proposals to legalize marijuana use.

PROPOSALS FOR LEGALIZATION   Since marijuana became illegal in 1937, both federal and state governments have generally prescribed severe penalties for its sale, possession, and use. In 1951 federal law provided mandatory minimum sentences of at least two years for the first marijuana offense, five years for the second, and ten years for third and subsequent offenses. In 1956 the minimum sentences were raised to five years for the first offense of sale or importation, and ten years for second and subsequent offenses. State penalties have been varied and generally severe. Until recently, penalties for first offenses ranged from two to twenty years, and fines up to $20,000. Second offenses carried penalties up to thirty years. Some states forbade probation or parole for convicted offenders, and in several states the death penalty was provided for sale to minors.[65]

By the late 1960s the lack of any substantial basis for classifying marijuana with narcotics and the futility of the federal government's policy of severe penalties for marijuana use had become evident. The federal law was changed to reduce the possession of marijuana for personal use from a felony to a misdemeanor, and the law that became effective in June 1971 permits judges to expunge the arrest records of persons under 21 who have fulfilled conditions of probation successfully.

The states are tending to follow the lead of the federal government. In 1973 Oregon abolished criminal penalties for possession of an ounce or less of marijuana and made it a civil offense similar to a traffic violation, carrying a maximum fine of $100. In 1975 Alaska legalized the use of marijuana at home, while continuing to prohibit its sale and public use of the drug. Eight other states have stopped arresting people for smoking marijuana or for possessing small amounts. New York's 1973 law, the nation's toughest, was supposed to eliminate drug traffic of all sorts; it provided possible 15-year prison terms for the private use or possession of marijuana. All the law did, apparently, was to clog up the court system with cases of small-time users or sellers and to prevent prosecutors from developing major cases.[66]

Proposals for the full legalization of marijuana use have come from a number of sources and have aroused bitter opposition. In 1970 the National Commission on the Causes and Prevention of Violence recommended the legalization of marijuana to persons over 18. The individual rights section of the American Bar Association urges decriminalization of "casual" marijuana use, and the National Commission on Marijuana and Drug Abuse and the American Medical Association have urged that felony penalties for the possession of "insignificant" quantities of pot be abandoned. Similarly, a 600-page study on *Licit and Illicit Drugs* by Consumer's Union recommended the repeal of all federal laws against the growing, processing, transportation, sale, possession, and use of marijuana. In late 1972 word leaked out of a federally financed private study of marijuana, concealed for six months by the Department of Health, Education and Welfare, which recommended official limited acceptance of marijuana use as an alternative to prevention. The government was urged to give up its "failure-ridden quest for a youthful society free of drug use—a proposed idyllic island awash in a sea of alcohol, nicotine, and legally prescribed drug-taking."[67]

The arguments of those who would legalize marijuana are typified by the conclusions of the National Commission on Marijuana and Drug Abuse. The Commission avers that marijuana use does not lead to the use of heroin, but does tend to involve users in a criminal drug-using counterculture. Legalizing marijuana would help take young marijuana users out of that counterculture, and thus reduce the element of secondary deviation. Further, 5 million Americans use marijuana at least once a week. To criminalize such a large proportion of the population is to render all sanctions ineffective. The rigid enforcement of laws against marijuana use has other unanticipated and harmful effects. By creating scarcity it drives prices up. This in turn attracts more pushers and eventually increases the supply. One former assistant United States attorney has concluded that the United States should have a regulatory structure for marijuana similar to but tougher than those used with alcohol and tobacco. Either private manufacturers or a government monopoly would be authorized to grow and package marijuana. Quality would be controlled. Government-licensed stores would sell it, imposing stiff taxes to keep it out of the reach of young people. Sale to persons under 18 would be illegal. Such a policy probably would increase experimentation with marijuana, but it would remove the "forbidden fruit" appeal and provide a convenient alternative to hard drugs.

The opponents of legalization believe that their antagonists are deluded. The more sophisticated opponents do not argue that marijuana use leads directly to the use of heroin, but point out that the drug-using counterculture shows little discrimination in its use of drugs, and users often also use amphetamines, barbiturates, and hallucinogens. Two studies are relevant. Erich Goode studied 204 marijuana smokers and found that 68 percent had tried at least one other drug at least once. Although most of these experimenters had used other drugs no more than a few times, and often only once, 13 percent had used heroin and almost 44 percent had tried LSD.[68] The second study found that only 6 percent of 106 marijuana users had experimented with heroin or morphine. Nearly three-quarters of them, however, had tried psychedelic drugs such as LSD or mescaline. Sixty percent of the subjects had used amphetamines and 44 percent had used barbiturates.[69]

Public opinion seems to be on the side of those who oppose legalization. In a California election in late 1972, for example, only 33 percent of those voting favored decriminalization for personal use and cultivation. A subsequent survey of a nationwide cross-section of 2,133 adults by the Opinion Research Corporation found that 53 percent favored either tougher penalties for marijuana use or keeping present laws as they are.[70]

SOCIAL FACTORS IN DRUG USE

Until recently very little rigorous research was done on social and personality factors associated with drug use; society at large found it relatively easy to ignore the use of heroin in ghetto, and particularly black ghetto, areas. Concerned professional persons described drug addiction as a symptom of rebellion against discrimination, futility, and frustration among minority group residents of slum areas. Physicians, seeking personality correlates of addiction, also wrote that addicts are "nervous, tense individuals with a great deal of anxiety and many somatic complaints . . . [some] are irresponsible, selfish, immature, thrill-seeking individuals who are constantly in trouble."[71]

Research after World War II confirmed that most narcotics users in the United States were minority group members between 15 and 44 years of age, and that many had been involved in criminal activity before addiction.[72] Some insight into why only some slum youth become addicted to narcotics, and into the factors that sustain them in addiction, was provided by a comparison of 37 New York City addicts with their nonaddicted siblings.[73] It found that the addicted siblings were earlier and more serious participants in street life and in the illegitimate opportunity structure that accompanies street life. Having been arrested and incarcerated, and thus having legitimate careers closed to them, they gained status among their drug-using peers by being knowledgeable and experienced in the use of drugs and by being successful in the hustling required to provide the money to support their habits. By contrast, their nonaddicted siblings eschewed the illegitimate world from an early age and sought conventional employment.

That drug use is learned in a particular social context has been confirmed by several studies of marijuana users. First, the predisposition to drug use is a function of the family and social situations in which youngsters grow up. Erich Goode reports a powerful relationship between liberalism in all forms and drug use. Students who attend large universities with high academic standards in large cities, especially if they and their parents have no religious connections, are more likely to be drug users. There is also a positive relationship between social class and drug use, and students from working-class families are more likely to use drugs if they attend schools that have middle-class student bodies. Parents who use alcohol are more likely to have children who try drugs, and the more the parents drink the greater is the likelihood. Similarly, parents who use prescription drugs such as barbiturates are more likely to have children who use drugs.[74]

These relationships indicate that marijuana use is a social phenomenon and that no assumptions concerning the alleged psychological maladjustment of users are required to explain it. Most users are introduced to marijuana by their friends, smoke with those friends, gain status by so doing, and reinforce both their behavior and that of their friends in the process. The social normality of smoking pot was shown by one study of 459 California high-school students; the researcher found that students who anticipated going to college were about twice as likely to have used marijuana as a comparable group who were not likely to attend college. The researcher concluded that the college-oriented youth acquire a perception of the college lifestyle that includes at least occasional marijuana use along with certain modes of dress, expression, and so on.[75] The second annual report to Congress on *Marijuana and Health* emphasizes the sociological nature of the process: "It is well recognized that marijuana use, like much other illegal drug use, occurs first in a social group, is supported by group norms, and functions as a shared social symbol. . . . The spread of marijuana through different segments of the society is aptly viewed as an example of the adoption of an innovation. A given individual ordinarily goes through a number of stages before adopting an innovation—awareness of the innovation, development of interest, evaluation or knowledge-seeking, and a trial period. Sometimes the practice is not permanently adopted, but is rejected or discontinued."[76]

Staff conference at Odyssey House drug rehabilitation center.
(United Press International)

TREATMENT PROGRAMS

Attempts to treat narcotic addiction have a long and generally unsuccessful history in the United States. The oldest programs are those of the two federal narcotics hospitals at Lexington, Kentucky, and Fort Worth, Texas, which were also the most highly regarded ones at least until the mid-1960s. The recidivism rate at these hospitals is difficult to determine but is certainly high, perhaps as high as 97 percent.[77]

The obvious failure of conventional treatments for addiction led to the development of therapeutic groups among drug users comparable to Alcoholics Anonymous. The model for these groups of former drug users was the original Synanon, which was established in California and now has eight offices from the Philippines to Puerto Rico to West Germany and over $30 million worth of assets.[78] Other successful groups include Daytop, Odyssey House, and Phoenix House. Although the details of their programs vary, generally they include three elements: (1) a kind of encounter group therapy; (2) a highly structured community; and (3) a reward–punishment system based on a simple behavioral psychology. Unfortunately, no independent investigation of the success of these groups has been conducted, so the claims of the groups themselves cannot be verified. Daytop boasts a success record of 85 percent based on "clean" graduates, and Odyssey House claims that 71.5 percent of its graduates stay clean for at least a year and a half.[79] Yet only 3 percent of addicts volunteering for treatment choose the therapeutic communities, and the drop-out rates from the programs average 60 percent. Two principal criticisms, other than a low success rate, have been leveled at the therapeutic communities. First, they do not make people independent but encourage continued dependency on the therapeutic community itself. Second, black groups argue that the encounter therapy is destructive of personal identity and that black people have too long suffered personality destruction at the hands of the larger society.

In 1964 two New York City physicians began conducting experiments, treating addicts with a new synthetic drug called methadone. Methadone, taken orally in strictly regulated amounts, prevents withdrawal symptoms when addicts stop taking heroin and keeps them on an even plane, experiencing neither euphoria nor lassitude. It also helps reduce the craving for other drugs, and if the addicts should try heroin again it prevents them from obtaining the high that they seek.

Methadone treatment programs have mushroomed, with an estimated 80,000 addicts enrolled in 460 public and private clinics in 40 states.[80] In the best clinics, medication is combined with counseling and occupational rehabilitation. In Boston 70 percent of the patients have jobs; in Washington, D.C., 65 percent of the regular patients do. Proponents of the programs believe that the crime rate among patients is greatly reduced. Abuses of the programs have developed, however, and serious problems have appeared.[81] A basic problem is that methadone itself is addictive. It is unlike most other drugs in that patients do not develop a tolerance for it, so increasing amounts are not required. Methadone is also much cheaper than heroin. Critics argue, however, that making addicts dependent on one drug instead of another is morally abhorrent, like shifting alcoholics from whiskey to wine. They also point out that when heroin itself was discovered in 1898, it was widely regarded to be a desirable substitute for morphine.

While some addicts use methadone to reduce their dependence on drugs, methadone does not automatically reduce the craving for other drugs. Methadone can also be injected intravenously to produce a kind of orgasmic rush almost as intense as that from heroin. Consequently, a methadone black market has developed. By enrolling in several treatment centers, addicts acquire extra supplies to sell or to inject. When the clinics seek to stop this by mixing methadone with fruit juice and watching the patients take it, many still manage to hold the liquid in their mouths until they can spit it into plastic bags for later sale as "mouthwash methadone." It is particularly distressing that black market methadone is sold to beginning drug users, who quickly become addicted and who are particularly vulnerable to a lethal overdose.

A fierce debate rages between advocates of therapeutic communities and advocates of methadone programs. Methadone advocates claim that the drug permits addicts to stabilize their lives and that it eliminates drug-related crime. They also point out that the cure rate for the therapeutic communities is very low and is inflated by backers of the communities who ignore the high drop-out rate. Advocates of therapeutic communities attack methadone maintenance on moral grounds, arguing that it is based on the illusion that a drug can provide a fast, magical solution to a complex social problem.

Probably the newest, and perhaps the most controversial, drug treatment program is the Florida-based SEED program, which is now expanding into Kentucky, Ohio, North Carolina, and Texas. SEED, developed by an exalcoholic, focuses on teenagers who have used a variety of drugs and who are placed in treatment either by their parents or by the courts. Modeled upon Alcoholics Anonymous and employing a crude version of behavior modification, SEED takes a large proportion of its clients against their will; uses peer-group pressure to force them to adopt a morality emphasizing love of self, love of others, love of family, love of God, and love of country; and virtually incarcerates them until they become compliant. As they accept SEED's ideals and are weaned from drugs, the teenagers are gradually returned to their families and to the community.

The rate of success claimed for the program is very high—almost 90 percent. Even SEED's most violent critics acknowledge that it works. What they object to is the deprivation of young people's civil rights as they are forced into treatment. Some critics also claim to know of youngsters who have developed severe psychiatric problems as a result of the treatment, but this has not been verified. At least two civil suits have been filed against SEED, which continues to expand and to earn the praise of distraught parents of teenage drug abusers, even as the controversy mounts.[82]

One of the great unsolved questions about drug abuse is whether it is self-limiting in most cases. The vast majority of drug users are young or middle-aged; what happens to users and addicts as they grow older? Even allowing for a high death rate and for the institutionalization of some, drug abuse is not the problem among older people that it might be expected to be. Some research indicates that many people give up drug use when they marry and become parents.[83] Alfred Lindesmith also reports that many addicts abstain for longer and longer periods as they grow older. Some of them move to smaller towns where drugs are not readily available. Most such people continue to think of themselves as exaddicts, however, and in that sense addiction is incurable.[84]

Prostitution and Homosexuality

PROSTITUTION

HISTORY OF THE PROBLEM   The phrase "the oldest profession" suggests that prostitution may be as old as humankind. The Bible condemns it as immoral, and Christ was criticized for being tolerant of prostitutes. Later the church accepted the inevitability of sin, until the reformers of the Protestant Reformation again demanded that prostitutes be punished. Despite religious disapproval, prostitution flourished in American frontier communities, and sporting houses operated without serious restraint in the cities. One famous club, the Everleigh House in Chicago, operated in a 50-room mansion where, at $50 and up, guests were served champagne from golden buckets and perfume gushed from fountains. American policy toward prostitution has vacillated, particularly in the enthusiasm with which antiprostitution laws have been enforced. By the early twentieth century moralist views prevailed, and prostitution became generally illegal. Today it is illegal in every state except Nevada, where it is tolerated in 15 out of 17 counties. Maine has eliminated prison terms for prostitution, and the city of San Francisco recently stopped prosecuting prostitutes. Unofficially, prostitution is practiced openly in virtually every major American city.

SIZE AND COST OF THE PROBLEM   The number of prostitutes in the United States is unknown and unknowable. Women move into and out of the life: some turn tricks to supplement their income from legitimate jobs, some are part-time amateurs, still others accept gifts instead of money, and so on. Without clearly indicating the basis for their judgment, several authorities hazard the guess that the number of prostitutes has changed little over the last several decades.[85] Police make approximately 100,000 arrests per year for prostitution, and there may be 500,000 full-time professional prostitutes. One team of investigators, projecting from statistics collected by Alfred Kinsey a generation ago, estimates that there are 315 million episodes of commercial sex per year, for payments to prostitutes amounting to $2.25 billion.[86]

SOCIAL AND PERSONAL FACTORS   How do women become involved in prostitution? How do prostitutes differ from other women? There is virtually no evidence to support the popular stereotype of innocent young girls being lured into prostitution by unscrupulous men. Probably very few women are initiated into sexual experience through prostitution. Rather, previous sex experience seems to be almost a prerequisite to entering the profession. The same conditions that encourage sex outside marriage and relatively promiscuous behavior are favorable for entrance into prostitution. The more promiscuous the woman and the more contact she has with persons involved in prostitution, the more likely she is to resort to prostitution.[87]

The youth counterculture of the early 1970s and the spread of drug use among teenagers probably increased the number of young and relatively inexperienced girls entering prostitution. Countercultural norms denigrating the alleged hypocrisy of straight society and its sexual hang-ups favored relatively widespread sexual contacts and eliminated fears of sex as such. Marijuana and drugs are believed to heighten sexual pleasure, and the seeking after such pleasure may become part of the group experience. Girls and women who become hooked on hard drugs commonly have no way other than prostitution to support their habits. Ironically, this combination of circumstances may be giving more credence to the likelihood of young girls being forced into prostitution than has been true for at least two or three generations. Manhattan's East Village has become notorious for the number of pimps who seek out naive girls and lead them into prostitution through a combination of promised love, drugs, and brutality. The number of such cases is unknown, but it is estimated that 500 or more young girls gravitate to the East Village each year.[88]

Situational factors loom large in leading some women into prostitution. Women in dire economic circumstances and without occupational skills sometimes find prostitution the path of least resistance. Wartime finds large numbers of women without histories of promiscuity resorting to prostitution under conditions of great hardship. Finally, the importance of situational factors is underlined by the larger number of women than men who turn to homosexuality in prison.[89]

Yet even under conditions of great stress, only some women will turn to prostitution. Presumably personality differences are involved. One study of 24 high-priced call girls in New York City showed that all had suffered emotional deprivation in childhood. None had been tied to their families with bonds of love and affection. All apparently sought emotional security in promiscuous behavior before becoming call girls, but they found little satisfaction from sex. Most of them regarded themselves as being unhappy and many depended on their pimps for companionship.[90]

TREATMENT OF THE PROBLEM   As in the case of drugs, there is controversy over whether prostitution can and should be stamped out. Those who argue for legal suppression maintain that the state has the obligation to make laws to protect the family and children. Furthermore, they allege that prostitution degrades and abuses women, particularly poor women who do not have the skill and training to compete in the legitimate occupational world. Random sexual encounters also inevitably contain elements of squalor and violence; prostitution and crime are intricately interrelated. Finally, they claim, legalization of prostitution has never worked. Most prostitutes will not register and undergo regular medical examination. Even medical scrutiny cannot stop the spread of venereal disease. Corruption also attends the legal regulation of prostitution, inviting organized crime to enter.

Proponents of legalization argue that the prohibition of prostitution has never worked. "Sin" cannot effectively be outlawed; efforts to do so lead only to the consumption of police time and effort, with the corruption of police being very likely. On both moral and practical grounds it is unwise to define prostitution as a crime. There is no victim, and the state has no business trying to regulate sexual activity between consenting adults.

Prostitution has the curious status of being one of the oldest and more persistent social problems in history, yet not being clearly a social problem in the sense that people feel that the problem can be solved. There is a widespread feeling that prostitution is too deeply rooted in human nature to eliminate. Recent evidence on the perceptions of prostitutes themselves supports this view. While society has defined prostitutes as desperately unhappy women who want and need help to change, it now appears that many of them earn good incomes, like their lifestyles, and would be loathe to switch occupations with secretaries or saleswomen. From a study of 269 prostitutes, Wardell Pomeroy reports that they were more sexually responsive to customers than formerly appeared to be true, good incomes were reported as a reason for entering prostitution, two-thirds of them reported no regrets, and one-fifth of them would advise other women to enter the life.[91]

HOMOSEXUALITY

HISTORY OF THE PROBLEM   Abundant evidence of homosexual practices is found in the literature and graphic arts of ancient civilizations. Definitions of homosexuality as a social problem and condemnations of it are almost as old, with the church being the most consistent opponent. The Old Testament, for example, condemns sodomists to death as perpetrators of an abomination against the Lord. In the New Testament they are denounced as transgressors of the natural order, and are "disinherited from the kingdom of God."[92] Most school children know of the biblical account of the destruction of Sodom and Gomorrah because of their wickedness, although children seldom are told that the primary incidence of that wickedness was the forcing of strangers to accept homosexual relations.

In medieval times Peter Damiani, in the *Liber Gomorrhianus*, condemned the spread of homosexual practices among the clergy, and Thomas Aquinas declared that homosexual acts are "contrary to the natural order of the venereal act as becoming to the human race."[93] Condemnation generally has continued to the present, although contemporary church leaders are likely to accept homosexuals as individuals while retaining their mission to return homosexuals to normality.

Civil law pertaining to homosexuality originally followed church law and generally has been consistent with it. As recently as mid-1971, 47 states had statutes defining homosexual acts as criminal behavior. By the mid-1970s, however, more than one-third of the states had dropped their bans on homosexual practices between consenting adults. Government agencies still tend to define homosexuals as security risks, and many police forces engage in outright persecution of them. The widespread use of *agents provocateurs* for the entrapment of homosexuals, the harassment of homosexual gathering places, and the use of hidden observation techniques are well known.[94]

NATURE AND EXTENT OF HOMOSEXUALITY   Perhaps no other social problem is so well hidden from public view as homosexuality. The vast majority of homosexuals live in fear of discovery and exploitation, with the consequence that data on homosexuality are fragmentary and of doubtful reliability. Although studies have reported on the incidence of homosexual behavior, most are too old or methodologically too inadequate to warrant summarizing here.[95] We shall concentrate on the two best studies, which come from the Institute of Sex Research.

Alfred Kinsey's 1948 report on the sexual behavior of approximately 5,000 white males contained what appear to be unbiased estimates of homosexual behavior among college-educated men.[96] It showed that 6 percent of the college-educated males had at least one homosexual contact by age 12, rising to 21 percent by age 15. Thereafter the rate slowed, reaching 27 percent by age 20 and 33 percent by age 25. These figures should be viewed cautiously, because they also indicate that homosexuality is concentrated among the unmarried. The vast majority of males marry and cease all homosexual activity after marriage.[97] The 1953 Kinsey report on female sexual behavior showed that female homosexual behavior is also concentrated among the unmarried. The accumulative incidence climbed from 5 percent by age 15 to 9 percent by age 20 to 16 percent by age 25.[98]

If the two Kinsey reports are taken together as a single study, then the second Institute study was one of 477 white males without college education who served as a control group in a study of male sex offenders. These men had never been convicted of any offense. They may be taken as a non-college-educated group to be compared with those described above. The accumulative incidence of homosexuality among them was 16 percent by age 12, 21 percent by age 14, and between 25 and 27 percent until at least age 30. The 34 percent of this sample who had postpubertal homosexual contact was remarkably close to the 37 percent reported for the sample of 5,000.[99]

Paul Gebhard concludes that between one-quarter and one-third of adult U.S. males have had homosexual contact since puberty, most of it in adolescence. Only 1 to 1.5 percent of married males are predominantly homosexual, while 12 percent of single males up to age 25, and nearly one-third of males who are still single by age 35, are predominantly homosexual. When these figures are weighted by marital status, 4 percent of white, college-educated, adult males appear to be predominantly homosexual.

Female homosexuality presents a different picture. Unlike males, females do not concentrate homosexual activity in adolescence but become more involved up to age 30, when the incidence levels out at 17 percent of the college-educated. For the whole female population, the total accumulative incidence is 10 to 12 percent. The incidence of predominantly homosexual females is less than that among males, being only 1 or 2 percent.[100]

Thus, the evidence shows that significant fractions of both the male and the female populations have some homosexual experience before marriage, but that after marriage most of them give it up. Among those who remain single, the accumulative incidence becomes higher with increasing age, with several million males and less than half as many females remaining predominantly homosexual for life.

The cause of homosexuality has never been adequately explained. One group of theories emphasizes the importance of biological predisposition, focusing on genetic, chromosomal, and/or hormonal anomalies. Studies of chromosomal and hormonal differences between homosexuals and heterosexuals have yielded negative findings, but as the research becomes more sophisticated many experts believe that significant relationships will be discovered for at least some homosexuals.[101] A second group of theories are based in psychoanalysis and view homosexuality as the product of pathogenic relationships with parents in early childhood. Both groups of theories employ a medical model, viewing homosexuality as a disease to be cured. Psychotherapy is the most widely used treatment, with generally inconsistent and unimpressive results. Aversion therapies, employing such techniques as showing the subject pictures of naked men and women and giving him (or her) mild electric shocks when viewing the same-sex photo, have recently become popular. Used often in conjunction with hormone treatments, these new modes have not been adequately evaluated yet.

A third group of theories, which does not deny the possible validity of the other two, is sociological and assigns a major role to social and situational factors. These theorists emphasize that much homosexual experience occurs during adolescence and does not continue into adult married life. They also point out that group norms regulate much adolescent experience.

Two demonstrators in favor of gay rights at the Democratic National Convention, New York, August, 1980.
(United Press International)

Albert Reiss, for example, has described a situation in which members of a delinquent gang engage in homosexual relationships with adults for pay without defining themselves as homosexual and without accepting homosexual behavior in any other context. Group norms define the sexual activities permitted, payment therefor, and the maintenance of contemptuous attitudes toward homosexuals.[102]

Situational factors also appear to account for the large numbers of persons of both sexes who adopt homosexual behavior in situations of isolation from heterosexual contacts, such as a term in prison. Many of these people have had no prior homosexual experience, nor do they continue it following their release. Moreover, homosexual behavior in prison is again clearly regulated by social norms. Among men, the active partner is not defined as homosexual and does not perceive his masculinity to be threatened.[103] Emotional involvement with partners is rare. The situation in women's prisons is controlled by a very different set of norms, but the normative system is equally obvious and effective.[104]

HOMOSEXUALITY AS A SOCIAL PROBLEM The almost universal tendency to view homosexuality as a medical problem has until recently obscured the nature of homosexuality as a social problem. Only within the past several years have its social problem aspects received systematic attention in the context that something might be done about them.

The social problem hinges on the use of the label *homosexual,* which has been used to create a pariah caste subject to the contempt of virtually all those who do not bear the label, and subject to harassment and persecution at the hands of all of society's official agencies. Despite evidence that one-third of males and one-tenth or more of females have some homosexual experience, that most of that experience has no deleterious effects on their lives or the lives of others, and that their homosexual contacts are confined to the young, unmarried years, society officially treats all homosexual acts alike and defines them as a major threat to the public well-being.

Most homosexual acts remain hidden, those who commit them living with the fear of persecution more often than with persecution itself. For that small percentage of the population that is predominantly homosexual, however, the threat of discovery has been great and the likelihood of persecution real. Although organizations to promote understanding of homosexuality and to protect the rights of homosexuals are not new, they remained small and obscure until the late 1960s, and many of the people who participated in them did so through aliases to disguise their true identities. As part of the upheaval of the 1960s, the Gay Liberation Movement arose to denounce society's discrimination against homosexuals, to seek understanding, and to demand equal treatment.

The term *Gay Liberation Movement* may imply more unity than there is in fact. Instead of one monolithic organization, there are separate organizations such as the Mattachine Society and the Daughters of Bilitis; the movement emphasizes fluidity, spontaneity, antiauthoritarianism, and decentralization. The Gay Liberation Front, established in 1969, has been replaced by a variety of local groups such as the Gay Activists Alliance in New York City, dedicated to implementing and maintaining gay rights. The core of the gay movement is Marxist in theory, arguing that the sexual caste system in modern society is based on institutionalized heterosexuality and the oppression of females. That caste system, which reinforces discrimination on the bases of social class and race, must be eliminated before homosexuals can gain their rights and full acceptance as people.

The movement challenges both the medical and scientific models that have underlaid society's approach to homosexuality up to now, arguing that they make invalid assumptions, lead to biased conclusions, and provide thinly disguised rationalizations for the persecution of homosexuals. Underlying the models, movement members say, is a culturally biased concept of "normal" behavior that comes from the Judeo-Christian tradition. It assumes that human development occurs through stages, propelled by instinctive biological forces that result ordinarily in genital heterosexuality. This analysis, they say, is basically moral rather than scientific, leading to the unwarranted conclusion that homosexuals are abnormal and need to be cured. The true roots of the problem lie, instead, in the societal definitions of sexual variation and in punitive attitudes toward it. The Gay Liberation Movement asserts its right to live without persecution, a claim that many "straights" accept. The movement also demands recognition of homosexuality, not as an illness or personality defect, but as an equally valid and legitimate lifestyle, a view that does not have wide acceptance.

The Social-Disorganization Approach

A common factor underlying the several social problems analyzed in this chapter is that they have all existed as problems since time immemorial. No breakdown in social norms need be sought to account for their presence. Instead, they seem to be deeply rooted in human nature and to have defied all attempts to uproot them. Because this is a textbook in the *sociology* of social problems, we have not made detailed analyses of the biological and psychological factors in each of these problems, but it is obvious that such factors are important and would help account for why some persons become mentally ill, drug addicts, and so on, while others do not.

Even here, however, analysis of the supports provided to individuals by the social system offers important clues. Ideally, each person should be so indoctrinated with the dominant group values that he or she will not be tempted to engage in deviant behavior. Traditionally, family ties and other primary group ties provided protection against the temptation to engage in disapproved behaviors, with community institutions such as church and school playing major supportive roles. Occasionally these agencies fail in their respective tasks, but it is significant that social deviance is least in evidence where family and community life are most satisfactory. Conversely, deviance is most obvious in areas and situations in which family and community life are not well organized.

We have pointed out in earlier chapters that community life functions most smoothly in rural areas, and that the anonymous, heterogeneous, mobile character of urban life is disruptive of many of the more traditional kinds of human relationships. Institutional commitments and arrests for all kinds of deviance are unusually high in urban blight areas, around military installations, and in communities that undergo boomtown conditions. Social isolation and extreme mobility are statistically associated with increased evidence of personality disorganization.

Of the problems discussed in this chapter, drug abuse has become much more common in recent years, while prostitution and homosexuality have at least become much more visible. The spread of drug use, particularly among young people, represents a logical extension of the indiscriminate use of aspirin, tranquilizers, amphetamines, alcohol, and other drugs among adults. What the older generation views as social breakdown, the younger generation believes to reflect adult hypocrisy. The apparent increase in streetwalking prostitution has already been described as closely linked to drug use. The new visibility of homosexuality presents a direct challenge to the traditional normative system. Homosexuals are saying that society has no right to stigmatize and persecute them.

The Value-Conflict Approach

Few would argue whether the forms of deviance discussed in this chapter are social problems. But many quarrel over what aspects of these situations constitute the problems, and over what the appropriate remedies are. Many of the details of the controversies have already been discussed and need not be repeated here.

Less than a generation ago, when the mentally ill were sequestered in custodial institutions and habitual drunks were given prison sentences, attempts to substitute medical treatment for incarceration were hailed as a great advance. Most of the public and probably most professionals, too, are still of this belief. Over the past decade or so, however, civil libertarians have made strong attacks on both civil and medical authorities for using hospitalization as a substitute form of incarceration and for depriving persons accused of being ill of their civil rights without due process of law. These advocates argue that while mental illness and alcoholism are problems, they are not diseases. The mentally ill and drunks should be accountable for their behavior just like everyone else, and if treatment is part of the solution to the problem, it should be purely voluntary.

A second area of controversy concerns whether the illegality of some behavior—marijuana use, prostitution, and homosexuality—does not create more problems than the behaviors themselves. Proponents of legalization argue that such "vices" provide safety valves, draining off tensions that might otherwise be expressed in even more antisocial behavior. Legalization of prostitution would discourage voyeurism and rape. Legal marijuana would drive down the cost of drugs and eliminate most drug-related crime. Legalized homosexuality would discourage blackmail, police corruption, and so on. Opponents make a strong case on the other side. Effective regulation, they say, is impossible, leading to the corruption of regulating authorities. Legalization allegedly would also greatly increase the number of people indulging in such vices, multiplying the human and monetary costs. Finally, they oppose legalization as abhorrent on moral grounds.

One specific form of this controversy concerns recurrent proposals that the United States try the British system of legalized heroin maintenance. The British system, based on the assumption that narcotic addiction is an illness to be treated by physicians rather than by police and courts, has permitted physicians to dispense heroin, morphine, and other drugs to patients whom they deem to need them. The system worked splendidly until the mid-1950s; there were only a handful of addicts, most of them women who became hooked following the prescription of drugs during lengthy illnesses. Then striking changes occurred. Young British males began to take drugs, not because they needed them but because they liked them. A drug-using subculture appeared. By 1968 the problem had grown to the point where the government limited the number of physicians who could prescribe drugs. Britain's addict population is still much smaller than ours, there is less black market in drugs, and there is much less drug-related crime, causing some authorities to believe that a similar system would work here. Others argue that recent experience has shown the British system to be a failure, and that such a program in the United States would produce as many as three or four million addicts.

Homosexuality is a social problem created by value conflicts—whether adults should be permitted to engage in such acts without punishment, and whether the homosexual life is an abhorrent deviation or merely an alternative lifestyle. Should homosexuals be "helped" to become heterosexual, or to become more comfortable in a homosexual life? As with all other social problems, value conflicts are central to the definition of the problem and to its treatment.

The Personal-Deviation Approach

Primary deviance plays a more prominent role in the definition and proposals for treatment of the social problems discussed in this chapter than it does in the analysis of problems stemming from race, urbanization, education, and so on. In the case of some mental illness and some homosexuality, genetic and/or chromosomal factors may be involved. Metabolic factors may also help account for why some drinkers become alcoholics and some do not. Few people would argue that hereditary factors cause drug addiction, but most people believe that addicts are psychologically deviant. Finally, while some would argue that prostitutes are as neurotic as addicts, a strictly social causation plays a larger role here. The analysis of biological and even psychological factors, in any event, goes beyond the scope of this book. Ours is a sociological analysis of social problems.

The role of secondary deviance, a product of labeling, is central to the analysis of these problems. Many persons who are labeled as mentally ill may actually have no disabling behavior abnormalities until the label *mental illness* is attached.[105] Then they may be variously tolerated, humored, shunned, treated, and incarcerated. Persons labeled as alcoholics may be treated in comparable fashion. The most devastating of these labels probably is that of *homosexual*, leading to scorn and punishment by most groups. Moreover, once these labels are attached they can seldom be completely escaped. Long after release from mental hospitals, former mental patients carry the stigma of mental illness, former addicts continue to carry the label of *junkie,* and so on.

Finally, some forms of social deviance are nurtured in special subcultures and countercultures that have developed to support them. The subcultural phenomenon is evident on the homosexual scene, as gay liberation has emerged to try to interpret homosexuality to the straight society. Countercultures, with norms directly opposed to the norms of the larger society, play large roles in drug abuse and prostitution. The social pattern that involves the use of illegal drugs tends to entice users into experimenting with various forms of drugs until serious physical, psychological, and social problems develop. The world of prostitution is closely connected with the world of drug use, but has its own system of relationships among prostitutes, their customers, their pimps, and the law.

Summary

The costs of mental illness in the United States are enormous: at least $36 billion per year in treatment costs and lost productivity. Approximately 3 million people are being treated, most of them outside hospitals. Epidemiologic studies show incidences of mental illness in the population ranging from 10 to 40 percent.

Controversy has emerged over the institutional and compulsory treatment of mentally ill persons, with opponents of current practices arguing that mental illness is a social problem rather than a medical problem and that the legal rights of persons charged with being mentally ill must be protected. Studies show legal and medical biases toward commitment, and that commitment is dehumanizing. Social class is important in diagnosis and treatment; lower-class patients are often discriminated against. Recent evidence contradicts earlier data from hospital admission records and indicates that mental illness rates are especially high among married women. The isolation of some women in their marital roles, their complete dependence on men, the low status accorded to housewifery, and discrimination against employed women all appear to help explain this relationship.

Two-thirds of adult Americans drink alcoholic beverages, and some 10 million of them are labeled as alcoholics. The total economic cost of alcoholism approaches $15 billion per year; alcoholism contributes to 85,000 deaths each year; and broken homes, lost jobs, and physical and mental health problems are additional costs. Drinking, long a moral issue in American society, has only recently been defined as a medical problem. Although the medical view of alcoholism prevails today, it is being challenged by dissident professionals who point out that alcoholism is not a physical disease, cannot be treated by conventional medical means, and should be viewed as a social problem. As evidence, they point out that alcoholism rates vary drastically by nationality, ethnic group, and religion. Social class influences the diagnosis and treatment of alcoholism in a fashion very similar to that of mental illness.

Drug addiction rates in the United States today are higher than they were at the end of World War II, and about the same as at the beginning of the century. There is little relationship between official efforts to cope with drug abuse and the use of drugs. Some 450,000 drug addicts require approximately $15 billion per year to support their habits. The rapid spread of marijuana during the 1960s greatly altered the drug problem. As many as 25 million Americans have tried the drug, and over 8 million use it currently. Although there is little evidence that marijuana is harmful enough to warrant such concern, legal penalties for its use have been severe. Bitter controversy exists over whether the drug should be legalized.

The number of full-time prostitutes in the United States is estimated at around one-half million and is not believed to have changed much in recent decades. Currently, drug use and the need to support drug habits may be linked to increased entrance of fairly young girls into prostitution. Personality maladjustment may be common among prostitutes, but situational factors appear to have much to do with many women's entering the life. Contrary to popular belief, many prostitutes do not seem too unhappy with their lot, and treatment programs for prostitutes have not had much success.

One-third of American men and one-tenth of the women have had some homosexual experience since puberty. Only about 4 percent of the men and 1 or 2 percent of the women are exclusively homosexual. Sociologists emphasize situational factors in homosexuality and the normative system that regulates it. In the late 1960s homosexuals began to assume a militant stance and to demand an end to their persecution. They have challenged the traditional medical and scientific analyses of homosexuality and have sought to define the problems as deriving from the larger society's repressive norms.

The anonymity and mobility of modern urban life both augment and render more troublesome the various forms of social deviance. Bitter conflicts exist over whether such problems should be dealt with by suppression or whether these behaviors are so deeply rooted in human nature that legalization would be the least undesirable alternative. Controversy is also emerging over the practice of forcibly incarcerating the mentally ill, drunks, and prostitutes. Finally, the process of labeling these deviants often compounds the deviance, and deviant subcultures and countercultures play special roles in the analysis of some of the problems.

Suggested Readings

BERRY, RALPH E., JR., and JAMES P. BOLAND, *The Economic Cost of Alcohol Abuse* (New York: Free Press, 1977). Employs different definitions of alcoholism to assess six different categories of economic costs. Considers policy implications.

GOODE, ERICH, and RICHARD TROIDEN, eds., *Sexual Deviance and Sexual Deviants* (New York: William Morrow, 1974). A comprehensive set of current readings on various aspects of sexual deviance, including prostitution and homosexuality.

LETTIERI, DAN J., ed., *Predicting Adolescent Drug Abuse* (Rockville, Md.: National Institute on Drug Abuse, 1975). A series of working papers by experts in the field. Explores various approaches to the prediction of drug abuse.

LINGEMAN, RICHARD R., *Drugs from A to Z: A Dictionary,* 2nd ed. (New York: McGraw-Hill, 1974). A leading reference book on the fields of drug use and drug abuse.

PERRUCCI, ROBERT R., *Circle of Madness: On Being Insane and Institutionalized in America* (Englewood Cliffs, N.J.: Prentice-Hall, 1974). A perceptive analysis of mental hospital careers, employing a labeling perspective.

PLANT, MARTIN L., *Drinking Careers: Occupations, Drinking Habits, and Drinking Problems* (New York: Methuen, 1979). Report of longitudinal research showing how changes in drinking patterns are linked to social and occupational groups.

VOGLIOTTI, GABE, *The Girls of Nevada* (Secaucus, N.J.: Citadel Press, 1975). A candid account of the development and operation of legal prostitution in one American state.

Footnotes

[1]*Time Magazine,* 7 July 1975, p. 44.

[2]*Gainesville Sun,* 15 Dec. 1974.

[3]*U.S. News and World Report,* 8 Mar. 1976, p. 5.

[4]*New York Times,* 21 Dec. 1975.

[5]Edwin M. Schur, *Crimes without Victims: Deviant Behavior and Public Policy: Abortion, Homosexuality, and Drug Addiction* (Englewood Cliffs, N.J.: Prentice-Hall, 1965).

[6]For the most authoritative account, see Albert Deutsch, *The Shame of the States* (New York: Harcourt Brace, 1948).

[7]Bertram S. Brown, *Trends in Mental Health: Conflict and Detente between Social Issues and Clinical Practice* (Washington D.C.: U.S. Government Printing Office, 1978).

[8]Daniel S. Levine and Shirley G. Willner, "The Cost of Mental Illness, 1974," *Mental Health Statistical Note* No. 125 (Feb. 1976), p. 1.

[9]B. Drummond Ayres, Jr., "Growth of Community Mental Health in Reducing the Number of Patients in Hospitals," *New York Times,* 30 July 1972, p. 36.

[10]Leo Srole et al., *Mental Health in the Metropolis: The Manhattan Midtown Study* (New York: McGraw-Hill, 1962).

[11]Benjamin Pasamanick et al., "A Survey of Mental Disease in an Urban Population: I. Prevalence by Age, Sex, and Severity of Impairment," *American Journal of Public Health,* 47 (1957), 923–29; and Benjamin Pasamanick, "A Survey of Mental Disease in an Urban Population: IV. An Approach to Total Prevalence Rates," *Archives of General Psychiatry,* 5 (1961), 151–55.

[12]John J. Schwab et al., "Concurrent Psychiatric and Medical Illness," *Proceedings of the Third International Congress of Social Psychiatry,* 4 (Sept. 21–27, 1970), 157–63.

[13]Dorothea C. Leighton et al., *The Character of Danger: Vol. III. Psychiatric Symptoms in Selected Communities* (New York: Basic Books, 1963).

[14]Thomas Szasz, *The Myth of Mental Illness: Foundations of a Theory of Personal Conduct* (New York: Harper & Row, Paul B. Hoeber, 1961).

[15]Edwin Kiester, Jr., "Dr. Szasz, The Devil's Advocate," *Human Behavior,* July–Aug. 1972, pp. 16–23.

[16]Thomas J. Scheff, "The Social Reaction to Deviance: Ascriptive Elements in the Psychiatric Screening of Mental Patients in a Midwestern State," *Social Problems,* 11 (Spring 1964), 401–13.

[17]David Mechanic, "Some Factors in Identifying and Defining Mental Illness," *Mental Hygiene,* 46 (Jan. 1962), 66–75.

[18]Dorothy Miller and Michael Schwartz, "County Lunacy Commission Hearings: Some Observations of Commitments to a State Mental Hospital," *Social Problems,* 14 (Summer 1966), 26–35.

[19]L. Kutner, "The Illusion of Due Process in Commitment Proceedings," *Northwestern University Law Review,* 57 (Sept. 1962), 383–99.

[20]Sara Fein and Kent S. Miller, "Legal Processes and Adjudication in Mental Incompetency Proceedings," *Social Problems,* 20 (Summer 1972), 57–64.

[21]Peter Breggin and Daniel Greenberg, "Return of the Lobotomy," *Washington Post,* 12 Mar. 1972; and Peter Breggin, "Neural Bases of Violence and Aggression," paper presented to the Houston Neurological Symposium, 10 Mar. 1972. For other data bearing on this problem, see James R. Greenley, "Alternative Views of the Psychiatrist's Role," *Social Problems,* 20 (Fall 1972), 252–62; and Henry J. Steadman, "The Psychiatrist as a Conservative Agent of Social Control," *Social Problems,* 20 (Fall 1972), 263–71.

[22]National Institute of Mental Health, "News Watch," June 1972, pp. 3–5.

[23]Erving Goffman, "The Moral Career of the Mental Patient," *Psychiatry,* 22 (1959), 123–42.

[24]Erving Goffman, *Asylums: Essays on the Social Situation of Mental Patients and Other Inmates* (New York: Doubleday, 1961), pp. 151–59.

[25]Robert J. Trotter, "Schizophrenia: Is It Hereditary, Is It Environmental or Is It a Combination of Both Factors?" *Science News,* 102 (22 July 1972), 58–59.

[26]Differences were found for different types of psychosis. The manic-depressive psychoses did not fit the pattern indicated, but showed almost random distribution throughout the city. See Robert E. L. Faris and H. Warren Dunham, *Mental Disorders in Urban Areas* (Chicago: University of Chicago Press, 1939); and H. Warren Dunham, *Community and Schizophrenia: An Epidemiological Analysis* (Detroit: Wayne State University Press, 1965).

[27]H. Warren Dunham, "The Social

Personality of the Catatonic-Schizophrene," *American Journal of Sociology,* 49 (May 1944), 508–18. See also R. Jay Turner and Morton O. Wagenfeld, "Occupational Mobility and Schizophrenia: An Assessment of the Social Causation and Social Selection Hypotheses," *American Sociological Review,* 32 (Feb. 1967), 104–13; R. J. Turner and John W. Gartrell, "Social Factors in Psychiatric Outcome: Toward the Resolution of Interpretive Controversies," *American Sociological Review,* 43 (June 1978), 368–82; and Blair Wheaton, "The Sociogenesis of Psychological Disorder: Reexamining the Causal Issues with Longitudinal Data," *American Sociological Review,* 43 (June 1978), 383–403.

[28]August B. Hollingshead and Frederick C. Redlich, *Social Class and Mental Illness: A Community Study* (New York: John Wiley, 1958). See also Jerome K. Myers and Lee L. Bean, *A Decade Later: A Follow-up of Social Class and Mental Illness* (New York: John Wiley, 1968).

[29]For recent analyses, see Allan Horwitz, "Social Networks and Pathways to Psychiatric Treatment," *Social Forces* 56 (Sept. 1977), 86–105; William A. Rushing, "Status Resources, Societal Reactions, and Type of Mental Hospital Admission," *American Sociological Review,* 43 (Aug. 1978), 521–33; and William A. Rushing and Jack Esco, "Status Resources and Behavioral Deviance as Contingencies of Societal Reaction," *Social Forces,* 56 (Sept. 1977), 132–47.

[30]Walter R. Gove, "The Relationship between Sex Roles, Marital Status, and Mental Illness," *Social Forces,* 51 (Sept. 1972), 34–44. See also Leona L. Bachrach, "Marital Status and Mental Disorder: An Analytical Review," Publication No. (ADM)-75-217 (Washington, D.C.: Department of Health, Education and Welfare, 1975).

[31]Barry A. Kinsey, *Statistical Summary of Alcoholism Rates,* mimeographed. See also Sylvia Porter, "A $15 Billion Hangover," syndicated column, 18 Oct. 1972.

[32]Mary Ann Michie, "U.S. Alcoholics Getting a New 'Bill of Rights,'" Universal Science News Service, 13 Aug. 1972.

[33]Ibid.

[34]Claude Steiner, *Games Alcoholics Play: The Analysis of Life Scripts* (New York: Grove Press, 1971).

[35]*Time,* 21 June 1976, p. 45.

[36]Don Cahalan, Ira Cisin, and Helen M. Crossley, *American Drinking Practices: A National Study of Drinking Behavior and Attitudes* (New Brunswick, N.J.: Rutgers Center of Alcohol Studies, 1969).

[37]"Alcoholism: Challenge to the Theory That It's a Disease," *New York Times,* 11 Apr. 1971.

[38]Charles R. Snyder, *Alcohol and the Jews* (Glencoe, Ill.: Free Press, 1958).

[39]Gerald Berreman, "Drinking Patterns of the Aleuts," *Quarterly Journal of Studies on Alcohol,* 17 (Sept. 1956), 503–14.

[40]Article in the *British Medical Journal,* quoted in *Time,* 26 Nov. 1951.

[41]Robert Straus and Selden D. Bacon, *Drinking in College* (New Haven, Conn.: Yale University Press, 1953).

[42]*Time,* 5 Nov. 1979, p. 71.

[43]Michigan Department of Public Health, *Myths about Drinking* (Lansing, Mich., n.d.). For analysis of the special problems of skid-row alcoholics, see Jacqueline P. Wiseman, *Stations of the Lost: The Treatment of Skid Row Alcoholics* (Englewood Cliffs, N.J.: Prentice-Hall, 1970).

[44]*U.S. News and World Report,* 12 Jan. 1976.

[45]R. G. Smart, W. Schmidt, and M. K. Moss, "Social Class as a Determinant of the Type and Duration of Therapy Received by Alcoholics," *International Journal of Addiction,* 4 (1969), 543–56.

[46]John Barbour, "Why Can't We Solve the Drug Problem?" Associated Press, 2 May 1971.

[47]Alfred R. Lindesmith, *The Addict and the Law* (Bloomington: Indiana University Press, 1965), pp. 99–100.

[48]Barbour, "Why Can't We Solve the Drug Problem?"

[49]United Press International, 1 Apr. 1972.

[50]*U.S. News and World Report,* 19 Feb. 1979, p. 29.

[51]Ibid.

[52]United Press International, 1 Apr. 1972.

[53]Dorothy Berg, unpublished compilation of Bureau of Narcotics and Dangerous Drugs, Dec. 1971. Reported in Subcommittee on Alcoholism and Narcotics of the Committee on Labor and Public Welfare, United States Senate, *Marijuana and Health: Second Annual Report to Congress* (Washington, D.C.: Government Printing Office, May 1971). p. 25.

[54]Gallup Poll, 18 Nov. 1979.

[55]Ibid.

[56]*New York Times,* 15 May 1977.

[57]James D. Preston, *A Survey of Drug Use among High School Students in Houston* (College Station: Texas A. and M. University), reported in Subcommittee on Alcoholism and Narcotics, Marijuana and Health, p. 30.

[58]Edward Colbach, "Marijuana Use by G.I.'s in Viet Nam," *American Journal of Psychiatry,* 128 (Aug. 1971), 204–7.

[59]H. Isbell, C. W. Gorodetzky, D. Jasinski, et al., "Effects of Δ⁹-Trans-Treta-Hydro-Cannabinol in Man," *Psychopharmacologia,* 11 (1967), 184–88.

[60]D. Hartmann, "A Study of Drug-Taking Adolescents," in S. Eissler, A. Freud, and H. Hartmann, eds., *The Psychoanalytic Study of the Child,* vol. 24 (New York: International Universities Press, 1969), pp. 384–98.

[61]S. Gershon, "On the Pharmacology of Marijuana," *Behavioral Neuropsychiatry,* 1 (1970), 9–18.

[62]Harold Kolansky and William T. Moore, "Effects of Marijuana on Adolescents and Young Adults," *Journal of the American Medical Association,* 216 (19 Apr. 1971), 486–92.

[63]Solomon H. Snyder, "Work with Marijuana: I. Effects," *Psychology Today,* May 1971, pp. 37–40, 64–66.

[64]*Science News,* 108 (13 Dec. 1975), 374; *Observer* Wire Reports, 27 Jan. 1976.

[65]Helen H. Nowlis, *Drugs on the College Campus* (Garden City, N.Y.: Doubleday, 1969), pp. 33–40.

[66]*New York Times,* 20 July 1975.

[67]Associated Press, 2 Nov. 1972.

[68]Erich Goode, "Multiple Drug Use among Marijuana Smokers," *Social Problems,* 17 (Summer 1969), 48–63.

[69]United Press International, 9 Nov. 1971.

[70]*Psychology Today,* Apr. 1975, pp. 39–40.

[71]Harris Isbell, *What to Know about Drug Addiction,* no. 94 (Washington, D.C.: Public Health Service, 1958), p. 2.

[72]John C. Ball and Carl D. Chambers, *The Epidemiology of Opiate Addiction in the United States* (Springfield, Ill.: Charles C Thomas, 1970).

[73]Daniel Glaser, Bernard Lander, and William Abbott, "Opiate Addicted and Nonaddicted Siblings in a Slum Area," *Social Problems,* 18 (Spring 1971), 510–21.

[74]*New York Times,* 14 Feb. 1972.

[75]Armand L. Mauss, "Anticipatory Socialization toward College as a Factor in Adolescent Marijuana Use," *Social Problems,* 16 (Winter 1969), 357–64.

[76]Subcommittee on Alcohol and Narcotics, *Marijuana and Health,* p. 31.

[77]*Communities in Action,* United States Office of Economic Development, 2 Feb. 1968.

[78]Synanon was racked with scandal in late 1978 and 1979, when its founder was arrested and alleged to have ordered the "rattlesnake" murder of an attorney who had been involved in law suits against Synanon. A host of charges, including alcoholism and ordering vasectomies and abortions for members of the organization were leveled. It is too early to know what effects these charges will have on the organization and its programs. (*New York Times,* 10 Dec. 1978, pp. 1, 20.)

[79]Anne M. Romond, Catherine K. Forrest, and Herbert D. Kleber, "Follow-Up of Participants in a Drug Dependence Therapeutic Community, *Archives of General Psychiatry,* 32 (Mar. 1975), 369–74.

[80]*New York Times Magazine,* 16 Mar. 1975, p. 16.

[81]Paula Holzman Kleinman, Irving F. Lukoff, and Barbara Lynn Kail, "The Magic Fix: A Critical Analysis of Methadone Treatment," *Social Problems,* 25 (Dec. 1977), pp. 208–14.

[82]Associated Press, 5 Jan. 1975.

[83]James W. Brown et al., "Turning Off: Cessation of Marijuana Use after College," *Social Problems,* 21 (Apr. 1974), 527–38; James R. Henley and Larry D. Adams, "Marijuana Use in Post-College Cohorts: Correlates of Use, Prevalence Patterns, and Factors Affected with Cessation," *Social Problems,* 20 (Spring 1973), 514–20.

[84]Alfred R. Lindesmith, *Addiction and Opiates* (Chicago: Aldine, 1968), pp. 51–52.

[85]See T. C. Esselstyn, "Prostitution in the United States," *Annals of the American Academy of Political and Social Science,* 376 (Mar. 1968), 123; Charles Winick and Paul M. Kinsie, *The Lively Commerce: Prostitution in the United States* (Chicago: Quadrangle Books, 1971), p. 5.

[86]*Time,* 23 Aug. 1971, p. 34.

[87]James H. Bryan, "Apprenticeships in Prostitution," *Social Problems,* 12 (Winter 1965), 287–97. See also Barbara Sherman Heyl, "The Madam as Teacher: The Training of House Prostitutes," *Social Problems,* 24 (June 1977), pp. 545–55.

[88]"White Slavery, 1972," *Time,* 5 June 1972, p. 54.

[89]David A. Ward and Gene G. Kassebaum, "Lesbian Liaisons," in John H.

486

Gagnon and William Simon, eds., *The Sexual Scene* (Chicago: Aldine, 1970), pp. 125–36.

[90]Harold Greenwald, *The Call Girl* (New York: Ballantine, 1959).

[91]Wardell B. Pomeroy, "Some Aspects of Prostitution," *Journal of Sex Research*, 1 (Dec. 1965), 177–87.

[92]Derrick S. Bailey, *Homosexuality and the Western Christian Tradition* (London: Longmans Green, 1955), p. 153.

[93]As quoted in Robert L. Katz, "Notes on Religious History, Attitudes, and Laws Pertaining to Homosexuality," in *Final Report and Background Papers of the National Institute of Mental Health Task Force on Homosexuality* (Washington, D.C.: Government Printing Office, 1972), p. 60.

[94]Edwin M. Schur, *Crimes without Victims* (Englewood Cliffs, N.J.: Prentice-Hall, 1965), pp. 77–82.

[95]These studies are reported carefully in Paul H. Gebhard, "Incidence of Overt Homosexuality in the United States and Western Europe," *Final Report of the National Institute of Mental Health Task Force on Homosexuality*, pp. 22–29.

[96]Data were reported for grade-school and high-school educated males also, but it was learned subsequently that these figures were distorted by the inclusion of persons with prison experience. We now know that such persons have more experience with homosexuality than do other persons.

[97]Alfred C. Kinsey, Wardell Pomeroy, and Clyde Martin, *Sexual Behavior in the Human Male* (Philadelphia: W. B. Saunders, 1948), as summaried in Gebhard, *Task Force on Homosexuality*, p. 24.

[98]Alfred C. Kinsey et al., *Sexual Behavior in the Human Female* (Philadelphia: W. B. Saunders, 1953), as summarized in Gebhard, *Task Force on Homosexuality*, p. 25.

[99]Paul Gebhard et al., *Sex Offenders: An Analysis of Types* (New York: Harper & Row, Paul B. Hoeber, 1965), as summarized in Gebhard, *Task Force on Homosexuality*.

[100]Gebhard, *Task Force on Homosexuality*, pp. 27–28.

[101]John Money, "Sexual Dimorphism and Homosexual Gender Identity," *Psychological Bulletin*, 74 (1970), 425–40.

[102]Albert J. Reiss, Jr., "The Social Integration of Queers and Peers," *Social Problems*, 9 (Fall 1961), 102–20.

[103]Gresham M. Sykes, *The Society of Captives: A Study of a Maximum Security Prison* (Princeton, N.J.: Princeton University Press, 1958).

[104]Rose Giallombardo, "Social Roles in a Prison for Women," *Social Problems*, 13 (Winter (1966), 268–88.

[105]In a recent experiment four psychologists, a psychiatrist, a pediatrician, a painter, and a housewife all feigned symptoms of mental illness to see whether they would be admitted to mental hospitals. The symptoms feigned consisted solely of reporting that they heard strange voices saying "empty," "hollow," and "thud." Otherwise all eight described their relationships with other people accurately. Not only were they admitted to hospitals as mental patients, but despite quickly reporting that their symptoms had disappeared, they were labeled as schizophrenics and kept hospitalized for between 7 and 52 days. In a further irony, other patients in the hospital discovered the ruse more often than did the hospital staff. See Sandra Blakeslee, "Eight Feign Insanity in Test and Are Termed Insane," *New York Times*, 21 Jan. 1973.

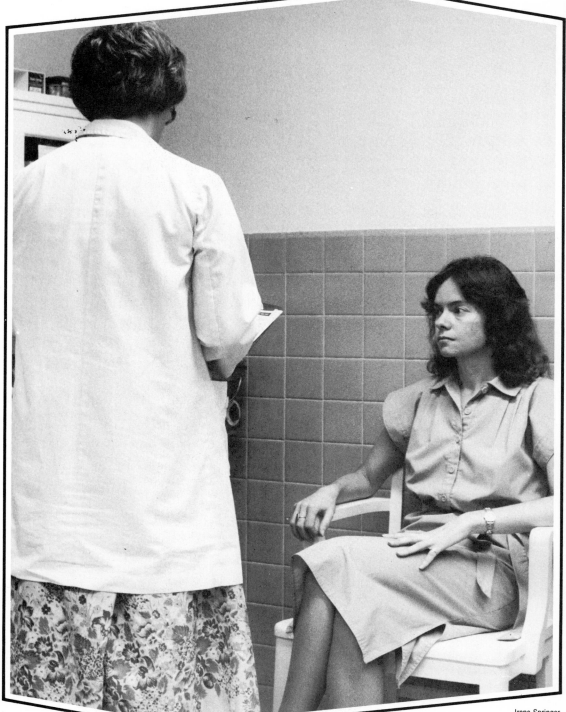

HEALTH AND MEDICAL CARE

17

If you had been a European sailor any-time from, oh, 1400 to 1700, say, the likeli-hood of your dying from scurvy would have been relatively high.

As we now know, scurvy is caused by a vitamin C deficiency. It produces general weakness, hemorrhaging, and ultimately death. It is a relatively rare disease today. A diet that contains almost any quantity of fresh fruits and vegetables will provide enough vitamin C to prevent the disease.

Cures for scurvy were discovered as early as the 1500s. The French explorer Jacques Cartier, who discovered the St. Lawrence River, was taught a cure for scurvy by the Indians in 1536. An English admiral, Sir John Hawkins, used citrus juice to prevent scurvy in 1593.

But citrus juice is expensive. Accord-ingly, in the words of the *Encyclopaedia Bri-tannica,* "Skippers and owners for a couple of centuries found it expedient to be skepti-cal." In short, in the absence of legal liability for the death of sailors, orange juice cost more than human life. And business then, as now, chose the cheapest path. For 200 years, sailors went on dying needlessly.

In 1747 a British naval doctor, James Lind, proved the relationship of citrus juice to the cure of scurvy and published his re-sults. Still no response from the medical es-tablishment, or the government, naval, or merchant shipping establishments.

Finally, in 1795 the British Admiralty got around to requiring its now-famous daily ra-tion of lime juice.

This story has been put together for us by Dr. Linus Pauling, in his revealing little book, *Vitamin C and the Common Cold.* But perhaps the most striking tidbit of Dr. Paul-ing's historical voyage is his report that the business community, represented by the British Board of Trade, didn't impose a sim-ilar regulation on itself—the merchant ship-ping companies—until 70 years after the Navy, in 1865![1]

Good health is the prime foundation of the "good life." A survey found that informants' self-reported health level is more highly associated with their total satisfaction with life than any other factor studied—age, education, sex, intelligence, marital status, or income.[2] And ill health is probably the greatest single cause of human suffering in modern society. In an average day in the United States, nearly two million persons of working age have no jobs because of disability, nearly another million with jobs are absent because of illness, and roughly one-fourth of the rest are working at less than full efficiency because of nondisabling illness. Although by no means can all illness be prevented or cured, our present mores define *any* ill health as an undesirable problem that commands our concern.

Health in the United States— How Good Is It?

Many U.S. citizens comfortably assume that as the wealthiest and, admittedly, the most progressive nation on earth, we must also be the healthiest. This is a pleasant but naive illusion. We have more doctors and hospital beds per 1,000 people than almost any other country,[3] and, according to the American Medical Association (AMA), our doctors are better trained and more competent than those of most other countries. Yet health statistics for the leading nations show that we lag far behind. Since 1938 the United States has slipped from eighth to sixteenth place in infant mortality and from fifth to seventh in the tuberculosis rate, and we now stand eighth from the top in crude death rate and tenth in expectation of life.[4] In no health statistic do we lead the world, and our health lag behind other leading countries is not diminishing. True, our health level has been improving, but that of other nations has been improving more rapidly.

Except among the aged, *most ill health is unnecessary.* People who eat and live sensibly and receive good medical care may still have occasional illnesses, but most of them will be in good health most of the time. Many years ago, five orphanages in North Carolina found that only 1.4 percent of their 1,138 former wards called in the World War II draft had been rejected, while the rejection rate for the entire state was 56.8 percent at the time of the study. This spectacular contrast was attributed to "sound nutrition and reasonably adequate medical care."[5] Such data show that America's health is in unflattering contrast to what it might be.

As defined by the World Health Organization, health is "a state of complete physical, mental and social well being, not merely the absence of disease or infirmity." Health is a product of many factors—genetic inheritance, economic status, life style, nutrition, accidental and environmental hazards, and medical care. The first of these—genetic inheritance—lies outside the field of social problems, at least at present. If and when we learn how to control genetic inheritance, or master the art of cloning (making multiple copies of the same person), then many issues will arise over who is to control these genetic processes and to what ends.[6] This problem may be near at hand, but it does not concern us yet. Each of the other factors is to some degree *social*, and deserves our attention.

Poverty and Social Class

Dozens of studies in past years reached the same dreary conclusion—the poor had more illness, received less medical care, and died several years earlier than the more prosperous. This has been proven so repeatedly and conclusively that we need waste no space in proving it again. Why does good health follow the dollar sign? To some extent poverty causes ill health. Poor housing and sometimes poor plumbing make it more difficult to keep clean. The poor suffer greater malnutrition—not so much through sheer lack of food as through lack of the proper foods. Actual hunger, although far from unknown in the United States, is not a problem for most of the poor, who are, in fact, more often overweight than the middle classes.[7] The diet of the poor runs heavily to starches and sugars—the cheap foods—and is sadly deficient in proteins, fruits, vegetables, and dairy products. While unwise food preferences may be an explanation in some cases, the high cost of the "protective" foods places them out of reach of the poor. The poor live in a world filled with violence and hazard, where death or injury through assault, fire, accident, or environmental pollution is a constant threat. The poor and the near-poor more often work at hazardous occupations. Illness and death stalk them every day.

Yet a recent study of the economics of ill health concludes that "many people . . . are poor simply because they are sick, but relatively few people . . . are sick simply because they are poor."[8] Thus poverty is far more often a *result* than a *cause* of ill health.

THE POOR AND MEDICAL CARE

Early studies made it painfully clear that the poor in the United States, who had the most illness, received the least medical care. This is true no longer, as table 17–1 shows. The poor still have more ill health but now receive more medical care than the rest of us. Some have suggested that the poor are getting wasteful amounts of medical services,[9] but this seems unwarranted, since the poor have more illness. It has also been argued that the poor get inferior care from hurried, indifferent doctors in hospital outpatient clinics, but since such clinics provide only 10 percent of the medical services to the affluent and 20 percent of the services to the poor, this is not a very convincing argument.[10] Clearly, the great gap between the health care of the poor and the affluent has largely disappeared.

Lifestyle and Health

In a number of places in the world, it is reported that many people live well beyond the century mark. Even allowing for possible error in reporting ages, it is clear than among some groups, people remain vigorous to re-

TABLE 17–1a   The Medical Care Gap for the Poor has Narrowed

		Poor	Nonpoor
Days of work loss from illness per year	1973	7.0	5.9
Physician visits per person per year	1964	4.3	4.6
	1977	5.8	4.7
Hospital admissions per 100 people per year	1964	14.6	14.8
	1977	15.8	9.3

SOURCES: 1964 data from *Health: United States, 1975* (Washington, D.C.: National Center for Health Statistics, 1975), p. 166; 1977 data from Harry Schwartz, "Health Care and the Poor," *Wall Street Journal*, 15 Feb. 1980, p. 16.

TABLE 17–1b   The Racial Health Gap Has Also Narrowed

Year	Expectation of life at birth, in years		Difference between white and nonwhite
	White	Nonwhite	
1950	69.1	60.8	8.3
1960	70.6	63.6	7.0
1970	71.7	65.3	6.4
1975	73.2	67.9	5.3

SOURCE: National Center for Health Statistics, *Monthly Vital Statistics Reports*, Vol. 25, No. 11, 11 Feb. 1977, pp. 8, 9.

markable ages. Studies of several such communities suggest that genetics is an unlikely explanation. There is no gene for longevity, only an absence of "bad" genes that predispose to disease. But all the long-lived groups share certain common experiences. They all do hard physical work with no retirement pattern, continuing to work at a gradually diminishing rate up to very advanced ages. Old people hold a high social status in all cases; growing old is a proud achievement, not a misfortune. Most people remain married, have active sex lives into advanced ages, and remain active in family and community life. They eat simple foods including many vegetables, and lead placid, unworried lives. When they finally quit working and become inactive, they die quickly.[11] A study of U.S. citizens who reached the age of 100 also found that, almost without exception, they did hard physical work, rarely retired completely, remained slender throughout life, drank moderately if at all, smoked sparingly if at all, and remained optimistic and unworried throughout life.[12] *It is clear that one's life patterns and practices are the most significant factor in one's level of health and well-being.* While it would be difficult to rank-order them, a number of characteristics of the American lifestyle are unhealthful, if not downright suicidal.

UNHEALTHFUL FEATURES OF THE U.S. LIFESTYLE

LACK OF EXERCISE   The urge to mechanize everything puts us on a conveyor belt to the cemetery. The automobile probably kills more people by carrying them than by crushing them. A few years ago we were chagrined to hear that children in the United States ranked far below European children in physical performance tests. The principal explanation was that European children walked, rode bicycles, and played vigorous games, while American children, when not being chauffeured by indulgent parents, were usually glued to the boob tube. (With greater affluence, European children may today be falling down to the level of American children.)

The recent popularity of jogging and physical fitness is a favorable health indication, and the rising popularity of the bicycle, aside from its environmental impact, is one of the best things that could happen to our health. Unfortunately, bicycle riding carries accidental hazards. But if only a penny from each highway-fund dollar were allocated to bikeways instead, our health level would rise while the problems of pollution, energy shortage, traffic congestion, and parking would be eased.

STRESS   The pioneering work on stress was published by Hans Selye in the 1950s.[13] In a single year nearly 6,000 reports on stress research were published. *Stress* should not be confused with *activity* or even with the speed and tempo of life. Speed and work do not necessarily produce stress. People with monotonous jobs suffer more stress and more illness than people with demanding but challenging jobs.[14] People who are busily active generally live to bury the indolent. An activity becomes stressful when it is pursued under intense time pressure ("I *must* finish this by Friday!"), or when it carries possibilities of humiliating or costly failure or is beset by constant worry and anxiety. Thus, it is not overwork that kills, but the pressure and anxieties sometimes associated with work. To cite one of hundreds of possible examples, airport air controllers, who direct aircraft approaches and landings from the control tower, work under constant knowledge that an error can cost the lives of hundreds of people—and a full two-thirds of them have peptic ulcers.[15] When American Indians leave the reservation, their blood pressure skyrockets.[16] Throughout the world, heart disorders and other diseases increase as societies modernize and industrialize.[17] As women compete more often with men for executive positions, their rates of ulcers, heart disease, and other stress-related illnesses are rising to the male executive levels.[18]

Major life changes are stressful. Not only are misfortunes likely to be followed by illness, but eagerly sought life changes—a marriage, a long-awaited promotion, a change of residence, an eagerly anticipated retirement—are also productive of stress-related illnesses (see table 17–2). It is beyond dispute that stress, unhappiness, loneliness, guilt, anger, and hostility are killers. In fact, unhappy family life has been called the greatest cause of illness.[19]

Until a century ago, most medicine was based on the idea that much illness arose from social and spiritual causes. Temporarily sidetracked by the

Coping with the stresses of life and work is a common problem in today's high-pressured world.
(Irene Springer)

discovery of germs and immunization, we are today rediscovering the importance of social causes of illness.[20] We now realize that unhealthy emotions directly cause some disorders and also reduce the body's ability to resist infection. The term, *holistic medicine,* describes the current effort to treat the entire person, not just the "case" or the "illness."[21]

SMOKING, DRINKING, AND DRUGS   There can no longer be any doubt that cigarette smoking shortens life expectancy—by more than seven years, according to one life insurance company estimate.[22] Not only is lung cancer rare among nonsmokers but a number of other diseases are also associated with smoking—heart disorders, ulcers, emphysema—and the list grows steadily as research continues.[23]

To some extent the statistical associations may be selective. There is some evidence that, as compared with nonsmokers, cigarette smokers tend to be more tense, restless, and insecure; less athletic and physically active; and more self-indulgent, immature, impulsive, reckless, and accident prone.[24] Such persons are less likely to have long and healthful lives whether they smoke or not. But selective factors cannot explain all the associations. For example, one medical study notes how female mortality rates have been

TABLE 17–2   Life Changes Bring Illness

Life event	Point value	Life event	Point value
Death of spouse	100	Trouble with in-laws	29
Divorce	73	Outstanding personal achievement	28
Marital separation	65	Wife begins or stops work	26
Jail term	63	Begin or end school	26
Death of close family member	63	Change in living conditions	25
Personal injury or illness	53	Revision of personal habits	24
Marriage	50	Trouble with boss	23
Fired at work	47	Change in work hours or conditions	20
Marital reconciliation	45	Change in residence	20
Retirement	45	Change in schools	20
Change in health of family member	44	Change in recreation	19
Pregnancy	40	Change in church activities	19
Sex difficulties	39	Change in social activities	18
Gain of new family member	39	Mortgage or loan less than $10,000	17
Business readjustment	39	Change in sleeping habits	16
Change in financial state	38	Change in number of family	
Death of a close friend	37	get-togethers	15
Change to different line of work	36	Change in eating habits	15
Change in number of arguments with		Vacation	13
spouse	35	Christmas	12
Mortgage over $10,000	31	Minor violations of the law	11
Foreclosure of mortgage or loan	30		
Change in work responsibilities	29		
Son or daughter leaving home	29		

When total point value is:	The odds of having a major illness or injury are:
Over 300	1 out of 2
200–299	1 out of 4
Under 200	1 out of 11

Based upon research on reported life changes and illnesses among 88 physicians. Adapted from Thomas H. Holmes and Minoru Masuda, "Psychosomatic Syndrome," *Psychology Today*, Apr. 1972, pp. 71 ff.

drawing closer to male mortality rates in recent years, and calculates that three-fourths of this is due to the increase in women smokers.[25] Dozens of such studies have removed all doubt about the consequences of smoking, at least among those who are not trapped in wishful thinking. Between 1964 and 1975, the percentage of smokers who agreed that "smoking is harmful to health" grew from 69 percent to 82 percent.[26]

The U.S. Department of Health, Education and Welfare estimates that 29 million Americans quit smoking between 1965 and 1975.[27] Cigarette smoking declined markedly among older people, especially among physi-

IS THIS WHAT YOUR KISSES TASTE LIKE?

If you smoke cigarettes, you taste like one. Your clothes and hair can smell stale and unpleasant, too.

You don't notice it, but people close to you do. Especially if they don't smoke.

And non-smokers are the best people to love. They live longer.

AMERICAN CANCER SOCIETY

This space contributed by the publisher as a public service.

(Irene Springer)

cians, most of whom quit. Meanwhile, smoking increased among young people, especially in the 13–15 age group. The greatest increase was among teenage girls, among whom pack-a-day smokers quadrupled between 1969 and 1976.[28] At present, however, teenage smoking is declining, falling by about one-fourth by 1979.[29]

Why were teenagers slower than their elders to turn from smoking? With no real evidence, we suspect that the time referent may be the explanation. From behaviorist psychology we learn that *immediate* rewards and punishments are most effective, while delay weakens them. To tell a small child, "I'll spank you tomorrow, maybe," would be useless. To a 13-year-old, the threat of cancer 40 or 50 years later has little impact. Forty years away is *forever*—four times as long as his or her entire life's recollections extend. Besides, to an exuberant teenager, a few more years of sedate old age may hold no great attraction. But to a middle-aged person, who recalls 20 years ago as though it were yesterday, 60 no longer looks very old or very far away.

Meanwhile, evidence of cigarette damage accumulates. The most recent addition is the discovery that smoking multiplies by six times the increased dangers of heart attack that accompanies the use of the contraceptive pill.[30] There is convincing evidence that cigarette smoking greatly speeds the aging and wrinkling of the skin;[31] possibly some who refuse to quit in order to lengthen their old age will quit to lengthen their youth. There is even a suspicion among sexologists that heavy smoking impairs sexual potency—just in case no other argument is persuasive.[32] Meanwhile, nonsmokers are becoming more aggressive in asserting their right to breathe clean air in public places, and bitter disputes between smokers and nonsmokers are common.[33]

The American Cancer Society suggests that all cigarette advertising (about $400 million a year) be disallowed as a business deduction, and that the government end its support payments (about $60 million a year) to tobacco growers.[34] Do you think these proposals are likely to be accepted?

Alcoholism is the most widespread, destructive form of drug addiction in the United States, with over 200,000 alcohol-related deaths a year.[35] The increase in alcoholism is shown by the death rate from cirrhosis of the liver, which rose 29 percent for men and 19 percent for women between 1964 and 1974.[36] This problem, treated in chapter 16, will not be detailed here. We must note, however, some features of the American lifestyle that are conducive to alcoholism: the pattern of "celebrating" by drinking heavily; the widespread attitude of tolerant amusement, rather than disgust, toward the intoxicated; the identification of heavy drinking (and smoking) with machismo (or with sexy sophistication) instead of with weakness, failure, social rejection, sexual inadequacy,[37] or immature self-indulgence.[38]

Figure 17–1
Ratio of death rates by cause for smokers and nonsmokers, male and female combined, 1978.
Source: State Mutual Life Assurance Company.

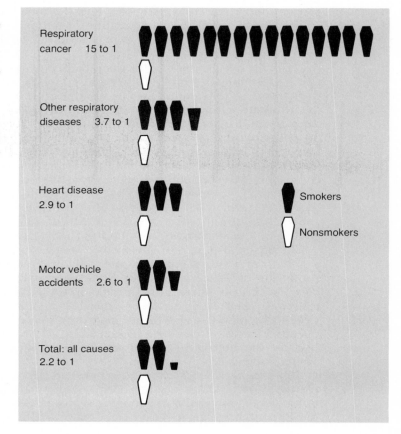

Drug addiction is also treated in chapter 16. Its health consequences are a matter of debate. It is unclear how much of the physical deterioration that often accompanies drug addiction is a direct effect of the drug use, and how much is due to the associations and living conditions that often accompany drug addiction (another illustration of secondary deviation). It is significant, however, that middle-aged and elderly drug addicts are uncommon. With rare exceptions, those who are not "clean" by middle age are dead.

A different kind of drug problem is overmedication with prescription drugs. The pill-for-everything pattern has made Americans the most over-medicated people on earth.[39] Critics have coined the term *iatrogenic disease* as a name for the damaging results of overmedication.[40] Some physicians use a hastily written prescription as a substitute for a thorough diagnosis. Most physicians write a prescription for every patient, because patients expect and want one. A physician who is competent and thorough enough to diagnose a condition accurately as needing no prescription thus *loses* prestige in the eyes of the patient. It is well known that persons whose parents are avid pill gobblers are themselves more likely to become users of illicit drugs. Thus, the overmedication of parents contributes to the drug problems of youth.

ALTERNATE LIFESTYLES AND HEALTH   There are so many different kinds and degrees of departure from traditional lifestyles today that it is difficult to generalize. There is not one counterculture, but many. Among the alternate behavior patterns more or less widely followed today are some that have health consequences.

(1) The *value system* held in some degree by a number of people is one that prizes immediate gratification and impulsive spontaneity over the cautious, long-range planning orientation toward life. This value system tends to encourage self-indulgence and unconcern for long-term consequences in the pursuit of immediate experiences and satisfactions.

(2) A more *casual sex life,* coupled with decreasing use of the condom, has brought venereal disease to an all-time high. Among young people venereal disease is exceeded by only the common cold in frequency. Gonorrhea is the most common serious venereal disease; new strains of gonnococci are appearing that are immune to existing antibiotic therapy.[41] Herpes simplex type II, for which there is no effective cure, now infects over 6 million Americans.[42] In all, there are about 20 different sexually-transmitted diseases in the United States, and most of them are at epidemic levels.[43]

It can be argued that alternative lifestyles expose people to less stress, anxiety, worry, social rejection, and guilt, and that this release from illness-producing pressures is healthful. This is possibly true, although it has not been established whether participants in these lifestyles actually experience less stress than other people. If the deviant norms of the counterculture were to become the general norms of the society, the possibilities of a reduction in stress levels might be enhanced. At present, some unhealthful aspects of the alternate lifestyles are well established, while the health gains are hypothetical.

(3) *Recreational risk-taking* is not new but it appears to be growing in popularity. Motorcycling, maddog skiing, hang-gliding, skydiving, and many other hazardous sports are gaining converts daily. Not all enthusiasts of these sports are danger-seekers, but many are. Our ethic of competitive ag-

gressiveness demands that a person distinguish himself in some manner. For some, challenging work fills the need for a sense of power and accomplishment. For the less fortunate, recreational risk-taking can fill this need. Most risk-takers are bored adults (the average age is 32 for snowmobile fatalities). One study found that "the snowmobiler most likely to get himself killed is a blue-collar worker in a dead-end job."[44] Danger relieves monotony. To require motorcyclists to wear helmets is probably futile: those who desire safety will wear them voluntarily; if one element of danger is removed, however, the risk-taker must seek another. One psychologist concludes that deliberate risk-taking, drug use, and sexual adventuring are all indications of a high-sensation-seeking personality, and suspects that there may be some biochemical or organic basis for such behavior.[45]

The risk-taking pattern has been primarily a male pattern but is appearing increasingly among females as well. For both sexes, deliberate risk-taking shades off through various degrees of careless or unthinking exposure to unnecessary risks. Accidents cause over 100,000 deaths a year (not all preventable, of course), and are the leading cause of death among teenagers.

Some people are highly accident-prone. Several studies have found that drivers who have repeated automobile accidents are usually undisciplined and unstable in their total life organization. As a group, they show high rates of divorce, unpaid bills, juvenile and adult court appearances, alcohol and drug abuse, venereal disease, job dismissals, and other signs of irresponsibility.[46] About one out of six American drivers fastens seat belts, which are ten times as likely to save your life as to trap you in a fatal situation. Studies show that belt wearers are significantly more likely to be educated, to go to church, to follow approved personal health habits, and to have a feeling of personal responsibility for what happens to them.[47] They are also more likely to obey traffic laws and to drive carefully instead of aggressively.[48] People drive the way they live—and some live longer than others.

Nutrition and Health

It is well known that dietary deficiencies will stunt physical growth, permanently lower the IQ of children, produce premature senility in older people, and produce a host of grave deficiency diseases in people of all ages. Perhaps half the world's people suffer from dietary deficiencies severe enough to cut years from their lives and make them physically incapable of doing a vigorous day's work at any time during their lives. The sad state of diet in the United States is less well known. Some Americans are too poor to eat properly, while many of the rest do not wish to. And the American diet is becoming worse, even as we grow more affluent. A Department of Agriculture study published in 1972 found that only half the American people had a good diet, and that this category had fallen by 10 percent during the preceding decade; meanwhile those eating a poor diet had risen by 5 percent, from 15 to 20. During the preceding three decades, the average American deleted 36 pounds of vegetables, 27 pounds of potatoes, and 48 pounds of fruit from the year's diet, while fats and sugar now compose three-fifths of the calories in the average American diet.[49] The past few years, however, have shown some improvement, with 1977 consumption of fats and sugars down slightly and vegetables up slightly over 1965.[50]

Nearly one-half the "meals" consumed by Americans are served by restaurants or institutions, and the proportion is rising. *Consumers' Research Magazine* comments:

> Commercial restaurants and many institutional dining areas exhibit four common characteristics: too much sugar, too much fat and salt, too little fiber and too many chemical additives, including monosodium glutamate.[51] ... Preparation in a central commissary [for frozen shipment to restaurants and institutions] with a "chemical preservative bath" applied to those fruits and vegetables which might change color or texture on standing or transportation, are poor contributions to human health and vigor. The extra processing and use of preservatives involve losses of nutrients which may be very important for a person who has to take his food day after day in an institutional eating place.[52]

"Home-cooked" meals are often no better, leaning heavily on "convenience" foods, which are heavily laced with chemical preservatives by manufacturers more concerned over long shelf life than with good nutrition or vitamin levels. It used to be said that people who ate a proper diet would have little need to waste money on supplementary vitamins. For people today who rely heavily on restaurant foods, convenience foods, and "snack" foods, nutritional deficiencies are a strong probability.

Anthropologists have noted for years that when native peoples shifted to a modern diet their health usually deteriorated, especially their teeth.[53] A study of an Eskimo population that quadrupled its sugar consumption in only eight years reported a startling rise in diabetes, atherosclerosis, obesity, gall bladder disease, and several other disorders.[54] Another study attributed many automobile accidents to the "pathologic drowsiness and hypoglycemia due to functional hyperinsulinism" arising from high sugar consumption.[55] During World War II sugar was rationed to save shipping space. To have continued rationing permanently would have saved lives but interfered with people's right to chew their way into their caskets.

OBESITY

Fat people are sick more and die sooner. One study of obese male industrial workers found that they took off nearly three times as many "sick days" as other workers.[56]

The causes of extreme obesity remain in dispute, with a number of genetic, organic, and hormonal theories under study.[57] There is a huge market for trick diets and the services of medical charlatans who promise painless weight loss. At any given time one or more "miracle reducing diet" books are generally on the best-seller list.[58] Without exception, such diet books are condemned by reputable nutritional authorities as misleading and medically irresponsible. All diet regimens that promise that you can "take it off" while "packing it in" are ineffective, dangerous, or both. Medically responsible books rarely if ever become best-sellers; if they tell all the truth, they promise too little and demand too much self-sacrifice to become highly popular.

People's food needs and metabolic processes vary widely; one person

Several years ago my daughter was attending a college where, as everywhere, students griped about the dormitory food. The dietitian believed that education should be relevant to the real needs of students, and she prepared menus to provide a scientifically balanced diet together, she hoped, with a learning experience in shaping their food habits in a healthful direction. She was operating on the false assumption that students want what is good for them, while the fact is that students—no less than most other people—want to eat whatever they like, whether it is good for them or not.

After a fashionably noisy student protest, the administration agreed that the students might be served by a food concession of their choice. Food service was taken over by a commercial concern that operated on the sound capitalistic principle that the way to make a lot of money is to give people what they want, and no nonsense about teaching good food habits. So the juices, vegetables, green salads, and citrus fruits largely disappeared from the menu, to be replaced with an abundance of nice fatty French fries, hamburgers, and sweet rolls, floating down a river of Cokes and milk shakes. The change was a complete success. The students quit grumbling about the food, the administration was happy to be off the hook, and the concessionaire made a lot of money. Everyone was happy except the dietitian, who kept muttering that such a diet would chop years from their lives.

Anecdote supplied by a friend of the author.

can lose weight on a diet that swells another. The only *healthful* way to lose weight is through increased exercise, reduced food intake, or both, under medical supervision. Unfortunately, a few medical racketeers are finding a fortune in the fat folds of gullible patients. They recklessly prescribe amphetamines, dangerous and addictive drugs. No known drug for reducing the appetite or redirecting bodily processes toward weight loss is both safe and effective. The Weight Watchers use group therapy processes in an attempt to reinforce members' adherence to a nutritious and well-balanced reducing diet, but many people find the diet monotonous and unappetizing. It is probably the most effective program for losing weight safely, but it requires a lot of self-discipline.

FOOD FADDISM

The belief that certain foods have magical powers is both ancient and popular. Food faddism is a faddist preoccupation with certain foods that are believed to have remarkable properties not recognized by scientific nutritionists. Food fad hucksters are omnipresent. Here, especially, one's credentials as an authority need to be carefully scrutinized. Some "nutrition authorities" have claimed spurious academic degrees and invented nonexistent "nutrition councils" to promote their books and lecture bookings. There are other books written by authors who have respectable scientific credentials, but who nonetheless go overboard into food faddism and are rejected by responsible nutrition scientists.[59] The list of food fads is long and constantly changing as food faddists shift to new discoveries—blackstrap molasses, yogurt, wheat germ, rose hips, granola, and whatever is "in" next.

The current health-food fad has spurred the opening of many health-food stores across the country.
(Irene Springer)

The therapeutic food theory—that certain foods have unique preventive or curative powers—is unproven and rejected by all scientific nutritionists. It is true, of course, that a deficiency of any essential food element will produce disease. For example, vitamin C deficiency produces scurvy, among other ailments, and lime juice will prevent scurvy. So will dozens of other fruits and vegetables. The body needs vitamin C, but the source of the vitamin matters not. No food has been shown to have any special preventive or curative value, beyond its basic food elements, vitamins, and minerals.

Most food faddism is harmless unless the diet is seriously unbalanced. A few freak diets limited to a very narrow range of foods, however, can be highly injurious. For example, the Zen Macrobiotic Diet consists mainly of brown rice, and has been condemned by the American Medical Association Council of Foods and Nutrition as "a major public health problem," certain to injure and possibly to kill those who follow it.[60] As is often the case with freak diets, the Zen Macrobiotic diet is only one expression of a comprehensive philosophy of life in which scientific authority is not seen as important.

Food fads are popular because they bring a feeling of certainty and simplicity to a complex, anxiety-laden, and ultimately losing battle—how to stay healthy, young, and virile. The typical food faddist is best understood by studying the members of social movements, the "true believers" that Eric Hoffer describes, who are seeking comfort, certainty, and reassurance in a troubled world.[61]

ORGANIC FOODS

The *organic food movement* is a true social movement,[62] combining a measure of sound nutritional science with a dollop of food faddism, sweetened by a delicious feeling that one is joining in a heroic battle against an unholy alliance of greedy, cynical exploiters. The term is confusing, since all foods that are grown rather than synthesized are organic. As commonly used, "organic" foods are those that are grown without pesticides or chemical fertilizers, with only natural manures or composted materials, and containing no chemical additives, preservatives, or emulsifiers. The term *natural* is often used interchangeably with *organic*.

The organic food enthusiasts' objections to pesticide residues and food additives have a sound scientific basis, although some may pursue this point to an unrealistic extreme. The organic food enthusiast's faith that "organically" grown food is more nutritious than commercially grown food is rejected by most food scientists as unproven. Although a few research articles claim to have found nutritional differences, most scientists reject this research as defective or inconclusive. The berry bush needs nitrates, but it apparently cannot tell whether its nitrates come from a bag or a manure pile, any more than the body can tell whether its vitamin C comes from an orange or a pill.[63] The theory that food grown on poor soils will be less nutritious is also rejected by food scientists. Poor soil grows smaller rutabagas, but ounce for ounce they are nutritionally the same as those grown in rich soil. Thus, to a considerable degree the organic food movement is based on scientifically disreputable theories.

Foods sold as "organic" are much more expensive than ordinary supermarket foods, and sometimes they actually are commercially grown and sold fraudulently. Since in the opinion of most nutritionists there really is no difference between them (except possibly in pesticide residues), nobody is hurt, just cheated.

In summary, nutrition is a highly important health determinant. Some people cannot afford a nutritious diet; many more cannot rise above a level of immature self-indulgence. Some are faddists or fanatics, usually harmlessly so but sometimes to their injury. And there are serious unsolved problems of food purity and food quality that affect all of us.

The result of inhaling cotton dust [in a textile factory] is known as Brown Lung. An Appalachian magazine, *Mountain Life and Work,* reported that in England, textile workers have been getting compensation for Brown Lung since 1961. In this country, it is still difficult to find doctors who recognize that the disease exists and who recognize its severity.

Richard Louv, "The Appalachia Syndrome," *Human Behavior,* May 1977, p. 42.

Environment and Health

Today pollution probably kills far more people than bacteria do in the advanced nations of the world. For many decades our environment has grown steadily more polluted with wastes, dusts, and deadly chemicals.

Occupational disease is not new. Slaves in Roman silver mines in Spain died at the rate of 20,000 a year, lasting an average of four years. Occupational diseases have usually been overlooked, minimized, and denied by vested interests that did not wish to recognize them.[64] Company doctors who diagnosed very many workers' illnesses as "occupationally induced" were soon replaced with more cooperative doctors.

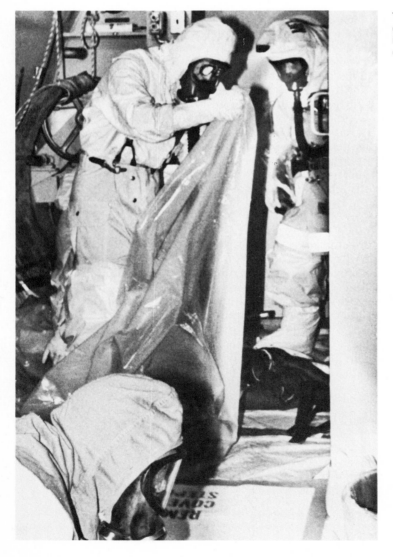

Three Mile Island nuclear reactor: an engineer places contaminated equipment into a plastic bag.
(United Press International)

Overwhelming evidence has now established that many workers are being poisoned and suffocated on the job, that their families sometimes suffer from contaminants the workers bring home on their clothes,[65] and that even unborn children may suffer birth defects from their parents' exposure to work hazards.[66] At least 26 commonly used chemicals have been definitely shown to be cancer-causing. The problem is growing; the variety of chemicals, dusts, and toxins in the work place has multiplied enormously, while a rising proportion of all workers are exposed to such hazards. Even farm workers are no longer safe from deadly poisons. The 1970 Occupational Safety and Health Act (OSHA) establishes the principle that no worker must work under unhealthful working conditions—but determining just what is unhealthful and following with effective enforcement is a sobering task.

Environmental hazards away from the workplace affect everyone. Evidence is steadily accumulating that many diseases are largely environmental. Some scientists believe that cancer is caused or at least triggered by the many pollutants, food additives, insecticides, radiations, and other environmental irritants that one can scarcely escape. Yet, although exposure to such pollutants has increased enormously in recent decades, the only significant increase in cancer has been in lung cancer, attributed to increased smoking. Thus the role of chemical carcinogens remains in dispute.[67] Deaths from bronchitis, emphysema, and asthma multiplied by two-and-a-half times between 1950 and 1973, partly because of increased smoking and partly because of increased air pollution.[68]

Although environmental concerns are sometimes dismissed as an elitist preoccupation, the truth is that pollution-related diseases strike most heavily at the poor, who more often live and work where pollution levels are the highest.[69]

To control environmental hazards is not simple. A single accident can produce a major regional hazard. For example, a few bags of a fire retardant chemical, PBB, were mistakenly mixed with cattle feed in Michigan. Thousands of cattle were destroyed, but thousands of people now have measurable concentrations of PBB in their bodies, and the effects are not yet known.[70] Nor will elimination of environmental hazards be cheap. A business may have to withdraw a profitable product or incur higher production costs. Consumers may be deprived of a product they enjoy, or may have to pay higher prices for it. And when a polluting factory closes, both the

The Environmental Protection Agency began testing the milk of human mothers in 1976. Preliminary results indicated that essentially all samples of mother's milk had detectable levels of PCBs [polychlorinated biphenyls]. Indeed, the average, 1.8 ppm, gives an infant seven times the amount permitted in cow's milk by the Food and Drug Administration. One nursing mother in Michigan had 10.6 ppm of PCBs in her milk, and that dosage approaches the levels that caused learning disabilities and hyperactivity in two groups of monkeys studied by Allen.

Robert H. Boyle and Joseph H. Highland, "The Persistence of PCBs," *Environment*, 21 (June 1979), 37.

stockholders and the workers suffer. For over a decade, both the managers and the workers of the Reserve Mining Company fought for their right to continue polluting Lake Superior, the water supply of Duluth, Minnesota.[71] Reducing environmental health hazards forces painful value choices upon all of us.

Medical Care and Health

Medical care is no longer the major factor in the health problem in the United States. The great inequalities in medical services to affluent and poor and to whites and blacks have largely disappeared. Very little illness today can be attributed to the victim's inability to obtain medical care. We have eliminated most ill health that can be prevented or cured by medical services. One careful study calculates that the most full and efficient use possible of present medical diagnosis and treatment procedures would reduce the American death rate by no more than 6 percent.[72] If cancer were completely eliminated, less than two years would be added to life expectancy.[73] Thus the possible contributions of medicine have been largely realized. Further health gains must be found in the other health factors: nutrition, health habits, lifestyles, and environmental hazards. Yet serious problems of costs and organization of medical services remain.

EXCESSIVE COST AND WASTE

In 1979 medical services cost the nation $216 billion, increasing by more than five times from the 1965 figure of $39 billion.[74] Medical costs now ab-

Figure 17–2
Medical care expenditures in the United States, 1965–79
Dollars not adjusted for inflation.
Data from *Time*, 28 May 1979, p. 61.

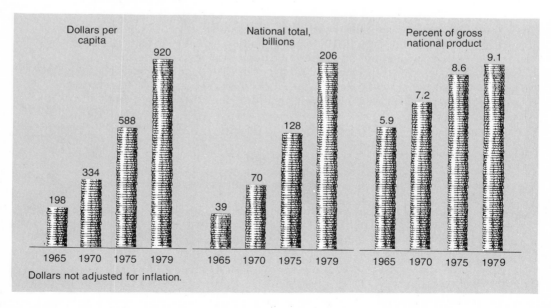

sorb over 9 percent of our national product, up from about 4 percent in 1940, and are expected to reach 10 percent—$250 billion—by 1981, even if no new medical programs are added.[75] Hospital costs have risen most sharply—increasing two-and-a-half times in ten years—with half the increase due to increasing services and half to increasing costs per unit of service.[76] Medical costs have been rising all over the world, but no country spends as much, either in dollars or as a percentage of its gross national product, as does the United States.

Waste and inefficiency, it is alleged, account for a significant part of the high costs of medical care. The *fee-for-service* system of physician payment encourages unnecessary services and the use of more expensive procedures (such as shots instead of pills).[77] Wherever the *salary* or *capitation* (flat fee per patient per year) methods of payment are used, costs are lower because "the unnecessary multiplication of procedures from financial motives" is reduced.[78] In Saskatchewan, Canada, when the fee-for-service and capitation systems operated side by side, the fee-for-service patients had a much higher rate of hospital admissions.[79] In England, where there is no financial incentive for surgery, the rate of surgery is only about half that in the United States; yet England's health level is well above ours.[80] One study found that "the medically indigent children of California (whose bills are paid from public funds) are having their tonsils removed at a *ten times higher* rate than are the patients of some group practice clinics which take care of nonindigent children."[81] Medical groups that require a second medical opinion before performing elective surgery report that less surgery is needed.[82] A recent congressional investigation concluded that approximately 2.38 million unnecessary surgical procedures, costing nearly $4 billion and leading to nearly 12,000 deaths, were performed in 1975.[83] The committee also found an interesting correlation between the volume of unnecessary surgery and the number of surgeons practicing in the area.[84] While there is sometimes a legitimate disagreement over whether a particular surgical procedure is necessary, there is little doubt that a certain fraction of all surgery in America is medically needless and wasteful.[85]

MALDISTRIBUTION OF MEDICAL FACILITIES

There is no longer a shortage of physicians in America,[86] but the physicians—one for each 500 persons in the United States—are unevenly distributed. Most in need of physicians are rural areas (826 rural areas have more than 4,000 people for each physician)[87] and inner city areas.[88] Most physicians choose their locations according to the availability of hospital and other facilities, the opportunity to earn a large income, the living amenities of the area, and the crime hazards[89]—and recently also according to the situation with respect to malpractice lawsuits.[90] Patient needs are not an important factor in the location of physicians. The desperate efforts of some communities to entice a physician with free offices, rents, and other benefits seldom succeed, while the maldistribution of physicians grows steadily more serious.

Increasing the supply of physicians has not corrected this maldistribution. The same preference factors still influence physicians' choices of location. Merely to continue to increase physician supply might simply inflate the total of unnecessary services received by people in well-staffed regions. Possibilities for relocating physicians according to medical needs include (1) recruiting medical students from the ghetto in the hope (probably unrealistic) that they will return to the ghetto to practice;[91] (2) requiring all physicians to practice for a term in a medical shortage area in exchange for their heavily subsidized medical educations; (3) offering financial inducements, through tax credits, free facilities, cash bonuses, and the like, for practice in shortage areas (the inducements would need to be enormous to overcome physicians' dislike of practice in the shortage areas);[92] and (4) reorganizing shortage-area medical care around hospital-based community medical networks with improved medical-technical facilities and intercommunity specialist referral.[93] None of these policies is being actively pursued at present, and the shortage areas grow steadily more deprived as old doctors retire with few young replacements.

THE UNEVEN QUALITY OF MEDICAL CARE IN THE UNITED STATES

Arguments over the level of quality of American medical care are numerous and acrimonious. Among the alleged imperfections are those discussed below.

ISOLATION OF PRACTITIONERS who work alone in scattered offices, is an alleged defect. Solo practice makes it more difficult to arrange for consultations, laboratory tests, and use of specialized equipment. Most important, the solo practitioner loses the exchange of knowledge and the stimulus toward professional excellence that come from an intimate working association with professional colleagues.

THE FEE-FOR-SERVICE SYSTEM is widely accused of not only increasing costs but also encouraging a low quality of practice. It emphasizes sickness rather than health. It gives multiplication of services primacy over keeping the patient well, encourages unnecessary and possibly harmful procedures, and gives the physician a financial incentive to retain a patient who should be referred to another physician better qualified to treat that particular patient.

LACK OF CONTINUITY AND COORDINATION impairs the effectiveness of some medical care. The fragmentation of medical care, especially as it is received by many of the poor, results in treating "cases" rather than persons whose personalities and medical histories are well known to the physician.

OVERWORK in the medical profession is a constant drain on its effectiveness. Physicians in general practice work an *average* of 60 hours a week—some work far longer—and sometimes their hours are irregular and their rest is broken. Physicians have a life expectancy several years shorter than that of other professional groups. A recent survey of physicians' needs found 40 percent listing greater ease of practice and 36 percent listing more free time as their greatest need.[94] It is not possible for an overworked profession to maintain the highest standards of professional service at all times.

MEDICAL INCOMPETENCE is far more widespread than is generally realized. The ethics of the medical profession forbid doctors from publicly criticizing one another's practice. This has two opposing consequences: (1) it helps pre-

> It is not uncommon for hospitals that have raised their standards and now scrutinize closely the credentials of all new doctors to have a few old practitioners who have had operating privileges for many years and who, for sympathetic reasons, are allowed to retain them. I wonder how the medical profession would feel about flying if an airline were to say something like this: "At least 90 percent of our pilots are fully qualified to fly modern jets. We do have a few fellows who've been with us since the days of the Ford Trimotor and who don't understand much about the newer planes, but whom we keep on for old times' sake. Don't worry about them, though. They'll all be dying off in the next 10 or 15 years."
>
> Alex Gerber, *The Gerber Report* (New York: David McKay, 1971), p. 104.

serve the patient's faith in his doctor, and this is known to aid in the patient's recovery; (2) it also protects the incompetent practitioner, whose patients (when they live) never learn how incompetent he is. A number of studies have shown that most patients are totally unable to judge the professional competence of their doctors, and that incompetent doctors have as large practices and earn as much money as highly competent ones.[95] A careful study 25 years ago of the practices of 88 North Carolina general practitioners found only 7 fully competent, 16 grossly incompetent, and the rest somewhere in between.[96] More recently the Federation of State Medical Boards concluded that about 5 percent (16,000) of the nation's physicians are definitely incompetent and should have their licenses revoked.[97]

There have been some recent improvements. Most hospitals today require tissue examinations following surgery to discourage the unnecessary surgery of the "eager cleavers." A 1972 amendment to the Social Security Act required that beginning in 1976, panels of physicians known as Professional Standards Review Organizations (PSROs) be established to monitor the professional practice of all physicians who receive federal funds. While relatively new, they hold promise. In one locality studied, hospital admissions dropped by one-half after a PSRO went into operation.[98]

Malpractice lawsuits, one type of penalty for incompetence, have multiplied recently as astronomical cash awards are no longer exceptional. But while the threat of a damage suit may make doctors more cautious, it does not necessarily make them more competent. Malpractice claims have increased costs to patients, because physicians raise their fees to cover higher malpractice insurance premiums. Costs are also inflated as physicians practice "defensive medicine," adding lab tests, consultations, and procedures that are not medically necessary but that would be useful in contesting a malpractice suit.[99] No less than one-fourth of a sample of physicians claimed to have quit using high-risk procedures, believing it safer to let a patient die naturally than to risk a procedure that might save but might also kill or cripple the patient.[100] While malpractice claims are doubtless fully justified in many cases, the wave of malpractice litigation has inflated medical costs without causing clear gains in the quality of medical practice. No really effective way of protecting patients from professional incompetence has been established for medical practice[101]—or, for that matter, for any other profession.

HOSPITAL INADEQUACIES   Many hospitals still do not meet the relatively lenient standards of the Joint Committee on Accreditation of Hospitals. Of 10,000 nurses who returned questionnaires to *Nursing* magazine, over one-third reported that they "would not, if they had a choice, be treated at their own hospitals."[102] This self-selected sample may exaggerate hospital defects, yet hospital error clearly is fairly common.

MEDICAL LABORATORY INADEQUACIES   lie behind many wrong diagnoses and premature funerals. Fewer than half the states require any license or test for a medical laboratory or a staff member. A laboratory technician named Straybourne Betts, listed on the staff of two mail-order laboratories, turned out to be a dog.[103] Until adequate licensing for labs and lab technicians is required, the quality of medical care will suffer.

MEDICAL QUACKERY   remains popular, profitable, and lethal. Quacks should be distinguished from health cultists. The *health cultist* is a nonmedical person who claims to give or receive cures through nonmedical, extrascientific therapies. Faith healing, Christian Science, Zen, Yoga, Rolfing, and a number of other philosophical systems are examples of health cultism. There is some evidence that the patient's health suffers from health cultism, but a proper examination of this topic is impossible within the space limitations of this chapter. The *medical quack* is a person who sometimes but not always has a medical degree and a license, and who uses an unscientific therapy while claiming that it is an advanced scientific procedure. Quackery is a pseudo-science, using scientific jargon and scientific-looking gadgets in the course of therapeutic procedures that are not grounded in any sound scientific knowledge. The quack can be recognized by his claim to possess a superior scientific therapy that the medical establishment, for purely selfish reasons, refuses to approve. While claiming remarkable cures, quacks refuse to cooperate in any evaluative studies of their therapy under proper scientific controls. Yet, although the quack is generally easy to recognize, public gullibility is great, and one recent survey finds that one-third of a national sample of people accepted a number of spurious remedies.[104]

Patients whose illnesses do not readily respond to orthodox treatment are highly susceptible to quackery. Persons who have (or imagine they have) cancer, arthritis, asthma, and vague, unspecified ailments are prime targets. Quackery also flourishes where orthodox treatment is unpleasant or demanding, as in the case of obesity. Often the patient's own physician is not very informative or sympathetic, while the quack *always* has an exceedingly sympathetic, reassuring bedside manner. The patients of quacks typically recall their doctors as having been cold and uninterested in them, while the quacks impress them with their great concern. Quacks are typically idolized by their patients; convictions for quackery are difficult to obtain, mainly because the patients (or their survivors) refuse to testify against the quacks.[105] The medical establishment has been active but not very successful in fighting quackery. Conviction is difficult and penalties are mild. If convicted, the quack generally pays a modest fine, moves to a new location, and starts hawking a new gadget or nostrum.

The list of imperfections could be extended, but the data above are sufficient to reveal grave inadequacies in American medical care. Clearly, the organization of medical services could be improved.

The Social-Disorganization Approach

The genial country doctor with his familiar black bag was fairly adequate for the medical needs of our great-grandparents. He knew relatively little medicine, because there was not much medical knowledge for him to learn. But most of the patients recovered anyway, and his earnest efforts and long nightly vigils earned him the respect and affection of his neighbors.

The spectacular growth of medical knowledge is revolutionizing the arrangements of medical practice. With the discovery of how disease is transmitted has come the realization that disease anywhere in the community is a threat to the health of all. This realization leads to the demand that health services be made equally available to all. Modern medical care involves many specialized fields and skills, and the traditional method of solo fee-for-service practice comes under fire as a major obstacle to high-quality medical care. The constant stream of new medical discoveries and treatments enables doctors to save many today who yesterday would have died—and also makes good medical care so costly that traditional methods of payment become unsatisfactory as expenses skyrocket.

In an earlier day, when medical practice was mostly guesswork in which many people had no faith and for which many people had no desire, it was logically consistent to view medical services as a purely private consumption item, which people might purchase if they wished and could afford it. But today, as a recent president of the AMA somewhat unhappily conceded, "We are faced with the concept of medical care as a right rather than as a privilege."[106] The forms of organization appropriate to an earlier period become woefully inadequate, once medical care becomes accepted as a basic human right.

Changes in the society also disorganize the traditional administration of health services. The growth of large-scale industry has led to industrial health service plans that sometimes infringe upon private practice.

Changing medical technology creates new ethical issues. The technique of organ transplants raises legal and ethical questions about the rights of donors and their families.[107] Medical technology has developed remarkable life-support procedures for keeping a human vegetable clinically "alive." This has aroused the right-to-die controversy over whether human vegetables should be preserved indefinitely or should be allowed to die naturally, as in the past.[108] The latter is sometimes called *passive euthanasia.*[109] The development of medications and surgical procedures for making overactive or violent patients more manageable has profound civil liberties implications. For example, would psychosurgery on violently aggressive blacks really be an attempt to help them, or would it be a low-cost substitute for basic social reform?[110] Some medical procedures are fearfully expensive, such as kidney dialysis and care for a Tay-Sachs child. This creates the agonizing problem of whom to treat and whom to let die, or the alternative of several billion dollars a year added to our tax bill. In medicine as elsewhere, change produces new problems.

The Value-Conflict Approach

Many of the value conflicts regarding medicine lurk behind opposing statements of alleged "facts." Defenders of the medical status quo point out that few who ask for free treatment are denied. Critics point out that the medical status quo discourages many from asking for the treatment they need. Both facts are true, and each implies a different value judgment. *How important is it that all should be offered complete medical care under conditions that strongly encourage all to ask freely for it? How important is it to preserve the current system of practice, which a majority of doctors prefer?* These questions of value lie at the heart of current medical controversy.

Is ill health among those too ignorant or too indolent to seek treatment a social problem? Some say, "No, it is their own fault!" Others say, "Yes, they must be educated to recognize their need and to demand treatment." If the life habits of the poor are an obstacle to their receiving effective medical services as those services are now organized, what should change? Should medical services be reorganized, or should the poor be required to change their life habits as the price of good health? For example, the hours that doctors and nurses like to work are not those when working-class people can easily come for treatment; so whose hours should be changed? The inner city poor will not travel very far for any service; if they must travel more than several blocks for medical care, they will rarely appear.[111] Should we simply let them suffer until they change their habits, or should we find ways of locating medical facilities in the neighborhoods in which they live? Such questions involve a number of value judgments about personal versus public responsibility, about taxes and public expenditure, and about the degree to which we should be "another's keeper."

Many other values compete with health values. Immature, self-indulgent habits of unwise eating, smoking, and drinking probably cause more premature deaths than all other causes combined; yet the American diet shows little improvement, while millions continue heavy smoking and drinking. Obviously, many people would rather enjoy life than prolong it. The counterculture, which values immediate satisfactions over deferred gratifications, is damaging to health in many ways. Sexual freedom has raised venereal and other genital diseases to epidemic levels. Many people who cannot "afford" doctor bills seem able to afford new cars and sporting goods. It is easier to obtain federal appropriations for the health of brood sows than for expectant mothers—sows are valuable, and farmers are organized while fathers are not! Until recently, far more U.S. women were killed by bungled illegal abortions than died in childbirth, and such abortions were largely responsible for the high maternal mortality rate in the United States. Recent legalization of early abortion brought a sharp decline in maternal mortality. But a furious controversy rages between those who maintain that it is wrong to kill a human embryo and those who maintain that it is wrong to force the birth of an unwanted child. Consequently, there is a determined effort to nullify the legalization of abortion. Pure food and drug laws mediate the bitter clash between the right of a business to seek a profit and the people's

THE SALUTARY SEVEN

Nedra Belloc of the [California] state public health department and Lester Breslow, dean of the School of Public Health at UCLA . . . queried 6,928 adults in Alameda County, California, about their living habits and health. They found that to a remarkable degree health and longevity are related to seven commonplace health practices. The salutary seven:

Eat breakfast.
Don't eat between meals.
Don't smoke cigarettes.
Stay within 10 percent of your proper weight.
Exercise regularly.
Don't drink to excess.
Sleep seven to eight hours a night.

The beneficial effects of the practices are additive. That is, someone who follows all seven is likely to be healthier than someone who follows six, and so forth. At age 45 a man who follows six or seven of the rules has a life expectancy 11 years longer than a man who follows fewer than four. A 70-year-old who follows all seven is apt to be just as healthy as a 40-year-old who follows only one or two.

Quoted by permission from A. F. Ehrbar, "A Radical Prescription for Medical Care," *Fortune,* Feb. 1977, p. 169.

need for protection against worthless, dangerous, or misrepresented products.[112] Thus, at many points health values conflict with other values, and a choice must be made as to which value to sacrifice.

The Personal-Deviation Approach

Of the many persons who practice poor health habits and are unaccustomed to seeking medical services, only a few are deviants; the rest merely reflect the normal behavior of persons in their social environments. The members of some groups or cults raise religious objections to medical services—these persons are conforming members of deviant groups.

When deviant persons are also emotionally disturbed persons, as they very often are, they are less likely to remain physically healthy for long. Various medical estimates define from one-half to three-fourths of all physical disorders as being wholly or partly caused by emotional disturbances. Today there is scarcely any disorder—not even cancer—from which emotional factors are definitely excluded as being of no importance. Accidents are far more common among maladjusted persons. Accident-prone drivers, for example, are typically immature, impulsive, irresponsible people who disdain rules and who cannot manage their jobs, their marriages, their finances, or their drinking habits.[113] Of course, not all deviants are disorganized or emotionally disturbed, and not all emotionally disturbed persons are deviant.

But deviation often carries emotional tensions, anxieties, confusions, and resentments that become active causes of a long list of physical ailments.[114] Much chronic illness is emotional in origin, and an endless succession of ailments strongly suggests emotional causation. When one is unconsciously using illness for an escape from responsibility, an appeal for affection, or a means of revenge, the "curing" of one ailment merely forces one to develop another. In this way, personal deviation is responsible for a certain proportion of ill health.

Many deviant persons are attracted by health fads, quacks, and absurd causes and controversies. Antivivisectionism (opposition to the use of animals in medical research experiments) cannot be explained on any rational basis; some emotional need must motivate the antivivisectionist. Personal deviation helps to explain a great deal of irrational behavior.

The Reorganization of Health Services

Changes in the nature of medical science and changes in our definition of medical needs are bringing changes in the organization of medical practice. Although many of these changes have been opposed by the AMA,[115] their development despite such powerful opposition suggests that there were compelling reasons for their adoption.

GROUP PRACTICE

In group practice a number of physicians combine their practices and office facilities, with central records and bookkeeping. They may be in *single-specialty group practice,* in which all members practice in the same medical area (such as pediatrics), or they may be in *multispecialty group practice,* in which general practitioners plus a number of specialists are included. Group practice may be *prepaid group practice,* using salary or capitation payment, or it may use traditional fee-for-service payment. Prepaid group practice effects greater cost savings but is not popular with physicians.

The greatest benefit of group practice may be the stimulus toward quality provided by the close working relationship with medical colleagues. The desire for colleague approval is a powerful motivation in any activity, including medical practice. As early as 1947 the New York Academy of Medicine stated,

> Close association with colleagues in such groups tends to maintain both ethical and technical standards. Solo practitioners, on the other hand, are "on their own" in these matters. It is one of the weaknesses of prevailing general practice that there is no means for maintaining standards, save within the broad limits set by licensure and the laws against malpractice. . . . But . . . outside pressure is not likely to prove effective and would certainly be resisted by physicians as being coercive. The merit of group practice is that it provides for some control of standards within the professional family. . . . Close association with colleagues also proves stimulating to the individual members.[116]

Despite its apparent superiority, group practice has been spreading slowly. Problems include the temperamental unsuitability of some physicians for group practice,[117] the early opposition and continuing lack of enthusiasm of the medical societies for group practice, the large cash outlay needed to set up a group practice, and in most cases the need for a large sponsoring consumer organization to provide financial backing and a core of patients.

PRIVATE HEALTH INSURANCE

At least four out of five people in the United States have some form of health insurance. About two-fifths of these are insured with Blue Cross plans, and the other insurance is divided among industrial and union programs, independent plans, and commercial insurance company policies. There is a wide variety of health insurance types in operation. Commercial insurance companies have long sold health and accident policies paying specified *cash benefits* to individual policyholders. As a means of meeting medical costs these policies are costly and inefficient; administrative costs consume over half of each dollar paid in premiums, and the size of the cash benefit bears no necessary relation to the cost of the treatment. Commercial insurance companies are now promoting the sale of both individual and group health insurance providing *service benefits* instead of cash benefits (that is, paying the actual cost of medical services, within stated limits, instead of paying *x* dollars per day of illness). For all commercial health insurance plans combined, administrative costs in 1976 consumed 26 cents of each premium dollar—17 cents for group policies and 53 cents for individual policies.[118]

Most of the plans, both Blue Cross–Blue Shield and insurance company plans, have roughly comparable coverage. They cover most hospital, medical, and surgical costs, sometimes dental costs, and usually part of prescription drug costs. There are always some limitations upon length and kinds of services covered, but the major part of the family medical expense is covered. Group enrollment is encouraged, usually employee groups, with the employer paying part or all of the annual fees. Individual enrollment is usually possible, but at higher fees.

How successfully does private health insurance meet people's health care needs? Such insurance paid slightly more than one-fourth of the national bill for personal health services in 1977,[119] and doubtless saved many persons from bankruptcy. Yet it has some serious limitations. Not all people can be covered, for the cost is beyond most of the poor, the migratory or seasonal workers, and the unemployed. Costs remain high, and efficiency of practice is not greatly improved under voluntary health insurance, since there are no important changes in the organization of medical practice. Inasmuch as the fee-for-service system of payment for medical care is retained, the tendency may be to *increase* costs rather than to reduce them. With health insurance or Medicare-Medicaid paying the bill, none of the parties involved—not the physician nor the patient, nor the hospital—has any incentive to try to reduce costs.[120] The physician is tempted to recommend unnecessary services, since the patient does not pay for them. The schedule of *maximum* fees the insurance plan will pay for specified operations tends to become the *minimum* surgeons charge, and sometimes the surgeon adds an additional fee for the patient himself to pay (a practice the AMA discourages). There are even instances of physicians billing the insurance plan for services never performed. Patients often seek hospitalization for services that could easily be handled outside, but that are covered by insurance only if performed in the hospital. At the insistence of health insurance officials, union officers, and state welfare officials, most hospitals have established "utilization committees" to attempt to control the problem of unnecessary hospitalization and surgery. In many ways, limited-coverage voluntary health insurance using fee-for-service payment tends to maintain and increase the cost of medical care and the somewhat inefficient organization of health services.

COMPREHENSIVE MEDICAL CARE PLANS AND HMOS

The comprehensive health care plans usually offer coverage that is somewhat more comprehensive than that offered by most private health insurance plans. For example, Group Health Association (Washington, D.C.) provides hospital care without dollar or time limits and covers practically all hospital-connected costs. It also provides unlimited medical and surgical care, including unlimited office calls, specialist services, maternity care, house calls (if deemed necessary by a GHA physician), prescription drugs (80 percent reimbursement after patient pays the first $50 during the year), and certain other services. These services cost (1980) from $680 a year for a single person to $1,713 for a family. A lower-cost plan with more limited coverage is also available.

Comprehensive health care plans differ from most private health insurance plans in that: (1) Comprehensive health care plans are usually "closed panel" plans, meaning that patients can choose only from those physicians who have contracted to serve the group's members. (2) Physicians are usually paid a salary rather than by fee-for-service.

The Health Maintenance Act of 1973 follows the model of the comprehensive health care plans, renamed Health Maintenance Organizations (HMOs). This act requires all employers of more than 25 employees either to offer private health insurance coverage or to set up or participate in local HMOs, which provide comprehensive medical and hospital services on a prepaid monthly fee basis. The act provides some federal funds to aid in organizing HMOs. By 1980 there were 225 HMOs serving about 8.2 million people in the United States, with membership more than doubling since 1971. About two-thirds of these HMOs operate on the group-practice model, while in about one-third the physicians see patients in their own offices.[121]

The *quality* of medical care provided by comprehensive plans is, according to their advocates, higher than ordinarily provided to most other people. Group practice is claimed to provide continuity of care, ease of consultation, and stimulus toward professional excellence. Preventive measures such as health examinations and immunizations are usually included and encouraged, and health education is actively promoted. Members appear to be generally well satisfied, and complaints are few.[122] A survey of 25 studies of HMOs conducted at Johns Hopkins University concluded that "in 19 instances the general quality of health care in HMOs was superior to that in fee-for-service or other settings . . . and none reported HMO care to be inferior."[123]

Efficiency is reported to be high, and costs are claimed to be lowered under these plans. Group practice is said to raise efficiency in the use of facilities, in arranging consultations, and in the use of the physician's time. Costs may be reduced through removal of the incentive for unnecessary services.

516

A review of all cost comparison studies made since 1950 found that total health care costs of HMO members averaged 10 to 40 percent lower than for persons with comparable private health insurance.[124] Most of these savings came through lower hospitalization rates—30 percent lower for HMO members than for persons with private health insurance.[125]

Savings are also made by supplying members with prescription drugs, bought at quantity discounts and using generic rather than higher-priced brand name drugs when available. The pharmaceutical industry claims that brand name products are superior to generic products—that they are more carefully quality-controlled and manufactured, and that "chemical similarity is not necessarily indicative of therapeutic equivalency." There is very little evidence to support the claim of superiority for brand name drugs. All drugs must meet Food and Drug Administration standards for purity, potency, and so on, and seizures for failure to meet FDA standards have been more numerous among brand name than among generic name drugs.[126] Many who have no vested interests involved do not believe that the brand name drugs are generally superior. Most government agencies, hospitals, and comprehensive group health care plans buy their drugs generically.

HMOs have their critics, however, who claim that the "savings" result from discouraging patient use through long waits and hurried consultations.[127] But the steady growth of HMOs suggests that such unhappy experiences are not too common.

MEDICARE AND MEDICAID

In 1965, after years of mounting concern over the inadequate health care of the aged, the federal government established a program of medical service for persons 65 and older, known as Medicare. It has two parts: a hospital care program, financed by social security taxes, and a medical care program for which voluntary enrollees pay monthly fees ($9.60 a month in 1980). Medicare is a federal insurance program, while Medicaid is a federal-state program of medical aid to the "medically indigent" of any age (low-income people and certain other categories, such as the blind or disabled). Each state sets its standards of eligibility and benefits, which vary widely. Both programs include the features of *deductibility* (the patient pays the first few dollars of expense) and *coinsurance* (the patient pays a certain fraction, currently 20 percent, of the rest of the bill). These features are intended to control costs, but they also make the program expensive for the very poor. Costs under Medicare/Medicaid have skyrocketed, because these programs were merely tacked onto the existing fee-for-service system of private practice and thus continued and compounded its costly inefficiencies. While the programs have been helpful to the aged and the poor, they have been complex, cumbersome, incomplete, wasteful, and highly vulnerable to fraud.[128] Many "Medicaid mills" were set up to offer unnecessary assembly-line services to the poor.[129] Outright frauds (billing for services not performed, illegal kickbacks from laboratories) are estimated to absorb at least one-sixth of all Medicare-Medicaid funds.[130] One economist calculated that only slightly over half the Medicare-Medicaid funds went to recipients in the form of increased services or absorption of bills they would have had to pay, with the other half enriching the medical establishment.[131] Medicare-Medicaid thus repeated the mistakes that other countries had made and corrected years ago. Its clumsy provisions were dictated by the political compromises necessary to get it enacted, not by any rational calculation of program efficiency.[132]

NATIONAL HEALTH INSURANCE

Every modern nation except the United States has some form of comprehensive medical care financed by taxation and available to the entire population. Compulsory national health insurance has twice been seriously considered in the United States, just before and after World War I and again during the Truman administration.[133] After heated public controversy and a spectacularly dishonest propaganda campaign by the AMA,[134] national health insurance was defeated. The AMA discounted the achievements of national health insurance in other countries. The facts are that national health insurance, in its several variants, has worked satisfactorily in other countries; that while there are some problems and discontents, neither the public nor the medical profession in these countries has any thought of dismantling it.[135]

For some years it has been announced annually that the United States was ready for national health insurance; a 1976 poll found 61 percent of the people in favor of compulsory health insurance and only 23 percent op-

The debate over a national health plan, of which Senator Edward M. Kennedy is a vocal proponent, continues to be waged.
(United Press International)

posed. Proponents seek such goals as (1) comprehensive care, with a full range of medical treatment and preventive medicine in an integrated program in place of the present fragmented patchwork of facilities and programs; (2) continuity of care, with each person having an assured, continuing contact with a physician of his choice; (3) accessibility and availability, with adequate facilities everywhere that people live in substantial numbers; (4) quality control, to ensure a higher level of professional competence as a minimum expectation; (5) universality, with full care available to everyone as a right; and (6) consumer participation in the control of the financial and organizational aspects of medical care.[136]

Some proposals are little more than fee-paying plans, retaining solo practice and fee-for-service payment. If enacted, such plans will multiply the wastes and frauds so clearly demonstrated by Medicare-Medicaid. If comprehensive medical care is to be available to all the people at reasonable cost, a basic *reorganization* of medical care will be needed.[137] Although "cost containment" is much discussed in the current medical economics literature, there is little confidence among economists that much will be accomplished.[138] As this is written, runaway inflation and fear of mounting federal deficits makes it unlikely that any new expansions of tax-paid medical care will soon be introduced.

Summary

Americans are neither the most healthy people in the world nor as healthy as they might be. Health is a product of many variables—genetics, diet, smoking, drinking, drug use, exercise, cleanliness and sanitation, the state of one's emotions, preventive medicine, and medical care. Most of these variables operate to the disadvantage of the poor, who have the most illness and the least of practically everything else. The poor are disproportionately nonwhite, and it is the blacks, the American Indians, the Puerto Ricans, and the Mexican-Americans who have the most ill health, accounting in part for the poor ranking of the United States among the nations.

Longevity studies show that people who work hard physically, eat and drink sparingly, and live placidly will generally outlive the rest of us. The conventional lifestyle of a great many Americans includes too little exercise, too much smoking and drinking, and a diet overloaded with salt, fat, sugar, and starch. Restaurant food, institutional food, and "convenience" foods are nutritionally deficient. Obesity is a health problem, but *all* painless reducing diets are either useless or dangerous. Food faddism and organic food fanaticism are usually harmless, but not always. Quackery siphons off medical funds and kills people who delay seeking scientific medical care. Occupational diseases remain widespread and underreported. Pollution-related diseases are a recently recognized problem.

Medical care in the United States is fragmented and relatively unorganized. It is widely accused of being excessively costly and wasteful, largely because of the incentive for unnecessary service inherent in the fee-for-service system, and medical facilities are not distributed according to medical need. The quality of medical care, while higher in the U.S. than in many other countries, is still impaired by a number of limitations.

The health problem can be analyzed in terms of the inability of traditional methods of medical organization and finance to handle efficiently the growing body of medical knowledge and meet changing medical needs—a so-cial-disorganization approach. The problem can be analyzed in terms of dif-fering value choices, as between health and self-indulgence, and different value judgments concerning the extent of medical needs and of desirable ways of meeting them—a value-conflict approach. The problem can be ana-lyzed in terms of the manner in which deviant personality organization con-tributes both to ill health and to debate about the problem—a personal-de-viation approach. Each approach contributes to a complete understanding of the problem.

Recent and current changes in American health services include the spread of group practice, private health insurance, comprehensive health care plans or health maintenance organizations (HMOs), and Medicare and Medicaid, while National Health Insurance continues to be a hotly debated proposal.

There are many other aspects of health problems—dental health serv-ices, mental health, chronic illness, the nursing home scandal,[139] the migrant-labor health problem, and others—to which this chapter gives little attention. But to discuss the entire health problem completely would require not a chapter but a bookshelf.

Suggested Readings

BATTISTELLA, ROGER M., and THOMAS G. RUNDALL, eds., *Health Care Policy in a Changing Environment* (Berkeley, Ca.: McCutchan, 1978). A collection of articles on various health problems.

BLANPAIN, JAN, et al., *National Health Insurance and Health Resources: The Euro-pean Experience* (Cambridge, Mass.: Harvard University Press, 1978). An analy-sis of the health care systems of several European countries.

BOYLE, ROBERT H., and JOSEPH H. HIGHLAND, "The Persistence of PCBs," *Environ-ment,* 21 (July 1979), 6–12ff. A brief account of how a dangerous chemical en-tered the human food chain.

DAVIS, KAREN, and CATHY SCHOEN, *Health and the War on Poverty* (Washington, D.C.: Brookings Institution, 1978). A survey of health care needs and policies for the poor, with good chapters on Medicare, Medicaid, and Recommendations.

ECKHOLM, ERIC, "Unhealthy Jobs," *Environment,* 19 (Aug./Sept. 1977), 29–38. A brief article on occupational health hazards.

ENOS, DARRYL D., and PAUL SULTAN, *The Sociology of Health Care* (New York: Praeger, 1977). A text on health care, with authoritative data on and analysis of most of the topics covered in this chapter. Highly recommended.

FELDSTEIN, MARTIN, "The High Cost of Hospitals—and What to Do about It." *The Public Interest,* Summer 1977, pp. 40–54. How existing health insurance has in-flated hospital costs, with a proposed alternative program.

GINSBERG, ELI, *Health Manpower and Health Policy* (New York: Universe, 1978). A discussion of problems and prospects for health policy.

GUMBINER, ROBERT, *HMO: Putting It All Together* (St. Louis: Mosby, 1975). A concise history of the founding and development of an HMO.

McMACY, JOHN C., and JAMES PRESLEY, *Human Life Styling: Keeping Whole in the Twentieth Century* (New York: Harper & Row, 1975). A popular prescription for healthful living.

MENDELSON, MARY A., *Tender Loving Greed* (New York: Alfred A. Knopf, 1974). A critical look at the American nursing home industry.

STUDLEY, JAMIENNE S., and DAVID G. WARREN, "Medical Malpractice: A Complex and Confusing Issue with No Easy Solution," *Vital Issues,* 25, no. 5, 1–6; reprinted in *Current,* Apr. 1976, pp. 23–31. An analysis of the medical malpractice problem.

———— , "Unhealthy Costs of Health," *Business Week,* 4 Sept. 1978, pp. 58–68; and "Health Costs: What Limits?" *Time,* 28 May 1979, pp. 60–68. Two popular articles on health care costs.

A number of popularly-written books have sharply criticized the organization and operation of the American health care system, among them: Barbara Ehrenreich and John Ehrenreich, *The American Health Empire: Power, Profits, and Politics* (New York: Random House, 1971); Rick J. Carlson, *The End of Medicine* (New York: John Wiley, 1975); Rex Dye, *The Hospital-Medical Racket and You* (Hicksville, N.Y.: Exposition, 1975); Selig Greenberg, *The Quality of Mercy: A Report on the Critical Condition of Hospital and Medical Care in America* (New York: Atheneum, 1971); Ruth Mulvey Harmer, *American Medical Avarice* (New York: Abelard-Schuman, 1975); Edward M. Kennedy, *In Critical Condition: The Crisis in America's Health Care* (New York: Simon & Schuster, 1972); Spencer Klaw, *The Great American Medical Show* (New York: Viking, 1975); Sylvia A. Law, *Blue Cross: What Went Wrong?* (New Haven, Conn.: Yale University Press, 1974); Daniel Schorr, *Don't Get Sick in America* (Nashville, Tenn.: Aurora, 1970); Victor W. Sidel and Ruth Sidel, *A Healthy State* (New York: Pantheon, 1978); Duane F. Stroman, *The Quick Knife: Unnecessary Surgery, USA* (Port Washington, N.Y.: Kennikat, 1979); James S. Turner, *The Chemical Feast* (New York: Grossman, 1970); Leonard Tushnet, *The Medicine Men: The Myth of Quality Medical Care in America Today* (New York: St. Martin's Press, 1971). For popularly-written defenses of the medical establishment, see Marvin H. Edwards, *Hazardous to Your Health: A New Look at the "Health Care Crisis" in America* (New Rochelle, N.Y.: Arlington House, 1972); Harry Schwartz, *The Case for American Medicine: A Realistic Look at Our Health Care System* (New York: David McKay, 1972).

Footnotes

[1]From an address by Nicholas Johnson, Federal Communications Commission, to the College of Arts and Sciences, The American University, 21 May 1972.

[2]Erdman Palmore and Clark Luikart, "Health and Social Factors Related to Life Satisfaction," *Journal of Health and Social Behavior,* 13 (Mar. 1972), 68–80.

[3]Except for Israel, which has a large number of refugee doctors.

[4]Source: United Nations, *Demographic Yearbook, 1978.* The ranking excludes from consideration a number of small areas, such as Monaco and the Faroe Islands, and all underdeveloped countries whose statistics are of doubtful accuracy.

[5]Dr. Clarence Poe, North Carolina Hospital and Medical Care Commission, quoted in Carl Malmberg, *140 Million Patients* (New York: Reynal, 1947), p. 27.

[6]John V. Tunney and Meldon V. Levine, "Genetic Engineering: Ethical Questions," *Saturday Review,* 5 Aug. 1972, pp. 23–29.

[7]Robert G. Burnight and Parker G. Marden, "Social Correlates of Weight in an Aging Population," *Milbank Memorial Fund Quarterly,* 55 (Apr. 1967), 75–92; Albert J. Stunkard, *The Pain of Obesity* (Palo Alto, Ca.: Bull, 1975).

[8]Harold S. Luft, *Poverty and Health: Economic Causes and Consequences of Health Problems* (Cambridge, Mass.: Ballinger, 1978), p. 15.

[9]Martin S. Feldstein, "The Medical Economy," *Scientific American,* 229 (Sept. 1973), 151ff.

[10]Harry Schwartz, "Health Care and the Poor," *Wall Street Journal,* 15 Feb. 1980, p. 16.

[11]Alexander Leaf, "Every Day Is a Gift When You Are Over 100," *National Geographic,* Jan. 1973, pp. 93–117; David Davies, *Centenarians of the Andes* (New York: Doubleday Anchor, 1975); Sula Benet, *How to Live to Be 100: The Life-style of the People of the Caucasus* (New York: Dial, 1976).

[12]George H. Gallup and Evan Hall, *The Secret of a Long Life* (New York: Geis, 1960).

[13]Hans Selye, *The Stress of Life* (New York: McGraw-Hill, 1956).

[14]"Boring Jobs Are Hardest on Health," *ISR Newsletter* (University of Michigan), Spring 1975, p. 3; Robert Friis, "Job Dissatisfaction and Coronary Heart Disease," *Intellect,* 104 (May–June 1976), 594–96.

[15]Sidney Cobb and Robert M. Rose, "Hypertension, Peptic Ulcer, and Diabetes in Air Traffic Controllers," *Journal of the American Medical Association,* 224 (23 Apr. 1973), 489–92.

[16]Alfred M. Braxton, "Blood Pressure Changes among Male Navajo Migrants to an Urban Environment," *Canadian Review of Sociology and Anthropology,* 7 (Aug. 1970), 189–200.

[17]David L. Dodge and Walter L. Martin, *Social Stress and Chronic Illness:*

Mortality Patterns in Industrial Society (South Bend, Ind.: University of Notre Dame Press, 1970).

[18]"Stress Has No Gender," *Business Week,* 15 Nov. 1976, pp. 73–74.

[19]John A. Schindler, *How to Live 365 Days a Year* (Englewood Cliffs, N.J.: Prentice-Hall, 1954); Thomas H. Holmes and Minoru Masuda, "Psychosomatic Syndrome," *Psychology Today,* Apr. 1972, pp. 71ff.

[20]Richard Trotman, *Social Causes of Illness* (New York: Pantheon, 1979).

[21]Donald A. Tubesing, *Wholistic Medicine: A Whole Person Approach to Primary Health Care* (New York: Human Sciences Press, 1979).

[22]*New York Times,* 28 Oct. 1979, sec. 4, p. 8.

[23]*Health Consequences of Smoking: A Report of the Surgeon General* (Washington, D.C.: Department of Health, Education and Welfare, 1971).

[24]Joseph A. Laoye et al., "A Cohort Study of 1,205 Secondary School Smokers," *Journal of School Health,* 42 (Jan. 1972), 47–52; Martin A. Jacobs, "The Addictive Personality: Prediction of Success in a Smoking Withdrawal Program," *Psychosomatic Medicine,* 34 (Jan.–Feb. 1972), 30–38; Jacob J. Lindenthal et al., "Smoking, Psychological Status, and Stress," *Social Science and Medicine,* 6 (Oct. 1972), 583–91.

[25]Harry W. Daniell, "Smokers' Wrinkles: A Study in the Etiology of 'Crow's Feet,' " *Annals of Internal Medicine,* 75 (Dec. 1971), 873–80.

[26]Gerald E. Markle and Ronald J. Troyer, "Smoke Gets in Your Eyes: Cigarette Smoking as Deviant Behavior," *Social Problems,* 26 (June 1979), 611–25.

[27]Department of Health, Education and Welfare, *The Smoking Digest: A Progress Report on a Nation Kicking the Habit* (Washington, D.C.: Government Printing Office, 1977).

[28]*Summary of Findings: From a Study about Cigarette Smoking among Teen-Aged Girls and Young Women* (conducted by Yankelovich, Skelly, and White, Inc., for the American Cancer Society, mimeographed), Feb. 1976.

[29]"Teenagers Curtail Smoking," *Science News,* 117 (1 Mar. 1980), 137.

[30]*Science News,* 111 (19 Apr. 1977), 233.

[31]Daniell, "Smokers' Wrinkles."

[32]Joyce Brothers, "What Can Be Done about Male Impotence," *Good Housekeeping,* July 1973, pp. 50–56.

[33]"Huffing and Puffing over All That Puffing," *Time,* 24 Apr. 1978, p. 59.

[34]*Business Week,* 11 Apr. 1977, p. 78.

[35]"The Sobering Cost of Alcohol," *Science News,* 114 (28 Oct. 1978), p. 293.

[36]*Statistical Bulletin* (Metropolitan Life Insurance Co.), Feb. 1977, p. 10.

[37]Daniell, "Smokers' Wrinkles."

[38]Jacobs, "The Addictive Personality."

[39]Victor R. Fuchs, "Improving the Delivery of Health Services," in Victor R. Fuchs, ed., *Essays in the Economics of Health and Medical Care* (New York: Columbia University Press, 1972), pp. 51–58.

[40]See Ivan Illich, *Limits to Medicine* (London: Marion Boyars, 1976).

[41]"The Penicillin Eaters," *Time,* 22 Nov. 1976, p. 53.

[42]*Business Week,* 30 July 1979, p. 79.

[43]See Walter S. Ross, "Our Unrecognized VD Epidemic," *Reader's Digest,* Nov. 1979, pp. 95–99, for a popularized account.

[44]David Klein, reported in Peter F. Greenberg, "The Thrill Seekers," *Human Behavior,* Apr. 1977, p. 19.

[45]Marvin Zukerman, "The Search for High Sensation," *Psychology Today,* Feb. 1978, pp. 38ff.

[46]Melvin L. Selzer et al., "Fatal Accidents: The Role of Psychopathology, Social Stress and Acute Disturbance," *American Journal of Psychiatry,* 124 (Feb. 1968), 1028–36; Thomas A. Puschock, "Driving Risks Usually Antisocial, Alcoholic," in Paul B. Horton and Gerald R. Leslie, *Readings in the Sociology of Social Problems* (Englewood Cliffs, N.J.: Prentice-Hall, 1975), pp. 52–53.

[47]Knud J. Helsing and George W. Comstock, "What Kind of People Do Not Use Seat Belts," *American Journal of Public Health,* 67 (Nov. 1977), 1043–50.

[48]"Study Shows Persons Who Don't Wear Seat Belts Are Also Riskier Drivers," *Associated Press,* 3 Mar. 1980.

[49]*Agricultural Statistics,* (Department of Agriculture, Al.47:975), 1960, pp. 208, 261; 1976, pp. 192, 251.

[50]Department of Agriculture, reported in *Psychology Today,* Apr. 1979, p. 104.

[51]Monosodium glutamate is a flavor enhancer, widely added to restore some hint of flavor to foods made pallid and tasteless by modern food processing. Many people are somewhat sensitive, and a few people are violently sensitive to this additive. See *New England Journal of Medicine,* 279 (11 July 1968), pp. 105–6.

[52]See "Restaurant Foods," *Consumer Research Magazine,* Mar. 1980, p. 10. Reprinted by permission of Consumer Research, Inc.

[53]Weston A. Price, *Nutrition and Physical Degeneration: A Comparison of Primitive and Modern Diets and Their Effects* (Santa Monica, Ca.: Price-Pottenger Foundation, 1945).

[54]Otto Schaefer, "Pre- and Post-Natal Growth Acceleration and Increased Sugar Consumption in Canadian Eskimos," *Canadian Medical Association Journal*, 103 (1 Nov. 1970), 1059–60.

[55]H. J. Roberts, *The Cause, Ecology, and Prevention of Traffic Accidents: With Emphasis upon Traffic Medicine Epidemiology, Sociology, and Logistics* (Springfield, Ill.: Charles C Thomas, 1971).

[56]Edwin Zarling et al., "Obesity and Illness Associated Absenteeism," *Obesity and Bariatric Medicine*, 6 (Nov. 4, 1977), 134–36.

[57]See Richard F. Spark, "Fat People," *New York Times Magazine*, 6 Jan. 1974, pp. 10ff.

[58]For example, Herman Taller, *Calories Don't Count* (New York: Simon & Schuster, 1961); Robert C. Atkins, *Dr. Atkins' Diet Revolution: The High Calorie Way to Stay Thin Forever* (New York: David McKay, 1972); Irwin Maxwell Stillman and Samm Sinclair Baker, *The Doctor's Quick Weight Loss Diet Cookbook* (New York: Bantam, 1973); Herman Tarnow, *The Complete Scarsdale Medical Diet* (New York: Rawson, Wade, 1979). All these books recommend the high-protein, no-carbohydrate diet that is rediscovered periodically in profitable best-sellers, but condemned as ineffective and dangerous by reputable nutritionists. See AMA Council on Foods and Nutrition, "A Critique of Low-Carbohydrate Ketogenic Weight Reduction Regimens: A Review of Dr. Atkins' Diet Revolution," *Journal of the American Medical Association*, 224 (4 June 1973), 1415–19.

[59]For example, a best-selling nutrition author is Adele Davis *(Let's Eat Right to Keep Fit; Let's Cook It Right; Let's Get Well; Let's Have Healthy Children)*, whose books have been unfavorably reviewed in medical journals. See Daniel Yergin, "Let's Get Adele Davis Right," *New York Times Magazine*, 20 May 1973, pp. 32ff.

[60]Council on Foods and Nutrition, "Zen Macrobiotic Diets," *Journal of the American Medical Association*, 218 (18 Oct. 1971), 397.

[61]Eric Hoffer, *The True Believer* (New York: Harper & Row, 1951).

[62]See Paul B. Horton and Chester L. Hunt, *Sociology*, 5th ed. (New York: McGraw-Hill, 1980), ch. 21, for a brief description of social movements.

[63]Ron Deutsch, "Where You Should Be Shopping for Your Family," *Today's Health*, Apr. 1972, pp. 1ff.

[64]See Paul Brodeur, *Expendable Americans* (New York: Viking, 1974).

[65]Alan Anderson, Jr., "The Hidden Plague," *New York Times Magazine*, 27 Oct. 1974, pp. 20ff.

[66]David Burnham, "Rise in Birth Defects Laid to Job Hazards," *New York Times*, 14 Mar. 1976, pp. 1ff.; see also George L. Waldbott, *Health Effects of Environmental Pollutants* (St. Louis, Mo.: Mosby, 1973).

[67]Joan Arehart-Treichel, "Chemical Carcinogens: Part of the Problem," *Science News*, 115 (23 June 1979), 411–14.

[68]*Health, United States, 1975*, p. 165. See also Lester B. Love and Eugene P. Seskin, *Air Pollution and Human Health* (Baltimore: Johns Hopkins University Press, 1977).

[69]Julian McCall, "Discriminatory Air Pollution," *Environment*, Mar. 1976, pp. 26–36.

[70]Edwin Chen, *PBB: An American Tragedy* (Englewood Cliffs, N.J.: Prentice-Hall, 1979).

[71]Wade Green, "Life vs. Livelihood," *New York Times Magazine*, 24 Nov. 1974, pp. 17ff.

[72]Palmore and Luikart, "Health and Social Factors," p. 142.

[73]Eli Ginsberg, *The Limits of Health Reform* (New York: Basic Books, 1977), p. 153.

[74]*Time*, 28 May 1979, p. 60.

[75]*Medical Economics*, 7 Mar. 1977, p. 32.

[76]*Health, United States, 1975*, p. 77.

[77]William A. Glaser, *Paying the Doctor: Systems of Remuneration and Their Effects* (Baltimore: Johns Hopkins Press, 1970), ch. 8.

[78]Ibid., p. 186; see also Alex Gerber, *The Gerber Report: The Shocking State of American Medical Care and What Must Be Done about It* (New York: David McKay, 1971), pp. 106, 164.

[79]Milton I. Roemer, "On Paying the Doctor and the Implications of Different Methods," *Journal of Health and Social Behavior*, 3 (Spring 1962), 4–14.

[80]David Mechanic, "The English National Health Service: Some Comparisons with the United States," *Journal of Health and Social Behavior*, 12 (Mar. 1971), 18–29.

[81]Gerber, *The Gerber Report*, p. 105.

[82]Frances Cerba, "Program Here

Finds 28 Percent of Surgery Unnecessary," *New York Times,* 15 Dec. 1974, pp. 1ff.; Andrew S. Markovits, "Why I'm All for Second Opinions on Elective Surgery," *Medical Economics,* 13 Dec. 1976, pp. 80–83.

[83]*Cost and Quality of Medical Care: Unnecessary Surgery,* Report of the Subcommittee on Oversight and Investigations of the Committee on Interstate and Foreign Commerce, House of Representatives, 94th Congress, 2nd Session (Washington, D.C., 1976, Y4In8/4:H34/25), pp. 5–6.

[84]Ibid., p. 4.

[85]Charles E. Lewis, "Variations in the Incidence of Surgery," *New England Journal of Medicine,* 281 (16 Oct. 1969), 880–84; Stanley Englebardt, "How to Avoid Needless Surgery," *Reader's Digest,* Dec. 1974, pp. 162–66.

[86]Harry T. Paxton, "Group Practice Jobs: Suddenly It's a Buyers' Market," *Medical Economics,* 26 Nov. 1979, pp. 27–34.

[87]Federal Bureau of Community Health Services, quoted in *New York Times,* 17 Oct. 1976, sec. 4, p. 7.

[88]William A. Rushing, *Community, Physicians, and Inequality: A Sociological Study of the Maldistribution of Physicians* (Lexington, Mass.: D. C. Heath, 1975), p. 216.

[89]G. V. Rimlinger and H. B. Steele, "Economic Interpretation of the Spatial Distribution of Physicians in the United States," *Southern Economic Journal,* 30 (July 1963), 1–12; Rushing, *Community, Physicians, and Inequality.*

[90]Norman S. Blackman, "How the Malpractice Squeeze Is Redistributing Doctors," *Medical Economics,* 5 Apr. 1976, pp. 71–74.

[91]Alan Gartner, "Health System and New Careers," *Health Service Reports,* 88 (Feb. 1973), 124–30.

[92]David Ellesh and Paul L. Schollaert, "Race and Urban Medicine: Factors Affecting the Distribution of Physicians in Chicago," *Journal of Health and Social Behavior,* 13 (Sept. 1972), 236–50.

[93]Rushing, *Community, Physicians, and Inequality,* pp. 216–19.

[94]Arthur Owens, "What Doctors Want Most from Their Practices Now," *Medical Economics,* 7 Mar. 1977, pp. 88–92.

[95]Lois Hoffman, "How Do Good Doctors Get That Way?" in E. Gartly Jaco, ed., *Patients, Physicians, and Illness* (Glencoe, Ill.: Free Press, 1958), pp. 365–81 (originally published as supplement to *Journal of Medical Education,*

1958); Kenneth F. Clute, *The General Practitioner* (Toronto: University of Toronto Press, 1963); Louis Lasagna, *Life, Death, and the Doctor* (New York: Alfred A. Knopf, 1968), ch. 3.

[96]Hoffman, "How Do Good Doctors Get That Way?"

[97]See "U.S. Doctors: About 5 Percent Are Unfit," *New York Times,* 1 Feb. 1976, sec. 4, p. 11.

[98]*Medical Economics,* 18 Feb. 1980, p. 242.

[99]Arthur Owens, "How Much Have Malpractice Premiums Gone Up?" *Medical Economics,* 27 Dec. 1976, pp. 102–8; also, *Medical Economics,* 28 May 1980, p. 177.

[100]James E. Ludlam, "Ways to Head Off a New Malpractice Crisis," *Medical Economics,* 7 Jan. 1980, pp. 35–48.

[101]Jamienne S. Studley and David G. Warren, "Medical Malpractice: A Complex and Confusing Issue with No Easy Solutions," *Vital Issues,* 25, no. 3, 1–6; reprinted in *Current,* Apr. 1976, pp. 23–32.

[102]*Time,* 17 Jan. 1977, p. 73.

[103]David Spencer, M.D., testimony before Senate Antitrust and Monopoly Committee, reported in newsletter of Sen. Philip Hart, Apr. 1967.

[104]Julian B. Roebuck and Bruce Hunter, "The Awareness of Health-Care Quackery as Deviant Behavior," *Journal of Health and Social Behavior,* 13 (June 1972), 162–66; Lawrence Farber, "The Quack Business: Still Booming," *Medical Economics,* 19 Apr. 1976, pp. 253–54.

[105]Beatrice Cobb, "Why Do People Detour to Quacks?" *The Psychiatric Bulletin,* 3 (Summer 1954), 66–69; Howard Lewis and Martha Lewis, *The Medical Offenders* (New York: Simon & Schuster, 1970), ch. 9.

[106]Milford Rouse, M.D., in *Journal of the American Medical Association,* 201 (17 July 1967), 169.

[107]Roberta G. Simmons and Richard L. Simmons, "Organ Transplantation: A Societal Problem," *Social Problems,* 19 (Summer 1971), 36–57.

[108]Joel H. Goldberg, "The Extraordinary Confusion over 'Right to Die,'" *Medical Economics,* 10 Jan. 1977, pp. 121–22.

[109]James Rachels, "Active and Passive Euthanasia," *New England Journal of Medicine,* 292 (9 Jan. 1975), 78–80.

[110]B. J. Mason, "Brain Surgery to Control Behavior," *Ebony,* Feb. 1973, pp. 62ff.

[111]Anselm Strauss, "Medical Ghettos," *Trans-action,* May 1967, pp. 7ff.

[112]Oscar E. Anderson, Jr., *The Health*

of a Nation: Harvey N. Wiley and the Fight for Pure Food (Chicago: University of Chicago Press, 1958); James Harvey King, The Medical Messiahs: A Social History of Health Quackery in Twentieth-Century America (Princeton, N.J.: Princeton University Press, 1967).

[113]Thomas A. Puschock, "Driving Risks,"; Paul J. C. Friedlander, "Medical Engineers Plot Road Safety," New York Times, 12 Nov. 1972, p. 37.

[114]For the pioneer work in emotionally induced illness, see Helen Flanders Dunbar, Mind and Body: Psychosomatic Medicine (New York: Random House, 1947).

[115]Roul Tunley, The American Health Scandal (New York: Harper & Row, 1966), ch. 7; Elton Rayack, Professional Power and American Medicine, 4th ed. (Cleveland: World, 1967), chs. 3, 5.

[116]New York Academy of Medicine, Medicine in the Changing Order (New York: The Commonwealth Fund and Harvard University Press, 1947), pp. 137–39; see also George A. Silver, A Spy in the House of Medicine (Germantown, Md.: Aspen Systems, 1976), pp. 186–91, for a general description of group practice.

[117]David Sheldon, "Are You Cut Out for Group Practice? Test Yourself," Medical Economics, 12 July 1976, pp. 59–66.

[118]Statistical Abstract, 1978, p. 555.

[119]Statistical Abstract, 1979, p. 102.

[120]Andrew S. Markowitz, "Health Insurers Won't Let Us Save Them Money," Medical Economics, 10 Jan. 1977, pp. 277–84; A. F. Ehrbar, "A Radical Prescription for Medical Care," Fortune, Feb. 1977, pp. 16ff.

[121] Data from U.S. Department of Health, Education and Welfare, Office of Health Maintenance Organizations, Fact Sheet, Jan. 1980.

[122]Madeline Leininger, Barriers and Facilitators to Quality Health Care (Philadelphia: F. A. Davis, 1975), pp. 66–68.

[123]Fact Sheet.

[124]Harold S. Luft, "How Do Health Maintenance Organizations Achieve Their 'Savings?' " New England Journal of Medicine, 298 (15 June 1978), 1336–43.

[125]Ibid. It should be noted that Luft does not attribute these savings to greater "efficiencies" of HMOs, and suggests other explanations.

[126]Hearings before the Subcommittee on Monopoly of the Select Committee on Small Business, U.S. Senate, 90th Congress, 1st Session (1967), Present Status of Competition in the Pharmaceutical Industry, Part I, p. 63.

[127]Elliott A. Krause, Power and Illness: A Political Sociology of Health and Medical Care (New York: Elsevier, 1977), "The Health Maintenance Organization: Breakthrough or Bad Dream," pp. 205–12.

[128]Karen Davis and Cathy Schoen, Health and the War on Poverty (Washington, D.C.: Brookings Institution, 1978), chs. 3 and 4.

[129]"The Medicaid Scandal," Time, 23 Feb. 1976, p. 37.

[130]"Medicaid's Sad Record," New York Times, 5 Sept. 1976, sec. 4, p. 1.

[131]Stuart C. Bruce, "Who Gains from Public Health Programs?" Annals of the American Academy of Political and Social Science, 399 (Jan. 1972), 145–50.

[132]Theodore R. Marmor, The Politics of Medicare (Chicago: Aldine-Atherton, 1973).

[133]George Rosen, A History of Public Health (New York: MD Publications, 1958), pp. 439–63.

[134]For accounts of this campaign, see Rayack, Professional Power, ch. 5; or any of the earlier editions of this textbook: 1955, pp. 452–54; 1960, pp. 541–43; 1965, pp. 621–23.

[135]Rosemary Stevens, Medical Practice in Modern England (New Haven, Conn.: Yale University Press, 1966); Jan Blanpain et al., National Health Insurance and Health Resources: The European Experience (Cambridge, Mass.: Harvard University Press, 1978).

[136]Alice M. Rivlin, "Agreed: Here Comes National Health Insurance," New York Times Magazine, 21 July 1974, pp. 8ff; Richard J. Margolis, "National Health Insurance—The Dream Whose Time Has Come?" New York Times Magazine, 9 Jan. 1977, p. 12ff.

[137]David D. Rutstein, Blueprint for Medical Care (Cambridge, Mass.: MIT Press, 1974); Robert F. Rushmen, Humanizing Health Care: Alternative Futures for Medicine (Cambridge, Mass.: MIT Press, 1975).

[138]Ginsberg, Limits of Health Reform, pp. 135–40; "The Unhealthy Costs of Health," Business Week, 4 Sept. 1978, pp. 58–68.

[139]Mary A. Mendelson, Tender Loving Greed (New York: Knopf, 1974).

Marc Anderson

CIVIL LIBERTIES IN AN AGE OF PROTEST

18

The wife and daughter of former Prime Minister Zulfikar Ali Bhutto and several political leaders were detained last night following President Zia-ul-Haq's decision to postpone elections indefinitely.

There was no official explanation for the action. But observers said its purpose was to stifle political activity . . . The offices of all the political parties, including their branches in various cities, have been sealed by the government. Sources said more arrests are expected.

President Zia has not indicated when the elections, scheduled for November 17, would be held. He announced yesterday that newspapers and magazines indulging in "anti-state propaganda" would be banned and all other domestic newspapers subject to censorship. The banned newspapers include publications which were supporting Bhutto's Pakistan People's Party.

The Government has issued a martial law regulation under which it may order printers, publishers or editors to submit any matter on a particular subject for scrutiny to a specified authority. It will include any material the publication or propagation of which is "prejudicial to the Islamic ideology or the sovereignty, integrity and security of Pakistan, or morality and maintenance of public order or the purposes of martial law."

Violations are punishable by up to 10 years in prison, fines or flogging not exceeding 25 strokes.[1]

527

There are perhaps two dozen countries in which freedom is firmly enough established that a news story like the foregoing would be unlikely to appear. There are perhaps another 50 countries (including all communist states) in which this story would not appear, because it would not be news. Where censorship and suppression of political dissent are routine and continuous, there is no freedom to suppress. That leaves nearly 100 countries in which people are neither "free" nor entirely "unfree," but fall somewhere in between.

Freedom House is a national organization that publishes an annual "comparative survey of freedom" in its publication, *Freedom at Issue.* The January–February 1980 issue reports that: "Freedom rose in 21 nations in 1979, and declined in nine. The number of free people reached a record high, although comprising only 37 percent of the world's population."[2] Freedom has been a rare flower throughout world history. In nearly all times and places the dungeon, torture chamber, and gallows awaited all who dared question accepted authorities and values. Today many Americans fear that our liberties are in danger. What is the American heritage of freedom, and what developments seem to jeopardize it?

The American Heritage of Freedom

> We hold these truths to be self-evident, that all men are created equal, that they are endowed by their Creator with certain inalienable rights, that among these are Life, Liberty, and the pursuit of Happiness—That to secure these rights, Governments are instituted among Men, deriving their just powers from the consent of the governed—That when any Form of Government becomes destructive of these ends, it is the Right of the People to alter or to abolish it, and to institute new Government. . . .

The Declaration of Independence and the Constitution of the United States were the work of men who were classical scholars. They were acquainted with the history and literature of ancient Rome and Greece and were fully familiar with the rationalist philosophy of the eighteenth century. They firmly believed in *natural rights,* that governments were humanly created (not divinely ordained) institutions for securing these rights, and that when governments fail to do this they should be reformed or overthrown. They believed that freedom of thought and expression were as inseparable parts of a divinely ordained natural order as was the law of gravity, and that any society that curtails these freedoms must suffer as surely as the person who violates the law of gravity.[3]

In framing the Constitution, and especially the Bill of Rights, these men sought to devise a government with the power to govern but without the power to oppress. They were highly aware of social change and of the need for adapting governmental institutions to a changing society. But remembering the bitter costs of change by revolution, they attempted to devise a government with built-in provisions for peaceful change—an experiment much of the world regarded as highly impractical. The provisions for peaceful change included not only a system of elections but also guarantees of freedom of speech, press, and religion, peaceful assembly, and political activity. In this way the people could secure a government of their choice at all times, and resort to armed revolt would be unnecessary.

THE BASIC ASSUMPTIONS OF AMERICAN DEMOCRACY

The attempt to harmonize orderly government with a free society rests on two fundamental propositions. The first is *the faith that truth defeats error,* that in the marketplace of free competition in ideas, truth will eventually triumph. Unless truth can win out over error in open contest, it follows that we must protect truth by suppressing error. Democratic government *must* rest on the assumption that the majority of the people, given free access to facts and unlimited opportunity to discuss them freely, will arrive at the right answers most of the time. Any attempt to prevent the expression of "wrong" ideas is a confession of doubt in the ability of the people to arrive at correct conclusions. If the majority of the people are "too dumb" to arrive

The Declaration of Independence.
(Culver Pictures, Inc.)

THE RIGHTS OF AMERICANS

The Right to the Essentials of Life

> The right to equal educational opportunity
> The right to equal employment opportunity
> The right to housing
> The right to welfare
> The right to special treatment
> The right to legal services
> The right to a habitable environment

The Right to Influence Government or Public Opinion

> The right to vote
> The right to participate
> The right to protest
> The right of association
> The right to publish
> The right of access to mass media

The Right of Personal Autonomy

> The right of privacy
> The right of religious liberty
> The right to control the use of one's body
> The right to use alcohol and drugs
> The right to travel

Rights against Government Process

> The rights of suspects
> The rights of criminal defendants
> The rights of prisoners
> The rights of juveniles
> The rights of mental patients
> The rights of selective service registrants

The Rights of Particular Groups

> The rights of women
> The rights of teachers and professors
> The rights of students
> The rights of unions and union members
> The rights of servicemen
> The rights of aliens

To which of the above is each person in the United States entitled?
How completely does each American now possess them?
How completely do citizens of other countries possess them?

Adapted from table of contents of Norman Dorsen, ed., *The Rights of Americans: What They Are—What They Should Be* (New York: Random House, 1971), pp. ix–x. Copyright © 1971 by Pantheon Books, a division of Random House.

at the right conclusions, then democratic government cannot endure and we may as well start considering what kind of dictatorship we prefer.

The second fundamental basis of democratic government is an implicit social contract in which *the majority gives up the persecution of the minority and the minority gives up the practice of revolution.* The majority agrees to tolerate the criticism and dissent of the minority (or minorities), while the minority agrees to seek power only through persuasion and political activity, not through violence. Such an unspoken agreement is necessary for orderly representative government. If the governing officials representing the majority seek to outlaw opposing political parties, jail critics, suppress critical newspapers, and so on, then it is no longer a free government, and the minority is justified in organizing a revolution. Conversely, if any members of the minority are unwilling to rely on persuasion, but use force and violence in attempting to gain power, they have sacrificed their claim to political freedom. In an authoritarian state where dissidents are not permitted to organize a political opposition, terrorism has some justification. But in a democratic state which tolerates a political opposition, terrorism is a confession that the dissenters cannot gain mass support. Thus the terrorists, for all their talk of "freedom," are trying to impose a minority view upon others by force and intimidation.[4]

Revolution, to our founding fathers, was justifiable in a republic only when the ruling powers interfered with the efforts of the minority to gain power through criticism, persuasion, and political activity; *if the government did so interfere, then revolution became a duty* ("it is their right, it is their duty, to throw off such Government . . ."). This is the real meaning of freedom—freedom for the idea one hates as well as for the idea one embraces. Unless people are free to express unpopular opinions and to support "dangerous" ideas without sacrifice of liberty, property, or employment, *freedom* is an empty word and free government an illusion.

It cannot be too strongly emphasized that our ancestors erected constitutional guarantees of freedom, not from any fondness for radicalism, but because they wanted *order.* Having lived through the chaos of revolution, they wanted a social order in which revolution would be unnecessary. They felt that free speech and unrestricted political agitation, even for the ideas they loathed, were a lesser threat to orderly government than the seething intrigues that the denial of freedom would provoke. Such a belief, together with a confidence in the people's wisdom, is reflected in Thomas Jefferson's First Inaugural Address:

> If there be any among us who wish to dissolve this union, or change its republican form, let them stand undisturbed, as monuments of the safety with which error of opinion may be tolerated, where reason is left free to combat it.

HISTORIC VIOLATIONS OF FREEDOM IN AMERICA

The popular idea of early America as a garden of liberty is a myth.[5] Not all of our ancestors shared the faiths that lie behind our constitutional guarantees of freedom. Alexander Hamilton's famous retort, "Your *people*, sir, is a great beast," expressed the views of a great many of the aristocracy. Aaron

RANKING OF NATIONS BY CIVIL LIBERTIES

Most Free 1	2	3	4	5	6	Least Free 7
Australia	Bahamas	Bangladesh	Bahrain	Argentina	Algeria	Afghanistan
Austria	Dominica	Bolivia	Comoro Is.	Bhutan	Benin	Albania
Barbados	Ecuador	Botswana	Cyprus	Chile	Burma	Angola
Belgium	Fiji	Brazil	Djibouti	China (Mainland)	Cameroon	Bulgaria
Canada	Finland	Colombia	Ghana	China (Taiwan)	Cape Verde Is.	Burundi
Costa Rica	France	Dominican Rep.	Guyana	Egypt	Central African Rep.	Congo
Denmark	Gambia	El Salvador	Kenya	Grenada	Chad	Czechoslovakia
Iceland	Germany (W)	Honduras	Kuwait	Guatemala	Cuba	Ethiopia
Ireland	Greece	Jamaica	Lebanon	Haiti	Equatorial Guinea	Germany (E)
Japan	India	Mexico	Malaysia	Hungary	Gabon	Guinea
Luxembourg	Israel	Nigeria	Mauritius	Indonesia	Guinea-Bissau	Iraq
Netherlands	Italy	St. Lucia	Morocco	Ivory Coast	Iran	Kampuchea
New Zealand	Kiribati	Senegal	Nepal	Korea (S)	Jordan	Korea (N)
Norway	Malta	Sri Lanka	Peru	Lesotho	Libya	Laos
Sweden	Nauru	Thailand		Liberia	Madagascar	Malawi
Switzerland	Papua New Guinea	Tonga		Maldives	Mali	Mongolia
United Kingdom	Portugal	Turkey		Nicaragua	Mauritania	Mozambique
United States	St. Vincent	Upper Volta		Panama	Niger	Somalia
	Solomon Is.			Paraguay	Oman	Vietnam
	Spain			Philippines	Pakistan	Yemen (S)
	Surinam			Poland	Rumania	
	Trinidad & Tobago			Qatar	Rwanda	
	Tuvalu			Seychelles	Sao Tome & Principe	
	Venezuela			Sierra Leone	Saudi Arabia	
	Western Samoa			Singapore	South Africa	
				Sudan	Syria	
				Swaziland	Tanzania	
				Tunisia	Togo	
				United Arab Emirates	Transkei	
				Yemen (N)	Uganda	
				Yugoslavia	USSR	
				Zambia	Uruguay	
				Zimbabwe Rhodesia	Zaire	

Source: Freedom at Issue, no. 54, Jan./Feb. 1980, p. 7. Copyright © Freedom House, 1980. Reprinted by permission.

Burr's revolutionary conspiracies received much support from persons who disliked the notion of representative government. Prosecutions and imprisonments for "sedition" were not uncommon. Scores of dissenters have been tarred and feathered; to burn the printing plant of an unpopular newspaper is an old American custom. Immigrants and racial and religious minorities have never enjoyed the full rights of citizenship or the equal protection of the law.[6] Radical political movements and efforts to organize labor unions have been opposed with injunction, intimidation, and violence. Even movements such as the feminist movement brought public ridicule and even physical danger to their supporters. Although American society has been far more tolerant of political unorthodoxy and dissent than most other nations, the record shows considerably less than complete toleration.

During several periods in American history, particularly severe waves of oppression swept over the land. During and immediately after the Revolutionary War, Loyalists were persecuted, beaten, tarred and feathered, and even lynched, and several thousand sought permanent refuge in Canada.[7] Next came the Alien and Sedition Laws, passed to help the Federalist Party silence its opponents at a time when the revolutionary ideals of the French Revolution seemed to threaten orderly governments everywhere. Another wave of intolerance accompanied the great slavery debate, with wholesale persecution of abolitionists. At the close of World War I, a return to isolationism, together with a "Red scare," produced a national persecution of communists, radicals, labor organizers, and nonconformists of nearly every sort—highly lawless, of course, and led by the nation's top law enforcement officer, Attorney General A. Mitchell Palmer.[8] More recent is the orgy of anticommunist witch-hunting of 1948–60, often known as McCarthyism although it extended far beyond the wild accusations of the unscrupulous Senator Joseph McCarthy from Wisconsin.[9] It included (1) congressional investigations, both federal and state, in which unsupported accusations of disloyalty were invited and publicized;[10] (2) antisubversive legislation, which sought to find some constitutional way to harass communists and other radicals; (3) loyalty and security procedures, under which suspected subversives were dismissed from a wide variety of jobs that supposedly involved national security;[11] and (4) blacklists of supposedly subversive persons and organizations, used to deny employment to all whom the blacklist compiler suspected.[12] While the hunt ostensibly aimed at communists, very few active communists were uncovered. The main victims were liberals, many of whom were drummed out of public life in disgrace for the crime of being honest liberals. By the early 1960s this wave of anticommunist hysteria had largely ended. In the preceding years, however, many innocent persons suffered, political debate was debased, and the nation suffered a degree of injury that will long be a matter of debate.[13]

In 1654 Peter Stuyvesant opposed granting civil rights to the first Jews arriving in America. "Giving them liberty," he wrote, "we cannot refuse the Lutherans and the Papists."

Newton Minow, quoted in *Time,* 24 Mar. 1975, p. 58.

HOW DEEP FLOWS THE STREAM OF AMERICAN LIBERTY?

Clearly the "American heritage of liberty" is a set of ideals, not a set of objective conditions. The ideals have never been shared by all or even most Americans. A favorite research exercise is to lift some phrases from the Constitution, the Declaration of Independence, or the Bill of Rights and, without identifying them, submit them to a sample of citizens for reaction. In the most recent example, over 70 percent of the sample signed a petition calling for repeal of the entire Bill of Rights.[14] A study following the student killings at Kent State University in 1970 found that half of a national sample of American men felt that shooting was "a good way of handling campus demonstrations," and that 20 percent felt that the police should shoot to kill.[15] James Michener has written of the violent hatred for the students felt by many of the local people following the Kent State killings.[16] If the number killed had reflected the feelings of the local population, the dead might have numbered 400, not 4. It is obvious that people are generally more intolerant and ruthless than their leaders. Historical moments of direct rule by the people have generally been blood baths.

During recent decades, however, the political tolerance of the American people has increased. A 1954 study of American political tolerance[17] was repeated in 1973.[18] As shown in table 18–1, American tolerance for nonconformity expanded substantially during this period.

Both these studies agree in exploding a popular myth. There is a romantic notion that "the people" are passionately devoted to liberty but are continually robbed of it by their wicked leaders. Both studies agree in finding that community leaders are considerably more tolerant of nonconformity than the general public, as shown in table 18–2.

How does it happen that we actually have more freedom and tolerance than the majority of our people seem to endorse? One reason is *inertia*. Our political system is designed to be *ultimately, but not immediately, responsive* to the public will. It takes 2 years to change the members of the House of Representatives, 6 years to change the Senate, and 20 or more to change all the members of the Supreme Court. Important legislative acts generally follow several years of debate, false starts, and abortive deliveries. This means that an outburst of public passion may have cooled before punitive legislative and judicial action find their leisurely way into operation. When campus dis-

TABLE 18–1   Tolerance for Nonconformity in the United States, 1954–73

National Cross-Section of Americans	1954 %	1973 %
Believe it "important to find out all the communists even if some innocent people should get hurt"	58	23
Would "allow a socialist to speak in your community"	58	72
Would "allow a socialist to teach in a college or university"	33	53

Adapted from Clyde Z. Nunn, Harry J. Crockett, Jr., and J. Allen Williams, Jr., *Tolerance for Nonconformity* (San Francisco: Jossey-Bass, 1978), pp. 37–39.

TABLE 18–2   Willingness to Tolerate Nonconformists, for Community Leaders and National Cross-Section, 1954 and 1973.

Sample	Tolerance scale scores:			
	Percent less tolerant	Percent in-between	Percent more tolerant	Number
1954				
Community leaders	5	29	66	1,500
National cross-section	19	50	31	4,933
1973				
Community leaders	4	13	83	649
National cross-section	16	25	55	3,539

Reprinted by permission from Clyde Z. Nunn, Harry J. Crockett, Jr., and J. Allen Williams, Jr., *Tolerance for Nonconformity* (San Francisco, Jossey-Bass, 1978), p. 51. Copyright © by Jossey-Bass, Inc., Publishers.

orders suddenly declined in 1970, hundreds of punitive legislative bills quietly died.

A second possible explanation is that community leaders tend to be *older, better educated, and more interested in public affairs* than the average citizen. All of these factors are clearly shown by both the Stouffer and the Nunn studies to be positively associated with greater tolerance for nonconformity.

A third possible explanation is the *responsibility and accountability* demanded of public leaders. Studies have shown that established civic leaders are more tolerant of dissent than the general public. Ordinary citizens are free to shout their hostilities and polemics without being forced to consider the consequences. Leaders must remember that every proposal has critics as well as proponents. If they wish to remain leaders, they cannot afford the luxury of "going off half-cocked." For example, consider this hypothetical dialogue:

"Anyone who works against America ought to be shot."

"Who is to decide who is working against America?"

Within four years after that first appearance [of Quakers in the United States in 1651] scores of Quakers had been stripped naked, whipped, pilloried, stocked, caged, imprisoned, laid neck and heels, branded and maimed; and four had been hanged in Boston by our Puritan forefathers.

Alice Morse Earle, *Curious Punishments of Bygone Days* (Chicago: Herbert S. Stone, 1896; reissued by Singing Tree Press, Detroit, 1968), p. 139.

"Well, the government, I guess."

"Suppose Mr. X should become president. Would you trust him to pick out the ones to shoot?"

"Of course not. He's a jackass."

"Suppose he became president and started shooting those who call him a jackass?"

"Well . . . that can't happen here."

"It has in a lot of places. Are you *sure* you want the government deciding whom to shoot?"

This oversimplified example may show why leaders are more tolerant than ordinary citizens. They are more fully aware of how any curtailment of basic freedoms may be turned against its sponsors. Therefore, they often defend freedoms that the majority of citizens would surrender.

Or it may be that the leaders simply have more wisdom than the followers. Some object to this as elitist, but it is nonetheless a possibility.

Current Civil Liberties Issues in The United States

The terms *civil rights* and *civil liberties* are often used interchangeably, and in fact a clear demarkation cannot always be made. Yet the words are not synonymous. *Liberty,* from the Latin *liber,* literally means "free." Liberty thus means a freedom from interference or restraint by others. The first ten amendments to the Constitution (the Bill of Rights) are mainly a list of the citizen's immunities from interference by the state. The term *right* may be used interchangeably with *liberty* to refer to a recognized privilege of acting in a certain way without interference or penalty, as in the case of free speech or freedom of religion. But the term *right* is also used to refer to a recognized privilege of making certain claims or demands on others that others are obligated to fulfill, as with the right to trial by jury or the child's right to parental support.

The list of current rights and liberties issues is long and constantly changing. Several major areas of controversy have been treated elsewhere in this book—racial equality, religious liberty, equal educational opportunity, women's liberation, rights of suspects and those accused of crimes, efforts to politicize the mass media—and will not be repeated here. Among other important issues are those of political extremism; the rights of property, dissent, and personal autonomy; the rights of the helpless; and the right to economic and status equality.

Political Extremism

No definition of political extremism will satisfy everyone. Most persons fancy themselves serenely seated upon the mount of wisdom, while on all sides the unenlightened are tumbling into the valleys of extremist excess.

TABLE 18–3   Support for Civil Liberties among College Students

Item	Libertarian response	Percentage giving libertarian response
The circulation of Russian or Chinese newspapers in this country should be restricted to scholars.	no	85
State governments should be able to pass laws making it illegal to speak against racial or religious groups.	no	85
Large-scale police round-ups of "undesirables" are proper as long as they detain only people with known criminal records.	no	83
The police are justified in holding a person with a long criminal record until they find enough evidence to convict him.	no	75
It unduly hampers police in their efforts to apprehend criminals when they must have a warrant before searching a house.	no	74
Legislative committees should not investigate the political beliefs of university faculty members.	yes	59
It is wrong for government investigators to take pictures of people listening to a street-corner speech.	yes	50
If a person is acquitted, and new evidence is later found that may prove him guilty, he should be retried.	no	34

Adapted from Clyde Z. Nunn, "Support of Civil Liberties among College Students," *Social Problems*, 20 (Winter 1973), 300–310 (survey of 437 undergraduates at University of Nebraska). By permission of the Society for the Study of Social Problems and Clyde Z. Nunn.

One common definition makes extremism the opposite terminals of the radical–reactionary continuum. In this analysis the extremists of the left wish to wipe out the existing system and replace it with a totally new one, while the extremists of the right wish to wipe out the present system through a return to an earlier one. Intermediate between them, the liberals and the conservatives wish to maintain the present system with varying amounts of remodeling and repair. Thus extremism is defined in terms of *goal:* the replacement of the present system with some alternative.

A different view defines extremism in terms of *means.* In this view extremists are those who reject rational persuasion and political action as the means of winning approval for their policies, but endorse violence, force, and other authoritarian means of getting their way. The two definitions converge, for those who are extremists by one definition often fit the other as well. Current forms of political extremism in the United States include the old left, the new left, and the radical right.

THE OLD LEFT

The old left includes many varieties of nineteenth- and early twentieth-century radicalism, including anarchism, syndicalism, and many versions of

Marxian socialism. *Anarchism* assumes that human nature is good unless corrupted by bad institutions, especially the state, which is the prime instrument of oppression and exploitation. Anarchism seeks justice and equality through the destruction of the state, by violence if necessary, and envisions a society of small cooperative groups reaching common agreements and knit to other such groups in a voluntary network within which each person and group is free of all compulsion or external control.[19] Many of these ideas are also shared by socialists.

While socialist ideas were a familiar feature of the intellectual atmosphere before Karl Marx, he organized socialist thought into a coherent theoretical system that has dominated radical thought for the past century. Although his writings, extending over many years, are not entirely consistent with one another, his *Communist Manifesto* in 1848 set forth the basic ideas of "classical communism:[20]"

1. The *labor theory of value,* a classic economic theory, held that all value was created by labor, whereas trade and distribution were nonproductive. Marx interpreted this to mean that all profits are stolen from the workers, and private capital is but an accumulation of past thievery. In expropriating private capital, the working class would merely be seizing stolen property as its rightful owner.

2. The *class-conflict* theory holds that the interests of the capitalist class and the working class are unalterably opposed, and that all history is but the record of class warfare.

3. The doctrine of *economic determinism* states that all other aspects of the culture are determined by its economic aspects. The methods of economic production and the system of ownership of the means of production (land, machines, resources) are said to shape and mold all other aspects of the culture into harmony with these economic aspects. Thus, Marx stated that under capitalistic ownership and operation of the economy, the family takes the forms and functions most profitable to capitalists; law, government, and the police are only devices for protecting the capitalists; warfare is only the effort of opposing groups of capitalists to steal resources and markets from one another; religion is but an "opiate of the people" promising them "pie in the sky" in exchange for earthly servitude; "bourgeois" morality is merely a body of superstitions to keep the working classes servile, while occasional crumbs of charity induce the poor to kiss the hands that rob them.

4. The *progressive misery of the proletariat* (the working class) is claimed to be inevitable under capitalism, where the rich allegedly grow richer and the poor grow poorer. Monopoly destroys small business, and the independent middle class of small business and professional people becomes proletarized, or converted into hired servants of the capitalists. Eventually, the workers become aware of their misery; the proletarized middle class comes to identify its interest with that of the workers; and capitalist rule is overthrown.

5. The *inevitability of violent revolution* stems from the refusal of the capitalist class to surrender its privileges. Political parties, elections, and the other trappings of representative government are said to be only a pretense that disguises the rule of the capitalists. Communism cannot be voted gradually or peacefully into power, for the capitalists will resort to force

to prevent it. Therefore, communism will eventually gain power through a violent revolution provoked by capitalist repression.

6. Following the revolution, a temporary *dictatorship of the proletariat* must ruthlessly exterminate all capitalist or bourgeois elements, lest they sabotage the regime or promote a counterrevolution.

7. After the generation or so of this dictatorship, the *classless society* or the state of true communism is supposed to emerge. The state, since it is only an instrument of capitalist oppression, should be unnecessary and should gradually wither away. The planning of production and other administration problems would be handled by local, regional, and national organizations of workers, and liberty and abundance would be enjoyed by all.

A detailed evaluation of communist ideology and of communism in practice would demand more space than this chapter affords.[21] Suffice it to say that some of Marx's ideas and predictions are not supported by the developments of the past century. For example, the "proletariat" has grown steadily more affluent, not more impoverished; the middle class shows no signs of being proletarized; the state shows no signs of withering away in communist countries. But Marx's thesis that capitalistic class exploitation is at the root of most social ills is the core of most radical thought today.

Marxist societies claim to be "democratic," but this does not include civil liberties, political freedom, or rule *by* the people; it is rule *of* the people by a party elite who claim to rule in the interests of the people. China's Chairman Hua Guofeng states:

> Democracy in China is a socialist democracy which means democracy of very wide scope enabling the people of our country to really be the masters of their own affairs. But I want our friends to know that we oppose anarchy and a use of democracy that prejudices the people's rights.
>
> And that is why, for example, we have declared in our laws that libel and slander are punishable by law and also that one cannot use democracy to stir up social disorders.[22]

Under such a definition, any criticism of officials or official policy is "libel and slander," and any attempt to organize political opposition is to "stir up

---

The London-based organization Amnesty International has earned a reputation as the world's public conscience on matters of political repression. Last week the conscience spoke again, with a wide-ranging, 219-page annual report on 96 countries. The report's major findings: the torture of political prisoners is nearly universal, the sinister practice by some governments of "disappearing" political opponents (arresting them clandestinely) is on the rise, and there has been a global increase in political murders.

Time, 24 Dec. 1979, p. 35.

social disorder," usually punished in China by banishment to a work camp for "reform through labor."

Although communist parties throughout the world share a common Marxist core, they differ considerably from one another. The present blood bath in Cambodia arises from a contest between rival communist movements, one supported by Russia and the other by China.[23] The Communist Party in the United States, thoroughly subservient to Russia, had some following in the 1930s and 1940s, but is today viewed as irrelevant by most American radicals.[24]

THE RISE AND STALL OF THE NEW LEFT

After 1920 the Communist Party brought some uniformity and doctrinal orthodoxy to the old left; the new left of the 1900s had no equally dominant center of influence. The term *new left* is applied to a wide variety of radical ideas and proposals that reject both the established society and the dogmatic rigidity of the Communist Party.[25] Among the roots of new left thought are the following:

ANARCHISM   Not all new leftists were anarchists, but anarchist ideas were prominent in the new left.[26] Its opposition to all bureaucracies, rules, regulations, compulsions, and involuntary restraints; its fondness for "doing one's own thing"; and its readiness to use violence against the establishment were all well within the anarchist tradition. The major goals of the new left—economic equality, personal liberty of action, minimum government through "participatory democracy"[27] were clearly anarchist.

MARXIST SOCIALISM   The new left followed the Marxist critique of capitalist society—that class exploitation lies at the root of racism, sexism, poverty, alienation from work, and virtually all other domestic problems; while wars and international conflicts are the inevitable product of capitalist imperialism.[28] Unlike Communist Party apologists, new leftists felt no need to try to make historical developments fit into Marx's system of successive evolutionary stages. Their Marxism is eclectic; they choose from Marx whatever seems to fit and ignore the rest.

The rise of the new left was greatly stimulated by the Vietnam War. Most Americans were slow to discover that the United States had become involved in a war of doubtful legality, with poor prospects for a satisfactory conclusion, and of a kind conducive to ugly atrocities as a routine mode of warfare.[29] Resistance to the war developed among all age groups, but especially among young people of draft age. It had a profoundly radicalizing effect; many war resisters had their first contacts with radical groups and ideas through war resistance activities.[30] While the war did not create the new left, it gave the new left a powerful assist.

The new left was notably lacking in blueprints for the future, beyond the expectation that replacing capitalism with a cooperative economic system operated as a participatory democracy will somehow solve most problems. The new left was thus not a political program as much as a set of ideas and feelings about society. One scholar, after surveying the extensive literature of the new left, claims that its main thought currents were: (1) *romanticism*, with utopian visions unsullied by any concessions to practicality; (2) *ahistori-*

cism, rejecting the lessons of history as meaningless; (3) *revitalization* of society through confrontations to purify it and redirect it to humane goals; (4) *communitarianism,* to end alienation through smaller communities operated as participatory democracies; and (5) *disengagement* from imperialist meddling abroad.[31]

The new left was most clearly represented by the Students for a Democratic Society (SDS), founded in 1960, and in its Port Huron Statement of 1962.[32] After reaching a high point of about 300 campus chapters and 8,000 members in 1969, the SDS dissolved into warring factions in 1970. Its most militant members formed the Weathermen, an underground revolutionary organization. Today the SDS is dead, the Liberation News Service is gone, the Weathermen are scattered, and the campuses are quiet.[33]

But the new left is stalled, not dead. The dedicated new leftists of the 1960s are now holding jobs; they have retreated from futile posturing and counterproductive violence into a period of reassessment, planning, and waiting.[34] Today college students are more moderate, while faculty members are more militant.[35] Marxist ideas have gained academic respectability; avowedly Marxist professors are now found in all major universities, and a section on "Marxist Sociology" meets annually as part of the American Sociological Association. Marxist textbooks and reference works are commonplace in the classroom. The new left has lost the battle for immediate revolution, but it may yet win the war.

THE RADICAL RIGHT

Like the new left, the radical right encompasses a number of groups and ideologies. All rightist groups share a loathing for communism, socialism, and liberalism, and a rededication to certain traditional American values. Among the principal concerns of most radical rightists are (1) *nationalism,* patriotism, with opposition to the United Nations, foreign aid, disarmament, and communism, and support for an aggressive foreign policy; (2) *individualism,* with praise for individual responsibility and the work ethic, and condemnation of welfare statism and egalitarianism; (3) *authoritarianism,* stressing obedience, law and order with swift and punitive justice for criminals and demonstrators, and prompt expulsion of dissenters from radical rightist organizations; (4) *moral and religious conservatism;* and (5) *racism,* with many but not all radical rightists opposing racial equality and nearly all highly critical of affirmative action, busing, and any other "compulsory" programs for racial equality.

One directory listed over 1,500 rightist organizations.[36] Many such organizations are no more than one person with a mimeograph machine and a mailing list. Many are mainly publication organizations with a newsletter and a subscription list but no active membership. A few, however, are active membership organizations; of these the John Birch Society is the best known.[37] Some of the membership organizations belong to the "responsible right"—organizations that are highly conservative or reactionary in their goals but responsible in their procedures. They believe in open debate and democratic processes and concede that their opponents are not necessarily traitors. The Young Americans for Freedom generally represent this point

Students for a Democratic Society (SDS) demonstrate in Chicago, on election day, 1968.

(Krystna Neuman, Photo Researchers, Inc.)

of view on the campus, and William F. Buckley, Jr.'s *National Review* carries this message nationally. But many organizations belong to the radical right. They are reactionary in their goals, wishing to reverse most of the social reforms of the twentieth century, and are irresponsible in their methods. They distrust open debate and the democratic process, believing that the government, the church, the schools and universities, and most of the press have fallen under the control of communist conspirators and sympathizers. They see all opponents as willing or unwitting communist collaborators.[38]

The radical right is basically a protest against most of the trends of modern society. Although it is sometimes called fascist, this label is not correct. While the radical right does resemble the fascists in its nationalism, authoritarianism, moral puritanism, and rejection of egalitarianism, liberalism, and rationalism, it differs from fascism in that it is authoritarian but not totalitarian. Both fascists and communists tend to be totalitarian, advocating that all important aspects of life be regulated by the government authority; not only politics and economics, but also education, family, art, recreation—virtually everything.[39] In China, for example, there was scarcely any daily action that one should take without considering the "Thoughts of Mao." (This veneration for Mao vanished quickly when Mao died, and China became slightly less rigidly totalitarian.[40]) The individualism of the radical right is flatly opposed to totalitarianism, and the role ascribed to government by radical rightists is definitely limited. Like the new left, the radical right at this moment appears to be relatively ineffective.

COMMON CHARACTERISTICS OF POLITICAL EXTREMISTS

While poles apart in most of their goals, the extreme right and the far left (both new and old) show certain similarities in outlook and tactics. Both reflect a self-righteous assurance of their purity of heart and motive while assailing the motives of their opposites. Whenever their rationalizations for their inconsistencies are questioned by others, they are pained and angry; yet they are ready with accusations of hypocrisy at the inconsistencies of others. Both attack centralized, bureaucratized government as oppressive. Both attack liberal democracy as incapable of justice, and both accuse the liberals and moderates of being intellectual prostitutes for the opposite side. Each charges that the basic institutions—government, church, school, the press—have been captured and subverted by the other side. Both accept a conspiratorial view of society in which bad happenings arise from the evil plots of others, and not from the operation of social trends or historical forces. Both see the people as the gullible pawns of evil conspirators. Neither has any faith in the judgment of ordinary people, but both believe that the people need firm guidance, which each set of extremists volunteers to provide. Both seek the politicization of the university, with themselves in the saddle and all dissenters expelled. Both distrust science, reason, and objectivity as inferior guides to truth, as compared with tradition (extreme right) or with a feeling for humanity (extreme left). Both are unable to recognize any facts that conflict with their ideology. Conflicting external realities are either rationalized or simply ignored, because their ideological systems are immune to any contrary facts. Both are willing to surrender some civil liberties (someone else's, that is) in pursuit of goals that are so "right" that any sacrifice is justified.[41]

Both apply a double standard in recognizing violations of civil liberties. Their concern for human rights is highly selective (or, as some would say, hypocritical). As one former Marxist notes,

> The left's indignation seems exclusively reserved for outrages that confirm Marxist diagnosis of the sickness of capitalist society. Thus there is protest against murder and repression in Nicaragua, but not Cambodia, Chile but not Tibet, South Africa but not Uganda, Israel but not Libya or Iraq.[42]

Read this backward and it describes equally well the double standard of the radical right.[43] More than one scholar has noted certain similarities between the attacks of contemporary extremists on "the system" and the attacks through which the left and the right cooperated to bring down the Weimar Republic and pave the way for Adolf Hitler in Germany.[44] Political extremism, which is basically a willingness to employ any means to achieve a goal, is a continual threat to the civil liberties of any society.

The Right of Property

No right has a more venerable tradition than the right to hold and use one's property and income. The Fifth Amendment states, "No person shall be . . . deprived of life, liberty, or property without due process of law; nor shall private property be taken for public use, without just compensation." Yet no right has been the subject of more debate, for the rights of property often conflict with other rights. My right to use my property for a chicken farm, a shooting gallery, or a night club has an impact on the rights of my neighbors. In practice, therefore, property rights are whatever the society agrees to tolerate. The rights of property owners have been limited by many zoning and licensing laws, by laws defining public nuisance, by taxation, and by many other laws and regulations. Property and income taxation are a form of partial confiscation by the state to serve some presumed public good.

For many years, efforts to abolish sweatshops, regulate factory safety, require minimum wages, and enact many other forms of social legislation were blocked or held unconstitutional as violations of the rights of property. It required a constitutional amendment to authorize the income tax. Today the principle that property rights may be curtailed for a greater public good is well established. The right to demand services, discussed later in this chapter, requires substantial inroads into property rights, as those with property and income are taxed for the benefit of those without property or income. The right to economic equality, which many leftists advance as the basic human right, would greatly curtail the historic right to hold property and income. Whether this is practical or desirable has been debated for centuries, and probably will be debated for centuries to come.

The Right of Dissent

Basic to the concept of democratic liberties is the right of dissent. To be real, this includes more than the right to *hold* dissenting views, even though in some places—China, for example—even this is forbidden. Many countries permit purely *private* expression of dissent (in homes, at tavern tables), but will punish any *public* expression of dissent through public address, publishing, or organizing an opposition. The right of dissent implies the right to express dissent in an open, public, systematic, organized manner. It thus includes the right to vote, to assemble peaceably, to speak freely, to publish, and to associate in formal organizations for the purpose of dissent. None of these freedoms exists in totalitarian countries, and not all of them are fully enjoyed by all citizens in even the liberal democracies.

Absolute freedom of speech is limited by the laws of libel, slander, and incitement to riot. A freedom to shout "fire!" in a crowded theater threatens others' freedom to stay alive, and a right to libel and slander would destroy others' right to preserve their reputations. Some compromises need to be made. While such necessary limits are not always easy to locate, the problem of dissent usually arises when some group or agency seeks to suppress the effective expression of ideas or facts that are offensive to them. For example, the Smith Act of 1940 and the Subversive Activities Control Act of 1950 were clearly intended to make it impossible for the Communist Party to operate by making *membership* a crime.[45] The right to protest has trod a stormy path strewn with many court decisions as to *where* and *how* one has the right to protest.[46] The right to vote would seem to be above argument, yet only in recent years has it become real for many blacks and other minority citizens in the United States. Throughout the Vietnam War, charges of giving aid and comfort to the enemy were regularly hurled at those who arrived too early at the conclusion that was eventually reached by the majority. The use of the right of dissent has always been an annoyance to some members of the society, and thus has been an issue in all societies claiming to respect it.

Dissenters are punished in all societies and all groups. Even dissenting groups are seldom tolerant of dissent among their members. Thus the radical leftist who suggests that welfare clients are mostly bums will receive about the same treatment as the radical rightist who argues that most welfare clients are not bums. The extremist attitude is intolerant of any dissent except its own. And in *any* group, deviation from group norms is greeted with some degree of disapproval and withdrawal of acceptance. Even groups that consider themselves highly tolerant of each member's right to do what he or she wishes are, in fact, tolerant of only *certain kinds* of deviation. A particular commune may accept a wide variety of sexual preferences but allow no deviation from the group norm of communally-shared income and property. *Informal* punishments—disapproval, ridicule, ostracism—are inherent in all group life, and are seldom an issue. It is the formal punishments and the limits of dissent that constitute the issue.

Punishments for dissent are many and varied. The dissenting scholar or

Anti-Nuke lie-in demonstration in New York City at the
1980 Democratic Convention.
(Marc Anderson)

writer may be dismissed, forbidden to publish, and be permitted to work (if at all) only as a menial laborer.[47] Or the dissenter may be exiled, as has happened to so many distinguished Russian writers.[48] A unique way of silencing dissenters in Russia is to confine them to psychiatric hospitals,[49] earning Russia the condemnation of the World Psychiatric Association in 1977. China has probably the most elaborate system of thought control in the entire world.[50] Only in free societies are dissenters even relatively secure from formal punishment for dissent.

CIVIL DISOBEDIENCE

Civil disobedience is a form of dissent in which people openly and publicly violate a law, and in most cases invite and accept punishment as a means of dramatizing their opposition.[51] Whether such deliberately unlawful protest is ethical for a responsible citizen has been a topic of much soul searching.[52] Whether the civil disobedient *must* accept punishment is also a matter of disagreement. Some claim that willing acceptance of punishment is necessary to make the law violation a moral act,[53] while others argue that no punishment is due for violation of an unjust law.[54] Sometimes punishment is avoided through mass civil disobedience, in which there are so many disobedients that identification, arrest, and prosecution are not practical. But most civil disobedients believe that the evasion of punishment would erode the moral basis for civil disobedience.

Another difficulty with civil disobedience is that it may be misunderstood by the public. The object of civil disobedience is to *persuade* the public to a changed point of view through the moving spectacle of people offering themselves for punishment on a matter of conscience. If most of the public perceives civil disobedience as just another kind of crime, the educational goal is lost.

DEMONSTRATIONS AND CONFRONTATIONS

Some tactics of dissent involve transgressions of civil liberties. *Peaceful demonstrations*, with marches, speeches, placard-carrying, and peaceful picketing, are legal forms of dissent that carry no threat to anyone's civil liberties. The *disorderly demonstration*, with disruption of meetings, shouting down of speakers, possibly some jostling, and often much obscene language, is clearly an illegal violation of others' right to assemble peaceably. At Yale University in 1974, students who disliked physicist William Shockley's views on race prevented him from making a public address by hooting, stomping, and shouting.[55] In this instance, one person's right to freedom of speech and assembly is trampled as others exercise their right of dissent. Both of the above tactics are generally classified as nonviolent, but they differ considerably in their civil liberties implications. The *obstructionist demonstration,* in which demonstrators fill an area with their bodies to disrupt an activity, originated in the effort of blacks (aided by whites) to claim rights already held under law, and was therefore entirely legal in purpose although often in violation of a law whose purpose was illegal. More recently, sit-ins have been staged to support the policy demands of the demonstrators. Such acts are an illegal trespass and interfere with others' right to proceed with their activities. The *violent demonstration*, with rock throwing, trashing, burning, and looting, is clearly illegal and a serious violation of the rights and liberties of others. The question of when demonstrations are effective, when they are ethical, and what are the ethical limits of demonstrations are topics of spirited debate. In a one-month period, Amitai Etzioni counted 216 demonstrations in the United States, of which 62 percent were nonviolent, 3 percent were obstructionist, and 35 percent were violent, with the violence being started by the demonstrators in half of the violent demonstrations.[56] Although the demonstration tactic is sometimes used by teachers, social workers, doctors, and other members of the establishment, it is especially suited to use by the powerless who despair of gaining consideration for their demands in any other way. There is some research evidence that "polite" protests are more successful in attaining their goals than violent protests,[57] but it is also clear that polite protests often receive only a polite brush-off. Herbert Gans suggests, for example, that the problems of the inner city cannot be solved under majority rule, since the rest of us will never vote the necessary funds for the benefit of an inner-city minority.[58] He suggests that whenever a minority is permanently ignored, demonstrations may be expected.

The law protects the right of dissent but grants no right to violate the law in expressing dissent. The laws protecting dissent are not always fully enforced, and American history is peppered with cases of persons and groups who were denied the right to assemble peaceably and discuss unpopular ideas. Sometimes the oppressor has been a private group, breaking up a meeting or applying pressure to deny access to a meeting place. Sometimes the oppressor has been the state, harassing suspected subversives with police surveillance, physical assault, arrest and prosecution, or in other ways preventing them from assembling and speaking freely.

The situation is complicated by the fact that dissenters sometimes *do* violate the law through illegal assembly, disorderly conduct, trespass, incitement to riot, assault, malicious destruction, arson, or the like. When they are prosecuted, is it for the violation of law or for the expression of dissent? When dissenters are victims of *unequal* law enforcement, and are prosecuted for actions that do not bring prosecution when committed by others, or are punished more severely than others, then a punishment for dissent can be inferred. For example, labor organizers or voter registration workers in some towns have found it utterly impossible to drive through town without getting a traffic ticket. An experiment showed that attaching a Black Panther bumper sticker to a car greatly multiplied the driver's probabilities of arrest for traffic violation.[59] The many prosecutions of Black Panthers on various charges, followed by virtually no convictions, strongly suggest official harassment.[60] (The lack of convictions also calls into question the frequent assertion at that time that blacks could not be fairly tried in the United States.) Many radical activists have been tried on charges of criminal conspiracy, and extremely few have been convicted, again suggesting a great governmental eagerness to "get" these dissenters.[61] The right of dissent includes no right to violate the law with impunity, but it does include the right to equal punishment for law violation—a right that is sometimes denied.

The Right of Personal Autonomy

To what extent do we have the right to live our lives as we wish without interference from others? The right of personal autonomy is not unlimited, for as it has been said, my right to swing my arm ends where your nose begins. The right of personal autonomy must always be balanced against the rights of others.

THE RIGHT OF PRIVACY

Implicit in American constitutional and statute law is the principle that the citizen has a right of privacy that the state must protect and may invade only because of pressing public need. Thus, trespassing upon property, peering into people's windows, and opening their mail are criminal offenses; police may not search people's premises without a search warrant; under many circumstances, an unauthorized publication of photographs or accounts of one's private life entitles one to collect damages for invasion of privacy. These and many other legal protections are provided.

Technological change has raised many new questions about the right of privacy. Many forms of electronic eavesdropping are available. Telephone lines can be tapped; miniature microphones and transmitters can be concealed in a light fixture, a switchplate, a tie pin, a cocktail olive; a spike transmitter can be shot into an outside wall from a gun; so many forms of bugging are available that it is safe to assume that if someone wants to bug you, he or she can do so. Bugging is used by police, FBI and CIA, business executives, government agencies, labor unions, husbands and wives seeking evidence of marital misconduct, and many others. Both bugging and debugging are established specialties, and one prominent debugger estimates that at least 10,000 illegal eavesdropping gadgets are in New York City at any moment.[62]

George Orwell's chilling novel, *1984*, foresees a society in which everyone is subject to continuous electronic surveillance.[63] That this may not be entirely fanciful is suggested by the prediction of the Commission on the Year 2000 that privacy may have disappeared by that year, and that someone may make a fortune by renting out a "privacy" room by the month, day, or hour.[64]

The problem of privacy assumes new dimensions because of the computer, with its almost unlimited capacity for storage and instant retrieval of data. For example, every personal check one writes is photocopied on both sides. It is technically feasible to have a central data bank in which details of the life of each person are stored—ancestry, school records, health history, arrests and convictions, marital history, financial history, armed services records, and practically everything else.[65] Such a data bank would have a great many uses: law enforcement, detecting tax evasion, personnel evaluations, credit checks, insurance company investigations, many kinds of scientific research, and so on. But the idea of having our entire lives thus recorded is disturbing. Who would have access to this confidential data? Would an item of long-past misconduct be recorded forever or eventually expunged? If false or incorrect information were stored, how would errors be detected and corrected? Many of us have had experience with credit bureau errors or computer mis-billings, and our difficulties in correcting these make us very uneasy about the idea of a national data bank. Nonetheless, a great deal of public and private snooping is being done, and the amount is growing steadily.[66]

The problem of privacy is not easily resolved. Electronic surveillance and computer storage might prove a far more effective behavior control than the fires of Hell ever were—but at what price? Electronic technology makes possible a far more perfect tyranny than Hitler was ever able to establish. What effects will the erosion of privacy have on people's mental health?

The Privacy Act of 1974 gives citizens the right to know what information about them is on file and to whom it is available, and to make correction of errors in the file. But this applies only to files kept by federal agencies, and even then not to such agencies as the FBI and the CIA.

A value choice must be made between personal privacy and bureaucratic efficiency, between the individual's need for some sense of privacy and the state's need to maintain law and order. This will be a perplexing problem that can never be solved to everyone's satisfaction.

THE RIGHT TO CHOOSE A LIFESTYLE

The idea of human dignity includes the right to freedom of choice in a wide range of life activities, limited, as always, by others' claim to the same right.

Thus, my right to carouse at midnight, to discharge firearms, or to drive while intoxicated is limited by others' right to sleep and stay alive. One's right to choose a lifestyle is also limited by the tolerance level of the community. Men with long hair and beards are far more acceptable today than a few years ago, and the choice of the gay life may carry fewer penalties in San Francisco than in Upper Sandusky, Ohio.

How great a freedom of choice of lifestyle should a society offer? Most societies have restricted people's choices far beyond any rational need to protect the rights or welfare of others. It is difficult to see how unisex clothing and obscene language carry any real threat to the health or safety of other people. It is esthetic ethnocentrism, not any rational hazard, that explains the penalties sometimes imposed for these "offenses." But how about hard drugs, free love, consenting adult homosexuality, or abortion on de-

Freedom of movement both within and outside the United States is a right which is often taken for granted.
(Irene Springer)

mand? Whether these are harmless to society is a matter of bitter public debate. The present trend is to decriminalize the "crimes without victims" and to widen the range of legally and socially allowable behavior. A generation ago, a faculty member "living in sin" faced instant dismissal from most universities; today one or more can be found in nearly every large department. But how far should the right to control one's body extend?[67] Suppose a small boy shows "feminine" characteristics and seems destined for homosexuality. Should one engage psychiatrists to cure his deviation from the norm, or would this be a denial of his right to choose his lifestyle?[68]

There is general agreement that one has no right to injure others; disagreement arises over what actions *do* injure others. Is the private ownership of handguns a constitutional right, or a danger to others that outweighs any possible benefits? Does one have the right to injure oneself? Does one have an unlimited right to smoke, eat, and drink too much, or to use drugs?[69] If I deliberately choose a high-risk lifestyle, and cripple myself, have I a right to food, housing, and expensive medical care at taxpayers' expense for the rest of my life? Should motorcyclists be required to wear helmets, motorists to wear seatbelts, or school children to have vaccinations? Again, the current tendency is to enlarge one's right to select a preferred mode of suicide in some respects, while narrowing it in others.

The right to select one's lifestyle does not, of course, include the right to demand that others approve the choice. My right to extend or to withhold my approval of the behavior of others is a right most people would concede. Those who make choices that outrage the moral or esthetic sensibilities of others must expect disapproval and social ostracism from those whom the choices outrage.

FREEDOM OF MOVEMENT

Americans take for granted the right to travel at will within the United States, to leave and re-enter the country, and to migrate freely to just about any country willing to accept them.[70] These rights are far from universal. At least a third of the world's people live in national prisons from which they can escape only in a hail of gunfire. In communist lands, even the *desire* to migrate is disloyal and treasonous, to be punished by instant loss of employment and other civil rights; or one may be permitted to travel abroad and then denied re-entry.

The right to travel has not always been observed in the United States. Indians were long confined to the reservations, and after the abolition of slavery blacks who wished to go north sometimes found it difficult to buy train tickets. During the 1950s a number of suspected subversives or security risks were denied passports until the Supreme Court finally instructed the State Department to cease applying political tests to the right to travel.[71] Sometimes Americans have been forbidden to travel to "unfriendly" countries, such as Red China or Cuba. The rationale is that the United States cannot provide services or protection to American tourists in countries with whom we do not have orderly diplomatic relations. There is a suspicion, however, that such travel restrictions were primarily a tactic in the cold war, with tourist safety more a pretext than a real reason. Again the issue is drawn—the right of the citizen to travel versus the right of the government to use the citizen as a pawn in international politics.

The Rights of the Helpless

There are a number of categories of people whose civil rights have been suspended or are otherwise unavailable to them. Prisoners suffer a loss of civil rights as part of their punishment. Recently the question has arisen whether prisoners, while in prison, may form political organizations, join labor unions, and receive normal rates of pay from prison labor. Would a strike by prison laborers be legitimate, or a form of punishable misconduct? As of this moment, the issue is unsettled.

Persons committed to mental hospitals also suffer a loss of civil rights. Children lack the civil rights of adults.[72] Juvenile courts were established as a therapeutic substitute for the adult court, to shift emphasis from determining guilt to finding helpful treatment for youths in trouble. Recently this concept has been attacked as unjust, and an effort is being made to give juveniles the legal rights of adult accused. Some see this as a step toward equal justice; others see it as a step backward into preoccupation with guilt and conviction procedures, and away from intelligent guidance. Similarly, behavior modification techniques appear to be successful with many mental patients and prisoners, but are under attack for violating the patients' or prisoners' rights since they must do what the therapist demands in order to get the rewards.[73] In all the above cases therapy and civil rights are in conflict, for the most effective therapy calls for some denial of the rights enjoyed by healthy, noncriminal adults.

The aged and the poor often are unable to claim their legal rights, because of ignorance, limited resources, and possibly intimidation. The legal services program of the Office of Economic Opportunity filed many class action suits intended to strengthen the poor in dealing with welfare agencies and business concerns. Because these test cases were often successful, the program aroused intense enmity and was soon discontinued.[74] The question of what rights each of these categories of the helpless should have will not easily be settled.

The Right to Demand Services

Most of the foregoing civil rights and liberties consist basically of the right to be let alone. They are rights of noninterference from the state or others. Another order of civil rights consists of rights to demand services for which others must foot the bill. These are "freedoms for," not "freedoms from." No such rights were stated in the Constitution; they developed later, justified by the "general welfare" clause.

For over a century each person has had the right to use public roads and public schools without paying any fees or charges for their use. In the 1930s the right to a minimum subsistence became recognized, and the welfare system developed. Within the past decade a right to medical care has been gaining recognition. Each of these changes has come after bitter debate and prolonged struggle. Some countries recognize a right to a far more extensive range of services and benefits than the United States. Whether or how far to extend them, and how to operate them, is a prime political issue in the United States.

Is there a right to equality in income and social status? Marxist and some other social critics argue that *any* substantial variations in income violate the principle of equal rights, and that all status inequalities ("elitism") should be cut to the bare minimum. To such critics most of this chapter has been irrelevant and trivial, for they view economic equality as the paramount civil right, with all others either secondary or unimportant.

It is difficult to predict how far we shall pursue the idea of economic equality. The principle that a democratic government may tax some people for the benefit of others is already firmly established. But there is considerable taxpayer resistance, and cutbacks in welfare programs always have broad popular support. Whether the idea of a serious attempt at economic equality will gain majority support is doubtful. *Equality of opportunity* is widely accepted as a desirable ideal. Is *equality of reward* a desirable goal? An attainable goal? Even a revolution may not answer these questions. Equality of reward has been sought many times in history, and never achieved for more than a moment or in small groups. Does this mean that it never will or can be?

The Social-Disorganization Approach

Like godliness and chastity, the right of civil liberties in the United States has been a value approved in theory but often ignored in practice. Throughout our history, legal and extralegal penalties have been exacted from the dissenter and the nonconformist. Although it is inconsistent with the ideal of civil liberty, vigilante action against nonconformists has been an integral part of the *organization* of American society.[75] Suppression of civil liberties, therefore, cannot be accurately described as disorganization.

But the disorganization of any aspect of the culture arouses anxieties, jeopardizes vested interests, inspires the questioning of established institutions, and stimulates many a forceful effort to silence these questionings and protect the status quo. Periods of disturbing change normally bring a crisis in civil liberties, whereas periods of relative cultural stability show fewer suppressions of liberty.

Changing technology, too, creates civil liberties problems. Electronic surveillance is widely possible. The portability of atomic weapons components or of biological warfare materials multiplies the potential destructiveness of the spy or saboteur, stimulating increased security precautions. Are the right of privacy and the right to travel hazards that our advanced society cannot permit? Is the regimentation of the anthill the price we must pay for the scientific marvels of the future?

The Value-Conflict Approach

The term *subversion* implies a value conflict. If all people shared the same values there could be no subversion. But people differ in the values they wish to preserve and in the means they think proper for preserving them. As indicated earlier, some wish to check communism while promoting liberalism, some wish to check both communism and liberalism, and some wish to promote communism while confusing and paralyzing liberalism. Some believe in civil liberties; some do not. At one extreme are those who follow Justice Oliver Wendell Holmes's "clear and present danger" doctrine[76]—that we should allow any *ideas* to be expressed and advocated, however repugnant, so long as there is no "clear and present danger" that violence will result. These people may join the American Civil Liberties Union and defend the right of all Americans, even those they despise, to express any views, even those they detest. At the opposite extreme are those who believe that only the "right" ideas are entitled to freedom of expression. When Russia's Andrei Vishinsky writes, "In our state, naturally, there can be no place for freedom of speech, press, and so on for the foes of socialism,"[77] many Americans need change only the last word to be in complete agreement. Between these two extremes fall many people with a vague general belief in civil liberties as an abstract ideal, but a willingness to curtail liberties whenever their own values are threatened.

The Personal-Deviation Approach

Extremists are deviants, for they reject the established order in favor of a wholesale change in the value system of the society. Does this deviation spring from a superior perceptive ability, or does it arise through a displacement of their emotional hostilities and frustrations?

There is considerable support for the idea that political extremism is a pathological emotional disturbance. Many extremists show a fanatical preoccupation with their cause; a suspicious distrust of other people in general; a lack of interest in normal pursuits, recreations, and small talk; and a strong tendency to divide other people into enemies and allies.[78] These are symptoms of an unhappy, neurotic personality. Morris Ernst and David Loth's study of American excommunists[79] finds that most of them were young people who were not yet settled in adult life, from comfortable but unhappy homes, intelligent and well-educated, but frequently unpopular people who had never really "belonged" until they found the Communist Party. Most suffered strong feelings of personal inadequacy and harbored hostilities or resentments against domineering parents. Many of the rank and file were idealistic, self-sacrificing, submissive, and unselfish. The total picture is that of unhappy, insecure persons who need a cause in which to lose themselves and from which to gain a sense of personal worth. The members were not much changed by their experience, retaining more or less the same personalities they possessed before and during their membership. In contrast to the idealistic young short-term communists studied by

Ernst and Loth, studies of hard-core party professionals by Gabriel Almond and Frank Meyer found them to be cynical, ruthless, and opportunistic.[80]

It has been difficult to conduct reliable personality studies of student radicals and black militants, who strongly resist any research that looks for the causes of social protest within the personalities of the protesters. Yet considerable research of this type has been done,[81] with disagreements so great that no typical profile can be drawn. And not all scholars agree that extremism is a pathological disorder. Some feel that extremism may be a normative response to rapid social change.[82] The association between extremism and psychopathology may vary according to the time and place setting. During a period of cultural stability and limited social change, it is most likely to be the emotionally disturbed who support radical extremism. But during a period of rapid social change when major value shifts are under way, many moderates may support radical causes. Thus the American Revolution had the support, not only of perennial malcontents like Tom Paine and Patrick Henry, but also of solid establishment types like George Washington, Alexander Hamilton, John Adams, Gouverneur Morris, and scores of others. Are we in such a period today, when emotionally secure and socially well adjusted persons will increasingly find that only the extremist answers make sense? Only time will tell.

There is another respect in which personal deviation is involved in civil liberties issues. Each of the many extensions of civil liberties and civil rights has been a deviation from traditional norms. Those who promoted those deviations were therefore deviant. Those who first promoted the right of children to free public education and the right of women to vote were subjected to much abuse and punishment, but are today revered as heroes and heroines. In time, those who promote the rights to birth control, abortion on demand, and voluntary euthanasia may also be revered. Without the action of a number of deviant crusaders, some of them rather unpleasant fanatics, our present range of rights and liberties would be less extensive. Among the present agitators seeking to extend our rights into areas not presently recognized—euthanasia, drug use, economic equality, status equality—only time will tell which will gain recognition as dangerous eccentrics or as cultural heroes and heroines.

Prospects

Human freedom is a world problem, not just an American problem. In much of the world the idea that the individual has rights that all should respect is utterly incomprehensible.[83] And many of the most severe critics of American imperfections are highly selective in their ability to recognize oppression elsewhere. In earlier years the United Nations Human Rights Commission was highly respected, but today a majority of its 32 member states are communist and third-world nations that are among the greatest violators of human rights. While trumpeting charges (sometimes valid) of human rights violations in the United States, the Union of South Africa, or Chile, the commission steadfastly refuses to investigate charges of human rights violations in communist and Third-World countries.[84] Until the composition of the United Nations Human Rights Commission is changed, not much progress can be expected.

Summary

The "American heritage of liberty" is made up of ideals that have never been fully realized. The implicit social contract in which the majority agrees not to persecute minorities and the minorities agree not to practice revolution has often been violated by both sides. *Political extremists*—the old left, the new left, and the radical right—disagree on goals but show considerable similarity in outlook and tactics. All are grave threats to civil liberties, which are always suppressed when extremists gain power.

Most societies recognize a *right to property,* but only within the limits defined by each society. *The right of dissent* grants certain rights of protest, but not the right to violate the law. *Civil disobedience* violates the law openly and generally accepts punishment as a means of dramatizing a protest. It gradually shades into *demonstration* and *confrontation,* which attempt to gain a goal through disrupting the activities of others. The *right to personal autonomy* includes the citizen's right to privacy, to choose a lifestyle and possibly even to injure himself, and freedom of movement; yet as with all rights, the allowable limits of the right to personal autonomy are in dispute. The rights of the helpless are a relatively recent concern, and sometimes rights are claimed that interfere with therapeutic goals. The right to demand services is another relatively recent concept whose boundaries are a major political issue. No right or liberty is absolute; all must be limited so that other persons' rights and liberties may be preserved. One person's freedom conflicts with the freedom of another, while freedom and equality are not fully compatible. The boundaries of the necessary compromises make the maintenance of civil rights and civil liberties a process of continual accommodation.

The social-disorganization approach notes that denials of liberty have been part of the organization of society, and that social change constantly disrupts existing accommodations. The value-conflict approach notes how value conflicts create civil liberties issues, especially between those who trust the people to make democratic choices and those who claim the right to impose choices on the people. The personal-deviation approach notes that many civil liberties issues arise as deviants propose new definitions that others oppose, and as extremists of the left or the right seek to impose their decisions on the society at the expense of a surrender of civil liberties. The content of recognized rights and liberties continues to change, and debates over their limits will be unending.

Suggested Readings

AMERICAN CIVIL LIBERTIES UNION, *Annual Report* (New York: ACLU, published yearly). A survey of the state of civil liberties in the United States, as seen by the American Civil Liberties Union.

BLOCH, SIDNEY, and PETER REDDAWAY, *Psychiatric Terror* (New York: Basic Books, 1977). Tells how dissenters in the Soviet Union are punished by commitment to psychiatric hospitals.

"THE COMPARATIVE STUDY OF FREEDOM," published annually in the Jan./Feb. issue of *Freedom at Issue,* publication of Freedom House, 20 West 40th St., New York 10018.

DORSEN, NORMAN, ed., *The Rights of Americans: What They Are—What They Should Be* (New York: Random House, 1971). The historical background and legal basis for each of our rights and liberties.

DOUGLAS, WILLIAM O., *An Almanac of Liberty* (Garden City, N.Y.: Doubleday, 1954). An almanac listing 365 incidents in the historic struggle for human liberty.

EBENSTEIN, WILLIAM, and E. FOGELMAN, *Today's Isms,* 8th ed. (Englewood Cliffs, N.J.: Prentice-Hall, 1980). A concise description and analysis of communism, fascism, capitalism, and socialism.

GERSHMAN, CARL, "New Left–New Face," *Freedom at Issue,* Mar./Apr. 1979, pp. 3–5; reprinted in *Current,* May 1979, pp. 23–28. A report on the current state of the new left.

GOLD, ALICE ROSS, et al., *Fists and Flowers: A Social Psychological Interpretation of Student Dissent* (New York: Academic Press, 1976). A detailed empirical study of student radicalism.

HARRIS, RICHARD, *Freedom Spent* (Boston: Little, Brown, 1976). Accounts of several recent victims of denial of civil liberty in the United States.

HOFSTADTER, RICHARD, and MICHAEL WALLACE, eds., *American Violence: A Documentary History* (New York: Alfred A. Knopf, 1970). Original documents describing many violent episodes in American history.

NUNN, CLYDE Z., HARRY J. CROCKETT, JR., and A. ALLEN WILLIAMS, JR., *Tolerance for Nonconformity* (San Francisco: Jossey-Bass, 1978). A replication of Stouffer's 1954 study of the degree of tolerance in American society.

SMITH, ROBERT ELLIS, *Privacy—How to Protect What's Left of It* (Garden City, N.Y.: Doubleday, 1979). A handbook on protection of privacy.

Society, Mar./Apr. 1976. Issue devoted to civil liberties issues.

TRAUB, JAMES, "The Privacy Snatchers," *Saturday Review,* 21 July 1979, pp. 16–20; reprinted in *Current,* Oct. 1979, pp. 9–18. How use of new technologies is destroying our privacy.

Footnotes

[1]From *South China Morning Post* (Hong Kong), 18 Oct. 1979, p. 1.

[2]Raymond D. Gastil, "The Comparative Study of Freedom–X," *Freedom at Issue,* no. 54, Jan./Feb. 1980, pp. 3–15.

[3]See Milton Mayer and Mortimer J. Adler, eds., *The Tradition of Freedom* (New York: Oceana, 1958), for selections from the writers who shaped American concepts of freedom and justice.

[4]The F.A.L.N., a Puerto Rican independence terrorist group, is an example. Puerto Ricans benefit economically from their ties with the U.S., and the independence movement cannot gain mass support. F.A.L.N. terrorist acts, from the attempted assassination of President Truman in 1952, through 100 bombings in the past five years, are the desperate attempts of an unsuccessful movement to gain attention. See *New York Times,* 16 Mar. 1980, pp. 1ff., 29.

[5]Leonard W. May, *Legacy of Suppression: Freedom of Speech and Press in Early American History* (Cambridge, Mass.: Harvard University Press, 1960); Hugh Davis Graham and Ted Robert Gurr, eds., *The History of Violence in America: Historical and Comparative Perspectives* (New York: Praeger, 1969); Richard Hofstadter and Michael Wallace, *American Violence: A Documentary History* (New York: Alfred A. Knopf, 1970).

[6]See John Higham, *Strangers in the Land: Patterns of American Nativism* (Brunswick, N.J.: Rutgers University Press, 1955), for accounts of persecutions of foreigners, Catholics, Jews, and other groups in America.

[7]Hofstadter and Wallace, *American Violence,* pp. 76–79.

[8]Robert K. Murray, *Red Scare: A Study in National Hysteria, 1919–1920* (Minneapolis: University of Minnesota Press, 1955); William Preston, *Aliens and Dissenters* (Cambridge, Mass.: Harvard University Press, 1963), ch. 8.

[9]Not to be confused with former Minnesota Senator Eugene McCarthy. For critical appraisals of Senator Joseph McCarthy, see Richard H. Rovere, *Senator Joseph McCarthy* (New York: Harcourt,

Brace & World, 1959); Seymour Martin Lipset and Earl Raab, *The Politics of Unreason* (New York: Harper & Row, 1970), ch. 6. For favorable appraisals, see William F. Buckley, *McCarthy and His Enemies* (Chicago: Henry Regnery, 1954); and Roy Cohn, *McCarthy* (New York: New American Library, 1968).

[10]See "Congressional Investigations," *University of Pennsylvania Law Review,* 106 (Nov. 1957), 124–27; Lillian Hellman, *Scoundrel Time* (Boston: Little, Brown, 1976).

[11]Association of the Bar of the City of New York, *The Federal Loyalty-Security Program* (New York: Dodd, Mead, 1956); O. Edmund Clubb, *The Witness and I* (New York: Columbia University Press, 1977).

[12]John Cogley, *A Report on Blacklisting: Vol. I, Movies; Vol. II, Radio-Television* (New York: Fund for the Republic, 1956).

[13]For example, China's rapid development of nuclear bombs was aided by several dozen Chinese scientists who were deported or hounded out of the United States during the communist witch-hunt. See William L. Ryan and Sam Summerlin, *The China Cloud: America's Tragic Blunder and China's Rise to Nuclear Power* (Boston: Little, Brown, 1967). The costly and unsuccessful war in Vietnam was, at least in part, a legacy of the communist hysteria. After President Franklin Roosevelt abandoned the hopeless effort to support the Chinese Nationalist Government of Chiang Kai-shek, he was denounced endlessly for "giving China to the communists." No president wanted to be charged with "giving Vietnam to the communists," so each made increasing commitments in Vietnam in what is now seen as a series of disastrous miscalculations. For an account, see David Halberstam, *The Best and the Brightest* (New York: Random House, 1972).

[14]"Taking Liberty," *Time,* 17 Dec. 1979, p. 35.

[15]Monica Blumenthal et al., *Justifying Violence: Attitudes of American Men* (Ann Arbor: Institute for Social Research, University of Michigan, 1972), p. 243.

[16]James A. Michener, *Kent State: What Happened and Why* (New York: Random House, 1971).

[17]Samuel A. Stouffer, *Communism, Conformity, and Civil Liberties* (Garden City, N.Y., Doubleday and Co., 1955).

[18]Clyde Z. Nunn, Harry J. Crockett, Jr., and J. Allen Williams, Jr., *Tolerance for Nonconformity* (San Francisco: Jossey-Bass, 1978).

[19]Giovanni Baldelli, *Social Anarchism* (Chicago: Aldine-Atherton, 1971); Gerald Runkle, *Anarchism: Old and New* (New York: Delacorte, 1972); Terry Michael Perlin, *Contemporary Anarchism* (New Brunswick, N.J.: Transaction Books, 1978).

[20]See Karl Marx and Friedrich Engels, *The Communist Manifesto,* first published in 1848 and available in many editions, for a concise statement of classic communist ideology. See Nikolai Lenin, *The State and Revolution* (New York: Vanguard, 1927), for a statement of communist technique of revolutionary action. For competent descriptions of contemporary communism, see Lyman T. Sargent, *Contemporary Political Ideologies* (Homewood, Ill.: Dorsey, 1975); and William Ebenstein and E. Fogelman, *Today's Isms,* 8th ed. (Englewood Cliffs, N.J.: Prentice-Hall, 1980).

[21]See Sargent, *Contemporary Political Ideologies;* Ebenstein and Fogelman, *Today's Isms.*

[22]Quoted in *South China Morning Post* (Hong Kong), 18 Oct. 1979, p. 9.

[23]See "Deathwatch: Cambodia," *Time,* 12 Nov. 1979, pp. 42–48; Sydney Schanberg, "The Death and Life of Dith Pran," *New York Times Magazine,* 20 Jan. 1980, pp. 16ff.

[24]American radicals consider that the brutalities and economic inefficiencies of the Soviet Union and her client states cast no reflection on socialism, because Russia is "not truly socialist." This is a handy excuse for the sins of any system. (For example, American militarism does not discredit Christianity, because the United States is not truly Christian; American social ills do not discredit capitalism, because the United States is not truly capitalist.)

[25]See Armand L. Mauss, "Lost Promise of Reconciliation: New Left vs. Old Left," *Journal of Social Issues,* 27, no. 1 (1970), 6–7.

[26]Runkle, *Anarchism,* ch. 8.

[27]"Participatory democracy" is the idea that each person should have the right to participate personally and directly in all decisions that affect him, somewhat in the manner of the New England town meeting. It is distinguished from "representative democracy," in which one participates through elected representatives. In a large society operating as a participatory democracy, small communitarian groups would be linked into a national network of cooperating groups. See C. George Benello and Dimitrios Roussopoulos, *The Case for*

Participatory Democracy (New York: Grossman, 1971); and Lyman T. Sargent, *New Left Thought* (Homewood, Ill.: Dorsey Press, 1972), ch. 6.

[28]See Howard Sherman, *Radical Political Economy* (New York: Basic Books, 1972); and Michael Hudson, *Super Imperialism: The Economic Strategy of American Empire* (New York: Holt, Rinehart and Winston, 1972), for highly scholarly presentations of these views. For opposing views, see Assar Lindbeck, *The Political Economy of the New Left* (New York: Harper & Row, 1971).

[29]Joseph Lelyveld, "The Story of a Soldier Who Refused to Fire at Songmy," *New York Times Magazine,* 14 Dec. 1969, pp. 32ff.

[30]Michael Useem, "Ideological and Interpersonal Change in the Radical Protest Movement," *Social Problems,* 19 (Spring 1972), 451–69.

[31]Gilbert Abcarian, "Romantics and Renegades: Political Disaffiliation and the Radical Left," *Journal of Social Issues,* 27, no. 1 (1971), 123–29. For a sympathetic presentation of the new left, see Christopher Bone, *The Disinherited Children* (New York: Wiley, 1977). For a critique, see Phillip Abbott Luce, *The New Left Today: America's Trojan Horse* (Washington, D.C.: Capitol Hill Press, 1971).

[32]George R. Vickers, *The Formation of the New Left* (Lexington, Mass.: Lexington Books, 1975).

[33]Philip G. Allback, *Student Politics in America: A Historical Analysis* (New York: McGraw-Hill, 1974); Edward E. Ericson, Jr., *Radicals in the University* (Stanford, Ca.: Hoover Institution Press, 1975); Seymour M. Lipset, *Rebellion in the University* (Chicago: University of Chicago Press, 1976).

[34]"New American Statement," *Current,* Jan. 1972, pp. 22–24; Margie Casady, "The Storm of the '60s: Where Have the Radicals Gone?" *Psychology Today,* Oct. 1975, pp. 62–65; Carl Gershman, "New Left–New Face," *Freedom at Issue,* Mar./Apr. 1979, pp. 3–5, reprinted in *Current,* May 1979, pp. 23–28.

[35]"The Cooling Campus," *Science News,* 111 (22 Jan. 1977), p. 58.

[36]*First National Directory of Rightist Groups, Publications, and Some Individuals* (Sausalito, Ca.: Noontide Press, 1962). This is now outdated, but apparently it has not been revised.

[37]Robert Welch, *The Blue Book of the John Birch Society* (Belmont, Mass.: Author, 1961); J. Allen Broyles, "The John Birch Society: A Movement of Social Protest of the Radical Right," *Journal of Social Issues,* 19 (Apr. 1963), 51–62; Lipset and Raab, *The Politics of Unreason,* chs. 8 and 9.

[38]Daniel Bell, ed., *The Radical Right* (New York: Doubleday/Anchor, 1964); Scott G. McNall, *Career of a Radical Rightist: A Study in Failure* (Port Washington, N.Y.: Kennikat, 1975).

[39]For analyses of fascism, see S. J. Woolf, *European Fascism* (New York: Random House, 1968); Karl Dietrich Bracher, *The German Dictatorship* (New York: Praeger, 1971); Renzo DeFelice, *Fascism: An Informal Introduction to Its Theory and Practice* (New Brunswick, N.J.: Transaction Books, 1976); and George L. Mosse, *Nazism: A Historical and Comparative Analysis of National Socialism* (New Brunswick, N.J.: Transaction Books, 1977).

[40]Seymour Topping, "China's Long March into the Future," *New York Times Magazine,* 3 Feb. 1980, pp. 29ff.

[41]For an analysis of similarities between right and left extremism, see Walter B. Mead, *Extremism and Cognition: Styles of Irresponsibility in American Society* (Dubuque, Iowa: Kendall/Hunt, 1971; David R. Schweitzer and James M. Elden, "New Left as Right; Convergent Themes of Political Discontent," *Journal of Social Issues,* 27, no. 2 (1971), 141–66; H. Clayton Waddell, "Common Features of Extremism's Ugly Faces," in Elmer West, Jr., *Extremism: Left and Right* (Grand Rapids, Mich.: Wm. B. Eerdmans, 1972), ch. 2.

[42]David Horowitz, "A Radical's Disenchantment," *Nation,* 229 (8 Dec. 1979), 587.

[43]A recent example of this double standard in operation appeared after folk singer Joan Baez, an anti-Vietnam War activist, published an open letter denouncing the new socialist government of Vietnam for its wholesale arrest and torture of political prisoners. (*New York Times,* 20 May 1979, p. 15.) To this, William Kuntzler, a leftist attorney, objected, saying, "I do not believe in public attacks on socialist countries, even where violations of human rights may occur." (*Time,* 11 June 1979, p. 21.)

[44]Walter LaQueur, "A Look Back at the Weimar Republic—The Cry Was 'Down with the System,' " *New York Times Magazine,* 16 Aug. 1970, pp. 12ff.

[45]See Nathaniel L. Nathanson, "The Right of Association," in Norman Dor-

sen, ed., *The Rights of Americans: What They Are—What They Should Be* (New York: Random House, 1971), pp. 231–51.

[46]Thomas I. Emerson, "The Right to Protest," in Dorsen, *The Rights of Americans,* pp. 218–30.

[47]See Carlos Ripoll, "Dissent in Cuba," *New York Times Book Review,* 11 Nov. 1979, pp. 1ff.

[48]Craig L. Whitney, "Exile for Sakharovs Chills Soviet Dissident Movement," *New York Times,* 27 Jan. 1980, sec. 4, p. 2.

[49]Sidney Bloch and Peter Reddaway, *Psychiatric Terror* (New York: Basic Books, 1977).

[50]Kenneth LaMott, "The Mao Solution," *Human Behavior,* Aug. 1977, pp. 20ff.

[51]See Gene Sharp, *The Politics of Nonviolent Action* (Boston: Porter Sargent, 1973).

[52]Carl Cohen, *Civil Disobedience: Conscience, Tactics, and the Law* (New York: Columbia University Press, 1971); William Sloane Coffin, Jr., and Morris I. Liebman, *Civil Disobedience: Aid or Hindrance to Justice* (Washington, D.C.: American Enterprise Institute for Public Policy Research, 1972).

[53]Cohen, *Civil Disobedience,* ch. 4.

[54]Howard Zinn, *Disobedience and Democracy* (New York: Random House, 1968), pp. 27–31.

[55]See "Free Speech at Yale," *Time,* 3 Feb. 1975, p. 6; "Freedom of Expression at Yale," *AAUP Bulletin,* 62 (Spring 1976), 28–42.

[56]Amitai Etzioni, *Demonstration Democracy* (New York: Gordon & Breach, 1970), pp. 8–9.

[57]Paul D. Schumaker, "Policy Responsiveness to Protest-Group Demands," *Journal of Politics,* 37 (May 1975), 488–521.

[58]Herbert J. Gans, "We Won't End the Urban Crisis until We End 'Majority Rule,'" *New York Times Magazine,* 3 Aug. 1969, pp. 12ff.

[59]F. K. Huessenstamm, "Bumper Stickers and the Cops," *Trans-action,* Feb. 1971, pp. 32–34.

[60]See Murray Kempton, *The Brier Patch* (New York: E. P. Dutton, 1973).

[61]See Murray Kempton, *Trials of the Resistance* (New York: Random House, 1970); Russell Baker, "The Injustice Department," *New York Times Magazine,* 23 Sept. 1973, p. 4.

[62]Bill Surface, "Keen Private Eye," *New York Times Magazine,* 11 Dec. 1966, pp. 121ff.

[63]George Orwell, *1984* (New York: Harcourt, Brace & World, 1949).

[64]Harry Kalven, Jr., "The Problem of Privacy in the Year 2000," *Daedalus,* 96 (Summer 1967), 876–82.

[65]James Martin and Adrian R. D. Norman, *The Computerized Society* (Englewood Cliffs, N.J.: Prentice-Hall, 1970).

[66]George W. Bailey, *Privacy* (Atlantic Highlands, N.J.: Humanities Press, 1979); David M. O'Brian, *Privacy, Law and Public Policy* (New York: Praeger, 1979); Robert Ellis Smith, *Privacy—How to Protect What's Left of It* (Garden City, N.Y.: Doubleday, 1979).

[67]Charles Lister, "The Right to Control the Use of One's Body," in Dorsen, *The Rights of Americans,* pp. 348–64.

[68]See Nicholas N. Kittrie, *The Right to Be Different: Deviance and Enforced Therapy* (Baltimore: Johns Hopkins Press, 1971); and Wayne Sage, "The Case of the Deviant Gender," *Human Behavior,* Sept. 1973, pp. 58ff.

[69]See Peter Barton Hutt, "The Right to Use Alcohol and Drugs," in Dorsen, *The Rights of Americans,* pp. 365–80.

[70]See Leonard B. Boudin, "The Right to Travel," in Dorsen, *The Rights of Americans,* pp. 381–98.

[71]Ibid., p. 390.

[72]Henry H. Foster, Jr., *A "Bill of Rights" for Children* (Springfield, Ill.: Charles C Thomas, 1974); Beatrice Gross and Ronald Gross, *The Children's Rights Movement* (New York: Doubleday/Anchor, 1977).

[73]Sharland Trotter and Jim Warren, "The Carrot, the Stick, and the Prisoner," *Science News,* 105 (16 Mar. 1974), 180–82; Peter L. Berwick and Larry A. Morris, "Token Economies: Are They Doomed?" *Professional Psychology,* 5 (Nov. 1974), 434–39.

[74]See "Public Corporation for Poverty Lawyers: Legal Services Program," *Business Week,* 15 May 1971, p. 52; "Why the Furor over Government Lawyers for Poor: Legal Services Program," *U.S. News and World Report,* 29 Jan. 1973, pp. 46–48.

[75]John W. Caughy, *Their Majesties the Mob: The Vigilante Impulse in America* (Chicago: University of Chicago Press, 1960); Richard Maxwell Brown, "The American Vigilante Tradition," in National Commission on the Causes and Prevention of Violence in America, *Violence in America* (Washington, D.C., 1969), ch. 5.

[76]Mr. Justice Holmes stated, and the full Supreme Court accepted the principle, that "The question in every case is whether the words used are used in such

circumstances and are of such a nature as to create a clear and present danger that will bring about the substantive evils that [the State] has a right to prevent." (*Schenck* v. *United States*, 249 U.S. 47, 52.)

[77]In *The Law of the Soviet Union*, 1948; quoted in John C. Wahlke, ed., *Loyalty in a Democratic State* (Boston: D. C. Heath, 1952), p. 45.

[78]See Elton Mayo, "Routine Interaction and the Problem of Collaboration," *American Sociological Review*, 41 (June 1939), 335–40; C. S. Blumel, *War, Politics, and Insanity* (Denver: World Press, 1950); Eric Hoffer, *The True Believer* (New York: Harper & Row, 1951).

[79]Morris Ernst and David Loth, *Report on the American Communist* (New York: Putnam, 1962), especially pp. 1–5.

[80]Gabriel A. Almond et al., *The Appeals of Communism* (Princeton, N.J.: Princeton University Press, 1954), based on intimate studies of 221 former American, British, French, and Italian communists; Frank S. Meyer, *Moulding of Communists: The Training of the Communist Cadre* (New York: Harcourt, Brace & World, 1961).

[81]For example, Kenneth Keniston, *Radicals and Militants: An Annotated Bibliography of Empirical Research on Campus Unrest* (Lexington, Mass.: Lexington Books, 1973); Alice Ross Gold et al., *Fists and Flowers: A Social Psychological Interpretation of Student Dissent* (New York: Academic Press, 1976).

[82]Dean S. Dorn and Gary L. Long, "Sociology and the Radical Right: A Critical Analysis," *American Sociologist*, May 1972, pp. 8–9; Christopher Bone, *The Disinherited Children*.

[83]See Ronald F. Bunn and William C. Andrews, eds., *Politics and Civil Liberties in Europe* (New York: Van Nostrand, 1967); Louis M. Colonese, *Human Rights and the Liberation of Man in the Americas* (South Bend, Ind.: University of Notre Dame Press, 1970); Susan Jacoby and Andrei Amalrik, "Rebel: The Cost of Dissent in Russia," *New York Times Magazine*, 29 July 1973, pp. 12ff.; and "The Dissidents v. Moscow," *Time*, 21 Feb. 1977, pp. 20–30.

[84]Daniel P. Moynihan, "The Politics of Human Rights," *Commentary*, 64 (Aug. 1977), 19–26.

Irene Springer

ENVIRONMENT AND SOCIAL POLICY

19

It is now generally agreed that the prevalent scrub vegetation of the Levantine highlands is the degraded remnant of an original cover of forest. Evidence of the degree and extent of the transformation has been accumulated by botanists, geographers, and other scholars in many parts of this complex realm. But the contrast between ancient and modern conditions is perhaps most strikingly evident on the humid, western versant of Mount Lebanon. From the earliest Egyptian and Mesopotamian documents (ca. 2600 B.C.) until the reign of Emperor Hadrian (A.D. 117–138) this area was known for its valuable timber. Today much of it is as barren as the mountains of the Sahara. Only scattered remnants survive of the once extensive stands of cedar, fir, and juniper, and most of the oak forests have been reduced to scrub. What did Mount Lebanon look like in prehistoric time, and how and why was its vegetation so greatly modified? To answer these questions, even tentatively, is to come to grips with processes that offer unrivaled evidence of man's ability to transform nature.[1]

An estuarine wetland can produce up to 242 pounds of food per acre per day all year long—all this, of course, without benefit of human labor. There isn't a farm in the world that can come near to such production. If the food were the kind that humans could consume directly without first letting it work its way up the food chain to the seafood that we eat, no one would have ever filled in or dredged a wetland.[2]

Gazing at the soaring columns of the ruined Temple of Poseidon, high on a point overlooking the sea approaches to Athens, and then peering across the surrounding arid, barren hills, the tourist may wonder, "How did such a harsh, barren land cradle the brilliant civilization of ancient Greece?" The answer is, It didn't! When Solomon imported the cedars of Lebanon for his temple, when Pericles was erecting the Parthenon, and when Alexander was scattering Greek cities across the ancient world, the lands bordering the Mediterranean were well watered, heavily forested, and far more fertile than they are today. Deforestation and centuries of land erosion have denuded the countryside of much of its vegetation, raised the average temperature, and reduced the annual rainfall, transforming most of the land into semiarid wasteland—beautiful to visit, but a wretched place to wrest a living from the land.

One of the most persistent myths of the modern sentimentalist is that ancient and primitive peoples somehow understood nature and lived in harmony with the land, while only modern people are heedlessly destructive. For example, Ashley Montagu writes,

> Just as the Wintu will use only dead wood, out of courtesy and respect for the living wood, most food-gathering and hunting people respect the land on which they live. Therefore they take only what they need to live on, and then, before they take too much to prevent natural restoration, they move on.[3]

A less sentimental observer might suspect that the Wintu burned dead wood because it burns more easily than green wood and moved on whenever game became hard to find. In contrast to such romanticizing is the fact that the slash-and-burn agriculture used widely throughout history is exceedingly destructive.[4] It is likely that ancient peoples hunted a number of species to extinction.[5] Many primitive peoples drove entire herds over cliffs and cornered and slaughtered entire bands of animals, leaving most to rot.[6] American Indians, sometimes eulogized as the "first environmentalists," actually treated the environment like most other people: whatever was scarce was treasured, and whatever was plentiful was wastefully used. After horses and guns made buffalo easy to hunt, the Plains Indians often slaughtered them wholesale, eating only the tongue and back meat, selling the hides, and leaving the rest to rot.[7] The Indians were making a good start at exterminating the buffalo when the white man took over the job.

Such slaughter continues today in Alaska and Northern Canada. According to one critic, "Recreation [for Alaskan natives] in some of these areas consists of getting drunk or high on drugs, getting on a snowmobile or in a boat, roaming the tundra or sea ice, killing groups of caribou or walruses and leaving much of the meat to spoil."[8] Ancient and primitive peoples damaged the environment less than modern people do because their numbers were fewer and their tools less powerful. At all times and places, most people have taken whatever they wanted with little thought of environmental consequences.

Today we are forced to consider our environment every time we pick up a newspaper. The Cuyahoga River catches fire and threatens to burn down Cleveland. In Tokyo the trees are dying from air pollution, and the Japanese are giving up traditional seafoods because hundreds have been killed or crippled by eating seafoods contaminated by industrial wastes. Workers are ordered out of a construction tunnel in Washington, D.C., because the air pollution in the tunnel exceeds legal limits—only to find that the air pollution measures twice as high at street level. Mother's milk in several east coast states tests so high in PCB contamination that, if it were cow's milk, it could not be sold for human consumption. Beaches are closed in many areas because sewage and sludge persist in floating ashore. Nearly every day brings another such environmental anecdote, convincing most people that a grave environmental crisis confronts us.

But not everyone. Many radical leftists object that the environmental movement is a conservative cop-out, a way of diverting people's attention from the real task of promoting revolutionary change; meanwhile, they charge, conservative forces "consolidate their control over national policy-making, bolster their hold over world resources, and escalate further cycles of useless economic growth."[9] This follows the familiar habit of extremists who angrily impugn the motives of all who do not share their priorities.

Indians hunting buffalo. Painting by George Catlin.
(Courtesy of the American Museum of Natural History)

While it is true that some environmental concerns, such as preserving wilderness areas and trout streams, are of no direct benefit to the urban poor, it is the urban poor who are the greatest victims of air pollution, noise pollution, crowding, garbage, vermin, and rodents.[10] In perpetuating the myth that environmental concerns are purely elitist, leftist extremists once again reveal their willingness to sacrifice the interests of the poor to the promotion of the revolution.

A somewhat more moderate level of criticism questions not the motives but the judgment of the environmentalists. In a well-known critique John Maddox charges (correctly) that some environmentalists have exaggerated recklessly in their shrill doomsday predictions, which are not grounded in scientific fact; but then Maddox answers with some factual inaccuracies of his own. For example, he drags out the hoary myth of the fertile tropical jungle lands ("1,000 million acres of cultivable land, enough to feed 1,000 million people . . .").[11] But tropical rain forest, for all its lush appearance, is notably poor in minerals; once stripped of the forest cover it quickly forms a hard, impenetrable crust utterly unsuitable for extensive cultivation.[12] Critics of the environmentalist movement are frequently as poorly informed as the environmentalists they scold.

Still other opposition to the environmentalist movement comes from vested interests with axes to grind. Ruthless despoliation is profitable to some people who are not eager to cut their profits. One coal mining executive remarked,

The conservationists who want strip miners to restore land are stupid idiots, socialists, and Commies who don't know what they are talking about. I think it is our bounden duty to knock them down and subject them to the ridicule they deserve.[13]

In contrast to such opinions, it is clear that the majority consider environmental concerns to be serious problems; witness a 1975 Opinion Research Corporation poll that showed 74 percent of a national sample willing to pay higher taxes and prices to protect the environment. The list of environmental problems is impressive: air pollution, noise pollution, thermal pollution, water pollution, energy shortages, flood control, food contamination and supply, land use, oil spills, pest control, population control, radiation hazards, recreational land use, recreational vehicle damage, resource exhaustion, sewage disposal, soil erosion, solid waste disposal, strip mining, water supply, wilderness preservation, wildlife protection, and still others. How have these problems arisen?

Origin of the Environmental Crisis

Environmental problems are not new. In the 1880s the streets of New York City were annointed with 1,250 tons of horse manure, 60,000 gallons of urine, and 40 dead horses each day.[14] But the gravity of environmental problems exceeds all earlier periods in our history. What causes this?

POPULATION GROWTH

Population growth carries growing pressures on resources. Until fairly recent times, few areas had enough people to make much impact on the earth. Now there are many such areas, with another 200,000 people added each day. It is undeniably true that if world population continues to grow at its present rate of about 2 percent a year for a few more generations, most of the world's people by then will share the wretched misery of the starving shanty-dwellers on the river banks of Calcutta. A few minutes' simple arithmetic will show how current rates of population growth cannot possibly continue for long. Nothing social scientists ever said is more predictably certain

Indiscriminate dumping of junk and other waste materials over a period of years has contributed to the serious problem of environmental pollution.
(Irene Springer)

than that *either birth rates will fall or death rates will rise,* in one painful way or another. The only uncertainty is, how soon? Without realistic population control over the entire earth, most of the environmental issues mentioned above will become academic—as pointless as complaining about the food service on a sinking ship. If human beings have any capacity to respond intelligently to the most obvious necessities, then the population explosion will be brought under control—hopefully in time to avoid total disaster. This problem is discussed at some length in chapter 9.

Is population growth responsible for the environmental crisis? In the 20 years between 1948 and 1968 the population of the United States grew by 43 percent, while pollution levels of various sorts increased by amounts ranging from 200 to 1,000 percent.[15] Obviously, population growth has played a modest role in the sudden emergence of the environmental crisis.

INCREASING AFFLUENCE

Each person in the United States enjoys a share of the gross national product equal to that of 38 residents of India. The U.S. standard of living, with its energy demands for automobiles and air conditioning, its mountains of packaging materials, and its piles of discards, has an impact on the environment that no other nation can match. Yet the increase in affluence does not begin to match the growth of the environmental crisis. Over the 1948–68 period, our gross national product (total, not per capita) rose by 126 percent, as compared with the up to 1,000 percent increase in pollution. Increasing affluence has played a significant role in the emergence of environmental problems, but clearly a secondary one. The steadily growing affluence of the less prosperous nations of the world, however, brings increasing environmental pressures. Other people are catching up in their capacity to despoil the earth.

PRODUCT TECHNOLOGY CHANGES

The main culprit is the spectacular changes in product technology, including the shift to disposables and the shift to nondegradables.

THE SHIFT TO DISPOSABLES   has been under way for many years. A century ago the average family threw away very little. Most needs were met through home production. Purchases were few, mainly locally produced, and seldom wrapped or packaged. The occasional paper bags, boxes, jars, and cans were saved and re-used repeatedly. Recycling is a concept with which earlier Americans were thoroughly familiar. Today nearly everything a family uses has passed through the market. Mass production and mass distribution require elaborate packaging. Many small items are overpackaged to discourage shoplifting. Returnable beverage bottles have been largely replaced by no-returns. Earlier hard goods were intended to last for generations, but modern manufactures, because of both flimsy construction and deliberate obsolescence through style changes, are not expected to last very long. The subassemblies of most appliances are designed not be be repaired, but to be replaced. Many articles are intended for only one use and instant discard—paper towels, paper diapers, facial tissues, plastic table service, cooking pans, even paper uniforms and bed "linens." All of these contribute to a growing mountain of things to throw away, but we are running out of any convenient place to throw them.

The nonreturnable beverage container is a striking example of the

568

wasteful shift to disposables. A nationwide return to deposit-and-return beverage bottles would reduce highway beverage container litter by two-thirds; produce estimated annual savings of at least 530,000 tons of aluminum, 1.5 million tons of steel, and 5.2 million tons of glass;[16] and also save 115,000 barrels of oil a day.[17] Seven states had passed bottle-deposit laws of some kind by 1980, and polls in these states show overwhelming popular approval.[18]

THE SHIFT TO NONDEGRADABLES   is also serious. Earlier trash was mainly ferrous metals, which rust away in time, or wool, cotton, paper, or wood, which burn easily and rot away fairly quickly. All these are easily degradable—that is, fire or decay rather easily transform them into relatively harmless natural elements.

There has been a massive shift toward products that are not easily degradable. "Tin" (actually steel) cans rust away in a few years in most climates, but aluminum cans, like diamonds, are forever. Plastics are widely used, both for packaging and in end products. Most plastics either will not burn at all (they just melt into a gooey mess) or give off clouds of poisonous gases. Synthetic textiles are popular with consumers, but most neither burn nor rot well. The shift to nondegradables has given consumers lovely new products and manufacturers lovely profits, but it has given society a monumental trash problem.

Changing production technology has also created a host of industrial waste problems. Factories produced very few toxic by-products before World War II. Today there are an estimated 32,000 toxic dumps around the country, with cleanup costs for *a part* of these estimated at $44 billion.[19] Many "disposal firms" contracted to collect and haul away toxic wastes from manufacturers who did not know—and did not wish to know—what became of them. The contractor would buy or lease a piece of vacant land somewhere, dump waste there until complaints accumulated, and then move on to a new location, leaving a chemical time bomb ticking away, slowing seeping into the ground water supply.[20] Hazardous waste disposal laws are now in effect in most states, but repairing the damage already done will be expensive.

THE ATTITUDINAL FACTOR

Ideas and actions are interrelated. Ideas support actions; actions create a need for supporting ideas. Certain widely held ideas and attitudes have contributed to the environmental crisis.

THE IDEA THAT GROWTH IS GOOD   is relatively recent. Throughout most of history, *stability* was the social idea. But centuries of rapid population increase and economic growth have cultivated a frame of mind in which *growth*—of population, wealth, or industry—is good, while lack of growth is unhealthy. Many people are reconsidering this notion. One highly prestigious group of social scientists and engineers has even suggested that unless population and economic growth are not merely slowed but brought to a full halt within a short time, a massive human die-off of several billion people can be anticipated.[21] Though this study probably overstates the case, it is clear that exponential growth (2, 4, 8, 16, 32, 64, . . .) cannot continue forever. At some point, either through choice or through default, we definitely shall return to the historic idea of relative stability as a test of the good society.[22] How soon we make this choice will largely determine whether we stabilize at a relatively comfortable level or at an anthill level of misery.

THE IDEA THAT NATURE EXISTS TO SERVE HUMANKIND   is far from universal. But the idea that God gave us the earth to use for our enjoyment is central to the Judeo-Christian tradition.[23] The Bible does not say exactly this, but states that God gave people "dominion" over the earth.[24] Persons engaged in profitable destructiveness have interpreted this as a divine sanction for their right to exploit the earth as they will. But dominion does not mean ownership with unrestricted right to exploit or destroy; it means sovereignty,[25] or exercising ruling authority in the interests of those who are ruled. The biblical charge authorizes people to rule, but not to ravish or despoil the earth. Environmentalists who seek a biblical basis for their environmental concerns can easily find it.[26]

THE DISRUPTION OF ECOSYSTEMS

For 20 years the people of Kern County, California, had waged unrelenting war against annoying predators: skunks, foxes, badgers, weasels, snakes, hawks, owls. Finally in 1924, the sheep herders hired a U.S. Biological Survey team to wipe out the coyotes. The 1926 food crop was the highest ever, but the following spring, an army of 100 million field mice surged from the dry lake bed, even killing and eating sheep in their hunger.[27] This is an example of ecosystem disruption.

An *ecosystem* is an interconnected web of living and nonliving things that interrelate in a relatively stable equilibrium. An ecosystem can be viewed as local (a swamp, a forest), regional (a river, a desert, an ocean), or even global (spaceship earth). Within an ecosystem, a number of life forms (insects, birds, animals, plants, and perhaps people) and nonliving entities (water, wind, air, sunlight, soil) are in constant interaction. A familiar example of an ecosystem in miniature is the sealed terrarium in which several plants live

Poor old Florida. Its benign climate and idiot population make it a haven for more ecological bad examples than the other 47 (or maybe 49) states combined. Asian "walking catfish" are spreading through its inland waters from a release point somewhere around Palm Beach. South American giant marine toads, a foot long and poisonous, are spreading from a release point around Miami. South American water hyacinths choke 80,000 acres of inland waterways. Australian "pines" grow so near the beach that their roots keep the few remaining sea turtles from digging nests in some areas. Exotic former pets, from little jaguarundis and ocelots to full-grown jaguars and American elk, roam uninhabited areas. A parrot, parakeet, or mynah bird on your bird feeder is not unusual enough for any but the most casual conversation. The state legislature just named a state insect for the first time—the European praying mantis!

Hundreds—some say thousands—of species of foreign flora and fauna have been introduced into Florida, some by accident, some by design. Almost all are either bothersome or harmful in one way or another. . . .

Dick Kirkpatrick, *Audubon*, Sept. 1973, p. 138.

within an air-tight glass enclosure, with a fixed amount of air and water entrapped therein, with only heat and sunlight coming from outside, while plant growth is limited to what the space, air, and water permit.

An ecosystem is not entirely stable. Drought, flood, or fire may change it suddenly; soil or climatic changes may alter it gradually; plant successions may occur, as when forests pass from young to mature to old and then to young again; temporary population explosions of a particular species may erupt. But there is a tendency to maintain a generally stable equilibrium, punctuated with these temporary population explosions, declines, and returns to equilibrium. For example, a hard winter kills off most of the members of a predator insect species; next there is a population explosion of the host species on which this predator feeds; this population explosion provides a rich food supply, and the predator species quickly rebuilds as it feeds on the host species and eats up this population explosion; then there is a die-off of the predator species, and an approximate equilibrium is re-established. Thus, a tussock moth outbreak generally collapses in a three-year pattern.[28]

The introduction of an alien species disrupts an ecosystem. In its native habitat each species has natural enemies and food supply limitations that keep it in check. When transported into a new environment that lacks these natural checks, an alien species may become a costly pest. Most of our serious pests—boll weevil, corn borer, fire ant, walking catfish, water hyacinth, Brazilian holly, Australian punk tree, Dutch elm mite, and many others—are alien imports. This is the reason for the strict border agricultural inspections, which foolish tourists sometimes seek to evade. The only effective way to control such pests often is to import their natural enemies—when this can be safely done.

Importation of an alien species is a tricky business, for it may not eat what we want it to eat. For example, rats (escaped from ships) became a great pest in Hawaii, where they had no natural enemies. Planters imported mongooses in 1883 to kill the rats. But the mongoose hunts by day while rats feed by night, so the mongooses killed few rats but decimated the island's ground-nesting birds and became pests themselves.[29] Most pests are alien species who have too few natural enemies in their new environment.

The elimination of a native species also disrupts ecosystems, by removing the natural enemy of other species. In India, where some snakes are poisonous, it is routine to kill all snakes on sight—and India loses an estimated one-fourth of its grain crop to rats and mice.[30] The efforts of sheep ranchers to eliminate coyotes in the United States and dingos (wild dogs) in Australia have fortunately been unsuccessful. Had they succeeded, the rodent population explosion would prove more costly to the sheep industry than the coyotes and dingos.[31] An interesting example of the domino effect of species extermination occurred in Borneo, where World Health Organization operatives sprayed DDT to eradicate malarial mosquitoes. While the mosquitoes were killed, other insects including cockroaches soon developed immunity and concentrated the DDT in their bodies. When geckos, the small lizards that abound in the area, ate the roaches, the geckos became ill and were unable to escape the cats, which died after eating the geckos. Disease-carrying rats multiplied, along with caterpillars that ate the thatched roofs so that the houses threatened to collapse. Normalcy returned when

> [W]hen DDT and two other chlorinated hydrocarbons were used exten-
> sively in pest control in a valley in Peru, the initial success gave way to a
> delayed disaster. In only four years, cotton production rose from 440 to 650
> pounds per acre. However, one year later, the yield dropped precipitately to
> 350 pounds per acre, almost 100 pounds per acre less than before the in-
> secticides were introduced. Studies indicated that the insecticide had de-
> stroyed predator insects and birds as well as insect pests. In fact, although
> the population of pest insects had decreased at first, the pest population
> soon recovered and flourished once again, this time quite resistant to the
> pesticides.
>
> Amos Turk, Jonathan Turk, and Janet T. Wittes, *Ecology, Pollution, Environment* (Philadel-
> phia: W. B. Saunders, 1972), p. 44.

the DDT was discontinued and planeloads of cats were parachuted into the area.[32]

A more monumental ecological disaster followed the completion of the Aswan High Dam in Egypt. Before its construction a distinguished Egyptian hydrologist accurately predicted some of its consequences; but he was fired and construction was begun. All the dire predictions came true, along with some consequences he did not foresee.[33] The dam failed to provide the expected amount of water for irrigation and power development because of underestimated seepage and because the large lake created wind systems that caused unexpected evaporation losses. Since the silt-laden Nile now drops its silt in the reservoir, Nile valley farmers must buy expensive imported fertilizers that are not even a good substitute for the volcanic silts that had made the Nile valley the most fertile valley on earth. The silt-free river, as it flows below the dam, now erodes the river banks and undermines bridges and barrier dams. The delta coastline is being eroded by changed sea currents. Lack of nutrients in the river water has decimated the marine life of the eastern Mediterranean, and is cutting the fish catch. The sardine catch, for example, has dropped by 18,000 tons a year. The increasing salinity of the irrigated lands can be controlled only by expensive procedures that will cost as much as the dam itself. An enervating parasitic disease, bilharzia (schistosomiasis), always endemic in Egypt, has increased nationally by 20 percent because there are no spring floods to flush away the snails that carry it. It is feared that malarial mosquitoes will become established and malaria will become endemic. The most sensible course of action would be dynamite the dam and hope for a return to the *status quo ante,* but this is not politically possible. So the Egyptians will have to endure the consequences of the most monumental ecological blunder in recent history. Not all dams are undesirable; some have been highly beneficial. Today, however, most desirable dam sites have already been dammed. The Bureau of Reclamation and the Army Corps of Engineers continue building dams, because this is what they are trained to do. But since few good dam sites are left, they build on poor dam sites,[34] wasting money and inflicting great damage on the environment.[35]

Small ecological disasters occur by the thousands. A ruggedly beautiful forest slope is strip mined into a spoil bank, oozing acid seepage into the streams. A meandering river is "channelized" into a big ditch, empty of fish, wildlife, or scenic value, whose function is to hurry the floodwaters down to the next stretch of river, where the carnage must then be repeated. A shoreline mine daily dumps thousands of tons of mine tailings into a lake, turning the water a sickly green for miles around, killing the fish, and sending lethal asbestos into the water intakes of cities many miles distant.[36] And 100,000 outlets spew sewage and industrial wastes into the drinking water of downriver communities, and from millions of acres of fertile farmland a thin layer of fertility is eroded each season. Ecosystem mayhem, arising from ignorance, greed, or both, is a constant factor in environmental degradation.

These are some general factors in the emergence of our environmental problems. Specific examples are now in order. Because a single chapter cannot treat each environmental problem in intelligent detail, we have selected an arbitrary sample of four problems for analysis.

A Sample of Environmental Problems

THE PESTICIDE PROBLEM

A single pair of houseflies, breeding and surviving undisturbed, would bury the entire earth many feet deep before most readers of this book would graduate from college. The only reason the insects have not inherited the earth is their habit of eating one another, with an assist from birds, reptiles, and others. It is this habit that pesticides disrupt.

Agriculture alters the ecosystem. Deforestation and cultivation tend to raise temperatures, reduce rainfall, and increase water runoff and soil erosion. Unless cultivation is pursued carefully the land is soon destroyed; yet there are lands that are still fertile after thousands of years of cultivation. The insect life of an ecosystem is profoundly affected by agriculture. With the change in plant species, some insects (and other species) decline while other species multiply. *Monoculture,* in which a large area is planted to a single plant species, provides an ideal opportunity for a population explosion of those herbivorous insects that feed on this particular plant.[37] Large-scale specialized farming thus creates a greater insect problem than the diversified farming of the past when fields were small, crops were varied, and numerous woodlots and fencerows provided habitat for birds and predator insects. Mixed forests or grasslands, with a variety of plants and insects, provide less opportunity for an insect explosion. In time the predator insects multiply and cancel the pest explosion, but meanwhile an entire crop may be lost. To meet the increased insect problem that modern agriculture has created, pesticides have been developed. At first they were chemically simple compounds such as lead arsenate, which killed a narrow range of insects and soon biodegraded into relatively harmless residues. About three decades ago chemists compounded a new family of chlorinated hydrocarbons, of which DDT is perhaps the best known. These insecticides were far more lethal, were long-lasting, and were broad-spectrum insecticides that killed every bug that moved, while appearing to be relatively harmless to humans and other animals. Their appearance was hailed as a modern miracle, as humanity's final triumph over the insect world. In World War II Americans sprayed DDT wherever they went, exterminating lice and mosquitoes and dropping malaria to the vanishing point.

The ecological backlash was not long in coming. These pesticides do not

573

biodegrade readily, but remain stable compounds for many years. They settle into the ground, entering the water supply and eventually the ocean. They accumulate in the fatty tissues of insects and fish and move up the food chain, concentrating as they go. It is not known just how much pesticide residue people can tolerate without damage. Since the DDT sprayed today takes many years—perhaps a dozen or more—to work its way up the food chain into our bodies, this means that if brain damage were established tomorrow as a result of pesticide exposure, another decade of exposure would still await us.

Spectacular declines in bird and wildlife populations routinely follow large-scale sprayings. A number of bird species are threatened with total extinction because pesticide residues cause the females to lay soft-shelled eggs which break before hatching.[38] Pesticides are now killing 2 percent more honeybees each year than are replaced in reproduction; another decade at this rate and serious crop losses from pollination shortages are predicted.[39] Fears of both human and animal damage have led to regulations restricting the use of DDT and certain other pesticides in the United States. Yet some use continues in the United States, while in most of the world there are no restrictions, and debate about the dangers and benefits of pesticides continues.[40]

A second difficulty in the use of broad-spectrum pesticides is that they kill both the pest and the predator. Thus they make the problem worse, for two basic reasons. One is that the host species greatly outnumbers the predator species, since a predator must eat many hosts each day to stay alive. Second, the predator generally has a longer life cycle than the host, with several host generations to one predator generation. As a result, an insecticide that kills 99 percent of both hosts and predators has worked to the advantage of the host species, which rebuilds more rapidly than the predator species (whose population may have been reduced so much that male and female cannot find each other to reproduce). Pesticide use demands continuing applications, with the natural enemies of the pest entirely eliminated and the pesticide as the only remaining control.[41]

At this point a third backlash factor becomes apparent. All species have some capacity to adapt to an environmental poison through selective survival. Suppose one application kills all but one in a thousand. These few survivors breed the next generation, of whom perhaps several in a thousand survive the pesticide. Of the third generation still more survive, until a resistant species has developed. By 1945 about a dozen insect species had become resistant to DDT; by 1976 the number of resistant species had risen to over 200.[42] Mosquito control has again become a crisis in some areas where malaria- and encephalitis-carrying mosquitoes have become resistant to virtually all insecticides for killing larvae.[43] Thirty years ago, America used 50 million pounds of insecticides a year and lost about 7 percent of our preharvest crops to insects; now we use about 600 million pounds and are losing 13 percent of our crop.[44] The more we use, the more we lose. It is clear that *primary reliance upon pesticides is a road to certain disaster*. The end of that road is not only Rachel Carson's *Silent Spring* [no birds][45] but an environment so poisoned that few species could survive.

What are the alternatives to insecticides? In some cases the answer is simply to keep calm and allow an insect outbreak to run its course. If not impeded, the natural enemies will often restore a balance within a year or two, whereas one area spraying may require annual spraying thereafter.

This is not to say that insecticides should *never* be used or that spraying a few rose bushes will trigger ecological disaster; but to make wide-area sprayings should be an expert decision, arrived at after informed consideration of all alternatives, not simply a conditioned reflex as has so often been the case. Nonpesticidal insect controls should become our routine means, with pesticides reserved for occasional emergency use.

Other alternatives are available. A rich and varied bird life is one. Another is the importation, cultivation, and release of natural enemies. If knowledgeably selected (an exceedingly important qualification), the predator multiplies rapidly while eating the pest and then, when its food supply is exhausted, it quietly dies off. Spraying with hormones can alter an insect's growth cycle so that it hatches at the wrong time and then either freezes or starves. Synthetic female sex lures can attract males for trapping or for sterilization and release so that they will mate fruitlessly. An area can be saturated with a synthetic sex lure so that males and females cannot find each other. Virus sprays can bring disease to a target insect without affecting other species. A resistant plant strain can sometimes be found or crossbred. Such biological controls offer the most promising alternatives to pesticides.[46] We have very little knowledge and experience to draw upon, and there is the disturbing possibility that insects may develop resistance to biological controls of some kinds. Yet it is the only alternative to disaster.[47]

The shift from pesticides is beset by four difficulties. One is that present knowledge is inadequate. Years of intensive research are needed before biological controls can replace insecticides. A second difficulty is that biological controls appear to offer fewer profit possibilities than insecticide manufacture. Chemical manufacturers can be trusted to continue pesticide research, but research on biological controls must be financed largely from public funds. Third, under the most optimistic estimate some short-term crop losses will be suffered during the change-over from pesticides to biologicals, for it would take some years for the natural enemies to rebuild. Finally, many people will need to change their habits of thinking and acting, and this is always difficult.

LAND USE

MINING   always makes a mess. Mines were historically places to which men were condemned, as to prison, and the life of a slave in the Roman silver

---

When noxious goatweed spread among the native grasses of the 19,000-acre National Bison Range, the Fish and Wildlife Service was forced to consider a spraying program. "That is absolutely a last resort on a wildlife refuge," says manager Robert Brown. "Aside from the ecological considerations, the cost of chemically treating weeds is prohibitive."

A record hatching of black beetles saved the government by devouring much of the insidious plant and stopping its spread. The cost of the spray program would have amounted to several thousand dollars. The beetles did the job free of charge.

Reprinted from *American Forests*, March 1980, p. 28.

mines of Spain averaged four years. Mining towns have always been among the most dreary of human settlements.

Modern technology has given us huge earthmovers and made strip mining possible. This mode of mining is cheap and fast, and the profits are enormous.[48] But strip mining turns a wooded hillside into a barren moonscape studded with puddles of acrid water. When a steep slope is strip mined, both that slope and much that lies below it are utterly useless throughout any foreseeable future. In arid regions such as the Western states, where millions of acres await the strippers, the slopes are often gentle but the rainfall is so sparse that a new vegetation cover will be difficult to establish. Where the slopes are gentle and the rainfall is adequate, it is possible to reclaim the land through leveling, fertilizing, and seeding it, at a cost that makes only a small dent in mining profits. Despite much talk and many promises, very little reclamation is actually done. Even the reclaimed land is seldom very useful. One study of a reclaimed grassland found that only 5 of the original 60 plant species had returned, mainly because of soil alkalinity.[49] Reclamation thus often does little beyond preventing further erosion of the all-but-useless land. Where slopes are steep or rainfall is inadequate, even this dubious reclamation is utterly impossible. Such land will be useless, not merely for a generation or a century but for a geological era.

The Surface Mining Mining Control and Reclamation Act of 1977 will abate the worst effects of strip mining, if it is enforced. A concerted attack on the new regulations as "too expensive" is now being pressed.[50] We must make a painful choice between costlier coal and despoiled land.

I have looked at "reclaimed" land from northern Pennsylvania to the southern end of the Alabama coal fields, and I have never seen a reasonably good job of restoration anywhere. I use as my standard English reclamation work which I have seen on two visits to that country. In England the topsoil is all saved. After the coal is taken out the land is put back in the pit layer by layer and then is compounded with heavy rolling machines. The topsoil is restored and the land is treated with limestone and fertilizer, sowed in grass and planted with huge trees brought from the national forests. If this is acceptable and responsible reclamation, then it is a certainty that it has no counterpart in the United States.

From a letter by Harry M. Caudill, published in *American Forests*, Aug. 1973, p. 2.

FOREST LANDS have many uses. They provide timber, wildlife habitat, and recreational and scenic values. It is less well known that forests manufacture a major portion of our oxygen supply; they sponge up rainfall and release it slowly, stabilizing the river levels and evening out the water supply; their presence moderates the temperature range and their cooling effect increases the rainfall. Their cover controls erosion and preserves the land for future generations. In the Amazon forest, for example, a hectare (2½ acres) of land may lose no more than three pounds of topsoil a year through erosion; when the land is stripped of its forest cover the erosion losses rise to 34 *tons* per hectare.[51]

Today the forest lands of Africa, Asia, and Latin America are shrinking by an amount equal to the size of Cuba each year. At this rate, most of the great forests of these continents will be gone by the end of the century, and much of this tropical land will become wasteland.[52]

Forest land management involves the balancing of many competing interests and values. *Tree farm monoculture* produces the most timber, but an even-aged forest of a single species offers little in scenic values or wildlife habitat and is far more vulnerable to pests and blights than a mixed forest. *Clear-cutting* (removing all trees and reseeding with a single species) also produces more timber than selective cutting, but allows more erosion. There is some question how many clear-cuttings a forest can survive before the land becomes unproductive.

GRASSLANDS cover much of the earth. They produce food and wildlife habitat, prevent soil erosion, and help stabilize the water supply. There are three major threats to grasslands. One is strip mining, since coal underlies much of our grasslands. Another is the unwise plowing of grasslands that are too steep, too dry, or too windy for cultivated crops. Stripping the grass cover exposes the land to erosion. A third threat to grasslands is overgrazing. When too many cattle or sheep eat the grass too short, edible grasses die out and are replaced by coarse grasses, sage, and scrub. These provide less effective cover, and the topsoil is soon lost to wind and water erosion. Millions of acres of productive grassland have been converted into eroded sagebrush wastes. The Bureau of Land Reclamation reported in 1974 that less than one-fifth of the grazing lands in the United States were in "good to excellent" condition.[53] In the absence of determined conservationist policy

Aerial view of Biology Gamma Forest. Death of trees at center was due to exposure of gamma radiation. The experiment is part of a program to investigate the long-term effects of chronic exposure of ecologic systems to radiation.
(Brookhaven National Laboratory)

the desert will grow ever larger. Most of the world's deserts are either created or greatly enlarged through human misuse. The Sahara, for example, has grown by an amount equal to the state of Texas in the past half-century, and is still growing.[54] The world's deserts are expanding at a rate of 14 million acres a year, a rate which would destroy one-third of our arable land within 25 years.[55] Properly used, forests, croplands, and grasslands last forever. Misuse them, and they become our graveyard.

> A letter sent by a county livestock association to Arizona congressmen last year resulted in the transfer of a BLM [Bureau of Land Management] manager out of the county. His crime? He fined three ranchers for having 1,058 more cattle grazing on BLM lands than their permits allowed.
>
> Russ Shay, "The Sagebrush Rebellion," *Sierra*, Jan./Feb. 1980, pp. 31–32.

ESTUARIES AND WETLANDS   are our most productive agricultural lands, although they are seldom recognized as such.[56] They provide spawning beds and food supply for seafoods, plus cover and food supply for some other forms of wildlife. Unfortunately, however, the seafoods are harvested far from the estuary, so the productivity of these lands is not immediately apparent. If the catch could be traced to the point of origin, these estuary and tidewater lands would be the most high-priced agricultural lands in the world. But since the shoreline owners receive no direct benefit from their productivity, it is more profitable to them to dredge and fill these lands and convert them into building sites and parking lots. Only recently has the great productivity of these "waste" lands been appreciated. Controls over shoreline development are being adopted, and such recklessly wasteful development may be curtailed.

SCENIC AND RECREATIONAL LANDS   are awash in controversy. Scenic and recreational values compete with maximum timber production, road construction, mining, dam and reservoir construction, and many other activities and values. In fact, scenic and recreational values compete with each other. Should the national parks be preserved as quiet, secluded places to view the unspoiled scenery and wildlife in solitude and grandeur, or should they be developed into high-density recreational areas, complete with expressways, resort hotels, ski runs, chair lifts, power boats, golf courses, supermarkets, and throngs of people?

Off-road recreational vehicles are one of the greatest menaces to land preservation. Some, such as snowmobiles, have some usefulness; others, such as trailbikes, have no use other than recreation. All are destructive. Snowmobiles pack the snow and kill the small wildlife living under the snow cover, break off small plants and trees, and allow their drivers to run animals to exhaustion. Trailbikes chew up the land; stripped of its fragile vegetation cover it erodes rapidly, silting up reservoirs and clogging irrigation systems.[57] There are few restrictions on off-road vehicle use and enforcement is extremely difficult. Much land has been destroyed by ill-considered use, but this is a unique example of land destruction for fun.

The discussion above by no means fully states the problems and issues of land use. Controversies over competing claims upon the land are unending. Public awareness of the issues is growing, and the move to develop and enforce comprehensive land use plans is gathering momentum. A few states have enacted land use acts and established land use commissions. The National Land Use Policy and Planning Assistance Act of 1973 provides federal funds to assist states in long-range land use planning.

WILDLIFE PRESERVATION

"It really doesn't matter one hell of a lot if the whooping crane doesn't make it." This remark by an environmentalist critic epitomizes one attitude toward wildlife. Another attitude appears in a national survey in 1978, finding that a majority of informants "favored protecting wildlife even at the expense of jobs, housing, and development projects."[58] Hundreds of species are already extinct, and hundreds more are headed for extinction. Does it really matter if there are fewer pretty birds to look at?

Wildlife species exist as parts of interrelated ecosystems. When an ecosystem is disrupted by the extermination of a species or the introduction of a new species, the result may be the disruption of the entire ecosystem. For example, the alligator is "the one animal that is absolutely essential to the balance of nature, to the survival of birds, animals, fish, trees, and all living things in the Everglades."[59] There are doubtless some species that can be removed from an ecosystem without injury, but this cannot always be known in advance.

In the case of plant species, the thousands of native plant species are the raw materials from which the plant geneticists develop new hybrids. The very productive new grain strains of the "green revolution" were possible only because there were dozens of native, genetically "pure" grains that could be crossbred. Recently several *thousand* varieties of native corn were screened in a search for insect-resistant corn, and several were found that will be crossbred with standard corn varieties.[60] Agronomists screened 618 types of cotton in developing a strain resistant to the lygus bug.[61] *No one knows which of the several million varieties of plant, animal, and insect life will someday be useful.* Extensive wild areas are needed to preserve the "bank" of native plant species with which plant scientists can experiment.

Wildlife faces many threats. We mentioned the pesticide menace above. Possibly the greatest threat of all is habitat change. Many species will live and breed only in a very special kind of habitat, and either starve or quit breeding if the habitat changes. Many timid species disappear when roads, airports, and snowmobiles invade their territory. Tree farms and other forms of monoculture offer fewer nesting places and food sources. Some species—coyotes, deer, starlings, pigeons—adapt readily to human presence, but many others—wolves, bighorn sheep, the larger cats, and many kinds of birds—do not.

"Sportsmen" who shoot anything that moves threaten to exterminate many species—wolves, eagles, grizzlies, and polar bears, for example. Ruthless slaughter extends well back into ancient times, but the snowmobile, all-terrain vehicle, and airplane can reduce hunting to the level of shooting fish in a barrel. In underdeveloped countries native poaching is decimating the elephant, rhinocerous, crocodile, tiger, leopard, and many other species. Some species of whale have recently become extinct, and all will be soon unless Russia and Japan, the principal whaling nations, can be persuaded to reduce the kill. Even though "there is no single product derived from whales that cannot now be synthesized at comparable cost,"[62] the whale kill continues because large capital investments and many jobs are involved. Apparently, Marxists and capitalists can be equally greedy.

For many years, the Division of Wildlife Services of the federal government conducted a "predator control" program, mainly to kill coyotes, a program strongly supported by sheep ranchers. Yet their reported lamb kill holds to a fairly constant 5–7 percent figure, regardless of predator control programs. These programs even fail to make any lasting dent in the coyote population, which promptly rebuilds since the coyote birth rate is highly affected by coyote population density and food supply. It is only in the killing of other wildlife (and domestic dogs) that the predator control programs are an unqualified success.

Some ranchers believe that the coyote does more good than harm to ranchers, by controlling rodents.[63] And there is a practical alternative to the coyote-killing program. One or two samplings of sheep-flesh bait laced with lithium chloride will condition coyotes to avoid sheep meat.[64] Experimentally this method has proven far more effective than coyote-poisoning, without the undesirable side effects.

In one of the few experiments on natural controls versus poisoning, a test plot in which rabbits and small rodents were intensively poisoned and trapped soon had a *larger* rabbit and rodent population than a control plot where there was no poisoning or trapping. In the test plot the poison killed many rodents, which were then eaten by predators (coyotes, weasels, birds, shrews, and the like), which then died, leaving the rodent population free to rebuild.[65] Obviously, we need much more research before the controversy

---

That crocodiles are useful for more than leather and meat has become apparent in places where they have been eliminated and their natural prey has multiplied unchecked. Rats and wild pigs grow up to damage gardens, and venomous snakes become a peril, since these animals safely can drink at rivers now that crocs are not hovering around. Undesirable catfish and lungfish, main croc diet items, increase and eat staple food fishes. In Madagascar stray dogs thrive and rabies spreads. With growing knowledge that the abominable crocodile has its good points, breeding farms and wildlife preserves may yet save it from extinction.

Reprinted from John Du Barry, *True Magazine*, Aug. 1973, p. 31. Copyright 1973, Fawcett Publications.

Eight Fund for Animals volunteers were put on trial last month on charges that they saved the lives of 1,000 seals by "painting" them with a harmless red organic dye that makes the fur useless for commercial purposes.

Under the so-called Seal Protection Act, the eight volunteers could be fined $5,000 for coming within a half-mile of the hunt and not killing seals . . .

Quoted from *Moneysworth*, March 1980, p. 4.

between ranchers and wildlife lovers can be settled on a basis of fact, not guesswork.

Fish are perhaps the most valuable form of wildlife, for seafoods provide a major fraction of the world's protein supply—all obtained without eroding an acre of land or polluting a single stream. World fish catch is heading steadily downward, due partly to water pollution but also to overfishing, and some of this fish catch is unfit to eat because of its cargo of toxins.[66] Jacques-Yves Cousteau claims that world marine life has declined nearly one-third in the past two decades. The haddock catch, for example, declined from 294 million pounds in 1929 to 160 million pounds in 1952, and to 12 million pounds in 1972.[67] Much commercial fishing is done in international waters where no law regulates the catch. Efficient new fishing fleets, equipped with electronic gear that schools of fish can seldom escape, are sweeping the oceans like enormous vacuum cleaners. In a few more years at present rates, most fishing areas will be producing only a fraction of their historic catch. International fishing agreements are difficult to negotiate and still more difficult to enforce, but the alternative is the steady loss of this ideal food supply.

ENERGY

Cheap energy is gone. We shall not "run out" of coal or oil in the way that a driver runs out of gas when the last drop is drained. Instead, as we exhaust the easily accessible deposits which can be developed cheaply and without great environmental damage, we move on to less and less desirable deposits—more difficult to locate, smaller, lower in quality, more expensive to develop, more injurious to the environment. Eventually, a point will be reached where mining or drilling *consumes* more energy than is produced. When this point is reached, all use of coal or oil as an energy source will end. There is no question *whether* this will happen; the only question is: *When?* And nobody knows.

Energy conservation might reduce our energy use as much as 25 percent without drastically changing our lifestyle.[68] Alternative energy sources are many: solar energy, geothermal energy, windmills, gas from biomass (garbage), wood as fuel, and such possibilities as hydrogen, direct solar conversion, ocean waves and tides, and others. The unproven technologies are highly problematical, while all the proven ones have serious limitations. Ex-

Firewood is the second largest threat to forests; 80 percent of the wood used in developing countries is burned for fuel . . . In parts of India, a family member must spend two days a week foraging for the family's wood. Illegal poaching of timber by armed poachers is being reported by Sudanese forest rangers; the wood will be marketed in the form of charcoal in urban areas. So bad are the wood shortages in Nepal and Haiti that already some peasants have cut back their diet of vegetables that require cooking, Eckholm reports. When wood cannot be found, families most often turn to burning animal dung, the only fertilizer most have to renew the soils that feed them.

"Wood Famine in Developing Countries," *Science News*, 115 (24 Feb. 1979), 119.

Solar energy is being investigated as one of the possible alternate energy sources for the future.
(Irene Springer)

tensive shift to wood fuel would increase air pollution. If all wood scraps are burned and none left to rot, this threatens long-range forest fertility. If wood use produces widespread deforestation, then soil erosion, climatic change, and eventual world famine will follow. Geothermal energy is limited to relatively few locations. Wind energy is dependable in relatively few places. The world's largest windmill, dedicated in 1979 atop Howard's Knob in North Carolina, has produced only a fraction of the expected electrical energy.[69] The most optimistic assessments of the possibilities of solar energy see it providing from one-sixth to one-third of our energy needs by the year 2000.[70]

Other alternative energy sources are being developed. Before long, we shall realize that "garbage" is too valuable to throw away. Various estimates place oil savings from garbage use as fuel at from 400,000 to two million barrels a day.[71] We are rediscovering some plants and trees with unrecognized possibilities as foods and fuels.[72] The return of the sailing ship on some sea routes seems to be a practical possibility.[73] Alternative sources, using the technology now known, cannot replace coal or oil, but they can help.

Meanwhile, a doubling of our coal use by 1985 is the current policy of our government. Among the costs would be: (1) millions of acres of wasteland created by strip mining of coal; (2) increased air pollution and increased "acid rain," possibly to levels curtailing food and forest growth;[74] (3) an estimated 12,000 deaths of mine and transport workers for each gigawatt of electrical energy developed from coal—six times more than the estimated radiation deaths from an equal amount of nuclear-generation capacity.[75] Coal is our only fuel available in the amounts needed during the next century, but its use clearly poses grave problems.

Unless there is a major scientific breakthrough in energy production— one which few scientists expect—the choices open during the next century or two appear to be these: (1) a return to a low-energy society with a preindustrial standard of living; (2) a great increase in coal use, with its environ-

In 1972, under orders from the Ontario government, Inco [International Nickel Company] constructed the tallest smokestack in the world, a "superstack" fully a quarter of a mile high. The intention was to disperse the sulphur dioxide over a wider area so that, as the wisdom of the day had it, the gas would become so diluted by distance that only harmless traces would fall to earth. Subsequently, this idea was picked up by many other polluters, particularly coal-fired generating stations in the U.S, as a cheap method of meeting clean-air standards imposed by the U.S. Environmental Protection Agency (EPA). Electric utilities even took advertisements in magazines to argue that reducing emissions—instead of spreading them farther—would result in fewer jobs, and they accused environmentalists of "taking the food from people's mouths to give them a better view of the mountains."

Unfortunately, as Colorado senator Gary Hart pointed out, "What goes up must come down. With acid rain, however, what comes down is much worse than what went up—worse in its potential damage to trees and crops, worse in its potential damage to freshwater lakes, fish and tourism, and worse in its damage to man-made objects." In fact, "high-altitude dispersion" turned out to be as effective as getting rid of your garbage by dumping it on your neighbor's lawn. Instead of falling on the Sudbury Basin, Inco's fumes were carried as much as 1,000 miles, oxidized in the atmosphere, and returned to the earth as acid rain.

Bill Damper, "Now Even the Rain is Dangerous," copyright 1980 by the National Wildlife Federation. Reprinted from the March–April issue of *International Wildlife Magazine*, pp. 17–18.

mental degradation and possibility of environmental disaster; (3) a continuing development of nuclear energy, along with its dangers.

The hazards of nuclear development are ominous: (1) radiation-induced deaths, estimated at 2,000 per gigawatt of generation capacity by the year 2000;[76] (2) the possibility of an unpredictable number of deaths from a nuclear accident; (3) the problems of nuclear waste disposal, as yet unsolved. Are these dangers greater or less than the dangers of a shift to greater use of coal? There is no data base sufficient to give a confident answer to this question.[77] Meanwhile, nuclear power development in the United States has slowed, while European countries are rapidly expanding their nuclear generation capacity. It may be many years before we know who made the wiser decision.

The foregoing sketches of only four of our many environmental problems—each no more than a bare outline—may give some idea of the wide range and complexity of environmental problems, and of the vast accumulation of data needed to analyze them intelligently.

The Social-Disorganization Approach

Environmental problems fit nicely into a social disorganization framework. Some environmental problems have developed because traditional patterns no longer work well because of technological change. The tradition of simply throwing away trash wherever handy is no longer satisfactory for the amounts and kinds of trash now produced. Likewise, burning is less satisfactory because many forms of modern trash do not burn easily or harmlessly. The traditions of fishing and hunting—take all you want—will now exterminate fish and game because of increased numbers of exterminators and because of more efficient killing technology. Mining laws and practices that were tolerable for deep shaft mining became ecologically devastating when applied to strip mining. Certain traditional attitudes—that the earth is ours to use as we wish, that resources are unlimited—are clearly suicidal in their impact today.

The Value-Conflict Approach

Virtually every environmental issue is at base, a value conflict—a choice between unlimited growth with a constant deterioration in the quality of life, and the limiting of growth to preserve the quality of life; between maximum timber production and scenic, recreational, and wildlife preservation values; between energy production and pollution reduction; between cheap strip-mined coal and higher-cost coal with land reclamation; between industrial pollution and higher prices for industrial products; between accepting nuclear risks with radioactive pollution and accepting coal-miner deaths and air pollution; between the convenience of disposables and a reduction of littering and solid wastes; between tolerating a polluting factory and accepting local unemployment; between clean air and the right to drive high-powered cars wherever we wish; between preserving a swamp area as a wildlife preserve and developing some profitable building sites—the list could be extended indefinitely, for every environmental issue involves a number of value conflicts. The solution to every environmental problem will require the sacrifice of a profit opportunity, the acceptance of a higher cost, or the sacrifice of some product or convenience we enjoy.

The Personal-Deviation Approach

This approach contributes little to an understanding of environmental problems. Most environmental problems arise, not from some deviation, but from ordinary people doing conventional things. As with all other problems, deviant persons sometimes become involved and often add to the confusion of the issue. A study of student support for Earth Day, an environmentalist rally in 1970, found that the student supporters were the student moderates, while both the leftists and the conservatives rejected environmentalist concerns.[78] The only personality study the authors could locate found that persons who are unconcerned over environmental issues tend to be intolerant of new ideas and high in need for personal safety.[79] Such persons are too numerous to be classed as deviant, just as those who are environmentally concerned are too numerous to be deviant.

Some Basic Considerations in the Treatment of Environmental Problems

It would be futile here to launch on an analysis of solutions to environmental problems, for each problem would demand a separate extended discussion that would overflow the covers of this volume. However, some general considerations that apply to all possible solutions may be developed.

ALL ENVIRONMENTAL VICTORIES ARE PROVISIONAL; MOST DEFEATS ARE PERMANENT   The successful blocking of a proposal to fill in an estuary, to develop a coastline, or to dam a river valley is provisional; it may be overturned tomorrow. But if the estuary is filled, the coastline is developed, or the river is dammed, for all practical purposes it is gone forever. No future victory of environmentalists can undo the change. The developers need to win only once, but the environmentalists must win *every time* if a section of the environment is to be preserved from reckless despoliation.

LOCAL INTERESTS RARELY SUPPORT ENVIRONMENTAL PROTECTION   Local interests generally favor whatever form of development will return the most in payrolls, land speculative windfalls, or quick profits. Local interests generally favor mining the minerals, cutting the timber, developing the land into profitable honky-tonks, and decimating the wildlife if it brings money into the

Bicyclists on Earth Day, 1980, Washington, D.C. The event highlights the many environmental problems of the day and the consequences of ignoring them.
(United Press International)

community. Local people are unimpressed by the argument that jobs lost locally are not gone, but merely transferred elsewhere, because the jobs are still lost *to them*. Local interests will even choose short-run profits over long-term economic gains. For example, if a river valley of spectacular beauty is logged, there will be jobs and local prosperity for a few years, followed by an economic collapse; but if it is made into a national park, it will return a steady and growing income from tourism for generations. Yet studies showing that a short-run sacrifice will be more than compensated by a long-term gain are seldom believed, because the short-run sacrifice is too painful. If local opinion had prevailed, there would be scarcely a national park, wildlife refuge, or wilderness area anywhere in the country. Although some local supporters usually can be found, most environmental victories come from mustering enough political clout from elsewhere to overpower the local opposition.

Environmental needs will demand many hardships of many localities. It is a genuine hardship to lose one's job in middle age, and find one's house unsalable because the local economy is destroyed. It may be both humane and politically necessary to find ways of compensating those who suffer economic hardship from environmental measures. This would force everyone to share the costs of environmental protection.

VOLUNTARY MEASURES ARE INEFFECTIVE   Few people will inconvenience themselves greatly as long as other people pollute and indulge themselves freely. No business will voluntarily incur heavy expenses for pollution abatement and place itself at a competitive disadvantage with its competitors. Either inducement or compulsion is necessary. Positive inducements, in the form of grants, subsidies, and tax credits, and negative inducements, in the form of special taxes and penalties, may induce many people to comply. Compulsion in the form of laws that forbid certain actions and require others is another approach. After suitable warnings, a manufacturer may be ordered to cease polluting the river and fined several thousand dollars a day as long as he continues. Such laws are difficult to enact, for they are strenuously and sometimes dishonestly resisted by those whom they are intended to control. They are even more difficult to enforce. Inspectors can be bribed, or strings can be pulled to ensure appointment of administrators who will be "reasonable." A control agency can be neutralized by keeping it so under-funded that it cannot possibly do its job. Public officials often support environmental protection with all the right words but with insufficient funds. And what elected official wants to be responsible for closing a factory and throwing hundreds or thousands of people out of work? When the taxpayers repeatedly refuse to vote the funds for a sewage treatment plant, how can they be forced to do so? Legal compulsion is a necessary route to environmental protection, but hardly an easy one.

Some existing laws and business practices actually *encourage* environmental destruction. The tax depletion allowances discourage recycling, since a depletion credit is given for freshly-mined raw materials but not for reclaimed ones. Thus our tax system rewards the wasteful. The existing freight rate structure also discriminates in favor of new raw materials and against reclaimed ones.[80] A reversal of this situation would greatly encourage recycling.

What combination of positive inducements, compulsions, and penalties will most effectively protect the environment? One scholar made a sophisticated analysis of four possible approaches to industrial pollution abatement: public education (educating people to support pollution abatement); judicial action (damage suits, fines, legal penalties); resource charge (imposing a tax upon those who use resources or pollute); and abatement subsidy (giving grants or tax rebates to reward pollution abatement). The study concluded that at least for industrial pollution abatement, the more effective means were resource charge and abatement subsidy.[81] But much more research and experimentation will be needed before the most effective means are definitely established.

CITIZEN ACTION IS CRUCIAL   If a government official must initiate every legal action against an environmental brigand, there will be no consistently effective environmental protection. All regulative agencies, left to themselves, tend to develop a cozy relationship with those they are supposed to regulate, and there is no reason to believe that the Environmental Protection Agency will be immune to this tendency. To be truly effective, environmental protection laws must empower any citizen to initiate a legal proceeding against a polluter or a proposal, even against a government agency, for government agencies are among the leading destroyers of the environment.[82]

We now have a substantial body of federal and state law for environmental protection, most of which allows for citizen-initiated action.[83] The Rivers and Harbors Act of 1899 gives the Army Corps of Engineers control over pollution of all "navigable waterways." Although originally concerned only with navigation, this law has recently been interpreted to cover river pollution in general. The Water Quality Act of 1965, the Clean Air Acts of 1963 and 1970, the Motor Vehicle Air Pollution Act of 1965, the Air Quality Act of 1967, the Environmental Policy Act of 1969, and the Water Pollution Control Act of 1972 are in the federal arsenal of legislation. The Environmental Protection Agency has broad powers to set and enforce pollution standards. For example, the law requires industries to use the "best practicable" procedures for water pollution prevention by 1977, and by 1983 to use the "best available" technology. *If fully implemented,* these measures will substantially reduce the pollution of the environment. But this is a big "if." Caught between citizens who want to clean up the environment and polluters who want to continue polluting, politicians often enact nice laws for environmentalists with nonenforcement for the polluters. When the crunch begins to hurt, the temptation to bend the standards is strong indeed.

ENVIRONMENTAL PROTECTION COSTS MONEY   Most environmental protective measures add to production costs, under either a capitalist or a socialist economy. The socialist countries are having environmental problems much like ours.[84] There are some instances where recycling will pay its way and where pollution abatement will recover enough salable material to cover expenses and perhaps even make a profit. Good candidates are trash recycling, biological controls in place of pesticides, and cancellation of many dam-building projects.[85] Proper disposal of toxic wastes costs far less than cleanup costs after careless disposal. Research may open more opportunities for "free" environmental protection, but not very many. Most environmental measures will increase costs and prices.

Costs multiply rapidly as pollution control approaches absolute purity.

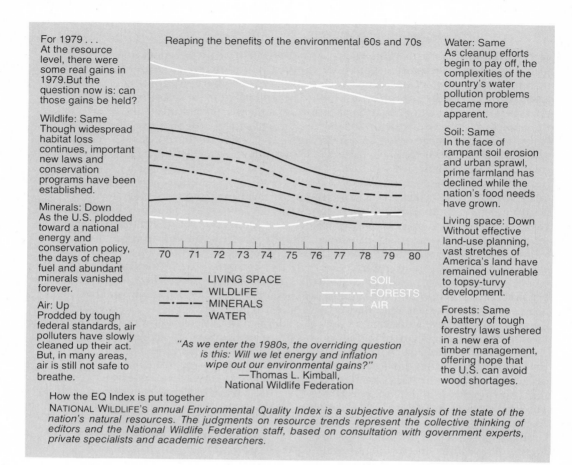

For 1979 . . .
At the resource level, there were some real gains in 1979. But the question now is: can those gains be held?

Wildlife: Same
Though widespread habitat loss continues, important new laws and conservation programs have been established.

Minerals: Down
As the U.S. plodded toward a national energy and conservation policy, the days of cheap fuel and abundant minerals vanished forever.

Air: Up
Prodded by tough federal standards, air polluters have slowly cleaned up their act. But, in many areas, air is still not safe to breathe.

Reaping the benefits of the environmental 60s and 70s

70 71 72 73 74 75 76 77 78 79 80

——— LIVING SPACE
– – – – WILDLIFE
–·–·– MINERALS
—— WATER

———— SOIL
–·–·– FORESTS
– – – – AIR

"As we enter the 1980s, the overriding question is this: Will we let energy and inflation wipe out our environmental gains?"
—Thomas L. Kimball,
National Wildlife Federation

Water: Same
As cleanup efforts begin to pay off, the complexities of the country's water pollution problems became more apparent.

Soil: Same
In the face of rampant soil erosion and urban sprawl, prime farmland has declined while the nation's food needs have grown.

Living space: Down
Without effective land-use planning, vast stretches of America's land have remained vulnerable to topsy-turvy development.

Forests: Same
A battery of tough forestry laws ushered in a new era of timber management, offering hope that the U.S. can avoid wood shortages.

How the EQ Index is put together
NATIONAL WILDLIFE'S *annual Environmental Quality Index is a subjective analysis of the state of the nation's natural resources. The judgments on resource trends represent the collective thinking of editors and the National Wildlife Federation staff, based on consultation with government experts, private specialists and academic researchers.*

Figure 19–1
1980 EQ SUMMARY
Reprinted from *National Wildlife*, February–March 1980, p. 36. Copyright 1980 by the International Wildlife Federation.

For example, to remove the first 50 percent of the pollutants may not be very costly; the next 25 percent costs far more; the final 10 percent may cost more than all the preceding 90 percent. How complete a pollutant removal do we wish to pay for? Should sewage effluent be purified to the drinking-water level? This is technically possible but exceedingly expensive. Or is a lesser degree of purification acceptable? This is a value conflict that will probably be resolved by accepting something less than absolutely pure water or perfectly clean air.

The costs of environmental protection will include the reluctant sacrifice of some conveniences and indulgences. Automobiles are growing smaller and less powerful. Returnable bottles are more nuisance than disposables, but this is one effective way to reduce litter and save precious resources. Air conditioning is a comfort we may have to learn to live without. The list of possible sacrifices could be extended for pages. The extent of the necessary sacrifices, and their priorities, are not yet clear, but there will be no environmental protection without sacrifices.

RESEARCH AND TECHNOLOGY ARE NECESSARY   We lack a great deal of the basic knowledge needed to clean up and protect the environment. We need more knowledge before we can replace pesticides with biologicals as our primary defense against insect pests. Experiments with plastics that self-destruct are under way, and an easily degradable plastic may be available before long. If we could discover an economical way to purify sea water (without using vast quantities of energy), our cultivatable lands would be greatly increased. A safe, nonpolluting way of unlocking nuclear power would do more to reduce environmental degradation than any other single discovery. What we need is not less technology, but *more,* if the world is to remain livable.

Prospects

All favor environmental protection—until they see the price tag! Then enthusiasm often wanes. All of the half-dozen environmentalist magazines founded in the great rush of enthusiasm surrounding Earth Day in 1970 have since folded, and the environmentalist movement has been reduced to its serious supporters. After several years of heady victories, in 1972 the environmentalists began suffering defeats. Environmentalists are now on the defensive, with the energy crisis being used as an argument for relaxing nearly all environmental safeguards.

Throughout much of the world environmental destruction continues unchecked. The world throws away or burns up more fertilizer each year than it uses—a practice which, if continued indefinitely, will doom the world to certain famine. Rising oil prices make kerosene too costly a cooking fuel for poor peasant peoples, who burn more firewood and are speeding the conversion of their semiarid lands into deserts.[86] In some places people burn animal dung for fuel instead of saving it for fertilizer, ensuring that next year there will be less food to cook. Although there are still a few optimists,[87] most scholars believe that the era of exponential economic growth and ever-rising standards of living has ended.[88] The human species is unlikely to die out; even the most catastrophic disaster would probably leave a few survi-

> The trends charted in this book do not point toward a sudden, cataclysmic global famine. What appears most likely, if current patterns prevail, is chronic depression conditions for the share of humanity, perhaps a fourth, that might be termed economically and politically marginal. Marginal people on marginal lands will slowly sink into the slough of hopeless poverty. Some will continue to wrest from the earth what fruits they can, others will turn up in the dead-end urban slums of Africa, Asia, and Latin America. Whether the deterioration of their prospects will be a quiet one is quite another question.
>
> Erik P. Eckholm, *Losing Ground: Environmental Stress and World Food Prospects* (New York: W. W. Norton, 1976), p. 187. Copyright © 1976 by Worldwatch Institute.

vors. A massive die-off within a few decades is more possible although not very likely. A greater possibility is a slow, steady degradation of the environment, together with a steady deterioration in the quality of life. Whether this will happen depends upon our value choices.

Summary

There is widespread public agreement that environmental protection is a major issue, although radical leftists consider it a conservative cop-out, and some other critics consider environmentalists' fears exaggerated. *Population growth* cannot continue endlessly, and control of population growth is essential for any program of environmental protection. Recent pollution increases in the United States have so greatly outrun population increases as to make population growth a secondary factor in our pollution problem. Likewise, *increasing affluence* is a secondary factor. *Product shifts to disposables and nondegradables* form the greatest single factor. The *attitudinal factor*—the idea that people own the world to use as they please—also shares responsibility. The *disruption of ecosystems* has produced many unforeseen consequences, most of them unfortunate.

Of the many environmental problems, this chapter outlined four in some detail. The *pesticide problem* arises because pests generally develop immunity to pesticides more rapidly than do the natural predator enemies of the insect pests. Thus, heavy use of pesticides sets up a vicious circle in which the more pesticides are used, the more are needed, with certain disaster as the conclusion. A shift to biological controls of insect pests is a necessary condition of human survival. *Land use problems* claim increasing attention, as agricultural land, forests, and grasslands are steadily destroyed by soil erosion, deforestation, unwise draining and filling, overgrazing, off-road vehicles, and other abuses. The *wildlife preservation* issue shows how even one of the least important environmental problems still has important implications. *Energy* problems are grave, involving difficult choices between values and opposing dangers.

A social-disorganization approach shows how old rules, practices, and attitudes are becoming increasingly inapplicable and destructive of the environment. A value-conflict approach emphasizes the many difficult value sacrifices that environmental protection requires. The personal-deviation approach is not very useful in the analysis of environmental problems.

Each environmental problem requires a separate cluster of solutions tailored to that problem. Some guiding considerations include the recognition that (1) environmental victories are provisional, while most defeats are final; (2) local interests generally favor jobs, profits, and development over environmental protection; (3) voluntary measures are ineffective, but must be accompanied by inducements and compulsions; (4) citizen-initiated legal actions are crucial; (5) environmental protection involves increasing costs; and (6) more research and technology are needed. The prospect is in doubt. A worldwide ecological catastrophe is unlikely, but a gradual deterioration of the quality of life is a distinct possibility.

Suggested Readings

AUCOIN, JAMES, "The Irrigation Revolution and Its Environmental Consequences," *Environment*, 21 (Oct. 1979), 17ff. Discusses the environmental effects of irrigation.

BOULDING, J. RUSSELL, "Coal: Savior or Demon?" *National Parks and Conservation Magazine,* June 1979, pp. 15–20. Examines the pros and cons of increasing our use of coal.

CAUDILL, HARRY M., *Night Comes to the Cumberlands* (Boston: Little, Brown, 1962). A moving account of how coal mining changed the Cumberland Plateau from one of the most lovely to one of the most depressing parts of America.

CITIZENS' ADVISORY COMMITTEE ON ENVIRONMENTAL QUALITY, *Annual Report to the President and to the Council on Environmental Quality* (Washington, D.C., published annually). An annual outline of environmental needs and policy recommendations.

DAHLSTEN, DONALD, "The Third Forest," *Environment,* July/Aug. 1976, pp. 35–42. A discussion of forest monoculture, pesticides, clear-cutting, and other forest problems.

DALY, HERMAN E., ed., *Toward a Steady-State Economy* (San Francisco: W. H. Freeman, 1973). The economics of replacing exponential growth with a stable economy.

DOUGLAS, DONALD H., "The Great Nuclear Power Debate: A Summary," *Science News,* 109 (17 Jan. 1976), 44–45. Brief summary of the pros and cons of nuclear power.

ECKHOLM, ERIC P., *Losing Ground: Environmental Stress and World Food Prospects* (New York: W. W. Norton, 1976). A readable treatment of world land waste and its consequences.

EHRLICH, PAUL H., and ANNE H. EHRLICH, *The End of Affluence: A Blueprint for Your Future* (New York: Ballantine, 1974). A dark view of the future, in contrast to Herman Kahn, below.

"EQ Summary," annually in Jan./Feb. issue of *National Wildlife.* An annual report on environmental gains and losses.

FIALKA, JOHN, "Running Wild," *National Wildlife,* Feb./Mar. 1975, pp. 36–40. An assessment of the environmental costs of off-road recreational vehicles.

HINDLEY, KEITH, "Reviving the Food of the Aztecs," *Science News,* 116 (8 Sept. 1979), 168–70. A look at some native plants which are more nutritious and better adapted to the locale than our western grains in nonwestern lands.

KAHN, HERMAN, et al., *The Next 200 Years: A Scenario for America and the World* (New York: Wm. Morrow, 1976). Argues that the pessimists are wrong and that the future is bright.

LAPEDES, DANIEL, ed., *McGraw-Hill Encyclopedia of Environmental Science* (New York: McGraw-Hill, 1976). A useful source book of basic knowledge.

MADDOX, JOHN R., *The Doomsday Syndrome* (New York: McGraw-Hill, 1972). The most popular of several "antiecology" books, arguing that the environmental crisis is greatly exaggerated.

MAZE, KENNEDY P., "The Great Kern County Mouse War," *Audubon,* Nov. 1977, pp. 158–60. An entertaining account of how an area was overrun with mice after people foolishly exterminated their natural enemies.

SPETH, GUS, "The Sisyphus Syndrome: Acid Rain and Public Responsibility," *National Parks and Conservation Magazine,* Feb. 1980, pp. 12–17. The causes and consequences of acid rain.

STERRETT, FRANCES S., "Careless Kepone," *Environment,* Mar. 1977, pp. 30–37. A true industrial poisoning horror story.

WOLFF, ANTHONY, "Building a Better Bug Trap," *New York Times Magazine,* 28 Nov. 1976, pp. 39ff. Entomologists find ways to use love instead of poison to control insects.

————, "The Nightmare Life without Fuel," *Time,* 25 Apr. 1977, p. 33. An imaginative essay on what the year 1997 might be like.

Footnotes

[1]Marvin W. Mikesell, "The Deforestation of Mount Lebanon," *The Geographical Review,* 59 (Jan. 1969), 1.

[2]Stephen Davenport, "Comeback of the Oyster," *New York Times Magazine,* 20 Dec. 1970, p. 31.

[3]Ashley Montagu, "The Aborigines," *International Wildlife*, Mar./Apr. 1973, p. 8.

[4]Jay G. Hutchinson, "Slash and Burn in the Tropical Forests," *The Environmental Journal*, Mar. 1973, pp. 10–13; James S. Packer, "Slash and Burn below the Border," *Smithsonian*, Apr. 1973, pp. 67–71.

[5]Paul S. Martin, "The Discovery of America," *Science*, 179 (9 Mar. 1973), 969–74; Dietrick E. Thomsen, "The Late Great Pleistocene Extinction: A Slothful Tale," *Science News*, 112 (10 Dec. 1977), 396–98.

[6]John G. Marshall, "Where Have All the Tuttu Gone?" *Audubon*, Mar. 1977, pp. 3–14.

[7]J. Baden et al., "Myths, Admonitions and Rationality: The American Indian as a Resource Manager," *Professional Papers in Political Economy and Natural Resources* (Bozeman: Montana State University, 1979); also John Aitkins, "Does Anyone Remember Rose Marie?" *International Wildlife*, May/June 1978, pp. 13ff.

[8]Lloyd F. Lowry (Alaska Department of Fish and Game), letter in *Audubon*, May 1977, p. 112.

[9]Katherine Barkley and Steve Weissman, *Ecocatastrophe* (San Francisco: Canfield, 1970), p. 16; see also James Ridgwood, *The Politics of Ecology* (New York: E. P. Dutton, 1970); Ritchie P. Lowry, "The New Religecology: Salvation or Soporific," *Social Policy*, 1 (July–Aug. 1970), 46–48; and Richard Neuhaus, *In Defense of People: Ecology and the Seduction of Radicalism* (New York: Macmillan, 1971).

[10]Daniel Zwerdling, "Pollution and Poverty," *The Progressive*, Jan. 1973, pp. 25–29; George L. Waldbott, *Health Effects of Environmental Pollutants* (St. Louis: C. V. Mosby, 1973); Julian McCall, "Discriminatory Air Pollution: If Poor, Don't Breathe," *Environment*, Mar. 1976, pp. 26–36.

[11]John Maddox, *The Doomsday Syndrome* (New York: McGraw-Hill, 1972), p. 83; see also Melvin J. Grayson and Thomas R. Shephard, Jr., *The Disaster Lobby: Prophets of Ecological Doom and Other Absurdities* (Chicago: Follett, 1973).

[12]R. J. A. Goodland and H. W. Irwin, *Amazon Jungle: Green Hell to Red Desert* (New York: Elsevier, 1975); Erik P. Eckholm, *Losing Ground: Environmental Stress and World Food Prospects* (New York: W. W. Norton, 1976), ch. 8.

[13]James D. Reilly, vice-president of Consolidated Coal Company, Pittsburgh, quoted in Harry M. Caudill, "Are Conservation and Capitalism Compatible?" in H. S. Helfrich, Jr., ed., *Agenda for Survival: The Environmental Crisis—2* (New Haven, Conn.: Yale University Press, 1970), p. 177.

[14]George H. Lewis, review in *Contemporary Sociology*, 6 (May 1977), 345.

[15]Barry Commoner et al., "The Causes of Pollution," *Environment*, Apr. 1971, pp. 25–29.

[16]Environmental Protection Agency estimate, in *Business Week*, 21 Feb. 1977, p. 85.

[17]Estimate of Environmental Action Foundation.

[18]*Reader's Digest*, Feb. 1980, p. 51.

[19]*National Wildlife*, Mar. 1980, p. 28–C.

[20]Janet Raloff, "Abandoned Dumps: A Chemical Legacy," *Science News*, 115 (26 May 1979), 348–55.

[21]Donella H. Meadows et al., *The Limits of Growth: A Report for the Club of Rome's Project on the Predicament of Mankind* (New York: Universe Books, 1972).

[22]See Herman E. Daly, ed., *Toward a Steady-State Economy* (San Francisco: W. H. Freeman, 1973), for a discussion of the economics of stability. See Suzanne Gowan et al., *Moving Toward a New Society* (Philadelphia: New Society Press, 1976), for a summons to return to a simple life.

[23]Lynn White, Jr., "The Roots of Our Ecologic Crisis," *Science*, 155 (10 Mar. 1967), 1203–7; Yi-fu Tuan, "Environmental Attitudes," *Science Studies*, 1 (Apr. 1971), 215–24.

[24]Genesis 1:26: "And God said, Let us make man in our image, after our likeness; and let them have dominion over the fish of the sea, and over the fowl of the air, and over the cattle, and over all the earth, and over every creeping thing that creepeth upon the earth."

[25]"Power or right of governing or controlling; sovereign authority; lordship, sovereignty; rule, sway, control, influence." *Oxford English Dictionary*, vol. 3, p. 597.

[26]Aharon Shapiro, "God, the Ecologist," *Environment*, Apr. 1976, p. 38.

[27]Kennedy P. Maze, "The Great Kern County Mouse War," *Audubon*, Nov. 1977, pp. 158–60.

[28]*American Forests*, July 1973, p. 9.

[29]Thomas Y. Canby, "The Rat: Lapdog of the Devil," *National Geographic*, July 1977, pp. 74–75.

[30]Zai Whitaker and Romulus Whitaker, "If They're Killers, What Good Are They?" *International Wildlife*, May/June 1977, pp. 12–16.

[31]"The Coyote Menace That Wasn't,"

Audubon, May 1976, pp. 138–39; "The Hated Dog," *Time,* 25 Nov. 1974, p. 123.

[32]"The Parachuting Cats of Borneo," *Science News,* 103 (31 Mar. 1973), 209.

[33]Claire Sterling, "The Aswan Disaster," *National Parks and Conservation Magazine—The Environmental Journal,* Aug. 1971, pp. 10–14; Amos Turk, Jonathan Turk, and Janet T. Wittes, *Ecology, Pollution, Environment* (Philadelphia: W. B. Saunders, 1972), pp. 35–37; "Egypt Turns to the U.S. for Help at Troubled Aswan," *U.S. News and World Report,* 6 Sept. 1976, pp. 37–38.

[34]Such as the Teton Dam in Idaho, which was an economic loser and an environmental disaster even before it collapsed, killing eleven people and causing $400 million property damage. See Dorothy Gallagher, "The Collapse of the Great Teton Dam," *New York Times Magazine,* 19 Sept. 1976, pp. 16ff.

[35]Arthur E. Morgan, *Dams and Other Disasters* (Boston: Porter Sargent, 1971); Richard L. Berkman and W. Kip Viscuse, *Damming the West* (New York: Grossman, 1973).

[36]Wade Greene, "Life vs. Livelihood," *New York Times Magazine,* 24 Nov. 1977, pp. 17ff.

[37]Donald Dahlsten, "The Third Forest," *Environment,* July/Aug. 1976, pp. 35–42.

[38]Daniel R. Zimmerman, "The Peregrine: America's Most Endangered Falcon," *National Parks and Conservation Magazine—The Environmental Journal,* Sept. 1972, pp. 4–10.

[39]*Science News,* 112 (10 Dec. 1977), 392.

[40]See Rita Gray Beatty, *The DDT Myth: Triumph of the Amateurs* (New York: John Day, 1973), for a defense of DDT use.

[41]Turk, *Ecology, Pollution, Environment,* pp. 45–46.

[42]Ibid., p. 45; *Science News,* 109 (14 Feb. 1976), 101.

[43]*Science News,* 103 (9 June 1973), 371.

[44]D. Pimentel et al., "Pesticides, Insects in Food, and Cosmetic Standards," *BioScience,* 27 (1977), 178–85.

[45]Rachel Carson, *The Silent Spring* (Boston: Houghton Mifflin, 1962).

[46]Hal Higdon, "New Tricks to Outwit Our Insect Enemies," *National Geographic,* 143 (Sept. 1972), 380–99; Frank Graham, Jr., "Plague the Pests," *Audubon,* Sept. 1975, pp. 64–87; Anthony Wolff,

"Building a Better Bug Trap," *New York Times Magazine,* 28 Nov. 1976, pp. 39ff.; Julie Ann Miller, "Helping Plants to Hold the Line," *Science News,* 112 (22 Oct. 1977), 268–70.

[47]Jerome Goldstein with Rill Ann Goldstein, eds., *The Least Is Best Pesticide Strategy: A Guide to Putting Integrated Pest Management into Action* (Emmaus, Pa.: JG Press, 1978).

[48]Harry M. Caudill, *My Land Is Dying* (New York: Dutton, 1970), ch. 8; Harry M. Caudill, *King Coal* (Boston: Little, Brown, 1976).

[49]*Science News,* 104 (21 July 1973), 37.

[50]"The Shifting Contour of the Strip Mine Law," *Business Week,* 17 Mar. 1980, p. 43.

[51]Goodland and Irwin, *Amazon Jungle.*

[52]Eric Eckholm, *Planting for the Future: Forestry and Human Needs* (Washington, D.C.: Worldwatch Institute, 1979); "Deforestation and Disaster," *Time,* 22 May 1978, p. 95.

[53]Steve Galligiole, "Deadly Overgrazing," *Defenders,* June 1976, pp. 161–63.

[54]Eckholm, *Losing Ground,* p. 61.

[55]Royce Rensberger, "14 Million Acres a Year Vanishing as Deserts Spread Around the Globe," *New York Times,* 28 Aug. 1977, pp. 1ff.

[56]Gladwin Hill, "Wetlands, Once Called Useless, Now Seen as Prime Resource," *New York Times,* 26 Aug. 1979, sec. 4, p. 5.

[57]Russell Heath, *Environmental Consequences of the Off-Road Vehicle* (Washington, D.C.: Defenders of Wildlife and Friends of the Earth, 1974); John Fialka, "Running Wild," *National Wildlife,* Feb./Mar. 1975, pp. 36–41.

[58]Megan Durham, "Survey Shows Americans Support Wildlife Conservation," *National Parks and Conservation Magazine,* Mar. 1980, pp. 14–16.

[59]Florida Game and Fresh Water Fish Commission, quoted in *Defenders of Wildlife News,* 47 (May/June 1972), 272.

[60]*Science News,* 107 (11 Jan. 1975), 22–23.

[61]Miller, "Helping Plants Hold the Line."

[62]Farley Mowat, *A Whale for the Killing* (Boston: Little, Brown, 1973), quoted from review in *Rodale's Environmental Action Bulletin,* 12 May 1973, p. 5.

[63]Dayton O. Hyde, "Man's Best Friend—The Coyote," *Defenders of Wild-*

life News, June 1974, pp. 221–23.

[64]*Science News,* 108 (23 Aug. 1975), 126.

[65]Robert R. Northway, "Prey–Predator Relations in the Sierra Nevada Foothill Range," *Defenders of Wildlife News,* 48 (Jan. 1973), 7–9.

[66]See W. Eugene Smith and Aileen W. Smith, *Minimata* (New York: Holt, Rinehart and Winston, 1975), for a harrowing example.

[67]Arthur Fisher, "The Living Sea," *International Wildlife,* May/June 1977, pp. 4–10.

[68]Steven J. Nadis, "An Optimal Solar Strategy," *Environment,* 21 (Nov. 1979), 4–14ff.

[69]*New York Times,* 9 Mar. 1980, p. 41.

[70]Nadis, "An Optimal Solar Strategy"; Robert Stobaugh et al., eds., *Energy Future: Report of the Energy Project at the Harvard Business School* (New York: Random House, 1979).

[71]"Moving to Garbage Power," *Time,* 9 Jan. 1978, p. 46; Eckhardt C. Beck, "Environmental Protection in an Energy-Conscious Economy," *USA Today,* Mar. 1980, pp. 40–42.

[72]Keith Hindley, "Reviving the Food of the Aztecs," *Science News,* 116 (8 Sept. 1979), 168–69.

[73]"The Wave of the Future: Shipping by Sail," *Business Week,* 21 Jan. 1980, pp. 66–67.

[74]Gus Speth, "The Sisyphus Syndrome: Acid Rain and Public Responsibility," *National Parks and Conservation Magazine,* Feb. 1980, pp. 12–17; Susan West, "Acid from Heaven," *Science News,* 117 (2 Feb. 1980), 76–78, and 117 (16 Feb. 1980), 106–8. Acid rain forms when the sulphur dioxide and nitrogen oxides from smokestacks and automobile exhausts combine with oxygen in the atmosphere to produce sulphuric and nitric acids. This falls as acid rain, which dissolves stone buildings, kills fish in lakes, and stunts plant and tree growth to a degree not yet fully measured.

[75]National Research Council's Committee on the Biological Effects of Ionizing Radiation, reported in *Science News,* 115 (12 May 1979), 310. See also Peter Beckmann, *The Health Hazard of Not Going Nuclear* (Golem Press, Boulder, Colo., 1976).

[76]Ibid.

[77]See Donald H. Douglas, "The Great Nuclear Power Debate: A Summary," *Science News,* 111 (17 Jan. 1976), 44–45, for a condensed summary of the arguments.

[78]A. Clay Schoenfeld, "National Earth Day: Where Are They Now," *Environment,* 21 (Dec. 1979), 4ff.

[79]Thomas C. Kinnear et al., "Ecologically Concerned Consumers: Who Are They?" *Journal of Marketing,* Apr. 1974, pp. 20–24.

[80]Peter Kakela, "Railroading Scrap," *Environment,* Mar. 1975, pp. 27–33.

[81]Eliot R. Hammer, "A Sociological Assessment of Alternatives to Industrial Pollution Abatement and Subsequent Implications for Policy Research," Ph.D. dissertation, Pennsylvania State University, 1973. Available from Photoduplication Department, Pattee Library, University Park, Pennsylvania. See also Organization for Economic Cooperation and Development, "Paying to Pollute," *Environment,* June 1976, pp. 16–20.

[82]See Joseph L. Sax, *Defending the Environment: A Strategy for Citizen Action* (New York: Alfred A. Knopf, 1971); Billie Shoecraft, *Sue the Bastards!* (Phoenix: The Franklin Press, 1971); William H. Brown, *How to Stop Corporate Polluters and Make Money Doing It* (San Francisco: Bellerophon Books, 1972).

[83]J. Clarence Davies III, *The Politics of Pollution* (New York: Pegasus, 1970), ch. 2; Arnold W. Reitze, Jr., "The Law of Pollution Control," in Terry R. Armstrong, ed., *Why Do We Still Have an Ecological Crisis?* (Englewood Cliffs, N.J.: Prentice-Hall, 1972); "The Law, the Polluter, and You," *Audubon,* Sept. 1973, pp. 121ff; James S. Cannon, *A Clear View: Guide to Industrial Pollution Control* (Emmaus, Pa.: Rodale, 1976).

[84]Leo A. Orleans and Richard B. Suttmeier, "The Mao Ethic and Environmental Quality," *Science,* 170 (11 Dec. 1970), 1173–76; Marshall I. Goldman, *The Spoils of Progress: Environmental Pollution in the Soviet Union* (Cambridge, Mass.: MIT Press, 1972); Norman Precoda, "Soviet Mine Wastes," *Environment,* Nov. 1975, pp. 15–20; Oliver A. Houck, "Lenin's Trees," *Audubon,* Mar. 1980, pp. 104–19.

[85]Boyce Rensberger, "Coining Trash: Gold Strike on the Disassembly Line," *New York Times Magazine,* 7 Dec. 1975, pp. 31ff.

[86]"Wood Famine in Developing Countries," *Science News,* 115 (24 Feb. 1979), 119.

[87]Herman Kahn, *The Next 200 Years—A Scenario for America and the World* (New York: William Morrow, 1976).

[88]Paul H. Erlich and Anne H. Erlich, *The End of Affluence* (New York: Ballantine, 1974).

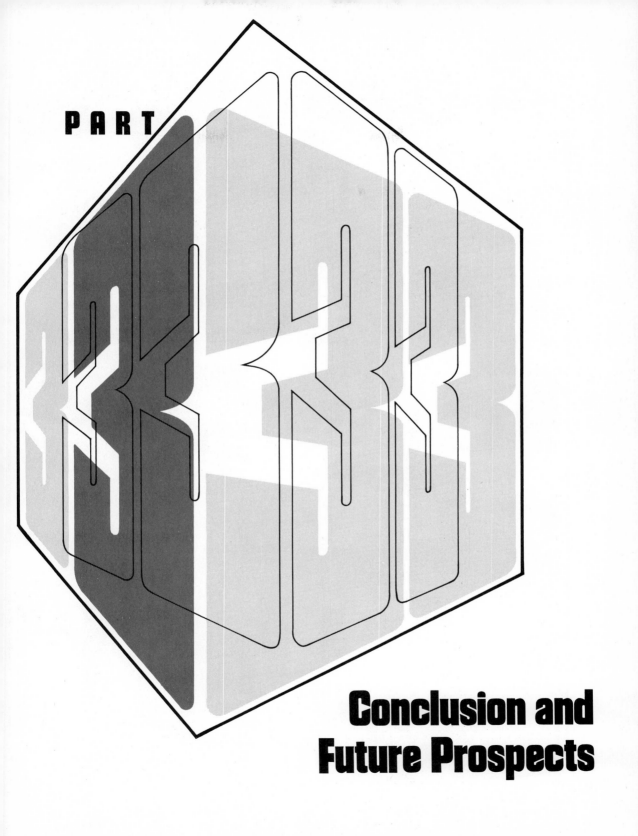

PART

3

Conclusion and Future Prospects

RETROSPECT AND PROSPECT 20

This is not the time for superficial solutions and everlasting elocution, for frantic boast and foolish word. For words are not deeds, and there are no cheap and painless solutions to war, hunger, ignorance, fear, and imperialist communism.—Adlai E. Stevenson

The trouble with Stevenson is that he makes everything too complicated. What we need are leaders who have clear, simple answers which are right every time.—A "letter to the editor" during Stevenson's campaign for the presidency

Here are two opposing views of social problems—the urbane view of the sophisticated scholar who sees the complexities, and the naive view of the layperson who wants simple, painless answers. In a world of revolutionary change, the answers are never simple or painless.

The Triple Revolution

A prominent business executive predicted in 1964, "Science and technology will advance more in the next 36 years than in all the millennia since man's creation."[1] Surely, we live in the period of the most revolutionary change in history. Some have termed this the period of the "triple revolution."[2]

1. THE CYBERNATION REVOLUTION   The use of tools, held in the human hand with the power supplied by human brawn, brought humankind out of caves and huts into civilized society. The industrial revolution shifted the tool from the hand to the machine; relieved of supplying the power, humans directed the machines and moved the work from machine to machine. The cybernation revolution includes two elments: automation and computer control. Automation connects a series of machines performing successive operations, with the work automatically moved from machine to machine; computers tell the machines what to do. Human beings build and service the machines and program the automated processes, while the computer (under complete cybernation) directs the actual operation of the machines and processes. This gives us almost unlimited productive capacity with less and less human labor.

2. THE WEAPONRY REVOLUTION   The weapons now being invented cannot win wars but can obliterate civilization. Total war has become obsolete as a method of resolving international disputes; yet wars continue, using "conventional" weapons, while every major nation feels that it needs more and more lethal weapons systems as a deterrent to other nations. So the arms race continues.

3. THE HUMAN RIGHTS REVOLUTION   The demand for human rights is worldwide. Women are shaking off male domination, subject races are claiming independence, and racial minorities are clamoring for a change of status. Even in communist countries, once the communist system is firmly established the demand for civil liberties arises.

The rising demand for civil liberties does not mean that a growing share of the world's people enjoy them. As we saw in chapter 19, the proportion of the world's people who enjoy civil rights has increased very little. Many former colonies, upon gaining their freedom, began oppressing their own minorities (or majorities). But the demand for human rights continues to be made almost everywhere.

The impact of the triple revolution upon society and culture will be greater than the impact of the industrial revolution. And, while the industrial revolution was two hundred years or more in the making, the triple revolution is maturing within a few decades. People's capacity to adapt themselves and their institutions to rapid social change is being tested as never before.

The Three Approaches to Changing Problems

SOCIAL DISORGANIZATION

Social problems arise from the disruption of traditional social systems by social change. The accelerating tempo of social change intensifies existing social problems and creates new ones. The recent revolution in Iran was, in part, a revolt against rapid social change. Every indication is that the tempo of social change will continue to accelerate, bringing an accelerating erosion of established authorities and controls. Group conflicts are intensified, with confrontations and disruption replacing petition, persuasion, and political organization as means of resolving disagreements. While a majority of American youth seeks reform within the framework of existing social and economic institutions, a noisy minority seeks their overthrow—with only the foggiest notion of what to put in their place.

Rapid social change is a new development in history. Never before have people had to adapt their social institutions to a continuously high rate of social change. Whether we can do so remains in doubt. Failure to deal successfully with our social problems could conceivably result in a growth of group conflict and disruption to the point of chaos, anarchy, and a paralysis of production and distribution, followed by mass starvation and a new "dark age." It is more likely, however, that failure to deal with social problems through democratic procedures would result in authoritarian rule, with ruthless suppression of dissent and extermination of persistent dissenters.

VALUE CONFLICT

Rapid social change intensifies value disagreements of many kinds. Values emerge from the social life of a people, and when their social life changes, their values change. But not all persons change their values at the same speed or in the same direction. For example, peasant thrift is a useful value in an economy of limited productivity; in a mass production economy individual thrift becomes a liability, for it is necessary for most people to spend most of their income if the economy is to operate. Most social scientists agree that large families are obsolete in a world of falling death rates, yet many people still revere certain religious authorities and values that rule out the most effective means of birth control. Thus, social change creates value conflicts.

The energy crisis is forcing many painful value choices upon us. Shall people be permitted to use as much energy as they can afford, or should their freedom to make certain choices—for powerful automobiles, vacation travel, air conditioning—be restricted? Should we be required to curtail energy use sharply, or should we risk the hazards of nuclear power?

A society can tolerate much value conflict, providing there is consensus on a few major values. Paramount to the survival of a democratic society is consensus on democratic means of decision making. If confrontation and disruption became the normal means of pursuing group interests, then either authoritarian rule or a new barbarism, or both, would seem inevitable.

For some years, popular faith in American institutions has been declining. Today it begins to appear that this decline may have "bottomed out." The most recent data show that although "trust in government" is still edging downward, as shown in figure 20–1, confidence in American institutions in general no longer shows a general decline, as shown in table 20–1. The prospects for keeping a minimum consensus on basic values is more promising now than it was a few years ago.

PERSONAL DEVIATION

When a scattered handful of persons are deviant, it makes sense to ask, "What's wrong with those nuts?" or, more academically, "What failures in the socialization process and in social control machinery resulted in these

Figure 20–1
Components of trust in government
Source: *ISR Newsletter*, Institute for Social Research, University of Michigan, Autumn 1979, p. 5.

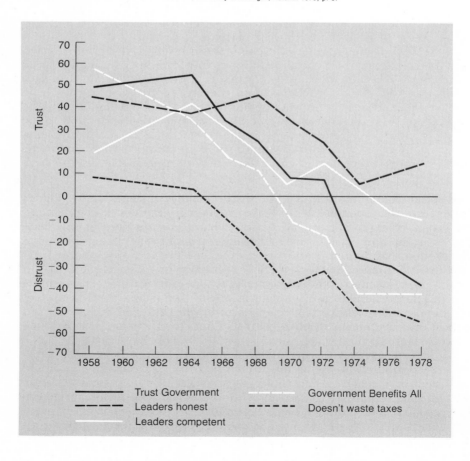

—————— Trust Government	– – – – – Government Benefits All
– – – – – Leaders honest	- - - - - Doesn't waste taxes
—————— Leaders competent	

Table 20–1   Public Confidence in Key Institutions in the United States

	Percent saying "great deal" or "quite a lot"				Percent change, 1973–79
	1973	1975	1977	1979	
The church or organized religion	66	68	64	65	−1
The military	—	58	57	54	−4
The public schools	58	—	54	53	−5
The newspapers	39	—	—	51	+11
The U.S. Supreme Court	44	49	46	45	+1
Television	37	—	—	38	+1
Organized labor	30	38	39	36	+6
Congress	42	40	40	34	−8
Big business	26	34	33	32	+6

SOURCE: *The Gallup Opinion Index*, No. 166, May 1979, p. 1.

few persons' failure to internalize the norms and values of the society?" This in turn leads to research into the deviant's background, family life, peer group experience, and personal frustrations and failures, to find possible explanations for the deviance.

When large numbers or entire groups of persons deviate from established norms and values, it is futile to seek purely individual explanations. Instead of asking, "What's wrong with those nuts?" we ask, "What's wrong with the society?" More academically, we ask, "What changes in the society have produced such an increase in the number of deviant persons who reject the traditional norms?"

Research focusing on deviant individuals (for example, comparing deviants with conformists) may give insight into who becomes deviant but will not explain the increase in deviance. Research into the social and cultural changes producing increased deviance is indicated. Not much of this type of research has yet appeared; so far, we have mainly speculative theorizing and impressionistic reports.[3] Possibly the youth rebellion and the "hip" culture should not be studied within the context of deviant behavior at all, but as examples of changing norms. For example, marijuana use is so widespread among youth that it is uncertain whether the total abstainer or the occasional user is the more "normal."

Not all deviation is bad; in fact, deviation is the process whereby new values and practices arise. A changing society requires a continuous adaptation of its norms and values, and individual and group deviation is a necessary part of this adaptive process. A century ago feminists were ridiculed as ludicrous deviants; today many of the goals for which they fought are so secure that the person who would question them is the deviant. Those deviants who first began practicing and advocating birth control were beginning a practice that *must* become a worldwide norm if humankind is to avoid breeding itself into starvation. Today those who advocate the acceptance of homosexuality as a legitimate alternative lifestyle are deviant. Are they pi-

I have worked much with the history of older civilizations and I believe they fell more because they failed to adjust to change than because they were undermined by it. American democracy had better learn to adjust to change or it, too, will be doomed.

The problem faced by Rome, and now by the United States, is the one that has perpetually faced organized society; how to hold on to the basic virtues on which the society was founded while adjusting rapidly to the change which it cannot escape.

The permanent American virtues would seem to me to include: respect for an honest day's work, a desire to do the right thing, a surprising capacity for investigation and improvization, a willingness to live under the rule of law, a willingness to contribute to the public welfare even if doing so requires heavy taxation, and a kind of naive trust in the destiny of the nation. Any program calling for the reinforcement of such basic virtues ought to be applauded and supported. But as much needed are programs which will help us to invent new concepts, and to decide which ideas are fertile and which are regressive.

It is the duty of our elected leaders to insure that our nation generates change, evaluates it, and assimilates that which represents progress. If they cannot do this, or if they are constitutionally opposed to all change, they should be retired from office, for if nations do not progress they perish.

James A. Michener, "One and a Half Cheers for Progress," *New York Times Magazine,* 5 Sept. 1971, p. 43. © 1971 by the New York Times Company. Reprinted by permission.

oneering a humane social norm, or contributing to role confusions and family disorganization?

When is deviation bad? Since by definition deviation is behavior that diverges from the norms and values of a social system, it can be answered only with reference to a particular social system. If one views the present social system (capitalism plus the welfare state under democratic rule) as worth preserving, then: (a) deviation is bad when it undermines the social system (crime, subversion, mass disruption); (b) deviation is good when it promotes reforms that are needed to keep the social system responsive to human needs (political dissent, reform movements, orderly demonstrations, civil disobedience under some circumstances, deviation from outworn codes or values). This test is not easy to apply, for it requires a judgment as to which reforms in the system are needed, and which deviations contribute to these reforms. For example, is a fairly high divorce rate a threat to the social system, or a needed adjustment to a highly differentiated, individualized society that places a high value upon mate love in marriage? Are the young unmarried couples who live openly together a threat to the family, or are they pioneering a sensible norm for approaching marriage? Is the ardent feminist who is campaigning for androgynous sex roles pointing the way to a more satisfying family life, or toward increasing frustration and role confusion? Any deviation is certain to be variously defined according to the values of those who judge it.

If one believes that the present social system should be overthrown, then any deviation that contributes to its overthrow is good. Within this context, deviations that produce reforms within the system would be bad, while those that paralyze it (closing down the university, harassing the police, interfering with recruiting for the armed services) would be good.

How about deviation that leads to the personal disorganization and demoralization of the deviant? Many juvenile delinquents become life-long misfits; many drug users become demoralized; persistent alcoholics drink themselves to death; and many sex deviants are unhappy. To those who wish to overthrow the social system such deviants are helpful. To the rest of us, any deviation that produces misery for the individual, without a redeeming benefit to the society, is a problem that deserves our sympathetic concern.

Much deviation, although it may be obnoxious to many of us, is socially inconsequential. Long hair and straggly beards may offend some people, but they harm nobody. The four-letter obscenities that some use as a substitute for expressive language really do no harm; their only effect is to deprive these words of their shock value by making them part of the common vocabulary, as has happened to many words that were once obscene. A considerable number of such harmless forms of deviation fill certain emotional needs without significant impact on the social system.

The prospect is that individual and group deviation will continue and possibly increase. Meanwhile, our facilities for treating individuals who are pathologically deviant are improving, and we can hope that the proportion of people whose lives are made permanently empty and miserable may show no increase, and may even decline. Deviation that regardless of intent has the effect of either reforming or undermining the social system will probably continue. Its ultimate effects may depend on our society's ability to make necessary adaptations rapidly and sensibly enough to avoid destruction.

Our Treatment of Problems Shows Some Successes . . .

Not long ago a book appeared claiming that conditions in America were better than critics picture them and citing data showing great improvement in many problem areas.[4] This book annoyed leftists who see nothing good about America and infuriated "problem entrepreneurs" who fear that evidence of improvement may undercut their fund appeals. Yet the simple truth is that not all problems are growing worse. Some problems are diminishing in severity, either because other social changes reduce the problem or because of effective social policies for treating it.

1. MIGRANT LABOR   Since John Steinbeck's *Grapes of Wrath* appeared in 1939,[5] the migrant labor problem has been studied and publicized but largely untreated. Each year a migrant labor force of several hundred thousand men, women, and children takes to the highways to harvest crops that demand a seasonal supply of unskilled labor. Their annual incomes are well below the poverty line. As agricultural workers they have been excluded from labor legislation that protected other workers. Their housing is often wretched and unsanitary, for it is hardly realistic to expect farm operators to provide pleasant housing for only a few days' or weeks' use per year. As migrants

who do not belong to the community, they have had little access to most social services. In short, they are among our most neglected minorities.

Today mechanical harvesters, together with the development of crop strains more amenable to mechanical harvesting, are rapidly displacing migrant farm workers. Thus, technological change is ending a social problem that we had little success in treating. True, there is a short-run problem of relocating the displaced farm workers, but this should last only a few years.

2. POVERTY AND INEQUALITY   In the developed nations of the world it is now possible to abolish poverty. A few countries—notably in Scandinavia—have come very close to achieving this goal. The United States lags behind but is catching up. While poverty is still real in America, and income inequalities are great, both have been reduced in recent decades. This trend toward equalizing incomes continues, mainly through progressive taxation and income transfers.

3. POPULATION GROWTH   In much of the world, birth rates are falling rapidly. The United States is now promoting population control in its foreign aid programs, and a number of countries, including India and China, are making a real effort to bring population growth under control. Recent improvements in contraception and abortion techniques have been helpful, and further improvements can be anticipated. While population growth is still the most grave world problem there are for the first time some grounds for hope that monumental disaster can be averted.

The introduction of mechanical harvesting has helped to eliminate the problem
of the migrant farm workers.
(United Nations)

4. ENVIRONMENTAL DEGRADATION After the grim tone of chapter 19 it may be surprising to find environmental degradation in this list of problems that are lessening. While the problem remains serious, a start has been made. The headlong, accelerating destruction of the environment has come very close to a standstill, although we have barely started to put into operation the policies for environmental protection. The outlook is clearly more favorable than it was a decade ago, if present momentum can be maintained.

5. DISCRIMINATION While discrimination may be growing in many parts of the world, it has been declining in the United States. The problem remains, as flagrant discriminations end and more subtle ones come under attack. But the continuing controversies over discrimination should not blind us to the great gains that have been achieved. Most issues of two or three decades ago have been resolved and dropped from public discussion (for example, voting rights, black access to public accommodations). Within a single decade feminists have made gains matched by few reform movements in history.

6. HEALTH The great gap between the poor and the prosperous in access to health care has virtually disappeared, and the gap in health levels has been reduced. The health problem today is one of costs, organization of services, and promotion of healthful habits.

. . . And Some Failures

For some problems we can claim no successes. Some problems are as frustrating as, or even more serious than, ever before.

1. CRIME Although the rate of crime increase appears to have slowed, crime remains at an all-time high. After decades of research and experimentation it is not clear that we are any closer to a solution.

> The traditional rewards of good pay, job security and a clean, safe plant will no longer suffice—the job itself will have to be changed so that a worker can feel pride and satisfaction while he is turning out the product and not only when he steps up to the cashier's window to get his pay envelope.
>
> Agis Salpukas, *New York Times*, 24 Dec. 1972, sec. 3, p. 3, in review of Harold L. Sheppard and Neal Q. Herrick, *Where Have All the Robots Gone?* (New York: Free Press, 1972).

2. ALIENATION FROM WORK seems to be a growing problem, with no clear solution in sight. Each age cohort of workers is more bitterly critical of "dehumanizing work."[6] Until very recently, studies of job satisfaction showed that most American workers were fairly well satisfied with their jobs,[7] and that levels of job satisfaction had been quite stable for some years.[8] But a 1977 survey shows a "slight but significant" decline in job satisfaction over

605

the preceding four years.[9] Despite the vaunted automated factories, there are still a lot of tiring, dirty, unpleasant jobs in mines, factories, slaughter-houses, and elsewhere.[10] Yet it is likely that the proportion of all jobs that are dehumanizing has never been lower. It is not that work has become more dehumanizing, but that younger workers are complaining bitterly about jobs their parents accepted gratefully, or at least passively.[11]

Perhaps because of rising levels of education, people who demand interesting and challenging work are increasing faster than such jobs are being created. A good deal of dubious Marxist rhetoric has been devoted to "worker alienation" in capitalist countries; yet patterns of worker satisfaction and discontent are strikingly similar in capitalist and communist countries.[12] The main difference is that in capitalist countries workers are free to quit and find other work (if they can).

Adequate treatment of this problem would demand a separate chapter. We can only note in passing that the problem is growing steadily more pressing, as shown by rising rates of employee turnover, absenteeism, wild-cat strikes, pilferage, sloppy work, and even sabotage. Management officials are fully aware of the problem and are experimenting with various attempts at "job enrichment," which to date do not appear to be very successful.[13] The problem is worldwide, probably increasing, and with no successful solution yet demonstrated.

3. TRANSPORTATION AND URBAN BLIGHT are interrelated problems that show no improvement. The private automobile (among other factors) is destroying

In recent years there has been a slight but significant decline in job satisfaction among this country's workers.
(Irene Springer)

the central cities, while the cities have enthusiastically cooperated in their own destruction. Either efficient public transportation must largely replace the automobile for daily commuter use in the larger cities, or they are doomed. This is but one of many aspects of the growing problems of transportation and urban blight.

4. THE ENERGY PROBLEM   is becoming more serious. Energy conservation is mainly talk, not a real program. Alternative energy technologies are not developing fast enough to avoid either a great drop in living standards or a choice between the dangers of increased use of nuclear energy and the dangers of increased use of coal.

5. PROBLEMS OF PRIVACY, LEISURE, AND RECREATION   are a growing concern, as discussed earlier. Perhaps still others should be added. Students of social problems are in no danger of running out of interesting pathological conditions to study.

Some Difficulties of "Solutions"

Why have social scientists, if they are so wise, not yet found "clear, simple answers" to social problems? There are several reasons.

1. INADEQUACIES OF KNOWLEDGE   Our knowledge of some problems is simply not adequate. We suspect that there may be some organic basis for at least part of our mentally ill, alcoholics, and possibly some criminals. But if so, it has not been definitely established. Because we cannot say exactly what causes crime, we must work with a number of possible causes, influences, and associations. No contraceptive is fully satisfactory for use among an unsophisticated population with limited motivation for family planning; until medical research develops one, population control in underdeveloped countries is difficult. A massive shift from pesticides to nonpoisonous pest controls is absolutely necessary for human survival, but little of the necessary knowledge has yet been discovered. We know of no way to generate electricity in the amounts desired without polluting the environment (either by burning fuels or by producing nuclear byproducts). For no social problem do we have all the knowledge we need.

It is also true that we do not use all the knowledge we have. We know how to treat sewage, yet most rivers are open sewers. We permit unregulated strip mining operations to ruin entire watersheds. We devote massive efforts to prevent use of marijuana, which most evidence suggests is relatively harmless, yet we make only a token effort to discourage use of cigarettes, which have killed millions. We know a great deal about the conditions encouraging crime, race conflict, and urban blight, yet we permit these conditions to continue. Our knowledge is far from complete, yet we have far more knowledge than we are using.

2. POPULAR IGNORANCE   Popular ignorance makes it difficult to implement policies that social scientists know would be helpful in alleviating some problems. Popular misinformation about property values and race is one of the

607

greatest obstacles to housing integration. Popular superstitions about drug addicts, sex deviants, and mental illness are barriers to their effective treatment. The antiurban bias and the myth that local government is more honest and efficient than federal government are obstacles to the sensible handling of many problems. There is a good deal of knowledge that social scientists have developed, but that cannot be fully used because so many of the public will not allow it to be used.

3. VALUE CONFLICTS   Many problems cannot be solved because there is insufficient value consensus. Problems such as gambling, prostitution, drug use, sex deviation or "immorality," and divorce cannot be solved because there is no general agreement on goals. Should prostitution be vigorously suppressed in an effort to exterminate it; or should it be recognized and regulated, in an effort to reduce the venereal disease, blackmail, and other consequences that accompany prostitution? Should public schools be integrated and racial balance promoted, or should black children attend black schools staffed and controlled by blacks? Neither blacks nor whites agree on this. *Solutions are impossible when value conflicts prevent agreement on goals.*

Even when there is agreement on goals, *value conflicts may prevent agreement on means.* Should sex education be provided by schools, or left to church and home (and peer group)? There is consensus that poverty is undesirable. Should poverty be attacked by a guaranteed annual income, by seeking to increase the work productivity and job opportunities of the poor, by scolding and starving the poor in a (futile) hope that they will work harder, or by some combination of these? Without considerable agreement on means, there can be no solutions.

4. VALUE SACRIFICES   There can be no solutions without value sacrifices. Paramount is the sacrifice of a value dear to the hearts of most of us—*money.* Most solutions are costly. To improve schools, rebuild cities, reduce poverty, and reduce pollution will cost a lot of tax monies. Solutions also impose costs upon persons and groups. Pollution abatement requires corporations to assume heavy costs for treatment of industrial wastes, and raises the consumer's cost of buying and operating an automobile. Should environmental concerns be sacrificed whenever jobs are at stake? Protecting a landmark, neighborhood, or park from the bulldozer means a more expensive and circuitous expressway, or a more costly and less conveniently located airport. Practically every solution requires someone to pay more taxes, suffer loss of job or income, or sacrifice an opportunity for future profits.

Many solutions also involve other kinds of value sacrifices. Racial equality requires whites to sacrifice both their economic exploitation of blacks and the psychological satisfactions of feeling and acting superior. Democratic family life requires men to relax their authority over women and to sacrifice the luxury of avoiding housework. Premarital sexual freedom, which some see as part of the solution for family problems, causes great anxiety and heartache for many parents, and for many young people as well. Most solutions involve sacrifice of values other than purely financial ones.

Future solutions may impose even greater value sacrifices. Farm production per acre may fall (at least temporarily) as the use of certain insecticides and fertilizers is curtailed. The privilege of private car ownership and operation may be restricted in the interest of energy conservation. The time may come when the "right" to have as many children as a couple may wish is limited. Such value sacrifices are certain to delay and possibly to prevent solutions from being adopted.

5. INADEQUATE EVALUATION OF SOLUTIONS   Rarely is a "solution" adopted after a number of trials have shown convincingly that it "works." Instead, a "solution" usually represents an act of faith by reformers, or a victory for a pressure group with an interest to defend. Often a "solution" acquires a momentum that raises it above the need for evaluation; since it is *right*, it *must* work. Thus, driver education in the schools, busing for racial balance, bilingual education, and legal suppression of drug traffic are programs that are above question, even though there is no convincing body of consistent evidence that they are achieving their goals. There is little evidence that the billions of dollars spent by the Law Enforcement Assistance Administration has had much impact upon the crime problem.

Rooney cites the skid row rescue missions as an example of programs that "succeed" only through failure. If they achieved their goals, their job would be ended, but their failure to achieve their goals is an argument for continuing and expanding them. Rooney notes that the Drug Enforcement Administration multiplied its personnel by 8 times and its budget by 32 times between 1965 and 1978, without reducing the availability of street drugs.[14] It is not suggested that program operators *wish* to fail, but their failure is seldom cited as a reason for abandoning an unsuccessful program. Instead, the usual answer is: "If it doesn't work, do more of it." Evaluation research, theoretically for the purpose of measuring program effectiveness, is usually conducted for the purpose of manufacturing support for the program's continuance and expansion. Our readiness to adopt huge but untested programs, and to continue unsuccessful ones, is a waste of private and public funds. It is finally dawning upon the U.S. Corps of Army Engineers that "shoreline erosion control" is an exercise in futility. Ocean waves and storms shift the sands around, and man-made jetties and seawalls simply make shoreline erosion worse. A more practical (and far cheaper) policy would be to buy up the shifting shoreline and let nature take its course, but such a sensible policy is meeting powerful political opposition.[15]

6. LACK OF INTEGRATION OF SOLUTIONS   Often a solution alleviates one problem while aggravating others. Our success in preventing disease and increasing life expectancy produced the population explosion. Programs of subsidized housing for the poor have not been integrated into a comprehensive program for their spatial distribution, education, income maintenance, or overall rehabilitation. In consequence, massive public housing projects that fill up with welfare poor, isolated from the rest of the community, have often become cesspools of crime and degradation. Our spectacular technological progress, our high standard of living, and our ingenuity in inventing new products have multiplied our pollution of the environment. Manufacturers have built automobiles that pollute the air less but use more gasoline, thus reducing one environmental problem while aggravating another. A half-century of flood control has not reduced average annual flood losses. The flood control projects greatly reduced the frequency and severity of floods, but they were not accompanied by any control over use of the floodlands. Consequently these lowland areas became valuable building sites and were

built upon, so that today's floods are more destructive than ever, and total flood losses have steadily increased.[16] Practically every solution, even if it works, brings new problems.

This does not mean that all solutions are useless. By any humanitarian values it is far better for the average couple to have only two or three children, all alive and healthy, than to have six or eight and watch half of them die. What this does mean is that solutions need to be integrated. Programs for death control must be accompanied by programs for birth control, otherwise we save people from a quick death from smallpox so that they may enjoy a slow death from malnutrition.

The little town of Whitesburg, Kentucky, spent $180,000 on a reservoir and water system, but even before it was finished the reservoir was completely filled with silt from upstream strip mining operations.[17] A reservoir or a flood control project unaccompanied by an enforceable land use program is wasteful. For one governmental agency to build urban expressways, creating traffic congestion and urban blight, while a separate and independent agency seeks to abate urban blight, is wasteful. Urban transportation (both private and public), urban blight, and urban and suburban land use are related problems, and must be treated within the context of a comprehensive metropolitan area authority if these related problems are to be handled successfully. Solutions must be integrated with one another to be effective.

Prospect—Armageddon or Promised Land?

The recitation of ills and troubles may obscure the fact that most Americans consider the quality of their lives fairly good.[18] A recent international Gallup Poll covering most of the noncommunist nations found that Americans are more content than most of the world's peoples.[19] What does the future hold?

It is dangerous for anyone, least of all a social scientist, to make confident predictions about the future. There is an impressive number of ways for the world to race to physical destruction.[20] Humankind may exterminate itself through nuclear warfare, decimate itself through reckless abuse of the environment, breed itself into Malthusian misery, or perhaps muddle through with a series of tardy, contradictory, and only partly effective solu-

---

Despite complaints about many aspects of their country, Americans, according to the Gallup Poll, appear to be considerably more satisfied with the quality of their life than most other people of the non-communist world. . . . "Presently efforts are being made to include Communist nations in the survey," the announcement said.

"Even among the lower economic groups in the United States," the poll found, "satisfaction levels for the items tested are higher than the national averages in the developing regions of the world.

"The nations with the highest per capita income almost invariably top every test of psychological well-being and satisfaction in major aspects of life."

New York Times, 7 Nov. 1976, p. 2.

tions. Or there is the possibility that we are learning how to deal more successfully with problems than did our ancestors. Far more knowledge is at our disposal today. Will we be able to resolve the value conflicts and accept the value sacrifices needed to use this knowledge?

It is easier to be optimistic if we retain the sense of perspective mentioned in the opening chapter. Present problems are grave indeed, but when has the world been serene and problem-free? The race problem remains unsolved, but was the outlook more favorable a century ago? The streets may be less safe than they were a few years ago, but we should remember that the idea that streets should be safe at night is a very recent one; throughout most of history no sane person ventured upon the streets at night without protection. Not all businesspeople are honest, but today's business executives are saints compared to their predecessors. The American colonies were the world's leading market for stolen merchandise, and colonial governors grew rich receiving bribes and selling protection, while leading families and prominent merchants organized pirate expeditions.[21] On the American frontier the fur trapper's greatest problem lay not in making his catch, but in transporting it to the fur buyer without being robbed on the way. Many a trio or quartet of prospectors set out, while only one returned months later, bearing a rich find and a suspicious account of the misfortunes that had befallen his partners. The "good old days" were truly good only in the fond imagination of those who don't know their history well. Compared to the realities of the past, the present with all its imperfections offers an encouraging contrast.

A bit of patience also helps maintain optimism. History shows that no social reform was ever accomplished without years of effort; that only after years or decades of fact-gathering, pamphleteering, organizing, petitioning,

The problem of atmospheric depletion of ozone layers is an example of an environmental problem which was speedily attacked and resolved.
(Irene Springer)

lobbying, and finally a bit of compromising, is any significant reform accomplished. Decades of effort lay behind such reforms as women's suffrage, workmen's compensation, social security, substantial federal aid to education, and the Civil Rights Acts of 1964 and 1968.

By contrast, one can find some examples of very prompt and sensible recognition and treatment of a problem. For instance, we first became aware of the fact of ozone depletion in 1974. Although this was denied by the chemical industry for two years, the restriction on the use of aerosol chlorfluoromethanes began in 1978.[22] Four years from identification of a problem to adoption of a practical solution is, historically speaking, almost instantaneous.

None can be sure what the future holds. Public confidence in the condition of our nation has faltered, at least temporarily, as shown in figure 20–2. It is likely that we shall never again see a period such as the quarter-century after World War II, when the living standards of the American people doubled in less than a generation. At present, the rising costs of energy, of raw materials, and of environmental protection all add up to lower productivity and falling living standards. Pessimism is in the air, with doomsday prophets much in fashion. Robert Heilbroner and E. J. Mishan see a nightmare future of resource shortages, nuclear blackmail, and wars to redistribute the world's wealth.[23] Herman Kahn sees a future of continued growth and rising prosperity.[24] L. S. Stavrianos foresees an end of affluence but is vague about what is to replace the present system.[25] Remember, however, that the ball-gazers are forever seeing us as teetering on the edge of the abyss. Predicted disasters rarely materialize. It is likely that we shall share neither the cornucopia of Kahn, the Götterdämmerung of Heilbroner, nor the socialist paradise of Stavrianos. A little of each seems a more likely prospect.

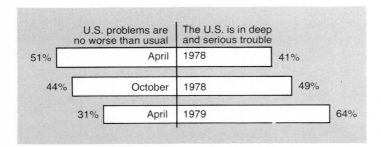

Figure 20–2
Public confidence in the condition of our nation has faltered
Source: National survey by Yankelovich, Skelly, and White, Inc., for Time, Inc. Reported in *Time*, 30 Apr. 1979, p. 18.

Summary

The modern world is experiencing a triple revolution—in cybernation, weaponry, and human rights. The consequences include increased social disorganization, intensified value conflicts, and increasing individual and group deviation (of which the youth rebellion was a prime example). Whether deviation is good or bad depends upon one's value judgments of contemporary society, and whether the deviation tends to preserve or destroy it.

A few problems are diminishing: changing technology is ending the migrant farm labor problem; we have had some success in reducing poverty and inequality; a substantial beginning at world population control has been made; promising efforts to ameliorate environmental problems are under way; most forms of discrimination in the United States have been eliminated or reduced; the health gap between the poor and the affluent has been greatly narrowed. On some other problems no success is evident: crime, alienation from work, transportation and urban blight, energy, privacy, leisure, and recreation. The search for solutions is complicated by the inadequacies of present scientific knowledge, by popular ignorance that prevents full use of our knowledge, by value conflicts that prevent agreement upon solutions, by unwillingness to accept the value sacrifices that solutions require, by a lack of realistic program evaluation, and by the need for integration of solutions if they are to be successful.

The future is unpredictable. A sense of historical perspective helps prevent panic, and a bit of patience helps us to be realistic. No complete or perfect solutions are possible, but a continued avoidance of passionate extremism, together with the use of humane intelligence, may still make the future better than the past.

Suggested Readings

BAIN, READ, "Our Schizoid Culture," *Sociology and Social Research,* 19 (Jan.–Feb. 1935), 266–76. A classic sociological essay, stating many of the value conflicts and inconsistencies in American social life.

BRODEUR, PAUL, "Aerosol Bombs: A Planetary Time Bomb," *National Parks and Conservation Magazine,* Feb. 1979, pp. 10–19. An example of rapid recognition and prompt treatment of a problem.

CAMPBELL, ANGUS, PHILIP E. CONVERSE, and WILLARD L. ROGERS, *The Quality of American Life: Perceptions, Evaluations, and Satisfactions* (New York: Russell Sage, 1976). An empirical study of the level of satisfaction with life for Americans of various ages, incomes, occupations, and life situations.

ETZIONI, AMITAI, "Shortcuts to Social Change," *The Public Interest,* Summer 1968, pp. 40–51; or, Amitai Etzioni and Richard Remp, *Technological Shortcuts to Social Change* (New York: Russell Sage, 1972). Argues that fundamental solutions to social problems are so costly that they are rejected, but that palliatives and piecemeal remedies have some value.

GAYLIN, WILLARD et al., *Doing Good: The Limits of Benevolence* (New York: Pantheon, 1978). Examines the question of how to take care of needy people without doing more harm than good.

KAHN, HERMAN, *The Next 200 Years: A Scenario for America and the World* (New York: Morrow, 1976); or *World Economic Development: 1979 and Beyond* (Boulder, Colo.: Westview Press, 1979). An optimistic view of the future of Western civilization.

KAUFMAN, WALLACE, and ORRIN PILKEY, *The Beaches Are Moving: The Drowning of America's Shoreline* (Garden City, N.Y.: Anchor Press/Doubleday, 1979). Tells of the wasteful effort to prevent the ocean from shoreline erosion; a case study in persisting in an ineffectual policy.

MICHENER, JAMES A., "One and a Half Cheers for Progress," *New York Times Magazine,* 5 Sept. 1971, pp. 9ff. A popular article classifying a number of recent inventions as either beneficial or harmful to the public good.

MISHAN, E. J., *The Economic Growth Debate: An Assessment* (London: George Allen and Unwin, 1977). A review of the progrowth and antigrowth advocates, ending on a note of pessimism.

ROONEY, JAMES F., "Organizational Success through Program Failure: Skid Row Rescue Missions," *Social Forces,* 58 (Mar. 1980), 904–24. A discussion of how and why unsuccessful programs are perpetuated.

ROSSI, PETER H., and WALTER WILLIAMS, *Evaluating Social Programs* (New York:

Seminar Press, 1972). A sophisticated analysis of the problem of testing social programs to see if they work.

———— , "The Future Economic Outlook," *Current*, Oct. 1979, pp. 19–33. Several brief essays on the state of the economy.

Footnotes

[1]David Sarnoff, "By the End of the Twentieth Century," *Fortune*, May 1964, pp. 166ff.

[2]Robert Perucci and Marc Pilisuk, *The Triple Revolution Emerging: Social Problems in Depth* (Boston: Little, Brown, 1971).

[3]J. L. Simmons and Barry Winograd, *It's Happening: A Portrait of the Youth Scene Today* (Santa Barbara, Ca.: Marc-Laird, 1966); Lewis Yablonski, *The Hippie Trip* (New York: Pegasus, 1968); Kenneth Keniston, *Youth and Dissent* (New York: Harcourt Brace Jovanovich, 1970); Theodore Roszak, *The Wasteland Ends* (New York: Doubleday, 1972); Seymour M. Lipset, *Rebellion in the University* (Chicago: University of Chicago Press, 1976).

[4]Ben J. Wattenberg, *The Real America: A Surprising Examination of the State of the Union* (New York: Doubleday, 1974).

[5]John Steinbeck, *The Grapes of Wrath* (New York: Viking, 1939).

[6]See "The Spreading Lordstown Syndrome," *Business Week*, 4 Mar. 1972, pp. 69–70; Andrew Levison, "The Rebellion of Blue Collar Youth," *The Progressive*, Oct. 1972, pp. 38–42; *Work in America: Report of a Special Task Force to the Secretary of Health, Education and Welfare* (Cambridge, Mass.: MIT Press, 1973).

[7]H. Roy Kaplan, "How Do Workers View Their Work in America?" *Monthly Labor Review*, 96 (June 1973), 46–48; H. Roy Kaplan, "Review Symposium on Work in America," *Sociology of Work and Occupations*, May 1975, pp. 188–93; Robert P. Quinn et al., *Job Satisfaction: Is There a Trend?* (Washington, D.C.: U.S. Department of Labor, 1974).

[8]Robert P. Quinn et al., *Job Satisfaction;* Angus Campbell, Philip E. Converse, and Willard L. Rogers, *The Quality of American Life: Perceptions, Evaluations and Satisfactions* (New York: Russell Sage, 1976), ch. 9.

[9]University of Michigan, Survey Research Center, quoted in *Business Week*, 4 July 1979, p. 152.

[10]See "The Dirty Work," *Wall Street Journal*, 16 July 1971, pp. 1ff.

[11]John Hoerr, "Worker Unrest: Not Dead but Playing Possum," *Business Week*, 10 May 1976, pp. 133–44.

[12]Arnold Tannenbaum, *Hierarchy in Organizations: An International Comparison* (San Francisco: Jossey-Bass, 1974).

[13]See "Motorola Creates a More Demanding Job," *Business Week*, 4 Sept. 1971, p. 32; J. L. Windle, "Motivation of Workers," paper presented to Indianapolis Personnel Association, 16 Nov. 1972, mimeograph from Department of Industrial Supervision, Purdue University; "Where Being Nice to Workers Didn't Work," *Business Week*, 20 Jan. 1973, pp. 99–100.

[14]James F. Rooney, "Organizational Success through Program Failure: Skid Row Rescue Missions," *Social Forces*, 58 (Mar. 1980), 904–24.

[15]Wallace Kaufman and Orrin Pilkey, *The Beaches Are Moving: The Drowning of America's Shoreline* (Garden City, N.Y.: Anchor Press/Doubleday, 1979); reviewed by Eric Salzman in *Sierra*, Jan./Feb. 1980, pp. 58–60; also Seth S. King, "Curbs on Development of Barrier Islands Proposed," *New York Times*, 23 Dec. 1979, p. 116.

[16]*A Unified Program for Managing Flood Losses*, House Document No. 465, 89th Congress, 2nd session, 1966; Arthur E. Morgan, *Dams and Other Disasters* (Boston: Porter Sargent, 1971).

[17]*The Mountain Eagle* (Whitesburg, Ky.), 23 May 1968, p. 1.

[18]Campbell, Converse, and Rogers, *The Quality of American Life.*

[19]"A World Poll on the 'Quality of Life,'" *New York Times*, 7 Nov. 1976, p. 2.

[20]Isaac Asimov, *A Choice of Catastrophes: The Disasters That Threaten Our World* (New York: Simon & Schuster, 1979).

[21]Hugh F. Rankin, *The Golden Age of Piracy* (Williamsburg, Va.: Colonial Williamsburg, Inc., 1968).

[22]Paul Brodeur, "Aerosol Bombs: A Planetary Time Bomb," *National Parks and Conservation Magazine*, Feb. 1979, pp. 10–19.

[23]Robert L. Heilbroner, *An Inquiry into the Human Prospect* (New York: Norton, 1974); E. J. Mishan, *The Economic*

Growth Debate: An Assessment (London: George Allen and Unwin, 1977).

[24]Herman Kahn, *The Next 200 Years: A Scenario for America and the World* (New York: William Morrow, 1976); Herman Kahn and The Hudson Institute, *World Economic Development: 1979 and Beyond* (Boulder, Colo.: Westview Press, 1979).

[25]L. S. Stavrianos, *Promise of the Coming Dark Age* (San Francisco: Freeman, 1976).

INDEXES

NAME INDEX

E

Earle, Alice Morse, 535
Ebenstein, William ,558, 559
Eckholm, Erik P., 520, 589, 591, 592, 593
Edelhertz, Herbert, 127
Edison, Thomas, 54
Edwards, Marvin H., 521
Efron, Edith, 441, 442
Ehrbar, A.F., 513, 525
Ehrenreich, Barbara, 520
Ehrenreich, John, 520
Ehrlich, Anne H., 591, 594
Ehrlich, Isaac, 158
Ehrlich, Paul R., 591, 594
Eisenhower, Dwight, 51
Eissler, S., 486
Elden, James M., 559
Ellesh, David, 524
Elliott, Delbert S., 154
Ellwood, Robert S., Jr., 217, 218
Emerson, Thomas I., 443, 560
Endres, Michael E., 248
Engels, Friedrich, 558
Englebardt, Stanley, 524
Enos, Darryl D., 520
Epstein, Edward J., 75
Epstein, Joseph, 192
Erickson, Maynard, L., 158
Ericson, Edward E., Jr., 559
Ernst, Harry W., 74
Ernst, Morris L., 444, 561
Esco, Jack, 485
Esselstyn, T.C., 126, 486
Etzioni, Amitai, 560, 613
Evans, Bergen, 74
Evans, J.C., 220
Everett, Bill, 442
Eversole, Pam, 441
Eysenck, Hans J., 313, 347

F

Fairlie, Henry, 25
Fantini, Mario, 274
Farber, Lawrence, 524
Farber, Stephen, 444
Faris, Robert E.L., 484
Farley, Reynolds, 351
Farnia, Amerigo, 376
Fausto, R., 158
Feagin, Joe R., 307, 345, 348
Feagle, Robert G., 24

Featherman, David L., 255, 272, 274, 374
Feender, Harold, 346
Fein, Sara, 484
Feinberg, Walter, 271
Feldman, Saul D., 377
Feldstein, Martin, 520, 521
Ferber, Marianne A., 374
Ferber, Michael, 128
Ferracuti, Franco, 154
Feshback, Seymour, 443
Fetterman, John, 307
Fialka, John, 591, 593
Fichter, Joseph H., 218
Ficker, Victor B., 44
Figlio, Robert M., 127, 154
Fincher, Jack, 270
Finn, Chester E., 271
Firey, Walter, 410
Fischer, Anita, 376
Fischer, David H., 373
Fischer, John, 410
Fisher, Arthur, 594
Fisher, Ben C., 444
Fisher, Charles W., 345
Fiske, Edward A., 271
Fiske, Edward B., 220, 274
Fitzpatrick, Joseph P., 346
Fogelman, E., 558, 559
Foner, Philip S., 348
Ford, Nick, A., 272
Foreman, Robert E., 153
Forrest, Catherine K., 486
Forslund, Morris A., 126
Fosdick, Harry E., 25
Foss, Dennis C., 25
Foster, Henry H., Jr., 192, 560
Fox, Vernon, 129
Fox, Robin, 75
Freberg, Stan, 443
Freeman, Ellen W., 193
Freeman, Jo, 373
Freeman, Richard B., 274
Frenkel-Brunswick, Else, 348
Freud, Anna, 486
Friday, Paul C., 156, 157, 158
Friedan, Betty, 180, 373, 375
Friedlander, Paul J.C., 525
Friedman, Jonathan, 374
Friedman, Milton, 18
Friendly, Fred W., 440, 443, 444
Frieze, Irene Hanson, 374
Friis, Robert, 521
Frumkin, Robert, 457

Frye, Jerry K., 442
Fuchs, Victor R., 522
Fuerst, J.S., 274
Fuller, Richard C., 40, 45
Fullinwider, S.P., 345
Furstenberg, Frank, Jr., 193

G

Gabrielson, Ira, 172, 173
Gabrielson, Mary O., 172, 173
Gage, Nicholas, 129
Gagnon, John H., 487
Gaitz, Charles M., 307
Galaway, Burt, 158
Galbraith, John K., 103, 305
Gallagher, Dorothy, 593
Galligiole, Steve, 593
Gallup, George, 521
Galton, Francis, 239, 241
Gannon, William, 219
Gans, Herbert J., 411, 547, 568
Gardiner, John A., 142, 156
Gardner, John, 97
Gardner, Martin, 74
Garrison, Martha L., 375
Garry, Charles R., 75
Gartner, Alan, 524
Gartrell, John W., 485
Gastil, Raymond D., 557
Gatti, Florence, M., 153, 154
Gaylin, Willard, 613
Gebhard, Paul H., 193, 476, 487
Gehlker, Gretchen, 127
Geiger, H. Hunt, 375
Geis, Gilbert, 152, 157
Gelles, Richard J., 164, 192
Gerber, Alex, 509, 523
Gerbner, George, 443
Gershman, Carl, 559
Gershon, S., 486
Giallombardo, Rose, 487
Gibb, Cecil A., 377
Gibbs, Jack P., 158
Gibson, Frank K., 157
Gilder, George F., 373, 376
Ginsberg, Eli, 520, 523
Gintis, Herbert, 270, 271
Giodano, Peggy C., 154
Gitlin, Todd, 410
Glaser, Daniel, 156, 486
Glaser, William A., 523
Glazer, Nathan, 351
Glazer-Malbin, Nona, 373

Troiden, Richard, 483
Troike, Rudolph, 273
Trotman, Richard, 522
Trotter, Robert J., 484
Trotter, Sharland, 560
Troyer, Ronald J., 522
Truzzi, Marcello, 219
Tsui, Amy Ong, 249
Tuan, Yi-fu, 592
Tubesing, Donald A., 522
Tuchman, Gaye, 440
Tullock, Gordon, 158
Tunley, Roul, 525
Tunney, John V., 521
Turk, Amos, 572, 593
Turk, Austin J., 127
Turk, Jonathan, 572, 593
Turlington, Ralph D., 274
Turner, James S., 521
Turner, Jonathan H., 306
Turner, R. Jay, 485
Tushnet, Leonard, 521
Tygert, Clarence E., 221
Tyler, Gus, 129, 346
Tyler, Ralph W., 273

U

Ungerleider, J. Thomas, 218
Uphoff, James K., 219
Useem, Michael, 559

V

Valentine, Jeanette, 273
Van den Berghe, Pierre, 376
Van Den Haag, Ernest, 158
Van Valey, Thomas L., 351
Vartan, Vartanig, G., 74
Vatter, Harold G., 306
Veblen, Thorstein, 18
Vener, Arthur M., 218
Venezia, Peter S., 155
Vickers, George R., 559
Vidman, Neil, 346, 349
Villemez, Wayne J., 127, 153, 350, 359, 374
Viscuse, W. Kip, 593
Vogliotti, Gabe, 483
Vold, George, 153, 155
Volkov, Solomon, 545
Vontress, Clement E., 272

W

Wachtel, A., 193
Wackman, Daniel B., 441
Waddell, H. Clayton, 559
Waehrer, Helen Youngelson, 373
Wagenfeld, Morton O., 485
Wagenheim, Kal, 410
Wahlke, John C., 561
Waldbott, George L., 523, 592
Waldo, Gordon P., 127, 157
Walker, Lewis, 345, 347
Walker, Stanley, 127, 128
Wallace, George, 425
Wallace, Michael, 559
Wallerstein, James S., 126
Wallis, Roy, 218
Walsh, D.P., 158
Walsh, Marilyn, 127
Walster, Elaine, 376
Ward, David A., 128, 156, 486
Ward, Hiley H., 218
Warren, Carol A.B., 154
Warren, David G., 520, 524
Warren, Jim, 560
Washington, Booker T., 321, 330
Washington, George, 555
Wasserman, Michael, 154
Waters, Harry F., 445
Wattenberg, Ben J., 614
Watts, Anita McFarland, 127
Weaver, Paul H., 440
Webster, Daniel, 25
Weed, James A., 351
Weinberg, Meyer, 350
Weinstein, David, 129
Weinstock, Edward, 192
Weintraub, Bernard, 346, 347
Weisberg, Arline, 270, 273
Weisbord, Robert, 346
Weisman, Carol Sachs, 348
Weiss, E.B., 24
Weiss, Robert S., 192
Weissman, Steve, 592
Welch, Robert, 50, 74, 559
Welles, Chris, 442
Wellisch, David K., 218
Weltfish, Gene, 345
Weppner, Robert S., 351
West, D. J., 153
West, Elmer, Jr., 559
West, Susan, 594

Westoff, Charles F., 192, 248, 249
Westoff, Leslie Aldridge, 192
Weston, Peter J., 374
Wheaton, Blair, 485
Whitaker, Ben, 347
Whitaker, Romulus, 592
Whitaker, Zai, 592
White, John W., 219
White, Lynn, Jr., 592
Whiteside, Thomas, 127
Whitney, Craig L., 560
Whitten, Les, 410, 411
Whyte, William F., Jr., 307
Wiley, Harvey N., 525
Wilks, Judith, 157
Will, Robert E., 306
Williams, E. Belvin, 76
Williams, J. Allen, Jr., 207, 534, 535, 558, 559
Williams, Ray R., 126
Williams, Walter, 613
Williamson, John B., 306
Willick, Denice H., 127
Willner, Shirley G., 484
Wilson, Clark, 158
Wilson, James Q., 153, 158, 348, 350, 351
Wilson, W. Cody, 444
Wilson, William J., 346, 347
Windle, J. L., 614
Winfrey, Carey, 217
Winick, Charles, 486
Winograd, Barry, 614
Wirt, R. D., 154
Wirth, Louis, 410
Wise, Arthur, 274
Wiseman, Jacqueline P., 485
Wiswell, Candace Hinson, 350
Wittes, Janet T., 572, 593
Wolf, Katherine, 349
Wolfe, Nancy, 192
Wolfe, Tom, 75
Wolff, Anthony, 591, 593
Wolff, Frank, 441, 444
Wolfgang, Marvin E., 127, 153, 154
Wolman, Diane, 249
Wood, James B., 221
Woolf, S.J., 559
Worchel, Stephen, 443
Wright, Sonia, 306
Wurdock, Clarence, 351
Wuthnow, Robert, 219, 221

SUBJECT INDEX